Balancing Green

Balancing Green

When to Embrace Sustainability in a Business (and When Not To)

Yossi Sheffi
With Edgar Blanco

The MIT Press
Cambridge, Massachusetts
London, England

This book was set in 10 on 14 pt Helvetica condensed and Sabon by Toppan Best-set Premedia Limited Printed and bound in the United States of America.

Library of Congress Cataloging-in-Publication Data is available.

ISBN: 978-0-262-03772-3

10 9 8 7 6 5 4 3 2 1

Contents

Preface

In this book, I offer a pragmatic take on whether, how, why, and to what extent businesses of all sizes are addressing environmental sustainability. Like my previous books, this one has its origins in extensive interviews with hundreds of executives at dozens of companies. The goal was not to argue for or against sustainability but to understand what, if anything, these executives were doing in this realm. The many examples in this book were selected to illustrate the diverse challenges, solutions, and implications of sustainability as a potential business goal, competing with the many other business goals that managers face. Rather than prescribe a specific course action, these examples enable business managers to draw their own conclusions about what might or might not work in their specific context and how far it makes sense to go.

This book takes an entirely agnostic view on the science of climate change because it may be irrelevant whether business executives either personally embrace environmentalists' arguments about "the challenge of our time" or if they believe it is a hoax. Companies, as entities that connect supply and demand around the world, have many stakeholders in the communities in which they operate who are interested in corporate profits, jobs, business growth, *and* sustainability. The business merits of sustainability are based on the fact that even the most ardent climate change skeptics in the C-suite face natural resource costs, public relations problems, regulatory burdens, and a green consumer segment. Thus, this book presents three main business rationales—cutting costs, reducing risk, and achieving growth—for corporate sustainability efforts. These three rationales underpin companies' struggles to bridge the gap between the conflicting constraints imposed and desires expressed by customers, competitors, employees, neighbors, investors, activists, local governments, and regulators.

The intention of this book is to describe and illustrate many of the choices companies face; their efforts up and down the supply chain; the tools they use to assess the impact of those efforts, both environmental and financial; and the multifaceted conflicts and collaborations between companies, NGOs, and government agencies. All these choices have to be taken in the context of other company objectives such as profits, product and service quality, risk management, and others. The book explores effective initiatives as well as wasteful ones, and it highlights the difficulties of accounting for the full life cycle of products and processes throughout the entire supply chain "from cradle to grave."

More than any of my previous books, this book's gestation has been long and arduous, owing to several deep gaps uncovered by this research. Our research team found that a multitude of companies claimed to pursue a variety of sustainability initiatives. Of course, when an MIT team interviews executives at a company, few would simply admit something such as, "We really don't care—we just do the minimum that our customers or regulators demand—and we put out some blurb to fend off NGOs. ..." We *did*, however, hear some frank opinions expressed, including one from a chief supply chain officer at a leading manufacturer, who declared, "We will do what customers demand and no more." Interestingly, two years later, that same executive asked us not to use this quote in the book, because the company was starting to change its stance. Another team of executives at a different company stated categorically, "If it reduces costs we will do it, otherwise we will not."

The long gestation process of this book allowed us to observe that more and more (yet by no means all) companies were starting to pay attention to environmental sustainability and do something to promote it. They were committing to, and often achieving, specific environmental impact reduction goals through myriad initiatives that targeted all phases of the product life cycle. These actions were carefully analyzed and constitute the majority of this book's discussion on *how* companies implement sustainable practices.

At the same time, environmental journalists and NGOs were decrying the many remaining examples of pollution, habitat loss, and rising CO_2 levels. Although it is easy to vilify companies as icons of cold-hearted capitalism, the picture is very different when one "walks in the shoes" of corporate executives. Keeping a company alive and growing is not simply a matter of satisfying Wall Street demands for profits. A successful company delivers something that its customers want or need while providing employment and supporting entire communities. For example, Walmart—the oft-criticized corporate behemoth—directly employs more than two million people and indirectly supports millions more. Its efficiency means that it can sell at "everyday low prices" to the one-third of the US population that visits its stores every week, and to the many more who make purchases online. The company single-handedly effected improvements in the sustainability of many products on a national scale. What was harder to understand was *why* companies pursued sustainability in the way they did.

The gap between companies' bright press releases that celebrate environmental stewardship and environmentalists' dark forecasts of planetary doom reflects a more complex reality. Sustainability is intimately connected with *supply chains*, the complex economic structures formed by companies that are using the global supply of natural resources to meet worldwide consumer demand.

The causes of this gap begin on the consumer side. Although a number of surveys show that most consumers *say* they want sustainable products, sales data show that only a small percentage are actually willing to pay more to buy sustainable products. This gap between "say" and "pay" puts companies in a difficult position. The position is made even more challenging by activists, journalists, and regulators who also demand (or command) sustainability from companies and attempt to punish transgressors.

The supply side exacerbates this gap. Most companies operate within the broad chasm between the environmental sensibilities of Western consumers and the economic priorities of developing countries that supply much of the natural, mineral, and energy resources consumed in the developed world. In the developing world (and in much of the Western world as well), the emphasis is on livelihood and economics rather than sustainability. Companies routinely violate their own country's laws, sometimes with the implicit "understanding" of the authorities, in the name of providing jobs. Thus, companies face seemingly incompatible requirements when accounting for sustainability, costs, and jobs. Most of the case studies in this book illustrate how companies are trying to navigate among these constraints and demands.

This book does not specifically address the social impacts of supply chains, such as child labor, fair pay, community welfare, or social justice issues. Nonetheless, many of the rationales and tools for addressing environmental challenges in supply chains carry over to social concerns as well. Many companies bundle their environmental and social initiatives under the general heading of "corporate social responsibility" or a broader definition of sustainability.

SUPPLY CHAINS IN THE CROSSHAIRS

Chapter 1 presents case studies of the rising influence wielded by NGOs, governmental regulations, lawsuits (including retroactive actions), and growing concern by customers, employees, and investors over environmental impacts. These external, sustainability-focused forces create economic incentives for corporate environmental initiatives. Thus, rather than debate whether responding to climate change is an ethical duty or not, this chapter gives a synopsis of the wide range of sustainability initiatives that can be justified using profit-motivated, business rationales alone. In particular, the chapter outlines the merits of sustainable practices in terms of cutting costs, reducing risks, and growing the company. The chapter also places sustainability in the context of the competing objectives and challenges facing any company. Even if sustainability is *a* priority, it is never the *only* priority.

Chapter 2 traces product supply chains. These supply chains play a crucial role in sustainability because the environmental impacts of many types of products are widely dispersed across the network of companies that convert raw materials into finished goods and sell them. Paralleling the chain of companies that make a product are the stages of a product's life cycle. The chapter outlines the impacts that occur as a product moves from cradle to grave. I examine sustainability from a supply chain perspective because the vast majority of environmental impacts and risks (and the associated potential improvements) take place outside the four walls of most companies, in their global networks of suppliers or in the actions of downstream customers.

Chapter 3 examines life cycle assessment (LCA), a methodology for estimating a product's total environmental impact. The examples illustrate the complexities of accounting for supply chain environmental impacts, as well as the potential for effective "hot spot" analysis. The chapter also addresses materiality assessment, which plays a crucial role in allowing companies to make sound business decisions about which impacts to tackle.

FUNCTIONAL SUSTAINABILITY INITIATIVES

The bulk of the book explores how specific subsets of managers in manufacturing, procurement, distribution, transportation, design, marketing, and upper management pursue sustainability initiatives within their particular domains. The wide-ranging dimensions of environmental sustainability (including greenhouse gases, energy, water, toxins, waste, and recycling)—coupled with the many opportunities to decrease impact in various parts of the life cycle— imply that companies have a very large number of possible avenues for improving sustainability rather than a single all-encompassing initiative. This leads companies to implement many different initiatives and to distribute their efforts across the organization and the supply chain.

Chapter 4 begins with sustainability improvements that occur *inside* the four walls of the organization, primarily in product manufacturing. These improvements focus on reductions in carbon footprint, water consumption, and toxin emissions by factories. Many of the initiatives cut costs as well as reduce environmental impact. The chapter lays the groundwork for the types of initiatives that supplier and customer companies might also take to reduce their own share of the impact.

Chapter 5 takes sustainability to the upstream supply chain; for most products, the majority of the environmental impacts and reputational risks are spread across the company's far-flung network of suppliers. The chapter looks at how companies such as IKEA and Starbucks manage deep supplier networks to reduce the risk of reputational damage. The chapter explores what companies do under challenging conditions, such as when agricultural and mineral commodities are produced in countries where environmental standards are lax and even the largest companies have little leverage.

Chapter 6 moves on to transportation and distribution, and to the very visible environmental impacts of moving materials and products around the world. The examples in the chapter show how companies can make significant reductions in greenhouse gas emissions through transportation management, vehicle efficiencies, and fuels. The chapter also considers the local environmental issues inherent in concentrated supply chain operations such as large seaports.

Chapter 7 follows the product life cycle (and the chain of companies) to the end-of-life of the product and beyond. It covers a range of measures, from postconsumer recycling to end-of-life sustainability improvements. These measures emphasize cost reduction, the recovery of value, the differential footprints (of recycled versus primary materials), and the complex economics of recycling. The chapter concludes with examples of companies or industries that are starting to "close the loop."

Chapter 8 delves into product design and engineering changes that can markedly affect environmental impact across the full product life cycle. In particular, it examines the environmental impact during the use of a product, a phase that typically dominates the total impact of goods that consume power, fuel, or water. The chapter also covers packaging design and design for recycling.

Chapter 9 discusses sustainability-related labeling, annual corporate social responsibility reporting, and other marketing communications. Because consumers' behavior, environmentalists' assessments, governments' oversight, and investors' risk analyses play key roles in companies' sustainability motivations, communication with these groups is essential for reaping the returns on these initiatives. The chapter outlines what kinds of communication might be productive or counterproductive, depending on the nature of the claims the company is making.

Whereas chapters 4 to 9 focus on subsets of sustainability from the narrower perspective of functional business areas, chapter 10 covers the larger management issues of introducing and coordinating sustainability initiatives across an organization. The chapter addresses management issues including initiative evaluation, culture, metrics, incentives, and collaboration with NGOs.

THE COMMITTED

The later chapters shift the focus from large companies that are *moving* toward sustainability to those (often smaller) firms that have always explicitly prioritized it and sell specifically to consumers who value it and are willing to pay higher prices. Chapter 11 presents in-depth case studies of three "deep green" companies: Dr. Bronner's Magic Soaps, Patagonia, and Seventh Generation. These companies exemplify potential future corporate practices, if sustainability becomes more highly prized, and they show how mission-driven firms can and do exert competitive and regulatory pressure on mainstream companies.

Chapter 12 examines the gap between large, shareholder-driven companies and their green-mission counterparts. Although the deep green companies profiled in chapter 11 have all been financially successful, their environmental impact pales in comparison to the much larger companies that dominate commerce and retail shelves. So, why are there green companies and large companies but only few large green companies? Chapter 12 explores the fundamental challenges of replicating deep green practices on a larger scale.

The final chapter investigates more thoroughly the trade-off between financial and environmental performance. Although the bulk of the book offers examples that are both sustainable *and* profitable, companies inevitably exhaust this low-hanging fruit and must make seemingly harder decisions that pit one performance dimension against another. Even so, the chapter demonstrates that companies do have ways to push the frontier outward in order to continue to deliver higher sustainability without reducing financial performance (or to increase financial performance without reducing sustainability).

Nuanced explorations of global supply chains reveal that sustainability is not a simple case of "profits versus planet" but is instead a more subtle issue of people versus people. It pits people looking for jobs and inexpensive goods versus people seeking a pristine environment. People who are worried about how to feed their families tomorrow come into conflict with people worried about future environmental disasters. These different people in many countries, coming from diverse socioeconomic classes and varied value systems, will not make the same choices in what they buy, what they supply, and how they feel about the confluence of environmental and economic issues. The challenge for companies lies in the fact that they must bridge these wildly diverse outlooks on the world and the environment. This book aims to help companies—caught in the middle of this debate by virtue of their globe-spanning operations—to satisfy conflicting motivations for both economic growth and environmental sustainability.

THANKS

As is the case with my other books, this work is based, in large measure, on primary research, including interviews all over the world with business and NGO executives. As a result, I owe deep thanks to the people who shared their time and expertise with the research team and pointed us in the right directions. Without them this book would not have been possible. The full list of individuals who helped this effort is given at the end of the book.

The people who helped with this effort directly include the main members of the research team: Dr. Alexis Bateman (now residing in California), who conducted many of the interviews; and Dr. Anthony Craig (now a professor at Iowa State) whose dissertation includes the banana case study described in chapter 3.

The contribution of Andrea and Dana Meyer of Working Knowledge in research and writing has been invaluable. The numerous hours of heated arguments with Dana helped shape the book as it tried to thread between environmental and economic concerns, while Andrea made sure that the writing worked. The editing was also shaped by Calais Harding at MIT.

Finally, my wife of 49 years (wow!)—Anat. I cannot imagine going through the past five decades with a better mate.

1

THE GROWING PRESSURES

Warren Buffett said, "It takes 20 years to build a reputation and five minutes to ruin it."[1] A single indelible magazine image, such as that of a very young Pakistani boy sewing a Nike soccer ball for reportedly 6 cents per hour,[2] can change public sentiment overnight. The 1996 image on the cover of *Life* magazine led to a "Boycott Nike" campaign, and the company lost more than half its market capitalization in the ensuing year.[3] It took Nike six years of demonstrated concerted corporate social responsibility efforts to regain the lost value.

Leading the campaigns to publicize and vilify corporations' environmental (and social) impacts are the many nongovernmental organizations (NGOs) spawned from the environmental movement. Examples include the World Wildlife Fund (1961), Greenpeace (1971), Rainforest Action Network (1985), and Conservation International (1987). These NGOs and countless others believe in the potential fragility of the environment—and they see the potential fragility of companies' brands as a means of pressuring companies to change.

"When Greenpeace reaches for its toolbox, it tends to find only one tool, and that's a mallet," said Scott Poynton, founder of The Forest Trust, "and it tends to beat people over the head with it. ... But it works, in the sense that it starts the process of change." He added, "I always say, people won't change unless they're uncomfortable. So, my view of Greenpeace is that they're serious agents of discomfort."[4]

AGENTS OF DISCOMFORT

On Haxby Road in the British city of York in 1932, the Rowntree factory reverberated with the sound of 500 women's voices singing *My Girl's a Yorkshire Girl.*[5] The factory belonged to chocolatier Seebohm Rowntree, and his workers—65 percent of whom were women—were singing while they worked. The women's voices rang out in unison as rich milk chocolate flowed from large vats onto confectionery-filled converter belts. Rowntree let them sing—indeed, encouraged it—based on the then-recent findings of industrial psychologists that music in the workplace improved productivity, alertness, and team interaction.[6] To that end, Rowntree also instituted employee suggestion boxes. One of the suggestions he received was for the company to make "a chocolate bar that a man could take to work in his pack up." To make the new chocolate bar more affordable for the working class, Rowntree's used long thin wafers enrobed in a layer of chocolate, reducing its costs by using less chocolate while keeping the traditional chocolate bar format.[7] Introduced as "Rowntree's Chocolate Crisp" in 1935, the four-finger wafer added "nicknamed KitKat" on its packaging and in ads in 1937.

When the J. Walter Thomson ad agency created KitKat's first television advertisement in 1957, the agency keyed into the idea of the "snap" of a breaking bar and combined it with previous ads showing KitKat as "the best companion to a cup of tea."[8] The tagline, "Have a break, have a KitKat" emerged and remains to this day. The "Gimme a Break" jingle that aired in 1986 quickly became firmly implanted in consumers' minds, so much so that a 2003 study found it was still one of the most common "earworms"—songs that people can't get out of their heads.[9]

Nestlé S.A. acquired Rowntree in 1988, when Rowntree was the fourth-largest chocolate manufacturer in the world.[10] By 2013, Nestlé had invested more than £200 million in the Rowntree business, making the York factory one of the world's largest and most successful confectionery factories, as well as the site for Nestlé's global research center for confectionery.[11] In 2010, Guinness World Records certified that KitKat was the world's most global brand, sold in more countries than any other that year.[12]

Minor Material, Major Headache

On March 17, 2010, Greenpeace released an online video parody of the KitKat commercial.[13,14] The 60-second clip opens with a bored office worker feeding papers into a shredder. Then, the screen turns red with the text, "Have a break?" Next, the worker opens a KitKat wrapper, but instead of KitKat's fingers of chocolate, he finds an orangutan finger—complete with tufts of orange hair. Two coworkers watch in horror as the worker crunches into the finger and blood dribbles from the corner of his mouth and onto his keyboard.

The video urged viewers to "give the orangutan a break" and "stop Nestlé buying palm oil from companies that destroy rainforests."[15] It closed with video of an orangutan in a tree, followed by an image of a single tree in a cleared field, symbolic of the deforestation wrought to make way for palm oil plantations. For a Facebook campaign, Greenpeace remade the candy bar's label to say "Killer" instead of "KitKat." Greenpeace used the power of social media to attack fast, far, and wide. In a matter of weeks, 1.5 million people had watched the YouTube video.[16] "Greenpeace's online campaigns ... are some parts coordination, some parts opportunity, and most importantly rely on people's support (through social media)," said Laura Kenyon, an online marketing and promotions specialist at Greenpeace International.

Nestlé first attempted to control the damage to the KitKat brand by demanding that YouTube pull the video for infringement of trademarks and copyright.[17] But attempts at censorship merely attracted more views of the video and an avalanche of consumer emails demanding that the company change its palm oil sourcing practices.[18] The company was featured on buycott.com, a website and mobile app that helps consumers "organize your everyday consumer spending so that it reflects your principles."[19] More than 20,000 members joined the boycotts against Nestlé.

The attacks surprised Nestlé, according to Poynton, not just because they were graphically hard-hitting but also because the company thought it had already been addressing the issue. The company had adopted a "no deforestation" policy when directly sourcing palm oil, committing that its palm oil would "not come from areas cleared of natural forest after November 2005."[20] In

2009, the company had even joined the Roundtable on Sustainable Palm Oil (RSPO),[21] a collaborative industry group formed in 2004[22] to transition palm oil into a sustainable commodity market.[23]

José Lopez, who was responsible for Nestlé's manufacturing at the time, voiced frustration with the campaign, saying that "you would have to 'look through a microscope' to find the palm oil in the snack."[24] Furthermore, Nestlé neither produced palm oil nor owned any farms near orangutan habitats, nor had it ever ordered the clearing of rainforests to increase production of palm oil. But one of its suppliers had. Chapter 5 delves into Nestlé's attempts to address the issue by canceling that supplier's contracts and why that response initially failed. "These cancellations did not really give the rainforests a break," Greenpeace wrote.[25] Keeping the pressure on, activists dressed as orangutans stood outside Nestlé's headquarters in Frankfurt, Germany. Other activists raided Nestlé's annual meeting later that year and even unfurled a banner inside the meeting itself.[26]

Although the effects of the campaign on KitKat sales are not publicly known, the company did agree to Greenpeace's demands to identify and remove any companies in its supply chain with links to deforestation after only eight weeks.[27]

Cut Off at the Source

Whereas Greenpeace tried to disrupt demand for Nestlé's products, NGOs also attack the supply side. In India, community groups accused the Coca-Cola Company and its subsidiaries of depleting and contaminating local water supplies.[28] Several protests, with as many as 2,000 people, picketed the gates of a 40-acre bottling plant in Plachimada in 2002.[29] In 2003, the high court of the Indian state of Kerala ordered the company to shut down its water wells, forcing Coke to close the plant. In August 2005, two months after Coke reopened the plant under a new license, organizers marched on the gates again, leading to four injuries and 43 arrests.[30]

As of 2017, the plant remained closed. In February 2011, the Kerala assembly passed the Plachimada Coca-Cola Victims Relief and Compensation Claims Tribunal Bill. The bill empowered a tribunal to decide a $48 million lawsuit against the company for alleged environmental and soil degradation, and for water contamination caused by overextraction of ground water. In 2014, a second plant in India—the Mehdiganj plant in the state of Uttar Pradesh—was ordered to close by the local Pollution Control Board.[31]

It Takes a Village

In the spring of 1969, residents of Woburn, Massachusetts, a small town 12 miles north of Boston, filed a petition with the mayor, attesting that water from city wells G and H was "very unpotable, very hard, and has a strong chemical taste."[32] They demanded the wells be shut down.[33] No action was undertaken until 1979, when the Department of Environmental Quality Engineering found that the two wells contained unacceptably high levels of "probable carcinogens" as defined by the US Environmental Protection Agency (EPA).[34] Anne Anderson, whose son had died of leukemia, discovered that six other children had died of leukemia within blocks of her home, a co-occurrence in time and distance that had a 1 in 100 chance of happening, according to the US Centers for Disease Control (CDC).[35] Anderson, her pastor Reverend Bruce Young, and 20 others formed a group and hired attorney Jan Schlichtmann to sue W. R. Grace and Company and Beatrice Foods, the companies allegedly responsible for the ground water contamination.[36]

The case spawned nearly two decades of publicity. A *60 Minutes* television exposé, titled "What Killed Jimmy Anderson?"[37] aired in 1986. The 1996 nonfiction book *A Civil Action* spent more than two years on the best-seller list[38] and became a 1998 movie starring John Travolta as Schlichtmann playing opposite legendary actor Robert Duvall. The legal proceedings stretched for nine years after the story began[39] and ended with an $8 million settlement.[40] Moreover, the US EPA, building upon Schlichtmann's work, brought an enforcement action against the companies and forced them to pay $69.5 million in cleanup costs.[41]

As this example demonstrates, NGO activism and community activism can feed off each other, with NGOs trying to foment community action and community action attracting NGO attention. By 2000, there were more than 6,000 national and regional environmental movement organizations in the United States, as well as more than 20,000 local ones.[42] NGO and community action, in turn, can lead to stricter regulations (see the section "Growing Regulatory Restrictions"). The Woburn case encouraged Massachusetts to pass its own "Superfund" act to force landowners to clean up toxic sites and to establish a statewide cancer registry to aid in the detection of pollution-induced cancer clusters.[43]

If You Can't Embarrass 'Em, Sue 'Em

Minnesota Power provides electricity to 145,000 customers in northeastern Minnesota, including some of the nation's largest industrial customers, namely paper mills.[44] In 2004, the company relied almost exclusively on coal to supply that electric power, and in 2005 it started investing millions of dollars to reduce emissions and improve efficiency of those coal-fired plants. Yet, in 2008, the US EPA cited Minnesota Power for Clean Air Act violations. The company responded that the instances where it exceeded limits were part of routine maintenance projects and therefore not subject to the requirements. The EPA and the company continued to trade legal arguments for the next six years.

The Sierra Club grew frustrated with the government's slow settlement negotiations with Minnesota Power.[45] The NGO dug through government-collected public data consisting of 3.5 million emission data points posted over a period of five years and found 12,774 deviations in the opacity[46] readings.[47] In March 2014, the Sierra Club threatened Minnesota Power with legal action,[48] claiming the company had violated the Clean Air Act by exceeding limits on particulate matter emissions. According to Michelle Rosier, the Sierra Club campaign organizing manager, "These serious violations call into question whether Minnesota Power is willing or able to operate its plants within the national safety guidelines for public health."[49]

Minnesota Power did not dispute the data but instead pointed out that its plants were operating within permitted limits 99.7 percent of the time.[50] Furthermore, opacity does not always indicate the release of any pollutants, because opacity "can be based on the weather—you put hot steam in cold air and it is going to have a higher opacity," said Pat Mullen, the company's vice president of marketing and corporate communications.[51] Even the government agreed: "This type of monitoring is quite complex and just because deviations are reported does not necessarily indicate that there are violations," said Katie Koelfgen, manager of the Minnesota Pollution Control Agency (MPCA) land and air compliance section.[52]

Despite the weakness of the Sierra Club's case, four months later, Minnesota Power reached a settlement with the EPA, agreeing to pay $1.4 million in civil penalties and to spend more than $500 million on emissions controls.[53] Al Rudeck, Minnesota Power's vice president of strategy and planning, explained the settlement: "From a reputation standpoint, it's never easy to see your name out in the paper this way. We take a lot of pride in our environmental stewardship. It's a bitter pill to swallow in terms of coming to settlement, but we felt it was in the best interest of our stakeholders."[54] Although environmentalists hailed the $500 million in mandated upgrades, the settlement included the $350 million that Minnesota Power had already invested since 2005. "Many of the emission control measures were implemented during the six-year discussions to resolve the [EPA's] Notice of Violation," the company stated in a press release.[55] The Sierra Club used a similar tactic against two utilities in Wisconsin in 2012 and 2013, winning settlements of $1.1 billion in environmental upgrades and $3.4 million in fines from the utilities.[56]

NGOs have brought countless other legal actions against companies, ranging from DuPont to Shell, which have cost these companies millions of dollars.[57,58] Affected groups and NGOs can use civil lawsuits to recover both compensatory and punitive damages. Moreover, some NGOs use these suits and their settlements to fund more legal action.[59] "Historically, there has been an uptick in citizen suit filings when there is something of a slowdown in enforcement," said Matthew Morrison, an environmental lawyer based in Washington, DC, and a former counsel for the EPA.[60]

Sustained Campaigns

NGO campaigns against companies can last years. The campaign against Nike's low wages at Asian suppliers[61] involved several

NGOs and media outlets and lasted more than a decade.[62] Forest-Ethics' *Victoria's Dirty Secret* campaign against the paper procurement policies of Victoria's Secret for its product catalogs[63] lasted two years and was joined by CampusActivism.org, Voice for Animals, Portland Independent Media Center, Treehugger, and many others.[64] The campaign ended only when the company agreed to use more recycled paper in its catalogs.

The moral of these stories is that targeted companies cannot expect that campaigns will quickly "run out of steam." When activist organizations decide to wage a campaign against a corporation, they typically raise funds and prepare for the long haul. According to Robert Beer, former director of the SmartWood program of the Rainforest Alliance, "They [the NGOs] all have different techniques, but they have critical mass. They have funding, funding for a particular cause, and they're pretty sophisticated in terms of understanding how to use the tools that are available to them. I think oftentimes businesses don't appreciate just how sophisticated they are. Then they walk into a firestorm."[65] Furthermore, the campaigns usually intensify over time as other groups join the crusade.

Nor do the activists stop when they achieve their stated goal. In their quest for true sustainability, their "goal posts" keep moving and the hurdles for companies keep growing higher. "After many of the world's leading electronics companies rose to the challenge of phasing out their worst hazardous substances, we are now challenging them to improve their sourcing of minerals and better managing the energy used throughout the supply chain," said Greenpeace campaigner Tom Dowall.[66]

WHEN COMPANY STAKEHOLDERS GET INVOLVED

Outside activists are not the only stakeholders motivating companies to consider environmental stewardship initiatives. Unlike NGOs, a company's economic stakeholders are directly aligned with the financial interests of the company—consumers, distributors, retailers, employees, and shareholders all benefit from the success of the company and bear risks if the company fails or is disrupted. This natural alignment can make the sustainability arguments of the company's economic stakeholders more persuasive for corporate managers than outsiders' arguments. Some of these insiders may believe that the threat of NGO attacks, regulatory change (see section "Growing Regulatory Restrictions"), or consumer backlash owing to environmental damage (see section "Vulnerability Is in the Hands of the Brand Holder") could hinder the success of the company.

Consumers: A "Green" Minority in a Sea of Apathy

Surveys by environmental groups and others find that more than half of consumers globally[67] and almost half in the United States[68] claim they would pay more for sustainable products. Yet, in 2012 Robert McDonald, Procter and Gamble's CEO at the time, suggested that only 15 percent of consumers were actually willing to pay more—and even then only a little more—for environmentally sustainable products.[69] As one commentator[70] suggested: "Green marketers have known this for a long time. Consumers will consistently tell surveys that they are willing to pay more for socially and environmentally superior products. But when they are alone in the shopping aisle and it's just them and their wallet, they rarely fork out more for 'green.'"[71] A 2014 study by the European Food Information Council confirmed this by concluding that although consumers understand sustainability, this understanding does not yet translate into changes in food choices.[72]

Although a cause-marketing agency reported that 91 percent of global consumers claim they are likely to switch brands to one associated with a good cause given comparable price and quality,[73] they often don't do so in practice for four possible reasons: First, consumers may not think other products are comparable, and other purchase criteria (e.g., a product's cost, features, and performance, or the retailer's location and service) are often more important than environmental issues. Second, consumers face costs or risks in switching to a different brand or retailer with which they are not familiar, especially in the case of complex products. Third, in a busy, media-saturated world, consumers may be unaware of a particular NGO campaign. Finally, some consumers may be "free riders"—they advocate boycotts in the hopes others will take part, while they continue to buy from the same company as always.[74] In fact, after growing rapidly through 2010, sales of green household cleaners and laundry products declined at a compounded annual rate of 2 percent from 2010 to 2014.[75]

Even though mainstream consumers were not buying green products in volume, surveys found that millennials (those individuals born in the 1980s and 1990s) may be more willing to pay for sustainable products than older consumers.[76] "We do not see this as a trend that will fade. Higher customer expectations are a permanent part of the future," said Mike Duke, Walmart's president and CEO, in 2009 in prepared remarks.[77] Yet, until retailers' sales data corroborate environmentalists' survey data, companies may be reluctant to invest in large-scale change or incur higher operating costs for environmentally sustainable products.

Customers' Changing Demands

Up until 2009, Ralph Lauren, the luxury apparel maker, had been untouched by the kind of public shaming campaigns waged against Nike and other apparel makers. Yet, the company faced pressure on sustainability issues that year when one of its customers, the retailer Kohl's, asked all of its suppliers for a sustainability scorecard. Kohl's had specific questions about environmental impacts, which required Ralph Lauren to conduct its first internal accounting of environmental issues. The retailer's demands did not end there. Each year, Kohl's asked increasingly complex and detailed scorecard questions. As a result, Ralph Lauren ramped up its internal auditing to meet those demands.[78]

As of 2013, Kohl's measured the sustainability practices and improvements of its 300 top suppliers on a quarterly basis and held annual supplier roundtable discussions on responsible practices.[79] Kohl's encouraged its suppliers to ask *their* suppliers about such practices, too. "We have a sizable group now asking their own suppliers sustainability questions. This is where we wanted it to go," said John Fojut, vice president of corporate sustainability at Kohl's Corporation.[80]

Kohl's demands of its suppliers arise from its concerns about consumer behavior. "Instead of having to react and adapt to someone else's priorities—like when some companies got surprised by the rising tide of consumer concern about social responsibility—[we're all discovering it's better to] get ahead of the curve and come together to agree on what's important and what progress we want to drive," Fojut said.

The Watchers from Within

Girl Scouts of America and their famous cookies came under scrutiny in late 2007 by two of their own.[81] Earlier that year, 11-year-old Rhiannon Tomtishen and 12-year-old Madison Vorva were researching orangutans to earn a Bronze Award for their troop when they stumbled upon the connection between the loss of orangutan habitat and the growth of palm oil plantations. After eliminating palm oil from their own diets, they were horrified to learn that palm oil was the second most common ingredient in Girl Scout cookies, which they were about to start selling.[82]

The girls began a five-year "Project Orangs" campaign to raise awareness of the issue.[83] Their campaign, however, encountered resistance from Girls Scouts USA's Amanda Hawmaker, who was in charge of cookie sales. Hawmaker argued that palm oil is needed to maintain taste, avoid crumbling, and delay cookie spoilage. Changes to the recipes could jeopardize sales, which could, in turn, jeopardize all the camps, field trips, and charities funded by cookie sales.[84]

Despite initial resistance, the girls achieved some progress after several years of campaigning. In the fall of 2011, Girl Scouts USA committed to buying Green Palm certificates (see chapter 5) in 2012 and to source sustainable palm oil by 2015. Acknowledging the role of the girls' campaign, Hawmaker said, "It is not our consumers who drove us to make this decision or expressed concern on the issue."[85] The Girl Scouts example demonstrates that even organizations with a wholesome image, which NGOs would be hesitant to target, are vulnerable—in this case, to campaigns by their own members.

Whistleblowers such as Mark Felt (Watergate),[86] David Weber (US Securities and Exchange Commission),[87] and Cheryl Eckard (GlaxoSmithKline),[88] are three among many who, over the years,

have exposed what they believed were unethical or criminal practices within their own organizations. Thus, while some attacks
come from external organizations, risks may lurk within each
organization's rank and file, if employees believe that their own
organization's behavior is objectionable.

Recruiting the Next Generation of Workers

The higher prevalence of environmental consciousness among
younger generations[89] means that a company's environmental reputation may affect its ability to recruit talent. "We know that it
makes a hiring difference when we're out recruiting at universities.
People ask about sustainability, and our recruiters do talk about
our packaging, so it is a draw for talent," said Oliver Campbell,
director of procurement at Dell.[90] A Rutgers University study of
worker priorities found that nearly half of college students (45
percent) said in 2012 that they would give up a 15 percent higher
salary to have a job "that seeks to make a social or environmental difference in the world."[91] Naturally, such responses to surveys
may or may not correlate with actual behavior, but they may be
an indicator.

When Shareholders Go Green

The concrete jungle of New York may be a long way from the real
jungles of Malaysia and Indonesia, but New York State Comptrol-
ler Thomas DiNapoli has campaigned on behalf of the New York
State Common Retirement Fund to change companies' palm oil
sourcing activities in order to reduce deforestation. In 2013,
DiNapoli filed a shareholder resolution requiring Dunkin' Donuts
to address the environmental problems associated with palm
oil production. He subsequently withdrew the resolution when
Dunkin' agreed to better reporting, sustainable sourcing, supplier
compliance, and to support a moratorium on deforestation.[92]
DiNapoli won similar concessions from Sara Lee Corporation in
2010 and J. M. Smucker Company in 2013. "Shareholder value is
enhanced when companies take steps to address the risks associated with environmental practices that promote climate change,"
he said.[93]

The New York State Common Retirement Fund is among a growing number of institutional investors concerned about environmental or social issues. Some of these institutions, such as NGO-affiliated and religious institutional investors, are pushing for environmental protection for ethical reasons ("doing good"). Others may be motivated by financial concerns (such as reducing the perceived risks and costs of unsustainable business practices).

At the very least, these investors seek better disclosure of potential risks lurking in companies' supply chains; the top five types of environmental proposals pushed by activist shareholders all call for reporting.[94] The CDP (formerly the Carbon Disclosure Project), which represents 822 institutional investors with $95 trillion in assets under management, induced thousands of public companies to disclose carbon, water, and waste impacts, and to report on their efforts to reduce these impacts[95] (see chapter 3). An analysis of 700 companies over a five-year period found that companies' perceived environmental risk was more affected by shareholders' environmental resolutions than by NGOs' attacks,[96] although it is unclear how many of these investors' actions were themselves motivated by NGOs' activities.

GROWING REGULATORY RESTRICTIONS

From the birth of the American nation in 1776 up until 1963, a total of five environmental protection laws were passed. The subsequent 40 years saw 27 new major environmental laws enacted—with the number jumping to 51 when occupational health and safety laws that restrict corporate activities are included.[97] Beyond accelerating the enactment of new laws, existing laws have been made more stringent. For example, passenger car emissions limits in the United States have been tightened from a limit of 3.1 grams of nitrogen oxides per mile in 1975 to 0.07 grams by 2004—a 98 percent reduction.[98]

Regulatory Requirements

As of 2016, most governments in the developed world have introduced and toughened regulations on corporate activities. Many of these regulations target specific air, water, and solid waste pollutants. Reports of man-made climate change have motivated governments to start regulating greenhouse gas (GHG) emissions from a wide range of sources. GHGs include CO_2 from the burning of fossil fuels plus a host of other gases such as methane, nitrous oxide (from fertilizers), refrigerants, and other gases with some CO_2-equivalent (CO_2e) effect on preventing heat from escaping the atmosphere. In 2007, the US Supreme Court ruled that emissions that cause climate change are subject to EPA regulations under the Clean Air Act, pending scientific findings that GHG emissions endanger public health and welfare.[99] The EPA's 2009 "endangerment finding"[100] established just that and led to further emissions regulations for power plants, industrial plants, and automobiles.[101]

The trend of rising regulation evident in developed countries may be taking hold in developing nations as well. The growing middle class in these countries is increasingly demanding clean air, water, and food, as well as preservation of the natural environment, which leads to more regulations and stricter enforcement. In April 2014, China started to combat its rampant pollution problems with some of its biggest policy changes in 25 years.[102] There was even speculation that the Chinese government might tax gasoline to finance electric cars.[103] Regulations, however, vary widely in their scope, rigidity, and associated costs.

Regulatory requirements range from disclosure demands, to "soft" requirements, to market mechanisms for inducing companies to act, to strict "thou shalt" laws that affect how companies manage sustainability (see chapter 10). Environmental regulations can even be applied retroactively.

Sins of the Fathers

In the 1940s, Hooker Chemicals and Plastics received permission from Niagara Power and Development Company to dump industrial waste into a never-finished canal in Niagara Falls, New York. Using accepted, legal practices of the time, Hooker drained the canal, lined it with heavy clay[104] and, during the 1940s and 1950s, dumped more than 21,000 tons of chemical waste into it.[105] Hooker then sealed the dump with yet more clay and dirt. In 1953, the Niagara Falls Board of Education bought the site for $1. Hooker disclosed the presence of the waste to the School Board and included an explicit indemnification clause in the deed for the land.[106]

Despite knowledge of what was in the ground, the Niagara Falls Board of Education then built an elementary school on part of the land and sold other parts for residential development. Construction removed some of the clay cap and breached the clay walls of the waste pit. In the 1960s, residents began to complain of odors and residues, especially when water levels rose after rains.[107] The neighborhood also experienced explosions caused by the leaching of chemicals into backyards and swimming pools. Love Canal, named for its 1892 promoter, would become one of the most infamous US environmental disasters.

In the late 1970s, testing of Love Canal uncovered a witches' brew of toxic materials in the ground, in basement sump pump water, in the air in houses, and in nearby streams. About 200 families in the immediate vicinity were evacuated. Subsequent studies revealed high rates of miscarriage, birth defects, mental illness, and various diseases among Love Canal residents, especially those living in wetter parts of the development.[108] Eventually, the government agreed to evacuate a total of 950 families who lived on and around the former landfill and to clean up the site.

Love Canal and other similar sites triggered the passage of the Comprehensive Environmental Response, Compensation and Liability Act (CERCLA) of 1980 (aka "Superfund").[109] The law tasked the EPA with forcing responsible parties to pay for, perform, or reimburse the government for cleanups.[110] Love Canal residents, the state of New York, and the federal government each filed lawsuits against Occidental Petroleum, which had bought Hooker Chemical in 1968, 15 years after Hooker had sold a permitted and properly disclosed dump site to the government.

Many legal scholars argue that the main responsible parties were the school board and the City of Niagara Falls, which failed to act with due caution.[111] Furthermore, Occidental Chemical's main defense was that it would be wrong to assess Hooker's actions in the 1940s and 1950s based on what is now known about toxic chemicals. The lawyers said Hooker's disposal techniques were "state of the art" at that time.[112] "You cannot be judging the conduct of people 40 years ago—when half of them are gone and they can't explain anything—by today's standards," said Thomas H. Truitt, the company's chief lawyer.[113]

Interestingly, CERCLA seems like a retroactive or *ex post facto* law that the US Constitution expressly forbids.[114] Several court cases have examined the constitutionality of CERCLA's retroactive aspects, such as United States v. Olin (1997)[115] and United States v. Monsanto (1988).[116] The US courts skirted the debate by finding that "the statute is not a punishment but rather a reimburse obligation, meaning that the statute is not retroactive and therefore not unconstitutional."[117] The US Supreme Court, however, has ruled that the Superfund law does not override state law if a state has a statute of repose in place. Statutes of repose (which have stricter deadlines than statutes of limitation) bar legal actions against an actor after a specific time period stipulated by the state has passed.[118] As of 2015, CERCLA continues to be applied to so-called brownfield sites, which are contaminated by long-past industrial uses. In total, Occidental Petroleum paid settlements totaling $249 million.[119,120] Between 1990 and 2015, the EPA collected more than $6 billion from multiple corporations to fund ongoing and future cleanup efforts.[121]

Other laws have similar retroactive aspects, albeit with some caveats. The WEEE (Waste Electrical and Electronic Equipment Directive) of the EU makes producers in an industry individually responsible for end-of-life products made after the introduction of the directive, but collectively responsible for end-of-life products made before the introduction of the WEEE.[122] Both CERCLA and WEEE demonstrate that staying within the letter of the law does not always indemnify a company from future liabilities when impacts are discovered, or, most importantly, when future laws are enacted.

The Hebrew prophet Ezekiel argued, "The son will not bear the punishment for the father's iniquity."[123] Yet these examples show that corporations can inherit liability for damages wrought by their predecessors. Moreover, even acting within the bounds of existing laws may not indemnify a company against future liabilities. These two issues create a unique open-ended legal risk.

VULNERABILITY IS IN THE HANDS OF THE BRAND HOLDER

In March 2017, a two-liter bottle of Coca-Cola sold for $1.59 at a Stop & Shop supermarket, twice the price of the retailer's own store brand.[124] Although Coke's formulation or ingredients may justify some price premium, much of that higher price arises from the trust and goodwill that customers feel for the Coca-Cola brand. The Coke brand name contributed about $23.5 billion in revenue to the company in 2013, making the brand worth roughly $54.9 billion, according to *Forbes*.[125] *BusinessWeek* estimated that brand reputation contributes more than 50 percent of the market capitalization of Coca-Cola, Disney, Apple, McDonald's, and others.[126] Internally, many of these companies place significantly higher estimates on their brand's worth.[127] The fragility of trust and goodwill make these companies vulnerable.

Examples of companies whose value has plummeted due to consumers' loss of trust in the brand abound. On September 17, 2015, German Chancellor Angela Merkel was pictured with top Volkswagen officials at the opening of the Frankfurt auto show. The next day the US EPA issued a notice of violation to VW over emissions cheating; the company's market value dropped 45 percent in short order.[128] Although EU regulators may have rigged vehicle emissions testing conditions to favor the finances of domestic automakers over EU urban pollution levels, such use of loopholes can become a noose around the manufacturer's neck if the "cheating" generates outrage.[129]

When toy maker RC2 recalled its iconic "Thomas and Friends" train sets due to lead in the paint, its market value was cut in half. One parent wrote: "Any trust I had with your firm is gone. I do not want any replacements. I want a refund. You have endangered my children."[130]

Risky Positions: Consumer-Facing Companies

At 9:45 p.m. on April 20, 2010, a blowout preventer supplied by Cameron International failed on an underwater oil well in the Gulf of Mexico. A Halliburton employee on the rig above the well was having a coffee and cigarette break at the time instead of monitoring the well.[131] High-pressure oil and gas rose up through the pipes and exploded when it reached the drilling platform, which was owned and operated by Transocean.

The explosion killed 11 workers, injured 17, set the surrounding ocean on fire, and started an 85-day televised saga during which more than 200 million gallons[132] of oil poured into the Gulf of Mexico for the entire world to see. Oil contaminated a thousand miles of beaches, marshes, and fragile ecosystems from Texas to Florida, causing environmental damage that is not yet fully understood.[133] Fishermen, shrimpers, and tourism businesses suffered millions of dollars in lost business and community impacts.

The well was jointly owned by MOEX Offshore, Andarko Petroleum, and British Petroleum (BP). However, BP was the majority owner of the well, the overall project manager, and the most well-known company associated with the disaster because it touched consumers directly through its retail outlets. Although Deepwater Horizon was the name of Transocean's vessel, the name became synonymous with BP and this environmental disaster. It is often overlooked in this saga that BP did not blunder into the Deepwater Horizon disaster on its own.

No single decision or company caused the explosive blowout, according to an MIT analysis.[134] Transocean, for example, provided a very poorly maintained rig and a crew who chose to disable basic safety precautions. Halliburton provided shoddy guidance and later tried to hide its culpability. Cameron supplied the failed blowout preventer. BP's leaders *did* err on the side of saving time and money instead of ensuring safety.

The true environmental and economic costs of the disaster may never be known, but it clearly took a heavy toll on BP. In 2012, the company agreed to pay $4.5 billion in penalties—including $1.26 billion in criminal fees—as part of a guilty plea.[135] As a result of that plea, the US EPA banned the company from US government contracts "until the company can provide sufficient evidence to the EPA, demonstrating that it meets federal business standards."[136] BP's final settlement cost the company $18.7 billion.[137]

BP's public image may take a very long time to fully recover. Following the disaster, the company's stock price plummeted from a high of $60.57 per share five days before the explosion to a 14-year low of $27.02 two months after it. By 2014, the company's stock price still hovered in the $40s and then sunk further, to the $30s, in 2017. BP gas station owners in the United States debated whether changing the brand name would help them recover lost sales (reportedly between 10 and 40 percent).[138]

BP's suppliers, on the other hand, did not suffer the same decline in market value. Cameron, Halliburton, Transocean, MOEX Offshore, and Andarko took only short-term financial hits. In fact, Halliburton's stock climbed through the end of 2010,[139] and by October 2013, its stock had reached a price nearly 50 percent higher than its pre-disaster peak. Consumers can't directly boycott Halliburton or Transocean. Companies that operate in the business-to-business (B2B) space are "behind the scenes" and out of the public spotlight. Even more so than consumers, corporate customers make procurement decisions that are based on cost, quality, capacity, and other fundamental operational factors. The environmental practices of many B2B suppliers tend to adhere to minimum regulatory compliance and the explicit requirements of their customers, "but no more," as one B2B executive declared during a 2015 interview at MIT.

Brands Are Vulnerable and NGOs Know It

NGOs can damage the brand image of consumer-facing companies because, unlike corporate customers, consumers tend to be more emotional and more easily mobilized through popular media and activist campaigns. It is not surprising, then, that 81 percent of nearly 1,000 supply chain executives surveyed in 2014 cited brand image concerns as a motivation for investing in corporate social and environmental responsibility.[140] A key rationale for proactive action to forestall attacks is the speed with which attackers can mobilize and damage a brand before the company can react.

"In the Information Age, customers have more access to information," said Robert Grosshandler, founder of iGive.com.[141] "They're more educated. They're no longer hidden from how their food is produced or how their iPods are made. And, because of things like social media, like-minded people more easily find each other, have their say, and effect change. There's a level of transparency that wasn't there before."[142]

Such attacks also support NGOs' goals of attracting donations by targeting high-profile companies. However, for every famous Nike or Nestlé campaign that affects company behavior, there are a hundred other campaigns that most people have never heard of, few care about, and that have almost no influence on either purchasing behavior or NGO donations. This may be the reason why activist organizations, such as Greenpeace, have resorted to more sensational physical disruptions of corporate events in an effort to increase publicity. Given the capricious nature of the media, there is always the chance that some heretofore-ignored campaign could go viral and lead to widespread media attention, new regulations, or investor activism.

In Me, On Me, or Around Me?

In a 2008 talk at the Sustainable Brands Conference, Bill Morrissey, vice president of environmental sustainability at Clorox, noted that "my environment" is more important than "the environment" to consumers.[143] And within the "my environment" category, consumers might consider whether the product goes "in me," "on me," or "around me." Companies that make food products face a higher scrutiny by consumers than companies that make, say, cosmetics and personal cleaning products. This may explain, for example, the recent growth of organic and "natural" food sales in the United States, which, while still a tiny fraction of total food sales,[144] more than tripled between 2004 and 2014 to $39 billion. And "on me" product companies, in turn, are more vulnerable than companies making less-personal products such as office supplies.

Consumer perceptions related to more distant "the environment" concerns depend on empathy. NGOs know that furry animals sell environmental causes better than scaly lizards. Deforestation for the development of palm oil plantations threatens thousands of unique species of plants, insects, and animals in the Indonesian rainforests,[145] but Greenpeace chose the orangutan to personify the threat. And the symbol for the World Wildlife Fund is the lovable panda, not the endangered snail darter fish.

TO BE OR NOT TO BE (AND HOW MUCH)?

The examples in this chapter show that companies' motivations for environmental responsiveness vary. Different companies operate in different echelons of the supply chain, deal with diverse consumer segments, face disparate vulnerabilities to activist attack, and are subject to varied regulatory exposures. This book examines the role of sustainability in business, focusing on supply chain management because, as shown throughout the book, environmental sustainability is a supply chain management issue. Pricewaterhouse-Cooper's 2013 Global Supply Chain Survey found that two-thirds of supply chain executives believe that sustainability will play an increasingly important role in global supply chain management.[146] But what is that role?

Although many companies espouse sustainability as a high priority, that high priority competes with other high priorities such as quality, cost, service, innovation, and growth.

The Dark Side of the Forge

High on the Darling Escarpment in the eucalyptus forests west of Perth, layers of Australia's iconic red earth cover layers of aluminum-based minerals known as bauxite. In 1961, Alcoa signed a number of 50-year government agreements (covering more than 7,000 square kilometers) to commercialize these bauxite deposits.[147] The company then built an entire supply chain in Australia to handle the mining, refining, smelting, and processing of that aluminum. In February 2016, Alcoa celebrated mining one billion metric tons of bauxite in Western Australia. Yet that prodigious volume of production came with a significant environmental footprint extending across all phases of aluminum production.

Alcoa's Huntly Mine, the second largest in the world,[148] is a ramifying web of mining cuts and wide dusty connecting roads spanning hundreds of square kilometers.[149] Each year, Alcoa logs another 600 hectares of forest and strips away the topsoil and overburden. Then, it blasts through the cap rock layer to reach and excavate the underlying layer of bauxite. Giant dump trucks, two stories in height, carry 190-ton loads of ore to a central rock-crushing facility. Up to 1.7 tons per second of crushed ore then travel down 23.4 kilometers of conveyor belt to the refinery.

The next stop for Alcoa's bauxite is visible from space as a giant red sore on the otherwise green plains between the Darling Escarpment and the Indian Ocean. The Pinjarra Alumina Refinery mixes the raw bauxite with a hot caustic solution to chemically synthesize and extract aluminum oxide (alumina) from the ore.[150] During the multistage process, four tons of bauxite become two tons of white alumina powder that will eventually be smelted into one ton of aluminum. Millions of tons of bright red waste residue sit in vast containment fields that span a nearly 3-kilometer by 3-kilometer area. Yet alumina—which has the same molecular structure as sapphire—is not aluminum.

Metal traders jokingly call aluminum "congealed electricity." A typical aluminum smelter has row upon row of hundreds of giant pots, each with hundreds of thousands of amps of electricity coursing through an 1,800°F molten mixture of alumina and cryolite flux. The cost of all that electricity is so high that aluminum makers often find it cheaper to ship the millions of tons of alumina to sources of inexpensive power rather than to smelt the aluminum near the source of the bauxite. One of Alcoa's 50-year agreements was for coal fields in southeastern Australia near Melbourne. Alcoa built the Port Henry smelter close to these inexpensive sources of power. This included what became a strip mine for brown coal (lignite) near the seaside town of Anglesea. As Alcoa's aluminum production volumes grew, the company built a coal-fired power plant on the site of the Anglesea coal mine, which subsequently provided 40 percent of the power demand for the Port Henry smelter.

In addition to Alcoa's footprint on the lands around the bauxite mine, alumina refinery, and those associated with power production, such as the Anglesea coal, Alcoa's demand for heat, power, and vehicle fuel leads to emissions of millions of tons of greenhouse gases and other pollutants into the air. Coal, and brown coal especially, has a higher carbon footprint than most other fossil fuels. Moreover, the very high sulfur content of the Anglesea coal made the power plant the third largest sulfur emitter in Australia.[151]

Even beyond the power and transportation impacts, Alcoa cannot help emitting greenhouse gases. Even if the company switched all of its refineries, smelters, and transportation to carbon-neutral sources (including, for example, hydroelectric, geothermal, biofuels, or solar), aluminum smelting still releases more than 1.65 tons of carbon dioxide per ton of aluminum because the electrolytic process consumes the large carbon anodes needed to conduct electricity into the molten alumina mixture.[152] Moreover, chemical reactions between the carbon anodes and fluoride compounds in the cryolite create perfluorocarbons (PFCs). Although survey data suggest that many smelters produce only a fraction of a kilogram of PFCs per ton of alumina, these particular PFCs are 6,500 to 9,200 times more potent than CO_2 as a greenhouse gas.[153,154]

The Other Side of the Story

"Because we are an extractive industry, sustainability needs to be front and center on the agenda," said Kevin Anton, Alcoa's first chief sustainability officer.[155] This manifests itself in three categories of initiatives at the company. First, Alcoa has worked to improve its carbon footprint, energy efficiency, water efficiency, and PFC emissions. Some 40 percent of the cost of aluminum is electricity consumed by the smelter.[156]

Between 2005 and 2015, Alcoa improved its production efficiency by 4.2, percent, saving money and reducing the company's greenhouse gas emissions by 25.9 percent.[157] In 2011, it ran 650 initiatives to reduce energy consumption and emissions that led to cost savings of $100 million, while meeting its GHG targets. PFC emissions occur when the alumina concentration in the pot drops and the electrochemistry of the reaction shifts from making aluminum to deleterious reactions between the carbon anode and fluoride compounds in the melt. Better process control of this so-called anode effect both saves Alcoa money and reduces these emissions. All such activities, which simultaneously save money and reduce environmental impact, are known as *eco-efficiency initiatives*.

Second, in celebrating the one billion metric tons of mining milestone, Alcoa Mining President Garret Dixon said, "We're very proud of this achievement and also our decades-long, internationally recognized land rehabilitation program—one of the most critical parts of the mining process which sees jarrah forest ecosystems restored."[158] Alcoa's published timeline of mining history in Australia highlights the company's decades of evolving efforts, spanning dozens of environmental mitigations, accomplishments, and awards.[159] The company has found techniques for preparing, resculpting, and landscaping the mining pits to increase the health of newly replanted forests. It has developed a program for the seasonal timing of new mining activities and careful shifting of removed topsoil (and the native seeds it contains) from new mine sites to rehabilitate old mine sites. These activities—which mitigate environmental damage, can forestall NGO attacks, community disapproval, and regulatory restrictions—are examples of what are known as *eco-risk management initiatives*.

Third, Alcoa highlights and markets the environmental benefits of using aluminum (which has one-third the weight of steel) to its industrial customers. For example, Alcoa sells various alloys of aluminum to vehicle makers as an environmentally superior alternative to steel, because each 10 percent reduction in vehicle weight improves fuel efficiency by 8 percent.[160] The company also touts the recyclability of aluminum, which helps reduce end-of-life waste and, at the same time, amortizes Alcoa's environmental impacts of primary production across a longer multiproduct lifetime.[161] These activities, which target "green" customer segments, are known as *eco-segmentation initiatives*.

Priorities

Yet, for all Alcoa's efforts to mitigate environmental impact, the company has to make sufficient profits and grow in order to remain a viable business. And because aluminum is a global commodity, Alcoa must remain cost competitive, which means using cheap power, such as Australia's brown coal, as one element of its strategy. In the same year (2010) that Alcoa reported "green light" status on its efforts to reduce CO_2 emissions,[162] it also inked a long-term deal with an Australian power producer for low-cost brown-coal-fired electricity that shocked environmentalists. "If power stations like Loy Yang are still operating in 2036, it will be all over for the climate," said Environment Victoria campaign director (and current CEO) Mark Wakeham.[163] At the same time, Victoria Premier John Brumby commented that the deal "secures jobs for Victorians."[164] This statement exemplifies one of the deep tensions that the environmental movement faces: Industry not only provides goods that consumers depend on but also provides jobs that communities rely on.

Overall, Alcoa sees itself as one of the "good guys" and cites many sustainability-related awards, such as its 15-consecutive-year tenure on the Dow Jones Sustainability Index (DJSI) of companies recognized for corporate responsibility and sustainability.[165] The company supports the Paris climate change agreement[166] and was among 13 well-known companies (including Apple, Walmart, GM, Coca-Cola, and UPS) that signed President Barack Obama's climate pledge to tackle environmental issues in their respective industries.[167] "If the product side wasn't there, maybe we wouldn't have the right to operate," said Alcoa's Anton. "But we do make products that make the world better and help build our social license to operate."[168]

The Business Steeplechase

The Alcoa example, as well as others in this book, shows that to be viable, companies must overcome three fundamental hurdles. The first hurdle is the marketplace. Alcoa has to be competitive and attract a sufficient volume of sales among its target customers. This means offering products and services that customers would want to buy, at a price that these customers are willing to pay, with a cost structure that allows for sufficient profit.

The second hurdle is the regulatory *bright-line*, which is defined by the clearly demarcated boundary between legal and illegal actions in all the geographies in which Alcoa has suppliers, facilities, or customers. To avoid government censure, companies must comply with all the myriad rules and regulations that often cover every aspect of their businesses.

The third, but less well-defined, hurdle is maintaining a "social license to operate."[169] In other words, in addition to the written laws of the land, companies must adhere to unwritten social norms of local communities, even though such norms may be ill-defined and constantly evolving. Protests against existing operations and resistance to new facilities can come from communities, NGOs, and other activist groups, and can result in business impacts, such as lost sales, short-term limits to growth, investor resolutions, and regulations that may limit the company's opportunities in the long run.

Goldilocks and the Three Bearable Views on Sustainability

John Fojut, of the Kohl's Corporation, found that the retailer's suppliers fall into three categories of thinking about sustainability. "They either consider [sustainability] part of their core values, or they see it as something that gives them competitive advantage, or they just see it as something they have to comply with," he said.[170]

For companies with "green" core values, such as Seventh Generation, Patagonia, or Dr. Bronner's (see chapter 11), environmental sustainability and financial performance align naturally, because their target customers are willing to pay more for responsibly produced goods or, in some cases, even accept lower product performance for the cause.

In contrast, for most mainstream companies, this strategy may be "too green," because they face customers with different priorities on the balance of product cost, product performance, and environmental impacts; or they have investors who are unwilling to sacrifice financial performance for the sake of environmental performance. These companies have to balance whether and how to pursue environmental initiatives, weighing resources and management attention against many competing demands (including, for example, product innovation, employee benefits, marketing, and expansion). As a result, most of these companies focus on environmental initiatives that are aligned with their shareholders' performance goals, such as increasing profits, mitigating risks, or gaining market share.

Sustainability at Scale

Large companies such as Walmart, Unilever, Nike, IKEA, Toyota, and Starbucks face significant challenges when implementing sustainability at scale. Walmart, for example, is actively engaged in promoting sustainable fishing practices. A Stanford University report predicted the collapse of wild seafood sources by 2050 without changes in fishing practices.[171] In 2006, to ensure the sustainability of its seafood supply chain, Walmart committed that by 2011 it would purchase only seafood certified by the Marine Stewardship Council (MSC). However, Walmart soon discovered that its $750 million per year seafood business vastly exceeded the global capacity of MSC-certified seafood suppliers. Yet, the company did not want to restrict its volume of seafood sales because that would merely cede market share to other less-sustainable retailers, an outcome that would serve neither the interests of Walmart nor the fisheries.

The company compromised on its 2011 goal and bought fish from non-MSC fisheries. At the same time, the retailer encouraged these noncertified suppliers to participate in Fishery Improvement Projects (FIPs),[172] with the intent of reducing overfishing and steering those suppliers toward MSC guidelines. But progress has been slow. A *Science* study found problems in two out of three FIPs in the developing world, and yet, one of the authors of the study said, "We don't want retailers backing away from these commitments—these are positive steps."[173]

Walmart worked with The Sustainability Consortium (TSC) and invited other major seafood buyers, representatives of suppliers, environmental groups, and academics to create a set of eight principles for alternative seafood certification programs known as Responsible Fisheries Management (RFM).[174] "When the Alaskan seafood industry wanted to move away from MSC to the RFM program, we respected their right to make that decision, but [they] still needed to respect our decision to source seafood from fisheries in a sustainable way," said Jeff Rice, Walmart's senior director of sustainability. Such debates between pragmatism and ideology would have delighted Voltaire, the French philosopher, who quoted the Italian proverb *il meglio è l'inimico del bene*: "the perfect is the enemy of the good."

The Holy Grail: More Economic Growth, Less Environmental Impact

Unilever's CEO Paul Polman pledged: "Our new business model will decouple growth from environmental impact. We will double in size, but reduce our overall effect on the environment. Consumers are asking for it, but governments are incapable of delivering it. It is needed for society and it energizes our people—it reduces costs and increases innovation."[175] Whereas simple efficiency improvements call for reduced resource consumption and emissions per unit of product or per dollar of sales, real sustainable growth requires an *absolute* reduction in environmental impacts across the entire company's processes and portfolio of products while growing its business.

The dual role of businesses' supply chains in creating both economic growth (including jobs) and environmental impact highlights a fallacy in the environmental activist-touted struggle of "profits versus planet." The environmentalists' narrative ignores the role of businesses and their supply chains in both employing people and delivering improved standards of living to humanity, especially to the billions of people who have yet to enjoy the plenty that modern industry can provide.

During Walmart's efforts to buy more sustainable seafood, Greenpeace contended that Walmart was not doing enough,[176] whereas Alaskan fishermen and state officials complained that Walmart was asking too much of them.[177] Thus, the real conflict is not "profits versus planet" but rather "(some) people versus (other) people." Therein lies the challenge. Even the most environmentally responsible companies must manage their supply chains to satisfy growing demand and provide jobs in the process.

The following chapters examine how companies have addressed the many competing priorities advocated by their shareholders, employees, customers, and communities in ways that balance environmental sustainability with profitable growth. Some environmental initiatives are undertaken because they align with the economic goals of the company. Thus, eco-efficiency initiatives—those that reduce costs—are launched when their financial returns exceed the company's hurdle rate. Eco-risk initiatives—those that reduce the risk of NGO, media, community, or regulatory attacks—can be justified in the same way that other risk management and insurance costs are. Finally, eco-segmentation—those initiatives that offer new green products to market segments willing to pay for them— are justified either as growth opportunities or as real options to ensure the company is not blindsided by future demand shifts or new regulations.

Some relatively small, usually private, companies do go beyond such considerations and are dedicated to environmental sustainability, selling to a segment of the market that is willing to pay a higher price or even compromise on quality to buy a sustainable product. This book describes several of these firms because they may offer insights into the future practices of mainstream companies if that future brings tightened regulations or changes in customers' preferences.

Throughout, this book discusses the business challenges created by environmental pressures in an era of growing economic pressures rooted in both competition and uncertainty. Companies need ways to assess, select, and manage long-term investments in sustainability while also managing their growth opportunities, as well as short-term challenges, such as margin compression, revenue stagnation, political unpredictability, and countless other immediate business pressures.

2

The Structure of Supply Chains

Greenpeace's attack on Nestlé for the use of palm oil in KitKat bars highlights a nearly universal characteristic of modern business: companies' heavy reliance on long supply chains that contain vast networks of suppliers of raw materials, refined ingredients, parts, and subassemblies. The term *supply chain* refers to a figurative linear chain of companies that extract raw materials, refine them, make parts, and assemble them into finished goods that are delivered to customers or distributed to retailers' shelves where they eventually make their way into consumers' homes. It also includes a vast array of intermediaries and service providers who move and store the material as well as handle the money and information involved.

In Nestlé's case, the company buys palm oil from a distributor who buys it from a refiner who buys crude palm oil from a mill who buys palm fruit from a middleman who in turn buys it from a plantation. The plantations that potentially create the environmental impacts sit deep within the palm oil supply chains.

The image of a neat chain of companies grossly oversimplifies the actual situation. Supply chains are actually networks, branching in many directions that include the many contributing upstream suppliers of any given ingredient and the many different downstream customers that rely on that same ingredient. For example, 40 percent of the palm oil in Indonesia comes from small farms.[1] Hundreds of thousands of palm fruit producers of all sizes send truckloads of palm fruit to palm oil mills that extract both the reddish palm fruit oil and the pale yellow palm kernel oil. Next, palm oil refineries remove impurities (degumming, bleaching, and deodorizing) and separate the different fatty acid components in the raw oil for various applications. The Palm Oil Refiners Association of Malaysia defines 14 different standardized palm oil products.[2] The various refined palm oil products then go to ingredient makers that produce edible oils and fats, saponified oils for soap, esterified oils for biodiesel, and dozens of other derivative products.

At each stage, middlemen might aggregate and mix sources of supply, accumulate inventories awaiting buyers, sell portions of their stocks, or transport bulk quantities to remote points of demand. Incoming oil flows into huge bulk tanks, commingling with prior batches before being sent to the next tier. With each stage, the location of the original palm oil plantation becomes less and less traceable, as oil from many plantations mixes together. By the time palm oil reaches Nestlé, almost any palm oil plantation in the world may have contributed to that particular batch. The complexity of the palm oil supply chain was a key reason Nestlé had trouble responding effectively to Greenpeace's attack.

Moreover, the KitKat product alone has 15 ingredients on the label,[3] which means Nestle has many distinct supply chains that provide chocolate, wheat flour, milk and milk by-products, vegetable fats, and other trace ingredients. Additionally, the vegetable fat in a KitKat might include any of seven different kinds of fat: palm kernel, palm fruit, shea, illipe, mango kernel, kokum gurgi, or sal. Even the plastic wrappers and cardboard boxes used for packaging the snack come from respective supply chains that trace back to oil wells and forests.

Almost every product has a complex interlinked *supply network* of contributing companies that spans the miners, growers, suppliers, manufacturing plants, transportation, warehouses, distribution, retailers, and the myriad supporting companies involved in the design, procurement, manufacturing, storing, shipping, selling, tracking, payments, customs, and servicing of goods. Many other raw materials (e.g., fossil fuels, wood products, conflict minerals, natural fibers, grains, tea, coffee, and cocoa) are aggregated from many sources as they are bought, processed, and sold on world markets. In the case of soap makers, the supply chain is even more opaque. Sodium lauryl sulfate, a common cleansing ingredient in soap as well as shampoo and toothpaste, can be made from palm kernel oil, coconut oil, petroleum, or a range of other oils.[4] Thus, buyers of this and similar ingredients may not even know whether the material was made from highly contentious palm oil, less contentious coconut oil, high-carbon-footprint petroleum, or another oil entirely.

Despite the oversimplification, the notion of a supply chain helps businesses think about management and sustainability in two ways. First, it reflects the general progression from raw materials to finished goods that occurs with accumulating environmental footprints and impacts along the chain, as more is done to the materials by more people in more places. Second, it highlights the idea of suppliers being a source of material and parts for manufacturers who make products and deliver them to their customers. At that level, the network is like a chain in that suppliers may have further suppliers up the chain and customers may have further customers down the chain. (The view of suppliers "upstream" and customers "downstream" is rooted in the riverlike direction of the flow of material, parts, and goods.) Each of these tiers of companies in the chain contributes to the total environmental impact of the product or service delivered to the final consumer.

To help firms design their internal business processes across different products, geographies, and networks, the Supply Chain Council (SCC) developed the Supply Chain Operations Reference (SCOR) model. The model, on its 11th version in 2013, classifies activities within each supply chain into one of six distinct high level (or "level-1") processes: *Plan, Source, Make, Deliver, Return,* and *Enable.*[5,6] *Plan* and *Enable* cover all the tasks of managing the business and the other four high-level processes. *Source* refers to the processes of procuring materials and parts from the upstream supply chain that go into the finished product. *Make* is the manufacturing process of converting sourced materials into finished goods. *Deliver* covers the downstream supply chain activities of warehousing, distribution, and transportation that fulfill customer orders. *Return* includes processes for handling defective products, repairs, and unwanted products.

MAKING A PRODUCT, MAKING AN IMPACT

Much of the environmental impact of any product depends both on *what* it is made of, and on *how* it is made. The "Make" process is the step in which a product's constituent parts are converted into finished goods via a series of manufacturing operations.

Exploding the BOM

Imagine a small, toy wind turbine—the child's version of the massive winds turbines such as those built by Siemens that are sprouting across the landscapes in many countries. The first step in understanding the environmental impact of making this toy is to analyze its bill of materials (BOM), which lists all the parts and the quantities of those parts required to manufacture a unit of the product. The BOM also includes information about how the parts relate to each other in terms of assemblies and subassemblies. Figure 2.1 depicts a 15-step process map with the 15 numbered parts listed in the toy's BOM and the respective manufacturing processes required to make the toy. Each part in the BOM is made using material, energy, and water; the process may also involve waste and emissions, thus accruing environmental impacts. A company's own manufacturing processes that make and assemble parts into a finished product will add to the total impacts accumulated along the supply chain.

This toy wind turbine has three major assemblies: the blade assembly, the nacelle assembly (the top portion that connects the tower to the blades), and the tower assembly. Workers start by making the three wooden blades (Part 1), which they first cut to the right size (Process 1) and then shape (Process 2) into shell molds (Part 2). They mold the rotor hub (Part 3) and combine the hub, blades, and shaft (Part 4) to make the blade assembly. A second group of workers creates the nacelle assembly by forming the plastic gearbox (Part 5), drilling mounting holes in the generator (Part 6), and attaching the parts together. They then combine the blade assembly and nacelle (Part 7) to create the upper housing assembly (Part 8).

A.

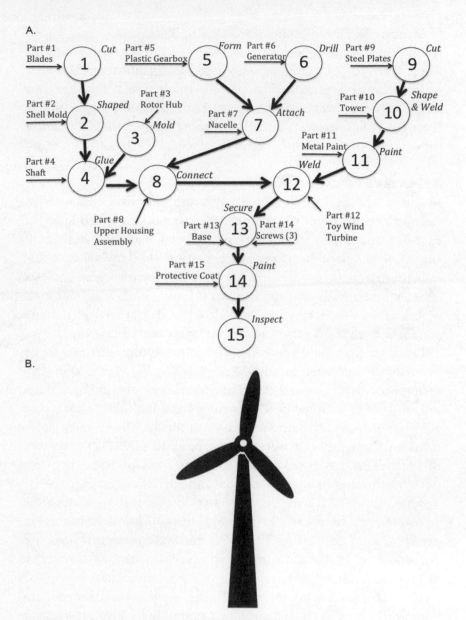

B.

Figure 2.1
Toy wind turbine and its bill of materials

Meanwhile, a third group of workers builds the tiny tower for the toy by cutting steel plates (Part 9), welding them together into the tower (Part 10), and applying a coat of metal paint (Part 11). They weld the upper housing to the top of the tower to make the toy (Part 12). Finally, they use three screws (Part 14) to secure the toy to its base (Part 13). A final protective coating of more paint (Part 15) produces the completed toy, which inspectors then check for quality.

Indirect Materials and Impacts

In theory, the BOM lists all the parts and materials bought from suppliers or made within the factory that go into a product. Yet BOMs actually leave out many of the incidental materials consumed or handled during the process of making a product. These indirect materials include an array of manufacturing consumables such as lubricants, solvents, cleansers, filters, and other materials that lurk in the factory's supply closet and are used in making products, even if the products are not made from these supplies.

From an environmental perspective, the two biggest categories of materials not listed in a BOM are energy and water. Manufacturing processes consume electricity for machinery, lighting, heating, and cooling. Some processes may consume fuels, such as the acetylene gas used to flame-cut the wind turbine tower parts, natural gas to generate hot water, or propane to power the factory's forklifts. The factory might use many gallons of water to wash parts, chemically treat parts, or cool industrial processes.

Thus, the BOM gives only a partial basis for calculating the environmental impacts of manufacturing. Although it implicitly specifies a unit of output of the finished product, it does not document other manufacturing outputs. Each item of the BOM, as well as indirect materials, might come with greenhouse gas (GHG) emissions, wastewater, and other by-products. Some manufacturing steps, such as painting or gluing, may give off toxic or smog-inducing vapors.

Did You Make It from Scratch?

In the 1920s, Ford's River Rouge plant was famous for owning and managing the entire car-making process. Raw materials straight from the earth went in one end of the sprawling factory complex, and finished automobiles rolled out the other end. The company owned iron mines, limestone quarries, coal mines, rubber plantations, and forests. Ford owned a fleet of barges and a railroad to ship materials from its mines to its plant. The company brought its iron ore, limestone, and coal to River Rouge to smelt into its own iron and steel. Ford brought sand to make glass and raw rubber to make tires. Ford even had its own electrical power plant on site to supply the factory and its 100,000 workers. Ford's 1920s strategy is known as *vertical integration*, in which a company strives to own many or all of the stages of production (and sometimes logistics and other services) throughout its supply chain. Had the environment been a concern when River Rouge was in operation, Ford could have documented the impacts of its entire process, including the 5,500 tons of coal burned every day, or the 538 million gallons of water used each day.[7,8,9]

The opposite of vertical integration is *outsourcing*—the use of outside suppliers for component items and services, even those the company had previously made and had the assets and know-how to make. Although Ford's goal with River Rouge was self-sufficiency, the factory still depended on no fewer than 6,000 outside suppliers for many specialized materials, components, and supplies.[10] Ford sometimes outsourced to supplement its own capacity. For example, Ford pioneered the use of soybeans in industrial products: By 1935, 60 pounds of soybeans went into the paint and molded plastic of each Ford car. The company eventually owned 60,000 acres of soybean farms, but these farms could supply only a fraction of all the soybeans needed. Thus, Ford bought the bulk of this raw material from outside growers.[11]

Over the decades, Ford moved away from vertical integration, outsourcing more and more production of raw materials and intermediate parts to outside suppliers. The biggest reason for outsourcing is to get the most competitive components and materials possible from specialized suppliers with economies of scale and special know-how in their respective industries. For example, carmakers spun off their internal parts-making divisions, such as Ford's Visteon and GM's Delphi, with the intention that these divisions would become more competitive and have better scale if they were exposed to market forces and sold parts to other companies.

By the dawn of the 21st century, outsourcing had become the norm as most companies focused on their "core competencies" and outsourced other functions. Still, some companies outsource less than others. For example, Samsung makes many of the parts—such as processors, memory chips, camera chips, and displays[12]—for the televisions, smartphones, and computer products it assembles. Cisco, by contrast, makes none of the parts that go into its many products. In fact, Cisco, and many other technology firms, such as Apple and Microsoft, as well as apparel companies such as Christian Dior and Nike, outsource virtually 100 percent of their manufacturing and then buy the finished goods in retail packaging from contract manufacturers. These highly outsourced companies typically only handle the design, marketing, sales, and supply chain management of their products.

Outsourcing brings the advantage of greater flexibility in choosing suppliers to meet changing volume and technology requirements, but also a disadvantage in that companies have lower visibility into, and control over, the processes deployed by those suppliers (and, in turn, their suppliers). The environmental impacts of *outsourced* manufacturing lie in the hands of suppliers.

The traditional criteria that most companies use in choosing suppliers include: (i) the quality of the part, materials, or services and the supplier's commitment to innovation; (ii) the full ("landed") cost of the items or service; (iii) the supplier's capacity to serve the volume required by the company; and (iv) the lead time for the order and the supplier's responsiveness.

As shown in chapter 1, however, a supplier's deficient environmental practices can negatively impact a company. Consequently, companies have begun to assess the environmental practices of suppliers or prohibit particular practices (see chapter 5). Yet, managing the environmental impacts of suppliers can be challenging as the suppliers, in turn, have their own suppliers, and those have their own suppliers, and so on up the chain. In many cases—and not only for high-tech brand names—the lion's share of a product's environmental impacts take place deep within the supply chain at the mines, farms, and oil fields that produce raw materials.

CONSIDER THE SOURCE

Unless the wind turbine toy maker is vertically integrated, each of the toy's parts will have come from one or more suppliers with respective environmental impacts. For example, the wood for the blades may have come from a sustainable tree farm or from an illegal clear-cut of old-growth forest. The steel for the tower may be recycled steel (low-impact) or virgin steel made from iron ore (high-impact). As these suppliers perform their own source, make, and deliver processes on their parts, they incur environmental impacts that accrue to the final product. Some suppliers might be in regions powered by coal-fired generators while others might rely on hydroelectric power, thereby affecting the carbon footprint of the electricity used by the supplier. Suppliers' physical locations may also affect land-use patterns, water availability, and legal regimes.

Multi-tier Supplier Networks
In contrast to the simple toy wind turbine with its 15 parts, a full-sized Siemens AG wind-turbine contains more than 8,000 parts[13] coming from manufacturers in at least six distinct industries operating in 177 countries.[14] Construction of the Siemens' turbine blades alone requires 50 to 60 suppliers and four or five principal steps.[15] Wind turbine manufacturing relies on supply chains that deliver a wide range of metals, polymers, and other materials, as well as electromechanical, electrical, semiconductor, and other types of parts. The turbines even contain agricultural products: plantation-grown balsa wood forms the lightweight core of each of the massive blades.

The 400 suppliers that ship parts directly to Siemens' wind turbine division are known as Tier 1 suppliers. Siemens selects all of its Tier 1 suppliers and negotiates contracts with them. These contracts formalize the delivered component's specifications, delivery terms, invoicing and payment terms, penalties, intellectual property provisions, reporting obligations, codes of conduct, and so on.

Tier 1 suppliers are often large- or medium-size organizations themselves. For example, one of Siemens' Tier 1 suppliers is Weidmüller, a 160-year old company that produces and sells €630 million of electrical and electronics components each year.[16] Weidmüller alone delivers more than three billion parts every year to its 24,000 customers, including Siemens. The supplier operates seven production sites with 4,600 employees around the world.[17]

Each of Weidmüller's parts has its own BOM, too. Like Siemens, Weidmüller also has a network of Tier 1 suppliers, with contracts specifying product and quality specifications, payment terms, intellectual property, and codes of conduct. Weidmüller's Tier 1 suppliers are referred to as "Tier 2" suppliers of Siemens, indicating the greater commercial distance between Siemens' and Weidmüller's direct suppliers. In the case of Siemens' wind turbines, the 400 Tier 1 suppliers have 3,000 suppliers who are Tier 2 to Siemens.[18] Direct suppliers to Siemens' Tier 2 suppliers are Tier 3 suppliers of Siemens. For products as complex as a Siemens wind turbine, there may be Tier 4, Tier 5, Tier 6 suppliers and even further, before reaching basic raw materials extracted from mines, oil wells, farms, and oceans. As the supply chain distance extends from the original equipment maker to the deeper tiers of suppliers, companies typically do not even know the identity of these deep-tier suppliers or the country of origin of the raw materials.

Moreover, Siemens also produces many other products, ranging from factory automation, building technology and medical devices to consumer products. In total, the company employs 370,000 people and does business in 190 countries around the world.[19] Its multiple supply chains across all its products span more than 90,000 Tier 1 suppliers and countless deep-tier suppliers.[20]

As companies, product offerings, and BOMs grow in size and complexity, it is not uncommon for a supplier to be both a Tier 1 and a Tier 2 supplier for the same manufacturer, sometimes unbeknownst to both of them. In addition, large companies in the same industry often buy from and sell to each other, serving as both supplier and customer to each other. For example, Siemens might buy industrial products from a supplier whose factory uses Siemens' factory-automation products. These hidden deep supply chain relationships typically cause no problems until disaster strikes.

Tears in the Deep Tiers

On April 24, 2013, horrific images saturated news outlets as more than 1,100 bodies were pulled from the collapsed eight-story Rana Plaza garment factory in Bangladesh.[21] Muhammad Yunus, the Bangladeshi Nobel laureate, wrote that the disaster was "a symbol of our failure as a nation."[22] Rana Plaza was not an isolated incident. Six months before this disaster, a fire at a different Bangladeshi garment factory, which was owned by Tazreen Fashions, killed 112 workers.[23] Such events in Bangladesh put a tragic human face on the repugnant conditions deep within some companies' outsourced global supply chains.

Paralleling the gruesome search for bodies buried under the rubble of Rana Plaza was the search for the Western companies behind the orders for the garments made in the collapsed factory. Most companies denied using suppliers who were operating in the structurally unsound building where employees were forced to work even after large cracks had appeared in the walls the previous day. Despite those denials, recovery workers found apparel in the rubble that had been ordered by many major retailers, including J. C. Penney and Walmart.

J. C. Penney, for its part, claimed that the company had no direct connection to any of the building's tenants. Yet Daphne Avila, a J. C. Penney spokeswoman, admitted the company did not "have visibility into our national brand partners' supplier bases," and that problem prevented the retailer from knowing more about where the clothes were being made. "This is something that we're actively working on," she added.[24]

In contrast, Walmart believed it had visibility and control over its supply chain. Walmart had fired Canadian jeans supplier Fame Jeans after it uncovered evidence that the supplier had ordered pants from one of the Rana Plaza factories in 2012, in violation of Walmart's policies. A Walmart spokesperson said, "This supplier, Fame Jeans, had told us there was no previous production at Rana Plaza ... our suppliers have a binding obligation to disclose

all factories producing Walmart merchandise."[25] Similarly, in the
case of the Tazreen factory fire, Walmart had banned Tazreen
Fashions from its approved supplier list after auditors hired by
Walmart inspected the factory and declared Tazreen to be "high
risk."[26] However, one of Walmart's other authorized suppliers sub-
contracted with *another* authorized supplier and then that sub-
contractor shifted the work to Tazreen.[27] Walmart terminated its
relationships with that supplier, too. Ultimately, name-brand companies such as Benetton, Mango, Bonmarché, Primark, The Children's Place, and others acknowledged their current or past use
of the suppliers operating in the collapsed structure.[28] Nor was
worker safety the only social concern in Bangladesh. When Pope
Francis learned that Bangladesh's minimum wage was only $40
per month, he said, "This is called slave labor."[29]

The Hidden Ingredients of Disaster

In mid-2007, in the wake of recalls hitting another toy maker, regulators lauded Mattel Inc.'s supplier control. "There are companies
that live up to their obligations to the government as well as to
consumers, and they are one of them," said the US government's
Consumer Product Safety Commission spokeswomen Julie Vallese
in reference to Mattel.[30] But even if a company takes steps to control deep-tier suppliers, supply chains are dynamic in nature, putting compliance at risk.

In early July 2007, testing by a European retailer revealed prohibited levels of lead in the paint and coatings on some Mattel toys.
Mattel immediately halted production of the toys, investigated the
cause, confirmed the problem, and announced a recall of nearly
one million toys of 83 different types in early August 2007.[31] Subsequent testing found other lead-contaminated toys, which forced
Mattel to recall another million toys that autumn.[32] The company
also paid a $2.3 million fine for violating federal bans on lead
paint.[33] More importantly, the incident tainted the brand in the
eyes of consumers and the media, causing a 25 percent drop in the
value of its stock during the worst of the recall incident.[34]

The fault occurred deep in Mattel's supply chain. A long-time
paint supplier to the company's Chinese contract manufacturer had

run short of the paint's colorants, quickly found a backup supplier via the Internet, and used that unauthorized source based on fraudulent certifications that the colorant was lead-free. The paint supplier did not test the new colorant because testing would have delayed production. Workers, however, noted that the new paint smelled different from the usual formulation.[35] "This is a vendor plant with whom we've worked for 15 years; this isn't somebody that just started making toys for us," Robert A. Eckert, CEO of Mattel, said in an interview. "They understand our regulations, they understand our program, and something went wrong. That hurts."[36]

How Toxic Taters Spoiled the Milk

The deep and interlinked structure of supply chains can lead to widespread contamination incidents. In October 2004, a routine test of the milk at a Dutch farm revealed high levels of dioxin, a dangerous and tightly regulated chemical. Dioxin is considered so toxic that a single gram of it is sufficient to contaminate 14 million liters of milk above EU safety limits.[37]

Initially, the authorities suspected a faulty furnace to be the cause—fire can create these substances—but further investigation finally uncovered the true, distant cause: the cow feed.[38] Specifically, the investigation revealed that in August 2004, McCain Food Limited's potato processing plant in Holland had received a load of marly clay from a German clay mine. Unbeknownst to both the clay company and the potato processing company, the clay had been contaminated with dioxin, which can occur naturally in some kinds of clay. McCain's plant made a watery slurry with the clay and used it to separate low-quality potatoes (which float in the muddy mixture) from denser, high-quality potatoes. Ironically, the reason McCain began using clay in the separation process was that a previous salt-water process had been outlawed for environmental reasons.[39] Fortunately, the dioxin did not contaminate the processed potatoes, which were used to make French fries and other snacks. Unfortunately, the dioxin did contaminate the potato peels that were converted into animal feed.

If most companies have many suppliers, most suppliers have many customers, too. Auspiciously, the EU's food traceability rules

include a "one step forward and one step back" provision for all
human food and animal feed companies.[40] Authorities traced the
contaminated peels to animal food processors in the Netherlands,
Belgium, France, and Germany, and then traced the tainted feed
to more than 200 farms.[41] Rapid detection and tracing in both
directions prevented any dioxin-tainted milk from reaching consumers.[42] Yet detecting the contamination after the fact was cold
comfort to the farmers who were forced to destroy milk or animals.

Location, Location, Location

Many agricultural commodities such as palm oil, bananas, coffee,
and cocoa grow only under specific conditions in a limited number
of countries. Other agricultural commodities (e.g., grains, soybeans, cotton, livestock, and wood) may have a broader geographic
range but still depend on adequate local water and fertilizers. Similarly, many economically important minerals, such as rare earths,
platinum group metals, tantalum, and graphite can be found only
in a limited number of sites.[43] Many of these regions face intense
social and economic tensions between preserving land for wildlife
and biodiversity on the one hand, or developing the land for production, such as agriculture or mining, on the other. Thus, the starting points of many supply chains—the raw materials producers—are
strongly tied to geography.

In contrast, businesses downstream in the supply chain have
more freedom to choose geographic locations for manufacturing
and distribution operations. Companies may choose to locate production facilities close to raw material supplies (e.g., a smelter near
a mine); close to sources of labor (e.g., low-cost or high-skill
regions); close to centers of demand (e.g., major population centers); in an industrial cluster location (close to other similar manufacturers); or in a location influenced by government (e.g., owing
to incentives and regulations). Although companies make these
decisions on either economic grounds (e.g., costs of land, labor,
local materials, and transportation) or strategic grounds (e.g., to
open new markets or create economies of scale), the decisions also
have environmental effects.

Countries vary widely in their base level of environmental
stewardship, which can reflect well or poorly on companies with

operations or suppliers in those countries. The Environmental Performance Index[44] is an independent measure of environmental sustainability at the country level. It was created by the Yale Center for Environmental Law & Policy and Columbia University's Center for International Earth Science Information Network, in collaboration with the World Economic Forum. The index measures both protection of human health and protection of the ecosystem. The former considers measurable health impacts, air quality, water cleanliness, and sanitation. The latter considers impacts on carbon footprint, agriculture, forests, water, fisheries, and biodiversity.[45] The 20 index indicators include both regulatory factors (e.g., pesticide regulations and habitat protection) and environmental outcomes (e.g., changes in forest cover and air quality). The index organizers rank countries and provide 10-year trend data. The 2016 report[46] ranked Finland first, followed by Iceland and Sweden, with the United States checking in at 26th place, Germany in 30th, and China lagging behind in 109th place.

DELIVERY: THE FOOTPRINTS OF A JOURNEY

A single part, such as the 75-meter-long blade of a Siemens wind turbine, can travel thousands or even tens of thousands of miles on its journey from raw materials to installation. The blades begin as 15- to 30-meter-tall balsa trees in Ecuador, planted four to six years in advance.[47] After the trees are cut, the lumber is processed in several steps. It must be cut, grooved, tiled, assembled into a blade shape, and then coated with layers of plastic netting. Eventually, it arrives at one of Siemens' four blade facilities in Europe, India, or Thailand. The semi-finished blade may make an additional trip to Spain, Finland, or the United States, depending on the final customer location, manufacturing capacity, and project timeline. Finally, the finished blade is transported to the installation site, which could be almost anywhere in the world.

Whereas the early parts of the journey can utilize standard trucks, rail cars, and shipping containers, the last steps of the journey rely on more specialized transportation. Each installation-ready blade can stretch as long as 75 meters (246 feet).[48] The loading, unloading, and transporting of individual blades is a logistical challenge that requires cranes, heavy tools, and specialized trucks that test the limits of road-based transport.[49] On every step of the journey, fuel goes into a tank, is burned in an engine, and GHGs and other emissions come out of an exhaust pipe.

Rudolph the Red-Nosed GHG Emitter

In the rush before Christmas, a toymaker might experience a surge in demand if its model wind turbine becomes the season's must-have toy. These last-minute orders mean the toymaker must suddenly order more parts from suppliers, get those parts, make more toys, and ship the toys to stores before the holiday. If the toymaker and its suppliers get enough warning, they can use ocean freight or rail transportation to deliver their wares efficiently around the world or across the country. Last-minute orders, however, provoke a flurry of warehousing and transportation activities. If time is short, the toymaker will switch to air freight when the toys "absolutely, positively have to get there overnight" (as the FedEx motto declares).

The rapidly declining costs of communications and the growing efficiency of logistics are enabling global trade and long supply chains. Overall, trade-related freight transportation accounts for more than 7 percent of all GHG emissions worldwide.[50] However, the total amount of transportation may be less indicative of environmental impact than *how* goods are transported. For example, air-freight emits more than 100 times the GHGs (in grams per ton-mile) than ocean freight.[51] The same amount of fuel needed to fly 150 tons of airfreight 5,000 miles at 570 mph can push 48,000 tons of ocean freight that same distance on a modern vessel at 22 mph.[52]

Backhaul: The Heavy Footprint of Empty Miles

Although it's easy to tally the fuel burned by a vehicle making a delivery, this may represent only half the footprint because of the need to reposition the conveyance. If a truck makes a trip from a supplier to a manufacturer fully loaded but then drives back to the supplier empty, the total footprint is almost double that of the one-way journey due to these "empty miles." Companies can reduce both the cost and footprint of a delivery by finding what is called a "backhaul load," in which the vehicle returns to its origin or another pickup point while carrying revenue-paying cargo. In that case, the emissions of the backhaul will be counted as part of the backhaul shipment.

The overall pattern of freight flows makes empty miles almost unavoidable. In most cases, more tons of materials are shipped *from* mines and farms than *to* mines and farms. Similarly, at most retail locations, trucks arrive full of goods and depart empty. Furthermore, in some cases the total weight of the flow in and out of a certain region is balanced but the modes used are not. For example, although most products are delivered to southern Florida by truck, most northbound freight from Florida (be it Florida's agricultural products or imports coming from the Port of Miami) move by rail. The result is empty miles for trucks returning north and empty container movements on the rails going south. Chapter 7 delves into this issue in further detail.

Movements of Money and Information

At the same time that materials flow down the supply chain, money generally flows up the chain when consumers pay the retailer, the retailer pays the distributor, the distributor pays the manufacturer, the manufacturer pays its suppliers, and so on through to the factory workers, farmers, or miners. This money flow—and its equitability and consistency—contribute to the welfare of the workers and communities at the heart of all supply chains. The Fair Trade movement seeks to ensure that all workers, especially those in developing countries, share in the bounty of the modern global economy.[53] The movement advocates for improved social and environmental standards through higher payments to workers and farmers for their labor and produce.

Another key supply chain flow is information in the form of forecasts, purchase orders, shipping notices, invoices, and other business and operational data. Information flows in both directions to coordinate activities across the supply chain. As shown in chapters 3, 5, and 9, these information flows play a major role in measuring and managing environmental sustainability.

Supply chain managers typically strive for both operational and strategic visibility. *Operational visibility* includes knowing where parts and products are as they move through the supply chain or wait as inventory in warehouses. Managers use these data to detect operational problems, manage the execution of plans, and handle supply and demand fluctuations. *Strategic visibility* includes knowledge of the multiyear capacity and technology road maps of the supply base. It is used to make long-term product, service, and supply network choices. Sustainability, in contrast, calls for *environmental visibility*—understanding all the suppliers, including deep-tier ones, who are involved in providing the goods and services required to make a product—as well as the environmental impacts of these supplied products and services. Companies use environmental visibility to assess (see chapter 3) and manage impacts. Environmental visibility also enables *transparency*, which is the ability to show outsiders—including downstream companies, certification bodies, NGOs, governments, sustainability-minded consumers, and investors—how the company is managing environmental impacts and risks. Transparency means that companies and consumers can access relevant information throughout the supply chain and know *who* makes and handles products and parts and *how* they are made, stored, transported, and handled.

CONSUMERS AND BEYOND

Even the most fuel-efficient cars can emit more than three times the carbon during their driving lifetime after they leave the factory than what was emitted during the manufacture of those cars.[54] Many types of products have significant environmental impacts during the *use phase* of their lives. The use phase consists of all the customer's activities and processes associated with the use of a company's products and services. The most obvious of these are energy-consuming products such as vehicles, appliances, HVAC (heating, ventilation, and cooling) equipment, and computers. Less obvious are products, such as shampoos, detergents, and cleansers that involve the use of hot water and consume both energy and water, as well as contaminate that water with additives. Chapter 8 discusses this in more detail.

Labels on many household products (such as paints, adhesives, and powerful cleansers) warn, "Use in a Well-Ventilated Area." The same ingredients that enable the high performance of these products may also pollute the air and harm the user through volatile and corrosive chemical gases. Analogous warnings cover accidental ingestion or contact with the skin and eyes.

The SCOR model of supply chains focuses on activities within a company's direct control, such as the sourcing, making, and delivering of a wind turbine, car, or shampoo. As such, this model lacks an important component that is crucial to assessing and managing sustainability: the use phase. Although these seem "out of scope" for SCOR, they do have an environmental impact, and the company that makes these products can affect that impact through the design and servicing of its products, as well as through messaging and marketing activities.[55]

Maintenance: Repair and Service Supply Chains

Maintenance is one reason why Siemens' role—and its environmental impacts—does not end with the final installation of the wind turbine. Siemens may issue a 5-year warranty for the turbine or agree to a 10- or 15-year service contract. To fulfill the warranties and service contracts, many parts must be readily available to repair a malfunctioning or damaged turbine. In 2013, Dr. Arnd Hirschberg, Siemens' supply chain manager for wind turbines, estimated that about 9,000 of Siemens' 2.3-megawatt turbines were in service around the globe, and parts were stocked to service each of them.[56] The company keeps as many as 25,000 different parts to service various wind turbine models, stocking as many as 1,500 units per part. Manufacturing, storing, and moving these parts is also part of the challenge of supply chain management and of calculating the wind turbine's carbon footprint: Full environmental assessment requires the mapping of hundreds of additional steps across the supply chain after the product has been delivered.

Interestingly, some companies have changed their business models from selling products to "servicizing" their offerings.[57] Instead of selling a product to the customer, the company provides the product's function as a service. For example, Michelin offers trucking companies a "pay by the mile" service for tires.[58] In other words, a trucking company may buy 100,000 miles worth of tire usage for a truck. Michelin goes beyond just delivering the tires: It also installs, maintains, replaces, and recycles the tires, guaranteeing that the tires will always be in good working order. Such an arrangement provides more business to Michelin and, at the same time, reduces the transportation company's business risk by turning fixed costs into variable costs. This business model also reduces the environmental footprint of trucking because good, correctly inflated tires—kept in optimal conditions by the tire manufacturer—have a longer life and less rolling resistance, leading to lower fuel consumption and fewer tire replacements.

Such arrangements improve the alignment between manufacturers and customers because manufacturers have strong incentives to build reliable products (leading to the environmental benefits of fewer product replacements), as well as incur less maintenance. Companies that have turned to such a business model include Xerox, through its managed print services,[59] Rolls Royce aircraft engines through its TotalCare solution,[60] and many others.[61]

Returns: The Reverse Supply Chain

In the SCOR model, the *return* process is the final operational step for the company and includes procedures for identifying malfunctioning products, deciding on the disposition of packaging, authorizing and scheduling product returns, scheduling return receipts, receiving the returns, disposing of the returns, and verifying and paying all parties involved. These processes require "reverse logistics"—the movement of goods in the opposite direction of the usual supplier–manufacturer–retailer–consumer chain.

The legal and environmental principle of extended producer responsibility (EPR)[62] potentially expands the volume of companies' returns processes. Under this principle, the manufacturer of a product has the social, and sometimes legal, duty to handle the disposal of all the products it makes, in perpetuity. EPR directives in the EU, for example, cover packaging, batteries, vehicles, and electrical and electronic equipment.

The returns process includes more than just the movement of goods from the consumer back to the company or to the company's hired vendor for managing end-of-life products. It also leads to new Source, Make, and Deliver activities if the company refurbishes and resells the used yet usable product, or deconstructs the product to extract valuable (or hazardous) materials, which are then recycled, detoxified, or disposed of in some sustainable way. Chapter 7 delves into these reverse supply chain management activities.

PLANNING AND MANAGING SUPPLY CHAINS

The four operational supply chain processes in the SCOR model are *Source*, *Make*, *Deliver*, and *Return*. The *Plan* and *Enable* processes, by themselves, have a negligible direct environmental impact, but these processes can be the most important levers in terms of the sustainability of many supply chains. Planning and enabling manage the performance of operational processes that consume resources and impact the environment.

These planning processes include decisions on how a product should be sourced, made, delivered, and returned. This means choosing the design, materials, and features of a manufactured good; identifying suppliers and service providers; and communicating expectations. The *enable* process includes the establishment of business rules, performance indicators, inventory policies, regulatory compliance processes, and risk assessment, to align with the business's strategic plans. It determines the general structure of the supply chain in terms of geography, markets, transportation, and distribution strategies.

Five Supply Chain Business Performance Attributes
In addition to the processes, the SCOR model recognizes five high-level performance attributes: cost, asset utilization, responsiveness, reliability, and agility.[63] The first two are internal-facing, whereas the last three are customer-facing metrics.

Discount retailers, such as Walmart, emphasize everyday low prices through *cost efficiency*. To achieve it, the company minimizes its variable costs and ensures that its sourcing, delivery, store operations, and all other supply chain-related activities are performed efficiently. Other companies emphasize *asset utilization*. For example, discount airlines also emphasize low cost but do so by maximizing utilization of their expensive assets—their aircraft. They use low prices to ensure high passenger loads, and they emphasize quick turnaround to maximize the aircraft's revenue-earning time (minimizing time spent on the tarmac). Many manufacturers use lean or just-in-time principles, modeled on the Toyota Production System, by working to minimize their inventories, thereby reducing the capital tied up in that inventory.

The last three metrics are customer-facing and measure various dimensions of service. First, *responsiveness* measures the time-dimension of service—how quickly the company can produce and deliver a customer's order. Amazon, for example, is pushing the boundaries of consumer responsiveness with one-hour delivery services in some cities by positioning inventory near population centers and working with urban delivery and courier services (in addition to using its own vehicles).[64] Similarly, fast food outlets often prepare food items before receiving an order, in anticipation of customers' requests so they can quickly serve made-to-order meals when customers arrive.

Second, *reliability* measures the certainty of products and delivery. Makers of lifesaving medical products have intensive quality control processes, often hold large amounts of inventory, and ensure on-time deliveries so that no patient ever goes without essential care or receives an incorrect or defective item.

Third, *flexibility* measures a company's ability to handle large changes in the volume or variety of products. It follows Leon C. Megginson's quote paraphrasing Charles Darwin: "It is not the strongest of the species that survives, nor the most intelligent. It is the one that is most adaptable to change."[65] Such companies often avoid owning inventory or assets that could become obsolete or could constrain the company's ability to serve volatile demand. Instead, these companies cultivate a varied portfolio of outsourcing partners who can produce as little or as much as the company needs.

Supply Chain Environmental Impact Metrics

Managing sustainability requires additional supply chain metrics to account for environmental impacts within and beyond the enterprise itself, namely the impacts of supply chain operations, including the use and disposal of the product. To this end, many companies measure, manage, and report improvements in various types of environmental impacts as part of, or in addition to, measuring and reporting financial metrics.

In support of these efforts, the 11th version of the SCOR model[66] includes "GreenSCOR" under its "Special Applications" section. GreenSCOR comprises a set of environmental metrics that can be measured at subprocess levels and aggregated into the model's plan-source-make-deliver-return-enable framework. GreenSCOR accounts for the carbon footprint, emissions, and recycling associated with each of its level 1 processes by using metrics for:[67]

- Carbon emissions (tons of CO_2e)
- Air pollutant emissions (tons, by pollutant)
- Liquid waste generated (gallons)
- Solid waste generated (tons)
- Recycled waste (percentage of all waste).

GreenSCOR's metrics, however, only measure one side of environmental impact; they only account for the environmentally impactful *outputs* of supply chain processes. The version of Green-SCOR in the 11th version of SCOR ignores impacts from the consumption of scarce and nonrenewable resources. Thus, a more complete set of SCOR-related impact metrics must encompass both emissions and consumption. Metrics for a supply chain's consumption footprint could include:

- Mineral consumption (tons, by material)
- Natural products consumption (tons, by natural product)[68]
- Water usage net of recycling (gallons)
- Land footprint (acres)
- Recycled inputs (percentage of all inputs).

Naturally, both emissions and consumption impacts can be weighted by their relative environmental burden and managed against specific regulatory or social-license-to-operate tolerances. GreenSCOR suggests that companies might track CO_x, NO_x, SO_x, volatile organic compounds (VOCs), and particulate emissions, which are the major types of emissions that the US EPA tracks and regulates. The impact of consumption metrics, such as water and land use, may be judged relative to local levels of water stress or the environmental sensitivity of the local habitat, respectively.

Metrics for Total Impact or Meaningful Change

These emission and consumption metrics can be expressed as total quantities across the supply chain or modified to measure progress on specific sustainability goals. Many companies normalize their total environmental impact over the total volume of production, so progress can be demonstrated even as the business grows. For example, AB InBev, the world's largest beer brewer, measures its water footprint in terms of the number of liters of water required to brew a liter of beer and works to improve water efficiency of all its brewing and bottling operations. Coca-Cola uses a similar metric. The British retailer Marks & Spencer chose to measure its transportation carbon footprint in terms of carbon per store. This metric aggregates the many contributing factors that affect its carbon footprint, such as changes in driver behavior, minimization of freight movements, replacement of inefficient vehicles, and the use of low-impact fuels.[69]

Companies under attack, or fearing attack for perceived environmental transgressions such as using unsustainable palm oil, create metrics and goals that measure the amount of sustainable palm oil they are buying, with the goal of becoming 100 percent compliant by some date. Aggressive goals, such as Unilever's objective to double sales while reducing impact, also call for measuring achievements in stark terms. For example, Unilever measures its progress on solid waste emissions not in terms of total tonnage sent to landfills or waste per unit of product, but in terms of the percentage of its factories that have achieved the "zero waste-to landfill" goal. This creates competition among its factories and a "race to the top" among factory managers.

Consumption and emission patterns take place at each stage of every supply chain. By uncovering what is happening to the environment in their names, companies can begin to decide whether and how to address these impacts.

3

Impact Assessment

In 2012, Friends of the Earth, a US environmental NGO, attacked major electronics companies, such as Apple and Samsung, over tin mining on the island of Bangka in Indonesia.[1] Bangka, along with a sister island and the surrounding seabed, provide about one third of the world's tin supply.[2] The NGO showed how the soft shiny tin has a tarnished record for being very hard on the environment. "Massive tracts of the island are stripped down to their tan sands, resembling images beamed back to Earth from Mars ..." proclaimed an August 2012 Bloomberg article.[3] In addition, while searching for tin offshore, illegal miners built thousands of floating shacks powered by diesel pumps to dredge tin ore from the seabed. The island's mining industry has contaminated rivers and damaged 65 percent of the area's forests and 70 percent of its coral reefs.[4] Unsafe working conditions, lack of clean water, and damage to centuries-old fishing ground have harmed the island's communities.

The tin supply chain is literally a melting pot, owing to the opaque web of smelters, brokers, and myriad middlemen who are involved in the global tin market. No one knows whether the tin in any particular Apple or Samsung smartphone or any other electronic product came from Bangka or not. For Apple and many other companies that outsource the manufacturing of electronics to contract manufacturers, the tin mines are at least five tiers deep in the supply chain, and yet, NGOs such as Friends of the Earth hold these companies responsible. Tin-based solder connects electrical components to circuit boards in virtually every electronic product on the planet, and that fact connects electronic product makers to solder suppliers, tin refiners, tin smelters, tin ore buyers, and mines around the world.

Because NGOs hold brand-name companies responsible not just for their own actions, but also for the actions of all their suppliers, environmental sustainability is first and foremost a supply chain issue. "Apple has started to recognize that supply chain problems start well before factories—the next step should be extending this scrutiny to other raw materials used in its products and packaging," said Julian Kirby of Friends of the Earth.[5] Tin in electronics isn't the only deep-tier sustainability issue that bedevils large swaths of the economy. Greenpeace's attack on Nestlé over palm oil cultivation practices (see chapter 1) similarly affects other food, cosmetics, and cleanser companies that depend on natural oils. Illegal logging potentially impacts all supply chains that handle wood, cardboard, or paper—essentially all products that require packaging.

Companies under attack often consider such activist actions unfair and unfounded, because these companies typically have no connection to the offending deep-tier suppliers and may not even know who they are. Yet, the lion's share of the carbon footprint of many manufacturers is indeed in their upstream supply chain: the processes of their suppliers, suppliers' suppliers, and so on. For example, the carbon footprint in the internal operations of brand-name makers of consumer discretionary products (such as apparel, automotive, home appliances, entertainment products, and others[6]) is only 5 percent of the total carbon footprint of these products, according to CDP.[7] Consequently, understanding and determining the environmental impacts caused on behalf of a company or a product requires assessing the entire supply chain "from cradle to grave."

FOOTPRINT ASSESSMENT: THE BANANA'S APPEAL

Bananas are the most frequently purchased grocery item in the United States.[8] They are also popular in the rest of the world: In 2013, more than 17 million tons of bananas were exported worldwide.[9]

The carbon footprint of bananas seems simple to assess, given that a banana has a single "part," does not require assembly, and comes in its own "packaging." Furthermore, bananas appear to have a simple supply chain with a few easy-to-trace major suppliers. Four of the five top banana exporters cluster in the warm and moist climate regions of Central and South America. Ecuador tops the list, followed by Costa Rica, Colombia, and Guatemala. Collectively, these four countries supplied 57 percent of the world's banana exports in 2011.[10]

When researchers at the MIT Center for Transportation and Logistics (CTL) assessed the greenhouse gas (GHG) emissions of the banana supply chain, they found that this simple product hides a bunch of complex issues. CTL partnered with Chiquita Brands International Inc. and Shaw's Supermarkets for several years to explore and calculate, in detail, the full carbon footprint of the average banana from Chiquita's plantations to Shaw's produce aisles.[11] The researchers documented each supply chain activity that generated greenhouse gases and estimated its emissions in CO_2e (CO_2 equivalent).[12] As it turned out, bananas were not quite the natural product they seemed to be, but rather a manufactured one due to the variety of processes involved in growing bananas and getting them to the retail shelf. These activities included various production processes, applied chemicals, and transportation.

Making Bananas

Originally native to Southeast Asia, bananas and their cultivation have spread to many tropical areas, such as Chiquita's Costa Rican plantations, which were the subject of the MIT study. Nature supplies the three main ingredients to making bananas: carbon dioxide, water, and sunlight. The banana plant removes carbon dioxide from the air and water from the ground as it grows. As each banana plant matures, it flowers and produces a cluster of 50 to 150 bananas hanging on a heavy stem. When people eat the energy-rich banana and metabolize it, they return the absorbed CO_2 back into the atmosphere. At first glance, this natural carbon cycle makes a banana appear to be carbon neutral. But it takes more than just air, water, and sunlight to make bananas, and it takes a lot more to deliver bananas to banana eaters.

Growing bananas successfully requires other inputs, such as fertilizers, as well as large amounts of organic matter and nutrients, such as nitrogen and potassium, along with pest-control products. For example, Costa Rican farms use translucent blue insecticidal bags to cover banana clusters, protecting them from a myriad of insects and pests that could ruin the fruit as it matures.

Six-Foot, Seven-Foot, Eight-Foot Bunch!

When a banana cluster reaches the right stage of development—still green, but approaching ripeness—farm laborers cut it down and take it to a sorting station. To transport bananas within the farm, workers hang them on an overhead metal track and manually pull a long line of banana clusters through the field. At the farm sorting station, workers divide the clusters by hand into supermarket-sized bunches. Bunches are then manually inspected for appearance and sorted by size. Any fruit with cosmetic imperfections is set aside for processing into products such as banana purees. Workers clean the remaining fruit in large water tanks and then transport the bunches to packing stations. Packers load the sorted and quality-controlled bananas into 40-pound boxes and stack 48 boxes on each pallet.

At the completion of the agricultural production stage, only 4.8 kg [13] of CO_2e (less than one-third of the total carbon footprint) per box of bananas has been emitted, on average. High levels of manual labor at the plantation imply modest electricity and fuel consumption by farm vehicles. These plantation operations contribute just 0.3 kg of CO_2e to the carbon footprint of a box of bananas. Production of the chemicals used at the farm, such as fertilizers and pesticides, emit 2.6 kg of CO_2e. Nitrogen fertilizers also cause the emission of nitrous oxide, a gas that is 300 times more potent as a greenhouse gas than CO_2.[14] Although only a few grams of N_2O per box escape, they are equal to 0.8 *kilograms* of CO_2e. Manufacturing the bananas' blue plastic pest-protection bags and cardboard boxes adds another 1.1 kg of CO_2e, bringing the total to 4.8 kg of CO_2e for each 18 kg box of bananas. But the banana's journey is far from over, which means the carbon footprint accounting is far from complete.

Come, Mister Tally Man, Tally Me Banana

At the end of the production line, workers load the one-ton pallets of bananas onto trucks to haul them east to the Costa Rican port of Puerto Moín, in Limón, on the Caribbean Sea. To prevent premature ripening, Chiquita chills its bananas for some stages of the journey. Plantation trips that take more than two hours from the farm to the port require refrigerated trucks. Trips of two hours or less need no refrigeration, so assessing the carbon footprint requires accounting for the two types of trips separately, because they generate different amounts of GHGs both from fuel consumption and from the GHG emissions from leaking refrigerants. On average, the trip from the farm to the port adds another 0.8 kg of CO_2e.

Once the bananas arrive at the port, workers load them into refrigerated shipping containers. Refrigerant gases used to chill the bananas during the journey add 0.9 kg of CO_2e. Each 40-foot container holds 20 pallets—more than 38,000 pounds of bananas or 960 boxes. Cranes then load hundreds of banana containers onto small, fast ocean vessels. Operations at the port contribute 0.3 kg of CO_2e.

At the time of the MIT research project, Chiquita used dedicated ocean ship carriers, the "Great White Fleet," in order to ensure freshness for the consumer.[15] The smaller ships used by Chiquita consume more fuel per ton of freight moved than do large freighters. In addition, Chiquita's vessels were routinely only partially loaded on the return trip (the southbound backhaul trip).[16] Despite the added costs, the need for freshness drove the required speed of the maritime system.

On average, ocean shipment for US-bound bananas added 3.6 kg of CO_2e, more than any other single activity in the supply chain. Overall, transportation and handling between the farm and US ports accounted for roughly another one-third of the bananas' total carbon footprint, or 5.6 kg of CO_2e per box. On average, by the time a box of bananas reaches a North American port, it has accumulated 10.4 kg CO_2e. The journey, however, still isn't over.

This Banana's Ripe for Delivery

At a port in North America, the banana containers are unloaded from the ship and transported to one of Chiquita's refrigerated distribution centers. At the distribution center, workers stack pallets of fruit in sealed ripening rooms that hold about one truckload each. A typical distribution center includes a half-dozen such rooms, each at a different stage of ripening. Shortly before shipping the bananas to retailers, Chiquita injects about one quart of ethylene gas into the room to restart the banana ripening process. Chiquita precisely controls the number of days of exposure to ethylene gas, ranging from two to five days, to achieve one of the three shades of green/yellow requested by its retail customers: hard green, green, or yellow. In some cases, Chiquita ships the fruit unripened, and retailers put the bananas in ripening rooms at their own distribution centers.

When the bananas reach the retailer's desired color, the retailer delivers the bananas to its stores. For example, each day at the Shaw's Greater Boston-area distribution center in Methuen, Massachusetts, thousands of boxes of bananas are loaded onto trucks with an assortment of other perishable items destined for Shaw's retail grocery outlets. In total, more than a million boxes of bananas pass through this distribution center each year.

Transportation from ports to the distribution network and on to the retail outlet adds an average of 2.0 kg of CO_2e to the carbon footprint of the fruit's journey. Additional emissions come from operations at the North American ports, ripening centers, and distribution centers, which contribute another 1.5 kg of CO_2e. Activities at retail stores, where consumers finally get their hands on the product, add another 2.3 kg of CO_2e. Disposing of the plastic and cardboard needed to protect the produce adds the final 1.2 kg of CO_2e. In total, the final carbon impact of the average 18-kg box of US-bound bananas is around 17 kg[17] of CO_2e. This is the average footprint of the banana up to the store shelf.

A Summary by the Numbers

Moving a banana box across the world from farm to retail store accounts for roughly 40 percent of the environmental impact.

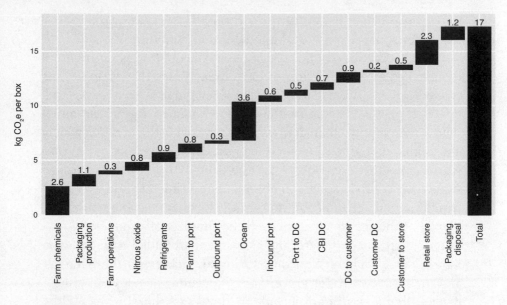

Figure 3.1
Carbon footprint breakdown of a box of bananas sold in the United States.
Source: A. Craig. "Measuring Supply Chain Carbon Efficiency: A Carbon Label
Framework." Diss., Massachusetts Institute of Technology, 2012.

Other impactful processes include the production of chemicals,
such as fertilizers and pesticides, which takes place in large manufacturing plants far from Chiquita's banana farms. Figure 3.1
shows the accumulated carbon footprint of the average box of
Chiquita bananas sold in the United States, split among its main
components.

Out of Scope

Finally, as comprehensive as the MIT analysis was, it limited the
scope of direct data collection to the primary actors to ensure trac-
tability. Even so, the researchers identified 56 primary materials
and processes across 16 major supply chain stages that were
required to grow a banana and deliver it from farm to consumer.
The banana supply chain is part of a much larger global commercial and industrial network that provides fertilizers, water, energy,
vehicles, packaging, and a myriad of other ingredients needed to
plant, grow, harvest, and ship the bananas. The fruit's carbon

impact also began before its growth on a farm: at fertilizer factories, forests, paper mills, coal mines, and power plants.

Using specialized Life Cycle Assessment (LCA) software[18]
designed to estimate environmental impacts [see the section "Life
Cycle Analysis (with Paralysis)"], the original 56 materials and
processes in the data collection phase expanded to include more
than 1,500 supply chain activities spanning the globe, all of which
are ultimately required to produce and deliver bananas. The software helped the researchers trace the contribution of each of these
supply chain processes and materials that ultimately add up to the
banana's final carbon footprint and, in turn, reveal the true complexity of the supply chain of even the simplest of products.

Even with the software, the assessment excluded a number of
minor items, such as the iconic Chiquita stickers on the bananas
and the plastic or paper grocery bags consumers use to carry their
bananas home. It did not include the bananas' share of the GHGs
emitted by shoppers' cars when they drove to and from the store. It
did not include the footprint of any electricity used by the consumer
to blend the banana into a daiquiri or bake it into bread, and it did
not include the footprint of methane emissions from the decay of
discarded bananas or banana peels. Although it may be argued that
these largely post-retail footprints are out of the control of Chiquita
and Shaw's, that does not stop NGOs, as well as governments, from
holding companies responsible for creating products that might
be used irresponsibly or have high impacts during use or disposal.
Chapters 7, 8, and 9 consider the opportunities companies have to
redesign their operations, products, or market messages to reduce
impacts in these later stages of the product's life cycle.

Your Footprints May Vary

As mentioned in the preceding sections, one would be hard-pressed
to find a seemingly simpler product to assess than a banana. Yet,
calculating the carbon footprint for even a "simple" product is further complicated by temporal and geographic variations of the
underlying supply chain. The estimated 17 kg of CO_2e is the *average* carbon footprint of a box of bananas grown by Chiquita in
Costa Rica and sold in the United States.

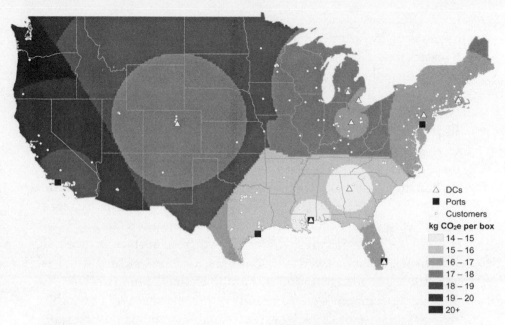

Figure 3.2
Carbon footprint of a box of bananas sold across the United States.
Source: A. Craig. "Measuring Supply Chain Carbon Efficiency: A Carbon Label
Framework." Diss., Massachusetts Institute of Technology, 2012.

In reality, each box of bananas has a very different carbon footprint depending on where in the United States, or around the globe,
the fruit is sold. For example, bananas sold in grocers in New
Orleans—near the port that is closest to the Costa Rican export
location—have a carbon footprint of only about 14 kg of CO_2e per
box. Bananas sold in Seattle—with a longer ocean voyage, lower
return-trip utilization, and longer (1,100-plus miles) drive from the
nearest distribution center—had a 21 kg carbon footprint per box.
Figure 3.2 depicts the variation in carbon footprint of Chiquita
bananas, depending on the locations of the domestic port of entry,
distribution centers, and retail customers across the United States.
The concentric circles reflect driving distances from distribution
centers, and the other boundaries reflect the service areas of different distribution centers.

The footprints for Chiquita's worldwide operation vary significantly across its network. The company manages hundreds of

farms and employs six ocean transportation services that unload bananas at five US and eight European ports. The company also operates nine distribution centers in the US and 11 in Europe, from which it supplies bananas to hundreds of retail chains that distribute bananas to thousands of retail outlets.

Water's the Matter with Bananas

Carbon isn't the only footprint of concern. Chiquita assessed its own *water* footprint of its bananas in a study analogous to the carbon footprint one.[19] Chiquita's assessment included separate estimates of the volumes of three categories of water. "Green water" is rainwater that naturally falls on Chiquita's land. In contrast, "blue water" is fresh water drawn from surface or ground water such as lakes, rivers, and aquifers. The use of green water is generally considered more sustainable than blue water use, although a company's consumption of green water will inevitably reduce the amount of blue water available to other downstream users. Finally, "gray water" is waste water emitted as run-off or sewage that might contaminate blue water supplies or require treatment of some type. All three types of water footprint affect downstream water users, such as farms, industry, and cities, as well as downstream wetlands and estuaries.

As with the carbon footprint of bananas, the water footprint of bananas varied significantly by location: from 440 to 632 liters per kilogram of bananas (53 to 76 US gallons per pound). Plantations in Costa Rica and Panama use less water and only use green water. Those in Honduras and Guatemala require more water and depend on blue water for artificial irrigation. Crop water accounted for 94 to 99 percent of the total water footprint, a pattern not uncommon for agricultural products. The remainder was process water that is used to cool and wash the bananas. This number, too, varied between 1.6 and 35.6 liters per kilogram of bananas, depending on the design of the washing system and the adoption of recirculation to reuse wash water. Chiquita also noted that the water footprint varies unpredictably from year to year as a function of rainfall, heat, humidity, and crop yield.[20]

Inside Footprint versus Outside Footprint

Although Chiquita owns much of the banana supply chain, its operations account for a little less than half of the banana's total carbon footprint. This is actually a relatively high figure due to Chiquita's "shallow" supply chain (including only two basic tiers) and the company's direct control over it. For many companies and many supply chains, the company's suppliers and customers along the supply chain contribute, on average, three times as much to a product's carbon footprint as the company's own operations.[21] As mentioned in chapter 2, this ratio is significantly larger for companies such as Cisco, Apple, Microsoft, and most apparel and shoe companies, who outsource most or all of their manufacturing and transportation activities. Also, as indicated in the introduction to this chapter, in the consumer discretionary product industry the footprint outside the company is 19 times greater, on average, than the footprint inside the company.[22] Carbon footprint and other environmental impacts are truly supply chain attributes.

The Greenhouse Gas Protocol[23] for assessing and reporting carbon footprints formalizes this notion of footprints inside and outside the company as a set of three scopes. Scope 1 carbon emissions are those that arise from sources that are owned or directly controlled by the company. Examples include furnaces, boilers, on-site power plants, fuel burned by the company's vehicles, and emissions of non-CO_2 GHGs, such as refrigerants, N_2O from fertilizer, and VOCs (volatile organic compounds) by the company's assets. Scope 2 includes indirect carbon emissions that arise from purchased electricity, heat, or steam used directly by the company. These depend on the carbon-intensity of electrical grid power and other third-party energy sources.

Scope 3 encompasses everything outside of the company's own operations, such as production of purchased material and parts and the provision of services by external vendors (such as transportation by vehicles not owned by the company). It also includes customer use and disposal.[24] It includes both the upstream and downstream parts of the entire supply chain, including end-of-life. In addition, Scope 3 includes the carbon footprint of capital goods, such as the company's factory equipment, office buildings, and vehicles that are not manufactured by the company. It also includes items such as business travel, employee commuting, franchises, and the carbon footprint of investments on the company's balance sheet (e.g., cross-holdings in another company). The protocol defines 15 categories of emissions within Scope 3 to facilitate comparable assessments and reporting across companies.

Note that the definitions of the three scopes by the Greenhouse Gas Protocol are not based on a supply chain view. In particular, such a perspective would segregate upstream impacts from downstream impacts. These are in fact commingled in Scope 3. Moreover, a supply chain angle would separate variable cost impacts from fixed cost impacts, but the Protocol also commingles the company's internal capital expense impacts into Scope 3. That is, the Protocol makes Scope 3 into a catchall that makes it hard for customers of a company to understand which of the company's impacts are ascribable to that customer.

LIFE CYCLE ANALYSIS (WITH PARALYSIS)

The assessment of the carbon footprint of bananas is an example of an LCA, which is the systematic appraisal of all of the inputs and outputs associated with sourcing, making, delivering, using, and returning or disposing of a product. Many consumers, companies, and policy makers wonder about the environmental impact of their choices: "Is it always better to buy a locally produced item than an item transported from afar?" (see chapter 5.) "Is a plastic pouch refill better than a traditional disposable plastic bottle for liquid products?" (see chapter 8). The intricacies of the analysis of the banana's footprint demonstrate that these simple questions rarely have simple answers, and simplistic intuitions can easily lead to incorrect conclusions. Only a comprehensive, systematic analysis of the product supply chain can ultimately lead to the right decision.

LCAs typically focus on a single category of environmental impact (such as carbon emissions, water consumption, or land use) as a prelude to understanding or mitigating that particular impact.

In the context of climate change, the most common LCAs estimate the carbon footprint of a product. LCAs gained popularity during the energy crisis of the 1970s and during the period of heightened environmental interest that followed in the 1980s.

An LCA is different from product life-cycle management (PLM)[25] in several regards. LCAs concern the material and environmental inputs and outputs of a single unit or specific quantity of a product. The scope of an LCA spans raw materials, parts, a unit of the finished good, consumer use, and on to the disposal of the unit under consideration. In contrast, PLM concerns the overall timing and management of a product, model, or SKU (stock-keeping unit). The scope of PLM spans R&D conception, engineering design, factory manufacturing, servicing, and eventual obsolescence of that type of product.

Tesco's Path to Footprint Assessment

In 1919, Jack Cohen started selling groceries from a stall in London's East End.[26] Five years later, he founded Tesco using the first three initials of his tea supplier, T. E. Stockwell (tea was Tesco's first own-branded product) and the first two letters of his last name. Tesco rose to the top of British retailing by focusing on its customers with innovations like loyalty schemes (the "green shield" cards), and using consumer-buying data to adapt early to consumer trends.[27] The chain grew both organically and through acquisitions, becoming the United Kingdom's largest retailer and the third largest in the world.

The grocer, however, did not have a good year in 2006. In that year the company was implicated in two scandals over the treatment of workers in Bangladesh factories,[28] including the use of child labor.[29] Moreover, when the National Consumer Council evaluated the UK's eight leading supermarket chains in 2006 on their environmental friendliness,[30] Tesco earned an overall score of "D," with a "D" on transport, a "C" on waste, and a "C" on sustainable farming. Fearing consumer backlash, Tesco rushed to respond.

In 2007—just as the fourth Intergovernmental Panel on Climate Change (IPCC) report stated that it is "unequivocal" that the earth's climate is warming—Tesco CEO Sir Terry Leahy stunned the press with his plan to seek or develop a carbon footprint label based on an LCA of the GHG emissions of every one of the 50,000 to 70,000 products Tesco sold. "Too often on issues like sustainability, Tesco has come to be portrayed as part of the problem," Leahy later said in prepared remarks to selected stakeholders.[31] "This could not be more wrong. When you want to reach and empower the many, Tesco is a big part of the solution, not the problem," Leahy added.[32]

Consumers have a new need, he argued. They want to live more sustainably, including making more environmentally conscious purchase decisions. Tesco's LCA-driven carbon footprint information on the label would empower consumers to reduce their carbon footprint by selecting less carbon-intensive products. "Our role as a business is to give them the information and the means to achieve this change," Leahy said.[33]

Around the same time, Walmart partnered with Environmental Defense Fund (EDF) to evaluate the carbon footprint of the supply chain for entire classes of its products. During a meeting at the company's Bentonville, Arkansas, home office, in front of an audience of 1,500 suppliers, associates, and sustainability leaders, Walmart President and CEO Mike Duke announced a plan to develop a "worldwide sustainable product index."[34] Duke echoed Leahy's enthusiasm as he spelled out a plan to document not only the carbon footprint of each product from more than 100,000 suppliers, but to also evaluate products for their consumption of natural resources, material efficiency, and their impact on people and communities.

Both announcements flabbergasted *Guardian* environmental commentator George Monbiot, who asked days after Leahy's announcement: "If Tesco and Walmart are friends of the Earth, are there any enemies left?"[35] The two firms, he noted in the same 2007 column, were holding themselves to "higher standards than any government would dare to impose on them."

True to its word, Tesco designed a black foot-shaped logo for its labels with a number informing consumers of the product's carbon footprint so that consumers could see—simply and directly—the environmental impact of the products they chose to buy.

They could then compare those products and, if they desired, purchase the one that would put less carbon into the atmosphere. Consumers might simply switch from one brand of milk to another, or perhaps they would give up their can of India-grown cashews in favor of a Cadbury product made closer to home with a lower carbon footprint. Furthermore, manufacturers might notice consumers' preferences for "greener" products and work to reduce their own carbon footprint, leading to a competition between manufacturers to be more sustainable, and resulting in industry-wide carbon emission reductions. In addition, consumers might flock to Tesco's stores, recognizing the company as a leader in providing consumers with environmentally responsible choices.

Meanwhile, the Carbon Trust was poised to introduce its own carbon footprint assessment service. The British NGO began operations in 2001 with the main goal of helping companies calculate and understand their carbon footprints.[36] In March 2007—just weeks after Leahy's announcement—the Carbon Trust added a carbon certification label to its portfolio of offerings.[37]

Given the proximity of the announcements and their similar goals, it made sense for Tesco to work with the Carbon Trust, according to Martin Barrow, head of footprinting at the Carbon Trust. Tesco and the Carbon Trust agreed to start by labeling a batch of about 100 products. That goal grew to 500, "and then the intent was to slowly expand," Barrow said.[38]

Footprints Take Footwork

To assign a number to each product's black foot label, the Carbon Trust developed and used an LCA standard known as PAS 2050,[39] which calls for a meticulous investigation into a product's complete life cycle.[40] The PAS 2050 manual illustrates the assessment process with a simplified example of a single croissant. Although intended to help companies understand the processes involved, the example also showed just how complex and laborious this process could be.

The croissant example included a multicolored flowchart with 25 interconnected processes representing inputs, outputs, conversions, storage, transport, and waste.[41] It included details such as any potential heating and freezing by consumers after they purchased the croissant, as well as the carbon produced by the packaging during transport and decomposition at a landfill. Each of the chart's 25 boxes required significant research and data collection.

Furthermore, the accompanying text admitted that the simplified chart entirely omitted butter, a key ingredient in flaky croissants and a major source of the pastry's carbon footprint. To include butter, the guide commented, would require accounting for the carbon footprint of the butter factory, the dairy farm that produced the milk, the hay fields that fed the cows, and all the associated transportation, handling, and storage processes.[42] Those cows might be in the UK or some other country—adding both to transportation costs and to variations in dairy operations practices. Moreover, the footprint might vary during the year if the cows grazed on nearby pastures in the summer but needed hay trucked in for the winter.

In summary, what Tesco and the Carbon Trust had agreed to do was to map the complete supply chain of every single product in the store and gather data on every supplier within these supply chains. These supply chains were not limited to Tesco's Tier 1 suppliers, with whom Tesco communicates on a regular basis. Tesco also needed to interview and gather data from deeper-tier suppliers. Helen Fleming, Tesco's climate change director, told *The Grocer* that it took "a minimum of several months' work" to calculate the single number to be placed on each black foot label.[43]

A First Batch, Then a Rough Patch
The first batch of carbon-labeled products landed on Tesco's shelves in August 2009 to much fanfare.[44] Store employees called attention to the labels by mounting special displays that jutted

perpendicular to the shelves. That, combined with the accompanying media spree, highlighted Tesco's efforts to the chain's consumers. Meanwhile, a collaborative team of Tesco employees and Carbon Trust consultants labored behind the scenes to prepare the next round of carbon labels.

On the surface, the plan seemed ambitious, yet achievable. A large and powerful retail chain with significant control over the market had partnered with a respected nonprofit to pursue a labeling plan that it believed its customers cared about. A framework for the project existed, and Tesco seemed to have the will to carry it through. But, in hindsight, the plan hinged on some wishful thinking.

The number of carbon-labeled products on Tesco's shelves never accelerated as intended. Leahy, who had been Tesco's CEO since 1997, left his post in March 2011.[45] Tesco ended the carbon footprinting program a year later, after labeling only 500 products.[46] The chain achieved a rate of only 125 products labeled per year.[47] At that pace, the company would have needed more than *seven centuries* to label all 90,000 SKUs in its stores.[48] And that is assuming, of course, that Tesco made no changes to its product assortment and that Tesco's suppliers made no changes to the ingredients or manufacturing processes of any of the labeled products during all those centuries.

Walmart's program did not fare any better. As Tesco's labeling program began to unwind, Walmart's labeling project also quietly died. In 2014, for example, the Walmart corporate page about the sustainability index included no reference to labeling products based on their environmental impact. Instead, it spoke of "developing a sustainable standard for products" in cooperation with The Sustainability Consortium.

Interestingly, despite the failure of Tesco's effort, its green image improved. Concurrent with the 2009 rollout of its newly carbon-labeled products, the Carbon Trust awarded the grocer its Carbon Trust Standard.[49] In giving the award, the Trust noted that Tesco had made significant progress in reducing its "carbon intensity."

Tesco's LCA plan failed because the company badly underestimated the effort required for each LCA and overestimated the response of consumers, other retailers, and product makers. In an attempt to explain the failure, Fleming said in her January 2012 interview with *The Grocer:*[50] "We expected that other retailers would move quickly to do it as well, giving it critical mass, but that hasn't happened." Tesco had hoped that the labels would change consumer behavior in ways that would motivate others to label their products, too. Consumers, however, were not buying the labeled products in larger numbers than unlabeled ones.

As the Chiquita example shows, an accurate LCA of the environmental impact of each product requires large amounts of data and extensive analysis. Cost estimates for a single footprint assessment range from $10,000 to $60,000 per product,[51,52] making it impractical unless the LCA technology and data collection become cheaper or other players join in the efforts.

Carbon Critics Become Label Libelers

Others thought Tesco's labels weren't good enough, demonstrating, again, that *il meglio è l'inimico del bene*: "The perfect is the enemy of the good" (see chapter 1). Environmentalists raised two main objections. First, the PAS 2050 methodology used by the Carbon Trust excludes some major categories of footprint. "In making a T-shirt, none of the machinery used to make it is taken into account [in PAS 2050], but this machinery can have an enormous carbon footprint. The efficiency of the machine is taken into account, but the impact of producing and maintaining the machine is not," said Dr. John Barrett from the Stockholm Environment Institute (SEI) at York University, UK.[53] Second, "a low carbon footprint on a product does not mean the product is entirely environmentally friendly. There could be other issues of deforestation, use of water, and social impact to do with the product," said Friends of the Earth food campaigner Richard Hines.[54]

"BIGGER THAN A BREADBOX ..."[55]

Companies can assess their approximate footprint without the excessive costs of tracing each ingredient across every link in the supply chain. A more pragmatic, although less rigorous, approach can be useful for uncovering "hot spot" areas (e.g., ingredients, locations, products, or processes) with the highest environmental impacts. These are the areas where mitigation initiatives may make the greatest difference or where the company has the greatest vulnerability of being attacked for its environmental impact. Several techniques provide footprint estimates that, while not precise enough to differentiate between, say, two brands of milk, can identify large hot spots, thus enabling pragmatic action.

Accelerating Assessment: Hot Spots in the Bill of Materials

"How much does your morning glass of orange juice contribute to global warming?" asked a January 2009 *New York Times* article about a study released earlier that year.[56] PepsiCo, in partnership with the Earth Institute at Columbia University, investigated the environmental footprint of 20 of PepsiCo's Tropicana Pure Premium orange juice products. The study concluded that the average 64 oz. carton of Tropicana Pure Premium orange juice sold in the United States was responsible for a 1.7 kg carbon footprint.[57] Thirty-five percent of that impact—the biggest hotspot—came from the fertilizer used to grow the oranges.[58]

The orange juice study was so successful that PepsiCo executives wanted to repeat it for all products across the company.[59] Instead of attempting a detailed LCA, however, Columbia and PepsiCo again partnered to create a new "fast" approach to LCAs that balanced the thoroughness of full LCAs with the speed and cost needed by PepsiCo. The technique begins with the bill of materials (BOM) for each product—1,137 of them in Pepsi's case—taken from the company's enterprise resource planning (ERP) system. It then matches the material data with known emissions factors for materials and processes to fill in a standard data structure of emission factors estimates. The data structure also includes an estimate of the accuracy of the emission factor for each material and process. For materials or processes with no readily available emission factors, the team developed a "generic" model for estimating the carbon impact based on attributes such as price,[60] weight, density, and type. Because the "generic" estimates included in the system are not as accurate as estimates based on specific data, analysts would do further assessments whenever a "generic" material was likely to be a significant contributor to the final carbon footprint of the product. That is, the company would spend effort on accuracy if the accuracy would make a difference to the overall footprint estimate.

This fast carbon footprinting procedure allowed PepsiCo to identify its carbon "hot spots" across its entire portfolio because, according to the Earth Institute team, "the approach dramatically reduces the number of required manual entries, up to approximately 1,000-fold." Another benefit of the system is that any updates of the central emissions database of any input—be it the carbon footprint of sugar or the adoption of lightweight bottles—are propagated to all products that use the material.

Specialized software applications can also speed footprint assessments. Applications such as SimaPro[61] and GaBi[62] come preprogrammed with databases like ecoinvent[63] that pull existing LCA studies from multiple sources. Although such LCA software enables faster insights, the applications rely on general data sets that are not specific to the processes, companies, or supplier locations studied. This increases the margins of error but can still provide an option for informed decision making, especially in terms of "order of magnitude" decisions.

Although fast footprinting cuts the time and effort of assessment and consequently enables analysis across a broad product portfolio, it still requires significant technical knowledge, time, and effort to develop. Other approaches require even less expertise to use, relying on far more accessible pieces of information within the organization: money flows.

Follow the Money

Ocean Spray, the Massachusetts producer of bottled juice drinks and fruit snacks, assessed its full supply chain emissions using an LCA variant called economic input-output life cycle assessment (EIO-LCA).[64] EIO-LCA provides an alternative to the kinds of laborious LCAs used in the banana and Tesco examples. EIO-LCA is less data intensive, but in many ways it can be even more complete.[65]

EIO-LCA builds on the work of Nobel Prize-winning economist Wassily Leontief, who divided the economy into sectors and traced the dependence between various sectors using trade data.[66] For instance, a box of Chiquita bananas requires a set of inputs such as chemicals at the farm, cardboard for the box, trucks for transportation, and numerous other materials, each coming from their respective sector or industry. Those inputs, in turn, have their own inputs, such as the steel and electricity needed to manufacture trucks that come from other sectors. Thus, each industrial sector can be characterized by the relative amounts of goods that it purchases as inputs from other sectors. These relationships create a tangle of interdependencies as they are traced up the supply chain. Truck manufacturers, for example, may purchase steel to build trucks, and steel makers may purchase trucks to transport their steel. Leontief developed a mathematical economic input-output model that tallied how a dollar of output produced by one sector depended on fractions of dollars of inputs from each of the other sectors of the economy, all the way upstream through the supply chain.

EIO-LCA extends Leontief's work by using sector-level environmental impact data. This environmental data is combined with the original Leontief EIO model to estimate environmental impact per dollar spent in each sector of the economy. Carnegie Mellon University offers a free version of the EIO-LCA model online for noncommercial use, as well as licensing the underlying data and methods.[67]

For Ocean Spray, the use of EIO-LCA meant that it could estimate the carbon footprint of its entire upstream supply chain using just the records of financial transactions from its ERP system. Working with MIT researchers, Ocean Spray collected data on all of its financial transactions for one year.[68] This included more than 400,000 transactions with suppliers, each of which was categorized and matched to one of the 500 economic sectors represented in the EIO-LCA model. The sector data and dollar value of the transactions were enough for a rough estimate of the carbon footprint of all the upstream activities.

EIO-LCA can be more comprehensive than the traditional LCA used by Tesco and Chiquita for three reasons. First, it automatically aggregates the environmental impacts in the depths of the supply chain that an LCA might miss owing to lack of visibility, such as if a supplier refuses to respond to a request for LCA-related data. Second, in using ERP data—not only BOM data—it encompasses more of the company's impacts, such as indirect materials and overhead activities. Finally, the use of cost data, instead of material quantity data, also implies that EIO-LCA includes the footprint of capital equipment, assuming that the cost of capital equipment is amortized into suppliers' and service providers' prices.

EIO-LCA is, however, less accurate than a deep LCA analysis, in that the economic input-output data only track aggregate interactions between industrial sectors and assume that all the products from a given sector have the same environmental impact per dollar cost. For example, fossil fuel diesel and biodiesel might be assigned the same impact per dollar if both are considered to be coming from the "fuel" sector. New sectors need to be created to reflect closely related materials that actually have significantly different environmental impacts per dollar. Another shortcoming of the EIO-LCA method is that it excludes downstream activities such as consumer use and disposal.

To get a more complete assessment, Ocean Spray combined its EIO-LCA approach with a traditional process-based LCA of its own operations and downstream activities, such as distribution, use, and disposal. Ocean Spray concluded that 71 percent of the total emissions came from purchased products and inputs (in other words, from the upstream supply chain), in line with industry averages. Another 17 percent came from downstream emissions related to distribution, use, and disposal of the products Ocean Spray sold. Only 11 percent came from Ocean Spray's own operations.

Like the simplified approach described in the previous section, EIO-LCA can help pinpoint processes that create significant environmental stress and which can be studied further for improvements. The combined approach is sometimes referred to as a hybrid LCA. It uses the faster and broader EIO-LCA for an initial screening[69] and then resorts to a more detailed study of high-impact areas using a standard, process-based LCA, such as those performed by MIT (on Chiquita bananas) or Tesco's efforts.

Real-Time LCA

Early LCAs, such as the Chiquita and Tesco examples, took months to perform, which limited their usefulness and financial feasibility. These LCAs cost too much and were out of date by the time they were completed. "Existing solutions do not allow carbon footprint measurements to be integrated within IT operations systems across the whole product life cycle, for each and every product," said Jean-Marc Lagoutte, CIO of Danone.[70] At the same time, the growing amount of LCA-related data (published analyses, sustainability vendor databases, and CDP disclosures) have increased the availability of environmental impact data that can be used in LCAs.

Danone, software provider SAP, and third-party experts developed a software system that takes BOMs and transactional ERP data, supplier survey data, and emissions factors data from a variety of sources[71] to quickly and (relatively) inexpensively estimate the end-to-end LCA of Danone's products. The companies do not detail the specific methodology used (which presumably involves simplifications similar to those in EIO-LCA or PepsiCo's "Fast LCA") or its accuracy (which is unknown).[72]

Each of Danone's country business units has a carbon master who is responsible, in part, for conducting this LCA twice a year. Using this system, Danone has assessed the end-to-end footprints of the 35,000 products that account for 70 percent of the company's revenues.[73] "By making this analysis part of our IT infrastructure, we gain valuable insights for decision-making; it becomes a catalyst for change in the company as a whole," said Myriam Cohen-Welgryn, vice president of Danone Nature.[74] Although the use of approximations may prevent accurate estimates of absolute emissions levels, SAP says the tool is a way to "highlight trends and rank-order emissions activities and supplier footprints to help identify opportunities for improvement."[75]

Stonyfield Farm Inc., a Danone subsidiary, found a new use for this system: analyzing the day-to-day changes in the LCA of the company's yogurt products.[76] With this system, Stonyfield claims to automatically estimate the end-to-end footprint of individual production orders. "Now we're able to get an immediate understanding of the climate impact of every single ingredient in our products as they're made, which allows us to both react quickly toward reducing impact and adjust our approach to making a continually lower-impact yogurt," said Wood Turner, Stonyfield's vice president of sustainability innovation.[77] However, it is not clear if the accuracy of the method allows for such an exact appraisal.

Collecting Data via Supplier Surveys

In 2012, the French cosmetics company L'Oréal pledged that by 2020 it would reduce its per-product waste and water usage, as well as the company's absolute carbon footprint, by 60 percent from its 2005 baseline.[78] To achieve such reductions, the company needed to understand the impact of both its own operations and those of its suppliers, which required a uniform approach to gathering and evaluating data regarding those impacts. "We use one scorecard, and that scorecard was developed by L'Oréal and CDP," said Miguel Castellanos, the company's environmental health and safety director.[79]

CDP is a UK-based nonprofit established in 2000 with a simple goal: to ask the world's largest companies to disclose their carbon emissions and share actions they are taking to mitigate this impact.[80] In 2002, when CDP sent out its first questionnaire, 221 of the 500 companies contacted responded.[81] By 2015, participation had grown to 4,500 companies, representing over 50 percent of the market capitalization of the world's 30 largest stock exchanges.[82] Part of the increase arose from the demands of institutional investors for companies to respond to the CDP questionnaires. In 2014, more than 767 institutional investors representing over US$92 trillion in assets[83] were behind CDP's information requests.

L'Oréal was an early respondent and in 2008 decided to go further. It joined CDP's supply chain program to encourage its suppliers, who might not be large or publicly traded companies and thus out of reach of the CDP, to report their emissions. By 2013,

Castellanos said, the company had sent CDP-based questionnaires to 173 of its suppliers, and 152 of them responded.[84] In that same year, the company sent a new L'Oréal/CDP scorecard investigating water usage to 17 of the company's suppliers; 15 of them responded.

Using the CDP's standardized reporting system allows suppliers to provide the same information, in the same format, to all their customers.[85] The comprehensive 17-page 2014 CDP questionnaire on climate change includes 86 questions covering management, strategy, policy, and communication of climate change risks, tailored to address inquiries of multiple customers and stakeholders. In addition, to make sure that all respondents calculate GHG emissions consistently, the CDP questionnaire leverages another level of standardization: the Greenhouse Gas Protocol mentioned earlier in this chapter.

ASSESSMENT IN THE USE AND POST-USE PHASES

An architect designing an energy-efficient building has many choices for structural materials, windows, insulation, lighting, and fixtures that will help minimize energy use and therefore the carbon footprint of the building as it is used by the occupants. In many product categories, a few simple metrics provide a good estimate of this use-phase footprint. With lighting, for example, the wattages of competing products with the same brightness provide an excellent estimate of carbon footprint: higher wattage options consume more electricity, which, in most locations, implies burning more fossil fuels.

Assessing the footprint of alternative hand-drying systems in the bathroom is harder than assessing lighting, owing to the heterogeneous options such as disposable paper towels, reusable cotton cloth rolls, hot-air electric dryers, Excel's Xlerator, and Dyson's Airblade (see figure 3.3). The first two options use no electricity in the bathroom but do require deliveries of disposable or reusable materials. The middle option is the ubiquitous old-design electric dryer, which was added to the choice set to provide a familiar baseline. The last two options have similar wattages, making the choice among these options not obvious without careful analysis.

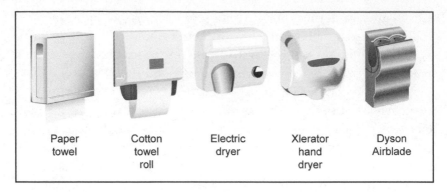

| Paper towel | Cotton towel roll | Electric dryer | Xlerator hand dryer | Dyson Airblade |

Figure 3.3
Hand dryers compared in MIT's LCA study

Assessing the Footprint of Drying Hands

Dyson, the maker of the Airblade, believed that its product was superior to the other four options in terms of its total life cycle carbon footprint. To justify these claims, the company commissioned the MIT Materials Systems Laboratory to conduct a careful and independent assessment of the footprint of manufacturing, servicing, and using the Airblade and the four other common hand-drying systems. In 2011, MIT published its assessment titled, "Life Cycle Assessments of Hand Drying Systems."[86] As a result of the study, *The Guardian* proclaimed, in November 2011: "Paper towels least green way of drying hands."[87]

Performing this assessment began with a series of important questions: what constitutes use; how will consumers use each product; what is the impact of each use; and what is the total amount of use? Assessing the use phase can be difficult. For example, whereas the upstream footprint involves hundreds or thousands of suppliers, the downstream side might encompass hundreds of millions of consumers.

First, the researchers chose the unit of usage to be a pair of dried hands. But this raised the question of what constitutes "dry." NSF International, an independent standards organization, defines hands as "dry" when they hold less than 0.1 g of residual moisture in a room-temperature environment.[88]

Next, the researchers had to estimate how people used each of the five methods to dry their hands. Using a variety of data from previous studies, the researchers determined that the average bathroom visitor uses two paper towels or one cotton towel to dry their hands. Electric hot air hand dryers take 31 seconds to evaporate the water on a user's hands. Both the Xlerator and the Airblade use a high-speed stream of air to blast droplets of water off the user's hands. Unlike the Xlerator, the Airblade focuses its 400 mile-per-hour stream of air into narrow sheets, or blades. The unconventional design requires users to draw their hands upward through the air blades. The Xlerator hand dryer required 20 seconds whereas the Airblade required only 12 seconds to dry a pair of hands—a significant improvement over other electric hand dryers.

To be able to fairly compare different choices, the researchers had to estimate an additional dimension of usage: how many pairs of hands would each method dry in its lifetime? The researchers used the five-year warranty typical for commercial electric hand dryers as the estimated life span of these products during which the dryer would be used 350,000 times.[89] With those usage estimates in place, measuring each method's inputs and their environmental impacts was the next step. In the case of hand dryers, this meant constructing a thorough list of all of the materials used to make and operate the machines—everything from metal, plastic, and adhesives to electronic components to the packaging in which the machines were shipped.

Each method had different usage footprint issues. Paper towels required a steady stream of paper, which might include some recycled content, and they also needed a waste bin and daily replacement of the bin liner bag. Cotton roll towels lasted an average of 103 uses before being replaced, but consumed bleach, starch, and hot water to wash the towels after each use. For both disposable and reusable towels, fuel consumed during towel delivery accounted for a large portion of their environmental impact. The Airblade machine itself, with its robust construction and advanced electronics, had high initial carbon emissions during the manufacturing process compared with the simple sheet metal box of the paper towel dispenser.

For the three types of electric hand dryers, the largest share of carbon footprint came from electricity consumed during usage (over 91 percent in the case of the Airblade[90]). This is where, as Dyson expected, its product outperformed all others. Not only did the Dyson Airblade draw electricity for a shorter time than its competitors, it drew less electricity when on. The Airblade drew 1,400 watts[91] during its 12-second blast. The Xlerator drew 1,500 watts for 21 seconds plus 1.5 seconds of half-power spin-down. The traditional hand dryer drew 2,300 watts for its 31-second cycle, almost five times the total energy used by the Airblade.

Ultimately, the study found that the Airblade did indeed have the lowest average carbon impact. The per-use carbon footprint for the plastic-bodied model, the study found, was just 4.19 g CO_2e; the aluminum-bodied model generated only slightly more: 4.44 g per use. The Xlerator had a 7.85 g per-use carbon footprint. Cotton roll towels generated 10.2 g per use; paper towels generated 14.6 g per use; and traditional hot-air electric dryers generated 17.2 g per use.

As with the banana LCA, the average numbers don't tell the whole story. In theory, the rankings of these choices might be different if the numerical values (e.g., the carbon footprint of electricity, time spent drying hands, number of hands dried over the life of the appliance) were different. To test this possibility, the researchers also performed a sensitivity analysis using a Monte Carlo simulation that compared the hand drying systems across a wide range of scenarios. They found that the Airblade was environmentally superior to the Xlerator in 86 percent of the scenarios and better than any of the remaining three drying systems in 98 percent or more of the simulated scenarios.

As in the case of Tesco's black foot carbon labeling project, the hand dryer LCA required considerable effort. The research team arrived at this and related conclusions after roughly 10 man-months of study. The report underwent a critical external expert panel review, whose feedback was incorporated into the final report. The final assessment report spanned 113 pages, complete with 42 charts, 48 tables, a 40-page appendix, and 3 pages of references. Dyson insisted on a strenuous assessment; strong claims about superior sustainability can attract allegations of bias or greenwashing from skeptical environmentalists (see chapter 9). Dyson "wanted the report to be bulletproof," said Jeremy Gregory, one of the report's authors.[92]

The Poisoned Product: Assessing Toxicity

Polycarbonate is a transparent thermoplastic polymer invented in 1898 but not commercialized until 1953. It is prized for its tough, shatter-resistant strength and its resistance to heat and flame. As a result, polycarbonate is a safer choice than glass and other plastics, making it ideal for a wide range of products from baby bottles to Blu-ray disks.[93] About one billion kilograms of polycarbonate are produced annually. Yet, although polycarbonate is not likely to shatter and physically harm users of these products, it is less clear whether the plastic might chemically harm them. Polycarbonate can contain traces of bisphenol A (BPA) from the manufacturing process and can release that BPA as the plastic ages or is exposed to heat, cleansers, or other substances. BPA is also found in many other products, such as some epoxy resins used in food cans and in many varieties of paper, such as those used for cash register receipts.

BPA is a very controversial chemical because in the human body it acts like the female hormone estrogen. Thus, it has the potential to affect the development of reproductive organs in fetuses, babies, and children; affect the reproductive performance of adult men and women; and affect the progression of some types of cancer. It has thus been categorized as an endocrine disruptor.[94] Research shows that people who handle these kinds of products (e.g., retail cashiers) accumulate detectable BPA levels in their blood.[95,96]

Various governments, including both the US and the EU, place some restrictions on BPA in food-related products but have not entirely banned its use. For example, BPA has been banned in baby bottles and sippy cups (in the US, the EU, and numerous countries in other regions).[97] Yet, consumer activist groups, such as the Natural Resources Defense Council and the US Public Interest Research Group, think these regulators have not gone far enough and are pressuring companies to stop using BPA entirely.

BPA is but one example of a widely used but controversial chemical. Each industry has its own alphabet soup of chemicals that have created concerns for regulators and NGOs.[98] These potentially toxic materials in the supply chain can affect the health of plants, animals, and people. Toxins include airborne emissions (e.g., mercury from coal-fired power plants, particulates from diesel-engine trucks, and sulfur emissions from ocean freighters), wastewater (e.g., cleansers, wash-water contaminants, solvents, eutrophy-causing ingredients, and pesticide run-off), and solid waste (e.g., electronics, metals, and plastics).

GOAL SETTING: FROM ASSESSMENT TO COMMITMENT

Assessing a company's environmental impacts serves many different purposes. L'Oréal used its assessment to define baselines for goals and then measure progress against that baseline. PepsiCo used assessment to identify "hotspots"—those areas of the company's activities, supply chain locations, or products that have particularly large environmental impacts—to help prioritize its improvement efforts. Tesco used assessment to create transparency of carbon footprints so that consumers could make sustainable choices. Dyson utilized assessment to make strong claims about its product's sustainability to the marketplace. Thus, assessment supports some combination of improvement (chapters 4 to 8), management of sustainability efforts (chapter 10), and as messaging concerning the company's sustainability (chapter 9). Implicit in these uses of assessment is an assumption that the measured impacts *matter*.

Materiality: Does It Matter to Me or to You?
As the largest chemical company in the world, BASF SE has significant environmental impacts of many different types and in many different locations. In order to most effectively improve sustainability, BASF needs to know which aspects of sustainability matter the most—both to the company and to its various stakeholders. To answer this question, the company performs an annual *materiality assessment*.[99] Through a set of workshops and interviews, the

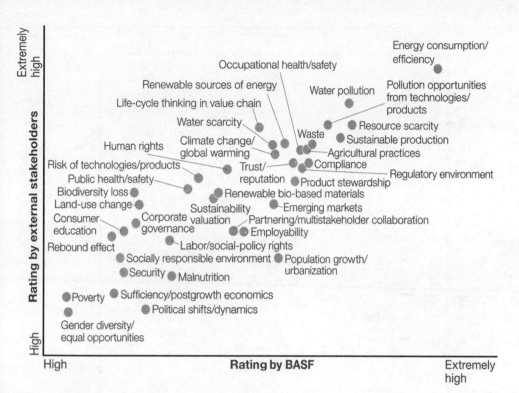

Figure 3.4
BASF environmental materiality assessment

company winnowed down a long list of potential impacts to 38 topics. Next, it surveyed 350 external stakeholders worldwide and 90 internal experts. The company collected data on the relevance of the 38 topics to BASF and to its external stakeholders, as depicted in figure 3.4.[100]

Different companies worry about different types of environmental impacts throughout their supply chain. Companies such as Apple, Tesco, and Chiquita focus on their carbon footprint; Coca-Cola, AB InBev, and Nestlé worry about water consumption, especially in drought-prone regions; and many companies that use agricultural products consider their land-use impacts, such as from growing palm oil, cotton, or coffee. Chicken of the Sea, the leading North American seafood supplier, uses internal versus external stakeholders' assessment, looking at 15 different topics. Each topic

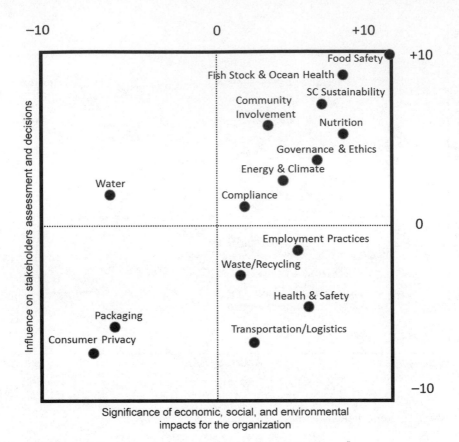

Figure 3.5
Chicken of the Sea's materiality assessment

was ranked between −10 and +10 in terms of materiality, leading to a chart similar to the one depicted in figure 3.5. A materiality assessment helps the company focus on important issues and set meaningful goals that matter to the company or its stakeholders.

By the Numbers, For the Numbers
In BASF's materiality assessment (figure 3.4), the highest-rated issue by both the company and external stakeholders was energy consumption or efficiency. Thus, a major focus of BASF's sustainability is *eco-efficiency* goals—reducing the quantity of resources consumed both to save money and curtail the environmental impact. These include 2020 goals to improve production process

energy efficiency by 35 percent and reduce GHG emissions per metric ton of sale by 40 percent relative to a 2002 baseline.

A company might define multiple numerical reduction goals to address its respective environmental impacts and cost components. For example, in 2013, toymaker Hasbro Inc. defined four numerical goals to achieve by 2020, all measured against a 2012 baseline. The four goals were: to lower global Scope 1 and Scope 2 GHG emissions from owned/operated facilities by 20 percent, decrease energy consumption at owned/operated facilities by 25 percent, cut water consumption from owned/operated facilities by 15 percent, and reduce waste to landfill at owned/operated facilities by 50 percent.[101] A well-formed environmental goal includes some dimension of sustainability (e.g., carbon footprint), a scope (e.g., owned/operated facilities), a target value (e.g., a 20 percent reduction compared to a baseline), and a time frame (e.g., from 2012 to 2020). In some cases, environmental goals might define an efficiency target rather than total reduction. For example, as mentioned in chapter 2, AB InBev and Coca-Cola define their water sustainability goals in terms of water efficiency—the number of liters of water needed to produce one liter of beer[102] or soda,[103] respectively.

Absolute Goals to Reduce Risks

Other issues in the materiality assessment might be of great concern to outside stakeholders but provide limited direct benefits to the company. Nevertheless, the risks of disruptions to reputation, demand, or supply arising from NGO action, regulation, community disapproval, or consumer boycott might motivate the company to incur higher costs in order to mitigate and manage these risks. *Eco-risk mitigation* goals and initiatives often include codifying, implementing, and enforcing restrictions against activities that might attract the attention of NGOs and the media, such as deforestation, hazardous waste dumping, and contamination by disfavored substances. These initiatives can also include design changes to eliminate known or suspected toxins associated with sourcing, making, using, or disposing of a product.

These environmental risks often lead companies to commit to an absolute goal within some time frame, such as Chicken of the Sea's commitment to dolphin-safe tuna, Campbell's goal to eliminate BPA from the linings of soup cans,[104] or McDonald's announcement to shift toward chicken raised without antibiotics.[105] Coca-Cola is committed to replacing every drop of water it uses. Other companies, such as Walmart,[106] P&G,[107] and General Motors[108] have "zero waste" goals. Rather than try to explain the basic concept of risk and to convince consumers, NGOs, or regulators that some level of a toxic substance or environmentally damaging activity is acceptable, these companies pledge to completely eliminate the contentious input or activity. To measure progress toward an absolute goal, companies typically assess the percent of products sold or percent of facilities that have achieved the goal in question.

Materiality to a Segment

A materiality assessment can lead the company to the realization that a subset of the market might care very much about particular attributes and be willing to prefer or pay for products that offer these attributes. For example, BASF's assessment (figure 3.4) noted stakeholder interest in issues such as pollution control, renewable bio-based materials, and agricultural sustainability. These are all issues that BASF might address through specific product lines and innovations. The result is *eco-segmentation* initiatives in which the company designs and sells products with one or more sustainability-related attributes, such as being energy-efficient, toxin-free, sustainably farmed, organic, or packaged in bio-based or recycled material. The higher costs of these products are typically defrayed through premium prices that green segment customers are willing to pay.

Other companies use eco-segmentation initiatives as part of their long-term risk management. The offering of Tide Coldwater laundry detergent and Pampers Cruiser diapers by consumer goods giant P&G allows the company to understand the technology and the market associated with green products. This knowledge positions the company to react quickly if and when consumers' preferences change or when regulations demand such products.

Getting Certified

"If there aren't fundamental changes in agriculture and fishing, then we won't have a business worth being in within one to two decades," said Antony Burgmans, chairman of Unilever. "No fish, no fish sticks," he added.[109] Grim assessments of the state of marine resources led Unilever to partner with the global conservation organization WWF in 1996 to create the Marine Stewardship Council (MSC), the first certification body for sustainable seafood.[110]

Both eco-risk mitigation and eco-segmentation initiatives may involve certification to provide independent evidence of the company's actions or product attributes (see chapter 9 for more on certification and labels).

Whereas environmental impacts, such as carbon footprint, water use, and energy are readily measured and managed via numerical reductions in the quantities of consumption or emissions, some categories of impacts have a strong nonquantitative element. For many categories of agricultural, natural, and food products, how a resource is harvested may matter more than how much of the resource is harvested. Thus, the goal might be codified not as a quantity to reduce, but rather as a complex set of practices or performance indicators to implement. For example, MSC certification requires a sufficiently high score on 31 performance indicators related to a sustainable level of harvesting of the target fish species, avoidance of environmental damage to other seafood species and marine habitats, and fishery management.[111] Certifications for agricultural crops, such as palm oil, cotton, coffee, cocoa, beef, and forest products include practices related to land use, water use, pesticides, fertilizers, harvesting, and waste management. These certifications are intended to ensure the future productivity of farm lands, forests, and oceans.

Feedback Loops: Assessments, Goals, and Improvements

By looking deep into both the upstream and the downstream of a supply chain of a product, including the consumer use and end-of-life phases, a company can assess where its environmental impact is the largest (and where it may be most vulnerable to accusations of excessive environmental impact). Such assessments can highlight opportunities for reducing the company's environmental impact or selling products that offer sustainability attributes. Unilever determined that its carbon footprint is divided very unevenly across the supply chain and life cycle of its products. On average, the footprint of a Unilever product is 29 percent from raw materials, 2 percent from manufacturing, 2 percent from logistics, 5 percent from retail, 62 percent from consumer use, and less than 1 percent from product disposal.[112] Such assessments help a company determine the locations and magnitudes of its environmental impacts, allowing it to design meaningful sustainability initiatives.

Assessment and goal definition are the first steps in a company's environmental journey. Sustainability initiatives can take place in any and all phases of a company's supply chain. These activities are discussed in the following chapters using the four operational processes of the SCOR model framework of *source*, *make*, *deliver*, and *return*, as well as in product design. Periodic reassessment— such as Danone's twice-a-year LCA—tracks progress toward meeting the company's goals for management, disclosure, and marketing purposes.

4

Making with Less Taking

As the English physician Sir Thomas Browne wrote in 1642, "Charity begins at home."[1] Likewise, sustainability also begins at home, and many companies look inward and focus their initial sustainability initiatives on self-improvement. "Developing and implementing sustainable manufacturing practices is an essential part of doing business today," said Michael Darr, plant manager at Bridgestone's passenger and light truck tire plant in Wilson, North Carolina.[2]

In most cases, these initial efforts align with the company's economic goals. Thus, improvements in the "make" process are often motivated by eco-efficiency considerations, including reducing the use (and therefore cost) of energy, water, and other inputs. These and other initiatives may also be motivated by eco-risk mitigation considerations, such as reducing or eliminating toxins in products or emissions, either of which could create expensive liabilities for the company or invite NGO criticism and attacks. This chapter emphasizes sustainability improvements in the manufacturing processes of a company's existing products, rather than changes to the products themselves (see chapter 8), changes in the raw materials and parts (see chapter 5), or changes in disposal (see chapter 7).

FROM THE TAMING OF FLAME TO THE SHAMING OF FLAME

A blazing fire can either be an untamed terror that consumes all before it or a comforting source of light and warmth that brings cheer on a cold winter night. At least half a million years ago, humanity tamed fire to harness this chemical process for an ever-growing number of applications.[3] Centuries of innovation have exploited the miracle of fire inside furnace boxes, beating pistons, and the twirling turbines of jets and power plants. The discovery of abundant fossil fuels, such as coal, oil, and natural gas, made energy cheap and plentiful, which fueled the modern world of industry and transportation.

As oil derricks drilled deep into the ground to extract black gold, so, too, did smokestacks, chimneys, and exhaust pipes rise into the sky. Emissions from the bright fires of early industry cast a dark pall over the landscape and sparked a wave of environmental laws after the Industrial Revolution. In response to regulation, engineers designed more efficient combustion systems that ensured more of the fuel was converted to useful heat. They also added a host of exhaust system add-ons, such as catalytic convertors, ash precipitators, and scrubbers, to further remove pollutants from exhaust.

Nevertheless, for all the control that humanity has exerted over this powerful natural reaction between air and fuel, it has failed to contain the most basic by-product of combustion: carbon dioxide. Each day, nearly 100 million tons of carbon dioxide flow into the atmosphere from the burning of fossil fuels in vehicles, factories, power plants, and other sources.[4] Those emissions have outstripped the present-day capacity of vegetation and other natural geochemical processes to absorb the excess CO_2, leading to a 27 percent increase in atmospheric carbon dioxide between 1960 and 2016.[5] The majority of scientists (but by no means all) believe that these emissions have been and will be responsible for significant climate change that could threaten the viability of agriculture and ecosystems.

Supply chains play a major role in the atmospheric buildup of CO_2 through the consumption of energy in both manufacturing and transportation. In the United States, industrial applications consume about one-third of all energy. Worldwide, industry consumes half of all energy. For that reason, many green supply chain initiatives focus on improving energy efficiency and reducing the carbon-intensity of energy sources. Under the Greenhouse Gas Protocol[6] described in chapter 3, these are, in large measure, improvements to Scope 1 and Scope 2 emissions. According to the US Department of Energy, "Energy efficiency is one of the easiest and most cost-effective ways to combat climate change, clean the air we breathe, improve the competitiveness of our businesses and reduce energy costs for consumers."[7]

Four Steps to Lower Footprints

In 2006, Siemens began implementing a "very German"[8] four-step approach to internal energy efficiency. The process begins with selecting a site for improvement, continues through an "energy health check," then moves on to an analysis of energy use, and ends with the implementation of a performance improvement contract between that Siemens facility and Siemens corporate headquarters.[9] This cycle of assessment and improvement is largely an eco-efficiency initiative.

At one of its Bavarian factories, Siemens installed €1.9 million in new energy-efficient equipment and processes. The program cut the factory's energy use by 20 percent and cut its carbon emissions by more than 2,700 metric tons of CO_2 per year.[10] Of course, a 2,700-metric-ton reduction at one factory is negligible in comparison to the 2,737,000 metric tons of CO_2 that Siemens emitted in 2013[11] and is infinitesimal compared with the 2013 global carbon emissions from fossil fuels of 36,000,000,000 metric tons.[12] The initiative does nothing to mitigate emissions at Siemens' tens of thousands of suppliers. And Siemens has thousands of business customers that use the company's products in ways that emit further carbon. However, the Bavarian factory improvement was only one of hundreds of initiatives undertaken by Siemens.

For example, at its factory in Newcastle, Siemens defined 13 individual initiatives in three categories: extension of existing building automation, modernization of measurement and control technology for the heating system, and installation of energy-efficient lighting. Siemens implemented its four-step energy saving process at its 298 major production and manufacturing plants worldwide. As a result, between 2010 and 2014, the company improved its overall energy efficiency by 11 percent and its CO_2 efficiency (output per unit of CO_2 emitted) by 20 percent.[13]

These examples show that sustainability is a broadly implemented process, not a "silver bullet" point solution; reducing
environmental impacts requires multiple points of intervention. In
other words, as any golfer knows, "you don't get to the green in
one stroke." Such is the case with many of the examples outlined
in this book, which exemplify the kinds of initiatives companies
are pursuing rather than exhaustively documenting every single
initiative.

Furthermore, many of these small changes are eco-efficient and
are, therefore, financially justified because they meet the company's return on investment thresholds. The Bavarian initiative paid
for itself in four-and-a-half years with projected annual savings of
almost €700,000.[14] The Newcastle improvements delivered a 27
percent internal rate of return (IRR).[15] In addition, each modest
success story (and its cumulative effect on impact reduction) contributes to eco-risk mitigation by demonstrating ongoing progress.

A 2006 study by the US Department of Energy (DOE) involving
200 energy savings assessments of steam or process heating systems utilized by manufacturers found that the average company in
the study could save $2.4 million a year on natural gas alone if it
implemented best practices in energy management or made modest
upgrades to systems.[16] Companies interested in superior energy
performance can pursue ISO 50001 certification, which is an international standard that specifies requirements for industrial energy
management systems.[17] The US DOE claims that companies that
achieve both ISO 50001 and the DOE's Superior Energy Performance (SEP) certification typically save 10 percent on their energy
costs within 18 months of SEP implementation.[18] Of course, such
studies do not test each environmental improvement against other
possible efficiency investments that companies could make or the
investment hurdle rate used by each company.

Beyond making improvements in the efficiency of each industrial process, companies can pursue more systemic solutions.

Cogeneration, Coproduction, and Verbund
Visit almost any factory and you will see pipes, ducts, and conduits
of all sizes carrying chilled water, hot water, steam, natural gas, and

electricity. Manufacturing processes often require various cycles of heating and cooling of ingredients, intermediate products, and finished goods. Much of the energy in a factory is consumed by attaining and maintaining the right temperature for all these industrial processes. Yet, many of these processes duplicate efforts, with one system consuming energy to chill down hot materials while another system consumes energy to warm cold materials. Moreover, the cooling towers and cooling ponds of electric power plants offer graphic evidence of the "wasted" heat produced in powering all these industrial heating and cooling systems.

To reduce such systemic waste of energy, Unilever spent about €28 million on a cogeneration program in Europe. Cogeneration, also called combined heat and power (CHP), is the intentional co-location of electricity generation and heat-dependent manufacturing systems. With cogeneration, Unilever captures more of the total energy latent in the fuel than a traditional power plant would and avoids the need for separate boilers. The program made both environmental and economic sense: it avoided 60,000 tons of CO_2 emissions and saved about €10 million a year.[19] Overall, cogeneration can be 20 to 60 percent more efficient than standard power plants.[20] "So we basically have a much cleaner energy generation, and it saves money," said Tony Dunnage, group environmental engineering manager at Unilever.[21]

BASF, the large German chemical producer, extended the eco-efficiency principle behind cogeneration to other *make* processes that produce significant quantities of by-products, such as those in the chemicals and agricultural products industries. BASF uses a holistic eco-efficiency practice of site-wide management of products and by-products, which it calls *verbund*, the German word meaning "combined," "linked," or "grouped." The largest of BASF's six verbund sites is located next to its headquarters in Ludwigshafen, Germany. The site integrates 160 production facilities interconnected by 2750 km of pipelines in a 10 square km campus. "At our verbund sites, production plants, energy and waste flows, logistics, and site infrastructure are all integrated," BASF claims on its website.[22] The strategy saves BASF more than €300 million annually.

Cogeneration and verbund take advantage of a supply chain that is more complex than the linear stages shown in the typical SCOR diagram. The verbund sites are a mesh in which each *make* step might consume multiple input materials (e.g., various raw materials and hot water) and produce multiple outputs (e.g., the intended product, valuable by-products, and cool water). Within this mesh, a by-product chemical from one production facility can provide a key ingredient to a second facility, while the second facility produces by-product heat used to power the first facility. With verbund, every production unit is potentially both a supplier and a customer of every other production unit. This holistic vision is also found in the *circular economy*: a sustainability concept borrowed from ecological sciences in which materials continually cycle in the environment (see chapter 7).[23]

Cogeneration and verbund require both large scale and breadth to be cost-effective. A smaller, more specialized chemical plant typically produces by-products in volumes that are too low to be economically viable for sale or further refinement, so they are typically burned for fuel or dumped. However, by integrating multiple large production facilities that can feed off each other's by-products, the volume of the by-products is large enough to justify storage and further processing, reducing the costs of subsequent manufacturing steps, and cutting by-product disposal costs. Yet, even the most efficient systems still need energy to drive manufacturing processes, which raises the issue of minimizing the carbon-intensity of these energy sources.

The Answer is Blowing in the Wind (and Shining in the Sky)

Starting in 2016, the winds sweeping across the hot dry plains of central Mexico have been helping General Motors build cars. The company signed an agreement with Enel Green Power to build a 34-megawatt wind farm to supply four of GM's Mexican factories. The new wind farm covers about 3 percent of the company's North American power needs and reduces GM's carbon footprint by nearly 40,000 tons annually.[24]

"There's also a good business case [because] prices for traditional power [in Mexico] are about a third greater than the United

States," said Rob Threlkeld, GM global manager of renewable energy.[25] In addition to the environmental benefits, GM will save about $2 million annually over Mexico's electricity rate.[26] "Using more renewable energy to power our plants helps us reduce costs, minimize risk and leave a smaller carbon footprint," said Jim DeLuca, GM's executive vice president of global manufacturing.[27]

Again, while such a reduction is trivial (vehicle manufacturing and assembly constitute only 4 percent of the total life cycle value of energy use and carbon emissions of a vehicle), it is but one effort among many potential renewable energy technologies being tested by the automaker. For example, two of GM's Ohio plants have multimegawatt rooftop solar arrays. "You don't often think of the Midwest when you think of ideal locations for solar, but reduced costs and increased utility rates have made sites like Lordstown and Toledo optimal locations to expand GM's use of solar power," Threlkeld said.[28] GM expects to get 12 percent of its total energy from renewables.[29] Overall, GM claimed to have achieved a 14 percent reduction in carbon intensity between 2010 and 2015.[30] Nevertheless, some companies are targeting 100 percent renewables.

Apple uses one kind of flat-panel product to supply power for another kind of flat-panel product. On the one hand, Apple buys hundreds of millions light-emitting display panels each year for its iPhones, iPads, and iMacs.[31] On the other hand, in 2015, the company pledged to invest $848 million in light-absorbing solar panels with First Solar's "California Flats Solar Project."[32] This commitment is part of $3 billion in investments by Apple in solar facilities in California and Arizona.[33] Those solar panels will power Apple's energy-hungry data centers that the company uses to fill the display panels of Apple users with apps, maps, videos, messages, and other data.

Apple has pursued renewables very aggressively, with the intent of reaching 100 percent renewables in its own operations. In 2010, Apple got 16 percent of its power for corporate, retail, and data center facilities from renewables. Like GM, Apple has tapped into a wide variety of renewables, including solar, wind, micro-hydro, biogas fuel cells, and geothermal sources.[34] Only four years later,

Apple's percentage usage of renewables in its own worldwide operations had climbed to 87 percent.[35]

Greenpeace even recognized Apple for its progress toward using
100 percent clean energy. The NGO gave Apple straight A's on all
four dimensions of Greenpeace's scorecard: energy transparency,
energy commitment and siting policy, energy efficiency and mitigation, and renewable energy deployment and advocacy.[36] "It's one
thing to talk about being 100 percent renewably powered, but it's
quite another thing to make good on that commitment with the
incredible speed and integrity that Apple has shown in the past two
years," said Greenpeace senior IT sector analyst Gary Cook.[37]

From Rubbish to Roadsters

The smell of decay from a landfill or sewage treatment plant can
also be the smell of an opportunity to reduce carbon intensity by
using biofuels. Many companies convert biomass waste (e.g., food
waste, agricultural waste, paper, and wood waste) into methane
that can then be used as fuel. Although BMW USA in Spartanburg,
South Carolina, does not produce significant biomass waste during
the production of cars, the car factory is located near a large municipal landfill. The decaying garbage gives off methane and various
other smelly gases. In 1999, BMW decided to harvest this gas to
run the energy-intensive operations at the plant. BMW's paint
shop, the single largest energy user in the factory, burns natural gas
for heating spray-booth air, paint-curing ovens, a regenerative thermal oxidizer (a pollution control device that burns off paint fumes),
and its energy center boiler.

The project required several capital equipment investments and
modifications. First, the carmaker built a 12-inch pipeline, 9.5
miles long, running from the landfill to the factory. This pipe delivers gas as the garbage in the landfill steadily decays. Because landfill gas (LFG) is not pure methane, it has a lower heating value than
fossil fuel natural gas. To accommodate the greater volume of gas
needed to deliver the required amount of energy, the project
required changes to many systems in the plant, such as larger pipes,
nozzle mixers, firing tubes, and blowers. BMW also added control
systems to easily switch between LFG and regular natural gas as
needed.

As of 2006, BMW Spartanburg got 63 percent of its energy from LFG. BMW originally justified the project based on a less than three-year payback from anticipated savings. Actual savings exceeded the original estimates. The project also reduces BMW's carbon emissions by 17,000 tons of CO_2 annually. In addition to the savings, the US Environmental Protection Agency awarded BMW with its Green Power Leadership Award in 2013.[38,39] For BMW, methane was a solution; for other companies, however, methane can be a problem.

The Footprints of Hoof Prints

When Stonyfield Farm, maker of organic yogurt, did its first LCA in the 1990s, it was shocked to find that fuel-burning trucks and power-hungry factories were not the biggest source of the company's carbon footprint. Rather, the beloved bovines that turn grass and organic grain into wholesome milk for Stonyfield belch vast quantities of enteric methane as a by-product of microbial digestion of plant material inside each cow. Methane is a potent greenhouse gas and has 30 times the long-term heat-trapping ability of CO_2. The average cow emits enough methane to equal the footprint of the average family car.

Many milk producers are aware of this crucial hotspot, and some are taking steps to mitigate it. Aurora Organic Dairy, for example, began to acquire land to grow feed for its cattle.[40] This allowed the company to control the type and quality of feed to maintain its organic standards, as well as control the cost. The feed has a direct impact on the amount of enteric emissions of cows. These emissions are responsible for 78 percent of the company's GHG emissions.[41] Aurora also acquired milk-processing capabilities, replacing a third party. In addition to reducing the dairy's carbon footprint, the control across the supply chain allows the company "the greatest traceability, most consistent standards and highest quality available."[42]

Reducing the Hothouse Effects of Chilling Gases

Keeping milk and other food cold on a hot summer day has a hidden environmental impact beyond the obvious energy consumed. Ironically, the most popular and "safe" gases that enable refrigerators to perform their chilling tricks are environmentally problematic. For much of the 20th century, refrigeration systems relied on chlorofluorocarbons (CFCs), because these gases were energy efficient, nonflammable, and had much lower toxicity than earlier refrigerants, such as ammonia.

The trouble starts when CFC refrigerants inevitably leak into the atmosphere during installation, maintenance, repair, disposal, and even during operation owing to imperfect seals in the equipment. The same inertness of CFCs that makes them prized for refrigeration and many other consumer, commercial, and industrial applications means that they could remain in the atmosphere for more than 100 years.[43] As the CFCs slowly break down high up in the atmosphere, they release chlorine that attacks the ozone layer that shields the Earth's surface from damaging levels of UV radiation.[44]

Late in the 20th century, environmentalists and then governments recognized that chlorinated and bromated hydrocarbons, including CFCs, were destroying the ozone layer of the Earth's atmosphere. The UN-mediated 1989 Montréal Protocol—considered the most successful environmental treaty to date—called for worldwide regulations on a broad range of ozone-depleting substances, including CFCs.[45] Governments around the world enacted regulations that steadily phased out both the manufacturing of CFCs and the use of equipment dependent on CFCs. In response, many companies turned to hydrofluorocarbons (HFCs) as ozone-safe, yet chemically similar, alternatives.

Unfortunately, CFCs, and even HFCs, create another environmental problem; a single ton of escaped HFCs could impact climate change as much as 14,000 tons of CO_2.[46] Although HFCs are certainly better for the ozone layer, they are potent greenhouse gases. Thus, activists began calling for a phaseout of HFCs too.[47]

In 2000, Greenpeace targeted Coca-Cola over the beverage maker's use of HFCs in vending machines and retail refrigeration units.[48] Refrigeration was responsible for 40 percent of Coca-Cola's carbon footprint.[49] Greenpeace parodied Coca-Cola's iconic polar bear ads by showing bears floating on melting icebergs and used Coca-Cola's distinctive cursive font to write "Enjoy Climate

Change."[50] The NGO specifically targeted Coca-Cola's sponsorship of the 2000 Sydney Olympic Games, which were purported to be green.

Coca-Cola began testing other technologies and rolled out its first HFC-free machine in 2002,[51] but its solution looked counterintuitive at first glance. Coca-Cola actually selected CO_2 as a refrigerant. "We talk about fighting fire with fire," said Bryan Jacob, director of energy and climate protection for Coke. "In the right application, CO_2 can be a solution to climate change," he added.[52] Carbon dioxide is a natural alternative that is nonflammable, relatively nontoxic, comparatively inexpensive, readily available, and eliminates 99 percent of direct emissions. By using CO_2 that would otherwise have been vented into the atmosphere, Coca-Cola sequesters greenhouse gases for the duration that it remains in the refrigeration system. In fact, in a document enumerating the growing threat of HFCs, Greenpeace itself recommends the use of CO_2 as a natural replacement to HFCs.[53]

By 2014, Coca-Cola had installed one million HFC-free units worldwide, with Europe and Japan being the market leaders in installations.[54] "Over the past decade we have invested more than $100 million to make our coolers better for the environment," said Jeff Seabright, vice president, environment and water for The Coca-Cola Company.[55] "We've made sustainable refrigeration the cornerstone of our climate protection and energy management efforts," he added. Still, Coca-Cola and its bottling partners had approximately 10 million HFC coolers and vending machines in place around the world.[56] On October 15, 2016, nearly 200 countries met in Rwanda's capital city of Kigali to hammer out an amendment to the Montréal Protocol to reduce the use of HFCs.[57]

If You Can't Reduce 'Em, Offset 'Em

Some impacts are almost unavoidable. During takeoff, an Airbus A380 guzzles as much as three gallons of jet fuel every second.[58] Heaving the 859,000-pound jet aircraft into the sky consumes prodigious amounts of fossil fuels. Although airlines are improving fleet fuel efficiency with newer aircraft, better engines, and operational improvements, these improvements are modest at best. The physics of airflow, as well as engineering limits on airframe and engine design, prevent larger reductions in fuel consumption by airplanes.

If a company cannot eliminate its own GHG emissions through better technology or better management, it can "outsource" the emissions reduction by purchasing "*carbon offsets*" that pay third parties to reduce emissions or sequester CO_2 elsewhere, thereby offsetting its own emissions. Carbon offset certification agencies use the money they collect from companies to fund projects around the globe that absorb or reduce carbon, such as planting trees in Africa or funding a hydropower project in Brazil.[59] Reductions in carbon emissions from these projects are then transferred to the paying organization and can be claimed to offset their own emissions.

Carbon offsets became an integral part of the 1997 Kyoto Protocol on climate change through the so-called clean-development mechanism.[60] If government regulations or public commitments require reduction of carbon emissions but technological or economic obstacles prevent direct compliance, then carbon offsets give businesses a viable way of complying. The net effect of using offsets is a reduction in the total carbon added to the planet's atmosphere at a lower cost for the economy than would be required for a company to do it directly. Carbon offsets help balance cost pressures with environmental pressures: If it is too expensive for a company to reduce its own carbon footprint by changing processes, machinery, or materials, the company, in effect, pays a third party to achieve the corresponding carbon footprint reduction at a lower cost elsewhere.

Some companies offer offsets to their customers as a service to their "green" customer segment. UPS, for example, offers "carbon neutral" shipping. The company estimates the carbon impact of each delivery and gives consumers the option to pay an offset fee. The company that sells the offset then uses that income to pay for carbon reduction projects such as reforestation and wastewater treatment.[61] Similarly, airlines, such as Lufthansa, Air France, and United Airlines, among others, let passengers buy carbon offsets.[62]

Although well intended, carbon credits and offsets have been criticized for letting polluters buy the appearance of sustainability without actually achieving it. Paying to clean up someone else's house is not the same as cleaning up your own house is the mantra of the critics. The eco-vacation company Responsible Travel began offering offset packages for customers in 2002. It cancelled the program in 2009 because, the company said, offsets can make customers feel virtuous while they engage in inherently destructive activities, such as flying a private jet or taking a helicopter tour. "The message was, 'Don't worry, you can offset the emissions,'" Responsible Travel's managing director Justin Francis told the *New York Times*. "But you don't really need to see Sydney from the air, do you? And you can travel in a commercial airliner."[63]

Despite their imperfections, carbon offset-funded projects can have positive effects. According to British NGO Climatecare.org, British insurance company Aviva Plc offset its carbon emissions and improved the lives of 200,000 people in Kenya and India by supplying them with technologies that allowed them to burn less fuel while cooking food or cleaning water.[64] According to the US NGO Conservation International, tree-planting projects funded with carbon offsets have a cascade of positive effects beyond carbon reduction. "These include the maintenance and regulation of water supplies, the prevention of soil erosion, protection of natural pollinators, and the provision of important non-timber forest products."[65]

A VOICE FOR THE BABBLING BROOK

What could be a more ubiquitous natural resource than crystal clear water? It falls naturally from the sky, pools on the ground, accumulates deep in aquifers, and steadily flows into rivers on its journey to the sea where it evaporates and begins the cycle anew. As abundant as water seems, it is scarcer than it appears. Although 71 percent of the Earth's surface is covered in water, 97.5 percent of it is corrosive salt water that is unusable for drinking, agriculture, or most industrial processes. Furthermore, over two-thirds of the remaining fraction of fresh water sits locked up in icecaps, glaciers, and permafrost.[66] According to a World Health Organization

2016 report, 663 million people lacked access to safe drinking water in 2015, and half a million people die every year as a result of consuming contaminated drinking water.[67]

The paradox of water is that it is priceless in both senses of the term: being essential to life and yet often considered an unpriced resource in that users in many locations can legally pump or divert unlimited amounts of water from lakes, rivers, and aquifers. According to Christopher Gasson, publisher of *Global Water Intelligence*, "Previously, water was treated as a free raw material," but that is changing.

"Water is to Coca-Cola as clean energy is to BP. ... We need to manage this issue or it will manage us," said Jeff Seabright, vice president of environmental and water resources, Coca-Cola Corporation.[68] Gasson added: "The marginal cost of water is rising around the world. Now, companies are realizing it can damage their brand, their credibility, their credit rating, and their insurance costs. That applies to a computer chipmaker and a food company as much as a power generator or a petrochemicals company."[69]

The Locality of Liquid Liabilities

Unlike GHG emissions, which create global impacts regardless of where the emissions occur, water scarcity (or plenitude) is a local or regional issue. For example, Brazil is home to the Amazon—the world's largest rainforest and river—and has been called the "the Saudi Arabia of water." All the same, 1,000 km south of that massive water supply, the 20 million people of the São Paulo metropolitan area and 40 percent of Brazil's industrial production face critical water shortages.[70] Similarly, in India, water has long been a "make-or-break" social, economic, and political issue because Indians, who account for 20 percent of the world's population, have only 4 percent of total renewable freshwater resources.[71] Farms and people in hot and dry regions need more water than those in cooler climes.

The Many Ways of Reducing Water

Many companies such as Coca-Cola, AB InBev, and Nestlé measure and manage water efficiency, which is the ratio of "water used" to "product produced." Given that a company like Coca-Cola makes bottled beverages, it absolutely cannot use less than one liter of water per liter of produced beverage, so it looks to other areas of water consumption within its production processes and facilities. Reducing the water footprint of syrup and bottling plants is a key part of that strategy. For example, the company found significant efficiency improvement opportunities in the cleaning processes for both bottles and the factory. It developed a new spray nozzle design that cleans bottles with less water.[72] The company also implemented air rinse systems to remove most of the dirty or soapy water from the bottles by using air blasts, much like those used in high-tech hand dryers.[73]

Similarly, water efficiency is the focus of AB InBev's water stewardship efforts. In 2002, the company needed 6.48 liters of water to manufacture each liter of beverage.[74] Then it implemented a wide range of water-saving initiatives at its breweries, such as controlling evaporation losses in the malting process, condensing the waste steam, and reusing treated wastewater for factory cleaning and other non-product uses.[75] By the end of 2014, AB InBev had achieved a ratio of 3.2 liters per liter, which implies the company could then produce double the amount of beer from a given amount of water.

"We're going to run out of water long before we run out of oil," said Peter Brabeck, chairman of Nestlé in an interview with the *Financial Times*.[76] Some 38 percent of Nestlé's factories reside in water-stressed regions,[77] a fact that has motivated the company to pursue nearly 500 water-saving projects as of August 2013. These initiatives have reduced company-wide water consumption by 10 percent, from 3.29 m³ per metric ton of product in 2010 to 2.89 m³ per metric ton of product by 2012.[78] Many of these efforts focused on 31 high-priority manufacturing facilities located in areas of severe water stress or that represented a significant portion of Nestlé's water withdrawals.[79]

Milking Milk to Evaporate Water Stress

Unlike energy, water is often only *borrowed* rather than *consumed* in industrial processes. For example, in Mexico, Nestlé built a new

"Cero Agua" (zero water) factory to make evaporated milk and other dairy products. The factory starts with cows' milk, which, on average, consists of 88 percent water. By condensing the steam coming from the evaporating milk and recovering that water, the factory can harvest 1.6 million liters of water per day. The recovered water is then used twice. First, it is used to clean the evaporating machines. Then it is collected, purified, and recycled a second time to be used for other cleaning activities in the factory and for watering the grounds. This water recovery and recycling process eliminates the need to tap the area's scarce groundwater.[80] It also illustrates that water can be an asset that is utilized multiple times rather than a consumable item.

Similarly, Nestlé's La Penilla candy factory in water-stressed Spain was a hot spot for water use. The plant used 72 cubic meters of water (or 72 metric tons) per metric ton of product, over 20 times more water consumption than the company-wide average. The company invested €1 million in multiple projects, such as installing a closed-loop refrigeration system with three new cooling towers that recycle water. The company also improved the regulation of water flowing into the milk evaporators to better achieve the required vacuum on the equipment. Finally, training helped too. "At the beginning, it was challenging to change the habits of the operators, who were used to working in a specific way," explained Ramon Montserrat, head of engineering and packaging services for the Iberian region. As a result of the new technology, improved processes, and employee retraining, the factory reduced its water consumption by 60 percent without affecting either energy efficiency or GHG emissions.[81]

Coca-Cola also reduced water use through the reuse of wash water. For example, wash water can be used to clean crates and floors.[82] The recovered wash water is carefully treated using existing technologies, including biological treatment in a membrane bioreactor, ultrafiltration, reverse osmosis, ozonation, and ultraviolet disinfection.[83] Other water reduction steps included improvements in water-based cooling systems, faster repair of water leaks, and replacing wet lubricants with dry or semi-dry ones.[84]

Of Quality and Quantity

The quality of incoming water also affects the water efficiency of some processes. At Nestlé USA's pizza division factory in Little Chute, Wisconsin, the municipal water supply was hard and alkaline. The company had to flush large amounts of water through its cooling system to avoid the buildup of energy efficiency-sapping mineral deposits. To tackle the issue, in 2012, the company invested in a water pretreatment system and a new control system for its four main ammonia refrigeration condensers. According to Nestlé, these systems save 7.4 million gallons of water annually and reduce sewer discharges.[85] As it turns out, the low cost of municipal water in Wisconsin meant that the effort saved a mere $50,000 in avoided water purchase costs and discharge fees.

The Pizza Division project was just one of 489 water-saving projects at Nestlé that same year, collectively saving 1.7 billion gallons of water and contributing to a 4.5 percent reduction in Nestlé's total water withdrawals that year.[86] "One of our sustainability goals here at Nestlé is to continuously improve water efficiency across our operations and reduce water withdrawals," said Louis Miller, utilities supervisor at Nestlé Pizza Division Little Chute. These water-saving initiatives help the company manage risks to the brand and to the company's social license to operate.

What Happens in the Brewery Doesn't Stay in the Brewery

AB InBev's in-house water efficiency improvements do not address the largest hotspot in the life cycle water footprint of beer: In addition to the 3.2 liters of water consumed at the brewery in making each liter of beer, growing barley consumes an average of 298 liters of water per liter of beer.[87] Even though 85 percent of these liters are green water, the company is working with farmers to improve water usage (see chapter 5). At the same time, AB InBev works on in-house production efficiencies that indirectly, but significantly, affect the agricultural water consumption per liter of beer. The company works to reduce so-called extract losses, which are the percentage of fermentable sugars left over after the brewing process.

Extract losses mean that the brewer must buy more high-water-footprint grain to produce a given volume of beer. In 2002, InBev's extract losses were almost 8 percent, which is to say that company had to buy 8 percent more grain than the theoretical brewing efficiency limit.[88] The company benchmarked the extract losses along with hundreds of other key performance indicators at 130 AB InBev locations and used best practices from the leading locations to set performance targets and improvements for lagging locations.[89] By 2013, the company had reduced these losses to 3 percent,[90] which represents a life cycle reduction in water use by 15 liters per liter of beer. This example illustrates that sometimes a hotspot in one part of the supply chain (e.g., irrigation water consumed to grow barley) may be tempered in another part of the supply chain (e.g., the brewer who improves the product yield from the supplied barley).

Manufacturing Inefficiency Means Wastewater Toxicity

AB InBev's extract losses had another significant effect—on the gray water emissions side—even though it was only 9 percent of AB InBev's water footprint. Extract losses mean that the breweries' wastewater contains more leftover sugars, which make the wastewater more of an environmental threat.[91] Sugars in the discharged wastewater cause bacteria to grow in water treatment plants and—if this waste is released into rivers, lakes, or oceans—the growing bacteria take oxygen out of the water and potentially kill fish and other animals living in the water.[92]

Reducing extract losses from 8 percent to 3 percent removed two-thirds of these waste sugars. To further reduce the amount of sugars in wastewater, AB InBev runs the effluent from the brewing process through a bio-treatment system, which serves two purposes. First, it removes these impurities from the water to help the company's wastewater meet water quality standards, thereby reducing risks and costs associated with wastewater. Second, the bio-treatment system produces biogas that helps fuel operations, as described in the BMW example earlier in the chapter, thereby cutting both energy costs and the beverage-maker's carbon footprint.[93]

A Round of Drinks on the House

In May 2015, torrential rains in Oklahoma and Texas reversed a five-year drought, but the muddy waters damaged municipal water systems and created a shortage of drinking water in some communities. In response, AB InBev subsidiary Anheuser-Busch halted beer production at its Cartersville brewery in Georgia to produce 50,000 cans of drinking water, which it gave to the American Red Cross.[94] "It's something we're uniquely positioned to do in a very timely period," said Rob Haas, manager of the Cartersville brewery that produces cans of emergency relief water a few times a year. The company did the same thing after hurricanes Katrina, Sandy, and Harvey. "Relief workers and people in the region are in need of safe, clean drinking water, and Anheuser-Busch is in a unique position to produce and ship large quantities of emergency drinking water," said Peter Kraemer, vice president of supply for the company. "Our local distributors help identify those communities most in need, and work with relief organizations such as the American Red Cross to make sure the water gets where it's needed," he added.[95]

That 50,000-can run was a tiny fraction of the million cans of drinking water produced by Anheuser-Busch for Hurricane Sandy in 2012, or the 9.4 million cans the company donated to relief agencies when Katrina and Rita devastated the Gulf Coast in 2005.[96] Since 1988, Anheuser-Busch has reported that it has packaged and donated more than 73 million cans of fresh drinking water in response to natural disasters of all kinds.[97] Although such acts of philanthropy exemplify social responsibility more so than environmental sustainability, they are part of Anheuser-Busch's broader corporate responsibility strategy that ensures that the company will maintain access to local resources, especially water. Anheuser-Busch and its parent, AB InBev, consume more than 39 billion gallons of water per year, which makes the company highly dependent on community and governmental cooperation.[98] Water stewardship is therefore the leading item in the brewer's materiality assessment.

Similarly, Coca-Cola's water stewardship and replenishment efforts include more than 382 community water projects to help protect watersheds, improve people's access to safe water, educate water users, and improve every person's water efficiency.[99]

Coca-Cola's access to water is contingent on community access to water. "If the communities around ... our bottling plants do not flourish and are not sustainable, our business will not be sustainable in the future," said Coca-Cola's CEO Neville Isdell.[100] In announcing Coca-Cola's worldwide initiative to conserve water resources in 2007, the CEO added, "Essentially the pledge is to return every drop we use back to nature."[101] The company reached its 2020 goal of being water-neutral in 2015.[102] The company's efforts, however, only cover water use in beverage manufacturing, bottling, and food service. They do not extend to the growing and production of ingredients, such as sugar.

No Free Lunch (Mostly)

Eleven of China's 31 provinces meet the World Bank's definition of water scarcity.[103] In response to this scarcity, China began building air-cooled power plants. As of the end of 2012, these plants made up 14 percent of China's thermal power generation capacity. That year, those same plants effectively avoided water consumption equivalent to about 60 percent of Beijing's total annual water use. Unfortunately, air-cooled plants have a lower thermodynamic efficiency than water-cooled plants and emit tens of millions more tons of CO_2 than water-cooled plants.[104]

Similarly, desalination offers another direct trade-off between water and energy. Locations with access to seawater can use energy to make fresh water. Half of all the world's desalination takes place in the Persian Gulf, where fresh water is scarce and oil is plentiful. "Desalination requires a lot of power ... we estimate that about four tonnes of carbon are emitted per million gallons of freshwater produced here," said Ivano Iannelli, CEO of the Dubai Carbon Centre of Excellence.[105] Given the high energy demands of desalination, the desalination plant in Beckton, East London, not only runs on biodiesel, including recycled fat and oil from London restaurants,[106] but is also designed to operate as an emergency backup system rather than to operate continuously.[107]

Some of the most successful and energy-efficient desalination plants are in Israel. The three plants built from 2005 to 2016 reversed Israel's water situation from dire shortages to having surplus water in the dry Middle East.[108] Israel's IDE Technologies built some of the largest desalination plants in the world using innovative new processes that require significantly less energy than previous plants. In 2017, the company was building desalination plants in California, India, Venezuela, and Mexico. Engineering breakthroughs, such as those of IDE Technologies, point to a rarely discussed aspect of environmental efforts and economic development. Technological breakthroughs such as carbon capture, artificial photosynthesis, solar geoengineering, cost-effective renewables, modern nuclear power, and other advances could change the current environmental calculus. Chapter 13 discusses the potential for innovation to upend assumptions that seem to link human consumption with environmental degradation.

While desalination plants trade a lower water footprint for a higher carbon one, in a few situations the two footprints can have synergistic relationships. For example, reducing the amount of wash water in cleaning processes also reduces the energy consumption used to heat that water. The example of AB InBev's extract losses and other similar wastewater treatment initiatives also demonstrate a positive coupling between carbon and water impacts: converting effluent into biogas mitigates both the company's gray water footprint and its carbon footprint.

FACTORIES GO TO DETOX

Acrid belching smoke, discolored run-off streams, foam-flecked rivers, and a smelly landscape of dead fish and skeletal trees make up the environmentalist's dystopia of the industrialized earth. Reality may not be as bad as the Hollywood cliché of mutants bursting forth from bubbling pools of industrial waste, but many of the industrial processes used for making metals, plastics, apparel, and paper do involve a witches' brew of heavy metals, corrosive acids, carcinogenic solvents, and toxic by-products. Manufacturers in many industries are starting to change their manufacturing assets or processes to reduce or eliminate toxins. These changes, however, may affect conversion efficiencies, costs, product performance, and customer acceptance.

The Frightening Story of Brightening

The bright white paper in every office and the white-coated card stock associated with consumer goods retail packaging of many products hides a pernicious skeleton in its closet: The chemicals often used to bleach naturally brown wood pulp are toxic. In the past, paper factories typically bleached raw wood pulp using elemental chlorine, a pale yellow-green corrosive gas. Unfortunately, the process produced significant quantities of dioxins,[109] which are some of the most toxic human-released pollutants in existence. Papermaking sludge, wastewater effluent, and the paper itself could contain both dioxins and AOX ("adsorbable organic halogens" that are a broad family of potentially toxic chlorinated by-products of the many different organic compounds in wood pulp). Dioxins could even leach into foods, such as milk, that are stored in chlorine-bleached paper containers.[110] Chlorinated AOXs have been on the European Commission's "black list" of toxic substances since 1976.[111]

In theory, paper makers could use any of a wide range of oxidizers to bleach brown pulp white, or they could convince customers to accept unbleached paper. Environmentalists advocated either unbleached paper or changing manufacturing methods to use oxygen, ozone, or hydrogen peroxide to create "totally chlorine free" (TCF) paper that generate no dioxin or AOX by-products.[112] However, converting papermaking operations to chlorine-free chemical processes requires significant capital expenditures, downtime, and employee training.[113]

Some papermakers, especially in Europe, built new factories using TCF papermaking methods.[114] For example, pioneering Swedish wood pulp maker Södra Cell developed Zero Chlorine Pulp and sold this paper to green companies who were willing to pay extra for it.[115] Most paper makers adopted a lower cost manufacturing process they dubbed "elemental chlorine free" (ECF). The process uses chlorine dioxide, which is actually a stronger bleaching agent. ECF reduces dioxins to "non-detect" levels and cuts AOX in mill effluent by 80 to 90 percent.[116] The lower cost and superior brightness of ECF paper led to it capturing 93 percent of the world paper market as of 2012.[117] Even Södra noted that market demand for ECF motivated them to use chlorine dioxide manufacturing methods in a new plant.[118]

Greenpeace and CorpWatch, however, sounded the alarm because ECF sounds like it is chlorine free but is not.[119] Greenpeace noted that data on low AOX was misleading because it was selectively picked from the most modern, so-called ECF-light plants, situated primarily in Nordic countries.[120] The moral is that partial improvements in a company's manufacturing processes, in terms of environmental performance, can still leave the company vulnerable to criticism.

Manufacturers in many different industries face similar issues of harmful ingredients or by-products in their manufacturing processes. For example, manufacturers who make, reprocess, or use aluminum often create a toxic sludge that requires special handling or disposal.[121] Semiconductor companies have problems with waste that contains fluorine, which prompted Oki Electric Industry, in Japan, to develop a two-stage chemical coagulation process to remove the chemical.[122] The top 20 sources of toxic pollution include mining and pesticides, which put these harmful footprints in the supply chains of any companies that depend on metals or agricultural products. The top sources of toxic pollution also include tanneries and apparel dyeing, as well as the manufacturing of pharmaceuticals, cleaning agents, and anticorrosion coatings.[123]

Waste Not, Want Not

While companies mentioned in the previous section reduced the toxicity of their manufacturing waste streams, others focused on reducing the total volume (and costs) of the waste stream in the first place. These companies utilized two main approaches: avoiding waste and recycling. "The biggest savings to be made in the waste arena are from not generating it in the first place," said Unilever's Tony Dunnage, "If we waste less, we're more efficient. If we're more efficient, we're more cost-effective."[124]

The second strategy reuses or recycles any unavoidable waste material either inside the company or through an outside contractor. In general, each scrap material, by-product, or off-spec product might have multiple uses, leading companies to find the highest-value uses that can handle the volumes generated. In part, BASF's verbund strategy addresses the challenge of reusing by-products by creating sufficient economies of scale of the production of by-products to justify further reprocessing into salable materials.

In 2007, P&G created the Global Asset Recovery Purchases (GARP) group, tasked with managing waste streams at sites around the world both to deliver cost savings and to increase reuse, recycling, and waste-to-energy generation opportunities. Solutions began to roll in. P&G's Budapest plant that made feminine hygiene products started to sell excess material to a cement kiln; Gillette's excess shaving foam materials were sold to companies that grow turf for commercial uses; scrap from US Pampers was converted into upholstery filling; and sludge from toilet tissue paper in Mexico was converted into low-cost roof tiles. The drive for waste reduction uncovered new sales opportunities for off-spec products: off-spec baby wipes are sold to veterinarians for animal care and off-spec detergent is sold to car washes.[125] According to James McCall, P&G's global product sustainability supply leader, the first five years of the GARP program (2007–2012) brought in an extra $1 billion to P&G.

Surplus or waste food offers even more challenges and opportunities. Marks & Spencer reduces food waste in its stores by reducing prices up to three times a day to clear short-shelf-life products.[126] Unsold yet edible food is often donated to charities.[127] In another example, Tesco introduced large boxes of strawberries to its stores and lowered the prices during February 2017; an unexpected warm period resulted in a glut of strawberries, and by moving large quantities of strawberries, the retailer helped avoid food waste at the farms.[128] In 2016, France banned food waste in supermarkets and most grocery stores, forcing food retailers to donate it to food banks and other charities.[129] Unfortunately, as a result of liability concerns and logistics difficulties, US food retailers toss out $47 billion worth of food, most of which is edible. This is despite existing US laws that encourage food donation through limited liability protection in the Emerson Good Samaritan Food Act of 1996,[130] as well as some tax deductions,[131] and the Federal

Food Donation Act of 2008, which encourages food donations by federal contractors.[132]

Overall, programs to eliminate toxic materials, improve efficiency, or find value in waste can markedly reduce the volume of materials sent for disposal and reduce costs at the same time. "More than half of our sites globally (approximately 130 sites) are at zero nonhazardous waste for landfill," said Unilever's Dunnage in an interview for this book. "Without any significant capital investment, we've saved more than €70 million in cost avoidance through the zero-waste program."[133] By 2012, Unilever reduced its manufacturing waste to half of its 2008 total and in 2014 it achieved zero waste to landfills in all its manufacturing operations. In 2015 it achieved zero waste from its other activities.[134] Reducing the volume of discarded material saved money because the materials originally had to be purchased or manufactured before they were ultimately discarded; therefore, reducing waste also reduces costs on the procurement and operations side.

From Toxic Waste to Watts

While BMW uses gases from a nearby community landfill to produce energy (see the earlier discussion in this chapter), other companies have found ways to turn their own costly industrial waste into valuable energy. At Unilever's Owensboro, Kentucky, facility, which produces pasta sauce under the Ragú and Bertolli brands, food waste is composted, blended for fertilizer, or converted into biogas through an anaerobic digestion process.[135] Anaerobic digesters are also used to mitigate the daily waste that results from batch switching at Ben & Jerry's ice cream production sites when changing production from, say, the Chunky Monkey to Cherry Garcia flavors.

Similarly, many industrial painting systems produce large amounts of volatile organic compounds (VOCs) from the solvents used to liquefy paint. In the past, companies typically abated this source of pollution by extracting the fumes from the painting area and passing them through an abatement incinerator that oxidizes the VOCs. These incinerators, however, require natural gas and emit CO_2.

Ford created a fumes-to-fuel (F2F) system that pulls VOCs from paint box air, concentrates the VOCs, and then burns them in a Stirling engine attached to a generator.[136] Instead of consuming natural gas to oxidize the fumes, the system produces electricity and reduces carbon emissions by 88 percent over a traditional incinerator.[137] Ford has estimated that the F2F life cycle cost is 20 to 35 percent of the cost of a traditional VOC abatement system.[138] Not only does the system save Ford money, but it also earned the company a US EPA Clean Air Excellence Award in 2003.

Ford continued to make improvements as it increased the scale of the system and installed it in other locations. Whereas the first pilot installation produced 5 kW, the system in Ford's Canadian Oakville plant will eventually produce 300 kW.[139] Oakville will use a third-generation version of the system that replaces the Stirling engine with a fuel cell to eliminate nitrogen oxide emissions. "The Oakville installation is the first of its kind in the world to harvest emissions from an automotive facility for use in fuel cell," said Kit Edgeworth, abatement equipment technical specialist for manufacturing at Ford Motor Company. "It is the greenest technology and offers the perfect solution to the industry's biggest environmental challenge traditionally."[140]

Manufacturing by Printing

In 2016, General Electric Company started manufacturing and selling the first jet engine parts manufactured by 3D printing, a method of additive manufacturing. A 3D printer manufactures items by printing layers of a building material—polymers, ceramics, metals, or cement—instead of a layer of ink. By printing layers on top of layers on top of layers, the printer slowly builds up a 3D object according to a digital plan.

While visiting the MIT Center for Transportation and Logistics, Philippe Cochet, chief productivity officer at GE, described the benefits his company reaps by using additive manufacturing at scale. GE's next-generation LEAP jet engine features 3D-printed fuel nozzles. The fuel nozzles are installed on engines that entered service in 2016. The metal-printed fuel nozzle is significantly lighter and many times stronger than the nozzle it replaced. What is significant from a supply chain management point of view is that it is a single component. Instead of procuring, receiving, and assembling 19 parts from 19 different suppliers, the new nozzle is printed in a single step. By 2020, GE plans to print 40,000 fuel nozzles per year.

Not only can the new nozzles be made to exact, complex specifications, but the technology also promises many environmental benefits, mostly stemming from waste reduction during the manufacturing process. Whereas traditional subtractive manufacturing starts with a large block of material and then cuts, mills, or drills away the unneeded material—thereby creating waste—additive manufacturing builds up the object, consuming the minimum amount of material needed to make the layers of the final item.[141] Moreover, 3D printing gives designers much more freedom to make unusual hollow parts that need less total material; GE's new jet nozzle is 25 percent lighter and five times more durable than its predecessor.[142] Finally, once the technology matures, it may also reduce transportation impacts because the parts can be "shipped" as a digital file to a printing facility closer to the point of assembly or consumption.

Although 3D-printing technology has not yet reached its full potential, it is one of the technologies that may reduce materials consumption, energy consumption, and waste in manufacturing processes.

Sustainability Outside the Four Walls

In 2015, at the same time that Greenpeace was lauding Apple for embracing clean energy[143] [see the section "The Answer is Blowing in the Wind (and Shining in the Sky)," earlier in this chapter], Truthout, an online investigative reporting organization, was vilifying the company for its high CO_2 emissions.[144] That two NGOs could come to such diametrically opposite conclusions about the company illuminates an important fact about corporate claims and about supply chains. Greenpeace's analysis focused on Apple's internal operations: buildings, data centers, and retail outlets owned by the company. These were the Scope 1 and Scope 2 emissions of the company.

In contrast, Truthout took a holistic approach and included Scope 3 emissions in its analysis: emissions in both the upstream and downstream supply chains associated with the manufacturing and use of Apple's products. For example, Apple's two leading Chinese suppliers, Foxconn and Unimicron, were accused not only of deplorable working conditions leading to employees' suicides[145] but also of polluting rivers and ground water with factory chemicals.[146] The NGO estimated that the vast majority (72.5 percent) of Apple's life cycle carbon footprint was in its suppliers' operations.[147] This is not surprising. As mentioned earlier, Apple does not make any of its computers, iPhones, iPads, or any other Apple product; it outsources all manufacturing to contract suppliers, mostly in China.

Truthout also asserted that Apple's products had a high footprint, not only during manufacturing but also during use. Even though Apple created energy-efficient data centers, consumers use apps connected to Facebook, Google, Samsung, Twitter, and millions of other websites and services that run on energy-intensive, non-Apple servers. Using Apple's own reporting, Truthout estimates that Apple's own facilities represent a puny 1.2 percent of the company's life cycle emissions.

For many companies, the carbon footprint, water footprint, and toxic emissions of the company's own operations are a small fraction of the total impacts of making the product. Moreover, as the examples of NGO attacks over various materials such as palm oil, tin, and paper show (see chapters 1 and 3), many environmental risks lurk outside the company's sphere of ownership in deep-tier suppliers that extract and process natural resources. Finally, many of the product attributes that green segment consumers seek (e.g., organic, natural ingredients, recycled, toxin-free, made with renewable energy) depend on the supply chain. Thus, in looking at these hotspots, many companies extend the focus of their environmental sustainability efforts to their suppliers.

5

The Sorcery of Sustainable Sourcing

Coca-Cola might be proud of its efforts to reduce its water consumption to 2.2 liters of water per liter of beverage. Meanwhile, the sugar beet farmers deep in its European supply chain are guzzling 28 liters per liter of Coke.[1] As mentioned at the end of chapter 4, for most companies, the life cycle environmental impacts and risks arise outside the company itself. Significant environmental impacts often take place in the deepest tiers of the supply chain that grow, harvest, or mine raw materials.

Awareness of the key role of suppliers in environmental impacts, efficiencies, and risks have led many companies to examine their upstream supply chain. In general, companies select and manage suppliers based on many criteria including cost, lead time, capacity, financial strength, quality, and reliability. With the rise of the environmental movement, many companies have begun to include sustainability as another factor in procurement decisions and supplier management. Not surprisingly, as with any performance dimension, companies vary widely in the weight they assign to their suppliers' environmental conduct.

As stated in chapter 1, brand owners seldom have control over, or even knowledge of, the identities of their deep-tier suppliers because many commodities flow through a web of intermediaries, subsuppliers, and brokers. Furthermore, each deep-tier supplier is likely to provide materials to many companies and sometimes to many industries as well, which further dilutes the opportunities for control. Coca-Cola does not have a direct relationship with the growers. In the EU, for instance, the company buys sugar from many different sugar refiners, and those refiners buy beets from thousands of beet growers. Moreover, in different regions, Coca-Cola buys sugar from multiple sugar suppliers using a variety of agricultural supply chains (beet, sugar cane, and corn). Even if the company knows the name of a distant supplier, it typically has no business relationship with that supplier and therefore cannot directly influence its processes.

THE SUSTAINABILITY WEAK LINKS IN THE CHAIN

As noted in chapter 2, Siemens' wind turbine division buys from more than 400 Tier 1 suppliers who, in turn, buy from more than 3,000 of their own suppliers, who are Tier 2 suppliers to Siemens. This is typical for large manufacturers, which often buy from hundreds to tens of thousands of suppliers across multiple industries, spread around the world. Ford Motor Company has about 1,500 Tier 1 suppliers and tens of thousands of deeper-tier suppliers. Flex, the contract manufacturer, procures 700,000 parts from 14,000[2] Tier 1 suppliers.[3] And Walmart has more than 60,000 Tier 1 suppliers[4] for the diverse merchandise that is displayed on its shelves.

The Limit of Influence

GRI (Global Reporting Initiative) is an independent standard for sustainability reporting.[5] GRI defines a company's environmental reporting boundary to include only supply chain partners over whom the company has financial control or influence, chiefly its Tier 1 suppliers. If a company has no influence over an upstream or downstream entity, that entity's impacts are excluded from the company's impact report.[6] Control or influence defines a practical boundary, because the company is more likely to obtain data and expect compliance from the entities that it can control or influence.

Nevertheless, the attacks by Greenpeace on Nestlé (see chapter 1) or by Friends of the Earth on Apple, Samsung, and other smartphone makers described in chapter 3 show that these NGOs do not accept lack of influence as an excuse for lack of improvement. And even if that seems unfair, these NGOs' "no excuses" tactics support their long-term goals. If companies could avoid taking responsibility for sustainability problems in their supply chain by avoiding control or influence, then they might be tempted to "outsource their impacts." Within the context of an LCA, every source of materials or services, no matter how indirect or outside the company's sphere of influence, is part of a company's broader environmental impact. Given the high costs of a detailed LCA, companies typically prioritize their efforts by looking for indicators of the suppliers and processes with the highest environmental impacts, the so-called hot spots in the upstream supply chain.

Looking for Risky Business

HP Inc., for example, considers several types of environmental risk indicators among its suppliers, using four risk categories. The first indicator is geographic location, because countries vary in their level of regulation and strictness of enforcement of environmental laws. Country risk can be estimated, for example, by the Yale Center for Environmental Law & Policy's Environmental Performance Index described in chapter 2. Second, HP considers the intrinsic sustainability risks of the processes performed by the supplier. Suppliers in heavy manufacturing, chemical-intensive conversions, labor-intensive assembly, and recycling are more likely to have higher environmental impacts than those in consulting services and software licensing. Third, the supplier's relationship to HP affects the likely risk: new suppliers, large-volume suppliers, and suppliers of HP-logo branded merchandise are considered riskier. Fourth, the company uses historical information from audits, press articles, external stakeholder (NGO) reports, incidents, and accidents to modulate its assessment of each supplier's risk. Out of 1,000 factories at 600 suppliers, HP identified 300 factories at 160 suppliers as high risk. These suppliers became the focus of the company's social and environmental responsibility (SER) program.[7,8]

Companies also worry about other kinds of supplier risks arising from events such as natural disasters, supplier bankruptcies, labor strikes, and political instability. A disruption to the supplies of a single part can halt all production at a factory. One of the principal strategies for mitigating these kinds of supplier disruption risks is sourcing from multiple suppliers to ensure a constant supply. Ironically, this actually increases the environmental risks to the company's brand. Each added supplier is one more chance for a "bad apple" that might be caught by NGOs or journalists. In most of these cases, it is the brand holder who will suffer the consequences, not the distant supplier. To balance these risks, companies use multiple sources where warranted and, at the same time, take steps to influence suppliers' behavior in order to reduce the chance of brand-damaging public-relations nightmares.

DISCLOSURE BEGETS DISCUSSION AND MITIGATION

The first step toward managing carbon emissions is to measure them, because in business *what gets measured gets managed.* "The Carbon Disclosure Project [CDP] has played a crucial role in encouraging companies to take the first steps in that measurement and management path," commented Lord Adair Turner, chairman of the UK Financial Services Authority.[9] In its strategic plan, CDP states, "Our theory of change is that measurement, transparency and accountability drive positive change in the world of business and investment."[10]

A Clear Path to Supply Chain Transparency
The rise of CDP reflects the concerns of stock market investors about environmental risks to companies' performance and investors' desire to make companies assess and disclose those risks. As mentioned in chapter 3, CDP elicited reporting by 4,500 large public companies in 2015,[11] and the scope of its disclosure questions has expanded to include carbon emissions, water footprint, response to climate change effects, and forestry issues.

Much of the growth of the CDP coverage came from its supply chain program, under which participating companies began recruiting their suppliers to join the program and to disclose their environmental impacts as well. As of late 2016, the CDP's supply chain program worked with 89 large corporations with $2.7 trillion in combined procurement spending.[12] Of the nine new members added to the CDP's supply chain program in 2015, two-thirds—including Lego Group, Kellogg Company, Toyota Motor Corporation, and Volkswagen AG—were asked by their own customers in 2014 to join the program and disclose their environmental impacts.[13] They, in turn, intend to hold their own suppliers to similar standards of disclosure.[14]

Nonetheless, not all suppliers are willing to participate: Nearly half of the participating companies' 7,879 suppliers failed to respond to their customer's 2015 climate change questionnaire.[15] Suppliers may be suspicious of customers who want to examine their (the suppliers') operations too closely, fearing that the disclosed information will be used to extract price concessions or to disintermediate the supplier.

From Supplier Disclosure to Sourcing Decisions to Supplier Management

Disclosed data on suppliers' environmental impacts can lead companies to make informed, if nonobvious, sourcing decisions in terms of total carbon footprint. For example, if a UK company asks its paper suppliers to disclose their carbon footprints, the company may be surprised to learn that a local supplier of recycled paper has a higher footprint than a Swedish supplier of virgin paper. The two suppliers' disclosures would reveal that the UK supplier's dependence on the coal-intensive UK power grid gives that supplier a much higher carbon intensity compared to the Swedish supplier that relies more on nuclear and hydroelectric energy to manufacture paper.[16,17] Thus, in this case, using the more distant supplier lowers the total carbon footprint, even though it requires more transportation.

Similarly, a Swedish food company might assume that the high carbon footprint of transportation means that local suppliers have a lower footprint than more distant suppliers. But asking suppliers to disclose their footprints might reveal that a local tomato supplier has a worse footprint than a Spanish supplier, because Spanish tomatoes are grown in open fields whereas the local products are grown in fossil-fuel-heated greenhouses,[18] leading to more than a tenfold higher energy consumption per kilogram of tomatoes.[19]

Some companies set incremental goals that favor sourcing from suppliers who disclose their impacts and work to mitigate them. For example, a 2014 CDP report quoted AT&T Inc. as saying:

"We set a goal that by the end of 2015 the majority of our supply chain spend with strategic suppliers would be with those suppliers who tracked their own greenhouse gas emissions and have specific greenhouse gas goals."[20] AT&T later reported achieving its goal one year ahead of schedule. Within the broader CDP program, the fraction of suppliers to CDP members who were setting emission targets had grown from 39 percent in 2012 to 44 percent in 2013 and 48 percent in 2014.[21]

The emphasis on sustainability in a company's procurement and supplier management policies varies among companies and among issues. At L'Oréal, for example, 20 percent of a key supplier's score is based on its performance on climate change impacts.[22] At Walmart, 5 percent of its buyers' performance evaluations are tied to sustainability, thereby giving said buyers some, if limited, incentive to modulate procurement decisions and encourage suppliers to improve sustainability.[23] Yet Walmart also has some zero-tolerance thresholds, as mentioned in the Bangladesh story in chapter 2.

More and more companies have supplier "codes of conduct" that include a combination of strict requirements (i.e., "zero tolerance" prohibitions) and softer quantitative expectations (e.g., a numerical scorecard with an expected minimum score). For example, AT&T asks suppliers to fill out a balanced Citizenship and Sustainability Scorecard with a 2017 goal that suppliers will achieve an average score of 80 percent, compared to 74 percent in 2015 and 63 percent in 2014.[24]

STANDARDS AND CHECKMARKS

Two slabs of wood may look identical in the natural beauty of their warm golden color and rich wood grain. They may have identical engineering specifications and pass every possible quality assurance test. Yet one piece of wood might have been carefully harvested from a sustainable tree farm and the other might have been illegally ripped from some country's national park lands. To a large extent, sustainability is less about what the product is—which can be tested at the buyer's receiving dock—and more about how the product is made, which can only be managed by monitoring and controlling suppliers' processes on site. These product provenance properties, known as "hidden credence attributes," are crucial to eco-segmentation and eco-risk mitigation and play a major role in how companies communicate with consumers and other stakeholders (see chapter 9). To set expectations for suppliers' behavior, many companies institute a supplier code of conduct, as well as implement audit, enforcement, and incentive mechanisms to increase suppliers' compliance.

Trying to drive the point home, Walmart's CEO Lee Scott surmised during a suppliers' conference in Beijing that, "A company that cheats on overtime and on the age of its labor, that dumps its scraps and its chemicals in our rivers, that does not pay its taxes or honor its contracts, will ultimately cheat on the quality of its products."[25]

It's IWAY or the Highway

IKEA relies on a global network of more than 1,000 suppliers that transform wood, textiles, foam, and metal into the company's signature easy-to-build furniture kits. In its 80-year history of lowering the cost of home furnishings, the company's reputation has been tainted by revelations that it was using political prisoner labor in communist-era East Germany in the 1980s[26] and revelations of illegal logging and deforestation in the 1990s.[27]

In 2000, IKEA implemented a comprehensive supplier code of conduct that it calls the "IKEA Way on Purchasing Home Furnishing Products," or "IWAY."[28] IWAY specifies additional requirements beyond the terms of the basic supplier contract governing the delivery of certain units of materials within certain quality, time, and cost parameters. These requirements encompass a range of environmental and social dos and don'ts. For example, they strictly prohibit direct discharge of untreated wastewater from production processes such as tanning, dyeing, surface treatment, and printing processes. IWAY environmental standards address outdoor air pollution, outdoor noise pollution, ground and water pollution, ground contamination, energy reduction, chemical handling, hazardous and nonhazardous waste, and the indoor work environment. Naturally, IWAY also includes many social responsibility requirements related to child labor, forced labor, worker wages, working hours, and working conditions.

The company had sought 100 percent compliance within five years (by 2005) but progress lagged. In 2009 the company announced a new strict three-year target that gave all suppliers until 2012 to reach full compliance.[29] When the deadline passed, 75 of the company's approximately 1,100 suppliers still fell short of the requirements. Those suppliers were immediately dismissed. "They were close—they were very close. Most of them were on 98, 99 percent fulfillment of the code of conduct, but we said it's only 100 percent that counts," said Jeanette Skjelmose, sustainability manager for IKEA during an interview for this book. "So, even if they were only missing one question, we said, 'Sorry. We have to end the contract with you,'" she added with fervor.

New suppliers do get a grace period of one year to reach full compliance but after that period they too are expected to be 100 percent compliant. For example, Xiamen Hung's Enterprise Co., Ltd., a Chinese firm providing "wire, cable, metal, and plastic components,"[30] labored for a year and a half to reach 92.6 percent of IKEA's requirements and became a qualified supplier in 2009. Once it had been awarded the business, however, Hung's was expected to meet the full IWAY code within one year of starting the contract. In late 2013, Hung's Enterprise listed 18 business partners on its website; IKEA was not among them.[31]

IKEA offers some flexibility to existing suppliers, but not much. If a supplier stumbles on an IWAY item, it has two weeks to outline a plan to correct the problem. IKEA requires the plan to include a description of what actions the supplier will undertake, who is responsible, and when the supplier will be in compliance.[32] Depending on the violation, the supplier may have up to 90 days to correct it. If the supplier fails to do so, according to Skjelmose, IKEA will phase out the supplier at the end of its contract. However, if the violation involves one of the eight core IWAY requirements[33] (which include severe environmental pollution; severe health or safety hazards; child labor; forced and bonded labor; business ethics; working hours; wages; and worker's accident insurance), IKEA gives the supplier also up to 90 days to correct the violation, but during that time the company will not take any delivery from the supplier.[34]

Unleash the Watch Dogs of Wariness

Kelly Deng, senior auditor for IKEA in China, is on the frontlines of ensuring IWAY is the way that suppliers actually operate. Typically twice a week she and a coworker will surprise one of IKEA's suppliers or subsuppliers with an unannounced on-site audit. They visit the facility and interview workers at random, which is a contractual requirement of IKEA.[35] Skjelmose explained: "If they should deny us access, we regard that as a violation of the IWAY norm. We classify that as a work deviation and stop orders from that supplier immediately." As a result of those strict penalties, Deng added, she is rarely turned away.

If a supplier is trying to hide IWAY violations, Deng knows what to look for, such as seeing a worker hurrying past while holding a stack of papers. Factory managers may sometimes falsify records, she said, and send a worker to smuggle the accurate records out of the building.

IKEA auditors typically spend two days at each site; in extreme cases, the auditors will arrive a day early or stay a day late to "stake-out" the facility and look for violations of IKEA's guidelines on environmental practices, maximum allowed work hours, and minimum rest days.

IKEA's inspections differ from those of many third-party auditors. Auditing firms keep costs low by giving a single auditor as little as one day to inspect a factory that may employ 1,000 or more workers. Sometimes, these auditors have received as little as five days of training compared to the three years of training required to become an inspector for the US Occupational Safety and Health Administration (OSHA). Some auditors merely fill out an inspection checklist that factory managers know about days in advance (enough warning in many cases for factory managers to hide any violations).[36]

In contrast, IKEA has 80 full-time auditors who do nothing else but audit suppliers and subsuppliers. According to Deng, the typical IKEA auditor has been on the job for five years. Deng herself has more than seven years of auditor experience at IKEA. "We audit all of our suppliers every other year," said Skjelmose,[37] "but in risky region, such as Asia, the audits are more frequent—usually once a year." The company requires that its suppliers disclose the names, addresses, and GPS coordinates of their subsuppliers' facilities. "We need to have it because we need to be able to go there unannounced," she added.

In addition to its own staff, IKEA hires third-party auditors to "verify" and "calibrate" IKEA's own audits. IKEA also formed a special "compliance monitoring group" composed of its most competent senior auditors. These expert auditors sample-audit suppliers' facilities after the other auditors have completed their jobs to ensure the uniformity of supplier operating standards in all regions. Overall, Skjelmose called it "the police watching the police."

Although IKEA's advanced auditing system has likely prevented some major social and environmental violations in its supply chain, the company did come under fire in 2012 from the Global Forest Coalition over logging of ancient forests in Russia.[38] Similarly, in 2013 IKEA was among a number of European companies found to have horse and pig meat rather than beef in their famous meatballs, as part of the infamous "horsemeat scandal" that engulfed Europe.[39] Operating a far-flung empire of more than 1,000 manufacturing suppliers, in addition to the many suppliers of non-direct materials and services, means that IKEA will likely stumble at times. However, Deng asserts that she has seen significant improvement in the environmental and social conditions of the factories she has visited during her tenure as an auditor.

All for One (Code) and One (Code) for All (Suppliers)

A possibly apocryphal tale tells of an inspector visiting a supplier and finding all the fire extinguishers mounted on vertical sliders on the walls. When the inspector inquired about this strange practice, the supplier replied that one customer demands that the extinguishers be mounted two feet off the floor, a second customer insists on a three-foot height, and a third customer requires a four-foot mounting point. The sliders enable the supplier to quickly shift the extinguishers to the right height for each customer's inspectors.

Proprietary codes, such as IKEA's internally developed IWAY, can work fairly well for the code's creator, as long as the company has sufficient influence over suppliers and the ability to dedicate significant resources for audit and reporting. The ultimate success of a company's code of conduct, however, hinges on the suppliers' willingness to sign contracts containing that code and to comply with it. Yet, most suppliers sell to many customer companies, and each proprietary code of conduct adds overhead costs and inefficiencies because of the minutiae of implementation, reporting, and audits associated with the many codes. In an industry such as electronics, in which a great many product-manufacturing companies purchase modest amounts of components from a great many parts makers, these suppliers have little incentive to acquiesce to proprietary codes of conduct and significant costs if they must implement multiple codes. In these cases, "Industry collaboration is the most effective way to raise standards," said Claudia Kruse, senior analyst, governance and socially responsive investing, at F&C Asset Management.[40]

For example, the Electronic Industry Citizenship Coalition (EICC) was formed in 2004 "to collaboratively implement a common supplier code of conduct for the technology industry."[41] The EICC is made up of "electronic manufacturers, software firms, information and communications technology firms, and manufacturing service providers, including contract labor."[42] The organization has grown to include more than 100 electronics companies with combined annual revenues of about $3 trillion and direct employment of 5.5 million people.[43] As of 2015, the EICC supplier code of conduct had evolved to version 5.0 and was available in 13 languages.[44]

The EICC's Code contains specific guidelines regarding labor, health and safety, environment, ethics, and management systems.[45] When EICC-member Flex signs a new supplier, the four-page Flex purchasing contract contains only a short "social responsibility" clause stipulating that the supplier "agrees to comply with the Electronic Industry Code of Conduct."[46] To the extent that a new supplier to Flex also sells components to other EICC members and is already EICC-compliant, compliance with Flex's contract is much easier than if Flex had its own proprietary code of conduct.

In addition to the industry-shared code of conduct, the EICC's Validated Assessment Process (VAP)[47] standardizes and pools audit efforts, reducing the costs of audits for both supplier and customer companies. The VAP "provides companies assurance in identifying risks and driving improvements and robust management systems for labor, ethics, health, safety and environmental conditions in the Information Technology supply chain."[48] The EICC program manages audit guidance, auditor training, audit review, and quality control, by which hundreds of auditors from nine firms execute the VAP protocol in more than 20 countries.[49] The EICC-ON website platform helps its members manage and share supplier sustainability data, such as audits, self-assessment questionnaires, and suppliers' corrective actions.[50]

Greater Common Good or Lowest Common Denominator?

Industry standards for codes of conduct may increase the number of companies that participate in supply chain sustainability management by standardizing performance metrics and reducing auditing process overhead. Such standards may satisfy corporate eco-risk goals in that the company can cite its compliance with standards to defend against criticism of its sustainability practices. However, environmentalists argue that industry codes may create weak standards relative to what individual companies might create for two reasons. First, if the standard is governed by the members, then sustainability laggards may impede adoption of more advanced practices. Second, if an industry has multiple standards bodies, they might compete for member companies by offering the easiest, least costly, and least rigorous code to implement. NGOs have criticized the EICC, saying, "Industry associations move very cautiously and operate on a lowest common denominator consensus."[51]

A weak standard creates a "checkbox mentality" by which both customer and supplier companies might claim to be sustainable without making substantive improvements in practices and impacts. Yet, industry standards have been successful in inducing more companies and more suppliers to consider environmental issues. This situation in which corporations claim progress in environmental sustainability and activists bemoan a lack of progress is sometimes termed "greenwashing" and "blackwashing," respectively. The former refers to exaggerated corporate claims of sustainability and the latter to exaggerations in activists' accusations of environmental destruction; both issues are discussed in chapter 9.

Pushing Higher Standards out into the Supply Chain

Both IKEA and the EICC expect Tier 1 suppliers to push the code of conduct out to Tier 2 and beyond. IKEA expects its Tier 1 suppliers to communicate IWAY to Tier 2 suppliers of production materials and for Tier 2 suppliers to sign a document acknowledging acceptance of the IWAY rules. The EICC explicitly states that suppliers must have "a process to communicate [EICC] Code requirements to [their] suppliers and to monitor supplier compliance to the Code," thereby giving original equipment manufacturers (OEMs) some assurance regarding the conduct of Tier 2 suppliers, although the EICC does not always audit subsuppliers.[52]

Interestingly, IKEA does not expect Tier 1 suppliers to push IWAY out to Tier 2 suppliers of overhead items such as electricity, fuel, office materials, indirect materials, and capital equipment.[53] These exemptions seem to suggest that IKEA is motivated mainly by eco-risk management concerns and that it believes it is unlikely to be the focus of an attack over issues in those categories of Tier 2 suppliers. In fact, even Tier 1 suppliers of indirect materials seem to operate under a lighter version of IWAY. The reason may possibly be that such suppliers are easier to replace in case they are caught in violations.

Similarly, HP is not trying to impose its code of conduct directly onto deeper tier suppliers. "You need to recognize that the companies supplying your suppliers tend to have limited resources, staff, and money," advised Bonnie Nixon Gardiner, global program manager for supply chain social and environmental responsibility at HP. "So it is important to work closely with your first-tier suppliers to diffuse best practice information out through the supply chain and support their efforts to audit and improve their suppliers," she added.[54]

From Audits to Alignment

A large-scale MIT study of 900 factories in 50 countries found that the traditional compliance model, defined by the power relationships of big multinationals over local suppliers, information collected through audits, and penalties for noncompliance, is not very effective.[55] Threats and audits tend to induce an adversarial relationship focused on minimum-effort compliance rather than a cooperative relationship of ongoing improvement. As a result of the audit mentality, suppliers may not see a need to "own sustainability," become proactive, inspect their own operations, disclose sustainability issues, or remediate them voluntarily.[56] Suppliers will do the minimum, but no more.

Furthermore, factories in the developing world have become adept at hiding problems or subverting the audit process. For example, a 2006 Bloomberg report details the story of Ningbo Beifa Group, a Chinese supplier of pens and pencils whose largest customer was Walmart. The supplier had failed Walmart's labor inspections three times. If the supplier had failed an upcoming fourth audit, Walmart would have terminated the company's contract, resulting in devastating consequences to the supplier. Rather than correct the problems, the supplier paid $5,000 to Shanghai Corporate Responsibility Management & Consulting, which taught Beifa how to falsify records and coached managers on how to answer the questions of Walmart's inspectors. Beifa passed the fourth audit. Apparently, numerous Chinese factories keep duplicate sets of books to fool auditors and train employees in how to respond to their questions.[57]

Given the high cost of either losing the business or becoming compliant, noncompliant suppliers may be tempted to bribe the auditor to ignore transgressions. A Chinese supplier representative commented: "The audit companies have the power to hurt the factory, so lots of bribery goes on."[58] Even a company's own audit teams can be corrupted because they typically draw employees from the community where the supplier factory is located. Finally,

Asian suppliers' fear of "losing face" intensifies the pressure to do anything to avoid getting caught.[59] As a result, some companies look for positive motivations that encourage suppliers to embrace sustainability.

HELPING SUPPLIERS HELP THE ENVIRONMENT

"While audits and corrective actions are essential, we believe the greatest opportunity for change comes from worker empowerment and education," said Jeff Williams, Apple's senior vice president of operations.[60] The large-scale MIT study mentioned in the previous section demonstrated that cooperation between buyers and suppliers was more effective than audit-and-sanction strategies.[61] The same large size and deep pockets of brand-owning companies that make them attractive targets for NGO attacks also enable these companies to lend their resources to improving their suppliers' sustainability. After reducing their own environmental impacts (see chapter 4), these companies can transfer what they've learned to their suppliers. Such *eco-alignment* initiatives are intended to encourage the spread of sustainability initiatives upstream and address deep-tier hotspots that are not under the direct control of the company.

From Auditors to Advisors

Based in part on the findings of the MIT study, Nike launched its *Project Rewire* in 2009, focusing on incentives in addition to regular compliance audits.[62] Suppliers were rewarded based on quality, on-time delivery, cost, and sustainability.[63] These four components are weighed equally in a manufacturing index, scoring suppliers as gold, silver, bronze, yellow, or red. As of 2013, 68 percent of Nike's 786 contract manufacturers were rated bronze or higher.[64] The highest achieving suppliers receive training on eco-efficiency issues (which lead to both cost reductions and sustainability improvements) such as waste and energy management. The goal is to engage and motivate suppliers to improve their practices on their own, instead of forcing them through penalties for noncompliance.

Cooperation with suppliers moves some of the responsibility for sustainability from the audit process to the supplier and aligns the supplier and customer goals. To align its goals with its suppliers, Levi Strauss & Co. has "a deal" with its suppliers. If the supplier proactively discloses a problem, then Levi Strauss does not count it as a violation and instead collaborates with the supplier to fix the problem.[65] However, if a supplier is caught falsifying records, Levi Strauss records that as a so-called zero-tolerance violation. In Levi's case, the penalties for zero-tolerance violations are not as strict as those of some other companies; Levi Strauss only terminates the supplier after two or three such violations.

Codes of conduct and audits can be used to set goals and collect information over time. That information then forms the basis for working with suppliers' factory managers on how best to tackle problems, transforming the role of inspector from enforcer to advisor.[66] Luen Thai Holding, a Levi Strauss supplier in Asia, finds that the Levi Strauss approach works well. However, they note that most of their other customers still use the audit and sanction model, rather than collaborative problem solving.[67]

If It Works for Us, It Will Work for Our Suppliers

In 2009, after Siemens had developed and successfully applied an in-house methodology for saving energy at its 298 factories (see chapter 4), chief sustainability officer Barbara Kux decided to share the energy-efficiency program with suppliers. Siemens estimated that its supply chain had roughly double the carbon footprint of the company itself.[68] In preparation for a 2009 sustainability summit, Kux shared all the details of her company's four-step method with the company's top 30 suppliers and suggested that each supplier apply the same approach with its own facilities; six did. In the days before the meeting, one of them was able to use Siemens' assessment methodology to identify a 12 percent energy savings potential.[69]

Encouraged by the early results, Siemens opened its energy reduction assessment methodology to all its suppliers through an online portal. "I call it the 'green Google.' A supplier can log in from the US or India, and just plug in his data, and then get a preliminary result," Kux said. The tool shows suppliers that sustainability can be profitable by lowering costs.

Some Siemens' suppliers saw immediate savings after using the tool and implementing the recommended changes. For example, Leoni AG, a €4.5 billion cable and harnessing firm headquartered in Germany, was able to reduce its CO_2 emissions by 800 tons/year through energy savings initiatives recommended by the Siemens tool.[70] It also saved more than €250,000 per year in energy costs as a result.[71] Overall, 80 percent of involved suppliers uncovered potential energy-efficiency improvements ranging from 9 to 20 percent.[72] As of early 2013, Siemens reported that more than 1,000 suppliers had participated in the program, identifying potential energy efficiency improvements averaging 10 percent.[73]

For Siemens, the benefit of engaging suppliers was threefold. First, Siemens' products would have a lower carbon footprint as a result of the greater environmental efficiency of both Siemens and its suppliers. Although the carbon savings were modest, they helped burnish Siemens' environmental record. Second, any reductions in energy consumption led to cost savings throughout the chain. Finally, as a company offering products that support environmental sustainability, such as factory technology, power supplies, facilities systems, and renewable energy systems, Siemens' suppliers could also then become customers: Siemens products are often recommended as part of its assessment tool.

Supplier Education and Assistance

Whereas Siemens shared its own green manufacturing methodologies with suppliers, Apple developed a range of educational systems to teach the workers and managers of its suppliers about environmental and social responsibility issues. In 2013, Apple developed an environmental health and safety (EHS) academy: an 18-month program, in cooperation with three universities, to train suppliers' managers, addressing a worldwide shortage of qualified EHS professionals. In 2014, Apple reported it had trained more than 2.3 million of its suppliers' workers on Apple's code of conduct and workers' rights. Its Supplier Employee Education and Development (SEED) program has expanded to 48 classrooms in

23 facilities—equipped with iMac computers, iPad tablets, educational software, video conferencing systems, and more. Since 2008, more than 1.4 million workers from suppliers have taken courses, free of charge, for personal development, and some workers have even received college degrees through the program.[74,75]

On water-related issues, Apple takes a more active role in helping suppliers reduce their impact as part of the company's Clean Water Program. "Through a series of regular assessments, Apple helped us to develop strategies for installation of water meters, a water-savings awareness campaign, wastewater reclaiming system, and proper storm water channels. As a result, we've saved 10 percent of our freshwater," said Colin Li, EHS and sustainability director, BU Mobile Devices & Substrates unit of AT&S of Leoben, Austria.[76] Piloted in 2013, Apple reported that the program grew from 13 initial supplier facilities to 265 in 2015.[77]

EARTH: THE ULTIMATE SOLE-SOURCE SUPPLIER

The 1972 book *Limits to Growth* by the Club of Rome[78] concluded that if (the then) present growth trends continue, "the limits to growth on this planet will be reached sometime within the next one hundred years. The most probable result will be a rather sudden and uncontrollable decline in both population and industrial capacity."[79] A 2014 Australian study[80] concluded that the factors tracked by the book (population growth, industrialization, pollution, food production, and resource depletion) match to actual statistics through 2014 very closely. Although the original book (and the recent study) have been controversial, ultimately, the Earth is a sole-source, base-tier supplier for all products and is typically Tier 1 or 2 "supplier" to industries such as food, apparel, and packaging. The potential environmental risk to business and society is that unsustainable agricultural and industrial practices will lead to a collapse of ecological systems through water scarcity, contamination, species loss, erosion, drought, and damaging weather conditions. This threat motivates companies to improve the environmental practices of suppliers of key agricultural ingredients.

"We are responsible for buying and using almost a quarter of the world's malt and barley," said John Rogers, global manager of agricultural development at AB InBev.[81] The company buys barley from a total of 20,000 growers who collectively cultivate a total of one million hectares.[82] "We have a lot of experience and expertise as a result, and we really want to make sure that we are bringing that experience and expertise out to that supply chain, to that grower so that we are creating that value at the farm level," he added.[83]

The company uses university researchers and 35 in-house agronomists to both help understand crop yield issues and to educate farmers. The company has created an online system (SmartBarley.com) in which 2,400 participating growers can anonymously compare their performance on 40 agricultural metrics with those of other growers around the world.[84] In addition to sustainability, the program focuses on the productivity of irrigation, fertilizers, and other efficiency practices aligning it with the farmers' economic goals.

Tea for Two

In 1895, William and James Lever founded Lever Brothers. Widespread cholera from unsanitary conditions in England motivated the brothers to transform the outdated soap industry by selling affordable, prepackaged soap to the masses.[85] The company, now known as Unilever, made its soap from glycerin and vegetable oils and branded it as Sunlight Soap.[86] Production expanded quickly,[87] and the accessibility of soap to people of all incomes improved hygiene and helped reduce illness throughout Europe.

As Unilever grew, William Lever's philosophy of improving public health defined the company's mission. The "doing well by doing good" motto[88] drove Unilever's development of sustainable supply chain practices as the company mushroomed into a diversified global consumer-packaged goods giant. More than a century later, that mission-focused internal culture and the company's ethical roots helped CEO Paul Polman and his chief supply chain officer, Pier Luigi Sigismondi, in their journey toward business-wide environmental sustainability.[89] This leadership has been reflected in ambitious commitments across the company's global and complex supply chains. In 2010, Unilever pledged to source all of its agricultural raw material sustainably by 2020. Unilever's tea supply chain illustrates the company's holistic approach to sourcing just one of its many raw materials.

Tea is the world's second most popular beverage (trailing only water);[90] the industry employs 13 million people cultivating nearly 5 million hectares of tea plantations in 45 countries.[91] Unilever—owner of Lipton, PG Tips, and several other tea brands—leads the tea market with a global market share of 12 percent, which is three times the size of its nearest competitor.[92]

Unilever buys about 90 percent of its tea globally, either directly from suppliers or via open market auctions. The tea comes from a combination of 750,000 smallholder tea farms and larger tea plantations.[93] In 2006, Unilever partnered with the Rainforest Alliance to develop a certification process for tea, and by 2015 the company announced that it had succeeded in sourcing all Lipton tea from Rainforest Alliance-certified growers.[94] In addition, it partnered with the Netherlands-based Sustainable Trade Initiative and the Kenya Tea Development Agency, to co-fund field schools to teach farmers a variety of sustainable practices.[95] These practices included improving water retention and the quality of the soil by leaving plant clippings in the field, as well as persuading farmers to plant fast-growing eucalyptus trees as a renewable source of fuel for heating and drying tea leaves.[96] Unilever's chief sustainability officer Gail Klintworth reported that between 2007 and 2012, the schools trained 450,000 farmers in preparation for Rainforest Alliance certification.[97]

The improved cultivation practices that Unilever teaches to farmers come from research at its own tea estates in Kenya and Tanzania.[98] The company's Kericho, Kenya, estate achieved the highest yield in the world at 3.5 to 4 tons per hectare. Its estate in Tanzania achieved yields of 3 tons per hectare, compared to a countrywide average of 2 tons per hectare.[99] Unilever is also pursuing genetic research to cultivate more sustainable tea varieties. "The ability to grow more tea on less land, further reduce the need for agrochemicals while boosting tolerance to drought and climate change is integral to this project," said Clive Gristwood, senior vice president for research and development of Unilever's Refreshment category.[100]

Mapping 120,000 Suppliers

"Coffee farmers are critical for us. We don't see them as a commodity, a faceless supply chain; rather they are people that we know, we know their families," said Kelly Goodejohn, director of ethical sourcing for Starbucks.[101] Starbucks' vision of having "a positive impact on the communities we serve—one person, one cup, and one neighborhood at a time," goes beyond its customers and extends to the far reaches of its supply chain, to the more than 120,000 farmers growing its coffee.[102] Starbucks not only promises to sell its customers the best coffee on the planet, but it also promises that the people who farm, pick, and process that coffee will be treated fairly on farms that have reduced environmental impact.

To ensure that it buys environmentally and socially sustainable coffee, Starbucks partnered with Conservation International[103] in 1999 to develop the Coffee and Farmer Equity (C.A.F.E.) program, a set of interlocking environmental, social, and economic guidelines for its coffee supply chain. Starbucks ensures that farmers meet its standards by gathering information on each farmer, including geocoding every plot, the identities of owners and workers, and information about the farming practices, including landscaping and biodiversity.[104] To become a Starbucks supplier, farmers and coffee processors must perform a set of mandatory practices, as well as a sufficient number of optional practices that give the farmer a high enough score on the C.A.F.E scorecard. Farmers who achieve even higher scores—by doing more of the optional practices—can become "preferred" and then "strategic" suppliers, which gives them enhanced pricing and contract terms.[105] These positive incentives for incremental improvements stand in contrast with mandate-oriented approaches, such as IWAY or the EICC code of conduct. They are more like the Levi's approach or Nike "Rewire" program mentioned earlier in this chapter; these programs also mix mandates and incentives.[106]

C.A.F.E. is more than just a scorecard; it conveys some 200 specific good practices (which it asks about in surveys), such as buffer zones of at least five meters from bodies of water, bench terraces to reduce erosion on steep slopes, the use of nitrogen-fixing cover crops, and protection for areas of high conservation value. Almost two-thirds of the C.A.F.E. scorecard items relate to environmental issues, while the rest are focused on social responsibility issues, such as working conditions, worker rights, worker benefits, worker wages, and child labor.[107]

The company employs 25 audit and verification organizations that visit and collect information about each farm.[108] SES Global Services, in Oakland, California, manages the quality and the integrity of the verification process. "They act as a second party to us that has oversight over the third parties," explained Starbucks' Goodejohn.[109] The findings of these audits generally lead to improvement efforts. However, some practices are governed by zero-tolerance mandates, including the use of banned pesticides, cutting down natural forests, and child labor.[110] These practices can cause Starbucks to immediately reject shipments and cancel contracts with the offending bean suppliers.[111]

These audited indicators let Starbucks measure progress toward its goal of 100 percent ethically sourced coffee (the number stood at 95 percent in 2013).[112] "Getting farm information from the last 5 percent is challenging because our supply chain constantly shifts," said Goodejohn, "but it is our commitment to reach the 100 percent goal and we continue to work towards it." The audits also help ensure the quality of the coffee and thus—like Unilever—align Starbucks' sustainability goals with its primary product quality goals. In 2015, Starbucks reached its maximum practical goal with 99 percent of its coffee ethically sourced.

Starbucks not only developed and implemented the system in its own operations, but it chose to make its system public for any grower, mill, or coffee company to use. "We've designed the program in a way that it's truly open source. None of the C.A.F.E. practices are secretive or not available. In fact, we purposely didn't want it to be a Starbucks proprietary program, because we felt that it really demonstrated best practices that would benefit farmers," said Goodejohn. "We wanted this to be open source to others, to other coffee companies."

After achieving the 99 percent ethically sourced milestone, Starbucks became a founding member, with other industry leaders, of the Sustainable Coffee Challenge, a call to action led by NGO Conservation International to make coffee the world's first sustainable agricultural product in the world.[113]

THE COMPLEXITIES OF COMMODITIES

In many lands near the Earth's equator, brilliant sunlight and copious rainfall create an exuberant biological riot of thousands of species coexisting in dense and mysterious rainforests. Plants of every shade of green reach for the sky and produce flowers and fruits of every imaginable color. Insects buzz, birds flutter, and animals rustle through the leaf litter or clamber in the high branches of these primeval forests.

Not surprisingly, both people and companies covet these highly productive lands to meet the increasing needs for food, agriproducts, minerals, and jobs for the planet's growing billions of people. Each year, farmers large and small tear down 7.3 million hectares of forest and replace it with regimented rows of oil palms, soy beans, other crops, or pasture.[114] The battle between the natural environment and the economic environment is fought by opposing battalions of soldiers comprising environmentalists (mostly through NGOs) on one side and consumers and workers (mostly through companies) on the other.

Good for You, Bad for the Environment?
Palm oil, extracted from the fruits and kernels of the tropical palm oil tree, is a vegetable oil used in everything from sweets and baked goods to soaps and cosmetics to biodiesel.[115] Its popularity and consumption surged in 2006 when the US Food and Drug Administration (FDA) began requiring that food labels list artery-clogging trans-fatty acids.[116] Palm oil was quickly identified as a leading replacement for trans fats because it was cheaper to produce than substitutes such as soybean oil. It is even environmentally superior on at least one key measure: the amount of newly cleared land needed to create new supplies of vegetable oil. Palm oil requires

only one-tenth to one-quarter as much land as other common oil seeds such as soy, sunflower, or rapeseed.[117,118]

When palm oil demand doubled between 2002 and 2014, suppliers sought large tracts of land in areas with the right climate. That climate exists in a band stretching seven degrees either north or south of the equator, according to Mohd Salem Kailany, senior vice president at Sime Darby Berhad, one of Malaysia's largest palm oil producers.[119] Kailany told the story of palm oil during a visit to the MIT Center for Transportation and Logistics in 2014. To meet increasing demand, palm oil farmers started clearing tropical forests, especially in Malaysia and Indonesia, on a massive scale. Those two countries came to supply as much as 85 percent of the world's palm oil. Yet, this same band swaddling the Earth's middle has thousands of unique species of plants and animals, including those very charismatic orangutans.

To clear the forest, farmers cut down all the trees and set them ablaze (a practice known as *slash and burn*). This process destroys the natural habitat of many tropical species, in addition to causing soil erosion and polluting both the air and the water.[120] Of special concern is the burning of carbon-rich forests and peatlands, which releases especially large amounts of GHGs. A joint study by Yale and Stanford universities estimated that palm oil plantation expansion would contribute more than 615 million tons of carbon dioxide to the atmosphere in 2020, an amount greater than all of Canada's 2012 fossil-fuel emissions.[121] Overall, deforestation around the world is responsible for an estimated 6 to 17 percent of the entire carbon footprint of the entire human race.[122]

Nestlé Cancels Contracts, but Does That Help?

Greenpeace's attack on Nestlé in 2010 (see chapter 1) was part of a wider Greenpeace palm oil campaign. It targeted many major consumer brands who were buyers of palm oil produced and sold by Golden Agri-Resources (GAR), the palm oil arm of the Indonesian conglomerate Sinar Mas Group.[123] Greenpeace also attacked name-brand companies who were using paper from Asia Pulp & Paper (APP), another subsidiary of Sinar Mas linked to deforestation.[124] As a result, in less than 12 months, Sinar Mas lost prominent customers including Nestlé, Unilever, Kraft, Burger King, and other Western companies.[125]

Even so, this loss of customers did not have an overwhelming financial impact on Sinar Mas and did little to satisfy Greenpeace, for two reasons. First, Nestlé represented less than 1 percent of Sinar Mas' revenue, and although Unilever is the largest single buyer of palm oil in the world, even it represented only 4 percent of the Indonesian conglomerate's revenue.[126] Buyers in Asia, especially China and India, where Greenpeace campaigns have limited influence, accounted for 89 percent of Sinar Mas' sales.

Second, the cancellation of Sinar Mas contracts by Nestlé and others did not mean that Sinar Mas oil stopped flowing to these Western companies. After Nestlé cut off Sinar Mas, Greenpeace mapped Nestlé's supply chain and discovered that Sinar Mas' palm oil was still finding its way into Nestlé's products through other palm oil suppliers. Palm oil from Sinar Mas plantations was being sold to other processors, refiners, and ingredient makers in the vegetable oil industry. "These cancellations did not really give the rainforests a break, because Nestlé continues to use Sinar Mas palm oil, as well as Sinar Mas pulp and paper products, via other suppliers like Cargill and APP," Greenpeace wrote.[127] Nestlé knew which bulk oil companies it was buying oil from, but it didn't know the plantations where that oil was coming from, according to Scott Poynton of The Forest Trust (TFT) "and they didn't know the practices ... going on out in those plantations."[128]

Sinar Mas Turns Over a (Partial) New Leaf

Although Sinar Mas could withstand the loss of the customers mentioned above, the public announcements, boycotts, and unfavorable press releases by these major Western companies were an embarrassment. Furthermore, these actions focused government, media, and community attention on the environmental damage caused by palm oil producers. Consequently, Sinar Mas' palm oil division, GAR, decided to act.

Early in 2011, GAR announced a commitment to a "Forest Conservation Policy," a first for a palm oil grower. The policy's principles included no development on primary forests, high carbon stock forests, or peat lands, and it agreed to have all its palm oil certified by RSPO (Roundtable on Sustainable Palm Oil) principles and criteria (see the next section).[129] To best achieve its conservation goals, GAR worked with Greenpeace and TFT to identify high carbon stock forest areas.[130] As a result, Greenpeace commended GAR's reforms as being progressive and leading the way for the palm oil industry.[131] Nestle, Unilever, and Burger King returned as customers.

Despite GAR's bold commitments, another Sinar Mas subsidiary, APP, did not follow GAR's example. Three years after GAR made its commitments, APP was accused of illegally logging an endangered rainforest in Riau, Indonesia.[132] According to Greenpeace, APP, "which is responsible for widespread deforestation to source paper and packing products, doesn't seem to realize that GAR's initiative is the way forward. Even with the revolt [of APP's practices] going on around the world, their commitments and announcements are not worth the paper they are written on."[133]

The RSPO Cracks a Tough Nut

Nestlé and many others realized that no single company could transform international agricultural practices on its own nor provide transparency across the entire complex supply chain of palm oil and its derivatives. Instead, a coalition of major palm oil suppliers and buyers, along with industry groups and NGOs, gathered to form the Roundtable on Sustainable Palm Oil. The Roundtable was the 2001 brainchild of the World Wildlife Fund (WWF) and was initiated by AAK UK Ltd, a developer of edible oils and fats; Migros, a supermarket chain; and Unilever. In 2013, RSPO members accounted for approximately 40 percent of global palm oil production,[134] and several member companies, including Carrefour, Unilever, Walmart, Nestlé, Johnson & Johnson, and P&G, have committed to sourcing only RSPO-certified sustainable palm oil.

To promote sustainable oil palm farming and overcome the problem of the opaque web of market participants, the RSPO developed the "GreenPalm" certificate program.[135] GreenPalm issues certificates, one per metric ton, to farms that meet the RSPO's sustainability standards for growing palm oil fruit. Companies interested in sustainable palm oil bid for GreenPalm certificates to cover part, and sometimes all, of the company's open market palm oil purchases. The money paid by the company for the certificates goes to the certificate-receiving farms, thereby covering the farmers' costs of using only sustainable practices and creating a financial incentive for other farms to utilize or convert to sustainable production.

In buying GreenPalm certificates, however, a company is not buying a particular ton of sustainable palm oil directly from a particular sustainable farm. Although GreenPalm guarantees that a ton of sustainable palm oil will be added to the global supply, the program does not create a separate supply chain to ensure that the specific palm oil received by a company came from sustainable sources. Thus, the GreenPalm approach restricts the claims that consumer brand companies can make about the oil in their products. However, the RSPO also offers certification for companies for using only sustainably produced palm oil; such certification requires identity-preserved or segregated supply chains, which can substantially increase costs.[136] GreenPalm exemplifies what is known as a "book and claim" system,[137] which is also used for purchasing renewable energy without the costs of a separate power grid to connect wind or solar farms to energy buyers.[138] It can also be viewed as an offset system, similar to carbon credits, but for palm oil.

Sometimes RSPO Gets No R-E-S-P-E-C-T

As with the EICC and offset practices, NGOs criticize the RSPO for not pushing far enough. Following a 2013 RSPO review of their principles and criteria and a proposed update of those standards, the WWF stated that "… because the review failed to accept strong, tough, and clear performance standards … it is, unfortunately, no longer possible for producers or users of palm oil to ensure that they are acting responsibly by producing or using Certified Sustainable Palm Oil."[139] WWF wanted the program to become more stringent on issues such as regulating GHG emissions and pesticide use at RSPO-certified farms. "Industry associations can only move as quickly as their least nimble members," bemoaned one NGO.[140]

In response, other initiatives have been formed to strengthen existing standards. For example, the Palm Oil Innovation Group, with members that include New Britain Palm Oil, WWF, and Greenpeace, aims to set ambitious standards, beyond the RSPO, in order to achieve higher levels of traceability and confidence in the sustainability of sources.

At the same time, the Indonesian government, in trying to balance environmental and economic concerns—especially for small palm oil farmers—created its own certification program: the Indonesian Sustainable Palm Oil (ISPO). Unlike the RSPO, which is voluntary and not widely adopted by Indonesian palm oil producers, ISPO rules are mandatory for these producers. However, the ISPO standards are even less stringent than the RSPO standards, and the compliance monitoring and enforcement mechanisms may not be rigorous.[141]

Still, the RSPO's certification isn't as toothless as some NGOs claim. When the RSPO suspended the sustainability certificates for the IOI Group, a large Malaysian palm oil producer and trader accused of failing to prevent its subsidiaries' involvement in deforestation in Indonesia, many companies suspended trading with the company. These companies included reputation-sensitive consumer brands such as Unilever, Nestlé, Kellogg, and Mars. Also included were other palm oil intermediaries such as Archer Daniels Midland, Louis Dreyfus Company, and even GAR. The news knocked 15 percent off IOI's share price and put the company under threat of a credit rating downgrade. "What we've seen is a strong and rapid response from the buying community and the financial community," said a GAR spokesperson.[142]

Overall, the RSPO remains the most widely recognized palm oil sustainability effort and gives companies, as well as NGOs, a venue for coordinating industry-wide initiatives and managing a viable financial mechanism to encourage sustainable palm oil production. Even the WWF recommended ratifying the updated RSPO standards, despite the NGO's own criticisms of that update.[143]

Agriculture: It's a Dirty Job, but Someone Has to Sustain It

Agricultural commodities in particular face significant environmental challenges on both the consumer and sourcing sides of the supply chain. On the consumer "in me, on me, around me" scale (see chapter 1) the products are often "in me" goods—the foods that people eat and care most about. At the same time, tea, coffee, palm oil, and other agricultural products have opaque upstream supply chains full of intermediaries and are too often marred by poor social and environmental practices. Moreover, agricultural products are often sourced from hundreds of thousands of small-holder farms, which is in contrast to many industrial sectors, such as mining or oil exploration, in which large, well-established firms provide the bulk of the supply.

A key factor in how companies handle these deep-tier environmental challenges arises from the primacy of the ingredients in the company's products. Coffee beans and tea leaves are the prime ingredients in the respective beverages made by Starbucks and Unilever. And, as with AB InBev's relationship with barley farmers, these brand-owning companies are major buyers—and sometimes the sole buyers—of the respective commodities from their suppliers. Thus, they may develop a strong relationship with the deep-tier growers of their product's primary ingredient for reasons of not just sustainability, but also product quality and productivity. The suppliers, in turn, are listening. The outcome of Starbucks' and Unilever's efforts has not only been environmental and social improvement but also increased yield for farmers and higher quality coffee beans and tea leaves.

In contrast to coffee and tea, palm oil is arguably a minor ingredient for companies such as Nestlé and Unilever; it is but one of many possible vegetable oils that they might use in their products. Furthermore, Nestlé and Unilever are minor customers to large palm oil refiners such as Sinar Mas. That difference between primary ingredient supply chains and minor ingredient supply chains gives Nestlé and Unilever less leverage to control the environmental impact of oil palm growers. Unilever may have a strong desire for more sustainable palm oil, but the company admits "our progress has been slower than we hoped and highlights that this journey to drive traceability and transformation is not an easy one."[144]

As challenging as controlling the environmental impacts of the upstream supply chain might seem, controlling the downstream supply chain is even more challenging. The moment a product leaves a company's four walls, the company may have little say over how business customers, distributors, retailers, and consumers handle it, use it, or dispose of it. Nevertheless, the total environmental impact of a product encompasses these downstream phases of the life cycle as well. Mitigating the downstream impacts during the use phase of a product can be particularly challenging. It involves some combination of product redesign (chapter 8), convincing customers to change their purchasing and use habits (chapter 9), and creating reverse supply chains for handling reuse, recycling, or disposal (chapter 7).

6

Moving More, Emitting Less

Kenyan coffee, Egyptian cotton sheets, German steel knives, Chilean sea bass, Florida orange juice, New Zealand apples, and Fijian spring water available in American stores exemplify the vast distances between suppliers and American consumers. In fact, the American Apparel & Footwear Association estimates that the United States imports nearly 98 percent of all apparel items.[1] But the globe-trotting "Made in ..." labels of apparel and other products reveal only the very tip of the proverbial iceberg. That German steel knife might be made from Brazilian iron ore, Kazakh chromium, Chinese molybdenum, and South African vanadium processed in a furnace heated by Russian natural gas.

PUTTING THE GO IN CARGO

A simple T-shirt can easily involve shipments moving more than 10,000 miles. The shirt may begin as cotton grown in western China near Urumqi, Xinjiang. Bales of cotton would then travel about 2,400 miles to the apparel manufacturing cluster in Shanghai. From there, shipping containers filled with shirts would go by ocean freighter some 6,500 miles to Los Angeles. In Los Angeles, a truckload of shirts may then travel to the shirt maker's distribution center in the Imperial Valley, Chicago, or the East Coast, as far as 2,800 miles away. From the manufacturer's distribution center, the shirt would travel hundreds of miles to the retailer's distribution center and then hundreds more miles to the retailer's store.[2]

And that's just a simplified version of the transportation path of a simple shirt. More complex apparel involves shipping various natural and artificial fibers from several countries, weaving the fibers in one country, cutting the fabric in a second, and sewing it in a third. Buttons, zippers, sewing thread, and dyes might come from other countries. Some products could have as many passport stamps and frequent flier miles as a seasoned traveler. In fact, given that the single largest export leaving from Los Angeles for China is raw cotton,[3] a Texas cotton grower's T-shirt made with his own cotton may have traveled nearly 20,000 miles to go from his fields to Chinese factories and back again.

Around the world, thousands of ships, hundreds of air freighters, and millions of rail cars and trucks carry $18.8 trillion in annual global merchandise trade[4] and carry even more in domestic trade. A careful look at any of those hardworking vehicles will reveal the telltale shimmer of hot, CO_2-rich exhaust gases streaming from their engines. Of all global carbon emissions, 5.5 percent—an estimated 2,800 megatons[5]—comes from logistics and freight transportation, according to World Economic Forum estimates. More than half of it comes from over-the-road freight transportation.[6]

The lion's share of the impact of the materials' movement in a given product's supply chain depends on the decisions of *shippers*, who are either the senders or the receivers of the goods and who dictate the transportation particulars. To a lesser extent, the environmental impact depends on decisions of *carriers*, who are the operators of transportation fleets. The shippers are the suppliers, manufacturers, distributors, and retailers who are the beneficial owners of the goods. They decide how much gets shipped, where it goes, how it is shipped, when it can be picked up at the origin, and when it must be delivered to the destination. Carriers manage the conveyances, the movement of cargo on those conveyances from origin to destination, the operating conditions of the vehicles, and the fuels they put into vehicles. They move the freight and deliver it in accordance with the shippers' instructions. In some cases, the same company takes on both the shipper and carrier roles, such as when a manufacturer or retailer operates its own fleet of trucks.

"One of the really great aspects of the freight space, and one of the reasons we think that freight is particularly ripe for carbon reductions today, is that there is such good synergy between cost and carbon reductions," said Jason Mathers, program manager, corporate partnerships program at Environmental Defense Fund (EDF).[7] Burning fuel is both the primary source of the environmental impact of transportation and a dominant cost factor in transportation economics. Thus, a greener transportation network is a cheaper transportation network, making fuel-saving initiatives easy eco-efficiency successes.

Fleet Fleets Have a Heavy Footprint

A shipment's journey of ten thousand miles begins with a single footstep, but the carbon footprint of that journey depends on the shipper's dictates on how the cargo moves, especially, as mentioned in chapter 2, on how fast it moves. The Natural Resources Defense Council (NRDC), an American NGO, illustrated the significant impact of these transportation decisions by detailing an apparel maker's hypothetical choices for shipping cotton and T-shirts from the Chinese cotton-growing region of Xinjiang to consumers in Denver, Colorado, in the United States. The shirt maker might choose truck or rail for the overland journey within China, air or ocean freight to cross the Pacific to Los Angeles, and then truck or rail for the overland journey to Denver. Based on these scenarios, the NRDC calculated that whereas the truck–air–truck option takes only about a week, the rail–ship–rail option takes four or five weeks. However, the former had 35 times the carbon footprint of the latter.[8]

Although vehicle emissions do vary significantly across different vehicle models and operating conditions, faster modes of transport generally use significantly greater amounts of fuel and have much higher carbon footprints. A 500 mph air freighter emits about 10 times more CO_2 per ton-mile than a 65 mph truck, and the truck emits about 10 times more CO_2 per ton-mile than a 20 mph ocean freighter. In addition to the carbon footprint differences, the various modes differ in other types of environmental impacts. Ocean freight has higher sulfur emissions, diesel truck and rail engines emit more particulates, and jet engines have higher NO_x emissions.[9]

Shippers can reduce their transportation footprints and costs by shifting from faster modes to slower ones.[10] Continental Clothing

Co., for example, slashed greenhouse gas (GHG) emissions for some of its products by 90 percent by implementing a "No Airfreight" policy.[11] Similarly, in 2008, Levi Strauss altered its international shipping routes to use less air and truck transport and more ocean and rail. Although the policy was motivated by cost concerns, many routing changes also decreased GHG emissions by 50 to 60 percent. JB Hunt, one of the largest US motor carriers, estimates that it saves 200 gallons of fuel and 2 tons of carbon emissions for each full truckload that it shifts to rail.[12] In 2011, United Parcel Service Inc. (UPS) saved more than 2 million metric tons of emissions by shifting some delivery volume from air to ground, and another 800,000 metric tons of emissions by shifting volume from truck to rail.[13]

Fiji Water Company changed its distribution patterns to reduce both costs and carbon footprint. Instead of shipping water to Los Angeles and trucking it to the major eastern US population centers, the company used ocean shipping through the Panama Canal to the Port of Philadelphia.[14] The new route reduced emissions by 33 percent while simultaneously cutting costs by 42 percent. However, the new route increased distribution lead time by about two weeks, but owing to the relatively predictable levels of demand for the bottled water, this resulted in neither a significant increase in inventories nor a degradation in level of customer service.[15] The company also uses a square bottle design for more efficient transportation.[16]

Slow and Steady Wins the Race to Low Cost and Low Carbon

Carriers can also affect their environmental impact by changing how they operate their vehicles. When bunker fuel prices doubled in 2008, ocean carriers started "slow steaming," operating vessels at less than their usual rated velocity. The nonlinear relationship between speed and drag means that slowing these vessels can save owners significant money and reduce GHG emissions. For example, operating a 12,000-TEU (twenty-foot equivalent unit) container ship at 18 knots instead of 20 knots can reduce fuel consumption by almost 30 percent per day of travel.[17] Of course, spending more time at sea offsets some of these savings: A trip from the port of Shanghai to the port of Rotterdam takes 25 days at 20 knots versus 28 days at 18 knots, a 12 percent increase in the labor and asset utilization costs[18] as well as increased inventory carrying costs for the shipper. It also increases travel time, adding 12 percent to the number of fuel-consuming days, which results in a net 22 percent fuel saving for the journey. The higher the cost of fuel, the more the savings on fuel justifies the added expense of a longer journey time. By late 2011, 75 percent of carriers surveyed had implemented slow steaming.[19]

The same relationship between speed and fuel efficiency extends to trucks. Limiting a truck's speed to 65 mph, instead of 75 mph, saves 15 percent on fuel over a trip.[20] This motivated US President Richard Nixon to propose a limit on highway speed during the 1973 oil price spike and supply disruptions. The subsequent law limited truck and car speeds to 55 mph, leading to modest overall fuel savings.[21]

In 2006, Mike Payette, director of fleet operations at Staples Inc., investigated ways to reduce fuel, costs, and emissions of the office supply retailer's fleet of delivery trucks. He changed the control software in one delivery truck to limit its top speed to 60 mph, monitored fuel consumption for 45 days, and found that average gas mileage climbed from 8.5 mpg to 10.4, a nearly 20 percent reduction in fuel consumption.[22] The retailer also tested an add-on aerodynamic nosecone, but it provided negligible improvement if the truck also had a speed limiter.

Changing the vehicle's top speed was very inexpensive because Staples only needed to change the vehicle's engine management software. Payette estimated it cost only $7 per truck for him to travel around the country and personally upload the new code into each vehicle. Staples' savings were immediate: According to the company, the change paid for itself in $3 million of fuel savings annually.[23] Staples did not even suffer any lost driver productivity because the time lost to slower speeds was offset by fewer fuel stops,[24] a finding confirmed by studies in Europe and Japan.[25]

Adding Time to Subtract Footprint
"If we have enough days in the supply chain, we can really be more environmentally friendly," said Russ LoCurto, senior vice president

of global logistics for Ralph Lauren. A slow-steaming ocean voyage from an Asian factory to the United States may take several weeks compared with the approximately 48-hour travel time using airfreight. Ocean shipping may significantly reduce shipping costs and emissions, but it adds weeks to the lead time and to in-process inventory carrying costs (while the conveyance is in transit). The added lead time for ocean shipping also requires the company to forecast sales further into the future. These forecasts are, inevitably, less accurate than the shorter-term forecasts that can be used to plan airfreighted shipments. The lower accuracy of the long-term forecast means the company must either accept a higher risk of lost sales or endure the costs of higher safety stock, including the risk of overstocked obsolete items.

Ralph Lauren focused its eco-efficiency efforts on switching as much of its store replenishment process as was practical to ocean freight instead of airfreight. The key was segmenting products by demand variability to determine which products could be sent by slower modes without taking on excessive inventory risks. For example, staple products, such as the company's signature Polo shirts, sell throughout the year, have relatively stable demand, and do not go out of style very quickly. As a result, Ralph Lauren can forecast demand for such items with sufficient accuracy over a longer term; adding a few weeks to the supply chain added little risk of lost sales or obsolete inventory. The global fashion company worked with Asian factories to build longer ocean shipping lead times into production schedules of these staple products.

In contrast, sales of seasonal or "fast fashion" garments experience the fickle whims of consumers, making long-range forecasting subject to large errors and resulting in high potential costs from overstocks or lost sales during their short selling season. Thus, the company continued to make and ship these garments as close as possible to their selling season and use airfreight as needed. Between 2009 and 2015, Ralph Lauren reduced its global air mix by 43 percent, reducing carbon by an amount equivalent to almost half of the company's footprint of its own operations.[26]

Many other companies shifted to slower transportation modes during the same period. Shifting freight among different modes, however—especially to slower modes—also requires coordination within the business and among transportation providers to ensure that shipments depart on time so that they arrive on time. To do this, Unilever implemented a "control tower" in 2009 to manage freight movements across 35 European countries. The system was built around an end-to-end transportation management system that delivers full operational visibility into the "three C's": customer service, carbon footprint, and cost. An example of managing delivery time with slower modes is Unilever's "Green Express" train line in Italy, which delivers ice cream from its Caivano factory near Naples to its Parma distribution hub in Northern Italy. This collaboration between Unilever, Trenitalia, and the Italian Ministry for the Environment takes 3,500 trucks off the road each year but requires tight coordination. "We have the scale and capabilities to better manage our logistics networks, improving our service costs while taking one in five trucks off the road in Europe," said Neil Humphrey, Unilever's senior vice president of supply chain for Europe.[27]

Taking Out Miles and Tons

In addition to changing the carbon intensity of ton-miles by changing the speed, shippers can change the "miles" part of the ton-miles equation through local sourcing. This is especially true for food, where the concept of "food miles" has been popularized by several NGOs[28] and environmental writers.[29] Whole Foods, Walmart, and other retailers have programs to "buy local," typically from suppliers in the same state or a modest distance of 100 to 200 miles from the store.[30] In addition to saving on transportation costs and emissions, Whole Foods and others view "buying local" as a social responsibility strategy, supporting local small businesses.[31]

Local sourcing does not always reduce the total life cycle carbon footprint of a product, however. As mentioned in chapter 5, the carbon intensity of the local power grid or the need for energy intensive production techniques in the local climate (e.g., natural-gas heated greenhouses) might more than offset any environmental impact savings from reduced transportation. One study found that New Zealand lamb meat shipped 11,000 miles to the UK actually had one-quarter the carbon footprint of local British lamb, owing to differences in what the lambs are typically fed in the two locations—lower-quality British pastures required supplemental feed, unlike New Zealand's clover-rich pastures.[32] Similar results were found for dairy and fruit products. Local sourcing may or may not be a good option; only a full life cycle analysis can tell for sure (see chapter 3).

Companies can also change the "tons" part of the ton-mile equation. For some products, the bulk of the items might be water or some other material that can be readily sourced in almost any location. Many beverage makers, for example, manufacture a concentrated syrup that is then shipped to a network of local bottlers for reconstitution and bottling for retail sale. Nevertheless, this strategy may involve a trade-off between reducing global CO_2 emissions and increasing local water consumption. Companies such as Coca-Cola and Nestlé have been criticized for locating bottling facilities in water-stressed locations; however, the strategy reduces the carbon footprint of the companies by reducing the ton-miles of heavy, filled bottles of beverage. Chapter 8 describes the case of dry shampoo in which the company redesigned its product to entirely avoid ever adding water.

FOR LESS FOOTPRINT, FILL MORE

What is *not* inside the millions of shipping containers, rail cars, and trucks that move around the world contributes a significant percentage of their total life cycle impact. For most conveyances, moving empty space also consumes large amounts of fuel (about two-thirds the fuel consumption of a full truck for a 40-ton tractor trailer). Much of the time, vehicles do not carry a full load of cargo. Statistics from the EU suggest that trucks move empty 24 percent of the time and only 57 percent are completely full when carrying a load.[33] Both shippers and carriers, as well as the environment, bear the costs of underutilized vehicles demonstrating, again, the congruence between environmental costs and financial costs in transportation.

Avoiding That Empty Feeling

As mentioned in chapter 2, the simple supply chain model focuses on the tons of goods flowing from suppliers to manufacturers to distributors and finally to retailers. But the trucks, containers, rail cars, and other vehicles that carried this cargo down the supply chain must return to pick up the next load. Often, they return empty; in many regions, very little freight flows from retailers back to suppliers. Reducing empty miles means finding what is termed "backhaul loads," which are shipments that happen to be going in the opposite direction—from the vicinity of the destination back to the vicinity of the original origin of the truck journey.

Faced with this problem, the retailer Macy's and the large motor carrier Schneider National joined the Voluntary Interindustry Commerce Solutions (VICS) Association Empty Miles program.[34] "The way the system works is retailers post empty miles," said Joe Andraski, president and chief executive officer of the association. "Others can review when those movements are and match them with their shipping needs." The VICS program and other programs like it help shippers (and carriers) identify instances in which the drop-off point of one shipper's load is close to the pickup point of another shipper's load so the truck does not have to wait or travel a long distance empty to get its next load. VICS is one of dozens of such online matching applications (including Uber Freight) that offer similar services for shippers and truckers. Shippers can post available loads, truckers can post available trucks, and both sides can search for nearby matches or participate in auctions that match loads to vehicles at a competitive price.

In the case of Macy's, the VICS program eliminated 21 percent of empty miles and saved the retailer about $1.75 million per year. "Filling empty miles with the VICS service is good for the economy, it's good for the environment, and it's healthy for those companies that know how to leverage it and leverage it effectively," said Steve Matheys, chief administration officer at Schneider National. "The Empty Miles Service creates an opportunity for us to limit the environmental impact of our day to day business operations," added Kevin Locascio, Macy's director of shuttle operations.[35]

Two Fruit Products Pass in the Night

In 2011, Ocean Spray opened a new distribution center for cranberry juice products in Lakeland, Florida. The center serves customers across Florida, Georgia, Alabama, and South Carolina, with products coming from Bordentown, New Jersey,[36] which is 1,100 miles away. Ocean Spray was using long-haul trucks to move product from northern cranberry growing locations to southern customers.

Shortly after the new distribution center opened, third-party logistics provider (3PL) Wheels Clipper approached Ocean Spray with an idea.[37] 3PLs provide an array of supply chain management services—typically integrated transportation, warehousing, distribution, and related information technology. Wheels Clipper was managing the movement of Tropicana refrigerated orange juice products from Florida to New Jersey using the CSX railroad. Noticing that Ocean Spray's facilities were less than 65 miles from CSX terminals, the logistics service provider offered to move cranberry juice products from New Jersey to Florida using the empty orange juice boxcars. This change could save Ocean Spray 40 percent in transportation costs and more than 65 percent in CO_2 emissions.

The proposal, however, faced three major obstacles. First, Ocean Spray was already working with another 3PL for its long-haul truck deliveries. Shifting from road to rail would require changing the contract with the existing provider. Second, Ocean Spray had never used rail in that portion of the network. Rail boxcars hold twice as many pallets as regular truck trailers and require one or two extra days of travel time. This would require Ocean Spray to change its transportation dispatching and inventory planning practices, in addition to ensuring product integrity during the rougher rail ride. Third, Wheels Clipper was moving orange juice products for Tropicana, one of Ocean Spray's competitors. For the arrangement to work, the rival companies would have to share a logistics service provider and communicate frequently to plan the timing and size of shipments. They would also have to notify each other when empty boxcars were ready to be loaded with their competitor's product.[38]

Despite the obstacles, Ocean Spray could not ignore the savings. In February 2011, Ocean Spray agreed to collaborate. Within 12 months, it had shifted 11,500 tons of shipments from truck to rail. The shift converted roughly 616 truck shipments into 308 boxcars. Although the cranberries had to travel 20 percent farther to be trucked to and from the CSX terminal, carbon emissions were less than one-third of the old level. All parties benefitted. Both Ocean Spray and Tropicana (which avoided empty backhaul movements) reduced both their transportation costs and their environmental impact. "It took us a little while to work through [the program]," said Kristine Young, who leads the Ocean Spray sustainability efforts, "but it has been a huge success. Internally, we talk about how we can [identify] other high-volume lanes where we might be able to find rail opportunities."[39]

Consolidation: Saving Costs, Saving Carbon

For motor carrier transportation, a full truck traveling the shortest-possible route between the origin and destination (a "truckload" or TL move) is both the most cost-effective and most environmentally efficient use of that truck. Yet shippers often face situations in which the shipment does not fill the truck, which leads them to consider one of three alternatives. First, they could send the truck partially full, but that would result in a higher transportation cost (and a higher carbon footprint) per ton-mile. Second, they could wait until there was enough freight going to that destination to fill the truck, but that would degrade the shipper's level of service to its customers, increase its (and customers') inventory carrying costs, and might be impossible in the case of perishable or time-sensitive goods. Third, they could use consolidation, in which shipments with different origins and/or different destinations are brought together in a tour, or "milk run," to share the truck's capacity over some portion of the route to reduce costs and decrease the carbon footprint per shipment relative to sending partially full trucks directly.

Sometimes shippers can consolidate freight themselves by creating milk runs that collect materials from multiple suppliers or deliver goods to multiple customers, but that tactic depends on the shipper's patterns of shipments. The prevalence of small shipments—and the economic incentives to fill trucks—have spawned an entire transportation sector of specialized carriers, known as less-than-truckload (LTL) in the US or "groupage" in Europe. These carriers pick up shipments, consolidate those heading in the same direction into full trucks, and then hand off the shipments through a series of hub terminals until they reach the destination city where smaller trucks deliver the shipments to their final destinations. Parcel delivery companies (such as UPS, FedEx, DHL, and the USPS) use a similar model with smaller vehicles handling urban pickup and delivery (utilizing so-called milk runs), larger vehicles handling intercity movement, and a network of hubs handling the sorting, consolidation, and deconsolidation of the parcels.

The dichotomy between "direct" (such as TL) and "consolidated" (such as LTL) carriers exists in every transportation mode, be it container ships, air freighters, or railroads. Even in passenger transportation, one can distinguish between taxi services (as well as Uber, Lyft, and the like) on the one hand, and urban mass transit services on the other. The former typically takes a single passenger directly from origin to destination, whereas the latter consolidates multiple passengers in the same vehicle. Consolidation also enables the use of larger, more fuel-efficient vehicles for movements between hubs. Consolidated transportation is painfully familiar to every airline traveler who has changed planes in a hub airport rather than flying nonstop. (This led to the saying about the busiest airport in the world: "When I die I am not sure if I will be going to heaven or hell, but for sure I will be changing planes in Atlanta.") Of course, the trade-off is that consolidation enables cost-effective, frequent service. So whereas LTL operations increase travel distance, travel time, and handling costs of a shipment, they compensate by more frequent departures, higher utilization, and lower costs (for small shipments). In addition, the carbon emissions per shipment are smaller compared with sending a large truck to carry a small shipment directly from origin to destination.

Unfortunately, much of the empty space in truckload transportation for partially loaded trucks owes to the industry's pricing structure. The competition between TL carriers leads to such low prices that even if a shipper has a load that can fill only one-third of the truck, it is cheaper, most of the time, to send it in a dedicated truck rather than to use an LTL carrier, resulting in a higher carbon footprint per ton shipped.

Taking Carbon out of Yogurt Deliveries

Suppliers of perishable or time-sensitive products cannot delay their shipments to achieve full conveyances—the products require high-frequency shipments of small orders. This was the dilemma facing Stonyfield Farm. The company was founded on the premise that it "serve as a model that environmentally and socially responsible business can also be profitable."[40]

When Stonyfield examined its total carbon footprint, it found that transportation of the final product was the third largest contributor (accounting for approximately 6 percent of the company's footprint) behind milk (approximately 80 percent) and packaging (approximately 11 percent).[41] While working on milk and packaging, Stonyfield carefully analyzed its outbound volumes, how it was shipping them, and where they were going. To collect the data, the company relied on Ryder Logistics, which operates Stonyfield's dedicated fleet and also manages the 30 for-hire motor carriers that Stonyfield uses.[42] "By reviewing six months of data, we realized a significant opportunity in consolidating our less-than-truckload (LTL) network into our truckload network," said Ryan Boccelli, Stonyfield's director of logistics.[43]

The company replaced the hub-and-spoke movements of the LTL network with more direct full truckload movements using multi-stop (milk run) deliveries in a destination region. Stonyfield also added time to subtract carbon. To enable full truckload delivery (on departure), the company instituted minimum order sizes for customers and began requiring 48 hours' advance notice of order revisions.[44] To further reduce its carbon footprint, the company also started to "think outside the truck," Boccelli said. In 2009, Stonyfield began shipping products to the Pacific Northwest using Railex, a weekly, refrigerated railcar service for food products.[45]

Stonyfield's multifaceted efforts improved many transportation-related metrics that affect carbon footprint. By requiring larger trailers and virtually eliminating less-than-full truckload movements, Stonyfield reduced the number of truckloads of product shipped by 13 percent between 2007 and 2008.[46] By consolidating loads, increasing order lead times, and rerouting, Stonyfield's fleet reduced empty miles by 15 percent in 2008.[47] In 2009, the US EPA honored Stonyfield Farm with a "SmartWay Excellence Award."[48] Overall, between 2006 and 2010 Stonyfield and its transportation providers reduced outbound transportation emissions by 56 percent, Boccelli said.[49]

Global Imbalance—Global Opportunity

A significant fraction of the empty mile problem arises from longer-term imbalances between production and consumption regions. For example, trade imbalances, such as the one between China and the United States, mean that containers full of merchandise move from Shanghai to Los Angeles, but little cargo moves in the other direction, necessitating the return of empty containers. Imbalances in freight volume create imbalances in shipping costs: the cost of shipping a container of freight back to Shanghai from Los Angeles can be half the cost of shipping a container from Shanghai to Los Angeles.[50] A carrier that knows its container or vehicle will be empty on the return journey typically offers that backhaul space at a steep discount and demands a premium for headhaul loads to destinations that offer little return freight.

This creates incentives for companies with Asia-bound freight to look for ways to use these low-cost backhaul containers. For example, agricultural commodities, such as grain and oil seeds, have traditionally been shipped via bulk ships. Now a small but growing amount of these US-to-Asia agricultural exports go via container.[51] The container that brought over T-shirts might take raw cotton back for the next shipment of shirts. An added benefit of the containerization of agricultural products is the preservation of the identity of the origin for each container-size batch, offering enhanced visibility into the exact source of the raw material.[52]

DRIVING GREENER VEHICLES

In general, shippers control the tons of freight, the approximate distance (through their sourcing decisions and their network structure), and the maximum allowable time in transit that affect transportation mode choice. Carriers, however, control the efficiency of these purchased movements between the shipper-defined origins and destinations. Vehicle choice, fuel choice, vehicle maintenance, driver behavior, and routing can all affect the environmental impact of a given freight movement.

UPS Meets Business Goals—With a Sustainability Bonus

UPS has long sought to reduce its energy use as part of its continuous focus on cost reduction initiatives. For example, after assessing the costs of delays and engine idling involved in taking left turns across traffic (in countries where vehicles drive on the right-hand side of the road), the company redesigned its routing software in 2003 to put a clockwise bias in the layout of pickup and delivery routes, increasing the number of right turns relative to left turns. The change reduced idling while waiting for oncoming traffic and led to faster completion of routes. In 2007, according to internal estimates, the policy saved the company 3.1 million gallons of fuel and 32,000 metric tons of carbon emissions.[53]

Many of the firm's most significant efficiency initiatives—such as the "reduced left turns" policy[54] mentioned in the paragraph above—were adopted for financial reasons, even as NGOs were also encouraging UPS to evaluate its environmental impacts. "Years ago, the focus was to reduce energy because it saves costs. Well, now, it's reduced energy because it saves costs and reduces our carbon footprint," said Scott Wicker, UPS chief sustainability officer. "The sustainability group really brings more focus to what we're doing."[55]

Other UPS innovations were put in place to offer a higher level of customer service. For example, UPS *My Choice* is an online service that allows UPS customers to manage deliveries to themselves. The service allows the customer to reschedule a delivery, reroute it to another address, authorize the driver to leave the package with a neighbor, hold the package at a UPS customer center, and so on. While offering high customer service, the program also avoids multiple delivery attempts, thereby saving costs and reducing the company's carbon footprint.

Driving Improvement by Improving Drivers

The American Trucking Association (ATA) estimates that as much as 30 to 50 percent of truck engine operating hours do nothing to move freight—the truck is idling.[56] At the Poland Spring division of Nestlé, a few simple steps reduced idling time by 70 percent between 2007 and 2009. "We didn't have to come up with elaborate rules," said Chris McKenna, the fleet manager at Poland Spring. "We just made suggestions and asked them [the drivers] to use their own best judgment." The company also posted a ranking of the 65 drivers in the break room. "Human nature—no one wants to be at the bottom of the list," added McKenna. To provide an added incentive, the company gave gift cards to the top 10 drivers.[57] Companies such as Coca-Cola, AT&T, and FedEx teach drivers to reduce fuel consumption in their fleets. They also reward drivers with recognition, special privileges, and sometimes money for better driving behavior. For Coca-Cola and others, a secondary outcome of improved driver behavior was a significant reduction in the number of road accidents.[58]

Many fleets use sensors and telematics devices on vehicles to continuously measure fuel consumption, vehicle activity, engine performance, and driver behavior.[59] Vehicle telematics can collect data on drivers' actions, such as heavy acceleration, using the wrong gear, or heavy braking. "UPS's telematics platform provides drivers with feedback in real time on their fuel-efficiency performance and suggests methods for improvement."[60] UPS estimates it reduced per-driver engine idling time from 122 minutes in 2011 to 48 minutes in 2012, saving the fleet 250,000 gallons of fuel.[61] As with other examples throughout this book, such savings are only a tiny fraction of UPS' total fuel consumption, but they are part of the general pattern in which companies implement many small changes that collectively can lead to significant reductions. Overall, UPS beat its 2016 goal of a 10 percent reduction in emissions (relative to a 2007 baseline) three years ahead of schedule.[62] Other companies are deploying technology to control idling, such as the use of automatic shutdown on locomotives at BNSF and other railroads.[63] The technology has even found its way into passenger cars employing automatic shutdown/start-up systems during idling.

Move It the SmartWay

In 2004, the US Environmental Protection Agency created the SmartWay program to improve the fuel efficiency of the transportation industry. The program spans multiple activities, including the development of tools for benchmarking operations, testing, equipment verification, and vehicle environmental rankings.[64] Participating organizations include shippers (retailers, manufacturers, and distributors) and carriers (trucking companies, railroads, and freight airlines) as well as logistics service providers and governmental agencies.[65] The program began with 15 motor carriers and grew over the following decade to include more than 3,000 carriers as well 600 shippers such as Nike, Whole Foods, and Chiquita.[66]

At its core, SmartWay offers tools to assess environmental impacts. Carriers (and shippers) can measure progress over time relative to industry peers. "Carriers collect information, such as fuel used, miles driven, truck and engine model year, and cargo payload and input it into the reporting tool to calculate freight environmental performance,"[67] explains the EPA in a guidebook for its partners. In addition, any operator of a tractor or trailer that meets certain technical specifications can be certified as a SmartWay carrier.

Next, the EPA uses six metrics to rank all the assessed carriers within each sector and mode category.[68] Although SmartWay does not verify information—it only aggregates carriers' data at the fleet level—it does randomly spot-check the reporting when calculating the rankings. The rankings are published so shippers can use them when selecting carriers. Some shippers also commit to increase the share of their business with both certified and top-ranked SmartWay carriers,[69] thereby providing market incentives for carriers to get certified, as well as to measure, disclose, and share their fuel-efficiency ranking.

Beginning in 2006, Chiquita became a SmartWay partner and boasted in its 2012 sustainability report that SmartWay-certified trucks handled 95 percent of the miles traveled in its North American operations.[70] Ana Lucia Alonzo, director of continuous improvement and sustainability for Chiquita commented, "We are committed to SmartWay." Similarly, Stonyfield Farm also committed to the program, shipping 100 percent of its freight using efficient SmartWay carriers, utilizing certified trucks that may be as much as 20 percent more efficient than standard trucks.[71]

At its 10-year anniversary on March 19, 2014, an EPA Smart-Way Transport Partnership press release estimated the total savings achieved by the program[72] at 1.4 percent of the diesel fuel used in trucking, with a corresponding savings on fuel costs and carbon emissions.[73] An exhaustive study of major US trucking fleets found that the fuel-saving technologies with the fastest adoption included adding skirts to trailers, using synthetic transmission oil, and installing speed limiters.[74] On average, the use of all these technologies reduced fuel consumption by more than 10 percent.[75]

Horses for Courses

The GHG Protocol uses a very simple model for truck emissions based on EPA estimates of the average CO_2 emissions per ton-mile computed across vehicle types and operating conditions (the EPA uses 0.297 kg CO_2e/ton-mile for this emissions factor).[76] With this aggregate emissions estimation model, the total emissions are simply the product of shipment weight, distance, and the emissions factor. However, using such a simple model can give the wrong results regarding some emissions-reduction opportunities, such as when tailoring specific vehicles to specific conditions, including shipment size, driving conditions, congestion, topography, and altitude.

The Swedish nonprofit Network for Transport Measures (NTM) aims to develop higher-fidelity standardized calculations for all transportation modes.[77] The NTM calculations and suggested fuel consumption factors are more specific to different vehicles, conditions, and fuels. For example, a 40-ton truck-trailer combination driving on a sea-level freeway is estimated to consume diesel fuel at a rate of 0.226 liters/km if empty. This figure climbs to a rate of 0.360 liters/km as the amount of cargo increases to full. A smaller, 14-ton truck consumes only 0.165 liters/km if driving empty on a freeway and 0.201 if full.

NTM's model assumes fuel consumption increases linearly with the load (starting with the weight of the empty truck), where the empty and full fuel consumption factors depend on the specific truck modeled. Emissions are then computed as the product of fuel consumption per kilometer from the graph, a fuel factor (e.g., 2.68 kg of CO_2e per liter of diesel burned[78]), and the distance traveled in kilometers.

Shippers and carriers can use emissions models such as NTM's to plan transportation movements that minimize both fuel costs and emissions.[79] For example, researchers at the MIT Center for Transportation and Logistics used stylized examples to show how re-sequencing a set of milk-run deliveries—so that the heaviest cargo would be delivered early in the journey—can yield environmental benefits. This scheme reduces fuel consumption during the remainder of the journey.

These researchers also worked with DHL in Mexico on assigning the right equipment to the right delivery tour in an urban area.[80] Even with constraints of equipment availability, timing of the delivery, and many other factors, the actual test reduced emissions by 3 percent. Although small, the result was equivalent to eliminating the emissions of 12 vehicles as compared with the baseline.

A more comprehensive model of fuel consumption and CO_2 emissions for trucking was developed by researchers at the University of California, Riverside.[81] This model is one of the most detailed, accounting for engine performance (including friction, engine displacement, and tractive power), mass of the vehicle, speed, acceleration, gravity, road slope, and more. When taking all these factors into account, the above-mentioned MIT study demonstrated that the effect of road slopes can dominate and that calculations accounting only for distance, speed, and weight that assume flat roads are missing an important factor. In fact, for some road slopes, the CO_2 emissions induced by the slope are substantially larger than the emission contribution resulting from the speed.[82]

The Right Power Source at the Right Time

In many freight vehicles, idling engines help maintain cabin temperatures, power the vehicle's ever-growing array of electronic devices, support departure readiness, or prevent cold weather damage to the engine. Unfortunately, these vehicles' large main engines are especially inefficient at idle speeds in which almost all of the fuel's extracted energy goes to overcoming the big engine's internal friction. One solution, used by Walmart and others, is to add an auxiliary power unit (APU) to their long-haul trucks. The APU is a compact system containing a very small diesel engine, generator, and air conditioner compressor. Such devices have been used on aircraft since World War I to power airplanes while taxiing, during maintenance operations, and other non-flight requirements. Adding APUs to Walmart's trucks saved an estimated 10 million gallons of fuel per year, according to the Rocky Mountain Institute.[83] The EPA estimates that long-haul trucks save an average of 8 percent in fuel costs and emissions by using APUs.[84]

An alternative to both engine idling and APUs is "shore power," a term taken from the maritime world. With this method, the vehicle connects to the local electrical grid and shuts down all onboard engines. To reduce emissions and pollution at port areas, ocean freighters can be outfitted to use shore power while docked. However, the technology requires coordinated investments in both the vehicles and infrastructure. The Port of Long Beach in California invested $200 million to install shore power hookups. The port is also committed to increasing the fraction of vessels serving the port using shore power, aiming to reach 80 percent in 2020 (see the last part of this chapter).

Adding shore power to a container vessel costs between $500,000 and $2 million.[85] Shore power is also expensive to use: $19,000 for three days of electricity in the Port of Oakland, for example. Moreover, shore power can add significant delays up to 13 hours to a ship's time in port, according to Lee Kindberg, director of environment and sustainability at Maersk Line. Because of these expenses and delays, carriers have retrofitted only a fraction of their fleets; as of 2014, Singapore-based APL had only added shore power to one-third of its container vessel fleet. Although limiting the number of retrofitted ships saves capital for the ocean carrier, it adds to its operating costs. The combination of having some ships outfitted for shore power and some ports that require it, while others do not, limits the flexibility of the shipping line. Because not all vessels can visit all ports, ship scheduling becomes constrained, reducing the line's ability to operate an optimal cost and service schedule[86] (see the section "Taming the Brimstone Beasts of Maritime Shipping Emissions").

The WAVE of the Future

In the long-term, innovations in engines and vehicles promise further gains in efficiency and reductions in emissions. When the Walmart Advanced Vehicle Experience (WAVE) concept truck drove from the Peterbilt Motors plant to a local airport for the unveiling ceremony in early 2014, it stopped traffic. "People were literally driving their cars off the road, trying to jump out and get pictures, and wanting us to stop so they could take pictures in front of it," said Elizabeth Fretheim, director of business strategy and sustainability for Walmart Logistics.[87] The narrow hatchet-faced cab placed the driver's seat in the center, perched on top of a teardrop-streamlined base that looked nothing like the utilitarian boxes of typical long-haul trucks.

The sleek sports-car-like sloping curves and advanced gadgets on the truck are all 100 percent functional—designed to avoid the fuel-sucking drag produced by the typical blunt-fronted truck.[88] The vehicle's carbon fiber trailer saves 4,000 pounds,[89] enabling the truck to legally carry that much more cargo. Nestled under the driver is a patented micro-turbine powering a battery-electric hybrid drivetrain. The air-cooled micro-turbine eliminates the weight and drag of a conventional radiator and can run efficiently on virtually any fuel, from natural gas to biodiesel. The development effort bundled innovations from 22 partner companies into one demonstration vehicle.[90] Walmart estimated that WAVE can increase fuel economy by 55 percent over long routes and even more over short ones, when its battery and hybrid drivetrain take over.[91]

According to Darren R. Jamison, president and CEO of Capstone Turbine Corp., "Walmart said they were looking for the truck of the future. They didn't want what the technology could look like next year."[92] Walmart's Fretheim explained: "It gave the company a license to think outside the box. It gave us confidence ... the ingenuity and the interest to pursue more bold innovation."[93] "It's important that we continue to work collectively on future innovations and challenge ourselves to look boldly at fleet efficiency in new and different ways," added Tracy Rosser, senior vice president of transportation at Walmart.[94] "It may never make it to the road, but it will allow us to test new technologies and new approaches," concluded Walmart president and CEO Doug McMillon.[95]

Many other innovations currently on the drawing board have the potential to reduce fuel consumption, thereby reducing costs and carbon emissions. These include *platooning*, in which one or more trucks tailgate extremely closely to a lead truck using high-speed electronic control of engines and brakes. Tests estimate platooning would reduce fuel costs for the trailing vehicle by about 8 percent and that even the lead vehicle enjoys up to a 5 percent boost in fuel economy owing to reduced drag behind its trailer.[96] Further technological developments that culminate in autonomous trucks can lead to fuel savings as a result of "always optimal" operation.[97]

In the air, Boeing developed the 787 aircraft to be 20 percent more fuel efficient than the 767 aircraft it is replacing. The savings come from using lighter materials (including 50 percent composites and 20 percent aluminum), new engines, lighter-weight batteries, and using electrically powered systems (instead of pneumatic systems that bleed high pressure air from the engines and rob the airplane of thrust).[98]

Bigger Vehicles Have Lighter Footprints

"One of the biggest challenges we face in the world today is how to meet the growing needs of a growing population while minimizing the impact that [it] is going to have on our planet," said Maersk Line CEO Eivind Kolding. Maersk designed the biggest (at the time) container ship ever because, for transportation carbon footprints, as well as operating costs, bigger *is* paradoxically better. At the time, fuel costs were high and rising, creating a strong incentive to reduce fuel consumption. Maersk dubbed it the Triple-E, short for "Economy of scale, Energy efficient, and Environmentally improved." With a hull as long as four football fields, the Triple-E can carry 18,000 TEU shipping containers while consuming 35 percent less fuel per container capacity than the already huge 13,100 TEU vessels entering service at the same time.

Everything about the Triple-E is massive. Two engines deliver a total of 86,000 horsepower to two 9.8-meter diameter 70-ton propellers. Each giant 910-ton engine has eight long-bore cylinders with a 3.4-meter stroke moving at a friction-reducing 74 rpm.[99] In guzzling a staggering 1,800 gallons of bunker oil every hour, the ship seems to have a high carbon footprint. Yet on a per ton-mile basis, the fully loaded ship is more than 10 times more fuel efficient than even some of the most fuel-efficient trucks of its time.[100]

At $190 million apiece, a ship like the Triple-E merits investment in all the latest energy-conserving equipment, such as a $10 million heat recovery system that offers a 9 percent improvement on fuel economy and emissions.[101,102] The ship was designed for efficient slow steaming of 22 knots from the start. "The lower top speed of the Triple-E vessels has a significant impact on the hull shape," said naval architect Troels Posborg. "It means we can build vessels with a larger capacity below the deck."[103] The result is both lower fuel consumption and greater cargo capacity. The Triple-E uses less total engine power than Maersk's previous generation, the 14,770 TEU E-class vessels, but it can carry 22 percent more cargo. The Triple-E did not hold the crown for the biggest container ship for long after its March 2013 debut; in December 2014, China Shipping launched the 19,000 TEU CSCL Globe.[104]

Other modes favor larger vehicles, too. Trucks with larger trailers, double-trailers, and triple-trailers offer 20 to 32 percent savings per ton-mile compared with smaller trucks.[105] And railroads in the US and EU are looking at efficiencies and other operating performance advantages[106] of longer trains.[107] Although their potential is promising, as mentioned earlier, larger vehicles deliver on their promise of a lower footprint per ton-mile only if their cavernous spaces are filled to capacity. "It's a simple logic, bigger is better," said Ulrik Sanders, global head of the shipping practice at Boston Consulting, "if you can fill it."[108]

An Emerging Standard?

As mentioned above, shippers (manufacturers, suppliers, distributors, etc.) determine the most important variables that affect the carbon footprint of transportation of their goods. They decide the origin and destination, shipment size, timing, and the carrier to use. Unfortunately, tracking transportation GHG emissions involves multiple methodologies across modes, countries, and programs.

In an attempt to provide a unified methodology, the Smart Freight Center,[109] a European-based nonprofit, convened the Global Logistics Emissions Council (GLEC). The GLEC developed a methodology across the multi-modal supply chain.[110] The methodology covers all modes of transport and combines existing methodologies and standards from each mode (air,[111] inland waterways,[112] sea,[113] rail,[114] road,[115] and transshipment centers[116]). Many of the mode-specific methodologies also incorporate SmartWay processes. The GLEC adheres to the Greenhouse Gas Protocol's framework of Scopes 1, 2, and 3 for corporate emissions data, ensuring that the total equals the sum of the parts. For example, a carrier's own Scope 1 and Scope 2 emissions are part of the Scope 3 emissions of the shipper or the logistics service provider (LSP) hiring the carrier's service. The scoping framework enables shippers to make transportation choices based on consistent emissions information.

FUEL TODAY, GREENHOUSE GAS TOMORROW

In addition to improvements in mode choice, conveyance utilization, routing, and fuel-saving vehicle features, shippers and carriers can reduce their carbon and emissions footprints by choosing different fuels. UPS, for example, had more than 5,000 alternative-fuel vehicles on the road as of 2014, including ones powered by compressed natural gas, liquefied natural gas, propane, and electricity. By 2017, UPS was planning to power 12 percent of its ground fleet with renewable fuels.[117]

Local requirements, as well as fuel availability and prices, determine carriers' choices. "As the world is changing and growing, different parts of the world have specific expectations as to how we address issues of congestion and climate change and air quality, so the requirements may vary based on where we are doing business," said Rhonda Clark, chief sustainability officer at UPS. UPS continues to try out new fleet solutions, such as using electric vehicles for short-range city deliveries in areas with high fuel prices.[118]

The Carbon Footprint of a Carbon Footprint

The laws of chemistry and thermodynamics dictate the limits on the lowest possible CO_2 emissions required to produce a kilowatt-hour of energy from different kinds of fuels. From this standpoint, natural gas outperforms diesel, and diesel outperforms coal. But chemistry doesn't tell the whole story. Some fuels involve hidden GHG emissions even before the fuel goes into the tank. In theory, natural gas power plants emit less than half the carbon dioxide of coal. In practice, natural gas is by itself a potent GHG: If even a small percentage escapes during the extraction, refining, delivery, and use of natural gas, the carbon footprint benefits may be negated.[119,120]

Similarly, environmentalists worry about hydraulic fracturing—the enhanced fossil fuel extraction technology more commonly known as fracking. NGOs such as Greenpeace have expressed "grave concerns" over issues of carbon, water use, contamination, health effects, and the secret chemicals injected into fracking wells.[121] Despite US EPA declarations that properly managed hydraulic fracturing wells are safe,[122] NGOs protests persist because key elements of well operations are exempted from EPA oversight.[123] The NGOs, however, do not take into account the political, security, and economic benefits of fracking to countries like the United States and others.

Taming the Brimstone Beasts of Maritime Emissions

The sooty black clouds billowing from a ship or truck's exhaust pipe vividly illustrate the other pollutants, besides CO_2, emitted by various vehicles. Sulfur compounds, a common contaminant of heavier fossil fuels such as diesel and bunker oil, burn inside vehicles' engines to form sulfur oxides (SO_x). The high temperatures in vehicles' efficient engines also convert atmospheric nitrogen into nitrogen oxides (NO_x). Both SO_x and NO_x are serious respiratory irritants, contributors to acid rain, large contributors to global warming, and have become regulated air pollutants. The world's approximately 90,000 ocean vessels emit about 20 million tons of SO_x per year. This is 250 times more than the SO_x emissions of all the more than 900 million[124] cars in the world put together.[125,126] In fact, *The Economist* reported that just 15 of the biggest ships emit more SO_x and NO_x than all the cars in the world.[127] Coal-fired power plants, and some manufacturing processes, such as ore smelters, oil refineries, and chemical plants, also emit SO_x and NO_x.

The MARPOL (short for "marine pollution") Convention is a growing set of international regulations created by the UN's International Maritime Organization (IMO).[128] Adopted in 1973, enacted through a protocol in 1978, and entered into force in 1983, MARPOL addresses maritime pollution by oil, noxious liquid substances, harmful substances, ship sewage, and garbage through a series of annexes. In 2008, the IMO[129] adopted the MARPOL Annex VI, which enacted tight standards regarding sulfur and nitrogen exhaust emissions from oceangoing vessels.[130] After January 2015, vessels could no longer use fuel containing more than 1,000 ppm (parts per million) sulfur in designated emissions control areas (the previous limit was 10,000 ppm).[131] In February 2017, the EU decided to include shipping in its emission-trading scheme starting in 2021; compliance will require expensive retrofitting of ships. Other modes of transportation, such as trucking and railroads, face similar or even more stringent local government restrictions on sulfur, mandating ultra-low-sulfur fuels of less than 15 ppm.[132]

For operations in some maritime Emission Control Areas (ECAs), both MARPOL and local regulations define much tighter restrictions.[133] Unfortunately, low-sulfur grades of marine fuel, such as marine gas oil (MGO),[134] increase operating fuel costs by 50 percent, making it uneconomical for full-time use. The low-sulfur fuels also create many safety and reliability risks for older fuel-handling systems and engines designed for high-sulfur fuels.[135] Ironically, the push for low-sulfur emissions in European ECAs might lead to more overall pollution by making fuel-efficient short-sea shipping more expensive than trucking.[136]

A-maize-ing Biofuel

What could be better than a fuel that promises to be both carbon neutral and immediately usable without needing investments in new vehicles with new engines? Across some 87.4 million acres of US farmland,[137] beams of bright yellow sunlight are transformed into rows of bright yellow corn kernels. After harvesting the corn, massive factories pulverize the grain, convert the cornstarch into sugar, and then convert the sugar into ethanol that may be used as a renewable fuel substitute for petroleum-derived gasoline in many types of engines. Around the globe, ethanol makers' most commonly used feedstocks are corn and sugar cane. However, the diesel engines used in trucks, railroad locomotives, and ocean vessels, as well as aircraft jet engines, rely on heavier fuels and must use other biofuels instead of ethanol.

At first glance, biofuels such as ethanol look like a perfect solution to the carbon footprint problems of gasoline-based transportation. The same amount of carbon dioxide released during the burning of biofuels was pulled out of the air during the growth period of these plants and thus, in theory, biofuels could be carbon neutral. But in practice, the production of biofuel relies on GHG-emitting energy sources (e.g., electrical power, natural gas for boilers, and fossil-fueled vehicles) and generates other GHGs, such as methane or nitrogen fertilizer emissions. Furthermore, life cycle assessments by the IPCC concluded that corn-based ethanol increases food supply risks.[138] The corn needed to fill the 25-gallon gas tank for a single car could fill the stomachs of almost 400 people for a day.[139] In short, true substitution of biofuel for fossil fuel means that the world's 1.2 billion vehicles compete with people and wildlife for food, land, and water.

Both ethanol and biodiesel can also be synthesized from cellulose extracted from inedible plant material such as agricultural waste, switchgrass, or wood, which mitigates the competition between hungry people and thirsty vehicles. Although cellulosic biofuel enjoys a more abundant range of feedstocks, serious technological obstacles have caused the industry to lag badly behind expectations. In 2007, the United States had mandated that 500 million gallons of cellulosic biofuel would be produced in 2012,[140] but production as late as the first part of 2016 was only running at a rate of 4 million gallons a year.[141]

Nonetheless, companies continue to pursue these fuels. Beginning in 2017, FedEx plans to buy 3 million gallons a year of cellulosic renewable jet fuel (out of a total of 1.14 billion gallons/year burned by the company's aircraft[142]) made by Red Rock Biofuels from leftover woody biomass.[143] Fulcrum Bioenergy aims even higher: It signed a long-term deal with United Airlines to produce biofuel from municipal waste for less than the prevailing cost of fossil fuel at five hub airports.[144] Ultimately, the system could produce a total of 180 million gallons of jet fuel per year. "Investing in alternative fuels is not only good for the environment, it's a smart move for our company as biofuels have the potential to hedge against future oil price volatility and carbon regulations," said United's executive vice president and general counsel, Brett Hart.[145]

Beginning in 2005, the US government embarked on a legislative and regulatory push to move the nation's transportation systems toward renewable fuels. More than 60 countries embarked on similar crusades,[146] all with the twin aims of improving energy security and reducing the net release of GHGs into the atmosphere. In support of the American version of this plan, legislators agreed on renewable fuel requirements, supported renewable energy startups, and subsidized domestic corn ethanol.

The Ethanol Shuffle

In 2011, a combination of market conditions and government policies in the United States and Brazil led to a perverse situation in which American firms sold subsidized corn-based ethanol to the Brazilian market and Brazilian firms sold sugar-based ethanol to the American market.

Brazilian sugarcane converts more effectively into ethanol than does American "dent corn"[147] (aka "field corn," which is generally grown for industrial uses and animal feed) because of the added steps in converting cornstarch into sugar prior to fermentation. According to the US EPA, sugar ethanol produced 61 percent lower emissions than traditional gasoline. In contrast, the EPA found that corn ethanol produced anywhere from 48 percent less all the way to 5 percent *more* emissions than did standard gasoline.[148] That significant edge meant that the EPA classified sugarcane-based ethanol as advanced biofuel, unlike corn-based ethanol. Thus, it was not held to the 2010 cap placed on corn-based ethanol. As a result, American suppliers began buying sugar-based ethanol from Brazil. Between July and October 2011, American fuel suppliers bought about 40 million gallons of Brazilian ethanol. Meanwhile, Brazil faced a domestic ethanol shortage (due, in part, to those market-fueled exports) and imported 123 million gallons of American corn ethanol. Thus, as a result of policies fostering corn ethanol in the United States, each gallon of that fuel benefitted from a 45-cent tax credit—in effect transferring 55 million American tax dollars into Brazilian gas tanks.[149]

Geoff Cooper, vice president of research and analysis for the Renewable Fuels Association, dubbed the strange phenomenon the "Ethanol Shuffle." "Picture the irony of a tanker full of US corn ethanol bound for Brazil passing a tanker full of sugarcane ethanol bound for Los Angeles or Miami along a Caribbean shipping route," Cooper said in comments published in *Ethanol Producer* magazine. "Remember, this is all being done in the name of reducing GHG emissions. But what are the real GHG implications of the shuffle? And what are the economic impacts?"[150]

Despite recognition of this folly, US internal political considerations have been blocking any attempt to correct the policy, because ethanol policies have been a boon to corn-producing states. For example, ethanol production has added about $20 billion to Iowa's economy since 2002 and increased the value of farmland in the state threefold.[151] Consequently, congressional efforts to correct the situation have gone nowhere.

Plugging into an Electric Future

Companies such as Frito-Lay, Coca Cola, and Duane Reade have invested in short-haul electric delivery trucks,[152] mainly for urban deliveries. Large trucking fleet operators, such as UPS and FedEx, have only adopted electric vehicles on an experimental basis or where government subsidies mitigate the extra capital costs of these vehicles.[153]

Electric vehicles offer the potential of zero-emission transportation, but only if the vehicle owner recharges the vehicle from a zero-emissions source of electricity. Otherwise, electrification simply shifts emissions from urban vehicles operating in the midst of population centers to potentially remote power plants. Thus, while an electric vehicle in Norway might have near zero emissions because 95 percent of the country's power comes from renewable hydroelectricity,[154] that same vehicle driven in Poland has significant emissions because 85 percent of Poland's power comes from high-carbon-emission coal.[155] In the long-term, however, stationary power plants have more cost-effective opportunities for boosting efficiency, controlling pollution, and sequestering carbon than do mobile pollution sources, aka vehicles. Interestingly, fracking has actually helped lower the carbon footprint of electric vehicles in the United States by increasing the percentage of power coming from natural gas.[156]

Unfortunately, the high cost and poor energy density of batteries makes electric vehicles infeasible for most long-haul freight transportation, including ocean, air freight, or long-haul trucking. Long-haul trains in Europe, Japan, and other countries often run on electricity supplied by catenary-wires running above the tracks.[157] In 2016, Siemens tested an electric truck concept that adapts catenary-wire electric technology to high-volume truck routes such as those associated with the ports of Los Angeles and Long Beach.[158]

SOOT BEGETS LAWSUITS: THE GREENING OF A PORT

All day every day, enormous ships glide into the ports of Los Angeles and Long Beach (LA/LB) to dock. Once the thick cables lash the ship to the dock, long-armed cantilever cranes pluck thousands of 20- and 40-foot-long containers from the ship's deck and load them onto rail cars and trucks to begin the process of distributing the cargo across the United States. In 2013, the combined LA/LB port complex ranked as the ninth busiest container port in the world.[159] In addition to delivering cargo, the ports deliver one million jobs to the Los Angeles area and generate more than $17 billion in direct and indirect sales in the local area.[160] Combined, the two ports handle 20 percent of America's incoming freight containers.[161] There is, however, an environmental price to be paid by residents living in proximity to the port complex and similar large-scale logistics clusters for this economic largess: It makes places like these ports a focus for environmentalists' actions.

Logistics Clusters: Globally Good, Locally Bad

The size and scale of the Los Angeles/Long Beach port complex is no fluke. The economics of transportation—the cost efficiencies of large vehicles and consolidated flows—often lead to hub-and-spoke networks. In many cases, such hubs develop around mode-change terminals, be they rail yards, ports, or airports. The natural nexus of activity at the hub then attracts more logistics and other industrial activities to grow into a logistics cluster. Logistics clusters are found in places like Shanghai, Singapore, Rotterdam, Memphis, São Paulo, and hundreds of others around the world.[162]

Such clusters, with their high hub-to-hub freight flows, improve the cost efficiency (and lower the environmental footprint) of global logistics for four reasons. First, the higher flows in and out of such a hub allow the use of larger conveyances, directly reducing CO_2 per ton-mile. Second, such conveyances are more likely to be filled, improving capacity utilization, which, again, reduces the carbon footprint per ton-mile. Third, the high volume of freight increases the frequency of cost-efficient (and eco-efficient) services from every origin feeding into the cluster and to every destination getting freight from the cluster. The higher frequency of service reduces schedule delays and enables shippers to switch to slower, less-costly, lower-footprint modes of transportation such as rail and intermodal. Fourth, the presence of several transportation modes within the cluster location lets shippers subdivide shipments into slow and fast modes rather than send entire shipments on a faster mode because some portion of a shipment has a tight deadline.

Some governments, such as Germany's, encourage and support the development of logistics clusters in order to shift more freight from trucking to rail (mainly using intermodal movements).[163] Rail

shipments produce about one-third to one-half of the carbon footprint of trucking.

Yet, even as the logistics cluster in the Los Angeles basin reduces
the global environmental impacts of freight movement, it increases
the local impacts. From this beehive of activity arises a black cloud
of diesel exhaust from the many ships that visit each year[164] and
the thousands of trucks that work in the port.[165] In 2011, the ports
of Los Angeles and Long Beach collectively handled 5,364 vessel
calls,[166] including 14.2 million TEUs of containers.[167] On average,
the 16 foreign vessels that unload at the ports every day produce
exhaust equivalent to about one million cars, as demonstrated by
the NRDC in a YouTube video.[168]

The ports' activities contributed to poor air quality in the South
Coast Basin Air District, which has been consistently ranked among
the worst in the United States.[169] "The vessels, the cargo-handling
equipment, the trucks and the trains—all were contributing to
the degradation of air quality and the health impacts associated
with that," said Bob Kanter, environmental director for the Port
of Long Beach.[170] The downside of one area handling 20 percent
of US inbound container traffic is that it gets a 20 percent share of
the nation's emissions associated with that traffic. The impacted
community,[171] home to more Americans than any other metropolitan area except New York City, took notice as the port grew
in size.

The Tide Turns Against Port Pollution

Concerns about the environmental impact of the port on LA basin's
citizens spurred both activist and government action. In 1998, the
California Air Resources Board declared that diesel exhaust was
a "toxic air contaminant"[172] and a carcinogen.[173] The ruling gave
the NRDC the legal leverage it needed to bring a 2001 lawsuit
against the ports on behalf of neighboring Los Angeles County
residents.[174] "As proposals for growth were starting to come in,
the NRDC started doing the math, and they saw that the potential health risk was going to grow," said Chris Cannon, director
of environmental management for the Port of Los Angeles. "They
basically stopped us and said, 'Wait a minute, you don't have a

plan here. You're asking us to bear the burden while you continue to grow and make all this money.'"[175]

In 2002, a three-judge panel halted the Port of Los Angeles' plan to build an additional container terminal for the China Shipping Company. The suit contended that diesel emissions at the port already endangered residents' health and that construction of an additional terminal would exacerbate this issue.[176] The appellate court agreed and the judges immediately halted any and all port expansion plans.[177] Responding to political pressure and community pushback of its own,[178] the nearby rival Port of Long Beach also began to explore environmental programs in 2003.

Strange Bedfellows: Partnering Between Rival Ports and NGOs

As in the case of industry associations such as RSPO (see chapter 5), addressing the challenges facing the ports and the communities required collaboration between competitors and adversaries. The Ports of Los Angeles and Long Beach compete for ship traffic. But in response to the pressure from NGOs and regulators, both ports dropped their independent efforts to reduce pollution. In 2006, they partnered with each other, NGOs, and regulatory agencies to create the Clean Truck Program and Clean Air Action Plan.[179] "We were always kind of at odds with the air quality regulatory agencies … and it wasn't helping anybody," Kanter said. "So, we basically held out an olive branch and said, look, we have the same goals in mind here. … How can we do it and work cooperatively?"[180] The plan not only represented unprecedented cooperation between two business rivals but also an unusual partnership with the NGOs and regulators that watched over both businesses.

The NRDC was not the ports' only ally throughout the development of the environmental programs. The ports also received support from the West Coast Collaborative and the South Coast Air Quality Management District. Where the ports' capacity or expertise fell short, these groups helped develop pollution-reduction programs while simultaneously planning for the ports' future growth. In 2013, the South Coast Air Quality District helped develop regulations that would take effect only if the ports missed the goals they had outlined for themselves.[181] The West Coast Collaborative helped by hosting a series of webinars on new technologies for reducing port and port-related emissions.[182]

The Port of Long Beach developed a strong relationship with environmental groups. "We had to walk the talk and demonstrate that we were good for our word, and we have. ... So, we gained credibility with the environmental community, and we've continued to build upon that by engaging them," said Kanter.[183] Although the ports nurtured a good working relationship with their former attackers and brought other collaborators on board, the path to that relationship was not always smooth. In 2008, the NRDC and the Coalition for a Safe Environment threatened to sue the Port of Long Beach for not reducing its environmental impact fast enough (the sides ultimately settled out of court).[184] "We don't always see eye to eye," Kanter said, "but one of the things we found is that we needed to educate them about what we were doing and what our challenges were. The education aspect can't be understated. We meet monthly with representatives of all of our major environmental groups and some of the minor ones. ... As a result, the resistance that used to translate into political pressure on us has backed off quite a bit."[185]

Clean Air Action Plan

For the 2003 injunction settlement, the Port of Los Angeles earmarked $50 million to fund a 50 percent reduction in diesel exhaust emissions from port operations by 2011.[186] To do so, the ports, the state, the air district, and companies that worked with the ports invested hundreds of millions of additional dollars in pollution-reducing programs.[187] The program also included guidelines and incentives to reduce ships' exhaust both near and in port. The port asked ships to slow steam at 12 nautical miles per hour or less as they approached the coast. After the ships docked, the ships used shore power.[188]

The ports offered carriers several compliance incentives for their sustainability programs. For example, ships that slow steamed into port got up to a 50 percent reduction in docking fees.[189] In addition, the ports created the Green Flag Award to publicly recognize companies with the best adherence to the new guidelines. According to

Port of Long Beach's Kanter, the award-winning companies started using this in their marketing materials.[190] By mid-2013, 99 percent of ship visits were compliant at the Port of Long Beach.[191] Nevertheless, the biggest initiative of the LA/LB ports centered on the complete overhaul of the ports' truck fleets, which were independently owned and operated.[192]

Clean Truck Program

In 2008, the ports launched the Clean Truck Program to transform the fleet of older, "dirty" diesel workhorse dray trucks that hauled cargo to and from the ports day in and day out.[193] At that time, approximately 16,000 trucks operated within the Port of Los Angeles alone, according to the Port's Chris Cannon. Those trucks were, on average, 11 years old, and many of them ran on minimal maintenance by small owner-operators who could hardly afford to buy a new vehicle.[194]

The ports used a "carrot and stick" approach to encourage a shift from old dirty trucks to new greener ones. In 2008, the ports added a $35 surcharge for every TEU picked up by a tractor trailer older than five years. The program mandated that all large trucks operating within port borders comply with the 2007 EPA emission standards for heavy-duty trucks. To help drivers comply, the port offers grants of up to $20,000 for drivers to purchase new vehicles. In total, the Port of Los Angeles awarded 2,200 grants totaling $41.6 million. The ports had planned to completely ban vehicles older than five years in 2012, but it never had to. Private carriers responded so quickly to the fees and incentives that they updated the entire 16,000-truck fleet before the end of 2010.[195]

The mandates did bankrupt some contract drivers, leading to community unrest over lost jobs.[196] "To be honest, there were some people (private trucks) that should have never been in business," Kanter said. "They were independent contractors, and they could drive that rig, even though it was held together by chewing gum and bailing wire. ... Those guys were driven out of business."[197] Some of those drivers brought unsuccessful lawsuits against the ports. In a twist, the NRDC—the same organization that had sued the Port of Los Angeles—provided legal defense for the ports' Clean Trucks Program.

Results, but Not the Final Results

The Clean Truck Program reduced truck-related diesel exhaust emissions at the two ports by more than 80 percent by 2010,[198] which was faster than the plan's architects had promised. "We set out initial goals for the Clean Air Action Plan, and we blew right by them in about four years instead of five or six years," said Christopher Patton, assistant director for environmental management at the LA port.[199] By 2012, total ship, truck, and other emissions for the port had fallen by about 76 percent.[200] The port invested almost $100 million in its clean air initiatives.[201] Private businesses working within the port invested an estimated $1 billion, mainly in replacement trucks, according to Cannon.[202]

"But we don't say we've arrived. We have some long-term air quality goals called our 'Bay Wide Standards,' which we still must meet," Patton declared.[203] The standards include reducing port-related emissions of NO and NO_2 by 59 percent, SO_x by 92 percent,[204] and diesel particulates by 77 percent, all by 2023.[205]

To achieve these new goals, both ports have continued their efforts. In 2010, the ports commissioned a hybrid-electric tugboat.[206] In 2012, the Port of Los Angeles announced financial incentives of as much as $1,250 per port call for carriers that used cleaner, more efficient ships.[207] In the same year, the Port of Long Beach tested electric vehicles on port grounds. In cooperation with Siemens, the port is testing an "e-highway" to electrically power trucks via overhead wires on the "heavily used and relatively short truck routes" that connect to rail yards less than 20 miles away.[208]

The ports' leaders are under no illusion that they have a conflict-free partnership with the NRDC and others. "They have a job to do, and it's to always keep pushing us," Cannon said, "and they've done a good job of pushing us. Every time we met one goal or requirement, then they wanted us to raise the bar, and we have progressively responded to that. Now, that may not always be the case, but they've been pushing us further and further in the direction of our stated goal, which is to become a zero-emission port. It won't be easy, but we welcome the challenge."[209]

Green Ports, World Tour: Taking It to the Next Step

Around the same time that the LA/LB ports were going through their efforts to reduce their environmental impacts, other ports around the world were attempting the same. The International Association of Ports and Harbors (IAPH), in consultation with regional port organizations, created a mechanism to support ports' environmental initiatives at its 2008 annual meeting in Los Angeles.[210] Following the meeting, 55 member ports signed on to the C40 World Ports Climate Declaration, in which they committed to jointly reduce their carbon footprint. The ports of Los Angeles and Long Beach were some of the first signatories.

Under the World Ports Climate Initiative (WPCI), member ports piloted various environmental initiatives including onshore power supply working groups, lease agreement templates with sustainability requirements, and a carbon footprinting working group.[211] Geraldine Knatz, former executive director of the Port of Los Angeles, served as the first chair of the WPCI during her presidency of the IAPH. The Port of Los Angeles, for example, presented its methodology for accounting for its GHGs inventory during the 2008 WPCI Los Angeles symposium and is an active member of the carbon footprinting working group.[212]

The WPCI also manages the Environmental Ship Index (ESI), which it rolled out in 2008 to catalog ships that "perform better in reducing air emissions than required by the current emission standards of the International Maritime Organization."[213] As a member of the WPCI, the Port of Los Angeles adopted the ESI and even took it a step further by introducing its own unique incentive program in 2012. "ESI is a voluntary program open to any oceangoing vessel that calls at the Port of Los Angeles," said Carter Atkins, an environmental specialist heading the ESI program. "It rewards operators for reducing emissions in port areas ahead of and beyond regulations through operational practices, investing in green technology, and deploying their cleanest ships to Los Angeles."[214]

7

All's Well That Ends Well

Many companies focus their sustainability efforts on reducing the impacts of sourcing, making, and delivering their products. This approach targets the so-called cradle-to-gate stages of the supply chain in that the company is focused on the origins and handling of the product up to the company's "gate," which is the point at which the customer takes possession of the product. But, as mentioned in previous chapters, some of the largest environmental impacts take place at the end of a product's life.

In 2008, the CBS investigative journalist Scott Pelley, visiting the city of Guiyu in southeastern China, uncovered a veritable post-apocalyptic wasteland within a sprawling area where 5,500 family workshops were handling discarded electronics.[1] Pelley was horrified. Acrid smoke tainted with lead and dioxin drifted into the air. Open vats of acid and chemicals, some stirred by hand, stripped metals off plastic parts. Smoky open fires melted solder off old circuit boards. Incinerators burnt off the plastic attached to the metal skeletons of PCs and other pieces of consumer electronics. Nearby drainage trenches carried heavy metals into local streams and rivers.[2] Air quality studies of Guiyu found elevated levels of lead and other atmospheric contaminants, which, based on well-documented research,[3] increase residents' risks of developing neurological, respiratory, and bone diseases.[4]

Guiyu is one of the largest electronic waste (e-waste) recycling facilities in the world. Yet China is not the only country where these hazardous electronic waste processing centers operate. Such unchecked recycling activities take place in many developing countries including India, Nigeria, Ghana, Ivory Coast, Benin, and Liberia.[5]

Revelations of the dangerous recycling practices found at many sites in the developing world tainted the green image of recycling. Moreover, images of gutted product carcasses at these e-waste recycling hellholes often showed the nameplates of popular electronics brands such as HP, IBM, Epson, Dell,[6] Apple, Sun, NEC, LG, and Motorola.[7] The environmental damage from unchecked waste processing has attracted increasing scrutiny from governments and environmental activists, resulting in increased business attention to managing what happens to products after consumers are done with them.

Managing end-of-life products, scrap, and waste does not always increase costs; in some cases, it can provide business opportunities through lower-cost materials, supply security, avoided costs of disposal, and avoided liabilities. Recycled aluminum, for example, offers a way to make more aluminum cans without investing in more aluminum mines and smelters. Furthermore, much of the cost of virgin aluminum is in the energy used to smelt ore into metal. A beer can made from recycled material requires 95 percent less energy to produce than one made from virgin material, according to the Aluminum Association.[8]

THE AFTERLIFE OF PRODUCTS

The opening of a new Primark clothing store provokes a feeding frenzy of shopping for fashionable frippery.[9] Primark specializes in selling trendy clothes at such low prices that anyone can be a fashionista.[10] The result is hyperfast fashion retailing with environmental impacts on both the upstream and downstream ends of the supply chain.

The frenzy of consumption at Primark's stores is backed by a frenzy of production at Primark's suppliers. On the upstream side, Primark's low costs mean that its suppliers—mostly in the developing world—pay workers a pittance to toil under deplorable conditions by Western standards (see the story of the Rana Plaza building collapse in chapter 2; Primark items were found in the rubble). On the downstream side, the fast-fashion retail model practiced by Primark and others also encourages consumers to buy large quantities of apparel and discard the cheap merchandise after only a few uses. However, bargain fashion is not the only source of discarded apparel. Some high-end brand owners prefer to destroy surplus inventory rather than cheapening their brand by marking it down, selling it through discount outlet channels, or donating it. These behaviors send 21 billion pounds of textiles to landfills each year.[11]

As the global population grows in number and in affluence, solid waste grows faster than any other environmental pollutant, *including* greenhouse gases.[12] The rate of waste generation has grown tenfold in the last century. The typical US resident uses and discards twice as many goods as they did 50 years ago[13] while US per capita GHG emissions have actually fallen slightly over the past 50 years.[14] Although the average person treats waste as "out of sight, out of mind," the problem is becoming increasingly visible. For example, in 2013 a barge loaded with six million pounds of garbage from an overfilled landfill in Islip, New York, floated aimlessly around the Atlantic Ocean for five months. After being rejected by six states and three foreign countries, it ended up in the headlines and right back where it had started.[15] And the Great Pacific Garbage Patch, a "floating junk yard on the high seas" stretches for hundreds of miles in the North Pacific Ocean. It is made up of non-biodegradable materials including plastic bags, bottles, and other products such as tires and computer parts.[16] It may be out of sight of land except for the dead seabirds and whales that wash up on beaches after ingesting fatal quantities of the flotsam and jetsam of modernity.

Although some companies are using more recycled material, most supply chains remain "linear," and most products end up in landfills or incinerators. In 2013, Americans generated approximately 254 million tons of municipal solid waste, about 4.4 pounds of trash per person per day.[17] Although recycling rates have grown from 8 percent in 1970 to almost 35 percent in 2013, the United States still trailed behind Germany (65 percent) and South Korea (59 percent).[18] Significant government efforts and programs are attempting to change consumer behavior and encourage recycling. For example, the EU is seeking a 50 percent recycling rate by 2020, primarily driven by increasing the recycling rates in countries like Spain (30 percent), Poland (29 percent), and Slovakia (11 percent), which had been lagging behind.

You Made It, You Dispose of It!

While working on his Master of Science degree in engineering physics at Lund University in 1990, Thomas Lindhqvist put forth a radical idea in a report to the Swedish Ministry of Environment.[19] He recommended that the organizations that profited from the production and sale of a product should also be held responsible for the costs of its disposal. Rather than foist the impacts of disposing end-of-life products onto municipalities, or engage in uncontrolled dumping, manufacturers would be expected to directly or indirectly handle these disposal tasks or costs.[20] This concept of extended producer responsibility (EPR) expands manufacturers' environmental responsibilities from "cradle-to-gate" to "cradle-to-grave."

Electronic waste in the EU is expected to grow from 9 million tons per year in 2005 to 12 million tons per year by 2020.[21] Worldwide, the total in 2012 was 50 million tons.[22] Owing to its residual value and its toxic risk if landfilled, e-waste is often exported from EU countries to developing nations where scenes like the uncontrolled processing in the city of Guiyu mar the landscape.[23]

To restrict hazardous handling of e-waste, the EU introduced the Waste Electrical and Electronic Equipment (WEEE) Directive in 2006, a performance-based (as defined in chapter 10) EPR regulation. The EU edict "puts the onus on distributors to accept WEEE from consumers on a one-to-one basis when selling new products, although Member States can deviate from this requirement if they can show that an alternative procedure is just as convenient for consumers."[24]

Other jurisdictions have implemented similar rules. In 2013, EPR regulations were in force in California for carpet, paint, and mercury thermometers. Canada, Japan, and several other countries require EPR for packaging, batteries, and hazardous substances.[25] In 2010, Brazil introduced its own National Solid Waste Policy (NSWP) based on EPR principles and WEEE regulations.[26] The

Brazilian policy applies to pesticides, batteries, tires, light bulbs, hazardous waste and associated packaging, lubricating oils and their packaging, and electronics products and components.[27,28]

Assessing End-of-Life Impacts

Companies assessing the impacts of postconsumer products can begin by examining the possible fates of these goods. Products may end up buried in a landfill, littered on the ground, dumped at sea, incinerated, or recycled into other products. Of prime concern are the potentially toxic effects that disposal may have on people, wildlife, land, and water. The toxicity assessment includes not only the manufacturer-specified bill of materials (BOM) ingredients of a given item but also the likely by-products emitted during waste handling. For example, the decay of foods and wood fibers (e.g., packaging) in a landfill can generate methane, a potent GHG. Metals, dyes, and chemicals in a product can break down and leach into groundwater. Incineration of some products, such as those made with PVC (polyvinylchloride), can release irritating particulates, as well as highly toxic dioxins. Of greatest concern are heavy metals such as mercury, lead, and cadmium, which can cause permanent neurological damage, especially in children. Other concerns include carcinogens such as arsenic, beryllium, cobalt, hexavalent chromium, nickel, and a host of dangerous petrochemical compounds.

The Three R's: Reduce, Reuse, Recycle

A now-ubiquitous icon on many cans, bottles, and packages hints at the main categories of corporate strategies for reducing the volume of waste arising from end-of-life products.

The recycling symbol—a Möbius strip triangle of arrows—encourages consumers to follow the "3R's": *reduce*, *reuse*, and *recycle*. The US EPA's "Solid Waste Management Hierarchy"[29] ranks the three R's by their environmental benefits. At the top of the hierarchy is *reduction*: minimizing initial resource consumption which curtails end-of-life waste production. Reduction activities take place in the other phases of a product's life, rather than at the end-of-life. *Reuse* seeks ways to prolong the life of the company's products, often involving secondary markets, sharing, and reverse supply chains by which companies refurbish and resell pre-owned products. It also includes the reuse of product components. Finally, *recycling* also requires a reverse supply chain, which moves used products to facilities where they can be deconstructed and their components reprocessed into their constituent raw materials that are then remanufactured into other products. Products made from recycled components are often marketed to "green customers." If none of the three R's are possible, end-of-life products are either burned to recover energy or disposed as waste in a landfill, which may incur costs of additional treatment.

PLAY IT AGAIN, SAM

Cars may be the most reused consumer product on the market and illustrate how the lives of products can be extended through resale. In the United States, used car sales outpace new car sales, with the average car having about three owners during its lifetime.[30] An entire industry of parts suppliers, parts retailers, service providers, dealers, and used cars appraisers serves this large market. Automakers even aid in resale through manufacturer-certified pre-owned vehicle sales as well as by managing supply chains of certified parts. Other durable goods that are readily sold and reused include trucks, aircraft, electronics, appliances, and tools.

Reuse: Natural Secondary Markets

Consumers often sell, give away, or donate a wide range of used household goods rather than discard them, according to an RMIT University survey of 306 Melbourne households.[31] Secondhand resale channels included traditional used items in secondhand retail shops, online exchange/reselling websites like eBay, newspaper ads, and special publications. The researchers also found that significant numbers of goods had been donated to charities or gifted to family or friends. And Australians are not alone in their impulse to get the most value out of their used household items.

Craigslist, with its local exchanges and no fees, grew from humble beginnings to become a major force in the market for consumer-to-consumer exchange and sale of secondhand goods. The company, founded in 1995 by Craig Newmark, started as a free email newsletter that listed events around San Francisco.[32] It evolved into a website on which anyone could post free[33] classified advertisements across a wide variety of categories seeking or offering everything from jobs to electronics to personal companionship. In the two decades following its creation, Craigslist has expanded to cover most major cities. In 2013, the site saw more than 1.5 million new posts globally each day,[34] with about two-thirds of the ads being items "for sale."[35] These posts generally connect buyers with sellers in the same region, city, or neighborhood, leading to face-to-face exchanges, and giving every person access to a large pool of buyers and a way to advertise and sell used items without transaction fees.[36]

Finding Gold in the Garbage

Companies can capitalize on rapidly changing technology products by supporting reuse of older technologies. For example, smartphones evolve rapidly, and some consumers only want the latest and greatest models. In fact, more than 100 million cell phones are discarded each year in the United States alone.[37] However, although last year's model might be passé to early adopters, many consumers don't mind an older model if the price is right. In 2011,[38] ecoATM, LLC in San Diego began installing kiosks at malls and other retail locations where consumers could sell back their used phones, tablets, or MP3 players and instantly receive cash. The transaction takes just minutes, and by September 2014, the company had installed 1,100 of the kiosks across the United States.[39]

The kiosks use machine vision and machine learning algorithms to determine the device's model and condition and then instantly match the phone with an industry buyer who has already agreed to a price. "Imagine a spreadsheet that's 8 columns wide and 4,000 rows deep," said Mark Bowles, ecoATM's founder. "And then you go through that 4,000 by 8 pricing matrix and you bid in advance on any one of those cells that you want. ... If you end up with the highest price in that pre-auction, then you win that cell."[40]

Yet ecoATM does not sell to just anyone. Bowles explained that ecoATM screens buyers for proper electronics disposal practices, as well as being "good business partners." The company holds on to the devices for 30 days to give law enforcement agencies time to recover them in case the device has been stolen.[41] Once that interval has passed, the buyer wires the agreed-upon payment and ecoATM sends the phones. The customer selling the phone, meanwhile, walked away 30 days earlier with cash in hand.

EcoATM is not the only player in this market. ReCellular began recycling cellphones from collection drives and later expanded into buying back individual phones by mail. In 2012, the company resold or recycled 5.2 million phones, up from the 2.1 million it handled in 2007.[42] In 2013, about 60 percent of ReCellular's stock was sold within the United States.[43] Furthermore, large retailers, notably Best Buy and Amazon, began selling refurbished phones, joining the recycling business opportunity.[44] Mainstream companies in the smartphone industry also participate in recycling and reusing. For example, both Apple[45] and Verizon[46] operate buyback services for smartphones.

Electric Car Batteries Get Their Second Wind
It's not every day that someone gets a call saying, "Give me your oldest batteries." But that's what suppliers and customers heard from Pablo Valencia, General Motors' senior manager of battery lifecycle management, when he wanted to test a new extended reuse concept in conjunction with the Swiss power technology giant ABB and Duke Energy, the largest utility in the United States.[47] Valencia realized that old products do not have to be used in the same way that they originally had been. Electric and hybrid vehicles require high performance from their batteries, both in terms of high power for vehicle acceleration and high total energy for vehicle range. "In a car, you want immediate power, and you want a lot of it," said Alexandra Goodson, business development manager for energy storage modules at ABB.[48] Unfortunately, as the battery ages, its performance on both dimensions declines, almost as if both the

car's engine and fuel tank were shrinking. But even if the battery can no longer deliver satisfactory power and range in a vehicle, it can still store and deliver significant amounts of electricity for other applications. GM's boxy demonstration unit showed that a cluster of five old Chevy Volt batteries could store and provide enough wall-outlet electricity to power three to five average American homes for up to two hours.[49]

This concept may be (a small) part of the solution to a looming problem in national electrical grids: the mismatch between electrical demand and the respective supply. The rising adoption of renewable power such as wind or solar adds unpredictable supply, and the recharging of electric vehicles adds new spikes to the demand. "Wind, it's a nightmare for grid operators to manage," said Britta Gross, director of global energy systems and infrastructure commercialization for GM. "It's up, down, it doesn't blow for three days." Moreover, if electric vehicles become popular, then tens of millions of commuters will be plugging in their vehicles at the end of the day, just as solar power output ebbs into night. "Our grid, and most electricity grids, are not really designed to handle that kind of rapid swinging. Storage can help dampen that out," said Dan Sowder, senior project manager for new technology at Duke Energy.[50]

GM is not the only automaker looking into secondary markets for used electric car batteries. Nissan North America, ABB, 4R Energy, and Sumitomo Corporation of America are building grid storage systems using old Nissan Leaf batteries. In addition, start-ups such as Green Charge Networks are selling prepackaged units of car batteries that enable commercial users, such as retailers 7-Eleven and Walgreens, to buy grid power when rates are low—to charge the battery packs—and then run their facilities off batteries when rates are high.[51]

From Cost of Disposal to Reusable Assets

Every day, Subaru's Indiana factory[52] receives truckloads of wheels secured by small temporary brass lug nuts. In the past, Subaru discarded these nuts—some 33,000 pounds a year. However, as part of its waste reduction program, Subaru started collecting and returning the lug nuts, working directly with its wheel supplier to reuse them until they are no longer serviceable, at which point they are recycled for brass material.[53]

Even the incidental materials used for packaging can offer an opportunity for reuse. Subaru returns Styrofoam forms used to cushion delicate components on their trip from Japan to Indiana so that they can be reused in future shipments. After five reuse cycles, the Styrofoam ends up in Japan, where 85 percent of it is recycled.[54] By converting consumables into assets, the cycle times become part of the sustainability metric: the faster the return of these assets (be it packaging, lug nuts, Styrofoam, or whatever) the higher their utilization and the fewer the number of consumables in the system.

Subaru's work to convert disposable items into reusable assets was part of a broad program to reduce solid waste. "People still think that it costs too much money to be environmentally friendly," said Denise Coogan, manager of safety and environmental compliance at Subaru of Indiana. "That's an antiquated idea. Waste is money: wasted time, wasted material. The first years cost us financially, but after you get over that hump, you see the [monetary gains] take off exponentially."[55]

The benefits of reusable containers may go even further. Office Depot Inc., for example, delivers some products in reusable plastic totes instead of cardboard boxes.[56] Estimates suggest that the useful lifetime of reusable plastic containers ranges from 5 to 20 years, with 4 to 25 uses per year.[57]

RECYCLING: THE REVERSE SUPPLY CHAIN

When a company's product can no longer be reused by another customer, the next step in the end-of-life handling hierarchy is recycling the item's constituent materials. Recycling involves "separating, collecting, processing, marketing, and ultimately using a material that otherwise would have been thrown away," according to the US EPA.[58] Unlike the supply chain for reuse, which may be relatively simple in routing reusable goods from one customer to another, the supply chain for recycling may be much deeper and loop back to the deeper supply chain tiers that handle raw materials.

Another large reverse flow stream is consumer returns of new products, which have always presented a challenge to retailers and manufacturers. "With returns, you are working against the clock. The longer the product sits in storage and more touch points it receives, the less value you may recover," said Ryan Kelly, senior vice president of sales, strategy and communications at GENCO, a FedEx company.[59] Companies must assess the returned item for damage and refurbish it for resale as needed, sometimes shipping it back to the manufacturer for proper handling. Dealing with returns has worsened with the growth of omni-channel retailing, in which consumers expect to be able to return online purchases to a retailer's local store. Not only is the return rate of online purchases higher than the rate for in-store purchases (18–25 percent versus 8–12 percent), but the local store may not even carry the returned item.

Where Downstream Becomes Upstream

Whereas retailers are the (downstream) end of the commercial supply chain of many products, they can also be the (upstream) beginning of the recycling supply chain for end-of-life products. For example, Staples sells new toner and ink cartridges and also provides convenient recycling drop-off bins for used toner and ink cartridges in its stores. To encourage recycling, the retailer offers a $2 reward per cartridge (with some restrictions) that can be used to buy more printer cartridges.[60] The result is a 73 percent recycling rate. Like Staples, other retailers promote recycling to encourage consumers to visit their stores. For example, some Best Buy programs provide gift cards in return for recycled products,[61] while customers who recycle ink and toner cartridges at Office Depot get rewards points that can be redeemed for merchandise discounts.[62]

Staples accumulates and consolidates the used cartridges and transports them (and other recyclables) back to its distribution center, using the backhaul capacity of its trucks. Some cartridges go back to the original manufacturer and others go to an e-Stewards certified recycling partner of Staples.[63] (e-Stewards is a global collective of individuals, institutions, businesses, NGOs, and governmental agencies "upholding a safe, ethical, and globally responsible standard for e-waste recycling and refurbishment."[64]) As of 2014, Staples was recycling 63 million cartridges per year.[65]

Retailers are not the only locations where downstream becomes upstream. In some cases, OEMs have their own direct collection programs using mail, prepaid parcel delivery services, or other customer service programs. For example, HP printer cartridges come with a special small, sturdy envelope with instructions to put the used cartridge in it and mail it (free of charge) to an HP processing center. IBM operates what it calls Global Asset Recovery Services (GARS), which offers collection of old IBM equipment from corporate customers and combines reuse, recycling, and safe disposal of discarded equipment.[66]

In some communities and for some materials, the collection stage of the recycling supply chain is integrated into the local solid waste collection process. These household and local business recycling programs are a key part of the supply chain for recycled glass, metal cans, plastic containers, paper, and cardboard.

The first positive outcome of recycling end-of-life products is a reduction in the volume of the waste stream. The natural rate of recycling of a company's products is a function of the ease of collecting them, the costs of recovering recyclable ingredients, and the value of the recovered materials. Actual recycling rates vary by material (98 percent of lead-acid batteries are recycled compared to 55 percent of aluminum cans[67]), as well as by country (recycling rates for plastic waste are 77 percent in Japan versus only 20 percent in the United States[68]). That which cannot be recycled ends up incinerated or buried in a landfill or washed out to sea.

New Supply Chain Partners for Collecting Recyclables

Lacking its own network of retail outlets, Dell created a channel for collecting e-waste by collaborating with Goodwill Industries, a 2,000-outlet charity that collects and resells lightly used merchandise.[69] Under the Dell–Goodwill partnership, consumers can drop off computers and other technology products, even non-Dell ones, at Goodwill's donation sites around the United States. The donated electronics are handled in one of three ways. First, Goodwill refurbishes and resells any newer devices that still have some life in them. Second, the modular nature of computers means that parts such as memory, storage, and peripheral cards can be sold for use in other PCs. Third, any otherwise unusable items or parts are carefully recycled by Dell.[70]

Dell's partnership with Goodwill also serves both companies' social responsibility goals. The increased stream of donations supports Goodwill's mission of helping people with disabilities by providing training in refurbishing PCs and working with technology. In addition, this program allows Goodwill customers to purchase relatively modern, functional technology at a low price.[71]

Dell uses two other programs to collect e-waste from its customers, a common pattern by which a company uses multiple collection streams to maximize reuse and recycling. Specifically, the company collaborates with FedEx on a free mail-in program. Whereas the Goodwill partnership accepts any kind of computer from any consumer, the mail-in program is restricted to Dell customers who can send in an old Dell or trade-in a non-Dell computer when they buy a new Dell.[72] For its large enterprise customers, Dell operates an asset resale and recycling services unit that manages the collection, resale, reuse, and recycling of an organization's computers. As of 2015, Dell had already recycled 1.42 billion pounds of electronic waste towards its stated 2020 goal of 2 billion pounds.[73]

The Asia–America–Asia Loop

Observers might wonder why some sections of the Port of Los Angeles look like a junkyard, complete with haphazard piles of rusting iron. As it turns out, this gritty corner of the port is a key link in a global reverse supply chain that moves recyclable materials and end-of-life products from areas of high consumption (e.g., the US) to areas of high production and demand for raw materials (e.g., China). Four of the top 10 exports from Los Angeles to China are recyclable materials: copper, paper or paperboard, aluminum, and iron or steel. Scrap materials are also a top-10 export from the Los Angeles customs district to South Korea, Taiwan, Germany, Malaysia, and Vietnam.[74] These materials flow overseas to reprocessors, parts makers, and product manufacturers. These reverse supply chains use the ports' low "backhaul rates," filling otherwise empty containers on their return trips.

REPROCESSING: A NEW LIFE FOR OLD INGREDIENTS

After collection, the next step in companies' recycling supply chains is the reprocessing of the waste and end-of-life materials into beginning-of-life ingredients for new products. In essence, reprocessing is the switchback turn where the reverse supply chain of recycling turns 180 degrees to connect with the forward supply chains of manufacturing, distribution, and retail. Many types of scrap metals and plastics can be readily remelted and directly reused as a raw material; other materials require more complex reprocessing steps. For example, e-waste contains many different materials that are "mixed, bolted, screwed, snapped, glued or soldered together; toxic materials are attached to nontoxic materials, which make separation of materials for reclamation difficult."[75] Trying to separate materials from e-waste without adequate technology can release heavy metals such as lead, cadmium, or mercury into the air, which is what takes place at Guiyu and the other unchecked sites in developing countries.[76]

For at least one category of material—plastics—a tiny change to product design has made reprocessing much easier. On most pieces of plastic, manufacturers have added an embossed or printed "3R" recycling triangle that also contains a code number.[77] Code numbers 1 through 6 identify the object as being made of one of six very common resins that can generally be recycled (although not all community recycling programs accept all types). In the recycling world, "7" is an unlucky number; the catch-all code for "other recyclable plastics." The code numbers help the sorting of plastics by type and help ensure the purity of the recycled plastics.

How Old Technology Becomes New Technology

Dell's partnership with Goodwill provides the computer maker with a supply of recyclable plastic. Dell separates, sorts, and inspects the plastic coming from electronics collected at Goodwill locations and then ships bales of certain types of recyclable plastic to its supplier, Wistron Corporation. Wistron shreds the return stream and blends it with virgin plastic to achieve the required structural integrity (in 2015, the mix had 35 percent recycled content). Then it molds the plastic into new parts for Dell.[78] By the end of 2015, Dell reported that 16 models of displays and three models of desktops were made with closed-loop recycled plastics.[79] "This initiative is designed to reduce the dependence on natural resources, as well as extending the value of end-of-life electronics," said Simon Lin, chairman and CEO of Wistron.[80]

HP recycles printer cartridges collected at drop-off points at retailers such as Staples, Office Depot, Office Max, and Walmart stores, as well as by mail directly from consumers, as mentioned earlier.[81] HP sends the returned printer cartridges to a recovery plant to be disassembled. Then, the plastic portions are shredded and sent to a facility in Québec, Canada, where they are mixed with flakes of discarded beverage bottles to create raw material for the next batch of cartridges.[82] The recycled resin is then sent to HP's cartridge manufacturing plants in Asia and Europe. As of April 2013, 280 million cartridges had been recycled, reducing a major waste stream and reducing the need for virgin material for new cartridges.[83]

In 2010, HP commissioned an independent life cycle assessment of its cartridge-recycling program.[84] The analysis compared the impact of the collection, transportation, and processing of used cartridges and other recycled plastic to the extraction and processing of oil and the production of virgin plastic. The study found that recycling had lower impacts on all 12 dimensions covered in the study, ranging from reducing toxicity 12 percent, to cutting carbon footprints and water use by 33 and 89 percent, respectively.

Through programs like these, Dell and HP are beginning to create closed-loop supply chains, reducing both waste and demand for new materials. Dell's closed-loop cycle generated 11 percent lower carbon emissions compared with the use of virgin plastics.[85] Ideally, end-of-life products could circulate endlessly back to beginning-of-life products—creating what the British environmental economists Pearce and Turner dubbed *the circular economy*.[86]

HP, for example, estimates that some of its cartridges have been recycled as many as 10 times.

Tons of Old Clothing Can Go to Tons of New Places

Although the secondary market for cell phones is a recent invention, some recycling markets, such as for apparel, have existed for generations and illustrate the more complex supply chains of a mature reuse and recycling system. Thrift shops, such as Goodwill and Salvation Army in the United States, and Oxfam and Scope in the United Kingdom, have long accepted donations of clothes to be resold in their shops. As the price of new clothing fell and fashion fads accelerated, Western consumers bought more new apparel and donated more old apparel to thrift stores, yet these shops can only sell a small fraction of the donated clothes locally. As Elizabeth Kline explains in her 2012 book *Over-Dressed: The Shockingly High Cost of Cheap Fashion*, the Quincy Street Salvation Army in New York City alone discharges six tons of unsellable clothes every day, and that quantity increases during the holiday season.[87]

Everything from hoodies to haute couture shows up in these donation boxes. To extract value from the stream of used clothes, thrift shop operators segregate the clothing by saleability. The nicest clothes go to boutiques that specialize in vintage styles. Mid-range items go to the organization's thrift shop. But the majority of the clothing, approximately 80 percent,[88] is sold by the ton to global brokers and processors, not to local individuals.

Processors, like Mac Recycling in Baltimore, buy from thrift stores and ship 80 tons of clothes each week to Europe, Africa, Asia, South America, and Central America.[89] Once there, still-usable clothes are sold again—sometimes with minor modifications. In India, for example, clothes sellers repurpose "many US women's nylon trousers into male laborers' trousers by cutting off the elasticated waistband, adding drawstrings and 'Adidas style' white stripes down the sides."[90]

Lower-quality pieces are "downcycled" into wiping cloths for industrial uses or shredded into fibers for carpets, insulation for cars or homes, or pillow stuffing. Buyers pay as little as $78 per ton—mere pennies per garment—for these discarded clothes.[91] Finally, about 1 to 3 percent becomes fuel to produce electricity.[92] At each stage, segregating the recycled material maximizes its value. At the same time, it displaces demand for higher-cost, higher-impact virgin products or raw materials for each segment of recycled material.

Upcycling: Handling a Pain in the Ash

Rising from the inferno inside a coal-fired power plant, choking hot gases loft clouds of pulverized dust—so-called fly ash—into the air. Until regulations prohibited it, fly ash flew up the smokestack, filled the air with particulates, and played a major role in the debilitating and lethal respiratory illnesses associated with coal-fired heavy industry. The advent of electrostatic precipitators enabled the capture of airborne particles but created another problem: what to do with the accumulating tons of fine gray powder. American coal-fired plants produce approximately 75 million tons of such fly ash every year.[93]

As far as the coal-fired power plant is concerned, fly ash is a hazardous waste that has negative value. It is a costly nuisance to store, transport, and bury in a landfill. Fly ash contains significant levels of various heavy metals that can contaminate ground and surface water. In 2010, 31 coal ash disposal sites were linked to contaminated groundwater, wetlands, creeks, and rivers in 14 American states.[94] When a fly ash containment pond was breached at a Tennessee Valley Authority electric generating plant in Kingston, Tennessee, in December 2008, the cleanup cost more than $1 billion.[95]

Even so, fly ash processing can be an example of converting an environmental liability into something of value. The high-temperature chemical reactions that occur inside a coal furnace are not unlike the high-temperature chemical reactions that take place inside a cement kiln. Depending on the type and the processing of the coal, fly ash can be used as a cementitious material in its own right or as a filler in concrete. As of 2010, about half of America's fly ash was used for cement and other similar applications.[96] CeraTech Inc., for example, is using fly ash reclaimed from coal-burning power plants as the primary input (up to 95 percent) of its cement.[97]

Fly ash is an environmental win for the cement industry, too. Producing a ton of cement by the standard process generates about a ton of CO_2 emissions.[98] As a "free" waste product, fly ash requires only negligible additional energy, resulting in little incremental GHG emissions, to create cement.[99] Each year, this and other uses of fly ash save an estimated 11 million tons of CO_2, 32 billion gallons of water, and 51 million cubic yards of landfill space, according to congressional testimony by the Electric Power Research Institute.[100]

Downcycling: From Foot to Field

In many cases, recycling old products or parts into new ones of the same kind is not economical or even feasible. One alternative is downcycling—recycling end-of-life high-value goods into lower-valued goods. For example, at more than 450,000 locations around the world, new and old Nike shoes meet in an unusual way—wearers of new Nike shoes play and compete on sporting field surfaces made from old Nike shoes. In 1993, Nike debuted the Reuse-A-Shoe program to recover used athletic shoes as well as the scrap left over from the shoemaking process.[101] Nike sliced and shredded recovered shoes into a material it called Nike Grind and sold it for surfacing high-performance tennis and basketball courts, running tracks, and other athletic surfaces.[102] By 2013, the program had recovered 28 million pairs of shoes and 36,000 tons of scrap, using it to cover playing surfaces around the world.[103]

In 2010, clothing retailer The Gap Inc. partnered with Cotton Inc.—a research and marketing company representing upland cotton[104]—to launch the "Recycle Your Blues" campaign. The campaign encouraged consumers to drop off their old pairs of jeans at any of the Gap's 1,000 participating stores. Participating consumers would get 30 percent off a new pair of Gap Jeans; the old jeans were converted into UltraTouch™ natural cotton fiber housing insulation. Cotton Inc. donated the material to underserved communities and to special housing projects such as the post-Hurricane Katrina rebuilding effort. Between 2006 and 2010, Gap collected

360,000 units of denim and used them to create fiber insulation for more than 700 homes.[105]

BTUs Are Better Than Nothing—The Ultimate Downcycling

In Denmark, 98 municipalities get household heat and electricity by burning garbage in 29 facilities across the country. For example, residents of the town of Hørsholm, an affluent northern suburb of Copenhagen, get 20 percent of their electricity and 80 percent of their heat from a carefully designed and managed garbage incinerator. "Constituents like it because it decreases heating costs and raises home values," said Mayor Morten Slotved.[106] About one-third (34 percent) of Hørsholm's trash goes to waste-to-energy incineration.

For unrecyclable kinds of urban waste, a well-managed waste-to-energy plant beats a landfill as the most environmentally friendly destination, according to a 2009 study by the US EPA and North Carolina State University.[107] Such plants use a complex sequence of processes and filters to remove or neutralize smokestack pollutants such as hydrochloric acid, sulfur oxides, nitrogen oxides, and heavy metals.[108] "The hazardous elements are concentrated and carefully handled rather than dispersed as they would be in a landfill," said Ivar Green-Paulsen, general manager of Denmark's largest waste-to-energy plant.[109]

Waste with a high percentage of organic material, such as food and agricultural waste, paper, wood, and sewage, can be biologically digested into renewable natural gas (RNG), which, in turn, can be used in logistics, manufacturing, and power production. For example, in 2015 UPS began using RNG at fueling depots in Sacramento, Fresno, and Los Angeles. The delivery company uses the equivalent of about 1.5 million gallons of RNG annually to fuel nearly 400 UPS compressed natural gas (CNG) vehicles in California[110] and plans to use 500,000 gallons a year in Texas.[111] According to the Bioenergy Association of California, the state has enough biomass waste to create RNG to replace three-quarters of the state's diesel needs.[112]

The Good and the Perfect

The previous three subsections illustrated ways of reducing environmental impact through the use of materials that would otherwise go to waste, be difficult to dispose of, or lead to environmental mishaps. Fly ash can be used to make cement, old Nike shoes can be used in Nike Grind, and hard-to-process waste can be used as an energy source. Nevertheless, in each of these cases (and many others), downcycling sparks complaints by environmentalists. For example, the downcycling examples of sneakers and jeans are lamented because they do nothing to reduce the impact of extracting virgin material for the manufacturing of new sneakers or jeans.

Such complaints might seem like perfectionist grumbling and another example of "the perfect is the enemy of the good" (see chapter 1). Alternatively, such criticisms may reflect fears that an interim solution will delay a long-term solution. A ton or so of fly ash may eliminate the need to emit a ton of CO_2 in the making of concrete, but that ton of fly ash is associated with 20 to 30 tons of CO_2 created in the burning of coal.[113] "In one sense, yes, you're using up this waste material. In another way, it's justifying the burning of coal as a fuel source," said Daniel Handeen, a research fellow at the University of Minnesota, Center for Sustainable Building Research.[114]

Environmentalists also criticize the burning of waste to produce energy. "Incinerators are really the devil," said Laura Haight, a senior environmental associate with the New York Public Interest Research Group. "Once you build a waste-to-energy plant, you then have to feed it. Our priority is pushing for zero waste."[115]

"We incinerate an enormous amount of waste in Denmark; waste which the Government could get much more out of by more recycling and better recycling," said Ida Auken, Denmark's Minister for the Environment.[116]

The Market Upside of Recycling

Recycling also adds to the base of supply of raw materials, which reduces material costs, price volatility, and availability risks, according to an MIT study of platinum markets.[117] Recycled materials suppliers provide a diffuse secondary source that is decoupled from the geopolitics of primary sources, such as in the case of the Chinese embargo on the export of rare earth elements and other cases of resource nationalism.[118] Moreover, for many materials, recycling consumes less energy than does primary extraction and refinement. This can decouple the price of the material from the volatile price of energy. Finally, recycling shortens the duration of price spikes because in times of high demand and short primary supply, recyclers can more quickly increase recycling capacity than miners can increase primary supply.[119]

Some companies have made a business out of recycling high-value materials. In 2012, the Belgian chemical company Solvay Group opened two rare earth metals recycling plants in France, extracting the material from used light bulbs, batteries, and magnets.[120] In 2013, the French company Veolia Environnement S.A. opened a recycling facility in Massachusetts to recover rare earth elements from phosphor powder, extracting it from fluorescent lamps, batteries, computers, electronics, and mercury-bearing waste.[121]

Recycling's Volatile Volumes

The downside of recycling as a business is that its economic viability is very sensitive to the cost of the virgin material. When oil prices plummeted in the second half of 2014, virgin plastic, which manufacturers prefer for technical reasons, became cheaper than recycled plastic and demand for recycled plastic plummeted. "People are just not willing to pay a higher price for the eco-friendly stuff," said Anne Freer, director at plastic bottle maker Measom Freer. "We try to use as much recycled as possible, but it really comes down to price."[122] What had been a money-maker for municipalities and plastics recyclers became a money-loser, with plants and other assets underutilized.

"At US$50 oil, anyone that does just plastics recycling is out of business," said David Steiner, chief executive of Waste Management Inc.[123] "Many in the recycling industry are hanging by the skin of their teeth," added Chris Collier, commercial director, CK Group, a plastics recycler.[124] Two German recyclers and a large British one went bankrupt in 2015 and others, such as Waste Management, are cutting back on recycling investments. "The bottom line is that what is recycled and what is not is directly linked to oil," said Tom Szaky, cofounder and CEO of TerraCycle Inc., which works with companies on recyclable packaging.[125]

WHEN GOVERNMENTS MAKE WASTE PAY

In some cases, end-of-life materials retain so much value that they support the formation of natural markets for their collection, separation, and reprocessing. For example, copper is the world's most reusable resource, according to the Copper Development Association Inc.[126] Relative to pure virgin copper smelted from mined ore, recycled copper retains 95 percent of its value because previous use and processing introduces only minor contamination.[127] Nearly three-quarters of copper used in new products comes from recycled material. In fact, old copper is so valuable and easily recycled that thieves steal copper pipe and wire from vacant houses, as well as transmission wire from power stations. The US Department of Energy estimates that copper theft causes nearly $1 billion in losses to US businesses every year.[128]

Nonetheless, not all end-of-life products and postconsumer materials have sufficient value to justify collection and recycling based on financial criteria alone. Some materials have high collection costs, high separation costs, or a low value of the recycled material, which implies that natural recycling markets fail to form and end-of-life waste accumulates. If that waste poses an environmental threat, then governments may regulate the disposal of the product.

A Fragile Aftermarket Shattered

Whereas price cycles may create temporary downturns for companies involved in recycling, changes in product technology can create permanent disruptions. For some five decades, almost all televisions and computer monitors used cathode ray tubes (CRT) to display images. Given the technology at the time, the same lead-containing glass that shielded viewers from dangerous X-ray radiation made the glass tubes an environmental hazard. CRTs could contain up to eight pounds of lead in the tube.[129] Due to lead's toxicity,[130] the

US EPA classified discarded CRTs as hazardous waste in the 1976 Resource Conservation and Recovery Act[131]—subjecting it to more stringent guidelines compared to other electronic waste. Initially, the Act was not a major burden because even as late as 2004, CRT processors could sell recycled CRT glass for as much as $200 per ton to firms producing new CRT televisions and monitors.

In the first decade of the 21st century, however, thin flat-panel displays rapidly replaced bulky CRTs in both the television and computer markets.[132] That fast turnover in technology created a toxic waste challenge. As flat-screen displays began to dominate the market for televisions and monitors,[133] CRT recycling grew more difficult, because the new displays did not use the leaded glass of CRTs. During the changeover, the EPA estimated that Americans discarded about 1.1 million tons of CRT televisions and monitors, of which fewer than 200,000 tons were recycled.[134] By 2013, the same companies that had earned $200 per ton had to *pay* more than $200 per ton to dispose of the same material.[135]

In the absence of a market for recycled leaded glass, CRT-collecting companies resorted to stockpiling them. In 2012, a routine inquiry by two inspectors from California's Department of Toxic Substance Control discovered a warehouse the size of a football field filled nine feet high with unprocessed CRTs.[136] In 2013, inspectors in Colorado and Arizona found similar scenes at abandoned warehouses that together contained more than 10,000 tons of CRTs and CRT glass.[137] In September 2013, a report titled *US CRT Glass Management* estimated that roughly 330,000 tons of CRT glass remained in storage in American facilities.[138]

In response to this market failure, state regulators in the US took a page from the EU's regulatory doctrine of extended producer responsibility (EPR; see the section "You Made It, You Dispose of It!" earlier in this chapter). They made manufacturers of new displays shoulder the financial burden of recycling old displays.[139] In Maine, for example, companies that handled discarded CRTs are asked to extract payments from the CRT's producer. According to the state's Title 38 law, "at a minimum, a consolidator shall invoice the manufacturers for the handling, transportation and recycling costs."[140] By 2013, in the absence of an overarching federal law,

22 US states had required technology manufacturers to pay for the cost of disposing their products—even when those products were sold long ago or by defunct competitors.[141] The spirit of these US state laws was similar to the 1980 Comprehensive Environmental Response, Compensation, and Liability Act (see chapter 1). This law allowed the EPA to identify the corporate descendants of historical parties responsible for particularly polluted patches of industrial land and force them to pay cleanup costs.[142] Such "after the fact" government actions are a version of EPR that is not grounded in law but rather in expediency. The potential for open-ended liability for environmental impacts discovered long after a product has reached end-of-life may induce companies toward more conservative eco-risk management initiatives such as the *precautionary principle*[143] that new materials and technologies are presumed guilty of harm until proven innocent.

Fix It or Tax It

Sometimes, small things can create big problems, as is the case with the smallest of energy products: batteries. At the end of their life, batteries become an unfortunate combination of useless, worthless, and toxic. Batteries' complex chemical ingredients can be difficult and costly to separate, and dumping them in landfills without any treatment can release toxic chemicals into the environment.[144] Recycling batteries costs at least 10 times more than burying them in a landfill.[145] Owing to the toxic nature of battery waste, many governments have regulated their disposal at the consumer level to force recycling. Despite the fact that California, for example, prohibits discarding batteries in household trash, Californians recycle less than 5 percent of the batteries they buy.[146]

The government of Belgium used the threat of a high eco-tax on new batteries to convince battery makers to collect and dispose of old ones.[147] An 800-member nonprofit consortium of battery producers called Bebat[148] handles battery collection and recycling. The program adds about 15 to 25 cents to the cost of each battery,[149] but that cost is only about one-quarter the cost of the threatened eco-tax that battery makers would pay if they do not achieve the government's ever-increasing recycling rate targets. To achieve the required rate, Bebat installed bright green collection boxes at 24,000 locations in markets, photo shops, jewelers, schools, municipal locations, and elsewhere to offer convenient battery drop-off points for consumers.[150,151] The consortium also paid for public information campaigns to ensure that the vast majority of consumers know about the recycling program.[152] As of 2015, Belgians recycled an estimated 56 percent of batteries.[153]

A Good Deposit Avoids a Bad Disposal

Prior to World War II, most beverage containers were made of glass and were too valuable to discard. Instead, they were part of a closed-loop supply chain that returned empty bottles to the local brewery, local bottler, or milkman for cleaning and refilling. After the war, beverage companies, especially in the developed world, started transitioning to single-use bottles and cans. One beverage company even advertised, "Drink right from the can: No empties to return."[154]

The Coca-Cola Company, after performing one of the first environmental LCAs in 1969, became more "comfortable" with the switch from glass bottles to plastic containers (see chapter 8).[155] Low-cost mass production of the new containers eliminated the need for collecting, cleaning, and refilling of used containers. But the generated waste was a different story. The manufacturers' interest in the disposable container ended as soon the customer purchased the drink, and the customer's interest in the container ended as soon as it was empty. Most consumers simply tossed their empties by the side of the road.

The resulting accumulation of litter so offended Vermont residents that, in 1953, the state instituted a four-year ban on nonrefillable beverage containers.[156] After lobbying from the beer industry, the ban was allowed to expire, but legislators in Vermont and many other states still sought a solution. In 1972, Vermont was the first of 11 states[157]—followed closely by California, Michigan, and Oregon—to pass legislation that instituted deposits, thereby creating a financial incentive to collect and return the empties.[158]

The containers remained single-use, but sellers were forced to add a surcharge of a few cents more for each bottle or a can. The state collected the money and then paid it to any individual return-ing the container, thus creating a market for empty bottles and cans. Anyone could claim the deposit at collection and redemp-tion centers, after which the containers were put into the recycling stream. In some cases, the poor and homeless collected the dis-carded containers to profit from the deposit. In other cases, whole-salers arose to collect the deposit and provide value added services to recycling plants.

On the whole, deposit mandates worked. Following the enact-ment of the mandates, 82 percent of covered beverage contain-ers sold in the state of California were recycled in 1992.[159] On average, the 10 states that require container deposits back to a store (California has thousands of special redemption locations) have glass container recycling rates of about 63 percent compared with a 24 percent recycling rate in non-deposit states, according to the Container Recycling Institute, which lobbies for such pro-grams. Moreover, because the containers are kept separate from the rest of the waste stream, the contamination level of recyclables in deposit-collecting states is less of a problem.[160]

CLOSING THE LOOP

Environmentalists dream of "closing the loop": recovering and recycling all the materials in the waste stream. Depicting the notion of the "circular economy," figure 7.1 illustrates a stylized supply chain and the various "backwards paths" that a product or its con-stituent elements can take back into the supply chain.[161]

In theory, the perfect closed loop (coupled with zero popula-tion growth, no increases in per capita consumption, and no prod-uct innovation) would mean that production and sales of new goods would require no additional mining or harvesting of the Earth's natural resources. Nor would the economy add waste or pollution to landfills, waterways, or the air. All waste and post-consumer materials would cycle endlessly back to suppliers, manu-facturers, and then on to the next generation of consumers. Under a closed-loop or circular economy, the concept of managing the "cradle-to-grave" supply chain would morph to "cradle-to-cradle."

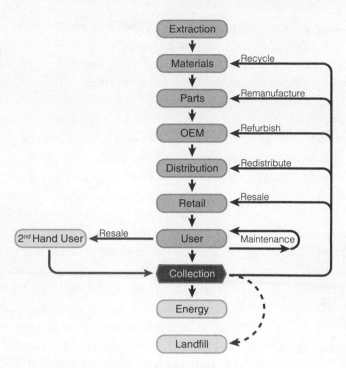

Figure 7.1
The circular economy

High Recovery-Rate Recycling

Johnson Controls International Plc, the world's largest supplier of automotive batteries, recycled its first battery in 1904—four years before Henry Ford introduced the Model T.[162] By 2015, the company recycled more than 97 percent of the lead-acid automotive batteries it sold in North America. From each returned end-of-life battery, the company can efficiently recover 99 percent of the materials and make new lead-acid batteries containing 80 percent recycled materials.[163]

Johnson Controls, having no direct relationship with end users of batteries, developed close business ties with retailers, auto shops, and junkyards to obtain a constant supply of waste batteries. The company built a reverse logistics operation optimized to collect old batteries every time it delivered new ones.[164] The company's reverse logistics and recycling systems are well established in North America, South America, and Europe (where it is known as ecosteps®), and the company is working to understand the economic and market conditions needed to implement or expand responsible recycling systems in other countries such as China.[165]

A key part of Johnson Controls' closed-loop strategy is the recycling of not just the lead but also the other materials of the battery,[166] thereby spreading the collection costs over more recycled elements. For example, Johnson Controls recycles the plastic housings of batteries to make new housings. It also recycles the acidic liquid electrolytes inside the battery and reuses them in new batteries or supplies them to makers of detergents and glass.

Sourcing 80 to 90 percent of its lead from recycled batteries protected the company from the volatility of lead prices on global markets. Between 2000 and 2010, lead prices oscillated between $500 per metric ton to as high as $4,000 per metric ton.[167] The price of recycling is less volatile, even though it is also rising due to increasingly stricter environmental standards on secondary lead smelters. In fact, in 2012, Johnson Controls announced an 8 percent increase in the price of lead-acid batteries in North America, citing the investment required to meet these new regulations.[168] At the same time, having a domestic supply of lead reduces the company's reliance on foreign lead producers such as China, Australia, and Peru,[169] thereby also insulating Johnson Controls from currency exchange rate volatility.

Municipal Waste Streams: The Final Frontier of Closing the Loop

Walmart aims to use three billion pounds of recycled plastic in the packaging and products it will sell by 2020 but is facing obstacles. "The problem is supply," explained Rob Kaplan, director of product sustainability at Walmart.[170] Similarly, Coca-Cola had a 2015 goal of using at least 25 percent recycled plastics in its containers, but scarce supply and high costs forced a downward revision of the goal. Much of the constrained supply of postconsumer plastic comes from municipal waste streams, which are an underdeveloped tier in the supplier base of the circular economy. Municipal waste collection is so diffuse and fragmented that neither Walmart nor Coca-Cola by themselves can readily remake the waste collection industry.

To encourage the growth of municipal recycling supply chains, a consortium of nine companies, including Walmart, Coca-Cola, P&G, and Goldman Sachs, created the $100 million Closed Loop Fund.[171] The Fund offers zero-interest rate loans to municipalities and private entities to develop more recycling infrastructure and services. These loans help waste-stream collectors and processors reduce the fraction of materials sent to landfill (thus reducing the amount they pay in landfill fees) and to add revenues from the sale of recycled raw materials. At the same time, the resultant increased supply of recycled raw material would enable the consortium companies to offer more products with recycled content.[172]

In another example of a direct partnership, Kimberly Clark Brazil collaborated with the mayor's office of Suzano, Brazil, to engage waste pickers.[173] The company provided training for local waste collectors and installed an extrusion machine that makes plastic sheets out of collected recycled material. The sheets are used in many different business applications, including the construction of garbage-collecting stations for Carrefour. According to Kimberly Clark's 2010 Sustainability Report, "This program demonstrates the feasibility of a solid waste reverse logistics system that is socially appealing and offers lower costs to the supply chain. All parties become responsible for the post-consumption stage through this system, which removes waste from the environment and channels it toward an environmentally sound destination."[174]

Taming the Greenhouse Gas Beast with Carbon Capture and Storage

The Dutch port of Rotterdam plans to become a major European hub for closing the loop on one of the primary culprits of climate change: carbon dioxide. In 2007, the Municipality of Rotterdam, the Port of Rotterdam Authority, the Rijnmond central environmental service agency, DCMR,[175] and the port business association, Deltalinqs, founded the Rotterdam Climate Initiative (RCI).[176] Building on the industrial and logistics cluster around Rotterdam, RCI aims to develop an integrated supply chain of CO_2 producers, CO_2 customers, and storage facilities, all interlinked by pipes, barges, and oceangoing ships. Ultimately, RCI seeks to turn Rotterdam into a hub that collects CO_2 from Rotterdam, Amsterdam, Antwerp, the Ruhr Valley of Germany, and many other Northern European sources of CO_2 and supplies the gas to a variety of CO_2 applications and sequestration facilities.[177]

For example, Dutch greenhouse operators routinely burn natural gas to generate CO_2, which increases the growth rate and yield of plants in greenhouses.[178] One of Rotterdam's early projects captured CO_2 from a power plant, oil refinery, and a bioethanol plant and then sold the CO_2 to greenhouse operators north of Rotterdam.[179] This project also reused an abandoned oil pipeline that happened to pass through the greenhouse agriculture areas in the Westlands of Holland.[180] As of 2011, the project supplied CO_2 to one-third of the area's greenhouses and is looking to expand the number of CO_2 suppliers.

To manage the CO_2 hub, Rotterdam is developing logistics infrastructure, including backbone pipelines and portside CO_2 loading facilities that will enable ships or offshore pipelines to take CO_2 to remote sequestration or application sites.[181] These remote applications include the use of captured CO_2 to aid in the extraction of more fossil fuels. Called *enhanced oil recovery*, it involves injecting CO_2 into an oil field reservoir, which drives the oil to the collection well and increases both the short-term extraction rate and the long-term percentage of the total reservoir that can be recovered.[182] Any CO_2 that comes back up with the oil can be recycled back to the injection site.[183]

It seems fitting that among the best places to sequester CO_2 are the same deep, impermeable rock formations that locked natural gas and oil underground for tens of millions of years.[184] "Of course, you need to pick sites carefully," said Sally Benson, Stanford professor of energy resources engineering and director of Stanford's Global Climate and Energy Project. "But finding these kinds of locations does not seem infeasible."[185]

Limits of Looping
Companies who want to close the loop in order to gain access to secondary sources of raw material, respond to EPR regulatory

trends, develop a deeper relationship with the end customer, or for purposes of reducing their environmental impacts face certain limits of closed-loop systems. Although making new products from materials recovered from old products seems simple in theory, many practical obstacles stymie full circularity. For example, the average mobile phone contains $16 worth of high-value metals such as gold, silver, and palladium, but current smelter-based recycling processes can only recover $3 worth of these ingredients.[186]

In some cases, contamination or impurities in the waste materials limits recycling.[187,188] Municipal waste streams, especially, often come with contamination problems that limit the value of recovered materials. "We get soiled diapers and dead animals on the line," complained James Devlin of North Carolina recycling facility operator ReCommunity.[189] For some clear plastics, contamination levels of only 0.0025 percent to 0.1 percent can create hazing of the recycled material.[190] Even for relatively uncontaminated materials such as scrap aluminum, purity is an issue, with different aluminum alloys acting like contaminants for other alloys. The result is aluminum makers must either dilute the recycled metal with virgin metal, which prevents complete circularity; use downcycling, in which higher grades of aluminum (e.g., aircraft and electronic parts) are recycled into lower grades (e.g., engine blocks); or pay for more expensive recycling processes to physically segregate alloys or chemically remove the impurities.[191]

Sometimes green tactics can have negative consequences elsewhere in the supply chain and impede circularity. For example, lighter-weight bottles, which reduce material use and other environmental impacts, can fool some recyclers' separation systems, which were designed on the assumption that plastic bottles are heavier than paper and cardboard packaging. Some new sustainable plastics, such as bio-derived polylactic acid (PLA), are not recyclable at all with current technology. Recycling creates environmental impacts, too. Ironically, reusing glass bottles makes Coca-Cola's water footprint worse in the developing world, where refillable glass bottles make up a large percentage of the volume, because carefully cleaning those returned bottles demands large amounts of water.[192]

Recycling also faces social and regulatory challenges. Cultural and social norms sometimes create barriers in the form of consumer habits, market resistance, and transaction frictions in getting discarded goods to a pickup point and recycling center. As mentioned earlier, the Japanese recycle 77 percent of their plastic waste, whereas Americans only recycle 20 percent of their plastic.[193] Regulatory policies might also have unexpected (and unintended) consequences on recycling. For example, the US Toxic Substances Control Act (TSCA) creates a compliance burden that discourages companies from attempting to recycle electronic waste.[194]

In other cases, unrelated regulations may interfere with closed-loop recycling. "We have looked in detail at the circular economy, and will continue to do so, but sometimes it feels like loops for loops' sake and in this instance, there may not be a loop," said Tim Brooks, LEGO's senior director of environmental sustainability.[195] On paper, LEGO's toy bricks seem like a perfect product for developing a closed loop system. The bricks are mostly made of a single material: ABS (acrylonitrile butadiene styrene) thermoplastic. In addition, LEGO bricks are abundant, with an average of 90 bricks per person on the planet, and they are also durable. But the toy industry is highly regulated with stringent health and safety issues that make the use of recycled material very limited.

End-of-Life Impacts Through Beginning-of-Life Solutions

Recycling—even closed-loop recycling—can't eliminate all environmental impacts. Many of the challenges with both the material footprints of new products and the economics of recovering materials from end-of-life products stem from decisions made during product design. Careful design and engineering can further reduce environmental impacts in the sourcing, making, and delivery processes, as well as reduce impacts when the product is ultimately being used by consumers.

8

Green by Design

Paraphrasing George Bernard Shaw, Senator Robert Kennedy said: "Some men see things as they are and say 'Why?' I dream things that never were and say 'Why not?'"[1] Moving from incremental sustainability initiatives to ones that create substantial reductions in environmental impacts requires changing the products themselves, and it sometimes involves far-reaching changes. It requires changing elements of the design such as the types of materials, the amounts of materials, and the manufacturing technologies. "Designers are the start of everything, and if we can educate the designer to make better choices, then they can become agents of change for the entire industry," said Hannah Jones, vice president of sustainable business and innovation at Nike.[2] Design and engineering with the environment in mind can lead to reduced impacts caused by sourcing, manufacturing, use, and disposal of the product.

Design, by its very nature, involves trade-offs among competing objectives such as costs, product features, product performance, quality, and manufacturability.[3] Starting at the end of the 20th century, many product designers and engineers were challenged with an additional objective: curbing environmental impacts by reducing material footprint, emissions, waste, and toxins. The goal is to "eliminate negative environmental impact completely through skillful, sensitive design," according to Jason McLennan, author of *The Philosophy of Sustainable Design*.[4]

These added goals may also involve trade-offs, even between different sustainability objectives, let alone conflicting with other business objectives. A new bioplastic might reduce the carbon footprint of making a product but *increase* waste if that plastic cannot be recycled. A new, more efficient car might go farther on a gallon of gas and spew fewer emissions but require sourcing higher-environmental footprint alloys that consume more energy during manufacturing. Eliminating a potentially toxic ingredient from a detergent might diminish cleaning performance and cause consumers to use more hot water or more of the product itself to achieve the same level of cleanliness.

MATERIAL SUBSTITUTION AND REDESIGN

Design engineers can choose among a spectrum of possible design variations to improve sustainability, from incremental adjustments to much larger transformations of the design and manufacturing processes. An example of an incremental design change is Pepsi-Co's thinner bottles for its Aquafina brand of water. The resulting bottles used less raw materials, required less energy to make and transport, and cost less to produce. To gain brand equity from the effort, the company ran a public relations campaign that branded the bottle as "Eco-Fina" and touted its environmental savings.[5] Other incremental design changes might involve substituting the materials used and only minor changes in the actual design and manufacturing processes to accommodate any slight differences in technical properties (e.g., using recycled plastic or bioplastic in place of traditional petroleum-based plastic).

A more complex change may involve substituting materials while retaining a similar design but requiring different manufacturing methods (e.g., plastic versus glass bottles). In many cases, a decision about the change of material may involve a total change in the supply chain and manufacturing processes, as was the case in Boeing's decision to use composites in the Boeing 787 and Ford's decision to use an aluminum body in its 2015 F150 truck.

Lastly, some changes require complete transformations of the materials, design, and manufacturing technologies and processes used to create the product (e.g., a one-piece woven product versus a multipiece assembled product or a complex 3D-printed engine part). Larger changes in design (e.g., a shift from internal combustion engines in cars to battery–electric drivetrains) can require changes not only to significant segments of the vehicles' and manufacturers' supply chains, but also to the infrastructure that supports the product during use (i.e., a new nationwide network of recharging stations).

Making a Material Difference

Many design-for-sustainability efforts focus on resource efficiency and on minimizing the full life cycle footprints of a product. This includes not just the environmental impact of sourcing the chosen materials and the manufacturing processes along the supply chain but also the use phase footprints of products. Thus, companies use a life cycle assessment to estimate how prospective materials and design choices impact various parts of the supply chain and stages of the product life cycle. In the 1960s, the Coca-Cola Company faced the question of whether or not to manufacture its own bottles and thus needed to know the trade-offs inherent in different types of bottle materials. The packaging manager for Coca-Cola, Harry Teasley, is generally credited with performing the first LCA in 1969 when he compared the environmental impact of glass and plastic bottles—a study that included life cycle impacts and ultimately upset conventional wisdom.

At the time, many people assumed that glass was the more sustainable material because it is more "natural" (i.e., requires fewer processing steps). However, after examining the full life cycle of the bottle, the company found that because plastic bottles are lighter, they required less energy to transport both from the bottle maker to Coca-Cola and from Coca-Cola to retailers. Moreover, Coca-Cola could produce plastic bottles in-house, reducing transportation distances. Importantly, plastic was also easier to recycle at the time.[6] As a result, Coca-Cola concluded that plastic would actually be better for the environment.

Another category of environmentally motivated design change focuses on eliminating toxic materials from the product and from the supply chain, either to mitigate risks or to create products that will appeal to more discerning consumers. For example, Apple announced in 2015 that it had eliminated PVC, brominated flame retardants, phthalates, beryllium, mercury, lead, and arsenic from components in many of its leading products, such as the iPhone 6, iPad Air 2, and MacBook.[7]

Materials Considered … Designs Considered

Nike uses about 16,000 different materials—many types of rubbers, plastics, foams, textiles, adhesives, for instance—all of which interact with each other and influence manufacturing alternatives. The company sources these materials from 1,500 global suppliers to make and deliver 900 million units of its products every year.[8] The apparel maker's material supply chain accounts for 56 percent of the company's greenhouse gas emissions and 83 percent of its total water consumption.[9] To aid complex material choice and design decisions, Nike collected data on suppliers' materials and the manufacturing processes involved, and it performed LCAs on a number of materials comprising the bulk of its products.[10] The company used the information to create its Material Assessment Tool (MAT), which led to Nike's "Considered" line of shoes, launched in 2005.

MAT is a software application that scores all materials used in manufacturing Nike shoes and ranks them based on their environmental footprint. MAT helps designers analyze any proposed product design and grade it on energy consumption, impacts of fabric treatments, use of solvents, and the amount of solid waste resulting from the use of that material.[11] A specific shoe design can gain points (as scored by MAT) and win a Considered award by, for example, eliminating the use of toxic adhesives, minimizing waste, or incorporating more environmentally sustainable materials. Nike's drive to identify and avoid the use of hazardous chemicals[12] is part of its goal to eliminate all releases of such chemicals across its global supply chain by 2020.[13]

By 2008, the company had regained much of its lost brand equity (see chapter 1) and remained untarnished by the kind of environmental assaults that struck Kimberley-Clark,[14] LEGO,[15] and countless others. In that year, Nike released the 23rd edition of its Air Jordan shoe, which was designed using the Considered process. While including recycled materials and minimizing solvent usage, the shoes meet or exceed all required performance attributes. Michael Jordan, the basketball superstar and Nike spokesman, was thrilled with the shoe's eco-friendliness and commented, "I want all my shoes made this way."[16]

Nike is also working to redesign the materials themselves. "We need new technology and new chemistry, new materials, to swap out with the old," said Hannah Jones, Nike's vice president of sustainable business and innovation.[17] In 2013, Nike hosted the LAUNCH summit. The gathering brought together 150 material scientists from business, academia, and NGOs together with NASA, the US Agency for International Development, and the US Department of State. The participants focused on catalyzing actions aimed at improving material and process sustainability.[18]

Smell This Shoe

Design choices that reduce impacts can go beyond changes in the bulk of the product, to include modifications in manufacturing processes and elimination of trace ingredients that affect the environment. In 1999, manufacturing a pair of Adidas shoes released 140 grams of VOCs (volatile organic compounds) from the primers and adhesives used to bond the parts of the shoe together.[19] VOCs can be toxic for workers, contribute to smog, and act as greenhouse gases. That "new shoe smell" is not good for the environment. To reduce VOCs, the company developed innovative manufacturing methods using bonding and cementing systems, such as water-based primers and reactive hot-melt adhesives.[20] As of 2014, VOC content per pair had dropped by almost 90 percent to 17.5 grams.[21]

Redesigning Design

For thousands of years, shoemakers designed and manufactured shoes by cutting out a pattern of pieces from flat sheets of materials such as leather, fur, cloth, rubber, and plastic, and then laboriously nailing, stitching, or gluing those flat pieces together to form the three-dimensional shape of the shoe. In 2012, Nike moved beyond this age-old paradigm to implement radical changes in *both* the design *and* the manufacturing processes of its shoes.

Rather than assemble a shoe from, say, 37 pieces (as in the case of the popular Nike Air Pegasus), the company developed a new shoe manufacturing system that replaced the Considered technology. Called "Flyknit," it makes shoes with just two pieces. Nike adapted the same technologies used in sock manufacturing to knit the entire upper part of the shoe as a single, formfitting piece that is then attached to a one-piece injection-molded rubber sole.[22] "There is no more cutting and stitching with this. The most labor-intensive part of the footwear manufacturing process is gone from the picture," said Nike Chief Executive Officer Mark Parker, who joined the company as a shoe designer in 1979. Overall, the new approach to design and manufacturing eliminates 50 percent of the often-contentious manual labor used in traditional shoe assembly processes. Also gone are all the little scrap pieces of material left on the cutting room floor. Nike says the Flyknit generates 66 percent less waste than the Air Pegasus.[23]

The Flyknit design process calls for very different skills compared with the traditional shoe design. With the traditional approach, designers selected many different pieces of various types of material to accomplish their goals of aesthetics, comfort, and performance. With Flyknit, by contrast, the designer uses special software to choose the patterns and density of the knots in the weave to achieve technical performance, comfort, and aesthetics. Whereas complex colorful patterns require many different colored pieces for a traditional shoe, the Flyknit's aesthetic pattern is almost unlimited. Weaving with threads of multiple colors and carefully controlling which of the colored threads appear on the surface of the shoe and which are buried in the weave allows for the creation of almost any pattern. Notwithstanding Nike's success, many seemingly straightforward material substitutions can be challenging.

Sacrificing Performance for Lower Impact

Phosphates play a key role in many industrial processes, consumer products, and agricultural fertilizers. Dishwashing detergent makers have used phosphates for decades to leave glasses spotless.[24] However, phosphates in wastewater can cause eutrophication: the overstimulation of algae growth in rivers, lakes, and oceans. In some cases, algae grow so rampantly that they remove all oxygen in the water and suffocate aquatic life.[25] In 2006, Washington state Governor Christine Gregoire signed the first state law banning phosphates in dishwashing detergents.[26] By 2010, legislatures in 17 American states had passed similar laws.

The spreading wave of prohibitions forced dishwashing detergent makers to redesign their products,[27] but the first phosphate-free reformulations were much less effective than the old formulas. "This is the worst product ever made for use as a dishwashing detergent!" one customer wrote in an online review after trying an early version of P&G's reformulated Cascade.[28] P&G consumers were upset at the underperforming detergent and the fact that it was not perfected in advance of the ban; they were not ready to sacrifice performance for the sake of aquatic life. Moreover, one early unintended consequence of the redesigned detergents was that consumers ran their dishwashers again and again, thus wasting energy and water.

Detergent makers kept working on the problem. P&G modified the initial nonphosphate formulas of some products in response to customer complaints, according to Susan Baba, a spokeswoman for Cascade. "As we learn more, we're finding out that there's a lot more variation than we saw in the labs," she said. One of the key complications, she added, was that P&G needed to use three or four substitute ingredients to match the performance that phosphates achieved on their own.[29] Over the ensuing years, dish detergent makers eventually solved the problem (as was the case with laundry detergents, from which phosphates had been removed years before).[30]

In other areas, sustainable solutions lag behind the market leaders. Although most natural household goods perform as well as chemical-based ones, not all of them do. Take, for example, the personal experience (actually, her baby daughter's) of a researcher involved in the Sustainable Supply Chains project at MIT that led to this book. For her, a "green" diaper made by a leading company did not perform nearly as well (in terms of absorption and leakage) as Procter & Gamble's Pampers or Kimberly-Clark's Huggies. In another case, the author and his wife tried a "green" dishwashing soap at home, resulting in the declaration that if the family had to continue using this product, then future dinners would consist of preprepared food served on paper plates. Lastly, the author's wife tried a drain-unclogging product called Green Gobbler (whose tag line is "Finally power meets green") on a stubborn sink. The sink did eventually unclog, but only after pouring in a standard chemical compound because several packs of the Green Gobbler did not do the job.

Safer Ingredients or Not?

Other product redesigns can be ensnared by conflicting safety data and the challenges of communicating complex scientific arguments to a lay audience. In 2009, Seventh Generation announced a reformulated dishwashing liquid as part of its commitment to remove 1,4-dioxane from its products.[31] The US EPA classifies 1,4-dioxane as a probable carcinogen.[32] As part of this commitment, Seventh Generation decided to switch from sodium lauryl ether sulfate (SLES) to sodium lauryl sulfate (SLS) in its products. SLES and SLS are both surfactants, and though SLES is considered safe for use, it can be contaminated with 1,4-dioxane during the production process.[33]

The switch to SLS raised concerns among a number of Seventh Generation customers, who believed SLS itself was a carcinogen. Despite the company's explanation and references to scientific data—including a specific statement regarding SLS from the American Cancer Institute—consumers continued to ask Seventh Generation to remove SLS from its products. The dilemma for the company, or any other company in this situation, is that if enough consumers believe a product is harmful, the company may have no choice but to change it even if there is no scientific basis for the claims.

A similar consideration caused General Mills Inc., the giant American food company, to announce that its Cheerios cereal will be free of genetically modified organisms (GMOs). The company took this step despite the consensus of hundreds of scientific studies finding that GMO crops harm neither people nor the environment.[34]

In fact, it seems unlikely that the company believes that GMO food is harmful; none of its other products are GMO-free. Instead, the company aims to capture the segment of consumers who believe that GMOs are harmful, without passing judgment on the issue. The company's GMO-free product addresses the gulf between scientific opinion (88 percent of scientists say GMOs are safe to eat) and public opinion (only 37 percent of US adults say the same).[35]

Designing a Green Product Line

While many companies redesign existing products to reduce impact, others create entirely new product lines with environmentally friendly attributes. In 2012, Walgreens released its "Ology" brand of home products that, at the time of its release, claimed to be the "first nationally accessible and affordable brand formulated to be free of harmful chemicals."[36] The product line included baby care, personal care, household cleaning, and paper goods.

Office Depot similarly launched "Office Depot Green," a line that included products with a large amount of recycled content. Nike's Considered and Flyknit lines as well as PUMA's "InCycle" line are also examples of products developed following the same strategy: the launch of a "green" product line to appeal to green customers and test the market potential of such products, while simultaneously burnishing the company's reputation. Chapter 12 delves more deeply into the challenges of such eco-segmentation strategies of investments in green products.[37,38]

Managing the Product Portfolio Life Cycles

"Value chains are very complex," said Charlene Wall-Warren, director of sustainability at BASF. "If you remove one material without really thinking through the alternative solutions and what is involved to get a product out into the marketplace, you run the risk that you might respond to a public perception issue, and not be doing overall the best thing from a sustainability perspective."[39] To deal with these complex issues, BASF developed a process to "systematically steer our entire portfolio towards more sustainable solutions supporting our customers' needs," said Dirk Voeste, vice president of sustainability strategy.[40]

BASF's Sustainable Solution Steering method categorizes the sustainability attributes of products into one of four best-to-worst levels: "Accelerator," "Performer," "Transitioner," and "Challenged." As of 2014, BASF classified 23 percent of the sales of its 60,000 product-application combinations as "Environmental Accelerators"—products that offer green market segment features by helping to improve the environmental footprint of its customers, or its customers' customers. The company is working to reach 28 percent of sales from "Accelerator" products by 2020.[41] According to BASF, the margins on these products average more than 10 percent higher than the company's average.[42] The bulk of BASF's sales (74 percent) come from "Performer" products that meet BASF's internal sustainability criteria. "Transitioner" products—accounting for 2.6 percent of sales—have sustainability issues for which BASF is in the process of implementing a known solution. "Challenged" products (0.3 percent of sales) have sustainability issues with no known solutions.

This categorization then drives improvements in sustainability. For example, BASF made polyfluorinated coatings that make paper greaseproof. Although EU regulators have generally recognized these compounds as safe, the long history of finding environmental problems with fluorinated hydrocarbons (e.g., the CFC threat to the ozone layer, and the potential toxicity of water-resistant materials such as those used on outdoor clothing) makes these compounds a potential sustainability risk. BASF expected that these chemicals could become prohibited at some time in the future, yet the company had no known alternatives for the application. Thus, it classified its polyfluorinated coatings as "Challenged" and began a research program to create an alternative. The result was not just one new alternative but two: a recyclable material and a biodegradable one. Because these new products not only eliminated the potential toxicity issues of polyfluorinated coatings but also improved the waste stream impacts for greaseproof papers, they were classified as "Accelerators."[43]

"To develop a sustainable solution that only covers green aspects is not enough. It also needs to be affordable and has to meet societal demands," said Andreas Kicherer, director of sustainability strategy at BASF.[44] Charlene Wall-Warren explained the goals and rationale for the Sustainability Solutions Steering: "Long-term, the businesses want to be able to bring to market the products that will be the highest growth and the more profitable solutions. It's challenging to get through all of the detailed work of the entire process. It [Sustainability Solutions Steering] took four years. At the end, it gave a very nice view and validated the business case of why, long term, the company should be considering sustainability in as systematic way as possible."[45]

DESIGN FOR DELIVERY: PACKAGING

"I get pictures from my president ... [of] this tiny little thing in this humungous box with a whole bunch of void fill," said Cynthia Wilkinson, Staples' director of supply chain sustainability.[46] *Consumerist*, a blog about consumers' frustrations, shared an August 2012 story of an office worker who ordered a batch of office supplies—including highlighters, pens, tape, and a tiny bottle of typewriter correction fluid—from Staples.com. The correction fluid arrived two hours before the rest of the order and came in a very large box. The blog entry lampooned Staples, noting that Staples' shipping department had so stuffed the big box with air pillows that it sounded empty.[47] *Consumerist* also published similar amusing customer stories about embarrassingly wasteful packaging from other e-commerce companies, like Amazon and Macy's.[48,49] "It is one of the top customer comments in our North American delivery business," said Wilkinson.[50]

Big Boxes and Small Items
Staples, as one of the five largest US Internet retailers,[51] spends considerable amounts on packaging to deliver its online orders. The company shipped between 650,000 and 1 million packages every day in 2013.[52] "One out of every $10 or $11 of sales is related to packaging," Wilkinson said. "So if you look at a $25 billion company, that's $2.5 billion. That's a lot of money and a lot of value."

With that in mind, Wilkinson introduced a new technology, called Packsize, into the warehouse. Packsize International LLC makes equipment that produces custom boxes on demand. Each machine can build 300 boxes per hour in any number of specified designs. At Staples' Secaucus, New Jersey, facility, the company installed five Packsize machines and programmed them for 100 different box sizes.[53] Specialized software calculates the best custom-built box for each shipment. The machine cuts a shape out of bulk cardboard, folds it into a box, and sends it down the conveyor network to workers who pick the order. The facility ships as many as 40,000 orders a day, including 30 percent in break-pack orders,[54] which consolidate small numbers of different products. This is where the Packsize machines are most valuable.[55]

During the 2011 pilot implementation,[56] Staples reduced the average cardboard used per box by more than 15 percent. Air pillow use declined by almost 60 percent. In addition, smaller boxes translated into better truck utilization. Wilkinson said that the new system reduced line haul costs—transportation from the fulfillments centers to the customers—by about 8 percent.[57] It also saved warehouse storage space: corrugated cardboard for the on-demand boxes requires less than 20 percent of the space needed for the previous pre-sized boxes.[58]

By March 2013, Staples had expanded the program to 15 of its 35 US fulfillment centers.[59,60] "The environmental impact is fantastic; the corrugated cost is fantastic; the customer satisfaction change has been pretty significant," Wilkinson said. "So it's definitely a win." Despite the additional equipment and training, Wilkinson said installing Packsize machines had no appreciable impact on labor costs. Wilkinson would not comment on the program's return on investment (ROI), but she said that the company would not have expanded the program if its ROI did meet Staples' global standards. However, minimizing the size of the box used to enclose a shipped product is only a first (internal) step.

From Independent to Coordinated Efforts

Packaging materials (and the associated environmental impacts) span multiple industries, on both the upstream and downstream sides of many companies' supply chains. At the retailing end of the supply chain, Walmart rolled out a packaging scorecard in 2006 to encourage manufacturers to reduce their packaging's environmental impact. In response, Cosco, the juvenile products brand of Dorel Industries, eliminated the bulky boxes for its child car seats and shipped them in clear plastic bags instead. Not only did the change reduce the volume of packaging material, but the car seats were now stackable, creating significant savings in transportation and warehousing costs.[61] Other infant car seat manufacturers copied the change. Through efforts such as these, Walmart reached its goal of reducing company-wide packaging by 5 percent[62] by April 2013.[63]

Amazon CEO Jeff Bezos said, "We've all experienced the frustration of trying to remove a product from nearly impenetrable packaging."[64] The online retailer had realized that traditional consumer goods packaging, designed to prevent in-store theft (e.g., large, hard-to-open, heavy plastic clamshells) or ease retail displays (e.g., oversized rack-hanger packaging), is irrelevant and undesirable for e-commerce. Changing the packages meant working with suppliers, such as Philips Oral Healthcare, to redesign their products' clamshell. "We've worked with both manufacturers and customers to design Frustration-Free Packaging that is easy-to-open, protects the product and reduces waste," Bezos said.[65]

Amazon introduced its Frustration-Free Packaging program in 2008.[66] By removing excess packing material, Amazon estimated that it eliminated more than 24.7 million pounds of material over the first five years of the program,[67] and customers responded: products with reduced packaging had a 73 percent reduction in negative feedback on Amazon.com.[68] For Philips, having better reviews at Amazon.com was a significant selling point. According to Stephen Cheung, senior consumer marketing manager for Philips Oral Healthcare, "It wasn't necessarily that the product was the issue, it was the unpack experience—you've got to get scissors and knives."[69]

In 2004, GreenBlue, an environmental NGO, formed the Sustainable Packaging Coalition (SPC) with nine founding partners, including Dow Chemical, Nike, and Starbucks, with funding from the US EPA.[70] To enable more sustainable packaging, the SPC developed a tool called COMPASS (comparative packaging assessment), which provides designers with two categories of estimates of environmental metrics: consumption metrics (fossil fuel, water, minerals, and biotic resources) and emissions metrics (greenhouse gases, human impacts, aquatic toxicity, and eutrophication).[71]

In addition to offering the assessment tool, the coalition fosters engagement across the supply chain between buyers and suppliers, and it supports shared packaging industry innovation. Although individual packaging-reduction efforts may be eco-efficiency initiatives—providing costs savings for manufacturers—these larger-scale coalitions are examples of multicompany coordination leading to *eco-alignment* in which a broad array of companies coordinate sustainability efforts for mutual financial and environmental benefit.

The Market Rules

Natural household goods company Seventh Generation faced a conundrum regarding the redesign of the packaging of the company's dish soap and hand wash products. A major retailer told the company of a new requirement to offer refill pouches for these items. At first glance, the pouches seem like an environmental win. According to Martin Wolf, Seventh Generation's director of product sustainability and authenticity, consumers perceive that refilling and reusing the plastic dispenser bottle is environmentally better than replacing the single-use traditional plastic containers each time. The main environmental benefit of the pouches is that per ounce of product, pouches use one-third the materials of single-use plastic containers: a pouch containing 36 oz. of product uses only 0.7 oz. of plastic compared to a traditional single-use plastic bottle holding only 25 oz. that requires 1.6 oz. of plastic. In addition, pouches are malleable, making them easier to ship and handle in comparison to rigid plastic containers.

When Wolf did an LCA comparing the two types of packaging, he was surprised. For all the green appearance of refills, the pouches have a high impact. They are typically made from 75 percent virgin materials and 25 percent bio-based materials.[72] They can't be recycled and are landfilled at their end-of-life.[73] In contrast, traditional plastic containers can be made with as much as 100 percent postconsumer recycled (PCR) materials, and those bottles can be recycled, although the prevailing recycling rate in the US is only about 30 percent. Seventh Generation's analysis found that under these material source and recycling scenarios, a single-use container with more than 57 percent PCR material was the better environmental choice despite using larger amounts of material. Because Seventh Generation sells the majority of its products in bottles already made with more than 57 percent PCR material (and sometimes as high as 100 percent), the best environmental decision was easy: do not use pouches.[74]

Despite the results of the LCA, the marketing team decided to offer the pouches to satisfy retailers' demands and consumers' perceptions. Seventh Generation products are displayed alongside other mainstream CPG competitors, and the company was not willing to risk consumer perceptions that Seventh Generation was less green, even if those perceptions were false. This decision demonstrates that even green companies bow to market forces and consumer perceptions, despite the higher environmental impact.

Concentrated Products, Smaller Footprints ... Smaller Shelf Space

In 1987, the Kao Corporation introduced a concentrated laundry powder aimed at urban Japanese consumers.[75] Many of Kao's target consumers live in small apartments and depend on public transportation to bring their groceries home. For these reasons, Japanese consumers wanted laundry detergent that was lighter to transport and smaller to store; Kao responded.

The company designed a new product, called "Attack," with a concentrated formula based on a newly discovered bio-enzyme with quadrupled potency. At the time, the typical box of powdered detergent weighed 4.1 kg.[76] Attack's increased potency allowed Kao to pack the same number of washes into a box that weighed just 1.5 kg and took up one-quarter of the space. Kao promoted the reduced weight and size to Japanese consumers through a marketing campaign with the slogan "a size that can be carried easily in one hand."[77]

Attack triumphed in the marketplace. Prior to its introduction, Kao and domestic rival Lion each controlled about 30 percent of the detergent market. In 1989, two years after the introduction of Attack, Kao's market share had risen above 50 percent.[78] The concentrated formula even reduced supply chain costs and environmental impacts (although this was not Kao's focus at the time), because the smaller containers meant less packaging and lower distribution costs. But significant changes, such as those, to a product's size, formulation, appearance, and use—which are necessary for such a substantial result—can be much harder than imagined.

Procter & Gamble, who also adopted concentrated formulas in Japan based on Kao's modifications,[79] attempted to transfer the same concept to the American market. In 1990,[80] the company introduced concentrated Tide Ultra powder, followed by liquid Tide Ultra in 1992.[81] To compete with Tide Ultra, other US detergent manufacturers also introduced formulations that required just a quarter cup (down from half a cup) of detergent per load of laundry.[82]

Despite the growing selection of concentrated detergents, Americans did not embrace them the way Japanese consumers had. Following several years of mixed results, sales of concentrated detergents fell by 30 percent by 1994.[83] American shoppers were apparently unwilling to pay the same price for a smaller box or bottle, even if it cleaned the same number of loads just as well as traditional non-concentrated formula products did. Worse, concentrated products suffered a glaring merchandising disadvantage because they cover less shelf space, making them less noticeable to consumers relative to their large box, non-concentrated competitors. Many detergent brands and retailers quietly curtailed their offerings of concentrated versions. As a result, concentrated detergents remained just a curiosity in the American market until 2005.

That year, Walmart began a major sustainability push and asked suppliers to reduce their packaging. The retailer debuted Unilever's 3X concentrated "All: Small and Mighty," in October 2005 with prominent end-of-aisle displays[84] and demonstrations at both Walmart and Sam's Club stores. In response to Walmart's call for reduced packaging, and to compete with Unilever, P&G developed concentrated formulations of all its detergent brands, and, by the end of 2008, the company had replaced all of its detergents brands with concentrated formulations. The redesign of liquid laundry detergent to a two-times concentrated formula reduced packaging by 22 to 43 percent. But the switch yielded even more. According to Kathy Claffey, P&G's manager of product design for environmental sustainability, the company could fit about 10,000 bottles of the new formulation onto a delivery truck compared to only 5,000 bottles previously,[85] leading to saving 60,000 truck-load moves annually, including five million gallons of diesel fuel per year.[86]

In a show of Walmart's scale and market power, the retail giant announced that it would cease stocking non-concentrated detergents by May 2008.[87] This move cemented the trend and allowed Walmart to capitalize on these advancements toward its target of reduced packaging. "Making this change will reduce water consumption by 400 million gallons and save more than 95 million pounds of plastic resin and 125 million pounds of cardboard a year," wrote Matt Kistler, Walmart's senior vice president of sustainability. "And thanks to Walmart's large purchasing power, its competitors are also expected to make the switch."[88]

Concentrated detergent was obviously a viable, eco-efficient alternative for everyone in the supply chain. Nevertheless, competition for display space and consumer misperceptions had created a disincentive for any one brand to lead the way. Only when Walmart forced the hand of all its suppliers did the entire detergent supply chain, including Walmart's retail competitors, reap the financial and environmental benefits. This is also an example of "choice editing." Walmart did not give consumers a choice of both types of products: It forced its customers' hands by removing less sustainable choices from the market.

The Mushrooming of Biomaterials

"When we started to listen to customers, and social media played a big role in this, we were getting beat up about some boxes that were too big," said Oliver Campbell, director of procurement for packaging and packaging engineering at Dell.[89] Dell implemented what it calls the "3 C's" for design of more sustainable packaging:

cube (reducing packaging size), *content* (being aware of what it's made of), and *curb* (limiting undesirable materials or processes).

One of the more maligned types of packing materials is the custom-molded foam inserts that cushion computers, electronics, and other high-value, precision products. These custom-shaped inserts have high environmental impacts on many levels, in that they come from fossil fuels, rely on potentially toxic ingredients such as formaldehyde and styrene, depend on foam-expanding propellant gases that are potent GHGs, and create bulky, nonrecyclable waste that is prone to becoming windblown or waterborne litter.

In 2009, Dell began exploring alternative sources for its packing materials.[90] "I grew up in a farming community in the rural Finger Lakes in upstate New York. I reached back to that agricultural experience and started thinking if there were some ideas we could steal out of agriculture," said Campbell.[91] "Sometimes Mother Nature has a few tricks up her sleeve, right?"[92]

One of the concepts Dell tried was "mushroom" packaging grown by Ecovative Design LLC, a biomaterials company.[93] Ecovative takes agricultural waste such as corn stalks, molds it into the shape of the desired foam cushion, and inoculates the object with a proprietary breed of mushroom spores. The fungus grows into the waste, consuming the material, and leaving behind a spongy mass of interlocking white fibers. Heating the mass kills the fungus and dries the object, creating a lightweight cushion of exactly the desired shape.[94] Mushroom packaging is completely biodegradable and reduces energy use and GHG emissions by more than 90 percent when compared to traditional packaging materials like polyethylene foam.[95]

Dell piloted the new technology in 2013 with the shipping of its PowerEdge R710 servers and found that the packaging outperformed polyethylene foam in damping vibration.[96] "It's bio-magic," said Campbell.[97] "We tested the entire supply chain, in terms of 'Does the product arrive there safe?' And that's the number one consideration, because if it arrives in a damaged condition it's the least sustainable solution," he added. Although the material seemed to work well, Dell was concerned about the lack of automation in the mushroom-growing process, doubting that Ecovative's process could consistently meet Dell's needs for scale at a competitive price.[98]

To reach scale, Ecovative licensed its technology to Sealed Air, the $7.8 billion maker of traditional packaging materials such as bubble wrap and air pillows. Sealed Air reopened a Cedar Rapids, Iowa, food plastic wrap factory that had been closed in 2009 during the financial crisis. The Iowa location provides ready access to a high volume of agricultural waste, and the company has pre-purchased corn stalks from farmers. "When they're ready to harvest their corn they're getting a second value stream from what was previously considered a waste," said Sam Harrington, Sealed Air's communications director.[99] Sealed Air was also planning to expand manufacturing of the material into Europe.[100] The sometimes underappreciated challenge of scaling sustainable solutions is discussed further in chapter 12.

As with many other innovations, bringing this concept to market required a partnership between an innovative design firm (Ecovative), a manufacturer who could provide scale (Sealed Air), and an OEM who was ready to implement new ideas (Dell). Before entering into this partnership, both Ecovative and Dell vetted each other. Dell's Campbell commented, "Usually in procurement we're interviewing suppliers. But it became very apparent in the meeting that he [Ecovative] was interviewing us. He was doing that because at the time he was talking to various other companies in the technology space, and he was trying to figure out whom to partner with."

LOWERING THE IMPACT OF USE

Worldwide, industry accounts for half of all energy consumption involved in making the products and services it provides. The other half of global energy consumption takes place when consumers and organizations use these products and services. Once in the hands of consumers, products such as appliances, lighting, tools, and vehicles consume electrical power, use water, burn fuel, or emit toxic substances into the environment. With many of these products, the use phase is responsible for the bulk of the product's environmental impact. In the wake of the energy crisis of the 1970s and subsequent energy price shocks, regulatory bodies began to require disclosure as well as product performance mandates. In the United States, regulations such as the Corporate Average Fuel Economy (CAFE) standards for vehicles,[101] the Seasonal Energy Efficiency Ratio (SEER) standards for air conditioners,[102] and the Energy Independence and Security Act (EISA) standard for light bulbs[103] require increasing levels of energy efficiency.

Do More with Less

Household appliances in the US account for more than 60 percent of residential energy consumption and 13 percent of the country's total energy consumption.[104] Because of both increasing minimum efficiency standards and mandatory efficiency labeling (see chapter 9), consumers can, and often do, buy more efficient versions of many household appliances. For example, the average refrigerator made in 2010 uses one-quarter the electricity of refrigerators made in 1972 despite being 20 percent larger.[105] Appliance makers have added better insulation, more efficient compressors and motors, and improved temperature controls.

Similarly, new high-efficiency washing machines use smaller amounts of water, which not only leads to water savings but also to energy savings owing to heating less water. The regulatory efficiency standards also reflect the coupling between the use-phase impacts of washers and dryers, motivating designers to increase the speed of the spin cycles of washing machines in order to remove more moisture and help reduce energy consumption by dryers.[106] Nor have appliance makers sacrificed on performance. According to *Consumer Reports*, washing machine cleaning performance has actually improved even as the machines became more energy and water efficient.[107]

The ever-shrinking size of semiconductor chip circuits, predicted by Moore's law, brings with it ever-improving energy efficiency as well. Smaller chips offer more computational speed per watt of electricity, and it is not just computer chips that have improved. Flat panel displays use one-third to one-half less power than the previous generation of bulky CRT monitors.[108] More efficient and more compact switching power supplies have replaced bulky, inefficient iron-core transformers. Solid-state storage drives have replaced the energy-intensive, spinning platters of hard disk drives. Many technology makers have strong self-serving use-phase efficiency incentives. Higher energy efficiency enables longer battery life with higher performance for thin, lightweight phones, tablets, or laptops, as well as offering corporate buyers energy efficiency for power-hungry data center products. The result is that 500-watt desktop PCs have evolved into 50-watt laptops and to 5-watt tablets and smartphones.

Low-cost, energy-efficient processors and sensors enable designers in many industries to create more efficient products. For example, washing machines can detect the volume of clothing in the machine and add just enough water to do the job. Humidity sensors in clothes dryers ensure the load gets dry without running longer than needed. Dishwashers can detect residual food debris in wastewater and regulate their wash and rinse cycles accordingly.

Similar gains are evident in the automotive industry; vehicles now use an extensive set of sensors to monitor airflow, fuel flow, temperatures, power, and emissions. An engine management computer carefully regulates all aspects of engine operations. The result is that carmakers can now design and manufacture relatively small engines—reducing vehicle weight and fuel consumption— that deliver very high power with both good fuel efficiency and very low levels of emitted pollutants. Between 1975 and 2013, the average engine power in cars and light trucks in the US increased 68 percent (from 137 hp to 230 hp) while average fuel economy nearly doubled (from 13.1 mpg to 24).[109]

Using Products Designed for Efficiency

Some design modifications require no changes in customer behavior or downstream supply chain processes. A more energy-efficient refrigerator or computer might be identical in performance and operating instructions to the less-efficient model it has replaced; it simply uses less energy. Others, such as a cold-water detergent, might involve some modest change to an otherwise familiar practice. Finally, some changes, such as electric vehicles, might demand both behavior changes (e.g., learning to manage the range of the vehicle and find charging stations), as well as concomitant consumer investments (e.g., installing charging facilities at home).

In addition to designing products for efficient downstream usage, companies may have to influence and educate consumers on the benefits and efficacy of new, environmentally responsible products, and how to use the product in a sustainable fashion. For example, dry shampoo[110] is a specially formulated spray or powder that absorbs excess oil from the hair and scalp, allowing for a longer period between wet hair washes. Unilever claims that it can replace a wet wash 60 percent of the time.[111] Consumers, apparently, do not believe the product has the same efficacy, value, or appeal; dry shampoo accounts for only 3 percent of the global market. (A staffer in my office tried the product and reported that it made her hair *look* like she washed it, but made her scalp feel worse than before.) Chapter 9 delves more deeply into how companies try to encourage customers to use sustainable products.

Rolling Out Products for Downstream Green

Component and raw material suppliers can redesign their products to improve use-phase energy efficiencies of the end products into which these components go. For example, Michelin conducted LCAs in 2001, 2003, 2009, and 2010 to understand the life cycle impact of its tires. In a 2012 report, Michelin stated: "Based on a standard 40,000 kilometers traveled, more than 92 percent of a car tire's health and environmental impact occurs during use, primarily as a result of its rolling resistance." The report said, "This proportion rises to 95 percent for a truck tire, based on a standard of 600,000 kilometers driven."[112] Rolling resistance accounts for up to 35 percent of a truck's fuel consumption, according to Michelin.[113]

As a result, Michelin focused the bulk of its environmental efforts on designing improvements to the rolling efficiency of its products. One such development, the Michelin *X One* tires, resulted in a 10 percent improvement in fuel efficiency. These tires do not reduce Michelin's direct (Scope 1 or Scope 2) environmental impacts or its costs. Nor do they improve the costs and direct impacts for the automakers, who are Michelin's customers. Instead, the tires' use-phase fuel cost reduction and environmental benefits accrue to the vehicles' buyers and operators who are the customers of Michelin's customers. In turn, the improvements in fuel efficiency contribute to the automakers' product sustainability claims and regulatory compliance (e.g., SmartWay truck fleet efficiency mentioned in chapter 6 or US CAFE standards for required fuel efficiency of cars).

Suppliers also create new materials and components that enable customer companies to create low-impact or green products. For example, BASF developed nearly 40 different new compounds such as chemicals used in solar cell production, coatings for wind turbines, higher-performance insulating foams, nitrous oxide pollutant decomposition catalysts, additives for lower-carbon footprint concrete, catalysts for the production of biodiesel, efficiency-boosting fuel additives, and many others. "We help our customers reduce their carbon footprints by offering innovative products for climate protection," said the company in its Carbon Disclosure Project application.[114] These products earned BASF some €6.7 billion in revenues (around 9 percent of BASF Group sales) in 2013.[115]

On May 9, 2005, General Electric chairman and CEO Jeff Immelt announced a new environmental initiative. "'Ecomagination' is GE's commitment to address challenges such as the need for cleaner, more efficient sources of energy, reduced emissions and abundant sources of clean water," Immelt said. "And we plan to make money doing it. Increasingly for business, 'green' is green. Ecomagination is about the future."[116] GE's Ecomagination initiative includes new high-efficiency power systems for locomotives, jet engines, and power plants.[117]

GE claimed that as of 2013, its Ecomagination program had generated more than $160 billion in revenue, in addition to a 34 percent reduction in GHG emissions and a 47 percent cut in freshwater use in its own operations.[118] Similarly, Siemens sells large quantities of renewable energy products such as wind turbines. In a 2013 interview, Siemens reported that products related to sustainability had generated cumulative revenues of €32.3 billion and saved 377 million metric tons of carbon emissions.[119]

However, the future viability of many of these sustainability-enabling products hinges on potentially capricious government policies. Although many redesigned products have eco-efficiency justifications, others—such as renewable energy sources, low-emissions vehicles, and biofuels—can depend on significant subsidies or economic distortions created by government regulations. For example, Elon Musk's companies (Tesla and SolarCity) benefited from an estimated $4.9 billion in government support, including "grants, tax breaks, factory construction, discounted loans and environmental credits that Tesla can sell."[120] In addition to access to carpool lanes and reduced electricity rates for vehicle charging in many states, a buyer of a Tesla vehicle enjoys $7,500 in income tax credits and an additional state income tax credit that varies; for example, in Louisiana it is between $6,900 and $9,500. If fossil-fuel prices remain low and regulators change their stance on environmental issues, then demand for energy-saving products might wane. On April 1, 2017, the government of Hong Kong slashed all tax breaks for electric vehicles. Sales of Tesla vehicles dropped to zero, demonstrating the sensitivity of these sales to government support.[121] Moreover, in many cases, sustainability claims do not withstand the rigor of an uncompromising LCA.

The Full LCA

Since Toyota introduced its Prius hybrid in 1997 in Japan,[122] growing numbers of drivers around the globe have traded in their traditional gasoline vehicles for this new class of fuel-efficient transportation. Under most driving conditions, hybrid cars achieve better gas mileage than standard engines by combining both a battery-powered electric motor and a small gasoline engine with a generator. Software manages the two motors, generator, transmission, and battery to maximize fuel efficiency by ensuring that the gasoline engine runs mostly at its optimal speed and load. Hybrids and electric cars cost substantially more than similarly sized traditional gasoline-powered cars. For example, a 2017 conventional Honda Accord was rated by the EPA at 29 miles per gallon in combined city and highway driving. By comparison, the hybrid Honda Accord achieved 47 miles per gallon, but cost $7,250 more.[123]

Whether such cars are eco-efficient—saving consumers money and the earth's environment—depends on both gas prices and driving habits. To break even financially, the Honda hybrid buyer would have to drive at least 177,000 miles if gas were $3 per gallon, and 265,000 miles if gas were $2 per gallon, which was the approximate gas price in the United States at the time of this writing. Yet if the consumer primarily drives the car on the highway, the break-even driving distance grows to 297,000 miles even with gas at $3 per gallon. And if the consumer used a loan to buy the more expensive car, they may never break even within the car's lifetime.[124] Many Americans chose such vehicles, but that choice may be less environmentally friendly than meets the eye.

In 2007, headlines declared "Tank vs. Hybrid: Is It Possible that a Hummer's Better for the Environment than a Prius Is?"[125] and "Prius Outdoes Hummer in Environmental Damage."[126] An LCA titled "Dust to Dust," performed by CNW Research Marketing, claimed the full life cycle impact of the diminutive Prius, the chariot of the environmental movement, exceeded those of the Hummer, even though the Prius had four times better gas mileage.[127] The firm's assessment attempted to account for the total life cycle impact of each automobile. Manufacturing a hybrid vehicle requires two engines, chemically complex batteries, and many additional high-tech components, generating significantly higher carbon emissions than manufacturing a traditional vehicle. However, the study contained many questionable assumptions and had inconsistencies that cast doubt on its findings.[128,129] It was also contradicted by other studies.[130]

Several subsequent studies revealed the complexity of the issue. For example, a detailed LCA performed by researchers at Keio University using data from Toyota concluded that electric vehicles may or may not be best, depending on the lifetime distance traveled and the country where the vehicle is driven. In Japan, hybrid vehicles with an engine displacement of 1500 cc that operated for 10 years became the greenest choice after 35,700 km per year due to Japan's reliance on nuclear power (the study was performed before the 2011 Fukushima disaster caused Japan to shut down most of its nuclear plants). In India, the coal-based electric grid rendered electric cars the dirtier choice unless they were driven more than 193,000 km per year.[131] Other studies highlighted the role of battery size on environmental impact: Plug-in electric vehicles with large batteries have higher impacts in production and poorer utilization during use because the car is carrying a heavy battery that is seldom fully used during the car's many short trips.[132] Nonetheless, the original publication, the controversy, and the subsequent studies did raise the media's consciousness on the importance of comparisons based on LCAs.

Even for conventional vehicles, the trend toward higher fuel efficiency—lower use-phase impacts—has come with increased impacts in the *source* and *make* phases. For example, lightweight aluminum—used extensively by Ford to improve the fuel economy of its new F-150 pickup truck[133]—requires seven times as much energy to produce as traditional steel.[134] Also note that in 1995 the carbon emissions during the use phase of a 1995 American car were eight times larger than the emissions of the manufacturing phase.[135] However, the use-phase carbon impact of a modern Tesla Model S, is only *twice* that of the manufacturing phase.[136] These examples highlight the common wisdom that "there is no free lunch." In other words, radical new designs intended to reduce environmental impact in the use phase may require higher environmental impacts in other supply chain phases.

Physics Is an Implacable Foe

Many of the design trade-offs in product performance and environmental impact arise from the fundamental physics of the universe or the chemistry of the Earth's atmosphere, which is 80 percent nitrogen. The same high pressures and high temperatures that make diesel and jet engines so fuel efficient also spawn acrid nitrogen oxides (NO_x) in the engine's exhaust. NO_x gases damage the human respiratory system, are GHGs, and contribute to smog and acid rain.[137] Tough new regulations on NO_x emissions by vehicles in Europe, and even stricter US regulations, forced automakers to add complicated systems to mitigate these emissions.

Although the new cars passed the strict emissions tests in laboratories, later investigations proved that not all automakers were successful in actually mitigating emissions. Beginning in 2013, John German, a senior fellow at the International Council on Clean Transportation (ICCT), tested emissions of diesel Volkswagen Jetta and Passat cars. He wanted to show that low emissions were possible so that the EU would toughen its diesel emissions standards to match the US. However, he found that under actual driving conditions—not laboratory conditions—the diesel-powered VW Jetta emitted 35 to 40 times the allowable emissions, making it worse than a heavy truck.[138] German filed a report with the US EPA.

Further investigation found no flaws in the testing but, instead, revealed massive fraud at VW. The carmaker's engineers could not get their emissions technology to meet the new requirements during normal driving conditions, and they resorted to cheating. They rewrote the engine management software to detect laboratory testing conditions (when the vehicle is run on a dynamometer and the steering wheel does not move) and retuned the engine's performance during the test in ways that no driver would like but that could pass the test. Between 2009 and 2015, VW installed this "test defeat" software in some 11 million cars, including half a million sold in the United States and six million sold in Europe.[139,140] The resulting scandal forced the CEO of VW Group to resign and several other top executives to be suspended. The stock lost more than one-third its value.[141] As of early 2016, the company faced a threat of more than \$48 billion in fines in US courts,[142] as well as dozens of lawsuits by car owners and stockholders worldwide. For example, South Korea banned the sale of all VW cars, indicted VW executives, and levied millions of dollars in fines against the company.[143] Similarly, the US has been pursuing criminal indictments against VW executives.[144]

DESIGN FOR RECYCLING

"The linear economy of the 20th century was based on taking material out of the ground and turning it into a commodity and then putting it back in the ground," said Sir David King, the UK Foreign

Office's special representative for climate change.[145] To break this circle, companies that design their products for recycling often go beyond just changes in materials or product. As with many of the examples in this chapter, these companies also change elements of their business relationships along their supply chains. In the case of recycling, many of these changes involve customers or other partners on the downstream side so the company can ensure that their recyclable products *are*, in fact, recycled.

Dismantling Products and Building Partnerships

The Herman Miller Company designed the "Mirra" chair with recyclability in mind through both material choice and design decisions. A full 96 percent of the plastic, aluminum, steel, and foam used in the chair can be recycled, and the chair's designers focused on making the chair easy to disassemble. Herman Miller provides a step-by-step instructional guide for disassembling the chair at its end of its life,[146] enabling recyclers to harvest as much reusable material as possible.[147] This, naturally, also makes it easy for users to replace parts as they wear out, thereby extending the chair's estimated 12-year life span.

Herman Miller's redesign and reengineering efforts were guided by its goal to reduce the environmental impact of its products without sacrificing value or quality. The redesigned chair helped boost the company's brand to boot by winning half a dozen awards in 2003 and 2004.[148]

To fully close the loop, Herman Miller partnered with Green Standards Ltd., a company that specializes in decommissioning furniture, and actively offers their services to its clients through its "rePurpose" program. The program also includes disposal management of products not sold by Herman Miller, from paper clips to copier machines.[149]

In another example of both product and supply chain design for recyclability, a coalition of four companies—office furniture company Steelcase, materials designer Designtex, textile manufacturer Victor, and recycled fiber maker Unifi—launched *Loop to Loop*, an upholstery for Steelcase furniture completely designed for a closed-loop supply chain. In addition to fiber innovations, the two-year collaboration included capital investments in Unifi's recycling facilities to make sure recycled fibers can be transformed into yarn for next-generation fabrics again and again.[150] Yet product design for recycling is only part of the story.

Product Life Cycle as Part of the Sales Cycle

A key player in all recycling initiatives is the customer, and that means that sales and recycling are linked. EMC Corporation,[151] a global provider of servers, cloud computing, virtualization, and other computer products and services, also offers equipment recovery services with every installation it sells. In 2012, it collected 10,000 metric tons of waste, of which it refurbished or resold 7.5 percent and recycled 90.1 percent. Some 2.2 percent of waste was converted to energy and a minuscule 0.2 percent was sent to a landfill.[152]

A recycling rate of 90.1 percent is nearly unheard of in the electronics industry because the complex amalgamation of materials used in electronic products makes recycling difficult. According to EMC, the company has achieved these high recycling rates by designing for it. "A truly effective take-back and e-waste program starts with product design," the company said.[153] "The easier a product is to disassemble, the easier it is to reclaim, recycle, and dispose of in a responsible manner."

The company was able to tie its recycling program to two important business benefits: security for its customers and increased sales for EMC. First, taking servers and storage devices back ensured the customer's data security. EMC guaranteed that all data on their old equipment would be permanently destroyed. Instead of merely erasing the data electronically and reselling the units, EMC shredded all data storage devices and recycled their fragments.

Second, the recycling program actually increased sales: Ezra Benjamin, principal program manager of EMC's Global Product Take Back and E-waste commented, "You might be surprised to learn that we consider the take back and e-waste process to be part of the sale. Much like at a car dealership, customers trade in old equipment when they buy new equipment. So, every sale generates used electronics coming back to EMC. Customers then get a discount on new gear and EMC can recover economic value from the old equipment."[154] Benjamin added that brand reputation and ethical practices also drove the decision, but the business benefits made it much easier to sell internally.

Cradle-to-Cradle Ownership

Interface Inc., a maker of carpeting, created "the industry's first completely closed-loop carpet recycling system."[155] When Ray Anderson founded the company in 1974, he did not have sustainability in mind. Then, in 1994, after two decades of operating the company conventionally, he read *The Ecology of Commerce* by Paul Hawken and had an epiphany. Anderson decided to refocus his business on the company's environmental legacy, aiming to develop a business that would be both profitable and conscious of what it would leave behind.[156] He even wrote a book of his own, *Mid-Course Correction: Toward a Sustainable Enterprise*, which detailed his efforts to remake Interface.[157]

The first of three new key elements of Anderson's transformation of his company was an innovative design of the carpet's pattern and installation methods to reduce waste. Interface designed modular square carpet tiles instead of the more conventional rolled or "broadloom" carpet. Carpet tiles were neither new nor unique, but Interface randomized the carpet pattern such that the tiles could be installed in any orientation. Interface's design choices sharply reduced the rate of scrapped carpet. Companies that install traditional broadloom carpet throw out as much as 12 to 15 percent of the material, because the installers cut the required odd-sized chunks out of the broad roll of material. That scrap rate drops to 3–4 percent with carpet tiles and to 1–2 percent with randomized tiles.[158]

Second, to ensure recyclability, the company not only makes the carpets from recycled material but also designs the weave and materials of the carpet itself to be easily recyclable. Interface takes each square of recovered carpet to a specialized facility where it is recycled into new carpet squares. Old carpet fibers become new carpet fibers. Old carpet backing becomes new carpet backing.[159]

Third, to ensure that carpet that *can* be recycled *is* recycled, Interface went one step beyond Herman Miller and EMC by changing its business model from selling carpets outright to a "servicizing" model. In this model, Interface does not sell the carpet to the customer. Instead, it provides a service that includes a lease on the carpet, installation, maintenance, upgrades, and recycling. What the customer buys is not a carpet but floor covering as a service. During the service period, Interface can take advantage of its random pattern tile design to selectively replace worn or damaged tiles. At the end of the lease, Interface rips out and recovers the carpet.[160,161] This business model gives Interface full cradle-to-cradle control over its products' life cycle.

As the examples in this and other chapters show, sustainability initiatives can have complex impacts on the product, its attributes, and how the product should be handled during its useful life and afterward. How companies inform customers and others of these complexities is the focus of the next chapter.

9

Talking the Walk: Communicating Sustainability

"The word on the street is everyone is selling the same food. Well, they ain't," Whole Foods co-CEO Walter Robb told *Fortune*, "I want to communicate the difference and sell the difference."[1] As chapter 3 discussed, the business rationale of environmental initiatives ranges from eco-efficiency (i.e., saving money by conserving natural resources), to eco-risk mitigation (such as forestalling environmentalist attacks and reducing political pressure for extreme regulations), to eco-segmentation (through sales of green products to green consumers). Moreover, the rationale behind any and all these initiatives may *also* include attracting investment from sustainability-minded investors.

Attracting green customers and green investors while avoiding attacks by NGOs and regulators requires that the outside world know about the company's sustainability efforts and their results, so that the company's brand and reputation will benefit.

Companies communicate their various sustainability initiatives and achievements through a variety of channels in order to reach different audiences. To reach consumers at the point of purchase, companies use product labels, designed to help consumers distinguish between ostensibly sustainable products and others, and feel virtuous because they are "doing something for the environment." Related marketing efforts can educate consumers about the company's sustainable sourcing, manufacturing, and transportation strategies, as well as the sustainable use and disposal of products. Companies use environmental reports or disclosure standards to tell investors, NGOs, the media, and regulators about goals, efforts, and outcomes of environmental impact reduction initiatives.

These kinds of communications can be a double-edged sword—a company's environmental claims help reap the business value of environmental sustainability efforts, but they can also invite increased scrutiny from skeptics and watchdogs. The age-old admonishment that one must "walk the talk" suggests the need for careful coordination between those who "manage the talk" (sales, marketing, public relations, investor relations, government lobbying, and senior management) and those who "manage the walk" (engineering and supply chain managers, including manufacturing, procurement, and logistics).

LABELS: YOUR MILEAGE MAY VARY

In a 2014 article, *The Guardian* demonstrated consumers' confusion in the simple task of buying eggs in a world where cartons now carry a cacophony of claims: "Cage-free or free-range? Free-roaming or free-farmed? Grass-fed, vegetarian-fed, or whole grain-fed? Antibiotic-free, biodynamic, hormone-free, non-irradiated, natural, organic, or pasteurized?"[2]

As companies noticed that consumers' environmental concerns could lead to improvements in market share or pricing for products marketed as environmentally friendly, they started to label products with green claims (or seemingly green claims). These included "natural," "recyclable," "biodegradable," "energy efficient," and so on. The variety of claims mushroomed, and with it consumer confusion and suspicion about the truth behind the labels.

To help clear up the confusion, the International Standards Organization (ISO) defined standards for three types of claims or logos on labels[3] as follows:

- Type I: A third-party logo linked to fulfillment of a set of environmental criteria based on life cycle considerations
- Type II: Self-declared claims made by companies about their own products (using non-misleading terms and accurate and verified data)
- Type III: A set of environmental data based on criteria put forward by a qualified third party, based on an LCA, and verified by the same or another third party.

The first two types of claims are aimed at consumers "walking down the aisle," while the third type could not be expressed in a logo but in a data set used in business-to-business exchanges.

Regardless, it is at the consumer level that most confusion and misinformation reigns.

Consumer Confusion?

Chapter 3 told the story of Tesco's carbon labels. The first batch of carbon-labeled products landed on store shelves in August 2009 to much fanfare.[4] Accompanying the rollout, Tesco polled its customers' carbon awareness. Only half understood the meaning of the phrase "carbon footprint,"[5] though that represented a significant increase from the 32 percent rate found in a similar survey from the previous year. The survey also concluded that half of the respondents who understood the term would alter their shopping patterns to buy products with lower carbon footprints, up from 35 percent in the previous year. In a "Green Blog" post noting the label rollout and poll results, the *New York Times'* James Kanter pointed to concerns that such labels would confuse customers.[6] Tesco, in a statement, dismissed that worry. Distressingly, one survey found that even if consumers *did* plan to alter their shopping habits, 30 to 40 percent mistakenly thought a higher carbon footprint number was better.[7]

"What does it mean to say a bag of chips contains 75 grams of carbon?" asked Steve Howard, CEO of the Climate Group, in a March 6, 2008, *BusinessWeek* article. "I have a PhD in environmental physics and it does not mean a thing to me." Not only does the absolute number have no intuitive meaning, but it also provides no insight into which manufacturer might be working the hardest to become more sustainable. This issue has not abated since Tesco's 2009 labeling efforts, which ended in 2012 after less than 1 percent of Tesco's products had been labeled.[8]

A 2013 survey found that 70 percent of consumers were confused by the messages companies use to talk about their corporate social responsibility initiatives.[9] "This information is really complex. Getting it reduced into a simple label for consumers is very challenging," said Elizabeth Sturcken, managing director at Environmental Defense Fund.[10]

Label Mania

If companies issue their own sustainability claims and labels (ISO Type II labels), they face natural skepticism about the company's motives and bias in evaluating its own products. In fact, only 46 percent of consumers surveyed said they trust brands to tell them the truth in their environmental messages.[11] In contrast, independent third parties (ISO Type I labels), especially those that are well-known and trusted, can help verify corporate "green" messages by providing standards, certifications, and auditing, as well as overcoming consumer skepticism.[12] Consequently, many environmental organizations have created eco-labels for a wide range of sustainability attributes.

This trend toward third-party labels may have grown to unsustainable levels, however. A 2014 compilation by the Ecolabel Index service[13] uncovered more than 458 eco-labels[14] from a range of groups including government agencies, leading NGOs, corporations, and small, regional nonprofit organizations. One of the reasons for the plethora of labels is that many of them have a narrow regional, category-specific, or issue-specific scope. The French government applies its carbon-specific labels only to products intended to be sold within the country's borders, although that does not prevent multinational companies from using the French label in other markets. The Carbon Trust may be more global than the French label, but it still only focuses on carbon emissions. The Marine Stewardship Council certifies only seafood. Some labels are especially narrow, such as the AvoGreen label, which focuses only on avocados and only on the use of "integrated pest management" in their cultivation.

To add to the potential confusion, not all eco-labels, even those issued by third parties, are created equal. Anastasia O'Rourke, cocreator of the Ecolabel Index, documented wide variations in the rigor required by different labels. Some call for products or companies to pass rigorous on-site, third-party verification of comprehensive standards, requiring adherence to dozens or even hundreds of nontrivial terms and conditions. For others, "It's like 'send us the money and we'll give you the [label] ...'" she said. "That's a little exaggerated, but not by much."[15] In fact, a 2010

TerraChoice report claims to show a green label bought online for $15.[16]

When "Organic" Leaves a Bad Taste in the Mouth

A 2010 University of California study[17] found that wineries that adhered to the standards for growing organic or biodynamic grapes, but which did not label their wines as "organic" (despite being certified), enjoyed an average price premium of 13 percent. In contrast, wineries that were certified and actually affixed the "organic" label to their bottles had to offer their wine at prices 20 percent below average, owing to beliefs among wine drinkers that organic wines are of lower quality. The reason may be that organic wines—which differ from wines that use organically grown grapes—do not add sulfite preservatives to their wines. Consequently, they are less stable over time and potentially decline in quality as they age.

Eco-labels can even cause a business to lose sales among certain consumer groups. A 2012 study published by the US National Academy of Science compared the sales of compact fluorescent light (CFL) bulbs, priced at $1.50 per bulb, with incandescent bulbs priced at $0.50 per bulb. If the CFL bulbs had a "protect the environment" label, then customers self-identifying as politically moderate or conservative were less likely to buy them.[18] If the CFL bulbs lacked the environmental label, then conservatives and progressives bought them in similar proportions. The study concluded that economic incentives are likely to drive consumers to buy CFL bulbs, because they save money in the long run. However, environmental messages may detract from this effect. Politically moderate and conservative individuals, who tend to put less trust in the government, may think that the purpose of the environmental message is to mask inadequacies on other performance dimensions of the pricier bulbs.

Limited Economic Effects of Labels

A survey of coffee drinkers in China found consumers would be willing to pay, on average, a 22 percent premium for a cup of Fair Trade labeled coffee.[19] Realistically, such surveys may overestimate the impact of labels: Survey participants tend to respond the way they think the survey creator wants them to respond, or they may want to appear progressive and caring. Data from actual product sales experiments, in contrast, show lower premiums for sustainability labels and sometimes no premium (or, as in the example above, a negative premium). British researchers, using an ordinary least squares model based on dozens of indicator variables, found the premium for Fair Trade coffee already on the market to be only 11 percent.[20]

A New England study of 26 grocery stores found that eco-labels had mixed effects on sales and price premiums. When a Fair Trade label was added to two previously unlabeled coffee varieties (one selling for $10.99 and the other $11.99 per pound), sales volumes of both increased by about 10 percent. When the prices of both coffees were raised by $1 per pound, sales volumes of the higher priced coffee remained elevated, whereas sales of the lower-priced coffee dropped by about 30 percent.[21] This result suggests that wealthier consumers may be willing to pay a premium for sustainable products, while more frugal consumers might use sustainability attributes only as a tiebreaker among equally priced products, rather than an inducement to pay more.

The effectiveness of a label may also vary with the type of product. Using data on Danish consumer purchases over a four-year period, Danish and American researchers found that the Nordic Swan label enabled a 10 to 17 percent price premium for toilet paper but no willingness to pay higher prices for Nordic Swan-labeled paper towels.[22] One possible explanation is that toilet paper has closer contact with the consumer's body and the eco-label might indicate higher safety and a lack of toxins, which may be more important in the case of toilet paper than in paper towels. In other words, the toilet paper had a stronger element of "on me" compared with paper towels (see chapter 1).

A 2014 study by the European Food Information Council (EUFIC) concluded that even though European consumers value sustainability and understand various eco-labels, such labels have only a minor effect on food choice. A survey of self-reported use of food label information found environmental impact information ranked 14th out of 16 categories. A conjoint analysis of food choices corroborated the label use finding in showing that nutritional attributes and price dominated consumer choice behavior. Again, not surprising given the "in me/on me/around me" framework mentioned in chapter 1. The study concluded: "Consumer understanding of sustainability does not yet translate into driving food choice." In other words, although consumers claim they care about sustainability, they care far more about other product attributes.[23]

These examples and others suggest that consumers may not be very different from corporations in how they assess the value of sustainability. The corporate sustainability ROI calculations discussed in chapter 10 imply that for many companies, sustainability initiatives must first and foremost be valuable enough to justify their costs—passing the company's hurdle rate for investments. Informal discussions with corporate sustainability executives suggest that sustainability acts less as an intrinsically valuable attribute and more as a tiebreaker in business decisions for all but the most dedicated green companies and consumers.

"Eco-labels just don't necessarily have a lot of sway with … mainstream consumers. There's a ton of them, hundreds … [and] most of them, to be honest, are pretty much meaningless," commented Keith Sutter, senior product director for Johnson & Johnson.[24] Confusion, irrelevance, and the high cost of the rigorous measurements of environmental attributes needed for accurate and comprehensive green labeling make some labels dubious investments. These problems arise from a fundamental property of the kinds of information conveyed on sustainability labels and the peculiar economics of labeling.

THE STICKY TRUTH ABOUT LABELS

Somewhere in every large grocery store is a wall of yogurt: arrays of clean white pots of fermented milk with bright labels and alluring images of fruit, happy cows, or a creamy spoonful laced with fruity chunks. The labels often sport words like "organic," "no pesticides," "hormone free," and "no artificial colors," as well as brand names and slogans. The labels also present presumably factual data about nutrition, ingredients, and allergens. In an ideal world, these multiple elements of the label would help consumers make wise and informed purchases among the large variety of choices. In the real world, many elements of the label are simply meant to entice consumers to purchase that particular yogurt.

This tension between objective information and subjective enticement affects many environmental attributes (e.g., carbon emissions, water use, land use, toxins, and recycling). A 2014 Nielsen survey of 30,000 consumers across 60 countries found that 52 percent of respondents say their purchase decisions are partially dependent on packaging—they check the labeling first before buying to ensure the brand is committed to positive social and environmental impact.[25] Such survey responses may or may not be indicative; the mixed effects of labels on consumer purchasing behavior show that exactly *how* consumers use labeling may not be straightforward.

What a Label Conveys

The diverse text and graphics elements found on a yogurt label, whether intended to inform or entice, illustrate the four categories of information on product attributes that consumers might use to guide their purchase decisions.[26] These categories differ in the extent to which consumers can verify the label's veracity.

The first and simplest are *search attributes*,[27] such as the weight of the yogurt, the price of the yogurt, and the form of the packaging. Search attributes are obvious tangible properties that consumers can personally evaluate in the store without ever buying or using the product.

Experience attributes are claims that the consumer cannot verify until after the purchase. These include the stated flavor of the yogurt, the claimed creamy texture, and whether any added fruit is on the bottom or mixed in. The consumer might experience a disappointing discontinuity between a label's image of large plump red strawberries glistening with morning dew and a cup of yogurt containing a few meager grayish-pink sodden lumps. The experience can help foster or degrade the consumer's trust in the label's other claims.

Intrinsic credence attributes[28] include the ingredients of the yogurt, calories, and protein content that are inherent to the product but cannot be readily evaluated by the average consumer, even after buying and using a product. Only someone with specialized equipment or access to a laboratory can verify these attributes. They are called *credence attributes*[29] because the consumer must give credence to the label and trust that the maker's supply chain delivered on those hard-to-test claims. Intrinsic credence attributes related to the environment may include the presence of controversial ingredients like palm oil (in a packet of crunchy granola sprinkles) or pesticides in the yogurt.

The final category is *hidden credence attributes*, which include almost all the environmental impact claims associated with making the product and bringing it to market. While most are stated, some may be implied, such as an image of happy cows in a green pasture under blue skies with the unstated implication that competitors' cows may live in dark crowded barns reeking of urine and manure. Almost all aspects of environmental sustainability discussed in this book are examples of hidden credence attributes. These include GHG emissions, water use, suppliers' environmental records, sustainable agriculture, local sourcing, hormone-free cows, and deforestation, among others.

Hidden credence attributes are factors tied to the history or provenance of the product that no test of the product itself can reveal. These attributes can only be verified by someone with detailed and trustworthy historical records of the product's sourcing, processing, and movement in the supply chain, which may be very costly, difficult, or (in many cases) impossible to acquire. Moreover, the degree of consumers' trust in the label affects a company's incentives to invest in sustainability beyond easy-to-justify eco-efficiency initiatives.

Lemons Are Not Green: The Cursed Economics of Credence

Sustainability attributes, especially of the hidden credence variety, suffer from the same unfortunate economic dynamics as do the quality attributes of used cars. George Akerlof won a Nobel Prize in economics for showing how asymmetries in what consumers and sellers can know about a product (e.g., whether a used car is a defective "lemon" or of high quality) affect the evolution of markets for that product (e.g., sellers' propensity to offer good versus defective vehicles). Without trustworthy, item-specific information, prospective customers will only pay for "average" performance. But that price would overpay for lemons, making the market unattractive for lemon buyers, and underpay for high-quality cars, making the market unattractive to would-be sellers of high quality cars. Consumers' inability to estimate the quality of the products would ultimately induce sellers of high-quality products to either leave the market or reduce their quality levels. This erosion of the high-quality end of the supply decreases the average quality level, leading to further price erosion and a potential downward spiral. Carried to the extreme, this phenomenon may damage the entire market as both suppliers and consumers flee the market and its declining prices and quality levels.

In the context of sustainability, if consumers cannot be confident that a product has the claimed environmental quality (e.g., a low carbon footprint, sustainable agriculture, shipping via biofuel hybrid trucks, or packaging made from recycled material), they will be reluctant to prefer or pay more for products making such "green" claims, even if those consumers prize green products. On the other side of the market, if manufacturers cannot garner a premium or additional market share for creating greener products, *they* will be reluctant to invest in developing, procuring, and manufacturing them. Similarly, they will not invest in a rigorous LCA or other certifications that communicate the green credentials of products. That is, if consumers cannot spot the lemons (or non-green products), soon lemons and non-green products will prevail in the market.

To counter the Akerlof effect in the used car market, high-quality providers can offer warranties, allow product testing, rely on product reviews from trusted sources, or seek product certification from trusted third parties. In the case of environmental attributes, warranties and product testing cannot ensure the status of hidden credence attributes. Thus, to communicate environmental qualities without being subject to Akerlof's curse, companies need to use labels that are both trusted by consumers and readily distinguishable from less trustworthy labels.

LABELS THAT WORK

According to Stefan Seidel, head of the PUMA group's corporate sustainability, marketing is at an impasse with sustainability: "Our marketing colleagues have said, 'Look, we have some of these great things for more sustainable products, but we are not really able to communicate them in an efficient way to the consumer because there are so many mixed messages.'" Once a sustainable product or process has been developed, the challenge is to find labels that the company can affordably implement and that consumers will recognize, trust, and value.

A Simple Seal of Approval

"When you put a Rainforest Alliance logo on a box of tea, and people trust that this is grown with good agricultural practices, the feedback we receive from consumers is that the tea actually tastes better," said Pier Luigi Sigismondi, Unilever's chief supply chain officer.[30] A trusted third-party seal assures consumers that the product has been grown and harvested using environmentally and socially responsible processes. "We see it as a business interest, because at the end you get premium tea leaves," Sigismondi added. The company features its tea sustainability efforts in its marketing campaigns around the world. In the United Kingdom, this increased its PG Tips' market share by 1.8 points. The company saw similar gains in Australia and Italy, although a more muted campaign in France failed to boost sales.[31]

In the wake of these gains, other tea brands moved to earn Rainforest Alliance certification. As a result, the NGO estimated in 2011 that it would certify as much as 25 percent of the world's tea crops by 2015.[32] The Corporate Sustainability Initiative attributed the rapid growth of the Rainforest Alliance certification, in part, to its easily recognized label and simple binary messaging: A product is either certified or it is not.[33] The Rainforest Alliance ensures the trustworthiness of the label's brand by placing strict limits on the use its trademarked logos. Not only must a company's product attain certification, but companies must apply for approval of each specific use of the Rainforest Alliance frog seal.[34]

In Scandinavia, the Nordic Swan[35] emblem is well-recognized and respected by consumers, according to Keith Sutter, senior product director for the sustainability arm of Johnson & Johnson, who secured the Nordic Swan label for its Natusan line of baby skin care products. The Nordic Swan label requires more time and effort than  most certifications to achieve and maintain.[36] To be considered for the label, a sanitary product brand like Natusan must answer 53 questions and provide supporting documentation. The certification process also includes on-site inspections and escalating requirements over time. The label does not convey any numeric information. Instead, its presence indicates that a product meets and maintains the green standards set by Nordic Swan.

In 1992, the EPA introduced the "Energy Star" label for home appliances. It works by "identifying the top performers and steering consumers towards them," said Ann Bailey, director of Energy Star product labeling.[37] For each appliance category, the Energy Star program periodically reevaluates the prevailing range of energy efficiencies  on the market and resets the threshold such that less than 50 percent of the products in each category could qualify for the Energy Star logo at any given time.[38] Companies interested in having their products considered for a voluntary Energy Star label then submit appropriate materials to the EPA for evaluation. Since its introduction, Energy Star has expanded to cover more than 60 product categories including refrigerators, dishwashers, lamps, personal computers, printers, and furnaces. In 2012, the EPA claimed[39] that close to 80 percent of Americans knew about the two-decade-old label and three-quarters of US households had used it to guide the purchase of a home appliance.[40]

As with Rainforest Alliance and Nordic Swan seals, Energy Star is a simple binary label and does not distinguish gradations of performance. All three achieve relatively high visibility by being simple, trustworthy, and available on a broad range of products.

Numerical Labels

Compared to Tesco's black foot carbon label, with its single number (grams of CO_2e), the EPA's vehicle fuel economy label is fiendishly complex, with no less than seven numbers related to the carbon footprint of a car. Nevertheless, the label is successful for three key reasons. First, the government-mandated label is universal and has been well-entrenched since 1975.[41] Consumers can readily compare any vehicle with any other vehicle, unlike the case of Tesco, which labeled only a tiny fraction of the items it carried. Second, the label expresses environmental impact in salient terms of costs and savings for the buyer rather than an abstract number such as grams of CO_2 released into the atmosphere. Finally, the label is defined and managed by the government, rather than the automobile companies themselves, or unfamiliar third parties.

The fuel economy label has grown even more elaborate in recent years.[42] Pushed by a congressional mandate,[43] the EPA began requiring automakers to measure other pollutants such as nitrogen oxides, particulate matter, carbon monoxide, and formaldehyde.[44] The EPA audits those measurements and performs some of its own[45] to compute two numerical ratings: one for GHGs and one for smog (on a 1–10 scale).[46]

A walk through any US appliance store reveals the analog of the fuel economy label for home appliances. Unlike the EPA's binary Energy Star label, the Federal Trade Commission's bright yellow "EnergyGuide" label is mandatory. It provides consumers with both estimated annual dollar operating costs of that model and a graphical depiction of how that model's cost per year compares to the range of costs of competing products with similar capacity and features. EnergyGuide labels are found on many types of appliances such as refrigerators, air conditioners, washing machines, dryers, hot water heaters, and furnaces.[47] Collectively, the categories of appliances covered by the EnergyGuide label account for over 60 percent of residential energy consumption, and 13 percent of total US energy consumption.[48,49]

Trustworthy Trust-Marks

Besides recognition, trust plays a major role in consumers' evaluation of eco-labels during their purchase decisions and companies' subsequent evaluation of investing in eco-labels initiatives. To be trustworthy, Rainforest Alliance and Nordic Swan use rigorous processes including on-site inspections.

The Energy Star and EnergyGuide programs are successful because they are backed by government agencies, which are generally perceived as unbiased. In that regard, corporate lobbying of the government about labeling can detract from this trust, as was the case with the US Department of Agriculture's (USDA) organic labeling guidelines. Miles McEvoy, deputy administrator of the USDA National Organic Program admits, "As the success of organic has expanded, there's been larger food companies that have gotten involved and there's been a fair amount of controversy about what is and what is not organic." The legislation regulating organic certification, along with a series of votes by the National Organic Standards Board,[50] allowed companies to use synthetic ingredients in USDA-certified organic products.[51] In response, US Senator Patrick Leahy of Vermont said that trend could "unravel everything we've done. If we don't protect the brand, the organic label, the program is finished," Leahy added, "It could disappear overnight."[52] If consumers do not trust the "organic" label enough to pay a sufficient premium for it, they will start the Akerlof lemon effect rolling.

Label Characteristics

The preceding examples suggest that effective labels must meet at least five basic criteria, as follows:

- Trustworthy: Consumers have to believe that the information is correct
- Meaningful: Clearly conveys some attribute of the product that consumers value and wish to know
- Simple and understandable: Consumers have to recognize and understand it (note that it can be based on a complex set of criteria and calculations, but the label itself has to be straightforward)
- Sufficiently broad: Widespread coverage so that consumers can easily find and compare products with that label
- Affordable: Relatively easy to measure, obtain, verify, and update continuously.

The examples of the attempts by Tesco and Walmart to create environmental footprint labels demonstrate that even the world's largest retailers failed based on affordability. A complete product LCA leading to a legitimate carbon label is too difficult and costly to develop. The Rainforest Alliance and Nordic Swan labels work because they use predefined questionnaires, rather than open-ended analysis of the entire supply chain.

To Claim or Not to Claim

For some credence attributes—both hidden and intrinsic—governments impose mandatory measurement, disclosure, and labeling requirements. Thus, the US government mandates, for example, fuel efficiency and emission labels on cars, and nutrition information on food products. Still, the vast majority of eco-labels (whether Type I or Type II) are voluntary.

In 2012, Apple Inc. decided to remove all of its products from the Electronic Product Environmental Assessment Tool (EPEAT), which is regarded as the main standard for personal computers[53] and is managed by the EPA's Green Electronics Council.[54] A compilation of approved "green" electronics, EPEAT evaluates and reports information about electronic products that use environmentally sustainable materials and processes."[55] The tool assesses computers on 28 environmental performance criteria and awards Bronze, Silver, or Gold designations if the product meets a sufficient number of criteria.[56] Apple felt that EPEAT's measures were outdated and did not include important criteria such as removal of toxic materials.[57] Thus, even though Apple had 40 Gold-level certified products listed,[58] the company removed all of them from the listings, claiming that their products far surpassed EPEAT's standards.

For exceptionally green brands such as Seventh Generation, the maker of sustainable cleaning products, labeling presents two challenges. The first is that any certification might lead consumers to believe that the company does that and no more, while in reality the company goes much further. "If two products are on a shelf and one meets the standard and one greatly exceeds it, the consumer doesn't know," said Martin Wolf, Seventh Generation's director of product sustainability and authenticity.[59] A second challenge is the overwhelming variety of available eco-labels and the limited availability of space on a product's packaging. "You don't want [the package] to look like NASCAR with all these logos on it," said Dave Rapaport, former senior director of corporate consciousness for Seventh Generation.[60] Limiting declarations, labels, and logos helps reduce clutter. Thus, the company limits the use of eco-labels on its packaging despite the fact that it surpasses the certification thresholds for many of them, ranging from organic to bio-based to using sustainable palm oil.

One of the conclusions from the studies of organic wine[61] and CFL bulb labels[62] is that taking sustainable actions, getting certification, and labeling are three separate steps that can be evaluated using three separate (and sequential) cost-benefit analyses. Sustainability initiatives by themselves may be justified based on cost efficiencies, some risk reductions, or human resources benefits (see chapter 10). Certification can be communicated in sustainability reports and on the company website to further reduce the risks of NGO attacks or onerous regulatory action. The final step of applying an eco-label to the products themselves might only provide added value if the label sufficiently enhances the product's desirability to green consumers while not having significant negative connotations for mainstream consumers.

CUSTOMER EDUCATION: THE MORE YOU KNOW ...

The Tesco example shows that sustainability can be a complex story. Sometimes the available space on a product's label is simply too small or too precious to communicate all that a company would wish to promote. Environmental issues are front and center for companies such as Stonyfield Farm, Patagonia, and Seventh Generation. These companies attract employees who believe in sustainability as a cause, and customers who are willing to pay for it. The companies have an extensive and personal story to tell—and that story cannot be summarized in a few words on a product label or with a simple graphic. These companies are committed to being transparent about their environmental progress across the supply chain, mistakes and all. That implies communicating a wealth of information to those consumers who value this degree and depth of information.

Transparency: What You See Is What You Get
"Customers want to hear more about transparency. They want to hear about provenance and where the food is from," said McDonald's Chief Executive Officer Don Thompson during an earnings call in October 2013.[63] Beginning in 2012, news reports highlighted an ingredient used in the processed meat industry called "mechanically separated meat" by the industry but referred to as "pink slime" by detractors. When a consumer asked McDonald's if they used this in McNuggets,[64] the company did more than just

say "no": it made a video detailing the McNugget manufacturing process inside one supplier's (Cargill) facilities. "Our latest videos aim to combat the misinformation and tell the truth about this iconic product—that Chicken McNuggets are made from chicken breast, a few seasonings, along with a natural proportion [of] skin, used both for flavor and as a binder," said Gema Rayo, McDonald's spokeswoman.

Other companies have voluntarily started to disclose additional information about the ingredients in their products. Clorox, for example, uses its website to summarize the kinds of ingredients in its "Green Works" line of cleaners. In some cases, it lists the actual ingredient, such as ethanol or alkyl polyglucoside. In others, it lists only the type of ingredient, such as "preservative," or "fragrance with essential oils."[65] Clorox did not apply the same level of disclosure to its mainstream cleaners. For example, in late 2013, the web page for Clorox Clean-Up Cleaner + Bleach included an "Ingredients & Safety" section, but it focused entirely on how to safely use the product and did not disclose the product's ingredients.[66]

The Story of Your Item

Whereas McDonald's and Clorox provide general information and stories about the types of ingredients and manufacturing processes used, some companies go beyond generic information to provide a very specific breakdown. In 2008, berry producer Driscoll's introduced a new program, "Follow Us to the Farm," letting consumers trace berries back to the specific farm and date of harvest for their berries. Each clamshell container of Driscoll's berries has a 16-digit code on the label that curious consumers can enter at the company's website. "Food safety is an utmost priority in our berry-growing operations, and clamshell-level traceability is a natural extension to our existing initiatives to ensure the integrity, consistency and quality of our products and services," said Miles Reiter, Driscoll's chairman and CEO.[67]

Other companies use QR codes—square patterns of dots that smartphones can scan— that take the consumer directly to the website encoded by the tag pattern. In Tesco's Lotus hypermarkets in Thailand, the retailer has put QR code tags on 80 percent of pre-packed fruit, vegetables, and meat. "They allow customers to see exactly where their food has come from—which farm and which batch—as well as nutritional information and recipe ideas to help customers to balance their diet; all with a quick scan from a smartphone," said Pornpen Nartpiriyarat, head of trading law and technical at Tesco Lotus.[68] Tesco's system was facilitated by Thai government standards that require traceability of animal and agricultural products.[69]

Companies also use these traceability labels to create a social connection between consumers and farmers[70] or fishermen.[71] NGOs use this same technology; Buycott.com offers an app that scans a product's label and informs consumers of the company's ownership and any boycott campaigns that the consumer can then pledge to join right from the app.[72]

Cold-Water Detergents Get the Cold Shoulder

About three-quarters of the energy consumption and GHG emissions from washing a load of laundry arise when the consumer heats the water.[73] For that reason, the biggest single contributor to P&G's corporate GHG emissions footprint is the energy used during machine washing.[74] To reduce that impact, P&G developed Tide Coldwater in 2005 and set a 2020 goal to have 70 percent of laundry loads done in relatively cold water.[75] Other manufacturers joined the fray; for example, Henkel released Purex ColdWater Ultraconcentrated.[76]

Consumers, however, have not been easily convinced. Tide Coldwater appeared on store shelves in 2005, but six years later the share of laundry done in hot water remained unchanged; Tide Coldwater sales were stagnant, despite P&G being the market leader.[77] Although Tide Coldwater was by far the best-selling cold-water detergent and accounted for $210 million in sales in the United States and Canada as of 2011, regular Tide outsold its cold-water cousin almost 8:1.[78] In fact, thermal energy is one of three secrets to cleaning clothes, along with mechanical energy and chemicals. To use less thermal energy, manufacturers turned to new chemicals and enzymes. But most consumers—even the environmentally

conscious Germans—were not convinced. "When you ask consumers, they currently don't see the immediate benefit of saving
energy," said Thomas Müeller-Kirschbaum, a senior vice president for research and development at Henkel, the German company that markets cold-water formulas under the Persil and Purex
brands.[79]

To increase adoption, P&G and others launched concerted consumer education efforts. These included a "30°C" (30°C = 86°F)
icon on laundry detergent packages (the average wash temperature
in Europe is 41°C, or 106°F[80]), an industry-led "I prefer 30°C" consumer education campaign, and a partnership
with appliance makers to include instructions on the benefits of cold water washing
with new washing machines.[81] Retailers and
garment manufacturers also participated.
Walmart, for example, has changed nearly
three-quarters of the labels on the clothing it

carries to say "machine wash cold" rather than "warm" or "hot."[82]
And Chip Bergh, CEO of Levi Strauss & Co., also encouraged
consumers to wash their jeans less frequently—he even suggested
never washing them; just occasionally freezing them to kill any
germs. (This may not be true; freezing jeans may put germs in a
dormant state, but it does not kill them.[83]) Berg made this statement during a May 2014 *Fortune* conference, while wearing the
company's iconic 501 jeans that, he claimed, were "a year old and
have never seen a washing machine."[84] The effort may be slowly
changing consumer behavior. Overall, between 2010 and 2014,
machine loads washed in cold water increased from 38 percent to
53 percent globally (led by Europe), according to P&G.[85]

P&G may have an easier time selling the cold-water concept as
an eco-efficiency initiative to financially minded institutional customers, such as hotels. The company launched its "Tide Professional Coldwater Laundry System" with a suite of four products: a
near-neutral pH detergent, a fabric softener, a bleach, and a white-
ness enhancer. The company claims that for the average 150-room
hotel, the product can reduce water use by 40 percent, energy use
by 75 percent, and linen replacement by 15 percent. The laundry

system won a 2015 Silver Edison Green Award, which recognizes organizations' efforts to reduce their carbon footprint and create "green collar" jobs.[86]

Cooler Shower Message

When Boots, a UK-based pharmacy chain, assessed the life cycle impacts of its shampoo, it found that 93 percent of the total impact took place during the consumer use phase, from the energy used to heat water.[87] New packaging released in 2007 included a Carbon Trust label and said, "You can help too. Using cooler water to wash your hair cuts CO_2 emissions, reduces your energy bills, and is actually better for your hair."[88]

Despite its best efforts, Boots witnessed little consumer recognition of the Carbon Trust label, and the pharmacy chain was unable to gauge whether its shampoo ads were causing any behavioral change. Only 28 percent of its customers seemed to have understood that the Carbon Trust label was linked to climate change. Moreover, almost half of the people surveyed confused it with Fair Trade, an entirely different label.[89]

Other corporate efforts to change consumers' behavior include Unilever's "Project Sunlight," which solicits and displays crowd-sourced ideas on a website.[90] These ideas include taking shorter showers (the "two songs" challenge), suggestions on recycling, air-drying hair, and so forth. Similarly, Levi's put a tag on its jeans, encouraging consumers to machine wash cold, line dry when possible, and donate when done with them.

CORPORATE SUSTAINABILITY REPORTS

BASF's 2014 annual report[91] illustrates another major category of sustainability communications—the annual reporting of environmental and social indicators of the company's performance to stakeholders. The principle audiences (and motivations) for this reporting include investors (to assuage environmental risk concerns and entice socially responsible investors), NGOs (to avoid attacks), and governments (to forestall heavy regulation). Although some companies publish separate "environmental sustainability"

or "corporate social responsibility" reports, BASF integrates its
financial, environmental, and social responsibility reporting into
one document. The company combines the two because they have
the same audience, allowing the company to present "how sustainability contributes to BASF's long-term success and how we as a
company create value for our employees, shareholders, business
partners, neighbors, and the public."[92]

Sustainability by the Numbers

Near the beginning of its annual report,[93] BASF presents a series
of "at a glance" numerical tables of various financial, social, and
environment performance indicators (including percentage change
from the previous year). The data includes 15 environmental sustainability metrics. Published consumption metrics include energy
usage, energy efficiency, total water consumption, and drinking water consumption. The company reports its total emissions
of GHGs, other air pollutants, nitrogen in water, heavy metals
in water, and organic substances in water as separate line items.
Other metrics cover emissions audits, spills, waste, and spending
on environmental protection.

The bulk of BASF's 276-page report intermingles discussions of
sustainability issues into presentations of the company's activities,
finances, and management issues. The report presents BASF's progress on 20 high-level goals for 2020, of which nine relate to sustainability. The report also delves into BASF's materiality analysis
of the environmental impacts important to the company and its
stakeholders (see chapter 3). Finally, the report cites BASF's sustainability accolades for the year, such as its 14th consecutive inclusion in Dow Jones Sustainability World Enlarged Index, which lists
the top 10 percent of companies in terms of their sustainability
credentials among the 2,500 largest companies in the S&P Global
Broad Market Index.

As mentioned in chapter 8, much of BASF's report focuses on the
company's efforts to produce products that improve the sustainability of its customers and *their* products. More generally, BASF's
report describes the "thorough analysis we conducted of our
products in more than 60,000 applications" using the Sustainable

Solution Steering method[94] to understand which products impact sustainability.

Going Public

As of 2015, only a few countries mandated sustainability reporting. In France, for example, Article 225 of the Grenelle II Act[95] required French companies with 500 employees or more to include third-party verified environmental, social, and governance indicators in their annual reports.[96] Although not actively enforced, the Grenelle II Act can be used as a basis for legal action by stakeholders. Other countries with similar policies include Denmark, South Africa, and China.[97] In most countries, unlike financial reporting by public companies, the reporting of sustainability efforts and performance by public companies is voluntary.

BASF prides itself on disclosure, citing its perfect 100 score on the Carbon Disclosure Leadership Index (CDLI) in its annual report. Moreover, BASF's annual report is just a gateway to further detailed reporting on sustainability issues in a section of the company's website dedicated to sustainability.[98] Publicly stated goals both inform outside stakeholders of internal commitments and foster external pressure on the company to meet those goals.

At UPS, such pressure to accomplish publicly announced goals is welcome, according to Scott Wicker of UPS, the vice president of global plant engineering and sustainability. UPS is proudly dominated by an engineering culture—metrics are the company's bread and butter. Along with other early adopters, the global logistics company started disclosing its environmental progress in 2003. According to Lynnette McIntire, UPS' manager of sustainability communications, this was a natural step. "We recognized that sustainability reporting was important and realized we could do this, because, in fact, we were already measuring all of these things," she said.[99]

Standardized Sustainability Reporting

Comparing the sustainability reports of any two companies highlights a current limitation of those reports and the challenge facing the stakeholders who read them. Whereas financial reports to investors have well-codified, regulator-approved international accounting standards for the structure of the report and the meanings of individual items in these reports, sustainability reporting is not standardized. In fact, a number of competing third parties offer different sustainability reporting frameworks.

A 2013 survey of sustainability executives found that the top three reporting frameworks are CDP (formerly known as the Carbon Disclosure Project), GRI (Global Reporting Initiative), and DJSI (Dow Jones Sustainability Indices).[100] CDP, for instance, claimed to have 5,000 companies reporting under its framework in 2014; it focused its efforts at that point on increasing reporting by suppliers. The GRI standards were being used by 80 percent of Fortune Global 250 firms, according to a 2011 survey performed by the audit, tax, and advisory services firm KPMG.[101] BASF and many other companies report under more than one framework, often in response to customer mandates to use a particular framework. To reduce duplication of efforts associated with reporting under the two different frameworks, the CDP and GRI have published a guide that aligns the two,[102] and DJSI announced that it will use the CDP's questions for the climate change portion of its survey.

TRUTH OR CONSEQUENCES (SOMETIMES BOTH)

"The truth is rarely pure and never simple," wrote Oscar Wilde,[103] a statement that applies doubly to both corporate claims of sustainability and activists' claims of corporate environmental malfeasance. The term "greenwashing" refers to misleading promotion of the environmental performance of a product or a company through selective or deceptive claims or messages. A quick online search of the term "greenwashing" uncovers a steady stream of journalists, activists, NGOs, and bloggers attacking companies for misrepresenting or overstating the sustainability of their products or corporate activities. Examples include articles calling out Sunlight's Green Clean laundry soap (promises "plant-based cleaning ingredients," in spite of the fact that the cleaning ingredients are 38 percent petrochemicals), Upper Canada's Eco Collection bath mitt (which uses harsh chemical processing to soften the mitt's bamboo fibers), and Eco Solutions' Organic Melt ice remover (the misleading label hides the fact that it is 97 percent mineral rock salt).[104] "It's like a tsunami of greenwash really," said Adria Vasil, a columnist and author of the *Ecoholic* book series.[105] The prevalence of greenwashing, or at least claims of greenwashing, may be why 88 percent of consumers believe companies share positive information about their corporate social responsibility efforts but withhold negative information.[106]

NGOs and journalists attack companies for greenwashing not only when the company makes false claims (which may actually result in lawsuits and fines over misleading advertisements). Even if the claims are true but the company falls short on other dimensions of sustainability, NGOs may claim that the company greenwashes by failing to be unbiased and transparent about both the good and the bad aspects of the company's actions. One company might tout its carbon footprint reductions but pollute local streams and rivers with toxic waste. Another might claim an eco-label certification that offers only weak protections of forests and habitat. A third might declare the environmental benefits of one ingredient in the product while ignoring the environmental impacts of other ingredients. Note that just being lax about the environment does not amount to greenwashing. Rather, putting a green spin on weak environmental performance is the essence of greenwashing.[107]

Outing the "Sinners"

In 2007, bottled water manufacturer Fiji Water announced plans to become "carbon negative" by offsetting 120 percent of its carbon footprint.[108] The following year, the company reported that it planted 250 acres of rainforest as a carbon offset under the guidance of Conservation International.[109] Although the company's press release disclosed that it would not achieve a 120 percent offset until the planted trees had grown for 30 years,[110] this detailed explanation of the long-term nature of the offset was not on the brand's labels. Fiji stated that the environmental nonprofit Conservation International guaranteed the quality of its carbon credits and that the consulting firm ICF International verifies its emissions data every year.[111] Nonetheless, environmentalists attacked Fiji's use of "forward credits," whereby the company claimed credits for future carbon offsets. Fiji Water was forced to recant its environmental claims in 2010, as a result of a California class action lawsuit regarding its claim to be "carbon negative."

In 2011, Fiji Water was again attacked for misleading labels. In the California First District Court of Appeal in San Francisco, Ayana Hill claimed that the image of a small green leaf on the Fiji bottle led her to believe that it was a third-party certification. She argued that this symbol made it seem that Fiji was claiming it was environmentally superior to its competitors, when in fact the symbol was meaningless.[112] As it did with the "carbon negative" label lawsuit mentioned earlier, Fiji settled the suit quietly and removed the leaf from the bottle.

SC Johnson & Son Inc. also settled two lawsuits claiming that the company's internally created and managed "Greenlist" logo misled consumers into believing that the logo had been issued by a trustworthy third party.[113] The Greenlist, which SC Johnson created in 2001, rated chemicals on a 0 to 3 scale, with 3 being best for the environment. In 2008, SC Johnson added a Greenlist logo to its Windex glass cleaner.[114] Within months, the first of two civil suits against the company was filed. One plaintiff noted that he and other customers paid a 50 percent premium for Greenlist-labeled Windex over similar products that didn't "misrepresent" themselves.[115] Note that the lawsuit did not attack the environmental qualities of the Greenlist ingredients themselves but instead focused on the perceived misrepresentation that Greenlist was an independent evaluator of the environmental claims. As a part of the resulting settlements, SC Johnson paid an undisclosed amount to the plaintiffs and removed the logo from its products, although the company still uses the list in promotional materials.[116]

After PepsiCo Inc. acquired the Naked brand of juices,[117] the company continued to advertise it as "all natural." Furthermore, it marketed it as "the freshest, purest stuff in the world." In 2011, plaintiffs filed a class action suit against the company, claiming that the drinks contained zinc oxide, ascorbic acid, and calcium pantothenate, in addition to genetically modified (GMO) ingredients (at odds with the "all natural" language of the labels). In July 2013,

PepsiCo agreed to settle the case, paying $9 million and ceasing to label the juices as "all natural."[118]

The Impossible Quest

To help prevent misrepresentation of environmental claims, the US Federal Trade Commission (FTC) released the "Green Guides" in 1992 and an update in 2012.[119] The Green Guides are designed to "help marketers avoid making environmental marketing claims that are unfair or deceptive."[120] Despite the FTC's best efforts to clarify marketing and label claims, the Green Guides may have actually worsened the complexity and confusion in defining these claims.

The Green Guides use hypothetical examples of products and potentially misleading labels to illustrate acceptable and unacceptable practices. In one sample scenario, they describe a window cleaner labeled as "Environment Approved" bestowed by a credible third-party organization based on passing 35 environmental indicators defined by that organization. But because the label suggests that the product is categorically better for the environment without specific qualification, it may be misleading to consumers. Instead, the FTC argued that a label must include moderating language such as "Virtually all products impact the environment. For details on which attributes we evaluated, go to [a website that discusses this product]."[121] Of course, such detail may doom any label, making it too long and complex.

After examining a draft of the FTC's Green Guides in 2010, the EPA pointed out that under this definition, the EPA's own label "Design for the Environment" would be misleading to consumers and subject to attack.[122] With two federal agencies at odds over what constitutes misleading claims, the boundary between acceptable and unacceptable labeling remains unclear, and so communicating environmental information is fraught with ambiguities and risks.

Green Groups: Red in Tooth and Claw

Although environmental NGOs want to project the image that they are fighting for the good of humanity, they also compete with each other for media attention, donor dollars, volunteers, and market share in the certification space. Both Rainforest Alliance and Fair Trade offer certifications for commodities such as tea, coffee, and bananas. Although both claim to address the social and environmental challenges facing farmers and farming, these two compete for companies seeking eco-label certification. The NGOs also disagree on some specifics of their respective certifications. The fair trade movement attacks Rainforest Alliance for not mandating fair prices to producers and higher wages for workers.[123] For its part, Rainforest Alliance cites studies showing that farms following its protocols enjoy higher agricultural yields that simultaneously reduce land-use impacts and increase the revenues and profitability of small-holder farms.[124]

When EDF partnered with Walmart (see chapter 10), other NGOs attacked it. This may illustrate legitimate disagreements over the ethics and effectiveness of different NGO strategies—EDF's collaborative strategy with Walmart aimed at effecting change from the inside versus Greenpeace's attack-from-the-outside strategy aimed at forcing a company to change. But these disagreements might also be environmental theater—scoring points with green supporters by appearing to be "greener" or more effective in their green efforts than the other NGOs. With so many different dimensions of sustainability (such as carbon, water, toxins, biodiversity, and waste), almost any company and even any NGO can be attacked for perceived shortcomings on some dimensions. The complexity of modern products and global supply chains—along with the incentives for activists, NGOs and journalists—makes it almost inevitable that someone will claim to find a problem somewhere along the supply chain, regardless of all efforts by the brand holder.

Terrorized by TerraChoice

In 2010, TerraChoice, an environmental consulting and marketing firm, released the third edition of a widely distributed and commonly cited report titled, "The Sins of Greenwashing," published in both English and French.[125] The firm looked for instances of greenwashing by documenting 12,000 claims on 5,300 products and evaluating each claim against seven criteria of environmental marketing, as defined by TerraChoice. If the claim failed one of the criteria, it was then categorized as one of seven "sins," such as "Sin of No Proof" or "Sin of Irrelevance."[126] The unsurprising result was TerraChoice found that 95 percent of products failed the evaluation and were guilty of greenwashing based on its methodology.[127]

However, in TerraChoice's race to convict companies of greenwashing, TerraChoice became guilty of many of the same "sins." TerraChoice offered no proofs of the companies' wrongdoing ("sin of no proof"); they derided deceptive claims ("fibbing") even though they are against the law anyway ("sin of irrelevance"); the report classified products as "sinners" without more information or identification ("sin of vagueness"); and so forth. Furthermore, all TerraChoice claims in the report were based on the opinions of TerraChoice's own researchers, rather than on unbiased outside data. These flaws and others were pointed out in a commentary by Joel Makower of GreenBiz, an environmental reporting website.[128] He noted that TerraChoice only provided unverified, subjective measures of how to classify products guilty of greenwashing. Corporations sometimes exaggerate their environmental sustainability credentials, but environmental organizations also sometimes exaggerate their cries of environmental malfeasance and greenwashing. "You are going to be accused of greenwashing whether you do or not," said Kathrin Winkler, senior vice president, corporate sustainability and chief sustainability officer at EMC.[129]

Blackwash

In early 2015, a viral video swept the Internet. "Kill the K-Cup" was an apocalyptic two-and-a-half-minute film depicting Keurig's K-Cup coffee pods raining down and destroying the Earth.[130] The video spawned a "KillTheKCup" hashtag on Twitter and led to copycat videos of people throwing their Keurig machines out of windows or bashing them with baseball bats.[131] The video relied on evocative statistical facts such as that the annual production of nine billion discarded K-cups would encircle the world 10.5 times. Yet this statistic relied on the innumeracy of the viewer, who may not realize that the Earth is so large that nine billion K-cups is only a scant one K-cup per 14 acres on Earth.

An article in *Mother Jones* derided K-cup users for not simply making a plain old pot of coffee,[132] not realizing that the standard drip coffee maker is actually environmentally worse than the K-cup.[133] Drip coffee makers require more energy and water per cup because they are often left on for hours to keep the coffee warm, and, typically, 10 to 15 percent of the pot is thrown out. Even worse, a drip coffee maker is less efficient at extracting the flavor of the coffee than the K-Cup and thus needs more coffee grounds per cup. When considering the full life cycle of coffee growing and coffee making, the invisible supply chain before the coffee gets to the consumer matters more than the visible pile of K-cups in the trash. In requiring more coffee grounds per cup, drip coffee makers have a higher impact on the sensitive ecosystems where coffee is grown (including deforestation for coffee plantations, water use, pesticide runoff, and carbon emissions from shipping coffee beans around the world).[134] Interestingly, an LCA found that instant coffee has the lowest carbon footprint because instant coffee factories extract flavor very efficiently, dried coffee crystals are lighter to ship than beans, and instant has the cup-by-cup convenience that avoids the waste of leftover old coffee in the pot.[135]

The attacks on K-cups could be termed "blackwash"—the flipside of greenwash—attacking companies who are actually selling products with reduced environmental impact, or attacking them for small and insignificant fractions of the impact of their products and their operations. This was also the complaint of José Lopez, who was responsible for Nestlé's manufacturing at the time of the Greenpeace attacks on KitKat. As mentioned in chapter 1, his comment was, "You would have to 'look through a microscope' to find the palm oil in the snack."[136]

Ironically, "misinformation campaigns by both corporations and environmental groups threaten to undermine efforts to conserve biodiversity and reduce environmental degradation," according to a 2009 paper published in the journal *Biotropica*.[137,138] The competing and overhyped claims and counterclaims erode consumers' trust in both companies *and* NGOs, hampering consumers' ability to interpret all types of hidden credence claims about sustainability.

Such mistrust may lead to the Akerlof effect, which may reduce companies' incentives to curtail their environmental impacts.

The Dance of Walk and Talk

Diageo Plc's experience illustrates the difficult interplay between *claiming* and actually *doing*, or "walking the talk."[139] In 2008, the global spirit maker announced eight environmental goals for 2015, including a 50 percent reduction in carbon footprint and wastewater levels. But when the deadline arrived the company had reached only a 33.3 percent reduction in carbon emissions and a 45.3 percent reduction in wastewater levels, and missed targets on five other goals. Friends of the Earth Scotland accused the company of failing "miserably." Diageo was further criticized for using corporate jargon when it said that these had been "stretch goals" and that sustainability was a "journey."

Even so, the company *did* reduce its environmental impact, despite falling short of its ambitious goals. "We set targets with a view to making a real contribution as to how the business performs not just now but where it needs to be for the world of tomorrow," said David Croft, global sustainability director at Diageo. If Diageo had set goals of a 25 percent reduction in carbon and wastewater levels, it would have been lauded for exceeding them.

This kind of criticism by environmental groups, journalists, and pundits makes companies more conservative in defining sustainability goals. At HP, Shelley Zimmer, who is responsible for social and environmental responsibility policy across all HP product groups, said, "We still say a lot less than what we are capable of. There's always the concern about greenwashing and not wanting to over-promise."[140]

Ultimately, to avoid being accused of greenwashing, a company's activities must place bounds on its communications. When Walmart embarked on its major sustainability push, CEO H. Lee Scott Jr. said, "It wasn't a matter of telling our story better. We had to create a better story."[141]

10

Managing Sustainability

When Michael Marks opened his first stall in a Leeds bazaar in 1884, his successful slogan was: "Don't ask the price, it's a penny."[1] His real success, however, came after he partnered with Tom Spencer in 1894. Marks and Spencer (M&S) grew rapidly thanks to continued retailing innovations[2] such as displaying stock on trays instead of behind the counter, buying directly from suppliers, emphasizing quality, and selling British goods under the St Michael brand (honoring Michael Marks).

Unfortunately, 110 years later, that illustrious history could not prevent a 73 percent fall in its stock price and an unwelcome buyout offer from rival retailer Philip Green. Rather than sell the company, the board installed Sir Stuart Rose as M&S's new CEO.[3] One of Rose's main strategies for reversing the company's fortunes was to align it with the growing environmental movement, turning it into a sustainability leader. In the summer of 2006, he took his top 100 executives to see former US Vice President Al Gore's movie, *An Inconvenient Truth*.[4] According to Rose, the executives' comments were, in a nutshell, "That was fantastic! What can we do?"

For M&S, that was just the start of a journey involving more than 100 different initiatives designed to whittle away at the retailer's many environmental impacts. Like many other business initiatives, sustainability projects face myriad "change management" challenges. Such projects involve coordination among internal stakeholders, balancing competing goals, justifying funding, and influencing the corporate culture. Furthermore, many environmental projects involve external supply chain elements, which only add to the challenge. As with any corporate initiative, a significant piece of the puzzle is in maintaining the momentum while simultaneously coping with internal and external changes.

AN ORGANIZATION'S PATH TO SUSTAINABILITY

The sixth century BC Chinese philosopher Lao-Tzu is quoted as having said: "A journey of a thousand miles begins with a single step."[5] Sustainability endeavors, like other efforts that target quality, innovation, diversity, or any other corporate goal, are journeys. For organizations undertaking this journey, that means making decisions regarding the destination, navigation, and actions along the way. Yet the motivation to begin the journey (see chapter 1), its origin, and the direction of that first step (chapters 4 through 8) may be markedly different for different companies even if they share similar end goals. The impetus for a company's sustainability efforts could be anything from a CEO's conviction, to a desire to reposition the organization, to a viral video attacking the company, to a customer's new mandate or the success of green competitors.

Green from the Top

When Doug Conant took the helm as Campbell Soup Company's new CEO and president in 2001, his first objective was to transform the company from a poor performer to a strong competitor and then to a leading enterprise.[6] To start out, Conant restructured the $8 billion company through both voluntary and involuntary departures of 300 out of its top 350 corporate leaders.[7] Initially, the turmoil spooked investors and the stock slumped from $33.56 at the start of Conant's tenure to a low of $20.40 by May 2003.[8] However, as the new management structure took hold and performance improved, the stock rose to $41.88 by 2007. Nonetheless, Conant was not yet satisfied with his turnaround legacy at the 145-year-old company.

Like Sir Stuart Rose of M&S, Conant decided that his next major transformation of the company would focus on converting sustainability from the internal musings of a few employees into a full-fledged corporate program that would boost morale and employee engagement.[9] He began with a major internal assessment of environmental impacts and with recruiting the right person to lead the charge. That person was Dave Stangis, who in 2008 became Campbell's first vice president of corporate social responsibility.[10] Starting off big and bold, the company committed to reduce the water and GHG footprints of its entire product portfolio by 50 percent by 2020, relative to a 2008 baseline.

With support from the board and the CEO, Stangis created the Sustainability Leadership Team, comprising senior executives in charge of functional areas such as supply chain, procurement, and agriculture.[11] The team created the "Sustainability 2020 Plan" and drove savings across the company. Dozens of initiatives were undertaken across the supply chain in areas such as agricultural process improvements, efficiency in factory operations, renewable energy, waste reduction, recycling, sustainable packaging, and logistics improvements. Between 2008 and 2015, these efforts collectively reduced GHG emissions by 23 percent and water usage per ton of food by 24 percent.[12] The various initiatives also saved the company more than $43 million across its manufacturing network.[13]

The key for Campbell's implementation of so many multifaceted initiatives was Conant's ongoing support during a time of change for the company. "In today's environment, with people getting pushed and pulled in so many different directions, if you really want to get traction with a CSR or sustainability effort, you have to lead from in front. The CEO has to make it a priority," Conant said.[14]

The importance of senior executive support for any corporate project has been echoed across many companies. EMC's Kathrin Winkler, agrees: "Disruptive change requires the CEO's active leadership."[15] She argues that without the support of EMC executives, sustainability initiatives would not have been embraced as fully as they were by business operations. Nevertheless, as important as top management support can be to large-scale change, many organizations begin their sustainability journey from the bottom up—at times in spite of the opposition or ambivalence of top executives. In fact, a 2010 *Economist* survey found that only 54 percent of sustainability efforts came from the top.[16]

Green Grassroots Efforts

In 2007, a group of about 40 environmentally conscious employees at online auction giant eBay shared pizza in the cafeteria at the company's San Jose headquarters and decided to start a "Green Team."[17] Their efforts went mostly unnoticed by senior management as the team pushed isolated initiatives such as installing recycling bins, solar arrays, certifying buildings through LEED (Leadership in Energy and Environment Design), and encouraging greener commuting choices. The Green Team operated without support from then-CEO Meg Whitman. According to Lori Duvall, eBay's global director of green, environmental initiatives were "just not [Whitman's] thing"[18]—a stance exemplified by Whitman's opposition to excessive environmental regulations during her failed 2010 California gubernatorial campaign.[19]

After Whitman retired in 2008, the Green Team convinced the company's procurement department to install the largest commercial solar array in San Jose, the heart of Silicon Valley.[20] John Donahoe became eBay's CEO and brought with him the idea that eBay was inherently green, because it was "the world's largest recycler,"[21] enabling millions of used products to find new homes.

In September 2013, eBay unveiled a new data center in Utah that included the single largest non-utility fuel-cell installation in the United States.[22] The company estimated that the fuel cell power would reduce carbon emissions by half relative to emissions from grid power.[23] In addition to allowing the data center to operate independently from the electrical grid, the fuel cells further cemented eBay's reputation as a green leader among technology companies.[24]

"I think it's because those grassroots efforts showed both the desire and advocacy of employees for eBay to care about this," said Caitlin Bristol, global manager of green for eBay. "The scale at which it was growing made it imperative that the corporate and executive team have a group and a person, particularly on the operations side, that could help to strategically funnel that good energy in the same direction," she added.[25]

Change Agents: Gaining Support from the Top and Bottom

Mark Buckley joined Staples in 1990 as vice president of facilities and purchasing. In that role, he pushed for some of the company's earliest sustainability efforts, such as starting to recycle paper and cardboard. "We convinced the company to basically sell all the compactors that we had purchased," Buckley said. In their place, Staples installed bailers so that the stores could "bail cardboard and paper, backhaul them to the mill and turn it into a revenue stream."[26]

Eco-efficiency initiatives like that fit with Buckley's deep personal passions, but he wanted to go further and create company-wide change beyond his functional responsibility. The challenge, Buckley said, was to frame environmental initiatives in the business language that his superiors and coworkers would understand. When the company considered upgrading lighting fixtures to save on electricity in one high-cost region, Buckley exploited the opportunity and sought approval for bigger changes. Instead of a one-off project for only the sites with the highest ROI, Buckley pitched a system-wide upgrade with long-term, system-wide cost savings, a framework he knew would resonate with the CFO.

He used the same approach to propose initiatives in which environmental improvements aligned with existing executive sentiments. In all these early "wins," Buckley said he was careful to frame them as cost-saving projects with an added environmental benefit, instead of focusing primarily on the environmental gains. This common-sense eco-efficiency approach paid off when Staples became motivated to embrace sustainability on a larger scale.

In 2002, Staples was facing the sharp end of a two-year-long environmentalist campaign spearheaded by the NGOs Dogwood Alliance and ForestEthics. The NGOs had criticized Staples for selling paper sourced from old-growth forests. The campaign included 600 demonstrations, a public service announcement featuring the popular music group REM, and a "Staples destroys forests" banner flown over Fenway Park during a Boston Red Sox game only 20 miles from Staples' corporate headquarters.[27] The company felt it had to act. Staples executives made the obvious choice and offered

Buckley the newly created position of vice president of environmental affairs.[28]

Buckley knew he had to convince Staples' entire workforce that
sustainability was worth their time. "In reality, there are always
people within an organization that don't understand the connection between environmental stewardship and core business goals
and strategies," he explained.[29] "It is important to create a culture
where environmental stewardship is part of everyone's job every
day. ... My advice for a large organization is to focus on creating
a cultural evolution versus a paradigm shift." The latter, he said, is
like flipping a switch. "A cultural evolution will affect broader and
more long-lasting change, but it does take time."[30]

As a result of Buckley's efforts, environmental sustainability began to find its way into many of Staples' programs. These
ranged from requiring suppliers to use less-wasteful packaging, to
saving cardboard by building custom boxes for each "break-pack"
delivery (see chapter 8). One of Buckley's famous cultural successes
came when Mike Payette, the company's fleet equipment manager,
personally traveled around the United States in 2007 to install
fuel-saving speed limiters on Staples' fleet of delivery trucks (see
chapter 6).

Staples went from being attacked in 2002 to proudly proclaim-
ing its various sustainability achievements in 2014, including
76.5 million ink and toner cartridges recycled globally, 75 percent renewable energy used for US operations, and the launch of
Staples' own green product line, Sustainable Earth Brand, across
Europe and Australia in 2012.[31]

EVALUATING POTENTIAL SUSTAINABILITY INITIATIVES

To a veteran corporate manager, a sustainability program is just
one more project clamoring for a slice of the organization's limited
attention, capital, and human resources. "Employees are precious
resources, allocated sparingly to initiatives," said Keith Sutter,
senior product director for the sustainability arm of Johnson &
Johnson.[32]

Gauging the business value of environmental initiatives often begins with a materiality assessment of the company's supply chain from raw materials to end-of-life (see chapter 3) to identify extensive usage of natural resources, significant environmental risks, or opportunities to serve green customer segments.

Once the areas of biggest impact or opportunity are identified, companies can use any combination of the three main categories of business rationale introduced in chapter 1 to evaluate, justify, and prioritize environmental initiatives. Although each of these three types offers its own respective value to the business, all three help with the company's brand. In particular, *eco-risk mitigation* is aimed at protecting the brand while *eco-segmentation* can enhance the brand in the eyes of green customers. Even *eco-efficiency* helps by creating easy wins on impact reduction that can be reported to consumers, NGOs, and investors.

Eco-Efficiency

As mentioned in chapter 1, *eco-efficiency* initiatives are those justified by reducing costs such as fuel, energy, water, materials, and waste disposal, while at the same time contributing to environmental sustainability. Companies can evaluate these initiatives using standard cost-benefit metrics such as ROI or payback period. At Unilever, for example, a waste-reduction initiative might be proposed because it contributes to the company's sustainability goals, but it will be evaluated on the same financial standards and required hurdle rate as any other proposed Unilever program.[33] Some companies bias their financial ROI calculations through either a relaxed hurdle rate or the addition of an artificial "shadow cost" of environmental impacts (see the section titled "Environmental Impacts in Financial Terms").

The term *eco-efficiency* was introduced in 1992 by the World Business Council for Sustainable Development.[34] Because these types of changes bring bottom-line results, they are the "low-hanging fruit" of corporate sustainability efforts. Justifying sustainability in business terms beyond cost reductions, however, means quantifying other kinds of value to the business.

Eco-Risk Mitigation

Eco-risk mitigation initiatives are those activities that explicitly aim to reduce the likelihood and magnitude of business disruptions caused by environmental issues. Thus they can, in principle, be evaluated in the same way as insurance or other business risk-reduction initiatives. Sustainability initiatives can mitigate a variety of risks including: NGO attacks (leading to business disruptions); unfavorable media coverage (causing reduced sales); investor actions (triggering changes in the board and senior management); and disruptive government regulations (resulting in higher costs, direct business restrictions, and even plant closures).

BlackRock—an investment firm with $4.89 trillion in assets under management—views climate change as creating several risks that investors (and companies) can no longer ignore. In BlackRock's assessment, the first of these are increased *physical* risks, which are based on predictions of the effects of climate change on weather, productivity, and economic growth. These risks are especially salient for companies that depend on specific agricultural products, such as Starbucks with coffee or AB InBev with barley and hops. Next are *technological* risks, in which various green technologies or know-how might impact the economic or competitive landscape of industries such as power generation and transportation. Third are *regulatory* risks, which might affect the costs of doing business—or even the permissibility of the business—in countries that have strong environmental political movements or that are experiencing high impacts. Last are *social* risks, as manifested either by changing consumer preferences or by pressure group activities to avoid high-impact products or companies.

Unfortunately, unlike the case of insurable events such as natural disasters and accidents, risk managers have scant reliable actuarial data for quantifying the likelihood of NGO strikes, consumer preference changes, or adverse regulatory changes. Even the possibility of physical damage from environmental impacts involves speculative extrapolations. As a result, the few available insurance policies have limited scope and high costs.[35] Thus, companies are left to manage these risks themselves using "just-in-case" or scenario-based justifications for risk mitigation.

In the early 1990s, BASF learned of the potential toxicity dangers of using bromine-based flame retardants in its polyamide plastic line. If incinerated, the material could produce highly carcinogenic dioxins in the smoke. The company took decisive action. "Less than six months after receiving an initial heads-up from management, the product was completely pulled from the market," said Carles Navarro, president of BASF Canada.[36]

Although it was "the right thing to do," the company's sales suffered. "There was literally nothing to offer our customers," said Navarro. Customers complained, and competitors that still sold polyamide with the toxin-generating flame retardant gained market share. It took two years for BASF to find a safe flame retardant that did not adversely affect the chemical and physical properties of the plastic. The company's strict eco-risk mitigation strategy meant it lost, but neither consumers nor the environment gained from BASF's caution, as competitors' toxic products captured market share. BASF, though, was not subject to reputational costs or attacks by environmentalists and the media during the period when it did not have the product on the market.

Exposure to environmentally motivated actions by activists or the media is particularly acute for three types of companies. The first are brand-name consumer-facing companies that rely on brand equity. Because consumers do not perform their own due diligence, they rely on NGOs and the media, who know that readers will identify with stories about brands they know, leaving these companies vulnerable to NGOs' antics and media campaigns. The second type are companies with "in me" or "on me" products, in which consumers may have heightened concerns about toxicity or safety (see chapter 1). Third are companies with many deep-tier suppliers that have labor-intensive processes, natural resource intensive processes, or operations in countries with lax governmental oversight. In insurance terms, all these companies face higher potential losses or higher likelihoods of environment-related attacks, which, in turn, justifies more investments in environmental risk mitigation measures.

The decision by brand-sensitive companies to invest in eco-risk mitigation has a relative dimension: NGOs are more likely to target environmental underperformers. NGO and media environmental performance scorecards can give rated companies some indication of their risks relative to their peers, which can influence a company's materiality assessment and eco-risk mitigation priorities. In essence, companies want to avoid being the "nail that sticks up" for publicity-eager NGOs. Such analysis can provide guidelines for minimum-required and maximum-reasonable investment (assuming that eco-risk mitigation is the sole green investment criterion).

Eco-Segmentation

Eco-segmentation initiatives are aimed at the green segment of consumers and seek revenue growth from price premiums and/or market share expansion from products explicitly designed or manufactured to minimize environmental impact. Paul Polman, CEO of Unilever said, "Our experience is that brands whose purpose and products respond to that demand—'sustainable living brands'— are delivering stronger and faster growth. These brands accounted for half the company's growth in 2014, growing at twice the rate of the rest of the business." They were also more profitable, according to Unilever.[37] US retailer Target reported a similar experience, with sustainable products producing superior growth even if not every customer was flocking to them.[38]

These investments, however, are not risk-free. The plunge into the green marketplace invites scrutiny from NGOs, media organizations, and consumer groups on the prowl for companies "greenwashing" their offerings (see chapter 9).

Another business rationale for introducing a line of green products—even if it does not lead directly to significant short-term growth—is for companies to experiment with the technology and learn about the green customer segment. In that sense, such eco-segmentation efforts include eco-risk management elements, ensuring that the company is not caught unprepared if government regulations or consumer preferences shift to require more sustainable products and services.

Environmental Impacts in Financial Terms

"We all enjoy the illusion of infinite supply and pay virtually nothing. We must acknowledge the true costs of protecting, treating and delivering water, and develop models that reflect that cost. We must begin to value water as the essential and precious resource it is," said Coca-Cola's CEO Muhtar Kent.[39] "If companies were to have to pay for the costs they created, it would actually wipe out profit," explained Richard Mattison, CEO of the sustainability research firm Trucost.[40]

To reflect the hidden environmental costs (externalities) of impacts, such as CO_2 emissions or water consumption, Nestlé and Unilever, among others, ascribe a "shadow price" to the environmental impacts in their ROI calculations. The shadow price is the estimated price of a good or a service for which a market does not exist, and thus true monetary values are unknowable or very difficult to calculate. Nestlé, for example, estimates the shadow price of water as $1 per cubic meter in wet locations and up to $5 per cubic meter in dry ones.[41]

PUMA, the German sportswear company, took the shadow price concept a step further and developed an "environmental profit and loss statement" in 2010. The EP&L estimates PUMA's costs to the planet (as if the Earth itself were a supplier) by accounting for the ecosystem services crucial to the business and its supply chain. The EP&L allows for year-over-year comparison in terms of a single metric that expresses the company's environmental performance in familiar financial terms.

To price these hidden costs, PUMA, working with Trucost, had to estimate two types of variables: the amount of PUMA's direct and indirect environmental impacts (the analysis went as deep as Tier 4 suppliers) and the environmental cost of a unit of each type of impact. PUMA found out that it generated a lot of waste—31 garbage trucks' worth of material waste for each 100,000 pairs of sneakers.[42] It also identified significant negative externalities across its supply chain, including greenhouse gas emissions, air pollution, and changes in land and water use. Next, Trucost estimated the shadow price of a unit of each type of impact. For example, it estimated that each ton of carbon dioxide cost £66, owing to its impact on human life, and that each hectare of destroyed tropical rainforest (related to PUMA's leather supply because Brazilian ranchers sometimes clear the rainforest to make room for cattle)[43] cost £1,352.[44]

PUMA's 2010 report detailed a total environmental impact of €145 million. "The total results revealed that if we treated our planet as we treat any other service provider, PUMA would have to pay €8 million to nature for services rendered to our core operations such as PUMA offices, warehouses, and stores in 2010 alone," said Jochen Zeitz, executive chairman of PUMA and chief sustainability officer of PUMA's parent company, Kering. "An additional €137 million would be owed to nature from PUMA's external supply chain partners that we share with numerous other companies."[45] At the level of products, Trucost and PUMA estimated that the typical pair of PUMA suede sneakers came with an unpaid environmental cost of €4.29, about 5 percent of the retail price.

"The raw material stage is really essential," according to PUMA's Seidel, "because that is where over 50 percent of the impact comes from."[46] For example, the procurement team used the EP&L approach to select recycled cotton instead of organic cotton because that optimized the combined financial and environmental costs, according to Seidel.

More broadly, the CDP reported in September 2016 that out of 5,759 companies responding to its climate change and supply chain information requests, 517 disclosed using an internal price for carbon as an accounting or risk management tool. Specifically, 147 companies embedded the carbon price in their systems, and 37 companies reported that such pricing affected their decisions.[47] Sprint Corporation, for instance, gives green initiatives somewhat relaxed financial hurdle rates, thus putting an implicit price on environmental impacts.[48]

Economics Rule

"The constitution is not a suicide pact" was a sentiment used by Justice Robert H. Jackson in his dissent of a 1949 US Supreme Court free-speech case, Terminiello v. Chicago, meaning that there were considerations more important than even the US constitution—the bedrock of the US government.[49] In business terms, one can use a similar argument that even when a company is aware of the environmental costs of its operations, corporate self-preservation and the need for profits and growth rule its decision-making.[50]

PUMA's EP&L revealed the high environmental costs of some materials, such as the leather used in its popular sneakers and the cotton in its athletic apparel. As a result, the company wondered whether it should eliminate such high-footprint materials,[51] but even for a business trying to be more environmentally conscientious, market imperatives prevail. "At the end of the day, we are a business and we have to make products that consumers want to buy," said Seidel. "In essence, if consumers want to buy leather shoes and if consumers want to buy cotton T-shirts, then there's no real way for us to change the consumer's behavior." And while PUMA still tries to minimize its environmental impacts, Seidel smiled, "we're not specifically targeting the Greenpeace member as a solid consumer."

Other companies see similar issues in the trade-off between financial health and environmental sustainability. "We want to be on the leading edge and not necessarily the bleeding edge," said Scott Wicker, chief sustainability officer at UPS. "That roughly means we want to be out there leading the way, but we don't want to kill the business in the process."[52]

In addition to taking many eco-efficiency steps, which are easy to justify financially, UPS dabbled in innovation initiatives in order to familiarize itself with sustainable technologies. UPS' 2013 truck fleet included more than 3,000 "compressed natural gas, liquefied natural gas, propane, hydraulic hybrid, electric, bio-methane, ethanol, composite vehicles, and hybrid electric vehicles."[53] These vehicles represented just 3.3 percent of UPS's vehicle fleet, because they can cost twice as much as traditional diesel trucks.[54] UPS justified the added expense as a set of experiments in ways to reduce the company's long-term reliance on petroleum.[55]

Wicker further told *Bloomberg Brief* in 2012 that although the company supports the development of jet-engine biofuels, he could not foresee them being used in the near future, because at the time they cost seven times as much as traditional jet fuel (see chapter 13). As biofuels became more affordable and available, UPS began utilizing more of them. For example, in July 2015, UPS announced a three-year biodiesel contract to help the company reach its goal of displacing 12 percent of the petroleum-based fuels in its ground fleet by 2017.[56]

This tension between economic growth and environmental impact goes beyond business. It also affects governments, especially (but not only) those in the developing world. Most governments understandably respond to the needs of their populations by focusing on economic growth and increased standards of living, rather than on environmental issues.

Creating Intangible Value: Attracting Workers and Suppliers

A 2008 global survey of 1,192 corporate executives suggests that many CEOs in the developed world believe that a reputation for corporate social responsibility increases a company's attractiveness to potential and existing employees.[57] The reason is that millennials are "the most socially conscious generation since the 1960s," according to a *Harvard Business Review* article on employee engagement.[58]

The effects of this are evident during recruitment, especially at "green" companies (described in depth in chapter 11). Patagonia, for example, receives an average of 900 applications for every job it posts,[59] significantly more than the average of 250 applicants per corporate job.[60] This gives the company a competitive advantage over less attractive rivals in being able to hire the best and brightest. David Bronner, CEO of Dr. Bronner's Magic Soaps, a natural care products company, said, "Because of the activist mission, we've attracted some amazing people and been able to increase our professionalism and expertise in business management—financial reporting, inventory control, sales."[61]

Good workers aren't the only ones companies want to attract and retain; they want to attract and retain suppliers as well. Husband and wife team Craig Sams and Josephine Fairley founded Green & Black's in 1991 with a passion for making chocolate sourced from fairly paid workers of sustainably managed cocoa farms.[62] The company collaborated with its supply chain partners in a way that acknowledged the mutual dependency of all stakeholders. The return on that investment came when demand for organic cocoa surged. The farmers responded in kind. "At a time when getting good-quality organic cocoa was practically impossible for most people, we sat with it piling up," said Sams.[63]

MANAGING BY MEASURING

Milton Friedman said, "One of the greatest mistakes is to judge policies and programs by their intentions rather than their results." Measuring the results of sustainability initiatives is a key part of managing them; audits and external certifications to ensure veracity are therefore essential. Moreover, the measured, validated results can then be used effectively in marketing campaigns and labeling (as discussed in chapter 9).

Picking Goals and Metrics

When Dell Inc. set out to reduce its environmental impact, it started with a blank sheet of (presumably recycled) paper. "We really stepped back and said, 'What do customers want?' We did a lot of tracking on [corporate] customer RFPs [request for proposals] and customer inquiries. We also did some market research with our customers to understand what the demands were. We spoke with a lot of our NGOs, government policymakers, and industry analysts before we wrote the plan," said David Lear, vice president of corporate sustainability. The 18-month materiality assessment combined internal review, dialogue with customers, and stakeholder collaboration, to create its "2020 Legacy of Good" plan in 2012.[64]

The resulting plan included 21 broad goals. Dell then created specific internal metrics to measure progress on each. In addition to metrics for the life cycle carbon emissions of individual key products, Dell measured the recyclable content used in the manufacturing of its computers; the recyclability of its packaging; the weight of electronics recovered for resale or recycling; and the fraction of renewable energy used by the company.[65] For each goal, Dell set a target based on a measurable performance indicator. For example, Dell aimed to recycle two billion pounds of electronic waste of any type or brand by 2020.

Other companies choose other metrics, befitting their biggest environmental "hotspots" and their materiality assessment. Rising awareness of climate change is motivating many companies to focus on carbon footprint indicators. In 2005, Walmart announced a 10-year target of reducing 20 million metric ton of greenhouse gas emissions from its global supply chain,[66] a target the company achieved on November 17, 2015.[67] Nestlé set a target of reducing direct water withdrawal per ton of product by 40 percent between 2005 and 2015,[68] achieving a 41 percent reduction in 2015.

Regardless of the issue of importance, a sustainability goal typically includes a *metric* (e.g., carbon footprint), a *scope* for that metric (e.g., manufacturing's carbon footprint), a *target value* or *increment* (e.g., 20 percent reduction), and a *timeframe* (e.g., from a 2010 baseline to a 2020 goal). To ensure progress toward their goals, companies set quarterly and annual key performance indicators that assess managers' performance.

Key Performance Indicators (KPIs)

Baxter Inc., the medical products and pharmaceuticals giant, began measuring GHG emissions in 1997 by subdividing aggregate emissions into more than a dozen KPIs. First, Baxter divided its GHG emissions into the Scope 1, Scope 2, and Scope 3 designations of The Greenhouse Gas Protocol.[69] Recall that Scope 1 emissions come from the organization's directly owned and controlled internal operations; Scope 2 emissions come from indirect sources such as purchased electricity, energy, and heat for internal operations; and Scope 3 emissions include all other indirect sources, be they suppliers, common carriers, service providers, distributors, and the use of products sold.

Baxter then realigned those three categories of sources to the structure of its supply chain to create three categories of activities: upstream (Scope 3), Baxter internal (Scopes 1 and 2), and downstream (Scope 3). In turn, each of the three categories included two to eight subcategories that could be separately measured and managed by the respective corporate functions. Managers in areas such as procurement, facilities, transportation, and others had responsibility for the specific KPIs that they could potentially influence.[70]

Measure, Improve, Copy ... Repeat

"We like metrics, tons of numbers," said Carlos Brito, CEO of the world's biggest beer company, AB InBev.[71] The company has a very competitive culture both at the plant and at the employee level. A system called Voyager Plant Optimization (VPO) is at the heart of the company's efforts to measure and improve all performance dimensions of producing beer and other beverages.[72]

In the context of sustainability, the company described VPO as "the centralized framework we use to benchmark our water and energy use, quantify performance gaps, identify and disseminate best practices and monitor our progress."[73] Using VPO, AB InBev can see the difference between its highest-performing plants and the rest. That lets the company both estimate the magnitude of the opportunity for improvement and focus on uncovering high-performance practices for replication by others.

For example, when AB InBev's team in China wanted to improve water and energy efficiency, they used VPO to find 700 good practices documented by other teams in the company's network of 130 breweries and soft drink facilities. As a result, the team achieved the company's largest region-wide reduction in water and energy consumption between 2009 and 2012 (38 percent and 30 percent, respectively). Moreover, the Chinese team also created some new effective practices of its own. For instance, the team drilled down into energy and water data to continuously benchmark utility usage across brewery departments. That practice was documented in VPO and subsequently adopted by plants in other regions.[74] Through monthly reporting and ranking of performance, regular team calls, and annual meetings to share and develop new ideas and expand the VPO practice database, AB InBev achieved or exceeded its three-year global environmental goals for 2012.[75]

From Metrics to Monetary Incentives?

Most managers believe that financial incentives drive behavior. In fact, the World Business Council for Sustainable Development (WBCSD) recommends incentive payments for achieving environmental targets.[76] For example, SC Johnson, the $10 billion home goods company, pegged part of the discretionary bonuses of 125 managers to their use of the company's "Greenlist" of low-impact ingredients (see chapter 9). The company policy requires improving the Greenlist rating of all product reformulations and rewards managers for pushing those reformulations.[77] Between 2001 and

2014, the fraction of the company's ingredients ranked in the "better" or "best" categories climbed from 18 percent to 44 percent.[78] "Just making it explicit and incentivizing performance had a great benefit," said Chris Librie, director of global sustainability at SC Johnson. "We would not have been able to achieve this if it had not been part of the objectives of senior people."[79]

According to Anca Novacovici, founder of Eco-Coach, "If sustainability is to become part of business operations and be successful in the long-term, it must be evaluated and tied to compensation at the executive level as well as organization-wide."[80] Unfortunately, as many HR professionals know, the problem with incentive systems is that they sometimes work too well. For example, Cisco had to scrap $2.5 billion of surplus materials in 2001 partly because managers maximized their incentives to deliver products quickly to customers and ignored the risks of ballooning inventories.[81] An improperly built incentive program can drive employees to act in their own short-term self-interest rather than in the broader, long-term goals of the organization. Incentive programs typically have elements of individual, team, and corporate performance to help balance these various goals.[82]

Companies vary in both whether and to what extent they link incentive pay to environmental targets as one of the company's many performance objectives (including margin growth, market share growth, quality, innovation, customer satisfaction, employee engagement, etc.). For example, Procter & Gamble does not include environmental sustainability achievements in its managers' bonuses. Intel links only 4 percent of employees' annual variable compensation to environmental goals,[83] whereas at Alcoa, "20 percent of our variable compensation plan was tied to achieving significant aspects of our sustainability targets," said Kevin Anton, chief sustainability officer at the aluminum maker.[84] At SC Johnson, only about 25 percent of the bonus-eligible top managers have a bonus objective linked to Greenlist.[85]

Interestingly, some environmentally committed companies disagree with the use of financial incentives for sustainability. "Achieving our environmental sustainability targets is not tied to our compensation," said Steve Lovejoy, senior vice president of

Starbucks Global Supply Chain organization. "It [sustainability] is what we believe in, what we signed up for, and what we are expected to do. Our CEO and our company have made public commitments on sustainability and we intend to meet them."[86] In 2014, nonprofit Ceres surveyed 613 publicly traded companies and found that 76 percent did not use financial incentives to guide sustainability pursuits.[87] In 2012, a Glass Lewis report found different results: 42 percent of evaluated companies linked some executive pay to sustainability, up from 29 percent in 2010.[88]

MANAGING WITHIN THE RULES

Government regulations affect companies' sustainability initiatives both at the level of what the companies tackle and how they tackle it. The four main categories of regulatory approaches described in this section span a spectrum from mild nudges to strict prohibitions. Although many regulations have a scope limited to the geographic jurisdiction of a particular government, others span the globe and the supply chain, such as the US Lacey Act, which prohibits trafficking in illegally harvested animals, plants, and wood products from anywhere in the world.[89]

Disclosure of Impacts and Risks

Many countries require companies to disclose the ingredients in food products, the fuel efficiency of cars, and the energy efficiency of appliances (see chapter 9) to consumers. Environmental disclosure requirements are the least onerous level of regulations—they focus on disseminating corporate information to investors and other stakeholders. For example, a 2014 EU directive requires large companies to report "on environmental, social and employee-related, human rights, anti-corruption and bribery matters."[90] In the United States, the Dodd-Frank Act mandates disclosure of companies' use of so-called *conflict minerals* (four metals linked to funding warlords in the Congo). The US Securities and Exchange Commission (SEC) issued guidance about disclosure related to climate change,[91] though enforcement has been minimal as of the end of 2014.[92] Although disclosure requirements do not directly force companies to change products or practices, they can expose a company to scrutiny by NGOs, the media, investors, and community groups.

Mandating Higher Environmental Performance

The second category of regulation—performance-based standards— is exemplified by the US Clean Air Act.[93] The law regulates air pollutants from mobile, stationary, and area sources through performance-based standards. These standards, based on available technologies and compliance costs,[94] vary widely. In some cases, the standards require using "reasonably available" technologies, while in other cases they mandate the "best available control technology." For example, the standard for automotive plants is tied to the top-performing 12 percent of comparable plants.[95] The US Congress also enacts stringent standards when it wants to push technology development through regulation. For example, the EPA's 2014 Tier 3 motor vehicle standards set high requirements for tailpipe and evaporative emissions for 2025, even though these could not be achieved with then-available technology.[96]

The Clean Air Act has often been referred to as one of the most successful federal environmental laws.[97] Its success was the result of a combination of clearly defined performance targets, real enforcement, and steep penalties for noncompliance. (Yet the law also added an estimated $21 billion a year in costs to industry and reduced productivity gains in heavy industry by an estimated 4.8 percent.[98])

Markets Mitigate Impacts

A third category of regulations set up financial incentives to change supplier and customer behavior. The simplest such mechanism is a tax on the objectionable product or activity. British Columbia, for instance, enacted a tax on the purchase and use of fuel within the province. An Irish tax on disposable plastic bags practically eliminated their use at retail outlets.[99] Taxes increase the cost of using a resource, thereby creating stronger incentives for eco-efficiency. Similarly, refundable deposits, such as those on bottles (see chapter 7), create incentives for customers to act sustainably. Such incentives, however, do not ensure a specific level of impact reduction.

In contrast, *cap-and-trade* is a government-mandated, market-based mechanism, which can regulate the total volume of environmentally impactful activities. Companies are granted an initial allowance for the regulated activity, such as the amount of CO_2 they are allowed to emit. Those that want to increase their volume of the regulated activity must buy more allowances from other companies who are willing to reduce their volumes. Naturally, companies that can easily reduce their volumes will do so and sell their surplus allowances for a profit. Companies that have especially valuable applications for the regulated activity might willingly pay a high price for more allowances.

Unlike a carbon tax, the cap-and-trade system is flexible—the price of carbon emission allowances rises automatically during periods of strong economic performance and plunges during downturns. A tax, although simpler to administer and understand, provides less flexibility.

Finally, the regulations, which are part of a cap-and-trade system, might stipulate a pattern of reductions, with each allowance permitting steadily less emissions, creating steadily increasing pressure to reduce the impact. Cap-and-trade has been the cornerstone of the European Trading System (ETS), the main tool used by the European Commission to combat climate change; it regulates about 45 percent of the EU's GHG emissions.[100]

Although the system helped reduce European emissions somewhat, the carbon market crashed in 2013 (the spot price of carbon plummeted from €25 per ton in early 2008 to only €3 per ton in 2013[101]). This was the result of giving too many permits to favored industries and companies to begin with, as well as the 2008 economic downturn and several other regulations and policies that required companies to reduce their emissions, creating a glut of permits just as the economy was tanking.

Avoid Where Strictly Prohibited
The fourth and most stringent form of regulations mandate a strict prohibition. For example, the EU's RoHS (Restriction of Hazardous Substances) restricts the use of lead, mercury, cadmium, hexavalent chromium, polybrominated biphenyls, and polybrominated

diphenyl ether in electrical and electronic equipment.[102] Prohibitions related to toxic materials affect product design, manufacturing, end-of-life handling, and disposal of hazardous waste.[103] Other regulations, such as the US Endangered Species Act (ESA), restrict land use, especially the conversion of land to industrial use.

In 2014, the US Fish and Wildlife Service invoked the ESA to declare 1,544 acres of land in St. Tammany Parish, Louisiana, as "critical habitat" for the dusky gopher frog.[104] The ruling potentially precluded all development on the land in order to conserve and recover the frog population numbering only 100 adult frogs. The Poitevent family, the area's largest landowners, sued, arguing the designation would cost them as much as $36 million dollars.[105] In August 2014, a district court in New Orleans sided with the Fish and Wildlife Service, preventing the family from developing their land. In July 2016, the 5th US Circuit Court of Appeals reaffirmed the decision.[106]

By 2017, 1,448 animal and 944 plant species were listed as endangered or threatened in the United States.[107] Many supply chains depend on large plots of land in specific locations for agricultural products (e.g., palm oil), minerals (e.g., ore outcrops), infrastructure (ports and roadways), and industrial parks. Environmental regulations such as the ESA and analogous regulations in other countries can prohibit land development, regardless of the economic consequences.

COLLABORATIVE SUSTAINABILITY

IKEA took 12 years to fully implement the IWAY supplier code of conduct—a task that required identifying hotspots of environmental impact often deep in the supply chain—and building a professional staff of 80 auditors. As companies struggle with increased scrutiny and a concomitant desire to increase their scrutiny of suppliers, many find that they lack the reach, understanding, and expertise to evaluate and manage the environmental practices of their suppliers on their own.

A Giant Moves

Walmart is a mammoth corporation.[108] It is the third largest employer in the world; only the US Department of Defense and the Chinese People's Liberation Army are larger. Walmart's size and economic footprint have long made it a target for criticism in a variety of arenas—worker pay, cost-cutting mandates on suppliers, and its impacts on local retailers—but activist attacks on the retailer's environmental practices never gained much traction. Despite that, the company began a campaign for sustainable environmental practices, possibly after a confidential 2004 report hinted that negative press might be curtailing revenue growth.[109]

In October 2005, Walmart's then-CEO Lee Scott vowed, "We can't let our critics define who we are and what we stand for."[110] The following July, Scott invited former US Vice President Al Gore to speak to 800 Walmart executives, managers, suppliers, and partners,[111] and used the opportunity to announce near-term concrete goals for Walmart's environmental commitment. The mega-retailer sought to reduce each existing store's and warehouse's carbon impact by 20 percent by 2015. During that same period, Walmart aimed to double the fuel efficiency of its transportation fleet of more than 7,000 semitrailer trucks.[112]

Given the broad scope of its goals and its scant experience in the environmental arena, Walmart reached out to the Environmental Defense Fund in late 2005.[113] EDF is a Washington, DC-based NGO, founded in 1967 with a mission to identify practical and long-term solutions for environmental challenges. The two organizations did not publicize the relationship at first; the *New York Times* finally reported on it four years later.[114] EDF's relationship with Walmart resembles that of a lobbyist pushing policy in Washington, according to Michelle Harvey, the senior manager who leads EDF's on-site partnership.

The partnership intensified in 2007, two years after its inception, with EDF opening an office across the street from the retailer's Bentonville, Arkansas, headquarters. As of 2014, the office housed three full-time EDF employees (including Harvey), all of whom are granted access to Walmart's headquarters. Harvey and her colleagues attend meetings inside Walmart, where they present EDF's concerns.

EDF's Bentonville personnel spend roughly 20 percent of their time meeting with Walmart employees, Harvey said, largely to build relationships and understand the challenges the company faces. That understanding, she said, helps EDF appropriately target its initiatives. EDF realized that about 90 percent of the retailer's environmental footprint takes place in its supply chain[115] among the 100,000 suppliers of the 140,000 types of products on its supercenters' shelves.[116] Through these relationships, EDF learned, for example, that buyers could affect supplier practices only during contract negotiations, which happen during a specific window each year for each product category. Sometimes this means that Harvey will talk to a buyer about an issue, despite understanding that the buyer may not act on it until many months later.[117]

While Walmart was using its clout to improve the environmental sustainability of its suppliers,[118] it also continued to improve its own environmental practices. In 2012, the company announced that it recycled more than 80 percent of the waste produced in its domestic stores. The company's favorability rating in 2012 reached 25 percent—about double its 2007 level[119]—according to YouGov's BrandIndex, which bases its ratings on 1.6 million annual US consumer interviews.[120] That improvement in public perception coincided with the company's ability to open stores in long-resistant communities around Chicago and Los Angeles.[121] The same year, the company's stock price surged to an all-time high of $75.81 per share after four years of stagnation.[122]

Managing Remote Environmental Efforts

Whereas Walmart engaged EDF for its broad environmental expertise, other companies seek a partner focused on a specific area in which the company lacks expertise or visibility. After Greenpeace waged a graphic viral video campaign against Nestlé's KitKat candy bar (see chapter 1), the Swiss company sought to understand and manage its palm oil supply chain. Because the company bought refined palm oil on world markets from large vegetable oil intermediaries rather than directly from palm oil growers or processors, it had little visibility into the oil's origins. The complex network of palm oil refiners, traders, and palm fruit mills hid the identities and practices of palm oil farmers in distant countries, such as Indonesia and Malaysia, from view in Nestlé headquarters on the shores of Lake Leman in Switzerland.

So, in 2010, Nestlé partnered with The Forest Trust (TFT), a leading NGO dedicated to deforestation and sustainable forestry issues. First, TFT worked with both Nestlé and Greenpeace, helping each understand what the other was willing and able to do. Later, TFT constructed supply chain maps for "almost all" of Nestlé's products that contained palm oil in the bill of materials.[123]

The following year, TFT helped the company implement a set of responsible sourcing guidelines for palm oil. Nestlé relied on TFT to visit the sites and negotiate with palm oil suppliers, with whom Nestlé had no direct relationships. Speaking generally, Scott Poynton, TFT's founder, said that his group uses its corporate partner as leverage to get a supplier to change its practices. "We bring the commercial power of the buyer," he said. "That's the change agent. That's the grease in the wheel."[124]

After concluding its supply chain work, TFT helped Nestlé communicate its improved sustainability to consumers.[125] To verify the claims, TFT employees personally visited palm oil field sites, as well as used local partners to audit the plantations. "We get our people out in the bush and have a look and report what's going on," Poynton said. Through these efforts over a two-year period, Nestlé changed from a Greenpeace-labeled pariah to having Greenpeace post an article thanking Nestlé for changing its policies.[126]

Following its partnership with TFT, Nestlé subsequently worked with other NGOs on 12 other commodities with complex supply chains, including soy, sugarcane, and cocoa.[127] Despite TFT's lack of involvement in those other efforts, Poynton said, "We think, well, this is absolutely terrific."

Picking the Right NGO

The challenge for companies seeking an NGO partnership is to find a compatible one that addresses the right problem, in the right way, at the right scale. After Greenpeace's attack on Nestlé's palm oil buying practices, Nestlé chose to partner with TFT instead of Greenpeace for several reasons. First, Nestlé felt the attack was unfair and unfounded, given its indirect connection to palm oil and its low-volume use of the ingredient. Second, Greenpeace has more of a reputation for aggressive campaigns against corporations rather than for fostering partnerships to improve environmental practices. Lastly, TFT had the expertise Nestlé needed in order to get deep into the global palm oil supply chain.

A report by EDF and the Global Environmental Management Initiative suggested that an NGO engagement includes three stages, not unlike any outsourcing arrangement.[128] First, the company crafts the overall design of the partnership and develops partner selection criteria. The parties can then negotiate a cooperation agreement with a clear plan, milestones, and cross-functional teams at different levels of management. The final stage measures and communicates the project's benefits. Although the arrangements, the scope of the effort, and the number of participants may vary, the report encourages businesses to align their strategy with the intended business outcomes.

Of Partnerships, Payments, and Perceptions

NGOs also face partner selection and partnership management challenges tied to the NGO's own brand image. Many company–NGO partnerships, while based on mutual collaboration, may include some company payments to the NGO. Such payments can raise ethical concerns and lead to criticisms of "greenwashing" (see chapter 9), reflecting poorly on both the NGO and the company. Some have criticized EDF as being too close to Walmart.[129] While EDF proclaims that it "does not take any money from corporations or corporate-run philanthropies with whom we work,"[130] the group accepted $66 million between 2005 and 2013 from the Walton Family Foundation (owned by the founder's family, which still has a large stake in Walmart). It represented a significant portion of EDF's operating budget.[131]

According to TFT's Poynton, the group warns its corporate members that the Trust will drive them through a bumpy ride if they are serious about reforming their practices, and he won't allow his group's brand to be used to "greenwash." In one case, he said, a large financial firm joined TFT, claiming it required sustainable practices in the businesses the firm funded. Less than a year later, Poynton said, TFT leadership decided the financial company was not serious and kicked it out of the TFT membership. "Basically, they just turned around and said, 'We'll give you $100,000 as a donation if we can stay members.'" Poynton said. "We said, 'We don't take donations. Yes, we're a charity, but we don't take donations. We work with companies to change their practices.'"[132]

In that respect, engaging with NGOs is different from engaging with traditional suppliers. It is more like engaging with the news media. Companies pay media outlets significant advertising dollars, yet any perceived influence of the company on the news media's coverage of the company may invite criticism. Thus, the culture in the mainstream media world is to separate the news and opinion coverage from the commercial advertisement business.

Similarly, a reputable NGO partner will often exhibit a strong sense of independence and will push back against a company's wishes. Greenpeace, for example, at one point attacked the RSPO and its member companies, with which it had been working closely, because the group's updated guidelines fell short of Greenpeace's expectations.[133]

An NGO's reputation also affects the reputations of sponsoring firms. In 2010, the Sustainable Forestry Initiative (SFI), a forestry certification program, was attacked by another NGO, ForestEthics, for "greenwashing" and being a shill for the paper industry.[134] In its report, ForestEthics claimed that the SFI was controlled by major paper and pulp companies and, among many other faults, "does not require any work to restore forests that are essential for the survival of rare wildlife."[135] Companies such as 3M, whose paper products were certified by the SFI, also came under fire.[136] In the years following the attack, 24 companies, including HP and AT&T, abandoned the SFI as a paper certifier.

The More the Merrier

Companies often employ multiple NGO partnerships to tackle the variety of environmental challenges they face. The types of partnerships may include one-on-one collaborations for tailored help on specific issues; an intra-industry collaboration to address an industry challenge; and/or an inter-industry collaboration spanning multiple areas. These collaborative models are not mutually exclusive, and many companies employ more than one in order to advance their environmental practices internally and across their supply chains.

Starbucks works with Conservation International to evaluate and improve its coffee supply chain; with the National Coffee Association for industry-wide sustainability issues;[137] and with Fair Trade International on matters pertaining to workers' rights across industries. Issues that are unique to specific business units are typically handled by direct partnerships with NGOs that have deep expertise in the specific areas under study, such as Starbucks' procurement team's partnership with the World Cocoa Foundation to improve the ethical sourcing of cocoa.[138] Starbucks also works with many other NGOs, environmental organizations, and industry groups.[139]

In contrast, IKEA engages its NGO partners mostly for their operational expertise. The global furniture company contracts with WWF and the Forest Stewardship Council to help its suppliers improve logging practices in accordance with the IWAY program. The company also solicits feedback on its sustainability ideas from representatives of several organizations, including Oxfam and Greenpeace. "We want them to challenge us and we want them to bring their competence to the table so the project can succeed," said IKEA's Jeanette Skjelmose. But, she said, IKEA would never allow its NGO partners to get between the company and its suppliers by outsourcing the audit function.[140]

When environmental challenges exceed the scale of the company or threaten to increase the costs of doing business or restrict operational capabilities, companies tend to work within industry alliances to pool resources and level the playing field. In other situations, they also work *across* different industries to increase leverage, pool innovation, achieve economies of scale, and include outside perspectives. For example, Nestlé, Coca-Cola, SAB Miller, and other companies joined forces with the International Finance

Corporation (the World Bank's private investment arm) to form the 2030 Water Resources Group to highlight the many dimensions of the water scarcity problem and find the least costly ways of tackling it.[141]

CORPORATE CULTURE

Unlike one-time projects, sustainability is a relentless quest, similar to the quest for quality, security, or resilience. Frequently, companies make public multiyear commitments spanning 5, 10, or even 20 years. In managing such long-term journeys, companies face many challenges that make it difficult to stay the course. Furthermore, sometimes the course needs changing, too. *Eco-culture* initiatives attempt to instill environmental awareness and encourage sustainability practices across the company.

Sustainability is more likely to take root in the organization if it is aligned with the company's overall mission or brand goals. Thus, *eco-efficiency* initiatives that save money on fuel, energy, and packaging fit well at Walmart and its overarching goal of "everyday low prices." At Starbucks, efforts to ensure the sustainability of its 120,000 coffee growers (see chapter 5) fit with maintaining its brand image as a caring company. At a more tactical level, the minimalist parts count and low material consumption of the Flyknit design (see chapter 8) support Nike's focus on innovation. Yet, even if sustainability goals align with broader corporate goals, companies might still face various hurdles.

Sustaining Sustainability

Stonyfield Farm started in 1983 as a small organic yogurt maker in New Hampshire serving mostly New England supermarkets. From the very beginning, it committed itself to a wide variety of environmental causes. By 2013, the company had grown significantly, reaching consumers as far away as California. To grow, Stonyfield hired many new employees, some of whom were not wedded to the same organic and eco-conscious values as the company's founders and early employees. "Our employees are no more interested or knowledgeable about environmental issues than the general population," said Nancy Hirshberg, the company's vice president of natural resources.[142]

To achieve its increasingly ambitious environmental goals, however, the company needed the active participation of all of its employees. Thus, the company launched the Mission Action Program (MAP) in 2006 to help employees understand the *why* and *how* of Stonyfield's environmental mission. "They learned about our company's impact on the environment and ways that they could help reduce environmental burdens both at work and in their personal life," wrote Hirshberg in a 2009 case study.[143] The program delineated Stonyfield's 11 environmental areas of focus,[144] ranging from milk production to "Stonyfield Walking Our Talk" (SWOT). The latter category encompassed small internal changes such as installing skylights in warehouses. Such actions resulted in minor changes to the company's environmental impact but reminded workers of the company's constant commitment.[145]

The program initially focused on the 10 percent of Stonyfield employees who managed operations, which were responsible for 95 percent of the company's carbon emissions.[146] In 2007, MAP grew to encompass the entire company. "From production line workers to executives, everyone had an opportunity to learn about global environmental issues, with a focus on climate change," wrote Hirshberg.[147] In 2008, Stonyfield went a step further and tied employee bonuses to the company's environmental performance.

One of the biggest challenges that Gary Hirshberg, Stonyfield's CEO at the time, faced was getting Stonyfield workers to think beyond eco-efficiency and instead use "truly sustainable thinking." He believed that this kind of internal mentality provided the organizational "personality" that helped the company attract "clients, customers, investors, and others outside the organization."[148]

Sustainability: Under New Management

In 2001, the French food conglomerate Danone acquired Stonyfield but has mostly stayed out of Stonyfield's daily operations and even tried to learn from its environmental practices. Stonyfield's organic milk and sugar are significantly more expensive than Danone's conventional ingredients, noted Hirshberg, "but my net margins are actually the same as or better than theirs."[149] This, he said, is because Stonyfield spends very little on advertising, relying instead on word-of-mouth marketing. The key, he believes, is the trust that Stonyfield's customers have in the company. "The flip side is that if we break that trust, we're toast."[150]

Similarly, British chocolate brand Green & Black's was able to keep its corporate social responsibility culture not only during a period of rapid growth but also after being acquired by Cadbury in 2005.[151,152] As described earlier, Green & Black's was founded on organic, fair trade, and sustainability principles. Green & Black's culture was even strong enough to influence Cadbury to pursue its own fair trade initiatives. In January 2010, while under Cadbury management, Green & Black's announced plans to use 100 percent Fair Trade chocolate across all chocolate bars and drinks.[153] According to Josephine Fairley, at a 2010 celebration dinner for outgoing Cadbury CEO Todd Stitzer, the retiring CEO turned to the Green & Black's founders and said, "I want to thank Craig Sams and Jo Fairley for showing Cadbury the way with fair trade."[154] In 2011, Cadbury announced an investment of more than £3 million over eight years in the Dominican Republic to support its pledge to expand its fair trade supply base.[155]

The company's progressive culture continued to be a business driver for its management even when Cadbury was acquired by US food giant Mondelez International Inc. in 2010.[156] In fact, Mondelez announced during a September 7, 2016, conference that the first of the three pillars of its growth strategy includes expanding the Green & Black's brand and adding many more sustainable snacks to its product line.[157]

On June 16, 2017, Amazon announced its acquisition of Whole Foods. Whole Foods is an upscale, progressive, and environmentally conscious food retailer. Amazon's success, by contrast, was based on relentless efficiency, low costs, and driving employees hard. While betting against Jeff Bezos, Amazon's CEO, is a fool's errand, the integration of the two cultures will provide an interesting case study in the power of sustainability commitments to survive corporate acquisitions.

The Ever-Moving Goal Posts

In 2007, Dell pledged to recycle two billion pounds of electronic waste by 2020, as described in chapter 7. By 2014, the company reported reaching one billion pounds. However, as Dell collected and analyzed data about recycled computers, it became apparent to Deborah Sanders, Dell's global director of consumer and commercial recycling, that the company was going to miss its 2020 target. "If you look at the desktop market, it is either flat or declining slightly, versus the rise of mobility products that continue to increase," said Sanders. The shift from heavy desktops to slim laptops and tablets meant Dell was in danger of missing its weight target, even though the number of units being recycled was on track. This prompted managers to not only increase their efforts by adding more donation points, but also to encourage consumers to return old equipment of any brand (not just Dell's), in any condition, to one of the more than 2,000 Goodwill locations across the US that were equipped to accept the used electronics.[158]

EMC Corporation tried to future-proof its goals through a careful definition of its metrics. "We at EMC believe that metrics need context," said EMC's Winkler.[159] Technological progress implies that although a new storage unit or server may be somewhat more energy-intensive to produce, it will likely have significantly more memory, higher processing speed, and higher I/O speed. Consequently, EMC normalizes footprint metrics to be per gigabyte, per input/output operations per second,[160] and per employee, rather than per product unit.[161] For example, EMC was one of the first companies to offer solid-state drives for enterprise storage systems; these drives use as much as 98 percent less energy per operations per second than older drives. They also use 38 percent less energy per terabyte of storage.[162] Not only do these metrics insulate EMC from future hardware technology changes, but they are also the same type of metrics used to improve the quality of EMC's products and are tied to the day-to-day decision-making of EMC employees.

Managing "Delayed Success"

Apple's success in eliminating many types of toxic materials from its products caused increased environmental pressure on other technology manufacturers. If Apple could eliminate brominated flame retardants (BFR) from its computer equipment, why couldn't others in the industry do the same? Nevertheless, when EMC's engineers tested Apple's BFR-free circuit board materials, the substitutes failed. The nontoxic substitutes that worked in consumer electronic products did not have the technical performance and reliability required for EMC's enterprise products, which are used in mission- and safety-critical systems in data centers, health care, aviation, and finance.[163]

The challenge of eliminating toxins from EMC products fell to Richard Murphy, vice president of global supply chain engineering. Even though the initial efforts to find substitutes failed, Murphy convinced his team to keep going, incorporating the lessons from the failures and trying again. It took two years of repeated attempts before the company found a BFR-free circuit-board material that met its strict specifications. When Murphy finally found a workable BFR-free solution, he faced another challenge. The new material required investments on the part of suppliers, meaning that it would have a high initial cost.[164]

By analyzing historical pricing trends for new technologies, Murphy was able to convince both EMC's suppliers and executives that as volumes increased, prices would decrease—and that it would happen soon enough to matter. "I won't say I wasn't elated when our supplier told us that the market for this new material was blossoming," said Murphy. Similarly, eliminating phthalates—chemicals used to make plastics softer and more pliable—from cables and cords followed the same development path: appearing technically challenging and economically risky at first but then fostering a market for the new material with commensurate declines in price and supply chain risks.

Murphy suggested two important lessons for companies faced with similar challenges. First, "projects that don't work the first time aren't failures. Rather, they're 'delayed successes,'" he said. Second, "when it comes to changing the industry, companies can't go it alone." For new materials and processes to become economically viable, the industrial ecosystem has to buy into the change, which involves using *eco-alignment* initiatives to convince suppliers, competitors, and customers. As more customers specify systems with the new sustainable feature, as more suppliers develop expertise and make it available, and as more OEMs use it, the economies of scale are likely to bring costs down.

Naturally, such a strategy has to be implemented slowly, bringing the entire ecosystem along. One of the lessons from Tesco's failed labeling effort (see chapter 3) is that charging ahead with a substantial change without preparing the groundwork for suppliers, customers, and service providers along the supply chain can lead to defeat and retreat from the efforts.

MANAGING A PLAN

After Marks & Spencer's CEO Stuart Rose convinced his top executives of the importance of sustainability, he challenged his team[165] to formulate a sustainability plan called "Plan A" ("because there is no plan B").[166,167] Unlike Sir Terry Leahy's drive to label every Tesco product with its carbon footprint, Rose went about it very differently. Rather than focus on complete LCAs of products—something that involved the entire supply chain—Plan A focused on multiple social and environmental issues across its own business. To keep the program moving forward, Rose created and chaired a committee so that "Plan A was part of the drumbeat, and every week I would raise the subject—the fact that I was the person chairing it meant that the senior managers at M&S had to come," Rose explained.[168]

When Rose presented Plan A to the M&S board, he didn't get much enthusiasm: "One-third of them probably thought I was batty, and probably only 10 percent or so wanted to do it."[169] Some investors protested the planned five-year £200 million potential hit to margins, but Rose stood his ground. In January 2007,[170] the company officially announced Plan A with 100 interlocking environmental pledges on a wide range of environmental and social sustainability issues organized into five pillars: climate change, waste, natural resources, fair partnerships, and health and well-being. Rose pledged to "complete Plan A without passing on any extra costs to our customers."[171]

From Centralization to Empowerment

In the beginning, M&S centralized authority on the assumption that the Plan A team would be the "most proficient and knowledgeable about sustainability to make sure that money was being spent in the right place," said Mike Barry, the firm's director of Plan A.[172] But centralization prevented employees from taking ownership of environmental initiatives. They were left "with a little begging bowl, needing to always ask for permission to invest it in A, B, and C, and we'd say yes or no. And they ended up doing Plan A grudgingly," he added. The whole idea of Plan A—doing multiple small changes where possible—was incompatible with central control. Moreover, employees did not fight for savings. "Their suppliers came along and said, 'Oh, yes, sustainable cotton, it costs 10 percent more,' and the buying group would say, 'Fine,' because there's a central pot of money to bail us out," Barry said.

To remedy the situation, the company decentralized decision-making and gave budget authority to thousands of people across the business.[173] "Now that it's their own budget, when a supplier starts with a 10-percent uplift, they say 'No, it's going to cost us nothing more,' and the supplier comes back and says 8 percent, and eventually, you'll get down to 2 percent or 3 percent. Because they own the budget, they are much more responsive to making sure that we're doing sustainability in a cost-effective way rather than in a subsidized way," Barry explained.

Decentralization gave employees license to identify a wider variety of opportunities. Barry asserted: "Once you wrap up this warm, emotional, save-the-planet banner around them, you empowered people as individuals to spot these multiple small sources of saving—a bit of energy there, a bit of waste there—that all have a relatively small dollar sign next to them, but when aggregated under the Plan A umbrella, suddenly you've got that magical $150 million of savings."

Linking Paychecks

Rose tied the annual bonuses of all M&S executives, down to the level of store managers, to meeting Plan A targets.[174] "Our store managers love a bit of healthy competition, so linking their bonus earning potential to their energy, water and waste performance, and issuing internal store league tables is very effective," said Munish Datta, head of facilities management and Plan A.[175] Plan A also became a way to identify high-potential employees who volunteered to be sustainability champions, signaling their ability to inspire others and lead change. The initiative was further embedded into the corporate culture through the company's leadership development course, in which employees work on current Plan A areas that need fresh thinking.[176]

Tracking progress required developing a Plan A management information system (MIS), because although sales data were available in real time, environmental performance data could be a year out of date.[177] The new MIS enabled monthly progress reviews of Plan A by the operating committee.[178]

M&S also changed how it calculated costs and returns on projects in several ways. It added an internal carbon price to projects;[179] it started using life cycle costing to reflect the lifetime costs of energy and maintenance; and it modeled how a project in one part of the store might affect other parts of the store (e.g., the effect of efficient lighting on heating and cooling).[180]

Influencing Suppliers and Consumers

Unlike many of the companies in this book, M&S excluded suppliers' carbon emissions from its footprint estimates and carbon neutrality goals, even though suppliers account for 60 percent of the company's carbon footprint. It reasoned that it would not be cost effective to quantify emissions for its more than 35,000 product lines.[181] Instead, M&S created a series of platforms to allow suppliers to share and implement best environmental and social management practices across all food factories. In concert with this, the company has been moving incrementally with a 2020 goal to have every product have at least one "Plan A quality," such as by meeting fair trade, sustainable raw materials, animal welfare, or healthier food standards.[182] By 2017, the company was well on the way with 79 percent of the items it sells having a Plan A story to tell.[183]

Rather than mandating a supplier code of conduct, Rose met privately with the CEOs of M&S's largest suppliers, explaining Plan

A's rationale. "Showcasing the business case for action is so much more powerful in terms of galvanizing change across the supply chain than any amount of documentation and codes of practice," argued Carmel McQuaid, head of sustainable business at M&S.[184]

To encourage best practices among suppliers, M&S set up a knowledge exchange for its 2,500 suppliers, which included working groups on specific issues such as refrigeration. Along with online systems, M&S hosts in-person sustainability conferences in the United Kingdom for suppliers, with the entire M&S board present to explain why Plan A matters, thereby signaling the plan's primary importance to the company.[185]

M&S's footprint reduction calculations also excluded the carbon emitted by customers while using or disposing of merchandise. Instead, the company created initiatives for specific hotspots such as: a "Think Climate, Wash at 30°C" campaign to educate consumers about washing their clothes at lower temperatures; carrying only appliances rated A or above according to the EU energy efficiency label standards; and creating a clothing recycling program called "shwopping,"[186] whereby M&S offered discounts in return for donated clothing.

Barry explained that "the average consumer's got 15 seconds at the point of purchase." Thus, instead of certifying and labeling each product, M&S pursued broad company-level certifications, such as being the first retailer to be certified on the Carbon Trust's Triple Standard on carbon, water, and waste,[187] as well as being the first major UK retailer to gain the ISO 50001 energy management certification.[188]

Results and Revisions

Plan A began with 100 commitments in 2007. These were a mix of internal social and environmental commitments, rather than extended supply chain commitments. By March 2010, the company had achieved 62 of the goals, was "on plan" for 30, and was "behind" or "on hold" for the remaining eight goals. M&S then added 80 new commitments to Plan A with an overall goal "to become the world's most sustainable major (multiline) retailer by 2015." Indeed, *Forbes* listed M&S as the top retailer among its lists of "The Most Sustainable Companies 2015."[189] In 2014, the firm announced a third version called "Plan A 2020" with a refreshed list of 100 commitments.[190]

Although Rose had warned shareholders that he planned to put £200 million into Plan A over a five-year period, eco-efficiency savings on energy and waste made the plan cost-positive in just two years.[191] By 2013, Plan A was adding £135 million annually to the retailer's profits.[192] In 2012, Decision Technology's annual Brand Personality survey found that Marks & Spencer had become the seventh "most green" brand in the United Kingdom, and the brand toward which Britons reported the most positive sentiment.[193]

In many ways, Marks & Spencer's branding success was the result of focusing its efforts on its own operations. However, to have a real impact on environmental sustainability, one has to include both upstream and downstream supply chain components, where most of the impact takes place. Even M&S's goal of having at least one Plan A quality for each product is quite modest when one considers all types of cradle-to-grave impacts. To achieve true environmental sustainability, every product needs several Plan A qualities.

Although many mainstream companies, such as M&S, pursue sustainability as one element among many other corporate initiatives (e.g., quality, value, and innovation), some generally smaller companies put sustainability at the very heart of their identities. These overtly "green" companies (and their environmental practices) may offer a glimpse into a possible future influenced by stricter regulation, greater activist pressure, or greater consumer interest in (and willingness to pay for) sustainable products.

11

Creating Deep Sustainability

On June 11, 2012, a bearded and ponytailed David Bronner locked himself and several cannabis plants inside a 64-square-foot steel cage in Washington, DC's Lafayette Square, directly north of the White House. He was trying to make enough hemp oil to spread on a piece of French bread. First, the police tried to cut the cage bars with bolt cutters, but failed. Next, the authorities attempted to haul the cage away with a tow truck, but that too failed.[1] It took police three hours to cut through the bars with a chainsaw, get to Bronner, and arrest him on charges of "blocking passage" and possession of marijuana.[2]

Anecdotes such as this may make David Bronner seem like just another protester for marijuana legalization, but he's actually the CEO (which in his case stands for "Cosmic Engagement Officer") of Dr. Bronner's Magic Soaps and is deeply concerned with environmental sustainability. Although most companies seek to maximize financial performance within the constraints of regulatory or social requirements, deeply sustainable companies, such as Dr. Bronner's, Seventh Generation, and Patagonia, flip these goals and constraints. That is, they seek to minimize environmental impact, subject to financial viability constraints. These "deep green" companies use their social and environmental strategy as branding and identity mechanisms—they sell to "green" customers and attract "green" job applicants.

DR. BRONNER'S MAGIC ALL-ONE

Whereas most CEOs assiduously avoid controversies, especially ones involving criminal prosecution by the humorless US Drug

Enforcement Administration (DEA), this wasn't Bronner's first run-in with the authorities. In 2001, he joined activists in front of DEA buildings nationwide to offer drug enforcement officers a taste-test comparison between hemp foods and poppy seed bagels.[3] In 2009, he was part of a group arrested while planting hemp outside of DEA headquarters.[4] In all three cases, he was protesting US policy prohibiting the growing of hemp, a strain of *Cannabis* closely related to marijuana but which lacks consequential amounts of marijuana's psychoactive chemicals.

During the Washington cage stunt, Bronner spokesman Ryan Fletcher said, "He's doing this action in part because he wants to be able to source that hemp oil from American farmers, rather than exporting his dollars to Canada."[5] Bronner wanted local sourcing, which is one of the tenets of the company's culture of environmental sustainability.

Spaceship Earth

Most corporations would be horrified by such radical behavior by the CEO, but the leaders of privately held Dr. Bronner's have always freely mixed activism with business practices, ever since the company's 1948 founding as a nonprofit religious organization.[6] Founder Emanuel ("Emil") Bronner (known as Dr. Bronner, despite lacking a formal doctoral degree), developed an "All-One!" vision to unify humanity on "Spaceship Earth." His voluminous writings on the morality of uniting all mankind (and the godliness of cleanliness) form a patchwork of fine print on the labels of the company's products.[7] After the founder passed away, and under IRS pressure, the company dropped its claim to be a religious organization. In the early 1990s, Bronner's son Jim took over, and in 1998 (after Jim's death), *his* son David Bronner assumed the role of CEO.

A dedicated activist, David Bronner continued his grandfather's legacy of change, by making Dr. Bronner's products as natural as possible while having the lowest possible environmental impact. Advocating for hemp cultivation has been part of this approach, citing the fast-growing plant as a renewable resource that provides high-quality fiber, edible oils, high-quality protein, and animal fodder.[8] In 1999, David Bronner replaced his soap's existing caramel coloring with hemp seed oil, which also creates a smoother lather.[9] That choice put him in conflict with US authorities, because DEA policies conflate hemp with marijuana, despite hemp's lack of intoxicating effects.[10] The law forced the Californian company to import hemp oil long distances from Canada, where the source crop can be legally grown.[11]

Given its sustainability philosophy, Dr. Bronner's does not make the same trade-offs that most public companies do when evaluating a project. "All of our deep ideas about sustainability and sourcing—all that extra expense, our charity as a company—is at the heart of our cost of goods sold," said Michael Milam, Dr. Bronner's COO.[12] "Once you build your supply chain like that, it doesn't become an option for swapping it out if things get tight." That commitment has been an integral part of the company for more than six decades, even during its brush with bankruptcy in 1985.

If You Can't Trace It

Hemp isn't the only environmental issue, or even the largest one, that Dr. Bronner's has tackled. In 2006, the soap maker started to align its supply chain with its beliefs by sourcing only certified Fair Trade ingredients through the Fair for Life program.[13] The company immediately ran into a challenge with coconut and palm oils, two of Dr. Bronner's largest ingredients by volume. The company's oil brokers could not verify the labor and environmental practices behind every batch of oil purchased. It was the same traceability issue that bedeviled many large companies, such as Nestlé and Unilever, which source from the global commodity market of palm oil (see chapter 5).

Bronner's response was to bypass the brokers and invest in vertical integration. The company built its own mill in Ghana and acquired a coconut oil processing facility in Sri Lanka. "There wasn't Fair Trade coconut oil, and so that's why we have a mill in Sri Lanka, specifically to have that," Milam said. Once the company owned the mill, it sourced coconuts only from local smallholder farmers, of whose practices the company approved.

Although vertical integration and direct control of the sources of raw materials reduced Dr. Bronner's environmental exposure in its supply chain, it increased both its business risks and its costs. Commodities are traded on world markets in order to pool risk and resources (including processing, transportation, and sales) of hundreds or thousands of small suppliers, thereby increasing efficiency and reducing the volatility of supplies and prices. In contrast, by having its own coconut oil and palm oil growers and mills, Dr. Bronner's Magic Soaps de-pooled that supply risk, exposing the company to shortages if its growers in Sri Lanka or Ghana had a bad year. In addition, Dr. Bronner's had to pay the start-up costs to get these small mills up to its standards. In the first years, the company even had to prepay for crops before they were planted. "We have to pre-finance the crops," Milam said in a 2013 interview.[14] "This forces us to be very good at projections." To minimize shortages or excess capacity, Milam explained that the company maps ingredient usage on a four-year horizon. "We can't just pick up the phone and get materials and expect that someone's going to get it for us."

Making a Point

In 2008, Dr. Bronner's Magic Soaps sued a group of competitors, chiefly the $11 billion cosmetics giant, Estée Lauder. The suit alleged that these companies were labeling products as organic even though they contained petrochemical ingredients.[15] Also named in the suit were Stella McCartney's CARE, JĀSÖN, Avalon Organics, Nature's Gate, Kiss My Face, and Ikove, among others. Dr. Bronner's specifically targeted ECOCERT, a European accreditation organization, that certified products as organic even if their organic content amounted to no more than 10 percent of the product.[16] Nevertheless, the companies were not breaking any laws because the USDA certification requirements for organic body products were not clearly defined.

Dr. Bronner's, whose products boast entirely organic ingredients, felt that the competitor's use of the organic label on products containing any amount of nonorganic ingredients was misleading consumers and diluting Dr. Bronner's own brand. The company did not want the organic label to become an "Akerlof lemon" (see chapter 9). Following the filing of the lawsuit, some companies quickly settled. For example, Juice Beauty Inc. agreed to change its product formulations. Whole Foods Market sided with Dr. Bronner's, telling the offending companies to fix the problem within 12 months or be removed from the retailer's shelves.[17] The lawsuit was dismissed four years later when a California federal court declared that the interpretation of USDA standards for organic certification was outside its jurisdiction. Dr. Bronner's, however, had already made its point both to its competitors and to its consumers at large.[18]

Just Say "No"

Emil Bronner, the eponymous founder of Dr. Bronner's, believed in "constructive capitalism," in which you should "share the profit with the workers and the earth from which you made it."[19] That belief underpins the company's emphasis on fair trade sourcing. It also led David Bronner to voluntarily cap the compensation of his company's executives—including himself—at $200,000 per year, or five times the salary of the company's lowest-paid full-time worker.

Dr. Bronner's uncommon business practices and radical leadership did not hurt its growth: The company grew from $6 million in sales in 2000 to $80 million in 2015, riding the expanding environmental movement. Along the way, the company said "no" to a lot of opportunities. In fact, during its rapid growth from the late 2000s to 2014, the company received so many buyout inquiries that CEO David Bronner threw them directly in the trash without looking at them.[20] "What we're doing is pretty radical; this is not feel-good sustainability, buying offsets and crap like that. This is taking on the Drug Enforcement Administration. My intention is never to sell," he said.[21]

Most companies dream of landing lucrative distribution deals with big retailers, but when Walmart approached Dr. Bronner's about a transaction, Dr. Bronner's said "no" to the world's largest retailer. According to David Bronner, he and other company leaders didn't like what "Walmart stands for."[22] Having Walmart as a customer may have significantly increased the company's revenue and reach but may also have created tensions with Dr. Bronner's core consumers and natural foods retailers.

PATAGONIA: WEARING ITS HEART ON ITS SLEEVE

Given Patagonia's emphasis on high-quality outdoor apparel, it is not surprising that the company aims to attract nature lovers as customers. Although chapter 1 cites evidence that the average consumer is not willing to pay a premium for more sustainable products, Patagonia's customers aren't average consumers. An analysis of the effects of the company's switch to higher-cost organic cotton in 1996 showed that Patagonia's customers continued to buy, paying a premium that exceeded the additional cost of that cotton.[23]

Patagonia's founder, Yvon Chouinard, has long prioritized sustainability over short-term financial gains in the company's business model. "Growth isn't central at all, because I'm trying to run this company as if it's going to be here a hundred years from now," he said.[24] "We measure our success on the number of threats averted: old-growth forests that were not clear-cut, mines that were never dug in pristine areas, toxic pesticides that were not sprayed," Chouinard wrote in his book *Let My People Go Surfing*.[25] Like Dr. Bronner's, Patagonia pushes other companies to "do the right thing." In 2002, Chouinard cofounded the group "1% for the Planet,"[26] which was modeled after a program he had started at Patagonia in 1985.[27] The group contributes 1 percent of total revenues to environmental causes. In 2017, the group's website listed 1,319 member companies.

"We operate on the credo that being in business and doing the right thing are not mutually exclusive," said Dave Abeloe, distribution center director for Patagonia. "For everything we do, we look at the impacts on the environment and try to figure out how we can lessen those impacts."[28]

Even so, lowering the total impact occasionally means using less sustainable materials. "We don't want to sacrifice quality for [short-term] environmental reasons," said Jill Dumain, Patagonia's director of environmental strategy. "If a garment is thrown away sooner due to a lack of durability, we haven't solved any environmental problems."[29]

The Footprint Chronicles

To bypass the confusion, mistrust, and "fog" associated with environmental claims and sustainability labels, Patagonia chose a bold approach. It took transparency beyond the ingredient level of "what's in this product's formula" to also reveal "who made this product." Frustrated by the state of eco-labels and corporate social responsibility reports, Patagonia launched the *Footprint Chronicles* on its website in 2007.

The Chronicles provide customers (and anybody else who cares to know) with detailed information about the supply chain for each of many of the company's products. Each product's page includes not only detailed features, materials, qualities, and customer reviews, but at the bottom of the page, Patagonia also shows the main suppliers involved in making the product, along with information about each of them. For example, according to the Chronicles, the Patagonia Windsweep 3-in-1 jacket is sewn by Maxport Ltd. in Vietnam, using fabric woven, dyed, and finished by Nantong Teijin Co. in China, with textiles supplied by TWE-Libeltex BCBA in Belgium and Everest Textile Co. Ltd. in Taiwan.[30]

In addition, the link to the Footprint Chronicles brings up a world map dotted with pins representing each of Patagonia's major supplier and manufacturing locations.[31] Clicking on a pin shows the activities at that location and information about what is made there, the composition of the workforce, and their history with Patagonia (see figure 11.1).

Patagonia has effectively made its supply chain transparent to anyone who wishes to verify the environmental or social claims the company makes about its products. Public response to the Footprint Chronicles has been overwhelmingly positive. Media outlets, ranging from business magazines to rock climbing community publications, have reported on the project, earning Patagonia positive exposure in its core market. Other progressive companies, including Seventh Generation, said they wished they could create something as transparent as the Footprint Chronicles.[32] Some

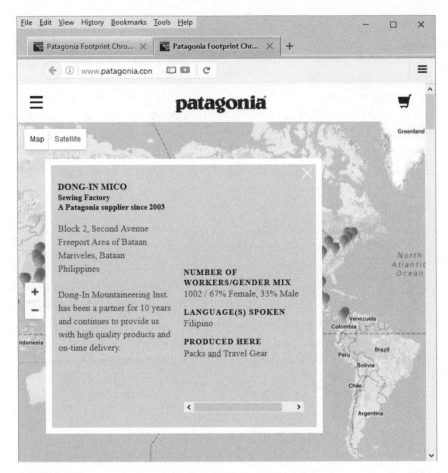

Figure 11.1
The Dong-In Mico site on Patagonia's Footprint Chronicles

companies followed suit, with applications such as Stonyfield's supply chain map,[33] using an MIT-developed tool *SourceMap*, a "social network" style representation of supply chains.[34]

As chapter 3 shows, even just collecting the data and keeping it current can be a challenge. Many deep-green companies try to show their customers the complete story behind the product they offer, intensifying the challenge of transparency.

Showing Everything, Warts and All

Radical transparency can become especially tough when the story is not very rosy. In 2009, Patagonia hired Indian firm Arvind Ltd.

to supply denim. The textile supplier had a reputation for environmental sustainability and fair worker treatment. As part of its supply agreement, Patagonia required Arvind to allow third-party factory audits. Patagonia also sent its new director of environmental and social responsibility, Cara Chacon, to investigate for herself, and she found some problems.

Following Chacon's visit, Patagonia published a photo slideshow titled, "Growing Pains," and added it to the Chronicles. The photos detailed not only the positive reasons why Patagonia chose Arvind, but also the supplier's shortcomings. On the plus side, Arvind had installed a system to cleanse wastewater so thoroughly that it could be safely discharged into the local sewer system.[35] On the minus side, Arvind had an unprotected concrete-edged wastewater drainage ditch, which created a safety hazard. Following Chacon's visit, Arvind installed a railing around the ditch's edge to prevent workers from falling in. Later, Patagonia posted a corresponding photo to prove it.[36]

Being open about environmental challenges, as well as successes, is a line the company *wants* to cross, according to Patagonia's Dumain. "If we started to squirm in our chairs a little bit, we were probably hitting the right point," she said when explaining the Chronicles. Patagonia strives to surpass the level of public disclosure exercised by most companies or any labeling program. That requires transparency from suppliers as well as communicating complex information to consumers. It means not only revealing the situation "as is"—a difficult task in its own right—but also showing the history of mistakes, corrective actions undertaken, and their consequences. Identifying specific worker safety or environmental issues at a supplier factory, and then demonstrating that they were remedied, does not neatly fit on a sticker or a hangtag.

Persistent Problems with Water Resistance

One issue Patagonia has had to address was the use of perfluorocarbon (PFC) fabric treatments, the manufacturing and use of which releases perfluorooctanoic acid (PFOA) as a by-product. Certain PFCs are prized for their ability to resist water, dirt, and oil. They have been widely used for many decades on products ranging from furniture, clothing, tents, car seats, and electronics, to grease-resistant food packaging such as microwave popcorn bags, fast-food wrappers, and pizza boxes.[37] Unfortunately, this resistance is a double-edged sword; these chemicals are also vilified for their ability to resist breakdown when released into the environment (from factories, during use, when washed, and in the waste stream). PFOA and other PFCs can accumulate in plants, animals, human blood, and even breast milk. A wide variety of studies suggests that some of these chemicals are hazardous, especially at high levels, and governments are steadily moving toward restricting their use.[38]

As more global attention was focused on the use of PFOA and other PFCs as water repellents in outdoor textile products, Patagonia chose to be transparent on the issue during the fall 2007 launch of the Footprint Chronicles.[39] The revelation did garner some angry comments, but it also won significant praise for the company's aggressive honesty. "Transparency defuses conflict," said Dumain. "Issues like PFOA, which might have led to confrontations, have instead prompted fruitful conversation."[40]

In the winter of 2012, Greenpeace published a report criticizing Patagonia and 12 other outdoor apparel makers over the presence of PFOA and various PFCs in the makers' clothing.[41,42] The attack surprised Patagonia, who felt it had been very open about the issue and was working to eliminate PFOA. In the aftermath of the attack, Greenpeace further criticized Patagonia's response for not promising a deadline for the removal of all PFCs.[43] For its part, Patagonia wrote, "We don't feel comfortable promising a path forward that hasn't yet been identified—that simply isn't fair given the complexity of this challenge."[44] Greenpeace's reply to this response was that "this is difficult to accept considering that PFC-free alternatives are already available on the market."[45]

Often businesses are accused of having a narrow, short-term mindset regarding environmental issues. Perhaps surprisingly, it may be Greenpeace who is taking the narrower, short-term view in fixating on just the impact of PFCs. Greenpeace claims that the alternative water repellant treatments are good enough, because "the decisive factor is optimal water repellency."[46] But Patagonia takes a broader view that none of the PFC-free alternatives have the durability of PFCs in resisting water, soil, and grease over time, which means current PFC-free jackets must be replaced more frequently.[47] The environmental impact of replacing a 360-gram jacket[48] that becomes quickly soiled or worn out exceeds the impact of about 0.0002 grams of PFCs found in that jacket.[49] Some within Patagonia wondered if there were people in Greenpeace who were sensationalizing an issue of little merit. Ironically, even while the dispute was taking place, Greenpeace was using Patagonia's products in the Arctic. (Greenpeace personnel were fighting oil drilling there.)

Patagonia, for its part, has tested dozens of possible PFC alternatives. It has switched its water-repellent fabric treatment to shorter-chain PFCs, which are not as contentious because their by-products are less bio-accumulative and less persistent in the environment than PFOA.[50] The company has said, "Patagonia's temporary solution, which is also being adopted by a number of manufacturers, is not good enough, but it's the best option we have found so far."[51] Patagonia continues to work with bluesign technologies, a Swiss company, and other apparel industry companies, as well as chemical suppliers and mills, to find alternatives. Patagonia has also made a strategic investment in another Swiss company, Beyond Surface Technologies AG, which is working to develop compounds with lower environmental impacts for outdoor apparel.[52]

Finally, there's no guarantee that PFC-free will actually be greener than PFCs. All of this has led Patagonia to some soul searching. Rick Ridgeway, vice president of external engagement said, "We started to wonder if we should even been [sic] making a product because it's that bad. ... This is a tension that goes on every day in our company. There isn't an apparel company in the world that considers environmental issues that doesn't face this issue. We like to dialogue with customers because some of these issues are so thorny that you can't address them without help."[53] Patagonia feels it does have a responsibility to produce the best possible products within all the trade-offs inherent in apparel manufacturing and then to be transparent about those choices and what is known about their impacts.

When Transparency Muddies the Waters

Patagonia's Footprint Chronicles revealed an especially challenging problem—it demonstrated consumers' limited comprehension of detailed sustainability-related information. When the site debuted, it included data on each product's carbon footprints, water use, and waste. However, the company found that many consumers didn't understand the implications or were overwhelmed by the level of detail. That data have since been removed.

"I think it was fairly new for people, and I think it was hard for people to question what we were saying," said Eliss Foster, senior manager of product responsibility at Patagonia. In that regard, Patagonia faced the same issue of data comprehension and comparability that bedeviled Tesco's "black foot" carbon label program (see chapter 9). Patagonia's competitors lacked the same level of disclosure, so Patagonia's customers could not compare and contrast impact numbers. The company intends to restore the environmental impact data when the apparel industry develops a standardized environmental impact measuring and reporting system. To support that outcome, Patagonia helped found the Sustainable Apparel Coalition, which is developing such a system[54] (see chapter 12).

Peak Transparency Means a Peek at Proprietary Data

The Footprint Chronicles also reveal Patagonia's inner workings to rivals and critics. In theory, competitors could "reverse engineer" Patagonia's products for commercial gain, because the Chronicles list each supplier's street address and details about materials, products, or parts made there. In addition, such full disclosure enables NGOs, government agencies, and journalists to easily investigate the supplier and connect it to Patagonia. Naturally, the latter is Patagonia's key rationale for the disclosure, and the company considers any resulting criticism to be an opportunity for improvement.

This transparency also extends upstream and flattens traditional walls around suppliers' proprietary information. Patagonia's Dumain said that some of Patagonia's suppliers initially balked at allowing public insight into their operations, "We have very blunt language of the good and the bad and what we think," she added by way of explaining the suppliers' reluctance. Nevertheless, Patagonia may have experienced less supplier resistance than other companies could have encountered, because the company has a good reputation and generous supplier remuneration practices. Even though Patagonia's volumes are relatively small with many of its suppliers, it pays more than many other apparel companies do for comparable products.

As the reputation of the Footprint Chronicles grew, many of Patagonia's suppliers began to see their inclusion in the Footprint Chronicles as a badge of honor. In 2013, only one of the company's suppliers had not been profiled. According to its mini-profile, the owners of Vietnamese sewing factory Maxport JSC asked for their details not to be included. Patagonia honored that request but added, "We consider Maxport's employment practices, as well as the quality of its work, to be among the best of all our suppliers."[55]

Although the Footprint Chronicles seem like a paragon of supply chain transparency, they are primarily limited to covering Tier 1 suppliers. Getting information about Tier 2 (and deeper-tier) suppliers is more difficult. To monitor Tier 2 suppliers in China and elsewhere, Patagonia works with bluesign technologies and several NGOs.[56]

Supplier Transparency Fosters Supplier Improvement

The Footprint Chronicles may have been intended as a consumer communications channel, but it also lets suppliers see each other's practices. "Because our suppliers like it, they watch it. They learn from it," said Randy Harward, Patagonia's quality director.[57] Harward believes that suppliers viewing other suppliers' practices and copying them has accomplished more within Patagonia's supply chain than almost anything else that Patagonia has done.[58] "It is beyond our wildest dreams successful," Harward said.[59]

In that regard, it is akin to the supplier and supply chain development efforts of Seventh Generation and of Natura (see chapter 12), in which these deep-green companies nurture the development of sustainable practices among their suppliers and throughout their industries. Dumain noted that a group of firms with progressive sustainability agendas—Stonyfield Farm, Aveda, Ben &

Jerry's, and Seventh Generation—have long informally shared best practices. "These companies have been working together for years to raise the bar," said Andrea Asch, manager of natural resources at Ben & Jerry's. "That's where Patagonia is with these Footprint Chronicles—that's the new bar."[60]

Sustainability Has Veto Power

Patagonia gives its sustainability and social responsibility associates "veto power" over the company's choice of suppliers. This veto power applies to Tier 1 and Tier 2 factories. Suppliers notify Patagonia about their intention to use a new candidate factory to fulfill a production batch. Patagonia then audits the supplier using a scorecard covering: (i) business aspects such as price, capacity, and delivery capabilities; (ii) quality; (iii) social responsibility; and (iv) environmental responsibility.

According to Patagonia's Chacon, in 2013 the company vetted the factories of 18 potential suppliers. Five of them were "approved" and 11 more received a "conditionally approved" status owing to low-, medium-, or high-risk issues (which could include either environmental or social issues), but no "zero tolerance" issues (such as child labor, forced labor, abuse, or harassment). Patagonia negotiated remediation of the identified issues with these conditional suppliers, usually before orders were placed. Two factories were vetoed for zero tolerance issues: child labor (in China, age 15) and refusal to admit Patagonia's third-party auditor into a factory (in Vietnam).

As mentioned above, Patagonia has been working with bluesign technologies, which categorizes textile industry chemicals as *blue*, safe to use; *gray*, special handling required; and *black*, forbidden under its standard.[61] Patagonia's requirement that more and more suppliers adhere to bluesign's specifications may result in "some changes to our supply chain," according to Steve Richardson, Patagonia's director of material development.[62]

Supporting Reuse

"DON'T BUY THIS JACKET"[63] is not the typical marketing slogan that most sales-hungry apparel companies would emblazon in a full-page *New York Times* ad (see figure 11.2) on Black Friday—the day after Thanksgiving in the United States and the country's biggest shopping day of the year. The ad encouraged consumers to buy second-hand Patagonia apparel instead. These used clothes were offered by independent eBay sellers under an arrangement between eBay and Patagonia.

This arrangement had its roots in 2011, when eBay started approaching major brands, like Patagonia, to develop portals through which reliable sellers could sell used products.[64] Patagonia signed on as part of the clothing company's larger "Common Threads" initiative, which promotes conscious consumption through resale, reuse, and recycling of Patagonia products. Sellers on eBay who want their auctions listed on Patagonia's website must pledge to "help wrest the full life out of every Patagonia product"[65] by buying used when possible and selling their Patagonia clothes when they're no longer in use.[66]

Figure 11.2

The *New York Times* ad

A November 2013 search on eBay found listings for 24,524 Patagonia items in 14 different product categories.[67] Sellers advertised their items with positive language like a "great lightweight jacket for layering"[68] or "maximum warmth with minimal weight." At the European launch of the joint program with eBay, Patagonia's Vice President Vincent Stanley joked that the eBay partnership may be a kind of customer loyalty program, but "it may be the only one in the world that is based not on more sales but perhaps on fewer."[69]

Most brand owners perceive sales of their used or refurbished goods as cannibalizing new sales. Caitlin Bristol, senior manager of global impact for eBay, commented: "We often get, as you might imagine, handfuls of cease-and-desists demands and angry calls, particularly from high-end luxury brands, about their products showing up second hand on eBay." For Patagonia, however, the calculus was different. These second-hand sales help Patagonia achieve its long-term environmental objectives. "The greenest product is often one that already exists," said Lori Duvall, global director of green at eBay. From 2005 to 2013, Patagonia recycled more than 56 tons of old clothing returned to its retail locations.[70] In 2013, the company began selling used Patagonia products directly at four of its stores.[71]

Interestingly, the initiative actually helped sales of new apparel in three ways. First and foremost, it was a testament to Patagonia apparel's durability. Second, for consumers worried about spending $400 on a new jacket, knowing that Patagonia provides a venue to resell the jacket in the future can help ease the purchasing decision, Duvall said.[72] Last, selling used clothing brings less affluent consumers into the brand's fold by enabling them to purchase less pricey second-hand products, creating long-lasting brand engagement. Thus, paradoxically, not only did Patagonia's "Don't Buy This Jacket" campaign not stunt its growth, the company grew by 27 percent by 2013, reaching $575 million in sales. In fact, the eBay initiative was so successful that an advertising industry publication questioned whether it was just a marketing ploy.[73]

SEVENTH GENERATION, LITERALLY

Seventh Generation's name comes from the Iroquois constitution (the "Great Law of Peace"). This Native American confederacy urged leaders to consider the impact of their actions on their descendants seven generations into the future.[74] The maker of household and personal care products was founded in Burlington, Vermont, and has taken a progressive approach to business since its earliest days in 1988.[75] Taking the long view on its products, Seventh Generation's leaders and employees have worked to push and pull the rest of the industry to act in an environmentally responsible mold.

"The old business model focused exclusively on profit is no longer viable, and the world needs to forge new economic and social systems built on sustainability," said John Replogle, CEO of Seventh Generation. He made this comment after the United Nations named his company a "Leader of Change" in 2011.[76] Jim Barch, director of research and development for Seventh Generation said, "I would argue that one has to examine the meaning of ROI in a broader context than is normal, because most companies are trying to show they've created wealth, when we're trying to show we are actually creating value."[77]

Radically Transparent

Many mainstream companies employ a phalanx of lawyers, marketers, and public relations experts whose sole duty is to prevent embarrassing stories or sensitive tidbits from escaping the fortress constructed around their proprietary information. "What people don't know, they can't protest" may well be the motto of these professional enforcers of corporate reticence. In contrast, Seventh Generation has long engaged in "radical transparency," which entails openness about the company's products and activities.

Whereas many companies have "secret formulas" or only disclose generic ingredient terms (e.g., "fragrance" or "preservative"), Seventh Generation publishes complete lists of all ingredients in each of its products. For example, the company's baby lotion lists 20 different specific ingredients.[78] Seventh Generation is confident about these disclosures because of its careful ingredient selection processes. "We adhere to the precautionary principle, meaning that substances are guilty until proven innocent in our eyes," said Heidi Raatikainen, associate scientist.[79] That is, the company is not satisfied with just an absence of evidence of toxicity—it looks for *evidence of absence* of toxicity. Jeffrey Hollender, the company's cofounder and former CEO, wrote, "Publicly sharing all our activities preempts the critics, and more eyes on the company's activities means more advocates and friends."[80]

This policy can cause problems with suppliers, however. Clement Choy, senior director of research and development for Seventh Generation, noted that some fragrance companies in particular are very nervous about disclosing confidential business information, such as their ingredients, for competitive reasons. However, he added, "part of our principle of working with a fragrance company is you need to tell us 100 percent what's inside, because we're going to put it on our bottle. And there were some fragrance companies that walked away from the table and said as a principle value, our values aren't aligned."[81]

Only a small percentage of Seventh Generation's customers actually want to know every ingredient in every cleaning product they bring into their home, according to Reed Doyle, the company's former director of corporate social responsibility. "We did it because we knew if we did it ... everyone else would be forced to follow," he said, "and that's exactly what happened in the cleaning products industry. ... This group called Women's Voices for the Earth went out there and pointed fingers at a lot of these guys [other cleaning product companies] and said, 'Hey, consumers have a right to know what's inside.'"[82]

Maybe My Warts Aren't as Bad as Yours
Like Patagonia, Seventh Generation believes that self-criticism can be healthy. Hollender once penned a critique of his company's own products and posted it on the company's website.[83] His competitors, he said, told Seventh Generation's retail customers of the self-critique.

Whereas competitors expected the self-critique to damage Seventh Generation's reputation, according to Hollender's account, many retailers responded by asking the competitors for their own self-critique. "The reality is, our [ingredient] list, as bad as it was, was better than the list that all our competitors had," he said during his presentation at the 2010 World Innovation Forum. "And in most cases, our competitors wouldn't even provide the buyer with a similar list."[84]

Snitching on Competitors
Similar to Dr. Bronner's, Seventh Generation also acts like an environmental activist at times. The company encourages environmental NGOs to test Seventh Generation's products against similar products from its competitors. Martin Wolf, Seventh Generation's director of product sustainability and authenticity, may even tip off an NGO that certain competing products contain an objectionable chemical, such as a known carcinogen.

In the short-term, these NGO-like actions serve the business interests of companies like Seventh Generation and Dr. Bronner's, earning them goodwill with their deep-green customers and putting competitors at a disadvantage. "As a result, we may come out on top," Wolf said. "But again, it's about how do we push the industry in the right direction." In the long-term, this strategy may raise the environmental bar for the entire industry, which is the ultimate objective of these deep-green companies.

Raising the Bar

In 2004, members of the American Cleaning Institute debated whether to add sustainability to the organization's core mission. Some members wanted to relegate sustainability to committee work that supplemented the existing mission. Seventh Generation's Wolf said, "I argued that no, you can't have a small box to the side called sustainability. It had to be core to the mission of the association. And they rewrote the charter of the American Cleaning Institute to include sustainability."[85]

In general, corporations lobby against tighter regulations that might force them to redesign products, increase costs, or limit innovation. However, some deeply sustainable companies actually lobby *for* regulation, as both a sustainability initiative and a competitive tool that creates a burden for less sustainable companies. To transform its industry, Seventh Generation joined with several NGOs on campaigns across the country to pressure state legislatures to regulate chemicals.[86] It teamed with notable environmental activist Erin Brockovich[87] and other companies like Stonyfield Farm as part of the Companies for Safer Chemicals Coalition.[88] Seventh Generation even sent its own scientists to legislative hearings to wage a protracted campaign to ban the use of phosphates in dishwashing detergents (see chapter 8).[89,90]

A Baby Attacks

In November 2009, a video was posted online featuring a babbling baby calling on other babies to crawl to Washington, DC. "Just put one hand in front of the other, followed by one knee in front of the other, and then sort of use your foot to scoot along," said the subtitled translation of the baby's babbling. "To Washington! In order to demand a law that will eliminate toxic chemicals found in household products," urged the infant activist.[91]

The video was part of a campaign called the "Million Baby Crawl" (a play on the 1995 "Million Man March"[92]). Adorable and infectious, it was nearly the polar opposite of the gruesome and poignant Greenpeace video attacking Nestlé's use of noncertified palm oil in KitKat bars (see chapter 1). The Million Baby Crawl video also featured a company product: the animated baby delivered its campaign speech from atop a literal soap box—one with a Seventh Generation label on it.

Beginning in 2009, Seventh Generation focused much of its activism on reforming the 1976 Toxic Substances Control Act (TSCA). The original act prohibited manufacturers from using substances not on the "TSCA inventory" without first providing the EPA with information on the chemical's impact on human health and the environment.[93] The original TSCA inventory automatically admitted about 62,000 chemicals already in use in American commerce without any testing at all. Nearly four decades after the old law's passage, the EPA had reviewed the health and safety of only about 200 of those grandfathered-in chemicals.[94] Seventh Generation urged legislators to increase the number of chemicals tested and to prevent adding new chemicals to the TSCA inventory without a thorough EPA review. Initially, the Million Baby Crawl campaign achieved very little formal legislative progress.[95] In 2016, Congress passed reform legislation that Seventh Generation said was "some improvement over current law, [but] it still falls short of our goals."[96]

Jumpstart Scaling

While Seventh Generation used legislation and competitive pressure to force other household cleaning companies to reduce their environmental impacts, the company also made it easier for competitors to do so. "We're willing to give up rights for the greater good," said Martin Wolf, of Seventh Generation. For example, a collaboration with Rhodia, one of the company's suppliers, found a biological source for a feedstock ingredient that had previously only been available from petroleum-derived sources. India Glycols, a supplier of plant-based bottles for Coca-Cola, had created a bio-based ethylene gas that Rhodia and Seventh Generation could use to synthesize cleansers. Even though Seventh Generation was the driving force behind the innovative use of the plant-based material developed by Rhodia, Seventh Generation did not demand a period of exclusivity from its supplier. "We said all we want to do is be first, and we'll do a co-announcement. And the co-announcement was probably more important to Rhodia than supplying us the couple million dollars' worth of plant-based chemicals,"[97] said Wolf.

While this open approach to research and development allows competitors to "catch up" quickly, it also offers Seventh Generation a subtle competitive advantage. It encourages suppliers to come to the company with new ideas, because they know that Seventh Generation will not pursue restrictive rights or exclusivity beyond a short period, which allows the supplier to grow revenues through broader sales of the new material. "It's amazing the type of collaborators we get that come to us and say, 'We want to work with you, because we see the speed to market, we see that you can bring things in a lot faster,'" said Seventh Generation's Choy. "There's a lot of different people that would probably never come to a $150 [million], $200 million company, but because of our way of going about business, I think there's an intrigue there that we can help prove concepts that will eventually lead to commercialization of that particular product of their platform."[98]

Seventh Generation is not alone in its innovation-sharing approach. Motivated by the same philosophy, Patagonia shared its development of Yulex bio-rubber extracted from the guayule plant, which entered the market in 2012.[99] Patagonia is using this naturally derived rubber to replace petroleum-derived neoprene in wetsuits and is sharing the technology, because the company is committed to increasing the environmental sustainability of the entire industry. Just like Seventh Generation's sharing arrangements, such a move encourages scaling of new material manufacturing, reducing its cost, and fueling further growth for Patagonia.

BALANCING ECONOMIC AND ENVIRONMENTAL CHALLENGES

Dr. Bronner's, Patagonia, and Seventh Generation exemplify what might be called "deep green" companies. These companies often sell premium-priced products backed by a story and the environmental credentials of the product or company. They serve a comparatively small customer segment that shares these environmental values and that is often willing to pay a higher price relative to mainstream offerings of similar performance.

Mainstream public companies face several challenges in replicating this model. Unilever CEO Paul Polman would likely lose his job if he caged himself in front of the White House or 10 Downing Street in the name of any environmental issue. David Bronner can do so because his customers and private owners are as committed as he is and even applaud such acts. Dr. Bronner's serves a narrow, eco-conscious market niche, while Polman must satisfy a wide range of customers, most of whom are more price sensitive than environmentally sensitive. Polman must also satisfy his public shareholders, bondholders, and the financial markets, who are crucial suppliers of the capital that Unilever requires to operate. These stakeholders may be generally less concerned with Unilever's social and environmental mission than they are with high returns on their equity investments and low-risk repayment of debts.

Regardless, Unilever *has* committed itself to environmental stewardship. In 2015 Polman declared, "In a volatile world of growing social inequality, rising population, development challenges and climate change, the need for businesses to adapt is clear, as are the benefits and opportunities." He added, "This calls for a transformational approach across the whole value chain if we are to continue to grow."[100] The company created a series of sustainable brands that have accounted for half the company's growth in 2014 and that grew at twice the rate of the rest of the business. Many green bloggers and publications picked up this statistic.[101]

The *Financial Times*, however, reported that some displeased shareholders perceived that Polman cared more about the environment than about the business. In an article titled, "Paul Polman's

Socially Responsible Unilever Falls Short on Growth,"[102] the paper cited revenue reductions in 2013 and 2014. It also noted that while the FTSE Consumer Goods Index grew by 80 percent during Polman's tenure, Unilever share price grew by only 40 percent during the same period.

Shareholders and Stakeholders

The trade-off between economic viability and environmental sustainability is at the heart of a long-running debate over the responsibilities of corporations and their decision makers. In a 1970 article titled, "The Social Responsibility of Business is to Increase its Profits," Milton Friedman, the noted Chicago economist, argued for the supremacy of the title's thesis.[103] For public companies, this requires serving their shareholders through ongoing growth of the company's stock price, dividends, and other financial returns. Friedman was reacting to a view that corporations also have social responsibilities to other stakeholders—their employees, the communities they operate in, the environment, and society at large, as articulated, for example, by Edward Freeman in his 1984 book, *Strategic Management: A Stakeholders Approach.*[104]

US investor protection laws side with Friedman's view, stating that the fiduciary duty of managers is to maximize shareholders' value. Although a company's managers have broad discretion under the doctrine of the business judgment rule,[105] they must ultimately serve as the stewards of their investors' financial resources. Note that within that context, eco-efficiency, eco-risk mitigation, and eco-segmentation initiatives are adequately aligned with shareholder interests. Managers may also engage in some level of philanthropic efforts as long as the outlays seem to support profit-driven strategies such as marketing or branding initiatives.[106] Despite all that, the companies in this chapter seem to go beyond these aligned activities when they reveal unfavorable facts about the company (radical transparency), aid competitors in becoming more sustainable (open sharing of competitive data and innovation), pay suppliers more than the minimum required, or forego lucrative business opportunities (eschewing large distribution deals or promising new raw materials, on sustainability grounds).

Although a company's failure to maximize shareholder value is not a criminal issue, it does portend a potential civil dispute between shareholders and management. Profit-preferring investors could potentially sue a firm in civil court for excessive investment in sustainability. Thus, the legal risks depend on investors' views on sustainability. Patagonia, Dr. Bronner's, and Seventh Generation are all privately held, which enables the companies to avoid such risks; their investors agree with the firms' priorities. In 2002, Patagonia CFO Martha Groszewski said, "It would be very difficult for us to be who we are [if the company were publicly owned]. The programs we support would be seen as unnecessary."[107] Former Patagonia Executive Vice President Perry Klebahn added, "There is not as much pressure for growth as if we were publicly traded."

A Different Corp.

One way for investor-backed corporations to engage in substantive amounts of activities other than profit-maximizing ones—be they environmental sustainability, social responsibility, or other philanthropic activities—is to change the company's legal structure. In April 2010, Maryland became the first US state to create a new type of corporate structure known as "Benefit Corporation," or "Benefit Corp."[108] Unlike standard corporations, with their legal obligation to shareholders' financial interests, a Benefit Corporation requires companies to have a general public benefit purpose and allows the company to codify specific environmental and social goals, in addition to and sometimes at the expense of preserving investors' capital and earning profits. Becoming a Benefit Corporation requires approval by the board of directors and shareholders; amendment of the company's bylaws; and reregistration of the entity. As of September 2017, Benefit Corporations could be formed in 33 US states[109] including Delaware, which is the legal home of half of all publicly traded companies in the country.[110] In 2016, Italy became the first country outside the United States to allow companies to register as *Societá Benefit* (a direct translation of the American term).[111]

The Benefit Corporation movement was spearheaded by B Lab, a nonprofit organization providing a certification known as

"Certified B Corporation" or "B Corp" that is distinct from the legal benefit corporation status provided by states. Unfortunately, the "B Corp" term is often used interchangeably (and mistakenly) to refer to both. The B Corp certification is similar to other credence-based labels (see chapter 9), in which companies pay a fee, complete a self-assessment questionnaire, attain a sufficient score on the assessment, submit supporting documentation, agree to make certain public disclosures, and allow for random on-site reviews.[112] As of July 2016, there were 4,099 Benefit Corporations,[113] and, as of September 2017, there were 2,109 certified B Corps worldwide.[114]

The confusion and overlap between Benefit Corporations and B Corps is twofold. First, the B Corp certification requires that companies that have the legal option to become a Benefit Corporation must do so within four years of certification (or get re-certified).[115] Second, Benefit Corporations must submit independent third-party reports about their environmental and social performance, and many have chosen B Lab's B Corp for this purpose. Note that only a formal, legal Benefit Corporation status protects managers from investors' lawsuits related to having goals other than maximizing shareholders' value.

Benefit Corporation status also provides protection for a company's environmental mission in the event of a hostile takeover bid. Without Benefit Corporation status, a buyout offer could tempt the shareholders and force the company into the hands of a "non-green" buyer. "The benefit corporation has allowed us to preserve our mission and culture against unsolicited tender offers. We don't have to worry that our board of directors might feel compelled to accept an offer that isn't in our overall best interests," said Jenn Vervier, director of strategy and sustainability at New Belgium Brewing Company.[116]

To B or Not to B (and Which B?)
The three green companies in this chapter have made somewhat different choices about Benefit Corporation status and B Corp certification. Patagonia became a certified B Corp in December 2011[117] and filed for Benefit Corporation status for five of its corporations

on January 1, 2012, the very first day the designation was available to California corporations.[118] "Patagonia is trying to build a company that could last 100 years," said founder Yvon Chouinard on the day Patagonia signed up. "Benefit corporation legislation creates the legal framework to enable mission-driven companies like Patagonia to stay mission-driven through succession, capital raises, and even changes in ownership, by institutionalizing the values, culture, processes, and high standards put in place by founding entrepreneurs," he said.[119]

Dr. Bronner's converted to a Benefit Corporation in July 2015[120] and became B Corp certified after that.[121] The company's new bylaws formally expand the company's goals to include (i) spending on public awareness of environmental and social issues; (ii) the purchase of Fair Trade and organic ingredients; (iii) equitable employee compensation; and (iv) indemnification of shareholders' activism on environmental and social issues. That last item essentially implies that the company can pay David Bronner's personal legal costs and fines when he tweaks the nose of US authorities over issues like hemp.

Seventh Generation is a founding member of the B Corp certification system. The company has been certified since May 2007[122] and received its latest certification in 2015.[123] However, Seventh Generation has not sought Benefit Corporation status, even though it has been available since 2011 in the company's home state of Vermont. Instead, the firm relies on clear language in the company's 2008 bylaws to define the firm's broader mission. The company has also gained outside investment from funds friendly to the company's mission, such as $30 million from Generation Investment Management Fund, which was cofounded by former US Vice President Al Gore.[124]

In September 2016, Unilever agreed to acquire Seventh Generation under terms that would maintain Seventh Generation's mission. "One of the things they really wanted to do is not impact or change who we are," said John Replogle, CEO of Seventh Generation.[125] Unilever took a similar approach when it bought Ben & Jerry's in 2000, allowing the ice cream maker to keep its corporate social and environmental mission. Unilever even supported Ben & Jerry's B Corp certification in 2012.[126]

Strategic Choices

The financial performance of a company, as viewed by shareholders, is most readily measured by a company's market capitalization, which is generally a function of three major factors. The first is the company's net present value of all future profits, which itself is a function of the investors' perceptions of the company's future revenues and costs. The second contributor to the company's total value is its assets, including tangible assets (such as buildings, inventory, cash, and payments owed by customers) and long-term intangible assets (such as patents, goodwill, and business methods). The third element, to be subtracted from the value of the company, is its liabilities, such as debts to bond holders, payments owed to suppliers, and money owed for lawsuits or other legal obligations. In general, shareholders prefer highly profitable, low-risk, fast-growing companies with valuable assets and minimal liabilities.

The environmental performance of a company, as assessed by the company itself or by NGOs and activists, is harder to measure and reduce to a single number. Not only are there many types of resource consumption, emissions, and toxicity impacts, but the impacts span the entire supply chain from suppliers to customers, around the world. There is no standard allocation mechanism related to environmental impact that can assign customer use or supplier footprint to a given company. Nevertheless, we aggregate all these dimensions in a notional "environmental impact" variable that reflects a company's net environmental effects.

Figure 11.3 depicts a company's space of possibilities on these two dimensions: environmental impact and market capitalization. The white area is the space of known and feasible operating conditions. The coordinates of any point in that space represent the outcome of how the company operates in terms financial and

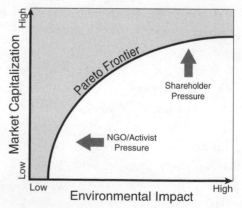

Figure 11.3
The Pareto Frontier

environmental performance. Points in the shaded area represent levels of performance that the company cannot yet achieve with known actions and current technologies. Investors would prefer companies to operate as high as possible along the vertical axis—in other words, to maximize shareholders' value. Environmental activists would like companies to operate as far to the left as possible on the horizontal axis—minimizing environmental impact.

All points on the boundary line between the white and shaded area in the figure—the Pareto frontier—reflect the best achievable performance levels of leading companies operating at the best possible levels of some mix of financial and environmental performance. Companies that have exhausted their low-hanging fruit of all the feasible initiatives face a trade-off of sliding one way or the other along the Pareto frontier. The slope of the frontier line reflects fundamental trade-offs between financial and environmental performance. The Pareto frontier is unique to each company because, in the short-run, it is a function of many contextual issues including the company's assets, the industry, its product designs, its supplier base, its distribution channels, and its customers.

The No-Go Zones: Non-viability and Noncompliance

Companies are not completely free to choose where to operate in the space depicted in figure 11.3. Every company faces constraints on both financial performance and environmental performance. In the long-term, businesses that consistently lose money are not economically viable. A company needs a minimum level of financial performance, over time, to cover expenses, attract capital, repay debts, compensate shareholders, accumulate reserves, and invest in its future. Green firms cannot continuously operate in the red. For example, Dr. Bronner's Benefit Corporation mission includes special public-benefit purposes that call for buying only sustainable ingredients "except when such certified ingredients are unavailable in sufficient quantities or are so cost prohibitive."[127] Similarly, Seventh Generation rewards employees for growth and profits, as well as sustainability.[128]

Likewise, the NGO attacks and government regulations cited in the first chapter illustrate that a company must attain some acceptable level of environmental performance. Governments can push companies toward lower environmental impact by tightening regulations. Most such actions are viewed by many companies as restricting their operating space, leading to inefficiencies and higher costs. Governments, however, have been willing to make this trade-off in the name of the common good when markets were perceived as failing to do it on their own.

In addition, as many of the examples throughout this book show, NGO attacks can be costly, motivating companies to be sufficiently environmentally responsible to forestall such potential attacks. Thus, both dimensions of performance have some bounds, which restrict the space of viable options, as shown in figure 11.4. (Of course, the lack of

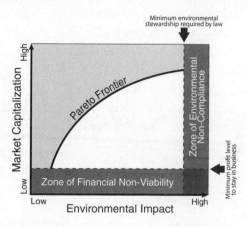

Figure 11.4
Meeting sustainability and financial goals

regulations or enforcement in some developing countries causes a corresponding absence of minimum environmental stewardship requirements. However, suppliers to Western companies may face customer requirements to limit environmental impacts.)

More Profitable, More Sustainable, or Both?

Most companies are not operating continuously along the Pareto frontier, because they are not doing all they can to achieve the best level of performance on either dimension. There are always more opportunities to reduce costs, mitigate risks, or boost revenues with new products or smart pricing. Analogously, most companies have further opportunities to improve supply chain resource efficiency, mitigate environmental risks across the life cycle, or boost the environmental qualities of their products. That is, most companies operate somewhere "below" the Pareto frontier at, for example, Point X in figure 11.5 and could move toward the Pareto frontier, improving either their financial performance, their environmental stewardship, or both. The direction of improving both dimensions (or improving one without degrading the other) is the zone represented by the grayed area in figure 11.5.

Figure 11.5 highlights the feasible region, depicting three different directions in which a company may choose to go. *P.Max* is the direction of maximizing profit at the expense of environmental performance. *E.Min* represents reducing environmental impact at the expense of profits, and the gray area represents directions that improve both goals.

Figure 11.5
Options for improving performance

Some companies, like those discussed in this chapter, move in the direction of the lower-left *E.Min* corner of the diagram—choosing higher environmental performance over higher financial performance. Benefit Corporation regulations provide a formal legal framework for companies to move "in the *E.Min* direction," reducing environmental impact at the expense of financial performance. In contrast, other companies tend to move toward the top-left *P.Max* corner of the diagram by maximizing shareholders' value while doing the minimum required to stay within the law and "out of trouble." This is the case with many B2B enterprises, which, because they operate "behind the scenes," are less susceptible to direct NGO pressure that can degrade consumer brands. Many of these companies will comply with the law and do what their customers require but no more. Of course, many other B2B companies, such as BASF, Siemens, and Alcoa, have significant environmental initiatives in place.

Numerous authors argue that profits and environmental sustainability are not at odds with each other and that companies can achieve both. This is certainly true if companies can pick performance improvements within the grayed region of figure 11.5, which allows them to move toward the Pareto frontier, improving on both dimensions. This is the case with initiatives motivated by eco-efficiency, eco-risk management, and/or eco-segmentation considerations. However, once companies reach the Pareto frontier, most of the low-hanging fruit, such as energy savings and waste reduction, as well as risk mitigation and new green product introduction, will have been harvested, and, without radical change, they will face unavoidable trade-offs between environmental and financial performance.

At that point, to further increase profitability, a company might, for instance, select factory sites or suppliers located in areas with lax regulations to avoid compliance costs. Alternatively, to further reduce impact, the company may need to place more onerous restrictions on suppliers, invest in expensive renewable energy or water conservation tactics, or design products with more sustainable but higher-cost materials. Pushing past the Pareto frontier to deliver both high financial performance and lower environmental impact requires a fundamental change.

12

The Travails of Scale

Although the deep-green companies described in the previous chapter have been quite successful, not a single one has captured a significant share of world markets.[1] A substantial gulf lies between these deep-green companies and the larger mainstream ones that dominate retailers' shelves. Dr. Bronner's sources its sustainable palm oil from its sister company, Serendipalm, which produces a mere 350 tons of palm oil per year.[2] By comparison, as the largest palm oil buyer in the world, Unilever purchases 1.5 million tons of palm oil and derivatives annually.[3] It would take Serendipalm almost 12 years of day-in day-out production to produce just a single day's supply for Unilever.

This massive gap in scale creates a corresponding gap in the effects of their efforts on palm oil sustainability, which is primarily concerned with mitigating the clear-cutting and burning of forests in Southeast Asia. No matter how much the diminutive Dr. Bronner's reduces its own environmental impact, the improvements will have little impact on the global palm oil market. In contrast, even a small, incremental 1 percent improvement in palm oil sustainability by giant Unilever may have more than 40 times the effect of Dr. Bronner's largest efforts. (Although even Unilever only purchases less than 3 percent of the global palm oil production.[4])

SUSTAINABILITY AT SCALE

Unilever's goal of sourcing all its palm oil from sustainable plantations is significantly more difficult to achieve than it is for Dr. Bronner's. In fact, the Rainforest Alliance lists limited supply as the first barrier to increased purchasing of certified sustainable palm oil.[5] This is an obstacle to sustainability for large companies and is a barrier to growth for smaller ones.

Fast Growing but Not Fast Enough

As part of its efforts to find more sustainable sources of packaging (see chapter 8), Dell approached Unisource Global Solutions, a small company that had been developing bamboo-cushioning technology. For shipments from China, where bamboo can be locally sourced, the material is more sustainable than cardboard because of bamboo's high yield and fast growth rate.[6] Dell developed the bamboo supply chain carefully, gaining Forest Stewardship Council certification in China. Oliver Campbell, director of procurement packaging, said, "I did not want to be the guy on *60 Minutes* taking bamboo out of the mouths of baby pandas."[7] By 2011, Dell was using bamboo in the packaging of 70 percent of its notebook computers,[8] and Unisource had more than tripled its sales.

Dell, however, was not the only company switching to bamboo as a more sustainable packaging material. As global demand for bamboo rose, prices rose to levels that Dell could not justify. "[We were a] victim of our own success I think. By popularizing bamboo, others really started to take a look at it," said Campbell.[9] In theory, surging prices for a material, such as bamboo, would eventually spur growth in supply and a reversion of prices back to the marginal cost of production. However, as the saying goes "in theory, theory and practice are the same. In practice, they are not."[10] In practice, the total global capacity for producing a material may be limited by natural resource constraints or land use regulations, such as anti-deforestation policies.

In 2015, Dell transitioned much of its laptop product packaging from bamboo cushions to cushions made from sustainably sourced paper and wheat straw. According to Dell, wheat straw became a less-expensive solution with comparable sustainability benefits.[11]

The Udder Challenges of Organic Growth

Using only organic milk is one of Stonyfield Farm's environmental commitments[12] (see chapter 6). Organic milk requires livestock raised according to organic farming methods in which the cows are allowed to graze on pesticide-free pastures, are fed only organic fodder, and are not treated with growth hormones. As demand for Stonyfield's organic yogurt grew, the company's demand for organic milk outstripped the local supply, and the company started sourcing organic milk from more distant states. When demand increased further, Stonyfield and other organic milk buyers faced mounting constraints. Organic milk production was not keeping pace with demand, owing to costs and delays inherent in the multi-year process of switching from conventional to organic production methods.

To switch to certified organic production, a dairy farm had to stop using pesticides for two to three years on pasture land, feed cows higher-priced organic feed for at least one year, and change its veterinary practices.[13] During this long transition time, farmers would likely face higher costs and lower yields but would not get a boost in the price of their milk until the transition was complete. This inability to source enough organic milk forced Stonyfield to convert two of its product lines from organic to conventional milk.[14]

In 2006, Stonyfield considered using powdered organic milk shipped from New Zealand to supplement its domestic supply. The company already used small amounts of powdered organic milk to offset inconsistencies in its incoming fluid milk, but the suggestion that the company might buy powdered milk from the other side of the globe upset some of Stonyfield's core consumers. In part, this discomfort came from CEO Gary Hirshberg's comment that powdered milk shipped from family farms in New Zealand would have a lower carbon footprint than chilled milk shipped from Wisconsin.[15] Some consumers feared that Stonyfield planned to make yogurt entirely from powdered milk, which was never part of the plan. The controversy began shortly after Danone increased its stake in the company to 80 percent, making Stonyfield more vulnerable to perceived sustainability issues. "We became the big bad guys! We knew that would happen once we did the Danone deal," said Nancy Hirshberg, former vice president of strategic initiatives.[16]

To protect the brand and "get back to its roots," Gary Hirshberg abandoned the New Zealand powdered milk idea.[17,18] Instead, Stonyfield Farm and Organic Valley (an organic dairy farm cooperative that is Stonyfield's main supplier of organic milk) invested in farmer education, recruitment, and outreach to add hundreds of new organic dairy farmers in the US to its supply chain.[19] As more organic milk became available, the company converted its entire line back.

As of 2015, the kinds of capacity problems that Stonyfield faced continued to plague many organic agricultural commodities such as eggs, corn, beans, soy, and chickens. "You can have great brands and great products, but if you don't have supply of [agricultural] products, you're going to be in trouble," said Irwin Simon, CEO of publicly traded Hain Celestial Group Inc., a $2 billion maker of organic and natural brands. The shortages have forced natural foods companies to hire full-time recruiters, offer technical training, finance farmers' conversion costs, offer up to five-year purchasing commitments, or start their own organic farming and livestock operations. "Supply growth isn't something that happens overnight," said Chuck Eggert, founder and CEO of Oregon-based Pacific Foods.[20]

Other certified ingredient supply chains have had similar growing pains. At one time, there wasn't enough fair trade sugar in the world for Green & Black's to increase production and keep fair trade certification across its entire line, said Dominic Lowe, the managing director for the company. The company also could not add a fair trade cherry chocolate bar because fair trade cherries simply did not exist.[21] Lowe said in 2009 that he was in talks with Fairtrade International to find ways to certify more ingredients. In 2010, as the fair trade movement matured, Green & Black's announced that it would convert all of its chocolate sold in Australia to fair trade by the end of 2011,[22] despite the sourcing challenges.

Both Stonyfield and Green & Black's faced business growth pressures from their respective parent companies. In the purchase and sales agreement of Stonyfield, Danone committed to keep Gary Hirshberg as CEO only as long as Stonyfield meets double digit growth targets.[23] And William Kendall, CEO of Green & Black's, said, "When Cadbury bought the business, it was growing at 'x' and Cadbury wanted that to be '3x.' They pushed it into America and went in so hard that the brand pretty much died out there."[24]

Growing Green

In April of 2013, members of this book's research team toured Dr. Bronner's world headquarters in Vista, California, which is colocated with one of its two production facilities. The tour lasted less than 30 minutes. In 2011, the same team visited a new Unilever distribution center in Cali, Colombia. Touring just this single cross-docking facility took a full hour, and that facility represented one portion of a single branch of Unilever's operations in only one country out of the more than 190 that it serves.[25] Unilever is literally more than a thousand times larger than Dr. Bronner's—169,000 multinational employees spread across the globe in 252 locations[26] versus 150 eco-minded Californians.

The enormous contrast between Dr. Bronner's and Unilever's size, geographic spread, and diversity creates a much greater challenge for Unilever when realigning its far-flung workforce to its strategic push for sustainable growth. "By any reckoning, this is one of the most ambitious 'change management' programs going on in any big company today," said Jonathon Porritt, a member of Unilever's external advisory board and founder of Forum for the Future. Commenting on Unilever's second annual sustainability report, he said, "As this report shows, progress is good, and some individual projects are hugely inspiring. But there is still a long way to go before the sustainable living plan is lived and breathed by every single part of the business."

The challenge is not unique to large mainstream firms; it also happens in small green firms as they grow. The story of Stonyfield Farm's challenge with maintaining its eco-culture as it grew to a mere 500 employees (see chapter 10) illustrates the difficulties of trying stay green during a period of fast growth. The examples of the multiyear paths to sustainability, including goals on 5- and 10-year horizons, which were mentioned at the start of chapter 10, show that change inevitably takes time in large organizations.

This challenge of inertia at scale also extends to consumers. Some 62 percent of Unilever's carbon footprint arises from consumer use of its products.[27] Even if Unilever could make itself and its supply chain totally carbon neutral, it would still fail to reach the company's goal of halving its environmental footprint. Convincing Unilever's two billion consumers[28] to use, for example, dry shampoos, cold-water cleansers, and more concentrated products is bound to take effort and time.

Green Investments

Green products involve, in many cases, higher ingredient costs than those of mainstream products. Furthermore, the restrictive ingredient lists and design criteria that are the hallmark of such products may make green products inferior to mainstream products on core performance dimensions (e.g., less effective cleansers or underpowered fuel-sipping vehicles). In turn, the higher costs and lower performance of some products attract only a small fraction of the customer base, leading to lower economies of scale in procurement, manufacturing, and distribution. Even if the green product succeeds, it may cannibalize the company's higher-profit mainstream offerings.

Given such downsides, companies serving mainstream consumers with successful mainstream products face what seems like an obvious investment decision. They'd rather put money and time into known, profitable, high-volume products that serve populous customer segments than into risky, less-profitable, low-volume products that may serve current noncustomers. Given that choice, these companies may choose to leave the green segment of the market to small niche competitors.

The existence of green companies that are willing to take these risks and create niche green products implies that mainstream companies may face what Harvard's Clayton Christensen termed *The Innovator's Dilemma*.[29] Christensen shows that large companies that ignore small, upcoming competitors—who may enter the market with inferior products, serving different market segments—are making a rational business decision in ceding those markets to the upstarts. However, they may be later threatened by those competitors as the upstarts' products improve and achieve more widespread adoption.

Christensen gives many examples, including the rise of the steel minimills and the success of Japanese carmakers, caused by large incumbent companies' natural preference for investment in seemingly successful existing products over risky niche products. Sustainable products could potentially follow Christensen's pattern. While the current market for sustainable products may be small, and some such products may be inferior and costly, this can change quickly due to a technological breakthrough (making green products better and cheaper), a change in consumer sentiment, a regulatory edict, or a court decision.

In trying to avoid the innovator's dilemma, several large companies have developed or acquired new products to serve the green segment of the market. To avoid internal rivalries with existing product lines, companies often maintain the green product as an independent business unit, regardless of whether it was internally developed or acquired. Examples of this include Clorox's acquisition of Burt's Bees, Danone's acquisition of Stonyfield, and Unilever's acquisition of Ben & Jerry's.

These strategic moves can be seen as experimentation and learning that helps nurture environmental-centric innovations, even if these products are not initially as profitable as traditional offerings. A year after acquiring Burt's Bees, Clorox launched Green Works (see the section "A Big Gorilla Dips a Toe"). Similarly, Danone launched its "Nature Commitment" in 2008, a program modeled after Stonyfield's business principles, including using Stonyfield's carbon metrics.[30] As these innovations develop, they establish connections with networks of like-minded environmentally driven suppliers, customers, and other stakeholders. These stakeholders, in turn, may infuse further ideas into the green product lines and the teams working on them, creating a virtuous innovation cycle that the original company can use.

Over time, research into and experimentation with bio-based materials and manufacturing methods can yield green products that can be sold on their merit, even though they may be more expensive and appeal to a narrow segment of the market. In May

2016, Procter & Gamble launched Tide Purclean laundry detergent and marketed it as the first bio-based liquid laundry detergent with the same cleaning power as regular Tide.[31] It was almost twice as expensive as regular Tide: a 50 oz. bottle of Tide, good for 32 loads, cost $7.47 on Jet.com, whereas a 50 oz. bottle of Tide Purclean, also good for 32 loads, cost $13.99. (By March 2017, the online price difference had shrunk to 40 percent—$10.99 vs. $7.92—either as a result of P&G's cost-learning curve or its attempts to "move" a product that was not selling well.) Such investments and experiments provide a *real option* for the company in case changes in either demand or regulations induce an increase in sales of sustainable products.

GETTING TO SCALE

The stories of Dell and Stonyfield show that scale is not always easy if the supply chain does not have the necessary capacity. Those stories also hint at the kinds of outreach, supplier education, and long-term contracting that companies can take on in order to grow their green business lines.

A Slow Ramp to a New Certification

Just as Unilever has sought to develop sustainable supplies of key commodities such as palm oil and tea (see chapter 5), it has also sought to acquire sustainable soybean oil in many of its manufacturing regions. Unilever buys 1 percent of all the soy in the world, mostly from the United States, Brazil, and Argentina.[32] In South America, the Round Table on Sustainable Soy certifies local farming practices to avoid deforestation, protect the lands of indigenous peoples, and prevent child labor. However, in the United States, these are not salient sustainability issues, and no similar certification existed when Unilever first began its push for sustainable growth.[33] The company had to create one.

Because Unilever did not buy soybeans directly, it enlisted the help of Archer Daniels Midland (ADM), the behemoth commodities trader that, with revenues of $62 billion in 2016, is actually larger than Unilever (€53 billion in 2016 revenues). Together, the two companies built a multimember team to ensure both credibility and technical ability. The team included two trade groups (United Soybean Board and the Iowa Soybean Association), two NGO scientific consultants (World Wildlife Fund and Practical Farmers of Iowa), and an alliance of agricultural companies that had developed software to assess farming practices (Field to Market).[34]

Rather than impose a code of conduct that farmers could simply reject by selling to other buyers, the group offered a simple but attractive deal: Give us data on your farm and we'll give you analytics on your farm's performance plus pay another 10 cents per bushel. Although the incremental payment was a token 1 percent premium,[35] hundreds of farmers signed up. "I like it," said soy grower Craig Pfantz who signed up in 2012. "What got me into it? To be honest? The 10 cent premium."[36]

The service also offers valuable feedback. "The ADM people were extremely helpful," said Iowa soybean farmer Greg Van Dyke. "They came to our farm and helped map out our profile in about a half-hour," he said.[37] Next, the software calculates a wide range of farm productivity and environmental impact metrics like the efficiency of water use, greenhouse gas emissions, and soil carbon levels.[38]

Unlike Patagonia's Footprint Chronicles (see chapter 11), Unilever was not forcing farmers to share their proprietary data with competing farmers, at least not directly. "One of the things that appealed to us was the confidentiality of the program," Van Dyke said. "All of our private information was kept private. And no one is looking over your shoulder."[39] The software aggregates and anonymizes the data. "At the end of the first year, we were able to see our individual numbers and got to compare them to averages of farms in our area," he said. "Unilever and ADM also shared feedback on how we compared to farms in other countries like Brazil and Argentina," Van Dyke added.

For the farmers, the program answers questions that are both financially and environmentally relevant. "How can they get better yields? How can they use less fertilizer? How can they just better overall improve their practices?" said Stefani Millie-Grant, senior manager, external affairs and sustainability at Unilever.[40] In general, more efficient farmers have more sustainable farms because they already are reducing fuel, fertilizers, pesticides, water, and contaminated run-off. Craig Pfantz, who farms more than 2,000 acres of corn and soybeans, said the knowledge gives him a clearer picture of his farm's "problem spots."[41] Millie-Grant continued, "They can look and see that maybe they've got one field that's using more nitrogen. And they can go back and say, 'Why is this different from my neighbors?' It's all about continuous improvement."[42]

As of late 2015, the program was still focused on voluntary performance improvement, not enforcement, because farmers can sell to whomever they choose. "We aren't telling them they're not sustainable or kicking them out of the program," said Clint Piper, the general manager for North American soybean processing at ADM.[43] "Right now it's about getting people in the program and sharing knowledge," he concluded.[44] As of 2015, the program had 250 participating farmers covering 288,000 acres,[45] which was less than 3 percent of Iowa's nine million acres of soybeans.[46] "We recognize that with our US sustainable soybean program, it is still early days," Unilever's Polman said.[47]

Plagiarism for Performance

Large companies often have dozens or hundreds of sites for manufacturing, distribution, and support functions. One manager at each of Unilever's 252 sites spends at least 50 percent of his or her time on environmental issues. To make the most of these independent efforts, the company created an in-house social network to help with the company-wide "copying" process.[48] Tony Dunnage, group director of manufacturing sustainability at Unilever, said, "It's copying not sharing," because just sharing knowledge does little good without action.[49]

The "copying" process is helping the company achieve its zero-waste goals. "So we know of our 20 ice cream plants, this many are at zero waste," he said. This information raises the question: "Well, why aren't all of them?" Dunnage added, "We had a lot of people say zero waste isn't possible at their plant due to lack of infrastructure or geography." Some regions lack a developed recycling industry, but some of these sites experimented with various waste-reduction and waste-to-energy systems. "As we started to share, other sites started to hold up the mirror and say, 'If they're doing it, why can't we?'" Dunnage said.[50] These systems for scaling best practices are relatively common in large multifacility corporations. AB InBev's Voyager Plant Optimization (see chapter 10) is an analogous system for encouraging the adoption of good ideas across multiple plant sites.

A Big Gorilla Dips a Toe

As mentioned previously, in 2007, Clorox bought Burt's Bees, a company focusing on organic personal care products.[51] Clorox, best known for Clorox Bleach, kept Burt's Bees as a separate business unit in order to learn from its environmental friendly processes and experiences. In 2008, Clorox launched Green Works—the first new product line in two decades for the 95-year-old company. Green Works was a family of 17 green cleaning products designed with natural active ingredients that competes with Clorox's main line of cleaning products.[52]

Following the Green Works launch, the US Better Business Bureau called upon Clorox to stop advertising Green Works to be just as effective as its chemical-based cousins. Although Clorox disagreed with the criticism, it did change its advertisements.[53] Buoyed by a $25 million-a-year advertising push in 2008 and 2009, the Green Works product line sales brought in $58 million a year in 2009. However, its price premium during a recession and doubts about its efficacy caused sales to fall to just $32 million in 2012.[54] In a move to bring Green Works to the mainstream customer, and to capture more "green" consumers, Clorox lowered Green Works' price.[55] It also launched a rebranding campaign in 2013 aimed at mainstream consumers[56] that claimed, "You don't have to be a trust fund baby to be green," and "You don't have to be perfect to be green."[57] In line with this campaign, Clorox moved the product out of the natural/organic aisle where it sat in competition with other green cleaners made by the likes of Method and Seventh Generation, to the mainstream household-cleaner section.

Green Works may have been a money-losing proposition for Clorox, given the R&D costs, the marketing campaigns, the specialized supply chain involved, and the meager sales. Despite the ups and downs, Don Knauss, CEO of Clorox insisted that "it was all about growth"[58] when Clorox launched its foray into sustainable products. For a company the size of Clorox, with $5.6 billion in annual sales, the Green Works product line can be considered "an experiment." "What's really exciting is that we're building knowledge and confidence within the rest of the company so that we can do the same things with a lot of our other product lines," said Jessica Buttimer, director of marketing for Green Works.[59]

What Big Fish Can Teach Little Fish

The scale and maturity of a large company can mean that a small company learns, too, about both sustainability and business. In talking about the Danone-Stonyfield deal, Nancy Hirshberg said, "I was stunned when we [Stonyfield] started working with them [Danone] because they have done unbelievable work in sustainability."[60] Giving an example, she added, "Our single biggest climate issue is enteric emissions from the cows and they helped us with that more than you can imagine." Danone also had the IT budget and staff to justify investment in advanced software for quickly computing LCAs, which is now used by both Danone and Stonyfield (see chapter 3). On top of that, the overlapping delivery footprint of the companies gave Stonyfield reduced transportation costs and impacts.[61] Gary Hirshberg, CEO of Stonyfield, said, "The real reason I did this deal was because I wanted to take this to the next level. They are out there feeding obviously a lot more people than we are, and what I'm trying to do is show other companies—the acquirer and acquiree—that everybody can win."[62]

Small green companies don't need to be acquired to learn something about business and scaling from larger ones. Just becoming a supplier—such as when Dr. Bronner's began selling to Target—can be enough. "Target's like a whole other ballgame," said CEO David Bronner. The retailer has high expectations of its suppliers and trains them on its business processes. "We had to go to Target

U, and our supply chain people had to really figure it out. But in being able to do that, now, we're able to supply pretty much anybody," he concluded.[63]

Why Did the Chicken Egg Buyer Cross the Road?

In addition to concerns over environmental emissions, some NGOs and consumers worry about the treatment of animals used to produce food. This includes the hundreds of millions of chickens confined in battery cages where they lay an estimated 75 billion eggs per year in the United States.[64] "The animal movement has battled this inhumane practice for decades on end," explained Wayne Pacelle, president and CEO of The Humane Society of the United States.[65]

In April 2016, Walmart pledged to "transition to a 100 percent cage-free egg supply chain" by 2025, but qualified that commitment as being "based on available supply, affordability, and customer demand."[66] The caveats and nine-year phase-in period reflect the challenges of scale. As of April 2016, only 10 percent of US production was cage free,[67] yet Walmart controlled 25 percent of the US food market.[68] Moreover, the retailer was competing with 57 other companies that are in the process of switching to cage-free eggs, including many major retailers (such as Target, Albertsons, and Costco), food producers (such as Unilever, General Mills, and Mondelēz), and restaurant chains (including McDonald's, Quiznos, Denny's, and Dunkin' Donuts).[69]

Switching to "cage free" is not as simple as opening the cages and letting the birds loose. Cage-free chickens require larger buildings of a different design than the current cage-based methods. Farmers invest millions of dollars in their chicken houses with the expectation that the buildings will last for 15 to 20 years. Replacing traditional chicken houses early would require large write-offs and costly investments that would increase the cost of egg production. Kathleen McLaughlin, chief sustainability officer at Walmart stated, "Our customers and associates count on Walmart and Sam's Club to deliver on affordability and quality, while at the same time offering transparency into how their food is grown and raised."[70] Unless egg buyers bid up the price of cage-free eggs, the transition will take decades as farmers slowly replace end-of-life battery cage buildings with cage-free designs over time.

A similar issue affects the rate of reduction of emissions from transportation. In the absence of strong external incentives (e.g., see the Port of LA story in chapter 6), the owners of older trucks and cars are unlikely to replace their vehicles with less-polluting models until the old vehicle reaches its natural end of life. Reducing environmental problems linked to long-lived assets takes time and money.

When Elephants Dance

When Walmart installed 105 megawatts of solar panels on the roofs of 327 stores and distribution centers, the company became the single biggest solar power generator in the United States.[71] To remain true to its commitment to low costs, the retailer contracted with installers—usually SolarCity Corporation—who put up the capital and then signed long-term power purchase agreements with Walmart. The long-term agreements gave Walmart below-market electricity rates and made it easier for the installer to secure low-cost financing for the project. Thus, Walmart off-loaded both the capital investment and the project's risk onto its suppliers. Naturally, those suppliers minimized their exposure by taking advantage of the federal government's generous subsidies for investments in alternative energy.[72]

The environmental initiatives of large companies, such as Walmart and Unilever, can have noticeable effects for three main reasons. The first is the scale effect, in which even modest improvements in their practices can have relatively large total impacts. Unilever buys 7 percent of the world's tomatoes and 12 percent of the world's commercial black tea, which implies that the company's efforts to convert these crops to drip irrigation could have a noticeable effect on total water use in the plantations.[73] Second, and more important, large companies attract a base of suppliers who are eager to cater to large companies' changing preferences. Walmart's insistence on concentrated laundry detergent (see chapter 8) broke the impasse by which no single detergent maker could successfully introduce this eco-efficiency initiative on its own.

"When Walmart, Unilever, and Procter & Gamble decided to introduce a 2X, they changed the industry," said Reed Doyle, former director of CSR at Seventh Generation. Third, commercial moves by large companies are likely to prompt corresponding efforts by competing companies.

EcoVadis, which scores supplier sustainability for large corporate procurement organizations such as Nestlé, Heineken, and Verizon, often sees this in action. "Purchasing managers and purchasing directors have huge leverage in terms of driving improvement," said Pierre-Francois Thaler, cofounder and co-CEO of EcoVadis.[74] In that sense, large players can become de facto regulators of the industries they dominate.

NOT BIG ENOUGH

As mentioned in chapter 3, part of Tesco's explanation of the failure of its labeling effort was the lack of participation of other retailers, preventing the project from reaching a critical mass of participants. For that reason, Walmart and Target jointly held the Personal Care Sustainability Summit in 2014 and 2015, bringing together some of the largest consumer product, chemical, and fragrance companies in that industry. The collaborative effort has been trying to assess the safety of personal care product ingredients and encourage the development of new, safer classes of chemicals. Laysha Ward, Target's executive vice president and chief corporate social responsibility officer, said, "We realize that we can leverage our scale, influence and resources to improve the way products come to market and drive transformational change for our business and society."[75]

It Takes a Village

Whether it's a behemoth like Walmart or a smaller green-mission company like Patagonia, no single corporation can ensure the sustainability of a product category, such as clothing. Every member of the entire supply chain—including suppliers, manufacturers, and retailers—influences the product's life cycle of environmental impacts. To address this broader challenge, Patagonia and Walmart recruited Nike, Target, Levi's, Li & Fung, and dozens of other apparel industry companies and stakeholders in 2011 to launch the Sustainable Apparel Coalition (SAC).[76] The coalition was formed with a vision to create "an apparel and footwear industry that produces no unnecessary environmental harm and has a positive impact on the people and communities associated with its activities."[77] By 2014, SAC included 44 suppliers, 30 apparel manufacturers, 16 retailers, 22 industry affiliates, and 20 nonprofit organizations, governments, and universities.[78] In total, SAC members accounted for 40 percent of global clothing and footwear sales.[79]

As part of its mission, the group created the Higg Index[80] by combining the Eco Index of the Outdoor Industry Association with Nike's Environmental Design Tool. "We've produced the Higg Index 1.0, essentially a self-assessment tool that companies can use for products to get baseline social and environmental information," explained Patagonia's vice president Vincent Stanley.[81] Launched in 2012, the index enables apparel companies to evaluate material types, products, processes, and facilities using a standard methodology across the supply chain.[82] "I was in China and Vietnam a few months ago and saw factories just starting to implement it," said Stanley in mid-2013.[83]

In late 2013, the SAC released the Higg Index 2.0, which is web based and gives the apparel and footwear industry measurement and benchmarking tools to drive supply chain improvement.[84] The online platform "allows companies to see where they are relative to their peers as a whole, and what we really hope is that this inspires a race to the top," said Jason Kibbey, SAC executive director, of the new platform. "It's a pretty strong incentive to improve, because no one wants to be at the bottom or the back of the pack."

"The next step is to really develop the standards so that a designer can look at it and decide if a certain dye or fabric is less environmentally harmful than another … to consider factors other than simply cost," Stanley said.[85] In the meantime, companies such as Columbia Sportswear, KEEN, Nester Hosiery, Icebreaker, and Korkers are using the index to make improvements in sourcing and manufacturing.[86]

In the long term, the index's ratings are also meant for public consumption, but, as of 2016, a public version of the index was still under development.[87] When finished, Patagonia plans to reintroduce environmental impact data to its Footprint Chronicles (see chapter 11). "We'll wait until the index has the metrics pieces ready before we put that back up," said Patagonia's Jill Dumain.[88] Ultimately, Stanley's vision for the SAC is for standardized tags on clothing to show the details of raw materials, labor standards, dyes, and finishes used to produce each item.[89]

"In our meetings you'll see the members are unbelievably collaborative and open about sharing their tools with the rest of the industry," Kibbey said. "Sometimes they're competitors, but I think everybody feels that with sustainability there's much bigger business gain to have from reducing risk overall in the supply chain, improving efficiencies, and developing innovation on a larger scale than from developing tools to be used only within the walls of your company. What you see from our members is a belief that company-based solutions alone are no longer capable of solving the sustainable challenges of our time nor are they cost effective, or efficient or just the right way to go anymore," Kibbey concluded.[90] In other cases, collaborations can even span multiple industries.

A PET Project

What do cars, beverages, shoes, detergents, and ketchup have in common? They all use polyethylene terephthalate (PET or PETE) plastics in the product or its packaging. Global production of PET, a type of polyester, exceeds 48 billion pounds—more than 6.5 pounds (about 3 kilograms) per person on Earth each year—and is used in making bottles, woven fabrics, carpets, buckets, and various kinds of molded plastic parts. Even Patagonia uses PET in its Capilene garments. Any plastic product marked with a recycling code of "1" (see chapter 7) is PET.

To increase the volume of renewable PET supplies, The Coca-Cola Company, Ford Motor Company, H. J. Heinz Company, Nike Inc., and Procter & Gamble Co. joined together in 2012 to form the Plant PET Technology Collaborative. The group carries out research and development on PET made entirely from plant-sourced materials.[91] Although Coca-Cola already has its PlantBottle Technology, the Collaborative hopes to increase the percentage of plant-derived feedstocks from PlantBottle's 30 percent to 100 percent.

In 2013, the effort expanded in scope to encompass all bioplastics, and it increased in size with the addition of Danone, Unilever, and the World Wildlife Fund (WWF), leading to the formation of the Bioplastic Feedstock Alliance.[92] A key element of the BFA's goals is to ensure that bioplastics production does not displace food production. To this end, Alliance members Heinz and Ford are testing the use of inedible tomato fibers left over from the more than two million tons of tomatoes used in Heinz ketchup. These fibers could be formed into wiring brackets or coin holders in Ford cars.[93] "Ensuring that our crops are used responsibly to create bioplastics is a critical conservation goal, especially as the global population is expected to grow rapidly through 2050," said Erin Simon of WWF.[94]

BIG AND SUSTAINABLE

The cosmetics industry has long been criticized for its practices, including the use of toxic chemicals and testing products on animals.[95] In contrast, Natura Cosméticos S.A. built its core mission around its Portuguese tagline of *bem estar bem*. The motto is a play on words with "bem estar" meaning well-being or good feelings and "estar bem" meaning to do something well or in the proper way.[96] The phrase conveys a sense of "well-being done well," which could be the Portuguese version of the well-known corporate social responsibility phrase "doing well by doing good." *Bem estar bem* signals the company's broader belief that its products should connect with consumers on physical, emotional, intellectual, and spiritual levels, and that the company's corporate strategy, principles, and beliefs should align with that eco-conscious concept.[97] Along the way, the company has expanded financial and environmental performance through innovation, aligning both its suppliers and its customers with its vision.

Antônio Luiz da Cunha Seabra founded Natura in 1969 with a very specific role in mind for his company and the products it offered. "It can be a way for people to express their emotions, their feelings, and a growing concern about the Earth's preservation and their quest for a harmonious development of human potential," said Seabra.[98] The company developed its Vôvó line of products, for example, in part to strengthen bonds between grandparents and grandchildren. The line included creams that grandparents and their grandchildren could massage into each other's hands and arms, as well as a memory album to encourage "playful dialogue, storytelling, and family closeness."[99]

"From the start, we have been intent on building a fundamentally different kind of company," said Luciana Hashiba, Natura's manager for partnerships and technological innovation, "one that succeeds in the marketplace ... by integrating the interests and consideration of our people, our customers, our communities, and the natural environment."[100] Natura also aligns itself with shareholders and the investment community by reporting its environmental performance quarterly, alongside its financial and social performance. The environmental reports are as detailed, commented, and explained—both achievements and failures—as its financial reports. "We want to reinforce the concept of a green economy as a rainforest economy," said Alessandro Carlucci, the company's CEO.[101]

Natura, however, is not a small, private company like those discussed in chapter 11. The company employs 7,000 employees and a direct sales network of 1.6 million independent consultants.[102] It is a public company traded on the Brazilian stock exchange with 2016 sales of R\$7.9 billion (approximately US\$2.5 billion, depending on the exchange rate at the time).[103] Natura does sustainability at scale.

Designing with Nature

When Natura's founders started their direct sales cosmetics company in Brazil in 1969, they knew they would never be able to compete with larger, more established cosmetic brands by trying to "find the right molecule in a lab."[104] Instead, they went out into the Brazilian rainforest to research natural ingredients—what Natura calls "biodiversity assets." For example, the Ekos line (see the section "One Ingredient at a Time") employs 14 different plant materials sourced from the rainforest.[105] Overall, Natura invests 3 percent of its revenue in R&D, a figure comparable to leading innovators such as Apple (also 3 percent),[106] and leading cosmetic companies such as L'Oréal (3.4 percent), and Procter & Gamble (2.5 percent).[107]

Natura embedded LCA into its product design process. In 2013, for example, it launched SOU ("I am"), a new line of personal soaps, shampoos, and beauty aids, combining low environmental impact, low cost, and strong customer influence—asking consumers to use every last drop of the product.[108] In 2005, the company transitioned away from petroleum-based ingredients in favor of natural oil harvested from Brazilian palms grown without the use of artificial chemicals. More than 90 percent of the company's dry raw materials come from natural resources harvested in the Amazon jungle.

The company even halted research into promising new ingredients on sustainability grounds. "We've discovered substances with potential use in the industry, but decided to abort the project because the operation was not sustainable," said Marcos Vaz, director of sustainability at Natura. "We would need a very large amount of plants to obtain the desired quantity of raw material."[109] For Natura, sustainable sourcing is more than just finding the right supplier. In many cases, the company creates new ingredient supply chains from the forest floor up.

One Ingredient at a Time

In 2000, Natura launched its Ekos cosmetics line, designed to use natural ingredients from the local Amazon rainforest. The Amazon's indigenous tribes have known of many of these ingredients for generations, but those tribes had little or no supply chain infrastructure for selling to mainstream companies and consumers. That did not deter Natura. "Instead of buying our raw materials from major intermediaries, we decided to purchase them directly from extractive communities throughout Brazil," said Marcos

Vaz, director of sustainability.[110] Doing so required significant effort.

When Natura considered creating a product that used priprioca, an Amazonian aromatic sedge (a botanical cousin of grass), the company found only one existing supplier. That supplier could produce only about 4 tons per year; Natura needed 40 tons per year. The most financially efficient way to build that capacity would have been to intensify sourcing from that single supplier, spurring larger-scale cultivation of priprioca and driving costs down through economies of scale. However, that would have jeopardized Natura's vision for sustainable sourcing from the Amazon jungle, which included preserving the natural capacity of the forest.

Instead, Natura searched for other Amazonian sites suited to growing and harvesting priprioca, ultimately settling on the outskirts of Campo Limpo, Boa Vista, and Cotijuba. The company helped 49 families in these communities start cultivating priprioca, both by giving them priprioca shoots to plant and by teaching them how to grow the plants in beds using natural fertilizers.[111] Finally, the company also identified a processor to extract the aromatic oil from the priprioca roots and a secondary processor to further refine the oil. Over the years, Natura has built similar supply chains for more than a dozen different natural ingredients, each of which began with sustainable cultivation and harvesting by local communities living in the rainforest.

As the company grew, it developed its own Active Ingredient Certification Program, which begins early in the procurement process. The program includes a survey of local conditions, creating a management plan, assessing environmental impacts, implementing the plan, and then continuously monitoring certified suppliers.[112] Many Brazilian farmers and ranchers had traditionally slashed and burned the rainforest to subdue the land; Natura banned that practice among its suppliers. To certify the sustainability of its ingredients, Natura used widely recognized certification protocols from the Biodynamic Institute (IBD), the Forest Stewardship Council (FSC), and the Sustainable Agriculture Network (SAN).[113]

Natura's insistence on sustainable sourcing from jungle communities did raise input costs for the Ekos line, but Natura has also been able to charge consumers a premium.[114] The success of the line proved what former director and shareholder Guilherme Leal said: "Our decisions are based on business strategies, and this adds value to products."[115]

Creating Stability

Natura's self-appointed role in creating new suppliers and supply chains for its natural ingredients puts it in a potentially awkward position of setting farmers' and processors' fair pricing for the cultivation, collection, and processing of these ingredients. To counter this, the company created a farmers association that can negotiate on behalf of individual farmers and deal with Natura on pricing, quantities, and other issues.[116] These associations increase the communities' access to other commercial opportunities. Furthermore, the company aligns all its supply chain partners through an "open value chain concept."[117] During product development and contract negotiations between deep-tier ingredient growers and intermediate-tier ingredient processors, Natura monitors discussions between the parties and ensures that each one knows every other party's costs. Natura aims for supply chain partners to agree upon fair profit margins for each participant along the supply chain—usually between 15 and 30 percent.[118] "One of the basic concepts of Ekos is offering economic gains for all the parties involved," said Ricardo Martello, the company's biodiversity raw materials procurement negotiator.[119,120]

As part of its social ethos, Natura works to insulate these Amazonian communities from the natural volatility in the market demand for Natura's products. Natura's direct-sales distribution model is a "very dynamic market," said Rodrigo Brea, procurement director for Natura. Such dynamism forestalls the 18-month projections and stable procurement volumes often needed for agriculture. "You have really small 30-family communities that are heavily dependent on what we buy from them," said Brea. "Part of our job is to make sure that all this craziness doesn't affect the rainforest communities, because they really can't react to the uncertainty."

To insulate rainforest communities from the "bullwhip effect" inherent in most supply chains,[121] the company commits to minimum purchase quantities independent of its final sales. It also realizes that when sales surge, the Amazonian communities cannot quickly scale up their output without disrupting the environment and their lifestyle. In those instances, the company promotes other products that use other ingredients, relying on its direct sales force to shape demand.[122]

Aligning Shareholders with the Mission

In December 2014, Natura became both the largest firm and the first public firm to become B Corp certified.[123] "Getting a public company to become a B Corporation had been a Holy Grail— and Natura's decision is hugely important. It's the beginning of a new relationship between shareholders and companies that, from my point of view, is both essential and inevitable," wrote Jeffrey Hollender, the founder and former CEO of Seventh Generation, in an email.[124] According to B Corp cofounder Jay Coen Gilbert, "Natura has not received any pushback [from its board]. When leadership engaged important shareholders early in the process, they affirmed that this was simply business as usual for Natura."[125] As of 2015, Brazil itself did not have a specific corporate structure analogous to a Benefit Corporation, although Brazilian law does assert that corporations have a social function that involves balancing between private and public interests. Sistema B, the Latin American counterpart of B Lab, had already certified 40 Brazilian firms by 2015.[126]

The Secret Sauce

The company's distribution model is well-suited to motivate mainstream consumers to care about the environment and buy Natura's products, despite the price premium. Inspired by the "Avon lady" model, Natura's 1.6 million "consultants" sell directly to consumers.[127] These consultants are often Natura's first consumers, driving sales through personal relationships and spreading Natura's social and environmental values.[128] They connect the customers to the "story of the product," something that Patagonia is doing digitally with the Footprint Chronicles. With Natura, however, the connection is personal. "There is a real pride in representing Natura's ethical standards, our high-quality products, and our support of broader social causes," said Luciana Hashiba of Natura.[129] This personal sales connection allows Natura to communicate the complex sustainability elements of its products and supply chain to consumers, avoiding many of the pitfalls of conveying credence attributes (see chapter 9).

Even though the company's brands command a premium, its vision of offering the "right price" extends to consumers. When Argentina suffered a currency devaluation in 2001, many cosmetic companies increased prices to protect profit margins. Natura did not. "We looked for ways to reduce costs and put ads in major magazines stating that we would keep our prices steady for the time being and would change them if and when local salaries were adjusted. The idea was to create a kind of social pact involving suppliers, employees, and customers, showing the Argentinean market that we were there for good and we expected profits in the long run," said Alessandro Carlucci, who was sales director of Argentina at the time.[130] In the following three years, Natura's revenues increased sixfold in the country.[131]

Natura's vision resonated with consumers. When Natura went public in May 2004, its annual sales were close to $500 million.[132] By 2009, Natura had achieved a 62 percent household penetration rate and a nearly 100 percent brand recognition rate in Brazil, with its domestic sales surpassing those of Avon and Unilever.[133] As of March 2017, Natura's market value was approximately US$9 billion;[134] in 2013, it was ranked by *Forbes* as one of the top 10 most innovative companies in the world.[135]

13

A Road to Sustainable Growth

When A. G. Lafley returned to Procter & Gamble as CEO in 2013, his mandate was to spur growth in the face of increasing competition.[1] "I am confident that we will deliver strong innovation, productivity, and growth to win with consumers, customers, and shareholders," he said when appointed.[2] Similarly, when Tom Mangas was named CEO of Armstrong Corporation, the $3 billion flooring manufacturer, a trade magazine quoted him as saying, "I'm going to ask a lot of questions and figure out how we can accelerate the growth."[3] Nothing in these statements is unique or surprising. As Bain & Company (and many scholarly articles) state, "For a business to survive, growth is an imperative, not an option."[4,5]

If a business is not growing it is dying, according to conventional management wisdom. Almost all companies need to grow to achieve the lowest long-term costs (owing to scale); to protect themselves from competitors growing in other geographies and adjacent markets; and to provide advancement opportunities for talented employees. Just as important are shareholders' and financial markets' expectations of increasing profits. Societies, too, live under a kind of growth imperative: to seek to improve the quality of life of their growing populations through the creation of jobs and the conversion of the country's natural resources into wealth.

A TALE OF TWO GROWTH STORIES

It was the best of times for growth, it was the worst of times for growth. Between 1994 and 2009, global GDP doubled[6] as the world's middle class grew to 1.8 billion citizens. In countries such as China, India, Brazil, and Mexico, more consumers gained increased purchasing power. Developing countries continue to industrialize and urbanize. The middle class is expected to grow to 3.2 billion by 2020 (approximately 41 percent of the world population) and 4.9 billion by 2030 (approximately 58 percent of the world population[7]), according to Mario Pezzini, director of the OECD Development Center.[8] These consumers strive for a "Western" standard of living that, in many ways, is defined by consumption.

The positive aspects of rising wealth come with a dark cloud of environmental impacts. Economic growth brings increased consumption of many natural resources such as water, minerals, forests, and sea life, as well as many kinds of emissions that can degrade these resources. In turn, the large companies, running the massive supply chains that use these resources, face pressure from NGOs, governments, and communities. "With the global middle class growing, we can all help to create solutions that use less water, less oil, less resources of all kinds. ... After all, our businesses can only be as strong and healthy as the communities that we proudly serve," said Muhtar Kent, CEO of Coca-Cola.[9]

Hot Growth = Hot Planet?

Rising wealth means rising energy production for electricity, industry, and transportation. With this prosperity comes growing GHG emissions; between 1970 and 2011, carbon emissions nearly doubled. China, for example, now emits more GHGs from fossil fuel combustion than the US and the EU combined.[10] Worldwide atmospheric levels of CO_2 rose more than 20 percent between 1970 and 2016.[11] If the 7.4 billion people alive in the world as of late 2016 attain the same standard of living as Americans, the world will need to almost quadruple its energy production.[12] Even if the world emulates energy-efficient Germany, the total would still need to double.

Concern about GHGs started in the 1960s when scientists uncovered a link between ancient climate fluctuations and atmospheric carbon dioxide levels. This concern was heightened when they also realized that CO_2 levels were rising quickly in the modern world.[13] Further data collection on both the past and present climate, as well as increasingly powerful climate models, led to ominous predictions of a significant rise in the Earth's temperature, the collapse of Antarctic ice sheets, and rise of sea levels. By 2001, the third report of the Intergovernmental Panel on Climate Change (IPCC) stated that global warming is "very likely," with possible severe consequences. The fifth IPCC report in 2013 cited a variety of climate-related changes already taking place, warned of acceleration, and stated that it is "extremely likely" that the main cause is human activity.[14]

Still, a minority of scientists question the accuracy of the IPCC climate projections, arguing that the measurements and models are not exact enough to form the basis of policy. Other experts argue that climate change is not caused by human activity but rather by natural or unknown processes.[15] Nonetheless, the majority scientific opinion resulted in a United Nations climate "Conference of Parties" (COP 21) in Paris in December 2015. At the conference, representatives of 196 countries agreed on a (nonbinding) resolution to limit global warming to 2°C by reducing net emissions of GHGs to zero during the second half of the 21st century. Such agreements, and the surrounding media attention, mean that consumers, investors, NGOs, and governments are likely to continue to demand that companies "do something" about the environment. In addition, companies are likely to be attacked if they are perceived as degrading the environment.

The amount of carbon *released* into the environment is not the only impact that worries activists, scientists, and policy makers, however. There is also concern of the resources that are *removed* from the ecosystem.

Dry Places on a Wet Planet

Half of India faces significant water stress due to population growth, overextraction, and pollution.[16] Worldwide, about 1.2 billion people live in areas of physical water scarcity and another 1.6 billion face economic water shortages.[17] At the same time, water is plentiful on the global level—the average volume of fresh surface water totals 3.5 million gallons per person.[18] Ground water (accessible by pumping) and salt water (usable with desalination) offers thousands of times more water in some areas. Unfortunately, pumping and desalination require energy, which, with current technologies, entails more GHG emissions. Physical, regulatory, and social restrictions on water consumption could affect many categories of companies beyond the obvious ones in the agriculture and beverage sectors because many power generation and manufacturing processes also depend on water for both cooling and cleaning.

Agricultural Aggravations

Between 1980 and 2013, demand for grain nearly doubled as more people could afford a more affluent diet, according to analysis by Syngenta.[19] One example of a newly affordable item for many was beer, which grew in global production by more than one-third between 2000 and 2011, largely driven by a 120 percent surge in production in China. Despite this increase, AB InBev, the world's largest brewer, told investors: "Climate change, or legal, regulatory or market measures to address climate change could have a long-term, material adverse impact on AB InBev's business or operations."[20,21] In recent years, heavy rains, droughts, and heat waves have all affected barley yields.[22] Climate change is forecast to make weather patterns more erratic, increasing the risk of crop failure.[23]

Brewers, and other agricultural commodity buyers, also face competition for arable land and water. For example, climate change-related policies in Germany are encouraging barley growers to switch to biofuel crops.[24] This can affect total supplies, affordability, and sales of beer, which is the world's third most popular beverage (behind water and tea). Nearly all food products (and a great many other products such as apparel, cleansers, cosmetics, and furniture) depend on agriculture that might be affected by climate change, water scarcity, pollution, and rising demand. Land-use policies, such as those associated with deforestation and biodiversity, also potentially restrict growth in production of commodities such as palm oil, soybean, and beef, or create obstacles to the extraction of mineral resources.

ON THE CUSP OF CATASTROPHE OR CORNUCOPIA?

Environmental activists call climate change "the challenge of our time."[25] Despite the inherent uncertainty and the complex assumptions underlying scientists' climate models, as well as occasional contradictory data, most climate scientists believe that climate change is occurring as a result of human activity.

Errors of Extrapolation

The Great Horse Manure Crisis of 1894 posited that London would be buried under nine feet of manure within 50 years, based on the exponential growth in the number of horses used in the city for personal and freight transportation.[26] In New York (where 150,000 horses were producing 2,000 tons of manure each day), the first international urban planning conference estimated that manure would reach third floors by 1930. What they did not foresee was that, by 1912, Henry Ford would develop the assembly line process to make affordable automobiles, obviating the manure problem. Crisis averted as a result of new technology.

In 1919, David White, chief geologist of the United States Geological Survey, wrote of US petroleum: "… the peak of production will soon be passed, possibly within 3 years."[27] His was the first of what has become nearly a century's worth of "peak oil" warnings. In 1980, the world only had 27.9 years of oil left,[28] and consumption was growing inexorably higher.

Fears of peak oil, volatile oil prices, and geopolitical stress between oil-producing countries and oil-consuming ones spurred investment and innovation, such as deepwater drilling and hydraulic fracturing ("fracking") that pull hidden oil out of old or previously infeasible fields. Innovations in geophysical sensing and computing allowed new oil fields to be discovered, and innovations in civil engineering enabled drilling in previously inaccessible areas. By 2013, despite 33 years of insatiable demand, reserves had grown to 49.5 years.[29] This significant growth in reserves contributed to the plunge in the price of a barrel of oil from $140 in January 2008 to $30 per barrel in January 2016.

There are numerous examples of forecasts rendered wrong as a result of an unforeseen technological development. In fact, some currently unforeseen future technology may be able to capture CO_2 and reduce its atmospheric concentration. Unfortunately, nothing like this seems to be on the current horizon. In fact, most scientific efforts are focused on reducing future emissions. Current experimental technologies like carbon capture and clean coal innovations are typically very expensive and require high energy inputs. The most promising avenue seems to be conservation and reduced use, which is the belief of many governments, NGOs, the mainstream media, and many consumers. As a result, one has to conclude, again, that regardless of personal beliefs and hopes, there are business reasons to pursue environmental initiatives.

The Deeper Tension

The tension between financial performance and environmental performance is sometimes cast as a conflict between short-term and long-term interests.[30] Many modern corporations practice what leading management thinker Peter Drucker warned about in 1986 when he wrote: "Corporate managements are being pushed into subordinating everything (even such long-range considerations as a company's market standing, its technology, indeed its basic wealth-producing capacity) to immediate earnings and next week's stock price."[31]

Despite corporate shortcomings, the anti-capitalist, anti-corporate rhetoric of many environmentalists is misplaced. In practice, socialist autocratic governments were significantly worse for the environment compared with their capitalist corporate counterparts, because the regimes' very survival depended on providing jobs and economic development. The former Soviet Union inflicted grave damage on the environment in Russia and the other Soviet republics in its quest for military and economic superiority.[32] And Venezuela is facing "serious environmental issues including vegetation loss, wrong solid waste management, and pollution of basins and reservoirs of water for human consumption," according to a 2016 article in the Caracas newspaper *El Universal*.[33] In socialist central-planning regimes, short-term thinking is rooted in rampant corruption and shortcuts taken to meet government mandates regarding quotas.

Short-term thinking bedevils government institutions in the developed world as well—the results of election-cycle politics, populism, lame-duck outgoing officials, and special interest group lobbying. Environmental impact seems to be less a function of any particular economic ideology and more a function of the fundamental purpose of all economies and supply chains to satisfy humanity's needs and wants. That purpose has inevitably led to the extraction of resources from the Earth and emissions of by-products.

PEOPLE VS. PEOPLE

In June 2015, the mayors of 22 communities in Northern Ontario and Québec held a press conference at Parliament Hill, followed by a series of meetings with federal ministries to address what they called "eco-terrorism."[34] At issue were attacks by Greenpeace and ForestEthics on product and retail brand owners who source paper made from trees harvested by those communities. The mayors argued that the groups were targeting their "way of life," using deliberate misinformation from organizations whose private politics have no regard for balancing the economic, social, and environmental sustainability of these northern communities.[35]

Although environmental activists portray sustainability as a battle of "profits versus planet"[36] or "shareholders versus stakeholders,"[37] those dichotomies of greed versus nature miss the deeper issue. The vilified financial profits and returns to shareholders are the monetary tip of a social iceberg in the form of (i) all the people whose livelihoods and communities depend on the supply chains of the maligned product or company, and (ii) all the consumers who want and rely on the products. Thus, the true tension between financial and environmental performance is not about shareholders versus stakeholders, but rather about (*some*) stakeholders versus (*other*) stakeholders, or (*some*) people versus (*other*) people.

The Sticky Business of Oil Sands

Alberta, Canada, has the world's third-largest reserves of oil, behind only Saudi Arabia and Venezuela.[38] But those 166 billion barrels of viscous crude oil lie locked in sandy formations that make extraction difficult and environmentally impactful. This results in open pit mines that scar the land where shallow layers of black oil sands can be dredged. Scattered nearby are more than 42,000 acres of toxic lakes[39] containing sludgy tailings that reek of residual oil from the processing of the oil sands. The ponds contain heavy metals such as lead, mercury, arsenic, nickel, vanadium, chromium, and selenium that potentially threaten both people and animals in the area.[40] To extract deeply buried oil sands, miners burn large quantities of natural gas to generate steam that is injected into the ground to mobilize the thick gooey bituminous deposits.[41] Overall, the energy required to extract and process oil sands adds 10 to 30 percent to the already high carbon footprint of regular oil.[42] Moreover, the process consumes several barrels of water for every barrel of oil produced.

"The most destructive project on Earth" is what Rick Smith, executive director of the NGO Environmental Defence Canada, calls these oil sands fields.[43] In 2010, ForestEthics began a campaign against US brand-name retailers and consumer goods companies, pressuring them to boycott fossil fuels derived from Canadian tar sands. "Unless you take action to take tar sands oil out of your footprint, you've got it in your footprint," ForestEthics campaign director Aaron Sanger told companies.[44] As the campaign gathered momentum, ForestEthics started publishing a growing list of companies that seemed to have agreed to its demands. The list included green companies such as Patagonia, Seventh Generation, and Whole Foods, as well as more mainstream companies, including Levi Strauss, The Gap, and FedEx (apparently without many of these companies' knowledge or consent).[45]

In rebuttal, the Alberta government published facts about the large economic benefits and modest environmental impacts of the industry,[46] which provided 30 percent of the GDP of the province. They touted the industry as the number one employer of indigenous (First Nations) people, its contribution to the provincial and Canadian tax base, and the estimated Can$2.5 trillion in revenues expected from existing and new projects over a 30-year period.

The government also argued that the industry was not as dirty as it was portrayed to be, noting that only 4,800 km^2 out of 381,000 km^2 of Alberta's boreal forest would be mined and that miners were recycling 80 to 95 percent of the water they used. The government also stated that oil sands producers had reduced per-barrel emissions by an average of 26 percent since 1990, with some achieving up to 50 percent reductions. Finally, the government pointed out that miners had already planted 12 million seedlings as part of required land reclamation efforts. The debate even had a semantic dimension, with environmentalists using the term "tar sands,"[47] whereas the industry used the less dark terminology of "oil sands" or the even more technically correct term "bitumen sands."[48]

The Canadian people were less measured in their reaction. "We invite Levi Strauss, The Gap, and the affiliates (as well as any other American/international company currently marketing their products in Canada that does not want to accept our 'dirty' money) to NO LONGER do business on Canadian soil. By all means, purchase your oil from regimes that provide NO human rights or environmental stewardship. Don't let the door hit your 'behind' on the way out," said a reader commenting on the story.[49] A nonprofit called Alberta Enterprise Group (AEG) launched a counter-boycott campaign on Facebook, urging Canadians to boycott the boycotters of Alberta's oil.[50] AEG vice president David MacLean said, "We want to push back on behalf of Albertans who benefit from this industry."[51]

Faced with heightened media coverage, some companies, who apparently did not consent to their inclusion in the ForestEthics list, clarified their position. Levi Strauss, The Gap, and Timberland criticized ForestEthics for including them on the NGO's anti-tar-sands list.[52] "We do not take a position opposing or supporting any fuel or energy source from any country or geography," said a Levi Strauss spokesperson. Timberland asked its transportation contractors to demonstrate that they were increasing the use of "low carbon fuels and avoiding carbon-intensive sources" but did not specifically boycott a "type or source of fuel," a spokeswoman told CBC News.[53]

The Big Picture: Quality of Living vs. Standard of Living

In 1978, the average Chinese citizen had an annual disposable income of only ¥343.40[54] (or about $200 at prevailing exchange rates at the time[55]). China was a very poor country with a stagnant, inefficient, centrally controlled economy that was relatively isolated from global markets. Then, in 1979, the Chinese government opened the country to foreign investment, enacted free-market reforms, and embarked on the fastest industrialization drive the world has ever seen.

In economic terms, the results have been stellar. Hundreds of millions of Chinese rose out of poverty and joined the middle class as income per capita grew almost 100-fold[56] to ¥33,616 in 2016.[57] Many observers believe that per capita income is actually much larger owing to the "gray economy" that flourished after the reforms. The fast and powerful rise of China out of poverty to become the second-largest (and soon to be the leading) engine of the world economy is one of the central stories of the late 20th and early 21st centuries. By 2025 the Chinese middle class is expected to include 700 to 800 million people,[58] about 50 to 60 percent of the projected Chinese population.

The story of China's economic miracle is also a story of China's significant environmental degradation.[59] Air pollution exceeds the EPA's "unsafe" levels many days of the year, especially in coastal cities. Water pollution taints 90 percent of the groundwater used for irrigation, and 60 percent of the groundwater beneath Chinese cities is described as "very polluted."[60] Farmland turned to desert and biodiversity dropped under the onslaught of deforestation and excessive agricultural development.[61] The wanton environmental destruction gave rise to "cancer villages," which are so polluted that just living there poses a significant cancer risk.

Outdoor air pollution may have contributed to 1.2 million premature deaths in China in 2010, subtracting an estimated 25 million healthy years of life from the population.[62] These mortality figures, however, are dwarfed by China's longevity gains. Life expectancy at birth in China increased from 65.5 in 1980 to 75.5 in 2013,[63] which represents an increase of 13 billion healthy years of life for the population. Shanghai's life expectancy—83 years—equals that of Switzerland.[64]

Over this entire period, many Chinese accepted the trade-off between increasing standards of living on the one hand and environmental degradation on the other. In fact, 350 million Chinese voted with their feet by moving to the country's booming, but polluted, cities.[65] And while environmentalists may lament China's policy choices, who should be the judge? Hundreds of millions of Chinese stakeholders chose (implicitly) higher standards of living (cars, housing, appliances, vacations, access to health care, improved education, and longer life span, among other things) over higher environmental standards. In the future, once the country becomes even richer, it may change its priorities, but its past and current priorities are clear.

The preference for better standards of living (or even just jobs) over environmental sustainability is not unique to China. "Apparel production is a springboard for national development, and often is the typical starter industry for countries engaged in export-oriented industrialization," wrote Gary Gereffi and Stacey Frederick in a 2010 World Bank Policy Research working paper.[66] The industry employs at least 40 million people worldwide and can provide increased purchasing power to lift people out of poverty.[67,68] At the same time, the Natural Resources Defense Council claims that "textile-making is one of the most polluting industries in the world."[69] It added that "a single mill can use 200 tons of water for each ton of fabric it dyes. And rivers run red—or chartreuse, or teal, depending on what color is in fashion that season—with untreated toxic dyes washing off from mills."

Unintended Consequences

Nearly two months before the Rana Plaza textile factory collapse (see chapter 2), Disney ordered an end to sourcing from Bangladesh and four other countries (Pakistan, Belarus, Ecuador, and Venezuela) based on audits and personal visits by senior executives. The company told the affected licensees that it would pursue "a responsible transition that mitigates the impact to affected workers and business." It implemented a year-long transitional period to phase out production by March 31, 2014.[70]

Others may follow Disney's departure from Bangladesh. If that happens on a large scale, it will severely damage the country's social and economic fabric. Garment manufacturing employs 3.6 million Bangladeshi workers. The United Nations Research Institute for Social Development said that, for women in particular, "working in garments, for all its many problems, was a better way to make money than what one had done in the past."[71]

Similar concerns about unintended consequences were raised during the early efforts to block conflict minerals—an effort to stop militants in some parts of the Congo from mining with slave labor to fund war efforts and atrocities (see chapter 10). Some smelters' initial response was to cease buying minerals from all of the Congo, but such a broad-brush approach was neither ethical nor responsible. "We got letters from the Congo and NGOs saying that there are 100,000 artisan miners in the Congo trying to earn money to eat," said Gary Niekerk of Intel, pointing out that not all of the miners work for the militants.[72] In the Congo, mining is one of the two primary legitimate sources of income available (farming being the other). "Putting a de facto ban on materials out of the Congo means that good people might starve," Niekerk said. Damaging the country's legitimate economy would only fuel further unrest.

Abrupt counteractions can have unintended consequences in which initiatives intended to reduce impacts can destroy livelihoods. If the target is a first world region, like Canada's province of Alberta, the affected populations can muster political support and fight back. Most people in the developing world have neither that option nor any other employment options. Consequently, a company's well-intentioned environmental actions can hurt many people. In addition, higher prices for sustainable goods pose more of a burden on the poor than on richer consumers.[73] Furthermore, biofuel mandates, which often use food crops such as corn and soybeans as a raw material, have induced higher food prices.[74]

Explaining the balancing act that companies have to perform, Mike Barry of Marks & Spencer said, "You've got to be constantly at the cutting edge of listening and engaging and triangulating trends and ideas."[75]

50 Shades of Green

"The challenge in setting standards and measuring progress is that there is no universally agreed definition for sustainability," said

Aron Cramer, president and CEO of consulting firm BSR, "and the standards that do apply vary by industry, commodity and even product line."[76] A Unilever spokesperson added, "There is no absolute measure of farm sustainability. It's a moving target."[77] As mentioned in chapter 4, well-written laws and regulations define what the legal profession terms a "bright-line"—a straightforward and easy-to-follow rule with a clear demarcation between acceptable and unacceptable behavior.[78] An action is either on the legal side of the line or not, with no ambiguity. Unfortunately, no such bright line exists between what is sustainable and what is not, which leads to disputes involving companies aspiring to be green.

Matt Rogers, a global produce coordinator for Whole Foods said, "We're really proud of the food we sell, and we know a lot about it, in general, and we want to share that with customers."[79] To that end, the company worked for three years with growers, distributors, certifiers, and topic experts to develop a 41-item questionnaire that scored the sustainability of farmers. The farmers' answers led to a prominent "Responsibly Grown" label listing a farmer's produce as unrated, good, better, or best.[80] Yet when the grocer debuted the label in 2015, some organic farmers complained that lower-priced conventionally grown produce sometimes got a better rating than their higher-priced organic fruits and vegetables. Both the *New York Times* and NPR reported on examples of conventional produce labeled as "best," while some nearby organic items were merely labeled "good."[81]

"Organic *is* responsibly grown, for goodness sake," said one dumbfounded fruit grower.[82] Five farmers wrote an open letter to John McKay, co-CEO of Whole Foods to say, "We are deeply concerned that Whole Foods' newly launched 'Responsibly Grown' rating program is onerous, expensive, and shifts the cost of this marketing initiative to growers, many of whom are family-scale farmers with narrow profit margins."[83]

In response, Edmund LaMacchia, the company's global vice president of perishable purchasing and the primary executive sponsor of the Responsibly Grown program, published a long point-by-point online reply explaining the company's motives.[84]

One of the cosigners of the farmers' complaint letter said, "I'm hopeful that, as it has in the past, Whole Foods will make some modifications."[85] Indeed, Whole Foods engaged with a nonprofit representative of organic farmers, California Certified Organic Farmers, to modify the program.[86] The changes included automatically giving more points to Certified Organic and Biodynamic producers and granting them at least a "good" rating while the growers adjusted to the system.[87]

"Becoming organic is a big investment of time and money," said Jeff Larkey of Route 1 Farms. "This ratings system kind of devalues all that—if you can get a 'best' rating as a conventional farmer using pesticides and other toxic substances, why would you grow organically?"[88] In truth, the Responsibly Grown rating system does not allow unfettered use of pesticides. When the rating system was updated, LaMacchia said: "Ecologically produced food can be defined in many different ways. We will also make room to recognize the contributions of other growing methods to the sustainable food supply." Although the updated system automatically awarded certified organic farms 88 points—covering 10 of the 41 questions in Whole Food's Responsibly Grown rating system—the "best" rating requires scoring 225 points (out of 300).[89] Getting a "best" rating also requires pollinator protection and industry leadership on pest management and environmental protection.

"There is no system, certification, production method or brand that adequately addresses all of the fast-moving issues that we need to understand," LaMacchia told organic farmers.[90] Rogers added, "None of that reduces the value of organic certification—it's just there are more things now on the table that we as buyers have to understand and address."[91]

A Rising Tide Becomes a Turning Tide

Historically, environmental regulations have often followed on the heels of development. In the US and EU, beginning in the second half of the 20th century, many kinds of pollution were halted and reversed, such as London's killer pea-soup smog,[92] Rhine River pollution,[93] LA smog,[94] and acid rain in the eastern US.[95] This trend has followed economic development around the world.

Although Western companies may have "outsourced their pollution" to the developing world in the short term, some argue that as these economies develop, their citizens will start demanding a healthier environment, leading to better environmental steward-ship.[96] The argument rests on a positive correlation between environmental stewardship and economic development once per capita income rises above some threshold—called the "environmental Kuznets curve." (However, detractors have questioned the methodology that led to these conclusions.[97]) In 2014, China passed the biggest changes to its environmental protection laws in 25 years, creating plans to punish polluters more severely in order to limit pollution of water, air, and soil linked to economic growth.[98] "The Chinese government is determined to tackle smog and environmental pollution as a whole," said China's Premier Li Keqiang in 2015.[99]

Beyond the acts of individual countries, the global community has also shown it can address global environmental concerns. The most successful environmental campaign—tackling the depletion of the atmosphere's ozone layer—culminated with the 1987 Montréal Protocol (see chapter 4). This protocol provided coordinated standards to phase out chlorofluorocarbons (CFCs) and related ozone-depleting compounds.[100]

Tackling climate change may be tougher than any of these examples. First, few places in the world are experiencing deleterious effects directly attributable to climate change, despite attempts to link higher average temperatures and weather fluctuations to the possible trend. Long-term computer forecasts about the weather are just not as convincing as choking smog or measurable ozone holes and UV levels. Between 1998 and 2013, global surface temperatures reportedly failed to track the predictions of climate-change models (even though they were still rising), stoking skepticism about the models. Second, whereas CFCs and other ozone-depleting chemicals were used in only small segments of the economy (e.g., refrigeration and aerosol products), GHG emissions are linked to almost every facet of human activity (agriculture, electricity, heating, transportation, and industrial processes). Finally, CFC substitutes were relatively easy to find and commercialize. Substantially curtailing GHGs is much harder and much more expensive than eliminating ozone-depleting chemicals.

Nevertheless, many companies are starting to address the risks and opportunities of climate change. While some do so because it is "the right thing to do," most do so to save money, reduce risks, or take advantage of new green opportunities. To mitigate future risks, Oxfam America created the Partnership for Resilience and Environmental Preparedness with collaborating companies—including Levi Strauss & Co., Green Mountain Coffee Roasters Inc., Starbucks, Swiss Re, and Entergy—to develop, refine, and share practices for resilience in the face of climate change.[101] Certain regions are starting to take advantage of current and anticipated changes. For instance, agricultural productivity and total production is increasing in Greenland, reducing the country's reliance on expensive imported food.[102] And in a twist of climate change fate, the melting of Arctic ice is enabling more sustainable transportation—ocean freighters can save almost 30 percent on time and fuel by sailing from China to Europe via the ice-free Arctic rather than by navigating the Suez Canal.[103]

Future (Non) Consumers

Consumers in the developed world—especially young ones—may be seeking fewer material goods, potentially reducing the material impacts of future consumers on the planet. According to Julie Hennessy of Northwestern University, who researched millennials' attitudes, "Nearly any possession you can think of stopped being an 'of course' and became a 'hmmmm' for millennials."[104] This is especially noticeable in the attitude toward car ownership[105]—in the United States, the proportion of 17-year-olds with drivers' licenses fell to less than half in 2010, down from more than two-thirds in 1978 [106]—but it is not limited to automobiles.

Millennials are investing in "experiences" rather than "things," which is why social networking, music services, YouTube, and the sharing economy thrive. Companies are responding by creating experiences—everything from sharing on Facebook to Walmart movie nights—shifting the material-intensive industrial economy toward a potentially less-resource-intensive service and information economy.

Consumption in the developed world may stop growing as standards of living rise and fertility rates drop. Already, some mature, high-consumption countries, such as Japan and Italy, are shrinking in population, and others would be shrinking without a steady influx of immigrants.[107] Estimates suggest that sometime between 2050 and 2100 the world's population may plateau at 10 billion,[108] although other estimates hint at continuing slow growth to anywhere between 9.6 billion and 12.3 billion by 2100.[109] Both estimates include many caveats that may point to even lower numbers.

MORE GROWTH AND LESS IMPACT

Large multinational companies that depend on global markets for both supply and demand to provide growth worry about potential disruptions or restrictions. "We thought about some of the megatrends in the world, like the shift east in terms of population growth and the growing demand for the world's resources. And we said, 'Why don't we develop a business model aimed at contributing to society and the environment instead of taking from them?'" said Paul Polman, the CEO of Unilever.[110] He even said, "I don't think our fiduciary duty is to put shareholders first."[111] In 2010, Polman committed Unilever to halving the environmental footprint of its products while doubling the size of its business.[112] It is an *eco-growth* target—growing the company's top line while shrinking its environmental impact.

The Push Toward Eco-Growth
Business-oriented eco-growth, of the kind that Polman desires, requires a very broad, multifaceted portfolio of initiatives to address the various types of impacts and the multiple sources. Figure 13.1 depicts the basis on which corporations may foster eco-growth, divided into *what* the initiatives seek to do (and why), and *who* they are aimed to influence. As described in previous chapters, companies can use a variety of *eco-efficiency*, *eco-risk mitigation*, and *eco-segmentation* initiatives to improve performance on both financial and environmental performance dimensions.

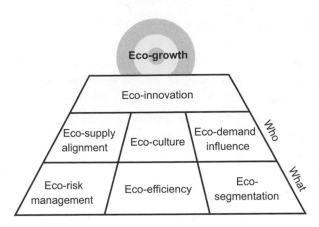

Figure 13.1
The elements of eco-growth

Each initiative can contribute individually to eco-growth while protecting and enhancing the company's brand. By reducing costs, eco-efficiency helps a company become more competitive while simultaneously reducing its environmental impact. By reducing risks of disruption to supply or demand, eco-risk mitigation reduces potential costs, losses, brand diminution, and barriers to maintaining a social license to operate and grow. By developing and promoting "green" products, eco-segmentation creates a real option for scaling costly or speculative sustainability practices, for testing green product concepts, for extending the brand to new consumers, and for priming customers' acceptance of sustainable products. As M&S's Barry said, "We are very much firmly in the view that sustainability is shifting from risk to opportunity, and that's happening very, very quickly."

The *who* layer of the eco-growth pyramid sees these three types of initiatives spread inward and outward to align all the supply chain stakeholders that affect both a company's environmental impact and its financial performance. The story of sustainability is the story of supply chain management. As illustrated throughout this book, the lion's share of a company's environmental impacts—be it emissions, resource consumption, or other impacts—usually lies outside the company's four walls. Moreover, an impact in one part of the supply chain (e.g., energy for hot water to wash clothes) may only be addressable by a different part of the supply chain (e.g., a chemical ingredient supplier who can make effective cold-water detergents). Thus, addressing impacts at the most cost-effective point requires a company to take on an expanded role in its industry. This also involves cooperation and communications with—as well as the education of—customers, the media, NGOs, and governments to assuage concerns about the company's efforts to manage environmental impacts efficiently.[113]

Eco-Culture: Sustainability Inside

As discussed in chapter 4, sustainability typically begins "at home" with reductions in the company's own footprint for manufacturing and overhead. Initially, these can be individual low-hanging-fruit projects such as replacing inefficient lights, recycling waste materials, or using fuel-efficient trucks. Achieving larger internal reductions might require more widespread efforts or more coordinated changes in product design, procurement, manufacturing, and marketing. Thus, if a company wishes to reach more aggressive sustainability goals, it will need to align a large fraction of its own employees with those goals. The eco-culture element in figure 13.1 refers to creating a corporate culture around sustainability similar to creating a corporate culture around any other strategic goal such as quality, safety, or service.

The challenge for large corporations is how to inculcate such a culture across the organization; the employees may span the globe, finding themselves in different time zones, legal frameworks, and national cultures. *Eco-culture* initiatives comprise both formal and informal practices. Formal practices include policies (including compensation), environmental KPIs, shadow prices of natural resources, and other rules set by the company's leadership. Informal practices include education; publicizing quick wins, challenges, and awards; and so forth. Such a culture encourages employees to watch for opportunities in their own and their coworkers' daily activities in order to create or support environmental initiatives. "At Walmart, we're working to make sustainability sustainable, so that it's a priority in good times and in the tough times," said Mike Duke, CEO, in 2009.[114]

Consider Apple CEO Tim Cook: When a shareholder group demanded Apple invest only in environmental measures that were profitable, Cook responded angrily, "When we work on making our devices accessible by the blind, I don't consider the bloody ROI. When I think about doing the right thing, I don't think about an ROI. If you want me to do things only for ROI reasons, you should get out of this stock." Apple shareholders applauded Cook's outburst and voted down the group's resolution.[115] Stories like Cook's angry response serve to polish Apple's green image, as well as foster a culture of service and sustainability among its employees.

Eco-Supply Alignment: Up the Supply Chain

As mentioned in chapter 4, however, Apple's green exterior hides a less green reality upstream in its supply chain, among its Asian suppliers (as well as in the use phase for its products). Glitzy brochures and triumphant claims aside, Apple is aware of the hidden carbon footprint hot spots in its supply chain. Beginning in 2008, Apple began training a growing number of suppliers' managers and workers on a range of environmental and social issues (see chapter 5). To further reduce the carbon footprint of its suppliers, in 2015, Apple partnered with suppliers to install four gigawatts of clean energy, including two gigawatts in China.[116] The company worked with its Asian contract manufacturers to change their manufacturing processes to increase usage of recycled aluminum and aluminum smelted using hydroelectric power. The company has also helped suppliers implement initiatives for energy eco-efficiency, water reduction, and waste reduction.[117] "This won't happen overnight—in fact, it will take years—but it's important work that has to happen," Cook pointed out in 2015.[118]

As with Apple, most companies have a large fraction of environmental impacts and risks that lie in their upstream supply chains. Thus they often attempt to align suppliers to environmental goals as described in chapter 5. These *eco-supply alignment* activities depicted in figure 13.1 include codes of conduct, transparency requirements, frequent audits, supplier education, economic incentives, and expectations that suppliers will push environmental objectives to the next tier of suppliers. Supplier alignment can target any of the three types of initiatives. Companies can align suppliers to eco-efficiency goals by requiring suppliers to report and reduce their energy use, carbon emissions, water usage, or other natural resource footprints. Supplier eco-risk initiatives might focus on prohibiting "zero tolerance" activities, such as deforestation (e.g., RSPO), particular pesticides (Whole Foods), or worker safety and work rules violations (IKEA and many others). Supplier eco-segmentation initiatives might involve certifications that materials or parts supplied allow the company to meet green label standards for its products. In many cases, however, effecting change in suppliers' processes requires industry-wide collaboration through consortia such as the Electronic Industry Citizenship Coalition (EICC) or RSPO.

One can assess companies on their level of process maturity for the role of sustainability in suppliers' management along the following scale (see figure 13.2).

Some companies manage their suppliers' environmental performance on their own, whereas others enlist the help of a third party, such as an NGO, certification body, or industry body. Companies such as L'Oréal, IKEA, Starbucks, Nike, and Patagonia have different levels of sustainability management depending on the supplier

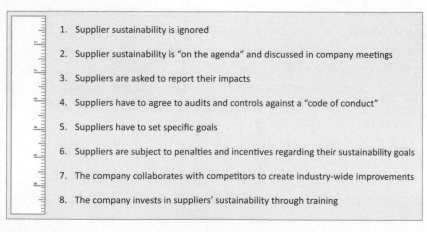

Figure 13.2
Suppliers' environmental management maturity model

type, as a function of the company's materiality assessment (see chapter 3) and supplier risk assessment (see the HP example in chapter 5).

A completely different element of supply eco-alignment is the attractiveness of sustainable companies to millennial recruits; in other words, the supply of human resources. As mentioned in chapter 10, many companies have seen evidence that millennials—who will be entering the workforce in large numbers in the second and third decades of the 21st century—are attracted to firms that practice social and environmental responsibility. These companies may attract a larger pool of applicants and therefore gain better employees. The competitive advantage created by such attraction is basic in that companies' most important assets are their employees, and superior employees create superior returns.

Eco-Demand Influence: Down the Supply Chain

Worldwide, industry consumes half of all energy produced. The other half of energy is consumed by the use of all the products created by industry. Pressure (and mandates) to reduce this total impact motivates companies to develop and market energy efficient products or change end-of-life disposal practices. To achieve this, companies combine new green products with marketing campaigns aimed at influencing consumers to buy and use them responsibly. Toyota made hybrid cars "cool" with the distinctive styling of the Prius and an aggressive marketing campaign. The carmaker has also attempted to influence consumers' behavior after they buy the car. The Prius gives real-time feedback to drivers on their driving habits, including fuel consumption and separate "eco-scores" for the driver's starting, cruising, and stopping habits.[119] Similarly, a range of companies, including detergent makers, appliance makers, apparel makers, and retailers, have tried to influence consumers to use cold water to wash clothing (see chapter 9).

Companies deeper in the supply chain also work to influence B2B customer behavior and product choices. Alcoa creates special lightweight alloys and products to improve the fuel efficiency of cars, trucks, and aircraft. BASF develops and markets specialty chemicals and materials for green product applications, which accounts for 23 percent of the company's sales (see chapter 8). These companies try to influence their customer companies to design and sell greener products, which (by no coincidence) are profitable for the suppliers of key materials needed to make these greener products.

Spreading Sustainability Outward

A company's alignment efforts can go beyond its own upstream and downstream ends of the supply chain to encompass others who affect resource consumption and impacts. AB InBev ranks water stewardship among the most important issues for both its business and its stakeholders[120] (see chapter 4). Although the beverage maker has worked to improve its own water use in places like Brazil, it recognizes that if the broader patterns of water use by others in the region are not sustainable, then AB InBev's access to water (or its social license to operate) might be disrupted. "With worsening droughts from the southwest United States to southeastern Brazil, scarcity presents enormous challenges that go beyond access, impacting the quality of health and socio-economic prosperity in our communities," wrote Carlos Brito, CEO of AB InBev.[121] This has motivated the brewer to go beyond efforts within the company and its supply chain, to take on a broader natural resource stewardship role in the region. These expanded eco-alignment efforts aim to harness the combined power of all players in an industry or region to work toward sustainability.

One element of AB InBev's water stewardship initiatives in Brazil focuses on restoration of the upstream areas of the watersheds surrounding the urban metropolis São Paulo. This work involves a complex public-private partnership with The Nature Conservancy, the area mayor's office, the Jaguariúna Bureau of the Environment, the Brazilian Agricultural Research Corporation, the Brazilian National Water Agency, and the Piracicaba, Capivari, and Jundiaí Watershed Committees.[122] These efforts target reforestation of riverbanks to reduce erosion and help control flooding. They also include improving soil conservation practices in area farms: deploying 195 water retention ponds, terracing 540 hectares, and readjusting 17 km of rural roads.[123] Watershed restoration in the region promotes better water retention in the greater São Paulo area. Not only does this help ensure continuity of water supplies, but it also reduces the threat of disruptions from flooding.

Another element of AB InBev's Brazilian water stewardship initiatives focuses on reducing water use by others, especially ordinary consumers, regardless of whether they drink the company's products or not. AB InBev and the Brazilian water utility Sabesp launched Banco Cyan (Cyan Bank) on Earth Day 2011. Twenty-six million consumers opened online accounts that help them track water usage, learn to conserve, and earn points toward discounts at online stores in Brazil.[124]

Efficient Supply Chain Management

Between 1980 and 2010, total ton-miles of freight in the United States grew by 36 percent.[125] Yet, at the same time, the percentage of the US GDP spent on logistics *declined* steadily from 15.7 percent in 1980 to 10.4 percent in 1995, and down to 8.3 percent in 2010.[126] The logistics industry had become significantly more efficient, which also enabled global merchandise trade to surge from 27.7 percent of global GDP in 1986, to 33.9 percent in 1995, and to reach 46.9 percent in 2010.[127]

The main impetus for the reduced cost of logistics services was the deregulation of the US transportation industry, followed by transportation deregulation in the EU and other regions. This trend was augmented by high fuel costs and environmental considerations that spurred the development of fuel-efficient trucks,[128] airplanes,[129] and ships,[130] as well as the adoption of fuel-saving operating procedures, such as slow steaming[131] and speed regulators on trucks.[132] Logistics facilities also adopted energy-saving devices, alternative energy sources, and reduced emissions technologies, all of which reduced costs. At the same time, better logistics management tools and processes (such as better coordination to minimize empty miles) reduced waste and cost, leading to higher efficiency and lower environmental impacts.

One of the most important trends that kept logistics costs from escalating with world GDP and the growth in international trade was the adoption of data capture, analysis, management, and communications tools. Digital information, besides directly replacing some manufactured print and music products, has also reduced the costs and, often, the environmental footprints of all manufactured goods. Timely information and precise control can help minimize the use of high-footprint expedited transportation; it can also lower safety stocks and help machinery perform optimally—all leading to both reduced costs and lower environmental impacts. When computers went from the desktop to the palmtop to embedded sensors with an always-on connection to the Internet, the enterprise management applications that efficiently ran administrative back-offices could be extended into the great outdoors where supply chains chiefly operate.

EXPANDING THE FRONTIERS OF PERFORMANCE

Once companies reach the Pareto frontier, the low-hanging fruit has been harvested. Decisions that led to better outcomes on both financial and environmental dimensions have already been taken, and at that point companies seem to be forced to make trade-offs between financial performance and environmental performance. But this frontier is only an absolute limit if decision makers have an unchanging set of options.

Fortunately, the world is not static. The set of options available to managers expands in two directions (see figure 13.3). First, innovation in the form of new management processes, new materials, and the inexorable advance of technology all expand the decision maker's space of options. Another source of innovation is suppliers, who may redesign or modify equipment to enable low-impact, high-efficiency, or low-risk manufacturing and transportation. Second, consumers' changing

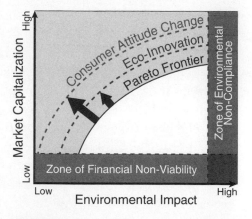

Figure 13.3

Expanding the Pareto Frontier

attitudes toward green companies and products (whether owing
to demand shaping by a company, a regulatory change, media
influence, or external trends) may make investments in sustainability more attractive and allow for premium pricing and/or market
share capture.

Such developments, when they come, allow companies to "push
out" the Pareto frontier and create new opportunities to achieve
both economic growth and a reduction in environmental impacts.

Creating Sustainable Growth

The common assertion that growth and environmental sustainability cannot coexist rests on two principle assumptions. The
first is that growth—such as revenue increases—must require
proportional increases in the material volume of products. But
eco-efficiency innovations might reduce the amount of material in
a product (e.g., concentrated detergent, lightweight plastic bottles,
aluminum-frame cars, and ever-shrinking consumer electronics).
Other innovations may increase the value of the product through
improvements in performance or service (e.g., customization of
products, "white glove delivery," software bundled with products),
leading to a higher price for a given quantity of physical product.
Furthermore, changing consumer preferences might favor more
services over owning more stuff. Finally, the Internet has enabled
both the sharing economy and growing online markets for secondhand products, which means more people get to use a given
product without the need to manufacture more of that product.

The second assumption is that higher material consumption
necessarily means corresponding increases in environmental degradation. At first glance this assumption seems true; making a ton
of cotton T-shirts seems to always require at least a ton of cotton,
with all the negative impacts that growing cotton entails. However,
innovations in irrigation, fertilizers, pesticides, and cotton breeding
can reduce the environmental impact of that ton of cotton. Recycling by consumers might mean that the one ton of new T-shirts
needs less than a ton of new cotton. Renewable energy initiatives
might replace carbon-intensive power used in the harvesting,
manufacturing, and transportation processes with carbon-neutral

alternatives. Eco-risk mitigation initiatives might reduce impactful activities (such as deforestation), substitute low-impact materials for high-impact ones (such as Patagonia's Yulex wet suit described in chapter 11), or phase out toxins.

Examples of new products that break the more-products–more-impact relationship include the array of hybrid and electric automobiles and machinery, which reduce the carbon footprint during a product's use phase. A specific example is Cummins' low-emissions diesel truck engines, which are cleaner, as well as more efficient and quieter, than the engines they replace.[133] The new engines opened new markets for Cummins in Europe and elsewhere.

Innovations can extend to manufacturing processes, such as Coca-Cola's redesigned bottle-washing spray equipment that reduces water consumption (see chapter 4). Raytheon Corporation's response to the evidence of ozone depletion caused by cleaning chemical solvents is another example. The company replaced a CFC-based cleaning agent with a semi-aqueous, terpene-based agent that was not only reusable but also increased product quality.[134] New manufacturing methods allow for radical redesigns of existing products to reduce their impacts (e.g., Nike's Flyknit shoe; see chapter 8). Finally, some companies might combine product and process innovations with new business models (e.g., Interface Carpet's cradle-to-cradle model; see chapter 8).

Regulations can affect many of these sustainability-related innovations, but they have to be correctly applied. Porter and van der Linde[135] argue that regulations mandating the use of specific technologies (e.g., a particular emissions-control device) can limit innovation. In contrast, environmental regulations that focus on achieving a measurable outcome (e.g., a limit on emissions) can spur innovation, thus pushing the Pareto frontier outward.

The Intrinsic Eco-Efficiency of Information

Although product supply chains and consumers' use of goods do require natural resources, the amount of resources required to produce value can decline. Ford switched from steel to aluminum to decrease weight and increase the fuel efficiency of its

F-150 pickup truck.[136] GE is investing $200 million to mass-produce ultra-lightweight high-performance materials to create higher-efficiency jet engines and gas turbines.[137]

Some of the greatest improvements in resource efficiency have taken place in consumer and business computing owing to Moore's Law. A modern-day tablet, such as an Apple iPad, has more processing power and functionality than a desktop PC of 20 years ago, yet it uses less than 1/10th the materials and 1/100th the electrical power. With the use of apps, a smartphone or tablet can replace dozens of previously separate consumer products (and their respective environmental impacts). Besides being a telephone, the device also acts as a camera, video recorder, walkie-talkie, GPS navigation aid, pocket calculator, wristwatch, game console, flashlight, hand mirror, appointment book, notepad, laptop, wallet, credit cards, and house keys, to name a few. The Internet, mobile networks, and digital delivery obviate most of the environmental impacts of manufacturing, distributing, retailing, and recycling of physical books, audio records, CDs, videotapes, DVDs, maps, and instruction manuals, as well as the furniture (bookshelves and filing cabinets) and floor space (and retail space) they formerly required.

In 2013, the UN reported that more people on Earth have access to mobile phones than toilets.[138] With cellular data networks available to six billion people, any country has the potential to jump from a preindustrial level of development to a postindustrial information economy. African countries are building cellphone networks and skipping the landline phase; they are using mobile payments without building bank branches everywhere; and they are in the process of skipping the PC revolution in favor of smartphones.[139]

Connecting the World

The growing availability of data and the declining cost (and increased accuracy) of sensors facilitates supply chain visibility—the ability to locate and track materials, parts, and products as they move around the world. Such operational visibility is critical for pharmaceuticals, food safety, sensitive defense parts, high-value products, and time-sensitive production and delivery processes. Companies invest in visibility for business benefits such as efficiency, reliability, and service that are enhanced by knowing where parts and products are at all times, anticipating delays, and allowing for better coordination of manufacturing and distribution activities.

Supply chain visibility systems can support tracking of hidden credence attributes, such as those associated with sustainability, by ensuring provenance. Companies can then use their operational visibility systems to manage and communicate sustainability information to those customers, consumers, and investors who want it, especially customers who must comply with government regulations (e.g., EU timber, US conflict minerals, among others). To communicate this information, companies can use online media, such as the interactive map Marks & Spencer created showing 1,230 suppliers in the retailer's food and apparel supply chains (which is reminiscent of Patagonia's Footprint Chronicles).[140] Such visual displays are currently static, but one can imagine a future dynamic layer depicting real-time information. Downstream information sharing may also help in managing responsible use and end-of-life issues. For example, GE has installed sensors in its jet engines, locomotives, and other products that send information back to the company about product usage and performance.[141] This enables GE to increase the operating efficiency, life span, and safety of its products, leading to both economic and environmental benefits.

On a more inspiring level, visibility can create a human connection between suppliers and consumers around the world, becoming a means by which rising standards of living foster rising concern for the environment. The near-universal availability of cellular phones[142] means that virtually every farmer, supplier, trader, factory, transportation carrier, retailer, worker, and consumer in the world can be connected at all times. The same tools that let FedEx or UPS track a package from origin to destination may help Starbucks track coffee from a Costa Rican farm to a consumer's venti latte, connecting the bean grower with the cup sipper. Such connections can help personify the impacts of supply chains and help accelerate a reduction of environmental impacts at both ends of the chain.

The Loops in the Chain

The linear economy of the 20th century was easy to understand. Goods flowed in one direction: downstream from supplier to manufacturer to retailer to consumer, and on to a landfill. However, as recycling and reuse efforts expand, consumers and customers become *suppliers*. Downstream end-of-life waste management efforts create new supply sources of materials for the upstream end of the supply chain.

Governments are contributing to this trend by enacting Extended Producer Responsibility (EPR) regulations (see chapter 7). These regulations include a combination of take-back requirements, disposal fees and deposit-refund schemes, recycled content requirements, and consumer education or labeling requirements. Between 1998 and 2007, more than 260 producer responsibility organizations that collect and/or recycle end-of-life products were established in Europe.[143]

Thus, government mandates and initial market forces are starting to shift companies (and supply chains) from the prevailing "take-make-dispose" paradigm to a "cradle-to-cradle" paradigm. Such thinking leads companies to adopt what EMC and Herman Miller (among others) call "design for disassembly." EMC accepts returns of all its branded products (see chapter 7).[144] Some returned products are reconditioned for internal deployment or donations, while others are harvested for remanufacturing. The company sends less than 1 percent of its postcustomer products and materials to landfills. Carpet manufacturer Interface Inc. went even further and changed its overall business model to obtain full control of its products throughout their entire life cycle (see chapter 8). Combined with innovative product design, Interface recovers, recycles, and reuses 98 percent of old carpet to make new carpet. "The circular economy has to be the better way forward. Every manufactured good in the future should be made so that it can be remanufactured," said Sir David King, the UK Foreign Office's special representative for climate change.[145]

As Unilever's CEO Paul Polman said, "Sustainability is contributing to our virtuous circle of growth. The more our products meet social needs and help people live sustainably, the more popular our brands become and the more we grow. And the more efficient we are at managing resources such as energy and raw materials, the more we lower our costs and reduce the risks to our business and the more we are able to invest in sustainable innovation and brands."[146]

Getting Green from Green Growth

At first glance, selling sustainability to business executives in the short term seems difficult. First, some executives might believe that the extent, timing, and impacts of climate change and other environmental risks are too uncertain to merit short-term investment. Second, they might believe that technological solutions will avert any potential catastrophe, as they have in the past, obviating the need to invest right now. Third, they might believe that long-term investment in sustainability does not serve the central short-term financial and competitive goals of the organization.

Nevertheless, even the most skeptical executive would still pursue some level of eco-initiatives; these initiatives are rooted in a business rationale that is independent of an executive's personal beliefs about the long-term future of the environment. The business rationale for eco-efficiency depends only on the inevitable cost savings of using fewer natural resources. The business sense behind eco-risk mitigation depends on the beliefs of the NGOs, media, and regulators who might attack non-green companies. It is also a rationale for recycling to protect against price increases and shortages. Finally, the business motivation for eco-segmentation depends on the beliefs of those consumers who might prefer green goods. It also socializes the organization to a possible future in which supplying green products will be required. Thus, even the most ardent climate change skeptics are likely to pursue some minimum level of sustainability efforts because those initiatives reduce costs, lower short-term risks, and reposition a company for potential changes in consumer attitudes or regulations.

Implementing sustainable practices falls on the shoulders of supply chain managers. The design and management of supply chains plays a dominant role both in creating and in mitigating the environmental impacts of sourcing, manufacturing, transportation, usage, and disposal of all products that sustain and improve peoples' lives. Supply chain management processes are caught in the crossfire between the tensions of economic performance, natural resource stresses, societally acceptable practices, and regulation. The debate regarding the acceptable trade-offs between human standards of living and prevalence of jobs on the one hand, and levels of environmental impacts on the other, has already begun, and it will affect the constraints and opportunities that companies face. Some inventive companies will find clever and profitable ways to beat these supposed trade-offs—innovating their way into eating the proverbial cake while having it, too. In 2011, Nike CEO Mark Parker told shareholders, "I believe that any company doing business today has two simple options: embrace sustainability as a core part of your growth strategy, or eventually stop growing."[147]

Notes

Notes to Chapter 1

1. http://business.time.com/2010/03/01/warren-buffetts-boring-brilliant -wisdom/.

2. http://www.reocities.com/Athens/Acropolis/5232/edmonton.htm.

3. Nike share price went from a high of $8.98 in February 1997 to a low of $4.34 in July 1998.

4. Interview with Scott Ponyton, Director of The Forest Trust, May 8, 2013.

5. Rowntree Ltd, Gaumont Sound Mirror, "Next Stop: York… Help yourself to some chocolates" 1932. Retrieved from: http://www.yorkshirefilmarchive.com/ film/next-stop-york-help-yourself-some-chocolates?destination=search/ apachesolr_search/chocolate?mode%3Dquick%26solrsort%3Dscore%2520 desc%252C%2520sis_cck_field_film_id%2520asc%26filters%3Dtype%253 Ayfa_film%26highl.

6. http://ezinearticles.com/?Music-in-the-Workplace&id=564815.

7. http://www.nestle.co.uk/aboutus/history/kitkat-is-named-after-a-man-called -christopher.

8. http://www.independent.co.uk/arts-entertainment/snap-those-fingers-1578753 .html.

9. Jessica Kovleraug, "When the Brain Grabs a Tune and Won't Let Go," *The New York Times*, August 12, 2003. Retrieved from: http://www.nytimes.com/2003/08/ 12/health/when-the-brain-grabs-a-tune-and-won-t-let-go.html.

10. Interestingly, in the United States, Kit Kat is made and sold by Hershey, not Nestlé, owing to a 1970 licensing agreement between Rowntree and Hershey. It is one of the top five brands of Hershey.

11. http://www.yorkpress.co.uk/news/10894637.Revealed__Secret_files_on _Rowntree_takeover/.

12. http://www.nestle.co.uk/aboutus/history/blog/posts/kitkatturns80.

13. *Huffington Post Green* (2011). "Dancing with Devils." Retrieved from: http:// www.huffingtonpost.com/scott-poynton/dancing-with-devils_b_837442.htm-l?view=print&comm_ref=false.

14. Greenpeace (2010). "Greenpeace Kit Kat Commercial: Ask Nestlé CEO to Stop Buying Unsustainable Palm Oil." Retrieved from: http://www.youtube.com/watch?v=1BCA8dQfGi0.

15. Greenpeace Video (2010). "Give the Orangutan a Break." Retrieved from: http://www.youtube.com/watch?v=QV1t-MvnCrA.

16. "The Other Oil Spill," *The Economist*, June 24, 2010. Retrieved from: http://www.economist.com/node/16423833.

17. Financial Times (2010). "Nestlé Learns to See the Wood for the Trees." Retrieved from: http://www.ft.com/intl/cms/s/0/f3459df2-6d15-11df-921a-00144 feab49a.html#axzz2e8duYYBX.

18. Jeremiah Owyang, "Greenpeace vs. Brands: Social Media Attacks to Continue," *Forbes*, July 19, 2010. Retrieved from: http://www.forbes.com/2010/07/19/greenpeace-bp-Nestlé-twitter-facebook-forbes-cmo-network-jeremiah-owyang.html.

19. Buycott (2013). Campaigns. Retrieved from: http://www.buycott.com/campaign/all.

20. Nestlé (2013). "Responsible Sourcing Guidelines: Palm Oil." Retrieved from: http://www.Nestlé.com/asset-library/documents/creating%20shared%20value/rural_development/2011-palm-oil-Nestlé-responsible-sourcing-guidelines.pdf.

21. Nestlé (2012). "Nestlé Committed to Traceable Sustainable Palm Oil to Ensure No-Deforestation." Retrieved from: http://www.Nestlé.com/media/Statements/Update-on-deforestation-and-palm-oil.

22. Roundtable on Sustainable Palm Oil (RSPO) (2012), History. Retrieved from: http://www.rspo.org/en/history.

23. RSPO (2013). Vision and Mission. Retrieved from: http://www.rspo.org/en/vision_and_mission.

24. The Economist, op. cit.

25. Gina-Marie Chesseman, "Nestle Responds to Greenpeace Pressure and Partners with the Forest Trust," *Triple Pundit*, May 19, 2010. Retrieved from: http://www.triplepundit.com/2010/05/Nestlé-responds-to-greenpeace-pressure-and-partners-with-the-forest-trust/.

26. Greenpeace (2010). "Greenpeace Protests at Nestlé Shareholder Meeting." Retrieved from: http://www.youtube.com/watch?v=s8kwVU5pujg.

27. http://www.greenpeace.org.uk/blog/forests/success-you-made-nestlé-drop-dodgy-palm-oil-now-lets-bank-it-hsbc-20100517.

28. Right to Water (2007). "Case Against Coca-Cola Kerala State: India." Retrieved from: http://www.righttowater.info/ways-to-influence/legal-approaches/case-against-coca-cola-kerala-state-india/.

29. "Indians force Coca-Cola bottling facility in Plachimada to shut down, 2001–2006," Global Nonviolent Action Database. Accessed March 17, 2015. Retrieved from: http://nvdatabase.swarthmore.edu/content/indians-force-coca-cola-bottling-facility-plachimada-shut-down-2001-2006.

30. Right to Water (2007). "Case Against Coca-Cola Kerala State: India." Retrieved from: http://www.righttowater.info/ways-to-influence/legal-approaches/case-against-coca-cola-kerala-state-india/.

31. "Indian Officials Order Coca-Cola Plant to Close for Using Too Much Water," *The Guardian*, June 18, 2014. Retrieved from: http://www.theguardian.com/environment/2014/jun/18/indian-officals-coca-cola-plant-water-mehdiganj.

32. Jonathan Harr, *A Civil Action* (New York: Random House, 1995), p. 23.

33. Melissa Fuchs, "Woburn's Burden of Proof: Corporate Social Responsibility and Public Health," *J. Undergrad. Sci.* 3 (Fall 1996): 165–170. Retrieved from: http://www.hcs.harvard.edu/~jus/0303/fuchs.pdf.

34. Eliot Marshall, "Woburn Case May Spark Explosion of Lawsuits," *Science*, 234, no. 4775 (1986): 418.

35. Evan T. Barr, "The New Age of Toxic Tort: Poisoned Well," *New Republic*, 194, no. 11 (March 17, 1986): 18.

36. Melissa Fuchs, "Woburn's Burden of Proof: Corporate Social Responsibility and Public Health," *J. Undergrad. Sci.* 3 (Fall 1996): 165–170. Retrieved from: http://www.hcs.harvard.edu/~jus/0303/fuchs.pdf.

37. http://iucat.iu.edu/iub/2861871.

38. http://loe.org/shows/segments.html?programID=98-P13-00050&segmentID=6.

39. http://serc.carleton.edu/woburn/woburntrialchrono.html.

40. Dan Kennedy, "Behind – and Beyond – the Hype Over a Civil Action: A Reporter Revisits the Scene of the Real Woburn Tragedy," *The Boston Phoenix*, December 17–24, 1998. Retrieved from: http://bostonphoenix.com/archive/features/98/12/17/WOBURN.html.

41. Woburn Toxic Trial Chronology, http://serc.carleton.edu/woburn/issues/woburn_trial_cronology.

42. Jason Carmichael, Craig Jenkins, and Robert Brulle, "Building Environmentalism: The Founding of Environmental Movement Organizations in the United States, 1900–2000," *The Sociological Quarterly* 43 no. 3 (2012): 422–453.

43. http://bostonphoenix.com/archive/features/98/12/17/WOBURN.html.

44. Dan Kraker, "Minnesota Power Reaches Deal on Coal-Fired Plants," *MPR News*, July 16, 2014. Retrieved from: http://www.mprnews.org/story/2014/07/16/minnesota-power-reaches-deal-on-coalfired-plants.

45. http://www.mnpower.com/Content/Documents/Company/PressReleases/2014/20140716_NewsRelease.pdf.

46. Opacity is the degree to which visibility of a background (i.e., blue sky) is reduced by particulates (smoke). See: https://ehs.unl.edu/sop/s-opacity_emissions.pdf.

47. Dan Haugen, "Sierra Club Says Minnesota Utility Violating Pollution Rules," *Midwestern Energy News*, March 25, 2014. Retrieved from: http://midwestenergynews.com/2014/03/25/sierra-club-says-minnesota-utility-violating-pollution-rules/.

48. Sierra Club (2014). "Minnesota Power Put on Notice for More Than 12,500 Clean Air Act Violations." Retrieved from: http://content.sierraclub.org/press -releases/2014/03/minnesota-power-put-notice-more-12500-clean-air-act -violations.

49. Ibid.

50. David Shaffer, "Sierra Club Alleges Minnesota Power Coal Plant Violations," *Star Tribune*, March 25, 2014. Retrieved from: http://www.startribune.com/ sierra-club-alleges-minnesota-power-coal-plant-violations/251962741/.

51. Ibid.

52. Ibid.

53. https://www.epa.gov/enforcement/minnesota-power-settlement.

54. Dan Kraker, "Minnesota Power Reaches Deal on Coal-Fired Plants," *MPR News*, July 16, 2014. Retrieved from: http://www.mprnews.org/story/2014/07/16/ minnesota-power-reaches-deal-on-coalfired-plants.

55. http://investor.allete.com/releasedetail.cfm?releaseid=860187.

56. David Shaffer, "Sierra Club Alleges Minnesota Power Coal Plant Violations," *Star Tribune*, March 25, 2014. Retrieved from: http://www.startribune.com/ sierra-club-alleges-minnesota-power-coal-plant-violations/251962741/.

57. *Huffington Post* (2013), "Shell's Arctic Drilling Vessels Violation Clean Air Act in 2012, Company to Pay Fine." Retrieved from: http://www.huffingtonpost. com/2013/09/06/shell-arctic-drilling-violations_n_3881226.html.

58. Joseph Popiolkowski, "DuPont to pay $440,000 fine in pollution settlement linked to Town of Tonawanda Plant," *The Buffalo News*, July 22, 2014. Retrieved from: http://www.buffalonews.com/city-region/town-of-tonawanda/dupont-to -pay-440000-fine-in-pollution-settlement-linked-to-town-of-tonawanda-plant -20140722.

59. Larry Bell, "EPA's Secret and Costly 'Sue and Settle' Collusion with Environ- mental Organizations," *Forbes*, February 17, 2013. Retrieved from: http://www .forbes.com/sites/larrybell/2013/02/17/epas-secret-and-costly-sue-and-settle -collusion-with-environmental-organizations/.

60. Neena Satija, "Fed Up With Government, Environmentalists File Lawsuits Over Pollution," *Texas Tribune*, February 23, 2014. Retrieved from: http://www .texastribune.org/2014/02/23/fed-government-environmentalists-sue-companies/.

61. Marc Gunther, "Under Pressure: Campaigns That Persuaded Companies to Change The World," *The Guardian*, February 9, 2015. Retrieved from: https:// www.theguardian.com/sustainable-business/2015/feb/09/corporate-ngo -campaign-environment-climate-change.

62. https://depts.washington.edu/ccce/polcommcampaigns/NikeChronology.htm.

63. ForestEthics (2001). "Victoria's Dirty Secret." Retrieved from: http://forestethics. org/news/ad-victorias-dirty-secret.

64. See, for example, a list of campaign support groups at http://corpethics.org/ article.php?id=1079.

65. Interview with Robert Beer, February 5, 2016.

66. http://www.bbc.co.uk/news/technology-15671823.

67. "Consumer Interest in Green Products Expands Across Categories," Cohn & Wolfe, June 8, 2011. Retrieved from: http://www.cohnwolfe.com/en/news/consumer-interest-green-products-expands-across-categories. Accessed March 21, 2015.

68. US Consumers Increase 'Green' Purchases; But Are They Willing to Pay More?" Harris Interactive, June 5, 2013. Retrieved from: http://www.prnewswire.com/news-releases/us-consumers-increase-green-purchases-but-are-they-willing-to-pay-more-210221081.html. Accessed April 1, 2015.

69. WSJ Interview with Robert McDonald, CEO of Procter and Gamble in March 2012. Retrieved from: http://www.wsj.com/articles/SB100014240527023046364045772995529364220 74. Accessed April 2015.

70. Gregory Unruh is the Arison Group Endowed Professor at George Mason University in Fairfax, Virginia.

71. Gregory Unruh, "No, Consumers Will Not Pay More for Green," *Forbes*, July 28, 2011. Retrieved from: http://www.forbes.com/sites/csr/2011/07/28/no-consumers-will-not-pay-more-for-green/.

72. http://www.sciencedirect.com/science/article/pii/S0306919213001796.

73. "2013 Cone Communications/Echo Global CSR Study." Cone Communications, 2013 Retrieved from: http://www.conecomm.com/global-csr-study. Accessed April 1, 2015.

74. http://www.iamz.ciheam.org/GTP2006/FinalpapersGTP2006/19final.pdf.

75. http://www.marketresearch.com/Packaged-Facts-v768/Green-Household-Cleaning-Laundry-Products-8825323/?progid=88505.

76. http://www.cnbc.com/2016/11/04/millennials-willing-to-pay-more-for-sustainable-better-quality-goods-nestle-chairman.html.

77. http://corporate.walmart.com/_news_/news-archive/2009/07/16/walmart-announces-sustainable-product-index.

78. Interview with Jay Kimpton, Russ LoCurto, and Dania Nasser of Ralph Lauren, October 29, 2013.

79. http://www.businesswire.com/news/home/20110524006289/en/Kohl's-Department-Store-Releases-Corporate-Sustainability-Report.

80. http://www.greenbiz.com/blog/2012/10/29/can-suppliers-meet-retailers-rising-sustainability-expectations.

81. NPR (2011). "Two Girl Scouts Want Palm Oil Out of Famous Cookies." Retrieved from: http://www.npr.org/2011/07/04/137539757/two-scouts-want-palm-oil-out-of-famous-cookies.

82. NPR (2011). "Two Girl Scouts Want Palm Oil Out of Famous Cookies." Retrieved from: http://www.npr.org/2011/07/04/137539757/two-scouts-want-palm-oil-out-of-famous-cookies.

83. *Huffington Post* (2012). "Girl Scouts Win U.N. Award for Efforts to Save Orangutans by Eliminating Palm Oil from Cookies." Retrieved from: http://www .huffingtonpost.com/2012/02/09/girl-scouts-win-award-united-nations_n _1265843.html.

84. NPR (2011). "Two Girl Scouts Want Palm Oil Out of Famous Cookies." Retrieved from: http://www.npr.org/2011/07/04/137539757/two-scouts-want -palm-oil-out-of-famous-cookies.

85. *Huffington Post* (2011). "Girl Scouts USA Respond to Campaign for Sustainable Cookies." Retrieved from: http://www.huffingtonpost.com/2011/10/07/girl -scouts-cookies-palm-oil-campaign_n_998437.html.

86. Bob Woodward, "How Mark Felt Became 'Deep Throat,'" *Washington Post*, June 20, 2005. Retrieved from: https://www.washingtonpost.com/politics/how -mark-felt-became-deep-throat/2012/06/04/gJQAlpARIV_story.html?utm _term=.c47fe550dff4.

87. Matt Taibbi, "SEC Rocked By Lurid Sex-and-Corruption Lawsuit," *Rolling Stone*, November 19, 2012.

88. Graeme Wearden, "GlaxoSmithKline Whistleblower Awarded $96m Payout," *The Guardian*, October 27, 2010.

89. http://www.msnbc.com/morning-joe/millennials-environment-climate-change.

90. Dell interview, April 18, 2014.

91. Cliff Zukin and Mark Szeltner, "What Workers Want in 2012," May 2012, John J. Heldrich Center for Workforce Development Rutgers, The State University of New Jersey. Retrieved from: https://netimpact.org/sites/default/files/docu ments/what-workers-want-2012.pdf. Accessed March 31, 2015.

92. Gina-Marie Chesseman, "Dunkin' Donuts Commits to 100% Sustainable Palm Oil," *Triple Pundit*, March 21, 2013. Retrieved from: http://www.triplepun dit.com/2013/03/dunkin-donuts-source-only-sustainably-produced-palm-oil/.

93. http://osc.state.ny.us/press/releases/mar13/030713a.htm.

94. http://paygovernance.com/activism-of-a-different-nature-social-investors-ad vocate-for-change-in-the-proxy/.

95. https://www.cdp.net/en-US/WhatWeDo/Pages/investors.aspx.

96. DOI: 10.1177/0003122412448796 http://asr.sagepub.com.

97. Timeline of major US environmental and occupational health regulation, https://en.wikipedia.org/wiki/Timeline_of_major_US_environmental_and _occupational_health_regulation.

98. Ann Johnson, "Environmental Regulations and Technology Development in the US Auto Industry," Washington Center for Equitable Growth, May 26, 2016. Retrieved from: http://equitablegrowth.org/report/environmental-regulation -technological-development-u-s-auto-industry/.

99. Climate Progress (2014). "7 Groups Attacking the President's Plan to Cure Pollution, Even Though It Hasn't Been Released Yet." Retrieved from: http:// thinkprogress.org/climate/2014/05/30/3442251/carbon-pollution-rule-attacks/.

100. EPA (2014). "Endangerment and Cause or Contribute Findings for Greenhouse Gases under Section 202(a) of the Clean Air Act." Retrieved from: http://www.epa.gov/climatechange/endangerment/.

101. Climate Progress (2014). "7 Groups Attacking the President's Plan to Cure Pollution, Even Though It Hasn't Been Released Yet." Retrieved from: http://thinkprogress.org/climate/2014/05/30/3442251/carbon-pollution-rule-attacks/.

102. Bloomberg (2014). "China Takes on Pollution With Biggest Changes in 25 Years." Retrieved from: http://www.bloomberg.com/news/2014-04-24/china-enacts-biggest-pollution-curbs-in-25-years.html.

103. Colum Murphy, "BYD Chairman: China is Weighing Tax to Help Electric-Car Effort," *Wall Street Journal*, August 29, 2014. Retrieved from: http://online.wsj.com/news/article_email/byd-chairman-china-is-weighing-tax-to-help-electric-car-effort-1409292914-lMyQjAxMTA0MDIwOTEyNDkyWj.

104. Eric Zuesse, "Love Canal: The Truth Seeps Out," *Reason Magazine*, February 1981. Retrieved from: http://reason.com/archives/1981/02/01/love-canal. Accessed March 3, 2015.

105. EPA (2012). "Love Canal: Region 2 Superfund." Retrieved from: http://www.epa.gov/region2/superfund/npl/lovecanal/.

106. A copy of the deed is available on http://commons.wikimedia.org/w/index.php?title=File:Hooker_Electrochemical_Quit_Claim_Deed_to_Board_of_Education.pdf&page=2.

107. EPA (2012). "Love Canal: Region 2 Superfund." Retrieved from: http://www.epa.gov/region2/superfund/npl/lovecanal/.

108. "Love Canal," Center for Health, Environment and Justice, Fact Pack P001. Retrieved from: http://chej.org/wp-content/uploads/Documents/love_canal_factpack.pdf. Accessed March 15, 2015.

109. EPA (2014). "Superfund Basic Information." Retrieved from: http://www.epa.gov/superfund/about.htm.

110. Ibid.

111. https://www.ncjrs.gov/App/Publications/abstract.aspx?ID=95622.

112. William Glaberson, "Love Canal: Suit Focuses on Records from the 1940's," *The New York Times*, October 22, 1990.

113. The last two sentences are a quote from William Glaberson, "Love Canal: Suit Focuses on Records from the 1940's," *The New York Times*, October 22, 1990.

114. http://www.law.cornell.edu/wex/ex_post_facto.

115. "USA, acting at request of the Administrator of the United States Environmental Protection Agency (EPA)," Plaintiff-Appellant, v. OLIN CORPORATION, Defendant-Appellee," http://caselaw.findlaw.com/us-11th-circuit/1316612.html#sthash.huH8W5kr.dpuf.

116. "United States v. Monsanto Co." http://elr.info/sites/default/files/litigation/19.20085.htm.

117. Cornell University Law School Legal Information Institute (2014). "Comprehensive Environmental Response, Compensation and Liability Act (CERCLA)." Retrieved from: http://www.law.cornell.edu/wex/comprehensive_environmental_response_compensation_and_liability_act_cercla.

118. http://www.bna.com/us-supreme-court-n17179891153/.

119. James Gerstenzang, "Firm Agrees to Settle Love Canal Suit: Pollution: Occidental Chemical will pay 2 government agencies for $129-million cost of cleaning up toxic waste site near Niagara Falls," *Los Angeles Times*, December 22, 1995. Retrieved from: http://articles.latimes.com/1995-12-22/news/mn-16926_1_love -canal.

120. Matthew L. Wald, "Out-of-Court Settlement Reached Over Love Canal," *The New York Times*, June 22, 1994. Retrieved from: http://www.nytimes .com/1994/06/22/nyregion/out-of-court-settlement-reached-over-love-canal.html.

121. http://www.epa.gov/enforcement/superfund-special-accounts.

122. http://ec.europa.eu/environment/waste/weee/pdf/final_rep_okopol.pdf.

123. Ezekiel 18:19–20, The Holy Bible, English Standard Version, Crossway Bibles (copyright 2001).

124. Peapod (2014). Retrieved from: http://www.peapod.com.

125. Forbes (2013). "The World's Most Valuable Brands." Retrieved from: http:// www.forbes.com/powerful-brands/list/.

126. See, for example, http://www.brandchannel.com/papers_review.asp?sp_id =357.

127. Private communication.

128. http://www.bloomberg.com/news/articles/2015-09-19/volkswagen-emis sions-cheating-found-by-curious-clean-air-group.

129. "To Stop Carmakers Bending the Rules on Emissions, Europe Must Get Much Tougher," *The Economist*, January 19, 2017. Retrieved from: http://www .economist.com/node/21714991.

130. David Leonhardt, "Lessons Even Thomas Could Learn," *The New York Times*, October 24, 2007.

131. Joe Carroll, "Halliburton Worker on Smoke Break Missed BP Well Data," *Bloomberg Businessweek*, December 7, 2010. Retrieved from: http://www .bloomberg.com/news/articles/2010-12-07/halliburton-worker-was-on-a-smoke -break-when-bp-spill-began-panel-is-told.

132. C. Ingersoll, R. Locke, and C. Reavis, "BP and the Deepwater Horizon Disaster of 2010." *MIT Sloan Management Review*, April 3, 2012.

133. *Huffington Post* (2012). "Gulf Oil Spill Timeline and the Ensuing Legal Cases Against BP." Retrieved from: http://www.huffingtonpost.com/2012/11/15/gulf -oil-spill-timeline_n_2139515.html.

134. C. Ingersoll, op. cit.

135. John M. Broder and Stanley Reed, "BP Is Barred from Taking Government Contracts," *The New York Times*, November 28, 2012. Retrieved from: http://

www.nytimes.com/2012/11/29/business/energy-environment/united-states
-suspends-bp-from-new-contracts.html?_r=0.

136. Campbell Robertson and Clifford Kraus, "BP May Be Fined Up to $18 Billion for Spill in Gulf," *The New York Times*, September 4, 2014. Retrieved from: http://www.nytimes.com/2014/09/05/business/bp-negligent-in-2010-oil-spill-us
-judge-rules.html?_r=0.

137. Terry Wade and Kristin Hays, "BP Settles 2010 US Oil Spill Claims for $18.7 billion," Reuters, July 2, 2015. Retrieved from: http://www.reuters.com/
article/us-bp-gulfmexico-settlement-idUSKCN0PC1BW20150703.

138. http://www.nbcnews.com/id/38493212/ns/business-us_business/#.Vove
PUaUKvA.

139. Google Finance (2012). Halliburton Company. Retrieved from: https://www
.google.com/finance?cid=16658.

140. K. O'Marah. "Supply Chain Leaders Must Own Sustainability." *SCM World*, February 27, 2015. Retrieved from: http://www.scmworld.com/Columns/
Beyond-Supply-Chain/Supply-chain-leaders-must-own-sustainability/.

141. http://knowledge.wharton.upenn.edu/article/from-fringe-to-mainstream
-companies-integrate-csr-initiatives-into-everyday-business/.

142. Ibid.

143. Bill Morrissey (2008). Leveraging Environmental Sustainability for Growth. Sustainable Brands 2008. Retrieved from http://www.sustainablebrands.com/
digital_learning/event-video/clorox-leveraging-environmental-sustainability
-drive-growth-bill-morris.

144. Total food sales in the United States amounted to about $5.3 trillion, making organic and natural foods less than 0.1 percent of the total. Retrieved from: https://www.statista.com/topics/1660/food-retail/.

145. "Illegal Palm Oil Plantations Threaten Protected Forests," WWF, June 26, 2013. Retrieved from: https://www.worldwildlife.org/stories/illegal-palm-oil-plan
tations-threaten-protected-forests.

146. PwC (2013). Next-generation supply chains: Efficient, fast and tailored. Retrieved from: http://www.pwc.be/en_BE/be/supply-chain-management/assets/
global_supply_chain_survey_2013.pdf.

147. http://www.parliament.wa.gov.au/publications/tabledpapers.nsf/display
paper/3814891cb116fb3fad8bb70f48257a770006604a/$file/4891.pdf. Accessed November 28, 2016.

148. http://www.aluplanet.com/eng/popup_news.asp?id_news=10704. Accessed November 30, 2016.

149. https://earthengine.google.com/timelapse/#v=-32.55779,116.12233,9.759,
latLng&t=0.83. Accessed December 1, 2016.

150. http://mininglink.com.au/site/pinjarra-alumina-refinery. Accessed December 1, 2016.

151. http://surfcoast.airaction.org/?p=483. Accessed November 22, 2016.

152. Derived from data on http://primary.world-aluminium.org/processes/anode -production.html. Accessed November 29, 2016.

153. http://www.world-aluminium.org/media/filer_public/2013/01/15/ fl0000127.pdf. Accessed December 2, 2016.

154. https://www.epa.gov/sites/production/files/2016-02/documents/pfc_generation .pdf. Accessed December 2, 2016.

155. Felicity Carus, "US Aluminum Giant Alcoa Says It's Leading the Way," *The Guardian*, October 19, 2012. Retrieved from: https://www.theguardian.com/ sustainable-business/us-aluminium-giant-alcoa-sustainability. Accessed November 27, 2016.

156. D. Todd, M. Caufield, and B. Helms, "Providing Reliability Services through Demand Response: A Preliminary Evaluation of the Demand Response Capabilities of Alcoa Inc." US DOE Report, January 2009. Retrieved from: https://www .ferc.gov/eventcalendar/Files/20100526085850-ALCOA%20Study.pdf.

157. Alcoa, "2014 Sustainability Highlights Report." Retrieved from: https:// www.alcoa.com/sustainability/en/pdf/archive/corporate/2014_Sustainability _Highlights_Report.pdf.

158. http://mininglink.com.au/site/huntly. Accessed November 30, 2016.

159. http://alcoa.p1.inter.alcoa.com/australia/en/info_page/mining_history.asp. Accessed November 28, 2016.

160. US Department of Energy, "Vehicle Technologies Office: Lightweight Materials for Cars and Trucks." Retrieved from: http://energy.gov/eere/vehicles/ vehicle-technologies-office-lightweight-materials-cars-and-trucks. Accessed December 9, 2016.

161. Alcoa, 2013 Australian Sustainability Highlights. Retrieved from: http:// alcoa.p1.inter.alcoa.com/australia/en/pdf/Sustainability/2013_sustainabilityhigh lightsreport.pdf.

162. https://www.alcoa.com/sustainability/en/pdf/archive/corporate/2010 _Sustainability_Highlights_Report.pdf. Accessed November 26, 2016.

163. "Alcoa Deal Will Secure Jobs: Brumby," *The Sydney Morning Herald*, March 2, 2010. Retrieved from: http://www.smh.com.au//breaking-news-national/ alcoa-deal-will-secure-jobs-brumby-20100302-pdv0.html. Accessed November 22, 2016.

164. Ibid.

165. http://news.alcoa.com/press-release/alcoa-named-sustainability-leader -dow-jones-indices-fifteenth-consecutive-year. Accessed December 6, 2016.

166. http://www.eenews.net/stories/1060022510. Accessed December 7, 2016.

167. Grant Whittington, "Big-Time Companies Hop Aboard the Climate Pledge," *Triple Pundit*, July 30, 2015. Retrieved from: http://www.triplepundit.com/ 2015/07/big-time-companies-hop-aboard-climate-pledge/. Accessed November 22, 2016.

168. Felicity Carus, "US Aluminum Giant Alcoa Says It's Leading the Way," *The Guardian*, October 19, 2012. Retrieved from: https://www.theguardian.com/

sustainable-business/us-aluminium-giant-alcoa-sustainability. Accessed November 27, 2016.

169. http://www.internationalresourcejournal.com/mining/mining_november _12/the_social_licence_to_operate_a_mine.html.

170. http://www.greenbiz.com/blog/2012/10/29/can-suppliers-meet-retailers -rising-sustainability-expectations.

171. http://news.stanford.edu/news/2006/november8/ocean-110806.html.

172. Brian Palmer, "Is the Demand for Sustainable Seafood Unsustainable?" *Pacific Standard*, May 7, 2015. Retrieved from http://www.psmag.com/nature-and -technology/is-the-demand-for-sustainable-seafood-unsustainable.

173. Ibid.

174. Clare Leschin-Hoar, "New Walmart Guidelines Put Alaskan Salmon Back on the Menu," *The Guardian*, January 24, 2014. Retrieved from: http://www .theguardian.com/sustainable-business/walmart-sustainable-seafood-alaskan -salmon.

175. Paul Polman, CEO, Unilever, http://www.managementtoday.co.uk/mt-inter view-paul-polman-unilever/article/1055793. Accessed January 21, 2016.

176. http://www.greenpeace.org/usa/happening-now-walmart-day-of-action-for -our-oceans/.

177. Lisa Demer, "Fishermen, state Officials Pushing Wal-Mart to Accept Alaska Salmon as a Sustainable Fishery," *Alaska Dispatch News*, published September 4, 2013; updated September 28, 2016. Retrieved from: http://www.adn.com/arti-cle/20130904/fishermen-state-officials-pushing-wal-mart-accept-alaska-salm-on-sustainable-fishery.

Notes to Chapter 2

1. http://www.undp.org/content/undp/en/home/presscenter/pressreleases/2015/ 03/11/indonesia-government-addresses-deforestation-challenges-in-its-aim-to -double-palm-oil-production-by-2020.html.

2. http://www.palmoilworld.org/about_palmoil.html.

3. http://www.kitkat.co.uk/content/kitkatcollection/FourFinger#4-finger-product -1.

4. http://chemistscorner.com/why-all-sodium-lauryl-sulfate-sources-arent-the -same/.

5. Supply Chain Council (2012). Supply Chain Operations Reference, Version 11.

6. The SCOR model includes a sixth high-level process called *enable*. It is a cross-cutting process matrixed with the other processes so that there is *enable source*, *enable make*, and so on. For example, supplier codes of conduct, which are discussed in chapter 5 would be classified as *enable* under SCOR. Much of the "Plan" chapter contains what SCOR calls *enable*.

7. http://www.assemblymag.com/articles/83966-special-section-the-rouge-an
-industrial-icon.

8. https://www.thehenryford.org/rouge/historyofrouge.aspx.

9. https://www.thehenryford.org/rouge/historyofrouge2.aspx.

10. https://www.thehenryford.org/rouge/historyofrouge.aspx.

11. http://www.soyinfocenter.com/HSS/henry_ford_and_employees.php.

12. http://www.samsung.com/semiconductor.

13. American Wind Energy Association. "Wind Power Challenges—Industry
Perspective." Presentation by AWEA Transportation Logistics Working Group, Re-
trieved from: http://midamericafreight.org/wp-content/uploads/Folladori_Wind
_Power.pdf.

14. Siemens (2013). "Siemens' Supply Chain & Sustainability." Presentation for
MIT-CTL Meeting February 2013.

15. Interview with Dr. Arnd Hirschberg, Siemens Supply Chain Manager for
Wind Turbines.

16. http://www.weidmueller.com/54004/Corporate/Corporate-Profile/cw_index
_v2.aspx.

17. Weidmüller corporate information. Accessed September 2013. Retrieved from:
http://www.weidmueller.com/bausteine.net/dav/showdav.aspx?domid=1031
&awpfad=http%3a%2f%2fcmswebdav.weidmueller.de%2fcms%2fcom_int%
2fCorporate%2fFact_Sheet%2f&rooturl=http%3a%2f%2fcmswebdav.weid
mueller.de%2fcms%2fcom_int&awname=Factsheet_Weidmueller_EN.pdf&type
=downloadfile&addmin_fd=2&sp=3&kompid=.

18. Interview with Dr. Arnd Hirschberg, Siemens Supply Chain Manager for
Wind Turbines.

19. Siemens (2013). Service Information. Retrieved from: www.siemens.com/
investor/en/service_information/faqs.htm.

20. Siemens AG, "Siemens SCM and CS at a Glance 2013," prepared for Dr.
Alexis Bateman, March 4, 2012.

21. http://www.bbc.co.uk/news/world-asia-22476774.

22. http://www.guardian.co.uk/commentisfree/2013/may/12/savar-banglades
h-international-minimum-wage.

23. http://abcnews.go.com/Blotter/fire-kills-112-workers-making-clothes-us
-brands/story?id=17807229.

24. ABC News (May 3, 2013). "Big Retailers Reassess Practices After Bangladesh
Building Collapse." Retrieved from: http://abcnews.go.com/Blotter/big-retailers
-reassess-practices-bangladesh-building-collapse/story?id=19097053#.Udoj
-D7F06E.

25. ABC News (2013). "Wal-Mart Fires Supplier After Bangladesh Revelation."
Retrieved from: http://abcnews.go.com/Blotter/wal-mart-fires-supplier-banglades
h-revelation/story?id=19188673.

26. http://online.wsj.com/article/SB100014241278873234019045781595121 18148362.html?google_editors_picks=true.

27. http://online.wsj.com/article/SB100014241278873234019045781595121 18148362.html?google_editors_picks=true.

28. http://www.bbc.co.uk/news/world-asia-22474601.

29. http://www.nytimes.com/2013/05/02/business/some-retailers-rethink-their -role-in-bangladesh.html?_r=0.

30. Louise Story, "Lead Paint Prompts Mattel to Recall 967,000 Toys," *The New York Times*, August 2, 2007. Retrieved from: http://www.nytimes.com/2007/08/02/ business/02toy.html?_r=1.

31. Ibid.

32. Joel Wisner, "The Chinese-Made Toy Recall at Mattel Inc.," University of Nevada Faculty Websites. http://faculty.unlv.edu/wisnerj/mba720_files/Mattel _case2.pdf.

33. http://money.cnn.com/2009/06/05/news/companies/cpsc/.

34. http://money.cnn.com/2007/10/12/markets/spotlight_mat/.

35. http://www.industryweek.com/blog/how-mattel-fiasco-really-happened.

36. Louise Story, "Lead Paint Prompts Mattel to Recall 967,000 Toys," *The New York Times*, August 2, 2007. Retrieved from: http://www.nytimes.com/2007/08/02/ business/02toy.html?_r=1.

37. See "Commission Regulation (EC) No 1881/2006 of 19 December 2006 setting maximum levels for certain contaminants in foodstuffs" at http://eur -lex.europa.eu/legal-content/EN/TXT/?qid=1419942037543&uri=CELEX: 02006R1881-20140701 for a listing of the contaminant levels permissible in milk.

38. http://www.utrechtlawreview.org/index.php/ulr/article/viewFile/URN%3 ANBN%3ANL%3AUI%3A10-1-101040/21 and http://www.fwi.co.uk/articles/ 12/11/2004/21719/dioxin-in-milk-scare-shuts-farms.htm.

39. http://archive.newsweaver.com/fsai/newsweaver.ie/fsai/e_article00034042864 e4.html?x=b11,0,w.

40. http://ec.europa.eu/transparency/regcomitology/index.cfm?do=Search.get PDF&2ZAqunybzgEqS2dzX8g/PeCXCTkEMvjCaXWhWTT3prm5SVAw47 eF02NzJJLXFBE77kGvLzo2Pu5uyjPyPE0HGhn1Yyu8a5hceFqN5ixnqYI=.

41. http://archive.newsweaver.com/fsai/newsweaver.ie/fsai/e_article00034042864 e4.html?x=b11,0,w.

42. http://ec.europa.eu/food/food/foodlaw/traceability/factsheet_trace_2007_en .pdf.

43. http://europa.eu/rapid/press-release_MEMO-10-263_en.htm?locale=en.

44. http://epi.yale.edu.

45. The index collects data separately on each one of these items.

46. http://epi.yale.edu/country-rankings.

47. Encyclopedia Britannica (2014). Balsa. Retrieved from: http://www.britannica.com/EBchecked/topic/50863/balsa.

48. James Holloway, "Siemens Unveils World's Largest Wind Turbine Blades," *New Atlas*, August 3, 2012. Retrieved from: http://www.gizmag.com/worlds-largest-wind-turbine-blades/23578/.

49. World Wind Technology (2013). "The Quay to Success: Transporting Modern Wind Turbines." Retrieved from: http://www.windpower-international.com/features/featurewind-turbine-transport-technology-poul-martin-wael-siemens-wind-power-emea.

50. http://www.itf-oecd.org/sites/default/files/docs/cop-pdf-06.pdf.

51. See, for example: http://www.nrdc.org/international/cleanbydesign/transportation.asp.

52. Derived from data on http://en.wikipedia.org/wiki/Boeing_747-8 and http://en.wikipedia.org/wiki/Maersk_Triple_E_class.

53. http://fairtradeusa.org/what-is-fair-trade.

54. http://www.csmonitor.com/Business/In-Gear/2014/0804/Which-is-greener-Old-car-or-new-car citing http://web.mit.edu/sloan-auto-lab/research/beforeh2/files/weiss_otr2020.pdf.

55. Yossi Sheffi (2015). "Responsible SCOR," Presented at the 2015 annual CSCMP Educators Conference, San Diego, CA.

56. Interview with Dr. Arnd Hirschberg, July 9, 2013.

57. http://sloanreview.mit.edu/article/sustainability-through-servicizing/.

58. http://www.michelintruck.com/services-and-programs/michelin-fleet-solutions/.

59. https://www.xerox.com/en-us/services/managed-print-services.

60. http://www.mro-network.com/analysis/2013/07/no-afterthought-rolls-royce-and-aftermarket/1345.

61. http://faculty.msb.edu/va64/ABChapter.pdf.

62. http://www.oecd.org/env/tools-evaluation/extendedproducerresponsibility.htm.

63. http://www.apics.org/sites/apics-supply-chain-council/benchmarking/scor-metrics.

64. http://techcrunch.com/2015/10/22/amazon-brings-its-one-hour-delivery-service-prime-now-to-the-san-francisco-bay-area/.

65. Leon Megginson, "Lessons from Europe for American Business," *Southwestern Social Science Quarterly* 44, no. 1 (1963): 3–13, at p. 4.

66. Supply Chain Council (2012). *Supply Chain Operations Reference Model*, Revision 11.0. (October). http://docs.huihoo.com/scm/supply-chain-operations-reference-model-r11.0.pdf.

67. http://www.apics.org/docs/default-source/scor-p-toolkits/apics-scc-scor-quick-reference-guide.pdf?sfvrsn=2.

68. Natural products might include fibers (wood, cotton, flax, hemp), seed oils (palm, soy, sunflower, etc.), grains and sugars, animal products (meat, leather, milk, eggs, fish), and specialty foods (chocolate, coffee, tea, spices).

69. http://planareport.marksandspencer.com/M&S_PlanAReport2015_Per formance.pdf.

Notes to Chapter 3

1. http://www.foei.org/press/archive-by-year/press-2012/new-report-smartphones -devastating-indonesian-island-people-forests-and-corals.

2. http://www.bloomberg.com/news/articles/2014-02-13/apple-supplier -responsibility-a-connection-to-illegal-tin-mining.

3. Ibid.

4. http://www.foei.org/press/archive-by-year/press-2012/new-report-smartphones -devastating-indonesian-island-people-forests-and-corals.

5. http://www.bloomberg.com/news/articles/2012-08-23/the-deadly-tin-inside -your-smartphone.

6. http://www.bloomberg.com/research/sectorandindustry/sectors/sectordetail .asp?code=25.

7. https://www.cdp.net/cdpresults/cdp-global-500-climate-change-report-2013 .pdf.

8. Bill Saporito, "Banananomics: Why You Can't Resist Some Rising Prices," *Time*, May 16, 2011. Retrieved from: http://content.time.com/time/magazine/ article/0,9171,2069034,00.html.

9. http://www.fao.org/economic/est/est-commodities/bananas/en/.

10. Food and Agricultural Organization of the United Nations (FAO). FAOSTAT: Trade Crops & Livestock Products—Banana Exports. Retrieved from: http:// faostat3.fao.org/home/index.html#DOWNLOAD.

11. A. Craig. "Measuring Supply Chain Carbon Efficiency: A Carbon Label Framework." Diss., Massachusetts Institute of Technology, 2012.

12. CO_2e stands for carbon dioxide equivalents. It is a quantity that describes the amount of CO_2 for a given mixture of greenhouse gases that would have the same global warming potential (GWP) over 100 years.

13. A. Craig. "Measuring Supply Chain Carbon Efficiency: A Carbon Label Framework." Diss., Massachusetts Institute of Technology, 2012.

14. http://epa.gov/climatechange/ghgemissions/gases/n2o.html.

15. Shipping was so critical in the banana business that the Great White Fleet was owned by Chiquita Brands International until 2007, when it sold the last of its vessels to Eastwind and NYK. See "Chiquita sells remaining Great White Fleet." Retrieved from: http://www.tmcnet.com/usubmit/2007/05/02/2577604.htm.

16. This problem has been more pronounced vessels serving the West Coast.

17. Ibid.

18. SimaPro LCA Software offered by Pre. Retrieved from: http://www.pre -sustainability.com/simapro-lca-software.

19. http://www.chiquita.com/Chiquita/documents/CSR/0924_Chiquita_WF _Final_09_12_12.pdf.

20. http://www.chiquita.com/Chiquita/documents/CSR/0924_Chiquita_WF _Final_09_12_12.pdf.

21. Y. Anny Huang, Christopher L. Weber, and H. Scott Matthews, "Categorization of Scope 3 Emissions for Streamlined Enterprise Carbon Footprinting," *Environmental Science & Technology* 43, no. 22 (2009): 8509–8515.

22. https://www.cdp.net/cdpresults/cdp-global-500-climate-change-report-2013 .pdf., page 21.

23. http://www.ghgprotocol.org/about-ghgp.

24. http://www.ghgprotocol.org/files/ghgp/Intro_GHGP_Tech.pdf.

25. https://en.wikipedia.org/wiki/Product_lifecycle.

26. Tim Clark, and Szu Ping Chan, "A History of Tesco: The Rise of Britain's Biggest Supermarket," *The Telegraph*, October 4, 2014.

27. http://www.bbc.com/news/magazine-23988795.

28. http://www.waronwant.org/attachments/Fashion%20Victims.pdf.

29. http://www.channel4.com/news/special-reports/special-reports-storypage.jsp ?id=3554.

30. BBC (2006). Supermarkets 'Not Green Enough.'" Retrieved from: http://news .bbc.co.uk/2/hi/business/5343488.stm.

31. Jim Ormond, "New Regimes of Responsibilization: Practicing Product Carbon Footprinting in the New Carbon Economy," *Economic Geography* 91, no. 4 (2015).

32. http://news.bbc.co.uk/2/hi/business/6276351.stm.

33. Terry Leahy, "Tesco, Carbon and the Consumer," Speech given to invited stakeholders at a joint Forum for the Future and Tesco event in central London on January 18, 2007. Retrieved from: http://www.tesco.com/climatechange/speech .asp on April 22, 2013.

34. Reuters (2009). "Wal-Mart Needs Industry Support For Green Labels." Retrieved from: http://www.reuters.com/article/2009/07/17/us-walmart-index -analysis-idUSTRE56G48N20090717.

35. George Monibiot, "If Tesco and Wal-Mart are Friends of the Earth, Are There Any Enemies Left?" *The Guardian*, January 22, 2007. Retrieved from: http:// www.theguardian.com/commentisfree/2007/jan/23/comment.supermarkets.

36. Carbon Trust (2014). About us. Retrieved from: http://www.carbontrust.com/ about-us.

37. Interview with Martin Barrow, Carbon Trust, Head of Footprinting, Business Advice.

38. Ibid.

39. PAS stands for Publicly Available Specification.

40. Carbon Trust (2008). "PAS 2050 Guide." Retrieved from: http://aggie -horticulture.tamu.edu/faculty/hall/publications/PAS2050_Guide.pdf.

41. Carbon Trust (2008). "PAS 2050 Guide." Retrieved from: http://aggie -horticulture.tamu.edu/faculty/hall/publications/PAS2050_Guide.pdf.

42. Ibid.

43. Ian Quinn, "'Frustrated' Tesco Ditches Eco-Labels." *The Grocer*, January 28, 2012. Retrieved from: http://www.thegrocer.co.uk/companies/supermarkets/ tesco/frustrated-tesco-ditches-eco-labels/225502.article.

44. James Kantor, "Does Carbon Labeling Confuse Consumers?" *The New York Times*, August 25, 2009. Retrieved from: http://green.blogs.nytimes.com/2009/08/ 25/does-carbon-labeling-confuse-consumers/.

45. BBC (2010). "Tesco Chief Sir Terry Leahy to Retire." Retrieved from: http:// www.bbc.co.uk/news/10262193.

46. Ian Quinn, "'Frustrated' Tesco Ditches Eco-Labels." *The Grocer*, January 28, 2012. Retrieved from: http://www.thegrocer.co.uk/companies/supermarkets/ tesco/frustrated-tesco-ditches-eco-labels/225502.article.

47. Adam Vaughn, "Tesco Drops Carbon-Label Pledge," *The Guardian*, January 30, 2012. Retrieved from: http://www.theguardian.com/environment/2012/ jan/30/tesco-drops-carbon-labelling.

48. In 2015 Tesco cut its number of SKUs in its stores to 65,000–70,000. See: http://www.esmmagazine.com/tesco-to-slash-nearly-one-third-of-products/8418.

49. Greenwise (2009). "Tesco Achieves Carbon Trust Standard." Retrieved from: http://www.greenwisebusiness.co.uk/news/tesco-achieves-carbon-trust-standard .aspx#.UwehuHnLA7U.

50. Ian Quinn, "'Frustrated' Tesco Ditches Eco-labels." *The Grocer*, January 28, 2012. Retrieved from: http://www.thegrocer.co.uk/companies/supermarkets/ tesco/frustrated-tesco-ditches-eco-labels/225502.article.

51. http://www.spiegel.de/international/business/attention-green-shoppers -carbon-confusion-a-540062.html.

52. http://upstreampolicy.org/whatever-happened-to-carbon-labeling/.

53. http://eandt.theiet.org/magazine/2008/20/calculate-carbon-cost.cfm.

54. Ibid.

55. "Bigger than a breadbox" is a traditional expression, used mainly in the US Midwest to indicate order-of-magnitude estimate.

56. Andrew Martin, "How Green is My Orange?" *The New York Times*, January 22, 2009. Retrieved from: http://www.nytimes.com/2009/01/22/business/22pepsi .html?_r=0.

57. Environmental Leader (2009). "Carbon Footprint of Orange Juice: 1.7 kg." Retrieved from: http://www.environmentalleader.com/2009/01/23/carbon-footprint -of-tropicana-orange-juice-17-kg/.

58. Andrew Winston, "Greening Pepsi, from Fertilizer to Bottles," *Harvard Business Review*, May 19, 2010. Retrieved from: https://hbr.org/2010/05/greening-pepsi-from-fertilizer.html.

59. Andrew Winston, "A New Algorithm for Fast Carbon Footprinting," *Harvard Business Review*, October 18, 2012. Retrieved from: https://hbr.org/2012/10/a-new-algorithm-for-fast-carbo.html.

60. Price information included in the approach is based on answers to questions such as "Given an assumed carbon price, would the costs for required upgrades (e.g., modified packaging and energy) be a worthwhile investment?" From: C. J. Meinrenken, S. M. Kaufman, S. Ramesh, and K. S. Lauckner. "Fast Carbon Footprinting for Large Product Portfolios." *Journal of Industrial Ecology* 16 (2012): 675.

61. Pre Sustainability (2014). SimaPro—World's Leading LCA Software. Retrieved from: http://www.pre-sustainability.com/simapro.

62. GaBi (2014). GaBi Sustainability Software. Retrieved from: http://www.gabi-software.com/america/index/.

63. Ecoinvent (2014). Discover Ecoinvent 3. Retrieved from://www.ecoinvent.org.

64. C. J. Meinrenken, S. M. Kaufman, S. Ramesh, and K. S. Lauckner. "Fast Carbon Footprinting for Large Product Portfolios." *Journal of Industrial Ecology* 16 (2012): 675.

65. C. Hendrickson, A. Horvath, S. Joshi, and L. Lave. "Economic Input–Output Models for Environmental Life-Cycle Assessment." *Environmental Science & Technology*, 32, no. 7 (1998): 184A–191A.

66. W. Leontief, "Environmental Repurcussions and Economic Structure—Input-Output Approach," *Review of Economics and Statistics* 52, no. 3 (1970): 262–271.

67. http://www.eiolca.net.

68. Jeong, Mendes, and Gregory (2010). Ocean Spray Cranberries Greenhouse Gas Emissions Inventory.

69. Suh et al., "System Boundary Selection in Life-Cycle Inventories Using Hybrid Approaches," *Environmental Science & Technology*, 38, no. 3 (2004): 657–664.

70. http://www.computing.co.uk/ctg/news/2165298/danone-custom-sap-track-carbon-footprint.

71. http://www.w.itcinfotech.com/erp/CarbonImpact.aspx.

72. Neither Danone nor Carbon Trust responded to repeated inquiries from the MIT research team.

73. http://docslide.us/documents/danone1pdf.html.

74. http://www.computing.co.uk/ctg/news/2165298/danone-custom-sap-track-carbon-footprint.

75. http://www.agdltd.com/Sales/pdflinks/2_SAP_CI_Solution_in_Detail_FINAL.pdf.

76. Although the base numbers may or may not be accurate, focusing on the changes reported by the system may point to actions, especially if the changes are significant.

77. http://www.greenbiz.com/blog/2013/01/15/stonyfield-farm-sap-measur e-carbon-footprint.

78. http://www.loreal.com/media/press-releases/2013/oct/l'oréal-announces -its-new-sustainability-commitment-for-2020-sharing-beauty-with-all.

79. Carbon Disclosure Project (2014). :Carbon Disclosure Project with Miguel Castellanos, Director of Environmental Health & Safety." Retrieved from: https:// www.cdp.net/en-US/Pages/cdp-supply-chain-broadcast-2014.aspx.

80. Andrew Winston, "The Most Powerful Green NGO You've Never Heard Of," *Harvard Business Review*, October 5, 2010. Retrieved from: https://hbr.org/ 2010/10/the-most-powerful-green-ngo.html.

81. CDP (2003). Carbon Finance and the Global Equity Markets. Retrieved from https://www.cdp.net/CDPResults/cdp_report.pdf.

82. https://www.cdp.net/Documents/CDP-strategic-plan-2014-2016.pdf.

83. CDP (2014). "CDP Investor Initiatives." Retrieved September 2014 from: https://www.cdp.net/en-US/WhatWeDo/Pages/investors.aspx.

84. L'Oréal (2013). Interview with Paul Simpson, CDP Chief Executive Officer. Retrieved from: http://www.lorealusa.com/sharing-beauty-with-all/producing -sustainably/interview-with-paul-simpson-cdp-chief-executive-officer.aspx.

85. Carbon Disclosure Project (2013). Reducing Risk and Driving Business Value: CDP Supply Chain Report 2012–2013. Retrieved from: https://www.cdp.net/ cdpresults/cdp-supply-chain-report-2013.pdf.

86. MIT Material Systems Laboratory (2011). Life Cycle Assessment of Hand Drying Systems. Report Commissioned by Dyson, Inc. Retrieved from: http:// msl.mit.edu/publications/HandDryingLCA-Report.pdf.

87. Rebecca Smithers, "Paper Towels Least Green Way of Drying Hands, Study Finds," *The Guardian*, November 11, 2011. Retrieved from: http://www .theguardian.com/environment/2011/nov/11/paper-towels-drying-hands-energy.

88. NSF International (2007). NSF Protocol 335—Hygienic Commercial Hand Dryers, NSF International, Ann Arbor, MI.

89. MIT Material Systems Laboratory (2011). Life Cycle Assessment of Hand Drying Systems. Report Commissioned by Dyson, Inc. Retrieved from: http:// msl.mit.edu/publications/HandDryingLCA-Report.pdf.

90. Carbon Trust (2013). Our Clients: Dyson—innovating product design for sustainability. Retrieved from: http://www.carbontrust.com/our-clients/d/dyson.

91. Recall that a watt is a measure of energy transfer per time unit (1 watt = 1 joule/second).

92. Interview with Jeremy Gregory.

93. Polycarbonate is used in baby bottles, water bottles, eyeglass lenses, food service containers, toys, sporting equipment, automotive headlight covers, aircraft

cockpit windows, bulletproof glass, theft-resistant retail packaging, compact disks, DVDs, and Blue-Ray disks.

94. Endocrine disruptors are chemicals that may interfere with the body's endocrine system and produce adverse developmental, reproductive, neurological, and immune effects in both humans and wildlife. See http://www.niehs.nih.gov/health/topics/agents/endocrine/.

95. http://www.sciencedaily.com/releases/2014/10/141022143628.htm.

96. http://www.watoxics.org/toxicswatch/handle-with-care-are-cash-register -receipts-giving-you-and-your-cashier-a-dose-of-bpa.

97. http://www.usatoday.com/search/bpa%20and%20baby%20bottles/.

98. In the dairy industry, concern over rBGH (bovine growth hormone) creates NGO and consumer pressure to make rBGH-free milk and milk products. In the broader food industry are concerns and regulations over GMOs (genetically modified organisms), food coloring, artificial flavors, and artificial sweeteners. For apparel companies, surfactants such as NPEs (nonylphenol ethoxylates) and stain-resistant additives called PFCs (perfluorinated chemicals) are of concern. Besides polycarbonate, other plastics or plastics additives have spurred NGO concerns or regulatory action about toxicity or hormone-like effects. These include PVC (polyvinyl chloride) and polystyrene, as well as common additives such as phthalates (a softening additive) and PBDEs (polybrominated diphenyl ethers used as flame retardants). In the transportation arena, concerns about PAH (polyaromatic hydrocarbons), PM2.5 (fine particulates), NO_x, and SO_x emissions create pressure on companies and facilities that have a high density of trucking and ocean freight.

99. https://www.basf.com/en/company/sustainability/management-and -instruments/topics.html.

100. http://www.mckinsey.com/insights/sustainability/bringing_discipline_to _your_sustainability_initiatives.

101. "Hasbro Announces 2020 Sustainability Goals; Company Aims to Reduce Environmental Impact of its Global Operations," *Business Wire*, September 12, 2013. Retrieved from: http://investor.hasbro.com/releasedetail.cfm?releaseid =790465. Accessed April 12, 2015.

102. http://www.ab-inbev.com/go/social_responsibility/environment/water_use .cfm.

103. http://www.coca-colacompany.com/setting-a-new-goal-for-water-efficiency.

104. http://www.breastcancerfund.org/media/press-releases/campbells-to-phas e-out-toxic-bpa.html.

105. Stephanie Strom, "McDonald's Moving to Limit Antibiotic Use in Chickens," *The New York Times*, March 4, 2015. Retrieved from: http://www.nytimes .com/2015/03/05/business/mcdonalds-moving-to-antibiotic-free-chicken.html.

106. http://corporate.walmart.com/global-responsibility/environment-sustain ability/waste.

107. http://www.plasticsnews.com/article/20150429/NEWS/150429899/p-g -official-talks-recycling-sustainability-and-zero-waste-goals.

108. http://www.triplepundit.com/2014/10/general-motors-expands-zero-waste -agenda-worldwide/.

109. http://www.unilever.com/mediacentre/pressreleases/2002/safety.aspx.

110. http://www.seafoodchoices.com/whatwedo/champions_unilever.php.

111. http://www.msc.org/documents/scheme-documents/msc-scheme-require ments/methodologies/Fisheries_Assessment_Methodology.pdf.

112. https://www.unilever.com/Images/uslp-unilever_sustainable_living_plan _progress_report_2011_tcm13.387588_tcm244-409863_en.pdf. Updated numbers provided by Alison Young, global communications—supply chain, Unilever.

Notes to Chapter 4

1. http://www.phrases.org.uk/meanings/charity-begins-at-home.html.

2. Bridgestone Americas, Inc., "Bridgestone Innovative Leadership Featured as Part of Sustainable Manufacturing Event," press release, March 26, 2015. Accessed December 23, 2016. https://www.bridgestoneamericas.com/es_US/news room/press-releases/2015/bridgestone-innovative-leadership-featured-as-part-of -sustainabl.

3. Claims for the earliest definitive evidence of control of fire by a member of *Homo* range from 0.2 to 1.7 million years ago. See, for example, Steven James, "Hominid Use of Fire in the Lower and Middle Pleistocene: A Review of the Evidence," *Current Anthropology*, Vol. 30, No. 1, 1989, pp. 1–26.

4. http://CO2now.org/Current-CO2/CO2-Now/global-carbon-emissions.html.

5. http://www.esrl.noaa.gov/gmd/ccgg/trends/full.html.

6. http://www.ghgprotocol.org.

7. US Department of Energy (2014). "Energy Efficiency." Retrieved from: http:// energy.gov/science-innovation/energy-efficiency.

8. Interview with Barbara Kux (2013).

9. Siemens (2012). CDP Webinar—Energy Efficiency for Customers. Munich, June 27, 2012.

10. Siemens (2013). "Energy Costs Reduced by Half a Million Euros." Retrieved from: http://www.siemens.com/innovation/en/news/2012/e_inno_1224_2.htm.

11. http://www.siemens.com/about/sustainability/pool/en/current-reporting/ siemens_ar2013_sustainability_information.pdf.

12. http://www.reuters.com/article/us-global-carbon-emissions-idUSBRE9AI 00A20131119.

13. http://www.siemens.com/about/sustainability/pool/en/current-reporting/ siemens_sustainability_information2015.pdf.

14. Siemens (2013). "Energy Costs Reduced by Half a Million Euros." Retrieved from: http://www.siemens.com/innovation/en/news/2012/e_inno_1224_2.htm.

15. 2013-05-23—Sustainability and Supply Chain Management at Siemens.pdf.

16. http://www.reliableplant.com/Read/6003/plant-energy-efficient.

17. http://www.iso.org/iso/home/standards/management-standards/iso50001.htm.

18. http://www.energy.gov/eere/amo/superior-energy-performance.

19. Interview with Tony Dunnage, Unilever Group Environmental Engineering Head (2012).

20. http://www.theguardian.com/big-energy-debate/2014/aug/20/denmark-district-heating-uk-energy-security.

21. Interview with Tony Dunnage (2012).

22. http://factbook.basf.com/BASF-The-Chemical-Company/Verbund.

23. http://www.ellenmacarthurfoundation.org/circular-economy.

24. http://www.wired.com/2015/02/gm-will-soon-use-wind-power-factories/.

25. http://media.gm.com/media/us/en/gm/news.detail.html/content/Pages/news/us/en/2015/feb/0217-windfarm.html.

26. http://www.triplepundit.com/2015/02/gm-wind-energy-mexico/.

27. http://www.wired.com/2015/02/gm-will-soon-use-wind-power-factories/.

28. http://media.gm.com/media/us/en/gm/news.detail.html/content/Pages/news/us/en/2014/Oct/1020-lordstown-chevrolet.html.

29. http://www.triplepundit.com/2015/02/gm-wind-energy-mexico/.

30. http://www.gmsustainability.com/at-a-glance/commitments.html.

31. http://www.macrumors.com/2015/01/27/apple-earnings-1q15/.

32. http://www.forbes.com/sites/maggiemcgrath/2015/02/10/first-solar-jumps-on-850-million-investment-from-apple/.

33. http://www.triplepundit.com/2015/02/apple-goes-invest-3-billion-solar-energy/.

34. https://www.apple.com/environment/pdf/Apple_Environmental_Responsibility_Report_2015.pdf.

35. Ibid.

36. http://www.greenpeace.org/usa/Global/usa/planet3/PDFs/2015Clicking Clean.pdf.

37. http://www.triplepundit.com/2015/02/apple-goes-invest-3-billion-solar-energy/.

38. http://www.epa.gov/lmop/documents/pdfs/conf/10th/harbison.pdf.

39. http://apps3.eere.energy.gov/greenpower/markets/certificates.shtml?page=2&companyid=578.

40. http://www.thefencepost.com/news/aurora-organic-dairy-expands-feed-capacity-in-weld/.

41. Aurora Organic Dairy (2014). GHG & Energy Report. Retrieved from: http://www.auroraorganic.com/pdfs/12_AOD_CCR_Energy-GHG.pdf.

42. Ibid.

43. http://www.atmos-chem-phys.net/13/2691/2013/acp-13-2691-2013.pdf.

44. http://www.epa.gov/ozone/science/process.html.

45. http://ozone.unep.org/new_site/en/montreal_protocol.php.

46. http://www.ipcc.ch/publications_and_data/ar4/wg1/en/ch2s2-10-2.html#table-2-14.

47. http://www.motherjones.com/blue-marble/2013/09/explained-90-seconds-hfcs-are-low-hanging-fruit-climate-action.

48. http://nvdatabase.swarthmore.edu/content/greenpeace-pressures-coca-cola-phase-out-hfc-refrigeration-olympic-games-australia-2000-2004.

49. http://www.forbes.com/2010/03/11/greenhouse-gases-refrigerants-technology-ecotech-coca-cola.html.

50. http://nvdatabase.swarthmore.edu/content/greenpeace-pressures-coca-cola-phase-out-hfc-refrigeration-olympic-games-australia-2000-2004.

51. http://www.forbes.com/2010/03/11/greenhouse-gases-refrigerants-technology-ecotech-coca-cola.html.

52. Ibid.

53. http://www.greenpeace.org/usa/pagefiles/58801/hfcs-a-growing-threat.pdf.

54. http://www.greenretaildecisions.com/news/2014/01/23/coca-cola-installs-one-millionth-hfc-free-cooler.

55. http://www.greenretaildecisions.com/news/2014/01/23/coca-cola-installs-one-millionth-hfc-free-cooler.

56. http://www.greenpeace.org/usa/en/media-center/news-releases/coca-cola-commits-to-climate-f/.

57. https://www.epa.gov/ozone-layer-protection/recent-international-developments-under-montreal-protocol.

58. http://www.srs.aero/wordpress/wp-content/uploads/2010/08/SRS-TSD-005-Rev-0-A380-Flex-Take-Off-Analysis.pdf.

59. Elisabeth Rosenthal, "Paying More for Flights Eases Guilt, Not Emissions," *The New York Times*, November 18, 2009. Retrieved from: http://www.nytimes.com/2009/11/18/science/earth/18offset.html?_r=0.

60. United Nations Framework Convention on Climate Change (2014). Retrieved from: http://unfccc.int/kyoto_protocol/mechanisms/clean_development_mechanism/items/2718.php.

61. UPS (2014). "Credentials for UPS Carbon Neutral." Retrieved from: http://www.ups.com/content/us/en/resources/ship/carbonneutral/credentials.html.

62. http://www.responsibletravelreport.com/component/content/article/2648-how-some-airlines-are-striving-toward-sustainability.

63. Elisabeth Rosenthal, "Paying More for Flights Eases Guilt, Not Emissions," *The New York Times*, November 187 2009. Retrieved from: http://www.nytimes.com/2009/11/18/science/earth/18offset.html?_r=0.

64. Climate Care (2014). "Aviva's Carbon Offset Programme Has Improved the Lives of 200,000." Retrieved from: http://climatecare.org/avivas-carbon-offset -programme-has-improved-the-lives-of-200000/.

65. Conservation (2011). "The Value of Forest Carbon Offsets: Tackling Climate Change, Protecting Biodiversity and Supporting Local Communities." Retrieved from: http://www.conservation.org/global/celb/Documents/2011.04.14_Value_of _Forest_Carbon_Offsets.pdf.

66. http://water.usgs.gov/edu/earthhowmuch.html.

67. http://www.who.int/mediacentre/factsheets/fs391/en/.

68. "In Hot Water," *The Economist*, October 6, 2005. Retrieved from: http:// www.economist.com/node/4492835.

69. http://www.ft.com/cms/s/2/8e42bdc8-0838-11e4-9afc-00144feab7de.html #slide0.

70. http://www.businessinsider.com/r-election-year-water-crisis-taking-a-toll-on -brazils-economy-2014-10?IR=T.

71. https://www.unglobalcompact.org/news/1811-04-24-2015.

72. http://www.trade.gov/competitiveness/sustainablemanufacturing/docs/Karas _Presentation_092310.pdf.

73. http://www.coca-colahellenic.com/sustainability/environment/water.

74. http://www.ab-inbev.com/content/dam/universaltemplate/abinbev/pdf/sr/ download-center/InBev_GCReport_05.pdf.

75. http://www.ab-inbev.com/content/dam/universaltemplate/abinbev/pdf/sr/ download-center/AmBev_GCReport_1.pdf.

76. http://www.ft.com/cms/s/2/8e42bdc8-0838-11e4-9afc-00144feab7de.html.

77. http://www.nestle.com/csv/water/water-efficiency.

78. Ibid.

79. Ibid.

80. http://www.environmentalleader.com/2014/10/27/nestle-factory-to-reduce -water-consumption-15/.

81. http://www.nestle.com/media/newsandfeatures/la-penilla.

82. Ibid.

83. http://www.environmentalleader.com/2012/07/10/coca-cola-recovery-system -can-cut-water-use-by-35/.

84. http://www.coca-colahellenic.com/sustainability/environment/water.

85. http://www.nestleusa.com/media/pressreleases/PizzaPlantReducesWater Usage.

86. http://www.nestle.com/media/newsandfeatures/la-penilla.

87. http://waterfootprint.org/media/downloads/Report47-WaterFootprintCrops -Vol1.pdf.

88. http://www.ab-inbev.com/content/dam/universaltemplate/abinbev/pdf/sr/ download-center/AmBev_GCReport_1.pdf.

89. http://www.ab-inbev.com/content/dam/universaltemplate/abinbev/pdf/investors/presentations/2010/Brief_of_Brewery_Tour.pdf.

90. http://www.ab-inbev.com/content/dam/universaltemplate/abinbev/pdf/investors/presentations/2013/14_Pete_Kraemer-Supply.pdf.

91. http://www.brewersofeurope.org/uploads/mycms-files/documents/archives/publications/2012/envi_report_2012_web.pdf.

92. http://extension.uga.edu/publications/detail.cfm?number=C992.

93. http://www.ab-inbev.com/content/dam/universaltemplate/abinbev/pdf/sr/global-citizenship-report/AB_InBev_GCR_2014.pdf.

94. https://www.nbcnews.com/news/us-news/anheuser-busch-halts-beer-production-provide-water-texas-oklahoma-storm-n366361.

95. https://www.washingtonpost.com/news/morning-mix/wp/2015/05/29/anheuser-busch-brewery-halts-beer-production-to-can-water-for-flood-victims/?utm_term=.334126a774f7.

96. http://anheuser-busch.com/index.php/our-responsibility/community-our-neighborhoods/natural-disaster-relief/.

97. http://www.ab-inbev.com/content/dam/universaltemplate/abinbev/pdf/sr/global-citizenship-report/AB_InBev_GCR_2014.pdf.

98. Ibid.

99. http://www.coca-colacompany.com/sustainabilityreport/world/water-stewardship.html.

100. Alexa Olesen, "Coca Cola Begins Water Conservation Bid," *Washington Post*, June 4, 2007.

101. Ibid.

102. https://www.washingtonpost.com/news/energy-environment/wp/2016/08/30/coca-cola-just-achieved-a-major-environmental-goal-for-its-water-use/.

103. http://www.economist.com/news/china/21620226-worlds-biggest-water-diversion-project-will-do-little-alleviate-water-scarcity-canal-too.

104. http://pubs.acs.org/doi/abs/10.1021/es5026454.

105. http://www.cnn.com/2012/01/20/world/meast/carbon-cost-water-uae/index.html.

106. http://www.water-technology.net/projects/water-desalination/.

107. http://www.wri.org/blog/2014/12/energy-gulping-desalination-can%E2%80%99t-solve-china%E2%80%99s-water-crisis-alone.

108. Rowan Jacobson, "Israel Proves the Desalination Era is Here," *Scientific American*, July 29, 2016. Retrieved from: https://www.scientificamerican.com/article/israel-proves-the-desalination-era-is-here/.

109. *Effluents from Pulp Mills Using Bleaching—PSL1*. Ottawa, ON: Health Canada and Environment Canada. 1991. ISBN 0-662-18734-2. Retrieved July 26, 2010. Catalog no. En40-215/2E.

110. Philip Hilt, "Carbon Found Leaching Dioxin to Milk," *The New York Times*, September 2, 1989.

111. http://apps.sepa.org.uk/spripa/Pages/SubstanceInformation.aspx?pid=143.

112. http://www.nrdc.org/cities/living/chlorine.asp.

113. http://www.pneac.org/sheets/all/paper.cfm.

114. https://legacy.risiinfo.com/magazines/February/2000/PPI/pulp-paper/magazine/international/february/2000/clean-up-chlorine-bleaching.html.

115. https://www.sodra.com/en/pulp/pulp-sustainability/.

116. https://legacy.risiinfo.com/magazines/February/2000/PPI/pulp-paper/magazine/international/february/2000/clean-up-chlorine-bleaching.html.

117. http://www.aet.org/science_of_ecf/eco_risk/2013_pulp.html.

118. http://www.sodra.com/en/pulp/Our-Pulp-Mills/Sodra-Cell-Varo/Expansion-Sodra-Cell-Varo/About-bleaching-with-chlorine-dioxide/.

119. http://www.corpwatch.org/article.php?id=4068.

120. https://www.risiinfo.com/magazines/February/2000/PPI/pulp-paper/magazine/international/february/2000/clean-up-chlorine-bleaching.html.

121. http://www.cbc.ca/news/world/red-mud-toxic-waste-of-aluminum-refining-1.906411.

122. http://www.oki.com/en/otr/downloads/otr-160-13.pdf.

123. http://worstpolluted.org/docs/TopTen2011.pdf.

124. http://www.businessgreen.com/print_article/bg/feature/2242656/case-study-unilever-reveals-secrets-of-zero-waste-campaign.

125. P&G (2014). "Global Asset and Recovery Purchases." P&G Internal Brief.

126. http://planareport.marksandspencer.com/M&S_PlanAReport2015_Performance.pdf.

127. http://www.bbc.co.uk/news/uk-24603008.

128. http://www.thegrocer.co.uk/home/topics/waste-not-want-not/tesco-launches-food-waste-hotline-to-aid-suppliers/549818.article.

129. http://www.theguardian.com/world/2016/feb/04/french-law-forbids-food-waste-by-supermarkets.

130. https://www.gpo.gov/fdsys/pkg/PLAW-104publ210/pdf/PLAW-104publ210.pdf.

131. Ibid.

132. https://www.gpo.gov/fdsys/pkg/BILLS-110s2420enr/pdf/BILLS-110s2420enr.pdf.

133. Interview with Tony Dunnage, Unilever Group Environmental Engineering Head (2012).

134. 2017 email from Tony Dunnage.

135. Ibid.

136. http://www.climatetechnologies.com/fumestofuel.html.

137. http://www.metalfinishing.com/view/2534/ford-motor-co-to-install-novel -paint-emissions-conversion-system/.

138. http://www.climatetechnologies.com/fumestofuel.html.

139. http://www.reliableplant.com/Read/8162/ford-eco-friendly-fumes.

140. Ibid.

141. http://www.3dsystems.com/sustainability.

142. http://www.techrepublic.com/article/how-ge-is-using-3d-printing-to-unleas h-the-biggest-revolution-in-large-scale-manufacturing/.

143. http://www.greenpeace.org/usa/wp-content/uploads/legacy/Global/usa/ planet3/PDFs/2015ClickingClean.pdf.

144. http://www.truth-out.org/news/item/30346-co2-emissions-growth-takes-a -bite-out-of-apple-s-sustainability-claims.

145. Eva Dou, "Deaths of Foxconn Employees Highlight Pressures Faced by China's Factory Workers," *Wall Street Journal*, August 21, 2016. Retrieved from: http://www.wsj.com/articles/deaths-of-foxconn-employees-highlight-pressures -faced-by-chinas-factory-workers-1471796417.

146. http://www.dailytech.com/Apples+Chinese+Suppliers+in+Trouble+for +Environmental+Pollution/article33103.htm.

147. http://www.truth-out.org/news/item/30346-co2-emissions-growth-takes-a -bite-out-of-apple-s-sustainability-claim.

Notes to Chapter 5

1. http://assets.coca-colacompany.com/68/24/f41f169c4923ad1c5f48e802fe0e/ 2011_europe-water-report.pdf.

2. Rachael King, "Flextronics Will Manage Global Supply Chain With New Real-Time Software," *Wall Street Journal*, July 7, 2015.

3. Tom Linton, Chief Procurement Officer, Flextronics.

4. http://articles.chicagotribune.com/2012-06-30/business/sns-rt-us-walmart -supplier-suspensionbre860004-20120630_1_wal-mart-stores-wal-mart-works -supplier-standards.

5. https://www.globalreporting.org/Pages/default.aspx.

6. https://www.globalreporting.org/resourcelibrary/GRI-Boundary-Protocol.pdf, p. 8.

7. https://www.instituteforsupplymanagement.org/files/RichterAwards/2008 Winner-HP.pdf.

8. http://h20195.www2.hp.com/V2/GetPDF.aspx/c03742930.pdf.

9. http://www.triplepundit.com/2010/11/carbon-disclosure-project/.

10. https://www.cdp.net/Documents/CDP-strategic-plan-2014-2016.pdf.

11. Ibid.

12. https://www.greenbiz.com/article/risk-data-revolution-and-life-post-paris-cdps-supply-chain-program.

13. http://www.greenbiz.com/article/cdps-supply-chain-program-now-2-trillion-plus-purchasing-power.

14. Ibid.

15. https://www.cdp.net/CDPResults/CDP-Supply-Chain-Report-2016.pdf.

16. Georgina Grenon, Director of Operations PSO at Booz Allen Hamilton, CTL (2007). "Achieving the Energy-Efficient Supply Chain."

17. Ibid.

18. http://ntl.bts.gov/lib/15000/15100/15145/DE97763079.pdf.

19. Ibid.

20. "Supply Chain Sustainability Revealed, Supply Chain Report 2014–2015." Accenture Report for the CDP.

21. http://www.cnbc.com/id/102582258.

22. https://www.greenbiz.com/article/risk-data-revolution-and-life-post-paris-cdps-supply-chain-program.

23. https://www.greenbiz.com/blog/2013/04/15/game-why-walmart-ranking-suppliers-sustainability.

24. http://about.att.com/content/csr/home/issue-brief-builder/environment/engaging-our-supply-chain.html.

25. Tom Mitchell and Jonathan Birchall, "Wal-Mart Orders Chinese Suppliers to Lift Standards," *The Financial Times*, October 23, 2008.

26. Nicholas Kulish and Julia Werdigier, "Ikea Admits Forced Labor Was Used in 1980s," *The New York Times*, November 16, 2012. Retrieved from: http://www.nytimes.com/2012/11/17/business/global/ikea-to-report-on-allegations-of-using-forced-labor-during-cold-war.html?_r=0.

27. Edward Kasabov and Alex Warlow, *The Compliance Business and its Customers* (New York: Palgrave Maximillian, 2012), p. 91.

28. IKEA Supply AG, "IWAY Standard: Minimum Requirements for Environment and Social & Working Conditions when Purchasing Products, Materials, and Services," 2012.

29. IKEA Interview with Jeanette Skjelmose, 2015.

30. Hung's Enterprise (2013). Company Profile. Retrieved from: http://hungs.salom.com.cn/hungs/english/Default.asp.

31. Ibid.

32. IKEA (2013). "IKEA Co-Workers On Site in the Factories." Retrieved from: http://www.ikea.com/ms/en_US/about_ikea/our_responsibility/working_conditions/ikea_on_site.html.

33. IKEA Supply AG, "IWAY Standard: Minimum Requirements for Environment and Social & Working Conditions when Purchasing Products, Materials, and Services," 2012.

34. Phone interview with Jeanette Skjlmose, April 28, 2017.

35. Interview with Kelly Deng, Senior Auditor for Ikea, December 12, 2013.

36. Stephanie Clifford and Steven Greenhouse, "Fast and Flawed Inspections of Factories Abroad," *The New York Times*, September 1, 2013. Retrieved from: http://www.nytimes.com/2013/09/02/business/global/superficial-visits-and -trickery-undermine-foreign-factory-inspections.html?pagewanted=1&_r =3&adxnnlx=1381428071-IR36jo9l9fQhwHXkB12DAA.

37. Phone interview with Jeanette Skjelmose, April 28, 2017.

38. Forbes (2012). "IKEA Under Fire for Clearing Ancient Russian Forest." Retrieved from: http://www.forbes.com/sites/eco-nomics/2012/06/06/IKEA-under -fire-for-clearing-ancient-russian-forest/.

39. http://www.huffingtonpost.com/2013/03/05/IKEA-horsemeat-meatballs_n _2811554.html.

40. http://www.hp.com/hpinfo/globalcitizenship/environment/pdf/eicc_pr1005 .pdf.

41. Ibid.

42. EICC (2014). About Us. Retrieved from: http://www.eicc.info/about_us .shtml.

43. http://www.eiccoalition.org/about/.

44. http://www.eiccoalition.org/standards/code-of-conduct/.

45. EICC Code of Conduct. Retrieved from: http://www.eiccoalition.org/media/ docs/EICCCodeofConduct5_English.pdf, September 2017.

46. Flextronics Standard Terms and Conditions of Purchase. Retrieved from: http://www.flextronics.com/supplier/StandardPurchasingTerms/Standard%20 Purchasing%20Terms_020613a.pdf, September 2013.

47. Also known as Validated Audit Process.

48. EICC (2012). Validated Assessment Process. Retrieved from: http://www.eicc .info/validatedauditprocess.shtml.

49. http://www.eiccoalition.org/standards/validated-audit-process/.

50. http://www.eiccoalition.org/standards/tools/.

51. http://www.raisehopeforcongo.org/node/250.

52. http://www.eiccoalition.org/media/docs/EICCCodeofConduct4_English.pdf.

53. http://www.ikea.com/ms/en_US/about_ikea/pdf/SCGlobal_IWAYSTDVers4 .pdf.

54. http://www.greenbiz.com/news/2008/01/17/hp-releases-green-supply-chain -guidelines.

55. Richard Locke. *The Promise and Limits of Private Power* (New York: Cambridge University Press, 2013).

56. Erica Plambeck, Hau Lee, and Pamela Yatsko, "Improving Environmental Performance in Your Chinese Supply Chain," *Sloan Management Review*, Winter 2012, pp. 43–51.

57. http://www.bloomberg.com/news/articles/2006-11-26/secrets-lies-and-sweat shops.

58. Erica Plambeck, Hau Lee, and Pamela Yatsko, "Improving Environmental Performance in Your Chinese Supply Chain," *Sloan Management Review*, Winter 2012, pp. 43–51.

59. Ibid.

60. http://www.apple.com/supplier-responsibility/progress-report/.

61. Richard Locke. *The Promise and Limits of Private Power* (New York: Cambridge University Press, 2013).

62. A. Porteous and S. Rammohan (2013). "Integration, Incentives, and Innovation: Nike's Strategy to Improve Social and Environmental Conditions in its Global Supply Chains. Stanford Initiative for the Study of Supply Chain Responsibility, White Paper.

63. A. Porteous and S. Rammohan (2013). "Integration, Incentives, and Innovation: Nike's Strategy to Improve Social and Environmental Conditions in its Global Supply Chains. Stanford Initiative for the Study of Supply Chain Responsibility," White Paper: 2.

64. Nike (2013). Sustainable Business Performance Summary. Retrieved from: http://www.nikeresponsibility.com/report/uploads/files/FY12-13_NIKE_Inc_CR _Report.pdf.

65. Erica Plambeck, Hau Lee, and Pamela Yatsko, "Improving Environmental Performance in Your Chinese Supply Chain," *Sloan Management Review*, Winter 2012, pp. 43–51.

66. Richard Locke, Matthew Amengual, and Akshay Mangla, "Virtue out of Necessity? Compliance, Commitment and Improvement of Labor Conditions in Global Supply Chains," *Politics & Society* 37 (September 2009): 319–351.

67. Erica Plambeck, Hau Lee, and Pamela Yatsko, "Improving Environmental Performance in Your Chinese Supply Chain," *Sloan Management Review*, Winter 2012, pp. 43–51.

68. Interview with Barbara Kux, 2013.

69. Ibid.

70. Siemens' Presentation to MIT, 2013.

71. Ibid.

72. http://www.bcsd.org.tw/sites/default/files/node/news/726.upload.2484.pdf.

73. http://www.siemens.com/press/en/pressrelease/2013/corporate/axx20130431.htm?content[]=CC&content[]=Corp.

74. http://www.apple.com/supplier-responsibility/empowering-workers/. Accessed December 21, 2016.

75. http://www.apple.com/supplier-responsibility/progress-report/.

76. http://www.apple.com/supplier-responsibility/environment/.

77. Ibid.

78. H. Donella, J. R. Meadows, D. L. Meadows, and E. E. Behrens. *The Limits to Growth, A Report for the Club of Rome Project on the Predicament of Mankind,* 2nd Ed. (New York: Universe Books, 1972).

79. http://www.clubofrome.org/.

80. http://sustainable.unimelb.edu.au/sites/default/files/docs/MSSI-ResearchPaper-4_Turner_2014.pdf.

81. http://www.sustainablebrands.com/news_and_views/collaboration/aarthi_rayapura/ab_inbev_working_growers_optimize_water_management_barl.

82. http://www.ab-inbev.com/content/dam/universaltemplate/abinbev/pdf/sr/global-citizenship-report/AB_InBev_GCR_2014.pdf.

83. http://www.sustainablebrands.com/news_and_views/collaboration/aarthi_rayapura/ab_inbev_working_growers_optimize_water_management_barl.

84. http://www.greenbiz.com/article/budweiser-miller-greening-big-beer-supply-chain.

85. Unilever (2014). "50 Years of Doing Well by Doing Good." Retrieved from: http://www.unilever.com.bd/aboutus/newsandmedia/news/50-years-of-Doing-Well-by-Doing-Good.aspx.

86. Unilever (2014). "Making Cleanliness Commonplace." Retrieved from: https://www.projectsunlight.us/stories/376475/Making-Cleanliness-Commonplace.aspx.

87. Jeannifer Filly Sumayku, "Unilever: Providing Enjoyable and Meaningful Life to Customers," *The President Post*, March 22, 2010. Retrieved from: http://www.thepresidentpost.com/2010/03/22/unilever-providing-enjoyable-and-meaningful-life-to-customers/.

88. Unilever (2014). "Our Culture." Retrieved from: http://www.unileverusa.com/Careers/insideunilever/howwework/ourculture/.

89. Alec Scott, "Unilever is Rethinking Capitalism: Why Doing Good is Good for Business," *Canadian Business*, November 19, 2013. Retrieved from: http://www.canadianbusiness.com/ceo-insider/unilever-tries-to-prove-corporate-charity-is-good-for-the-bottom-line-and-the-world/.

90. http://onward.nationalgeographic.com/2014/04/28/the-worlds-top-drink/.

91. https://www.iisd.org/pdf/2014/ssi_2014_chapter_14.pdf.

92. Tropical Commodity Coalition (2013). "Tea." Retrieved from: http://www.teacoffeecocoa.org/tcc/Commodities/Tea/Industry.

93. http://www.unilever.com/sustainable-living/the-sustainable-living-plan/reducing-environmental-impact/sustainable-sourcing/sustainable-tea-leading-the-industry/.

94. Unilever (2014). Timeline: 2000–2009. Retrieved from: http://www.unileverusa.com/aboutus/ourhistory/2000s/.

95. CSRWire (2013). "Partnerships & Policies: Creating Sustainable Models at Unilever." Retrieved from: http://www.csrwire.com/blog/posts/936-partnerships-policies-creating-sustainable-models-at-unilever.

96. R. Henderson and F. Nellemann (2011). "Sustainable Tea at Unilever." Harvard Business Case study.

97. CSRWire (2013). "Partnerships & Policies: Creating Sustainable Models at Unilever." Retrieved from: http://www.csrwire.com/blog/posts/936-partnerships -policies-creating-sustainable-models-at-unilever.

98. R. Henderson and F. Nellemann (2011). "Sustainable Tea at Unilever." Harvard Business Case study.

99. Ibid.

100. http://www.unilever.com/sustainable-living/the-sustainable-living-plan/ reducing-environmental-impact/sustainable-sourcing/sustainable-tea-leading-the -industry.

101. Interview with Kelly Goodejohn, Director of Ethical Sourcing, Starbucks, May 2014.

102. Starbucks (2014). Being a Responsible Company. Retrieved from: http:// www.starbucks.com/responsibility. Accessed April 2014.

103. Starbucks (2011). Starbucks Company Timeline. Retrieved from: http:// globalassets.starbucks.com/assets/BA6185AA2F9440379CE0857D89DE 8412.pdf.

104. http://www.conservation.org/campaigns/starbucks/Pages/default.aspx.

105. http://www.coffeehabitat.com/2012/02/starbucks-cafe-practices -assessment/.

106. https://www.gsb.stanford.edu/sites/gsb/files/publication-pdf/non-teaching -case-study-nike-strategy-improve-global-supply-chain.pdf.

107. SCSglobal Services & Starbucks (2014). List of Indicators that Require Documentation for C.A.F.E. Practices V3.2. Retrieved from: http://www.scsglobal services.com/files/cafe_requireddocumentationv3-2_010214_0.pdf.

108. Interview with Kelly Goodejohn, Director of Ethical Sourcing, Starbucks, May 2014.

109. Ibid.

110. Starbucks (2013). "2013 Global Responsibility Report—Goals and Progress 2013." Retrieved from: http://globalassets.starbucks.com/assets/98e5a8e6c7b1435 ab67f2368b1c7447a.pdf.

111. https://www.scsglobalservices.com/files/c_a_f_e_practices_v3_4_zero _tolerance_with_edits_110615_scs.pdf.

112. Starbucks (2013). "2013 Global Responsibility Report—Goals and Progress 2013." Retrieved from: http://globalassets.starbucks.com/assets/98e5a8e6c7b1435 ab67f2368b1c7447a.pdf.

113. https://www.starbucks.com/responsibility/sourcing/coffee.

114. http://www.livescience.com/27692-deforestation.html.

115. Sime Darby (2013). "Palm Oil Facts & Figures." Retrieved from: http://www .simedarby.com/upload/Palm_Oil_Facts_and_Figures.pdf. Accessed November 2013.

116. Stephanie M. Lee, "Environmental Advocates, Dieticians Leery of Palm Oil," *San Francisco Gate*, September 17, 2013. Retrieved from: http://www.sfgate.com/health/article/Environmental-advocates-dietitians-leery-of-palm-4822518.php#photo-5195192.

117. Amanda Hill, Al Kurki, and Mike Morris. "Biodiesel: The Sustainability Dimensions." A publication of ATTRA—National Sustainable Agriculture Information Service. (Butte, MT: National Center for Appropriate Technology, 2010), pp. 4–5.

118. Yelto Zimmer, "Competitiveness of Rapeseed, Soybeans, and Palm Oil," *Journal of Oilseed Brassica* 1, no. 2 (July 2010): 84–90.

119. It should be noted that Sime Darby did not clear extra land when palm oil became popular. Instead it repurposed some of its existing plantations but did not resort to forest clearing.

120. K. Obidzinski, R. Andiana, H. Komarudin, and A. Andrianto. "Environmental and Social Impacts of Oil Palm Plantations and their Implications for Biofuel Production in Indonesia." *Ecology and Society* 17, no. (2012): 25.

121. http://www.upi.com/Science_News/2012/10/08/Food-oil-production-environmental-threat/21921349720330/.

122. http://www.nature.com/nclimate/journal/v2/n3/full/nclimate1354.html.

123. *The Economist* (2010). "The Other Oil Spill." Retrieved from: http://www.economist.com/node/16423833.

124. http://www.greenpeace.org/international/en/campaigns/forests/asia-pacific/app/.

125. *The Economist* (2010). "The Other Oil Spill." Retrieved from: http://www.economist.com/node/16423833.

126. Ibid.

127. Gina-Marie Cheeseman, "Nestle Response to Greenpeace Pressure and Partners with the Forest Trust," *Triple Pundit*, May 5, 2010. Retrieved from: http://www.triplepundit.com/2010/05/nestle-responds-to-greenpeace-pressure-and-partners-with-the-forest-trust/.

128. Interview with Scott Poynton.

129. Yale-NUS (2013). "Case Study: Golden Agri Resources and Sustainability." Global Network for Advanced Management.

130. Greenpeace (2012). "Greenpeace Scorecard on Palm Oil Producers." Retrieved from: http://www.greenpeace.org/international/en/publications/Campaign-reports/Forests-Reports/Palm-Oil-Scorecard/.

131. Greenpeace (2012). "GAR Sets the Bar High in Indonesia Deforestation." Retrieved from: http://www.greenpeace.org/international/en/news/Blogs/making-waves/gar-sets-the-bar-high-in-indonesian-deforesta/blog/40823/?accept=a8a25a942160a7d25f38265ffddaecda.

132. Mongabay (2014). "Company Accused of Logging Endangered Rainforest Trees in Breach Of Timber Legality Certificate." Retrieved from: http://news.mongabay.com/2014/0107-dparker-april-triomas.html.

133. Greenpeace (2012). "GAR Sets the Bar High in Indonesia Deforestation."

134. Eco-Business (2013). "Palm Oil Industry Key Culprit Behind Deforestation, Haze in Indonesia." Retrieved from: http://www.eco-business.com/news/palm-oil -industry-key-culprit-behind-deforestation-haze-indonesia/.

135. Green Palm (2013). Overview. Retrieved from: http://greenpalm.org/en/ what-is-greenpalm/overview.

136. http://www.rspo.org/files/docs/rspo_factsheet_scc.pdf.

137. http://greenpalm.org/about-greenpalm/what-is-green-palm.

138. http://greenpalm.org/about-greenpalm/why-greenpalm-makes-a-difference/ book-and-claim-supply-chain-model.

139. WWF (2013). "WWF Statement on the Review of the RSPO Principles & Criteria." Retrieved from: http://awsassets.panda.org/downloads/wwf_statement _revised_rspo_principlescriteria_april_2013.pdf.

140. http://www.raisehopeforcongo.org/node/250.

141. http://voices.nationalgeographic.com/2014/01/28/indonesian-sustainable -palm-oil-future-fact-or-farce/.

142. https://www.ft.com/content/aac0151e-2f13-11e6-a18d-a96ab29e3c95.

143. WWF (2013). "WWF Statement on the Review of the RSPO Principles & Criteria." Retrieved from: http://awsassets.panda.org/downloads/wwf_statement _revised_rspo_principlescriteria_april_2013.pdf.

144. http://www.unilever.com/sustainable-living/what-matters-to-you/transforming -the-palm-oil-industry.html.

Notes to Chapter 6

1. https://www.wewear.org/cornerofficeviews/imports-work-for-us-manufac turing/.

2. Pietra Rivoli, *The Travels of a T-Shirt in The Global Economy: An Economist Examines the Markets, Power, and Politics of World Trade*, 2nd Ed. (Hoboken, New Jersey: Wiley, 2014).

3. http://www.portoflosangeles.org/pdf/Los-Angeles-Trade-Numbers-2013.pdf.

4. https://www.wto.org/english/news_e/pres14_e/pr721_e.htm.

5. One megaton = one million tons.

6. http://www3.weforum.org/docs/WEF_LT_SupplyChainDecarbonization _Report_2009.pdf.

7. http://www.forbes.com/sites/justingerdes/2012/02/24/how-nike-wal-mart-an d-ikea-are-saving-money-and-slashing-carbon-by-shipping-smarter/.

8. NRDC, "Clean by Design: Transportation," last revised on 2/5/2012, http:// www.nrdc.org/international/cleanbydesign/transportation.asp. Accessed on February 7, 2015.

9. http://www.ipcc.ch/ipccreports/sres/aviation/index.php?idp=64.

10. http://www3.weforum.org/docs/WEF_LT_SupplyChainDecarbonization_Report_2009.pdf.

11. http://www.nrdc.org/international/cleanbydesign/transportation.asp.

12. http://www.jbhunt.com/responsibility/sustainability/innovations/.

13. http://sustainability.ups.com/media/2011-sustainability-report.pdf.

14. N. Andrieu and L. Weiss. "Transport Mode and Network Architecture: Carbon Footprint as a New Decision Metric" (master's thesis, MIT Supply Chain Management, 2008).

15. Ibid.

16. Fiji Water (2014). Packaging. Retrieved from: http://fijiwater.sg/giving-back/environment/sustainable-practices/packaging/.

17. http://www.people.hofstra.edu/geotrans/eng/ch8en/conc8en/fuel_consumption_containerships.html.

18. http://ports.com/sea-route/port-of-shanghai,china/port-of-rotterdam,netherlands/.

19. http://www.bairdmaritime.com/index.php?option=com_content&view=article&id=13224.

20. http://www.bridgestonetrucktires.com/us_eng/real/magazines/ra_special-edit_4/ra_special4_fuel-speed.asp.

21. Later analysis demonstrated that most of the fuel saved was owed to reduced travel during this period, not reduced speed. In addition, the limits were relevant only on interstate highways while much of the national fuel consumption takes place on city and other small streets in stop-and-go traffic. As a result, it was later relaxed.

22. http://www.brightfleet.com/blog/2012/interview-with-mike-payette-at-staples-about-speed-limiters-fuel-economy-and-safety/.

23. Mark Buckley, VP Environmental Affairs, Staples. "Implementing Sustainability at Corporate Level." Presentation at MIT CTL "Crossroads 2010: Building Supply Chains that Deliver Sustainability" symposium held on March 25, 2010 in Cambridge, MA.

24. http://www.brightfleet.com/blog/2012/interview-with-mike-payette-at-staples-about-speed-limiters-fuel-economy-and-safety/.

25. Ibid.

26. http://phx.corporate-ir.net/External.File%3Fitem%3DUGFyZW50SUQ9MjkxMzQ3fENoaWxkSUQ9LTF8VHlwZT0z%26t%3D1.

27. http://www.logisticsmgmt.com/view/whats_your_supply_chain_priority1/sustainability.

28. https://food-hub.org/files/resources/Food%20Miles.pdf.

29. James McWilliams, "Food that Travels Well," *The New York Times*, August 6, 2007.

30. http://usatoday30.usatoday.com/money/economy/2008-10-27-local-grown-farms-produce_N.htm.

31. http://www.wholefoodsmarket.com/local.

32. James McWilliams, "Food that Travels Well," *The New York Times*, August 6, 2007.

33. http://www3.weforum.org/docs/WEF_LT_SupplyChainDecarbonization _Report_2009.pdf.

34. http://www.nrdc.org/international/cleanbydesign/transportation.asp.

35. http://macysgreenliving.com/media/_CustomMedia/EmptyMiles _cs_092809.pdf.

36. CTL (2013). Case Studies in Carbon-Efficient Logistics: Ocean Spray— Leveraging Distribution Network Redesign. CTL + Environmental Defense Fund.

37. Ibid.

38. Ibid.

39. Ibid.

40. https://books.google.com/books?id=gRS0WkCRiKsC&pg=PA85&lpg=PA85 &dq=stonyfield+%22educate+consumers+and+producers+about+the+value +of+protecting%22&source=bl&ots=jEH3ocg7nz&sig=UFnczQuBrMhjmZva ZHByS0ST2n8&hl=en&sa=X&ved=0CB8Q6AEwA2oVChMI9qWrv7 _YxgIVhnY-Ch34FQ46.

41. http://westcoastcollaborative.org/files/meetings/2008-04-15/StonyfieldFarm Presentation.pdf.

42. http://www.supplychainquarterly.com/topics/Logistics/scq200904stonyfield/.

43. http://www.inboundlogistics.com/cms/article/supply-chain-visibility-now-you -see-it/.

44. http://www.supplychainquarterly.com/print/scq20100126reduce_supply _chain_carbon_footprint/.

45. http://www.supplychainquarterly.com/topics/Logistics/scq200904stonyfield.

46. Ibid.

47. http://yosemite.epa.gov/opa/admpress.nsf/8b770facf5edf6f185257359003fb 69e/fb1ea32cc9d99d1d8525764a0055e6c0!OpenDocument.

48. Ibid.

49. https://nrf.com/news/retail-trends/eco-transport.

50. https://www.tc.gc.ca/eng/policy/report-research-ack-tp14837e-chapter8 -1661.htm.

51. http://www.ugpti.org/pubs/pdf/DP272.pdf.

52. http://cornandsoybeandigest.com/issues/containers-move-high-value-exports -when-do-containers-work-best-grain-buyer-and-grower.

53. http://alicia-arnold.com/2012/01/20/creativity-how-right-turns-saved-one -company-3-million/.

54. Tom Long, "Right Turns Make the Most Out of Gas," *Boston Globe*, July 10, 2008. Retrieved from: http://www.boston.com/news/local/articles/2008/07/10/ right_turns_make_the_most_out_of_gas/.

55. Interview with Scott Wicker, 2013.

56. http://des.nh.gov/organization/divisions/air/tsb/tps/msp/irc/categories/overview.htm.

57. http://business.edf.org/files/2014/04/poland-spring.pdf.

58. http://www.greenbiz.com/blog/2014/09/18/what-sharing-economy-can-learn-fleets.

59. Lauren Fletcher and Grace Lauron, "How Can Telematics Help Your Fleet?" *Automotive Fleet*, February 2009.

60. http://www.automotive-fleet.com/channel/fuel-management/news/story/2013/07/ups-sustainability-report-details-savings-of-1-3-million-gallons-of-fuel-in-2012.aspx.

61. http://www.greenbiz.com/blog/2014/09/18/what-sharing-economy-can-learn-fleets.

62. https://www.whitehouse.gov/the-press-office/2015/07/27/fact-sheet-white-house-launches-american-business-act-climate-pledge.

63. http://www.bnsf.com/communities/bnsf-and-the-environment/green-technology/.

64. EPA (2014). SmartWay for Countries. Retrieved from: http://www.epa.gov/smartway/forcountries/index.htm.

65. EPA (2014). SmartWay. Retrieved from: http://epa.gov/smartway/about/index.htm.

66. SmartWay (2014). Partners and Affiliate Lists. Retrieved from: http://www.epa.gov/smartway/about/partnerlists.htm.

67. US EPA (2013). SmartWay Transport Partnership: Driving Data Integrity in Transportation Supply Chains. Retrieved from: http://epa.gov/smartway/forpartners/documents/dataquality/420b13005.pdf.

68. https://www.epa.gov/smartway/smartway-carrier-performance-ranking.

69. https://www3.epa.gov/smartway/forpartners/documents/logo-use/sw-tractor-trailer-logo-usage-instruction-07-29-2015.pdf.

70. Chiquita (2012). "Chiquita Brands International Corporate Social Responsibility Report." Retrieved from: http://www.chiquita.com/getattachment/4dedce2f-c4ac-4183-9e14-c87a6202e511/2012-Corporate-Responsibility-Report.aspx.

71. http://www.mmta.com/document_upload/SmartWay%20and%20Truck%20Drivers.pdf.

72. RubberNews.com (2014). "EPA Celebrates 10th Anniversary of SmartWay." Retrieved from: http://www.rubbernews.com/article/20140320/NEWS/140329996/epa-celebrates-10th-anniversary-of-smartway#.

73. https://www.rita.dot.gov/bts/sites/rita.dot.gov.bts/files/publications/national_transportation_statistics/html/table_04_05.html.

74. Jill Dunn, "Study: Fuel Efficiency Efforts Pay off for Carriers," *Commercial Carrier Journal*, September 8, 2014. Retrieved from: http://www.ccjdigital.com/study-fuel-efficiency-efforts-pay-off-for-carriers/.

75. http://nacfe.org/wp-content/uploads/2014/06/June-26-TE-Workshop-Master-Little-Rock-061614.pdf.

76. GHG Protocol Calculation Tools (2011). GHG emissions from transport or mobile sources. Available at http://www.ghgprotocol.org/calculation-tools/all-tools. Accessed: March 11, 2011.

77. https://www.transportmeasures.org/en/.

78. www.ghgprotocol.org/files/ghgp/tools/co2-mobile.pdf.

79. J. Velázquez-Martínez, J. Fransoo, E. Blanco, and J. Mora-Vargas. "The Impact of Carbon Foot-Printing Aggregation on Realizing Emission Reduction Targets," *Flexible Services and Manufacturing Journal* 26, no. 1–2 (2014): 1–25.

80. J. Velázquez-Martínez, J. Fransoo, E. Blanco, and K. Valenzuela-Ocaña. "A New Statistical Method of Assigning Vehicles to Delivery Areas for CO_2 Emissions Reduction," *Transportation Research Part D: Transport and Environment*, 43 (2016): 133–144.

81. M. Barth, T. Younglove, G. Scora. "Development of a Heavy-Duty Diesel Modal Emissions and Fuel Consumption Model." Tech. Rep. UCB-ITS-PRR-2005-1, California PATH Program, Institute of Transportation Studies, University of California at Berkeley.

82. Velázquez-Martínez, J. Fransoo, E. Blanco, and K. Valenzuela-Ocaña. "A New Statistical Method of Assigning Vehicles to Delivery Areas for CO_2 Emissions Reduction," *Transportation Research Part D: Transport and Environment*, 43 (2016): 133–144.

83. http://www.rmi.org/Walmartsfleetoperations.

84. http://www.cggc.duke.edu/environment/climatesolutions/greeneconomy_Ch3_AuxiliaryPowerUnits.pdf.

85. Eric Kulisch, "Shore Power Disruptor?" *American Shipper*, September 17, 2014. Retrieved from: http://www.americanshipper.com/Main/News/Shore_power_disruptor_57985.aspx.

86. Interview with Lee Kindberg, Director, Environment and Sustainability at Maersk Line, August 12, 2015.

87. Interview with Elizabeth Fretheim, August 13, 2015.

88. http://corporate.walmart.com/_news_/news-archive/2014/03/26/walmart-debuts-futuristic-truck.

89. http://www.corporatereport.com/walmart/2015/grr/2015_WALMART_GRR.pdf.

90. http://corporate.walmart.com/_news_/news-archive/2014/03/26/Walmart-debuts-futuristic-truck.

91. http://www.latimes.com/business/la-fi-walmart-truck-20150920-story.html.

92. Ronald D. White, "Wal-Mart Test Trucks Aims to Slash Fuel Consumption on Big Rigs," *Los Angeles Times*, September 20, 2015. Retrieved from: http://www.latimes.com/business/la-fi-walmart-truck-20150920-story.html.

93. Interview with Elizabeth Fretheim, August 13, 2015.

94. http://corporate.walmart.com/_news_/news-archive/2014/03/26/walmart-debuts-futuristic-truck.

95. https://worldindustrialreporter.com/attention-walmart-shoppers-weve-created-futuristic-transport-truck/.

96. http://www.nrel.gov/transportation/fleettest_platooning.html.

97. https://www.trucks.com/2016/04/07/autonomous-trucks-improve-safety-fuel-economy/.

98. http://hero-aviation.com/post.php?post=37.

99. http://www.globallogisticsmedia.com/articles/view/majestic-mrsk.

100. http://www.peterbilt.com/about/media/2014/396/.

101. http://www.ship-technology.com/projects/triple-e-class/.

102. http://www.greencarcongress.com/2011/02/maersk-20110221.html.

103. https://www.yumpu.com/en/document/view/7803715/slow-steaming-the-full-story-maersk/7.

104. http://www.dailymail.co.uk/news/article-2861908/Monster-sea-size-four-football-fields-world-s-largest-container-ships-sets-maiden-voyage-China.html.

105. https://www.npc.org/FTF_Topic_papers/3-Truck_Transportation_Demand.pdf.

106. http://www.internationaltransportforum.org/jtrc/DiscussionPapers/DP201312.pdf.

107. http://www.railjournal.com/index.php/freight/marathon-sets-the-pace-for-longer-freight-trains.html.

108. Danny Hakim, "Aboard a Cargo Colossus," *The New York Times*, October 3, 2014.

109. http://www.smartfreightcentre.org/.

110. http://www.nucms.nl/tpl/smart-freight-centre/upload/SFC_GLEC_Framework.pdf.

111. https://www.iata.org/whatwedo/cargo/sustainability/Documents/rp-carbon-calculation.pdf.

112. http://www.imo.org/en/OurWork/Environment/PollutionPrevention/AirPollution/Documents/TechnicalandOperationalMeasures/MEPC.1_Circ.684_Guidelines for Voluntary use of EEOI.pdf.

113. http://www.imo.org/en/OurWork/Environment/PollutionPrevention/AirPollution/Documents/Circ-684.pdf.

114. http://www.ecotransit.org/download/EcoTransIT_World_Methodology_Report_2014-12-04.pdf.

115. https://standards.cen.eu/dyn/www/f?p=204:110:0::::FSP_PROJECT:32935&cs= 12646506D5D79DADCB74CA2C32A2DAA45.

116. http://www.green-logistics-network.info/en/download/reports.

117. http://www.nytimes.com/2015/07/30/business/ups-agrees-to-buy-46-million-gallons-of-renewable-diesel.html.

118. Andrea Newell, "UPS Drives Toward 1 Billion Miles with Alternative Fuels," *Triple Pundit*, July 30, 2015. Retrieved from: http://www.triplepundit.com/2015/07/ups-drives-toward-1-billion-miles-alternative-fuel/.

119. http://www.ucsusa.org/clean_energy/our-energy-choices/coal-and-other-fossil-fuels/environmental-impacts-of-natural-gas.html.

120. http://www.afdc.energy.gov/vehicles/natural_gas_emissions.html.

121. http://www.greenpeace.org/eu-unit/Global/eu-unit/reports-briefings/2012%20pubs/Pubs%202%20Apr-Jun/Joint%20statement%20on%20fracking.pdf.

122. http://www.wsj.com/articles/the-epa-fracking-miracle-1433460321.

123. http://thehill.com/policy/energy-environment/213635-gao-wants-epa-to-do-more-on-fracking-wastewater.

124. The number of passenger cars in use worldwide was 907,051 in 2014. In the same year, there were 329,253 commercial vehicles in use. See https://www.statista.com/statistics/281134/number-of-vehicles-in-use-worldwide/.

125. John Vidal, "Health Risks of Shipping Pollution Have Been 'Underestimated,'" *The Guardian*, April 9, 2009. Retrieved from: http://www.theguardian.com/environment/2009/apr/09/shipping-pollution.

126. http://forum.woodenboat.com/showthread.php?174072-Pollution-and-shipping-is-this-correct.

127. http://www.economist.com/news/finance-and-economics/21718519-new-ways-foot-hefty-bill-making-old-ships-less-polluting-green-finance.

128. International Maritime Organization (2014). "International Convention for the Prevention of Pollution from Ships (MARPOL)." Retrieved from: http://www.imo.org/About/Conventions/ListOfConventions/Pages/International-Convention-for-the-Prevention-of-Pollution-from-Ships-(MARPOL).aspx.

129. The IMP is the UN agency responsible for the safety and security of shipping and the prevention of maritime pollution by ships.

130. EPA (2008). "International Maritime Organization Adopts Program to Control Air Emissions from Oceangoing Vessels." Office of Transportation and Air Quality: EPA420-F-08-033.

131. http://www.imo.org/en/MediaCentre/HotTopics/GHG/Documents/sulphur%20limits%20FAQ.pdf.

132. http://www.epa.gov/otaq/fuels/dieselfuels/.

133. http://www.epa.gov/diesel-fuel-standards/diesel-fuel-standards-rulemakings#locomotive-and-marine-diesel-fuel-standards.

134. Caltex (2011). "Marine Gas Oil (diesel)." Retrieved from: http://www.caltex.com.au/sites/Marine/Products/Pages/MarineGasOil.aspx.

135. http://www.steamshipmutual.com/downloads/Risk-Alerts/RA44ECA_ULSFuelOilChangeoverProceduresDec14.pdf.

136. http://ec.europa.eu/environment/air/transport/pdf/Report_Sulphur_Requirement.pdf.

137. http://www.agcensus.usda.gov/Publications/2012/Online_Resources/Highlights/Farms_and_Farmland/Highlights_Farms_and_Farmland.pdf.

138. http://www.forbes.com/sites/jamesconca/2014/04/20/its-final-corn-ethanol-is-of-no-use/#40434d2a2ca2.

139. Ibid.

140. https://www.cadc.uscourts.gov/internet/opinions.nsf/A57AB46B228054BD85257AFE00556B45/$file/12-1139-1417101.pdf.

141. http://www.forbes.com/sites/rrapier/2016/04/26/a-cellulosic-ethanol-milestone/.

142. http://investors.fedex.com/news-and-events/investor-news/news-release-details/2015/FedEx-Corp-Accelerates-Aircraft-Retirements/default.aspx.

143. http://www.sustainablebrands.com/news_and_views/cleantech/mike_hower/fedex_purchase_3_million_gallons_jet_biofuel_annually.

144. http://centreforaviation.com/analysis/oil-prices-are-down-so-why-is-united-airlines-buying-into-biofuels-symbolic-or-sound-strategy-233866.

145. http://apex.aero/2015/07/07/united-fulcrum-investment-biofuel.

146. http://www.forbes.com/sites/jamesconca/2014/04/20/its-final-corn-ethanol-is-of-no-use/.

147. USDA (2012). Commodity Image Gallery: Yellow Dent Corn (Maize). Retrieved from: http://www.gipsa.usda.gov/fgis/educout/commgallery/gr_ywdtcorn.html.

148. EPA (2010). "Chapter 2: Lifecycle GHG analysis" in: Renewable Fuel Standard Program (RFS2) Regulatory Impact Analysis, EPA-420-R-10-006, pp. 298–502. Retrieved from: https://www.epa.gov/sites/production/files/2015-08/documents/420r10006.pdf.

149. Holly Jessen, "Ethanol Shuffle Based on 'Questionable Assumptions,'" *Ethanol Producer Magazine*, December 13, 2011. Retrieved from: http://www.ethanolproducer.com/articles/8424/ethanol-shuffle-based-on-questionable-assumptions.

150. Ibid.

151. http://www.businessweek.com/articles/2013-12-19/ethanol-support-in-congress-under-threat-corn-farmers-worry.

152. https://igel.wharton.upenn.edu/wp-content/uploads/2012/09/2012_0601_IGEL_Supply-Chain-Sustainability_LR.pdf.

153. Ibid.

154. https://en.wikipedia.org/wiki/Electricity_sector_in_Norway.

155. http://data.worldbank.org/indicator/EG.ELC.COAL.ZS?year_high_desc=true.

156. https://www.washingtonpost.com/world/electric-cars-and-the-coal-that-runs-them/2015/11/23/74869240-734b-11e5-ba14-318f8e87a2fc_story.html.

157. http://energyskeptic.com/2014/electrification-of-freight-rail/.

158. http://www.gizmag.com/siemens-ehighway-of-the-future-concept/22648/.

159. http://www.portoflosangeles.org/about/facts.asp.

160. PMSA (2008). Trade and the Economy: Economic Impact. Retrieved from: http://www.pmsaship.com/economic-impact.aspx.

161. Memo to Members of the Congressional Subcommittee on Highways and Transit (2010). Hearing on Assessing the Implementation and Impacts of the Clean Truck Programs at the Port of Los Angeles and the Port of Long Beach. Retrieved from: http://www.gpo.gov/fdsys/pkg/CHRG-111hhrg56421/pdf/CHRG-111hhrg56421.pdf.

162. Yossi Sheffi, *Logistics Clusters: Delivering Value and Driving Growth* (Cambridge, MA: MIT Press, 2012).

163. Ibid.

164. http://www.portoflosangeles.org/about/facts.asp.

165. https://www.portoflosangeles.org/ctp/ctp_Cargo_Move_Analysis.pdf.

166. US Department of Transportation Maritime Administration (Released 2013). Vessel Calls Snapshot, 2011. Retrieved from: http://www.marad.dot.gov/documents/Vessel_Calls_at_US_Ports_Snapshot.pdf.

167. Colliers (2012). "North American Port Analysis: Preparing for the First Post-Panamax Decade." Retrieved from: http://www.colliers.com/-/media/Files/MarketResearch/UnitedStates/MARKETS/2012%20Q2/Colliers_PortReport_2012q2_final?campaign=Colliers_Port_Analysis_NA_Aug-2012.

168. YouTube (2006). "Terminal Impact: Activists block construction of a massively polluting cargo terminal and create the world's first green container shipping facility in its place." Retrieved from: http://www.youtube.com/watch?feature=player_embedded&v=qOUbj1ssjKs#at=63.

169. US House of Representatives (2010). Hearing on "Assessing the Implementation and Impacts of the Clean Truck Programs at the Port of Los Angeles and the Port of Long Beach," May 3, 2010.

170. Interview with Bob Kanter, Environmental Director for the Port of Long Beach.

171. http://articles.latimes.com/2002/feb/10/local/me-smog10.

172. California Air Resources Board (1998). "The Report on Diesel Exhaust" Retrieved from: http://www.arb.ca.gov/toxics/dieseltac/de-fnds.htm.

173. Ibid.

174. National Resources Defense Council (2001). "Improving Air Quality in an Urban Neighborhood." Retrieved from: http://www.nrdc.org/ej/partnerships/air.asp.

175. Interview with Chris Cannon, Director of Port Environmental Management, and Christopher Patton, Assistant Director of Port Environmental Management Port of Los Angeles.

176. NRDC (2002). "Appeals Court Stops China Shipping Terminal Construction." Press Release. Retrieved from: http://www.nrdc.org/media/pressreleases/021030b.asp.

177. American Bar Association Supreme Court Preview, No. 11-798, p. 2.

178. Port of Long Beach Interview.

179. NRDC (2008). "90-Day Notice of Intent to Initiate Action Under the Resource Conservation and Recovery Act, 42 U.S.C. §§ 6901 *et seq.*" Retrieved from: https://www.nrdc.org/sites/default/files/air_08020601a.pdf.

180. Port of Long Beach Interview.

181. Air Quality Management District (2013). "AQMD Approves Clean Air Plan Amendment to Ensure Ports Mean Clean Air Goals." Retrieved from: http://www.aqmd.gov/news1/2013/bs020513.htm.

182. West Coast Collaborative (2013). "Marine Vessels & Ports Sector." Retrieved from: http://westcoastcollaborative.org/wkgrp-marine.htm.

183. Interview with Bob Kanter, Environmental Director for the Port of Long Beach.

184. NRDC (2008). "Port of Long Beach Faced Federal Lawsuit over Empty Promises of 'Greener' Operations." Retrieved from: http://www.nrdc.org/media/2008/080206.asp.

185. Port of Long Beach Interview.

186. The Port of Los Angeles. Community Mitigation. Retrieved in 2012 from: http://www.portoflosangeles.org/environment/mitigation.asp.

187. Joint Press Release (2006). "Nation's Two Largest Ports Debut Plan to Target Air Pollution Health Risks." Retrieved from: http://www.portoflosangeles.org/Press/REL_CAAP.pdf.

188. Ibid.

189. Port of Long Beach Interview.

190. Ibid.

191. Port of Long Beach (June 30, 2013). Green Flag Incentive Program Monthly Report. Retrieved from: http://www.polb.com/civica/filebank/blobdload.asp?BlobID=10913.

192. Interview with Chris Cannon, Director of Port Environmental Management, and Christopher Patton, Assistant Director of Port Environmental Management Port of Los Angeles.

193. Joint Press Release (2006). "Nation's Two Largest Ports Debut Plan to Target Air Pollution Health Risks." Retrieved from: http://www.portoflosangeles.org/Press/REL_CAAP.pdf.

194. Interview with Chris Cannon, Director of Port Environmental Management, and Christopher Patton, Assistant Director of Port Environmental Management Port of Los Angeles.

195. Port of Los Angeles Interview.

196. Consumer Federation of California (2008). "Foreclosure on Wheels: Long Beach's Truck Program Puts Drivers at High Risk for Default." Retrieved from: http://consumercal.live.radicaldesigns.org/downloads/Foreclosure%20on%20Wheels.pdf.

197. Port of Long Beach Interview.

198. US House of Representatives (2010). Hearing on "Assessing the Implementation and Impacts of the Clean Truck Programs at the Port of Los Angeles and the Port of Long Beach," May 3, 2010.

199. Port of Los Angeles Interview.

200. Environmental Leader (2012). "Port of Los Angeles Cuts Emissions as Much as 76%." Retrieved from: http://www.environmentalleader.com/2012/08/07/port-of-los-angeles-cuts-emissions-as-much-as-76/.

201. Memo to Members of the Congressional Subcommittee on Highways and Transit (2010). "Hearing on Assessing the Implementation and Impacts of the Clean Truck Programs at the Port of Los Angeles and the Port of Long Beach." Retrieved from: http://www.gpo.gov/fdsys/pkg/CHRG-111hhrg56421/pdf/CHRG-111hhrg56421.pdf.

202. Interview with Chris Cannon, Director of Port Environmental Management, and Christopher Patton, Assistant Director of Port Environmental Management Port of Los Angeles.

203. Port of Los Angeles Interview.

204. Refers to types of sulfur and oxygen containing compounds such as SO, SO_2 and SO_3, among others.

205. San Pedro Bay Ports (2013). Clean Air Action Plan: San Pedro Bay Standards. Retrieved from: http://www.cleanairactionplan.org/programs/standards.asp.

206. Environmental News Network (2010). "World's First Hybrid Tugboat Reduces Emissions at California Ports." Retrieved from: http://www.enn.com/pollution/article/42038.

207. Environmental Leader (2012). "Port of Los Angeles to Pay Carriers for Using Low-Emission Ships." Retrieved from: http://www.environmentalleader.com/2012/05/07/port-of-los-angeles-to-pay-carriers-for-using-low-emission-ships/.

208. Cargo Business (2014). "California Gives Siemens' e-Highways Program the Green Light." Retrieved from: http://cargobusinessnews.com/news/techwire/Tech_Archives/080814/index.html.

209. Port of Los Angeles Interview.

210. World Ports Climate Initiative (2014). "About Us." Retrieved from: http://wpci.iaphworldports.org/about-us/index.html#How%20WPCI%20Began.

211. World Ports Climate Initiative (2014). "World Ports Climate Initiative." Retrieved from: http://wpci.iaphworldports.org/index.html.

212. World Ports Climate Initiative (2014). World Ports Climate Initiative." Retrieved from: http://wpci.iaphworldports.org/data/docs/carbon-footprinting/CF_Lisa%20Wunder.pdf.

213. World Port Climate Initiative (2014). "Environmental Ship Index." Retrieved from: http://esi.wpci.nl/Public/Home.

214. Latitude (2013). "Going Green Pays Off." Retrieved from: http://www
.portoflosangeles.org/latitude/article.php?a=221&p=/March_2013/articles/
Going_Green_Pays_Off.

Notes to Chapter 7

1. http://www.cbsnews.com/news/following-the-trail-of-toxic-e-waste/.

2. http://old.seattletimes.com/html/nationworld/2002920133_ewaste09.html.

3. S. Tong, et al. "Environmental Lead Exposure: A Public Health Problem of Global Dimensions." *Bulletin of the World Health Organization* 78, no. 9 (2000).

4. Anna O. W. Leung, et al. "Heavy Metals Concentrations of Surface Dust from E-Waste Recycling and Its Human Health Implications in Southeast China." *Environmental Science & Technology* 42(7) (2008): 2674–2680.

5. http://www.usnews.com/news/articles/2014/08/01/e-waste-in-developing
-countries-endangers-environment-locals citing http://pubs.acs.org/doi/abs/10
.1021/es5021313.

6. http://www.cnn.com/2013/05/30/world/asia/china-electronic-waste-e-waste/.

7. http://www.greenpeace.org/international/en/news/features/e-waste-china
-toxic-pollution-230707/.

8. The Aluminum Association (2012). "Aluminum Can Extends Lead as Most Recycled Beverage Container: Aluminum Can Recycling Rate Reaches 65.1 Percent."Retrievedfrom:http://www.aluminum.org/AM/Template.cfm?Section=2012
&CONTENTID=33554&TEMPLATE=/CM/ContentDisplay.cfm.

9. http://www.coventrytelegraph.net/news/coventry-news/primark-sparks
-shopping-frenzy-3121054.

10. According to *The Economist*, quoting research firm Sanford C. Bernstein, the average selling price for women's clothing at Primark is a little more than a third of the price at the fast fashion retailer H&M.

11. http://www.marketplace.org/topics/business/ive-always-wondered/what-d
o-stores-do-unsold-merchandise-0.

12. Daniel Hoornweg, Perinaz Bhada-Tata, and Chris Kennedy. "Environment: Waste Production Must Peak This Century," *Nature* 502 (2013): 7473. Retrieved from: http://www.nature.com/news/environment-waste-production-must-peak
-this-century-1.14032.

13. Betsy Taylor and Dave Tilford, "Why Consumption Matters" in Juliet Schor and Douglas Holt, *The Consumer Society Reader* (New York: The New Press, 2000).

14. http://data.worldbank.org/indicator/EN.ATM.CO2E.PC?locations=US.

15. Keith Wagstaff, "WATCH: The Garbage Barge Without a Home," *The Week*, May 6, 2013. Retrieved from: http://theweek.com/articles/464713/watch-garbag
e-barge-without-home.

16. http://www.mnn.com/earth-matters/translating-uncle-sam/stories/what-is-the-great-pacific-ocean-garbage-patch.

17. US Environmental Protection Agency. "Municipal Solid Waste Generation—Fact and Figures for 2011." Retrieved from: http://www.epa.gov/osw/nonhaz/municipal/pubs/MSWcharacterization_508_053113_fs.pdf.

18. https://www.statista.com/chart/4470/the-countries-winning-the-recycling-race/.

19. T. Lindhqvist and K. Lidgren. "Models for Extended Producer Responsibility" in Ministry of the Environment, *From the Cradle to the Grave — Six Studies of the Environmental Impact of Products* (7-44) Ds 1991: 9.

20. C. Morawski and R3 Consulting Group (2009). "Evaluating End-of-Life Beverage Container Management Systems for California." Retrieved from: http://www.bottlebill.org/assets/pdfs/pubs/2009-BeverageSystemsCalifornia.pdf.

21. European Commission (2014). Waste Electrical & Electronic Equipment (WEEE). Retrieved from: http://ec.europa.eu/environment/waste/weee/index_en.htm.

22. STEP (2014). StEP WorldMap 2012 data. Retrieved from: http://www.step-initiative.org/index.php/overview-world.html. Accessed August 2014.

23. Population Reference Bureau (2013). "The Human and Environmental Effects of E-Waste." Retrieved from: http://www.prb.org/Publications/Articles/2013/e-waste.aspx.

24. European Commission (2007). "Extended Producer Responsibility Principles of the WEEE Directive: Final Report." Environmental Study Report by Okopol GmbH Institute for Environmental Strategies, The International Institute for Industrial Environmental Economics, and Risk and Policy Analysts.

25. CalRecycle (2013). "Product Stewardship and Extended Producer Responsibility (EPR): Policy and Law." Retrieved from: http://www.calrecycle.ca.gov/epr/PolicyLaw/default.htm#World.

26. EPA (n.d.) "Brazilian National Solid Waste Policy." Retrieved from: http://www.epa.gov/jius/policy/brazil/brazilian_national_solid_waste_policy.html.

27. Ibid.

28. Although the policy is ambitious, its implementation has been lagging. For example, the regulation does not clearly identify who should be responsible—the government or industry— for the cost of the reverse logistics for the collection of end-of-life goods.

29. https://www.epa.gov/smm/sustainable-materials-management-non-hazardous-materials-and-waste-management-hierarchy.

30. http://www.cnn.com/2008/LIVING/wayoflife/09/19/aa.used.car.fun.facts/.

31. R. Lane, H. Ralph, and J. Bicknell. "Routes of Reuse of Second-hand Goods in Melbourne Householders," *Australian Geographer*, 40, no. 2 (2009): 151–168.

32. John Naughton, "Websites that Changed the World," *The Guardian*, August 13, 2006. Retrieved from: http://www.theguardian.com/technology/2006/aug/13/observerreview.onlinesupplement.

33. Excluding job postings, which involve a modest fee.

34. TheServerSide.com (2011). "The Craigslist Dilemma: A Case Study for Big Data and NoSQL Solutions." Retrieved from: http://www.theserverside.com/feature/The-Craigslist-Dilemma-A-case-study-for-big-data-and-NoSQL-solutions.

35. https://3taps.com/papers/Craigslist-by-the-Numbers.pdf.

36. The site only charges for job posting at six major US cities and a small fee for apartment rental listing in New York. All other listings are free.

37. http://www.att.com/Common/merger/files/pdf/CPFS_EarthDay/CPFS_Enviro_FS.pdf.

38. EcoATM (2013). Press Releases. Retrieved from: http://www.ecoatm.com/press-releases.html.

39. Mike Freeman, "ecoATM ramping up recycling footprint," *The San Diego Union-Tribune*, September 11, 2014. Retrieved from: http://www.utsandiego.com/news/2014/sep/11/ecoATM-outerwall-redbox-recycling-mobile-phones/.

40. Interview with Mark Bowles, ecoATM founder.

41. Ibid.

42. James R. Hagerty, "Entrepreneurs Find Gold in Used Phones," *The Wall Street Journal*, February 24, 2011. Retrieved from: http://online.wsj.com/article/SB10001424052748704520504576162431091194572.html.

43. The company went bankrupt in 2013.

44. Best Buy (2012). Refurbished Phones. Retrieved from: http://www.bestbuy.com/site/olstemplatemapper.jsp?id=pcat17080&type=page&qp= percent20cab-cat0800000~~nf711 percent7C percent7C5265667572626973686564&list=y&nrp=15&sc=phoneOfficeSP&sp=-bestsellingsort+skuid&usc=abcat0800000.

45. http://www.wired.com/2013/08/apple-trade-in/.

46. http://www.verizonwireless.com/landingpages/device-trade-in/.

47. http://news.nationalgeographic.com/news/energy/2012/11/121116-second-life-for-used-electric-car-batteries/.

48. Ibid.

49. Ibid.

50. Ibid.

51. http://fortune.com/2015/06/15/electric-car-batteries-reuse/.

52. This factory makes both Subaru and Toyota vehicles.

53. Los Angeles Times (2011). "A Really Green Plant: Subaru of Indiana Automotive Makes Cars—Not Garbage. Retrieved from: http://sections.latimes.com/altvehicles/2011/04/#?article=1229857.

54. http://www.youtube.com/watch?v=mDOD-qa05mM.

55. Ibid.

56. Supply Chain Brain (2013). "Less is More: Office Depot Cuts Supply-Chain Waste." Retrieved from: http://www.supplychainbrain.com/content/index.php?id=7098&type=98&tx_ttnews percent5Btt_news percent5D=20702&cHash=da03e20e36.

57. R. Simon, E. Rice, E., T. Kingsbury, and D. Dornfeld (2012). "A Comparison of Life Cycle Assessment (LCA) Software in Packaging Applications." Laboratory for Manufacturing and Sustainability, University of California, Berkeley.

58. Environmental Protection Agency (2013). "Reduce, Reuse Recycle, Buy Recycled." Retrieved from: http://www.epa.gov/region9/waste/solid/reduce.html #recycling.

59. David Maloney, "Many Happy Returns?" *DC Velocity*, December 2016, pp. 39–44.

60. http://www.staples.com/sbd/cre/products/ink-recycle/index.html.

61. http://www.bestbuy.com/site/Electronics-Promotions/Online-Trade-In/pcmcat133600050011.c?id=pcmcat133600050011&DCMP=rdr3384.

62. http://www.officedepot.com/a/content/loyalty/recycling-program/.

63. http://www.environmentalleader.com/2013/11/05/staples-alcoa-endorse-e-stewards-standard-version-2-0/.

64. http://e-stewards.org/about-us/the-e-stewards-story/.

65. http://www.staples.com/sbd/cre/marketing/about_us/documents/global perfsummary-2015.pdf.

66. http://www.ibm.com/financing/us-en/solutions/asset-recovery.

67. https://www.theguardian.com/environment/2011/dec/29/japan-leads-field-plastic-recycling.

68. http://www.theguardian.com/environment/2011/dec/29/japan-leads-field-plastic-recycling.

69. http://www.dell.com/learn/us/en/uscorp1/corp-comm/us-goodwill-reconnect.

70. Ibid.

71. Ibid.

72. http://www.dell.com/learn/us/en/uscorp1/corp-comm/getfreeat-homepickup?c=us&l=en&s=corp&cs=uscorp1.

73. http://i.dell.com/sites/doccontent/corporate/corp-comm/en/Documents/fy15-cr-report.pdf.

74. http://www.portoflosangeles.org/pdf/Los-Angeles-Trade-Numbers-2013.pdf.

75. E-Stewards (2013). "What's Driving the E-Waste Crisis." Retrieved from: http://www.e-stewards.org/the-e-waste-crisis/why-does-this-problem-exist/.

76. Greenpeace (2009). "Where Does e-Waste End Up?" http://www.greenpeace.org/international/en/campaigns/toxics/electronics/the-e-waste-problem/where-does-e-waste-end-up/#a4.

77. https://www.google.com/search?hl=en&site=imghp&tbm=isch&source=hp&biw=1586&bih=873&q=3R+recycling+triangle&oq=3R+recycling+triangle&gs_l=img.3...2048.11262.0.11630.21.4.0.17.17.0.93.349.4.4.0....0...1ac.1.64.img..0.9.356...0.OhS3tDR8b2c#hl=en&tbm=isch&q=3R+recycling+code+for+platics&imgrc=G6TwsV8ZiSc8KM%3A.

78. http://i.dell.com/sites/doccontent/corporate/corp-comm/en/Documents/fy15-cr-report.pdf.

79. http://i.dell.com/sites/doccontent/corporate/corp-comm/en/Documents/fy15-cr-report.pdf.

80. http://www.wistron.com/press/news_releases/news_2014_05_20.htm.

81. Market Watch (2013). "HP Empowers Customers to Print Responsibly with New Products, Expanded Recycling Options." Retrieved from: http://www.marketwatch.com/story/hp-empowers-customers-to-print-responsibly-with-new-products-expanded-recycling-options-2013-04-16.

82. *Triple Pundit* (2012). "HP Cartridge Recycling is More than a Shred Ahead." Retrieved from: http://www.triplepundit.com/2012/04/hewlett-packard-printer-cartridge-recycling-smyrna/.

83. Market Watch (2013). "HP Empowers Customers to Print Responsibly with New Products, Expanded Recycling Options."

84. Four Elements Consulting, LLC (2010). "Life Cycle Environmental Impact Assessment." Retrieved from: http://www.hp.com/hpinfo/newsroom/press_kits/2010/ecoachievement/RPET_LCA_whitepaper.pdf.

85. http://i.dell.com/sites/doccontent/corporate/corp-comm/en/Documents/fy15-cr-report.pdf.

86. David W. Pearce and R. Kerry Turner, *Economics of Natural Resources and the Environment*. (Baltimore: Johns Hopkins University Press, 1989).

87. E. Kline, E. *Over-Dressed: The Shockingly High Cost of Cheap Fashion*. (New York: Penguin, 2012).

88. NPR (2013). "The Global Afterlife of Your Donated Clothes." Retrieved from: http://www.npr.org/blogs/parallels/2013/05/21/185596830/the-global-afterlife-of-your-donated-clothes.

89. Ibid.

90. M. Crang, A. Hughes, N. Gregson et al. "Rethinking Governance and Value in Commodity Chains Through Global Recycling Networks," *Transactions of the Institute of British Geographers* 28 (2011):12–24.

91. E. Kline, E. *Over-Dressed: The Shockingly High Cost of Cheap Fashion*. (New York: Penguin, 2012).

92. H. Nguyen, M. Stuchtey, and M. Zils, "Remaking the Industrial Economy," *McKinsey Quarterly*, February 2014.

93. http://breakingenergy.com/2014/02/18/can-coal-fly-ash-waste-be-put-to-good-use/.

94. http://earthjustice.org/sites/default/files/library/reports/ej-eipreportout-of-control-final.pdf.

95. http://www.concreteconstruction.net/concrete/fly-ash-threat.aspx.

96. http://www.concreteconstruction.net/concrete/fly-ash-threat.aspx.

97. Jean Rogers, "4 signs of Sustainability from Oil, Gas and Mining Companies," *GreenBiz*, November 5, 2013. Retrieved from: https://www.greenbiz.com/blog/2013/11/05/4-sustainability-trends-oil-gas-mining.

98. http://epa.gov/climatechange/wycd/waste/downloads/fly-ash-chapter10-28 -10.pdf.

99. http://epa.gov/climatechange/wycd/waste/downloads/fly-ash-chapter10-28 -10.pdf.

100. http://democrats.energycommerce.house.gov/sites/default/files/documents/ Testimony-Ladwig-EE-Drinking-Water-Coal-2009-12-10.pdf.

101. CSRWire (2004). "Gold Medal Soccer Mia Hamm & Briana Scurry Help NikeGO and the US Soccer Foundation Dedicate Soccer Field." Retrieved from: http://www.csrwire.com/press_releases/24944-Gold-Medal-Soccer-Stars-Mia -Hamm-Briana-Scurry-Help-NikeGO-and-The-U-S-Soccer-Foundation-Dedicate -Chicago-Soccer-Field.

102. Ace Surfaces (2013). "Nike Grind." Retrieved from: http://www.reboundace .com/nike-grind-recycled-surfaces-FAQ.php.

103. Nike (2013). "Reuse-A-Shoe." Retrieved from: http://www.nike.com/us/en _us/c/better-world/stories/2013/05/reuse-a-shoe.

104. Gossypium hirsutum, also known as upland cotton, is the most widely planted species of cotton in the United States, constituting some 95 percent of all cotton production there.

105. http://www.gapinc.com/content/attachments/sersite/SR percent20Full percent20Report.pdf.

106. Elizabeth Rosenthal, "Europe Finds Clean Energy in Trash, but US Lags," *The New York Times*, April 12, 2010.

107. http://www.wte.org/userfiles/file/Better percent20to percent20burn percent20or percent20bury.pdf.

108. http://www.engineering-timelines.com/why/lowCarbonCopenhagen/ copenhagenPower_03.asp.

109. Elizabeth Rosenthal, "Europe Finds Clean Energy in Trash, but US Lags," *The New York Times*, April 12, 2010.

110. http://www.environmentalleader.com/2015/05/06/ups-becomes-larges t-renewable-natural-gas-user-in-shipping-industry/.

111. https://pressroom.ups.com/pressroom/ContentDetailsViewer.page?Concept Type=PressReleases&id=1455110888923-689.

112. http://breakingenergy.com/2014/12/05/renewable-natural-gas-helps-reduc e-emissions-policy-support-needed/.

113. http://transparency.perkinswill.com/Content/Whitepapers/FlyAsh_White Paper.pdf.

114. Tom Elko. "Green Enough for 35W concrete, Toxic Coal Ash is Also Used on Farms," *Twin Cities Daily Plant*, April 7, 2009. Retrieved from: https://www .tcdailyplanet.net/green-enough-35w-concrete-toxic-coal-ash-also-used-farms/.

115. Elizabeth Rosenthal, "Europe Finds Clean Energy in Trash, but US Lags," *The New York Times*, April 12, 2010.

116. http://www.internationallawoffice.com/newsletters/detail.aspx?g=a178c0d3 -39f6-492c-8ff0-c8bc65b479ec.

117. E. Alonso, F. Field, and R. Kirchain, "Platinum Availability for Future Automotive Technologies," *Environmental Science & Technology* 46(23) (2012): 12986–12993.

118. http://www.sei-international.org/mediamanager/documents/Publications/ SEI-2014-DiscussionBrief-China-Rareearths.pdf.

119. Ibid.

120. http://www.solvay.com/en/media/press_releases/20120927-coleopterre.html.

121. Rare Earth Investing News (2013). "REE Electronics Recycling Being Explored." Retrieved from: http://rareearthinvestingnews.com/14967-ree-electronics-recycling -being-explored.html.

122. Georgi Kantchev and Serena Ng, "Recycling Becomes a Tougher Sell as Oil Prices Drop," *Wall Street Journal*, April 5, 2015.

123. http://www.afr.com/business/energy/oil/plastic-recycling-is-hit-by-the-fall -in-oil-prices-20150503-1mypyr.

124. Georgi Kantchev and Serena Ng, "Recycling Becomes a Tougher Sell as Oil Prices Drop," *Wall Street Journal*, April 5, 2015.

125. http://www.cbsnews.com/news/why-recycling-economics-are-in-the-trash -bin/.

126. Copper Development Association Inc. (2013)." Copper—the World's Most Reusable Resource." Retrieved from: http://www.copper.org/environment/ lifecycle/g_recycl.html.

127. Ibid.

128. http://www.cnbc.com/id/100917758.

129. Ian Urbina, "Unwanted Electronic Gear Rising in Toxic Piles," *The New York Times*, March 18, 2013.

130. Mayo Clinic (2011). "Lead Poisoning." Retrieved from: http://www .mayoclinic.com/health/lead-poisoning/FL00068.

131. EPA (2013). Regulation of Cathode Ray Tubes. Retrieved from: http://www .epa.gov/osw/hazard/recycling/electron/.

132. C. Morawski and R3 Consulting Group (2009). Evaluating End-of-Life Beverage Container Management Systems for California." Retrieved from: http:// www.bottlebill.org/assets/pdfs/pubs/2009-BeverageSystemsCalifornia.pdf.

133. M. Realff, M. Raymond, J. Ammons, "E-waste: An Opportunity," *Materials Today* 7, no. 1 (2004): 40–45.

134. EPA (2007). "Management of Electronic Waste in the United States: Approach Two. Report."

135. Ian Urbina, "Unwanted Electronic Gear Rising in Toxic Piles," *The New York Times*, March 18, 2013.

136. Ibid.

137. E-Scrap News (2013). "Breaking News: Abandoned Warehouses Full of CRTs Found in Several States." Retrieved from: https://resource-recycling.com/e-scrap/2013/08/23/abandoned-warehouses-full-crts-found-several-states/.

138. E-Scrap News (2013). "Avoiding the Old Maid: Causes and Cures for CRT Glass Stockpiling in the US September 2013."

139. Ian Urbina, "Unwanted Electronic Gear Rising in Toxic Piles," *The New York Times*, March 18, 2013.

140. Maine Legislature. Chapter 16, Title 38. 1610: Electronic Waste.

141. Ibid.

142. EPA (2011). Superfund 30th Anniversary Timeline. Retrieved from: http://www.epa.gov/superfund/30years/timeline/index.htm#.

143. http://unesdoc.unesco.org/images/0013/001395/139578e.pdf.

144. E. Olivetti, J. Gregory, and R. Kirchain (2011). "Life Cycle Impacts of Alkaline Batteries with a Focus on End Of Life. A study conducted for the National Electrical Manufacturers Association." MIT Materials Systems Lab.

145. Mathew Weaver, "Q&A: Battery Recycling," *The Guardian*, May 5, 2006. Retrieved from: http://www.theguardian.com/world/2006/may/05/qanda.recycling.

146. Waste 360.com. (2013). "California Considering Battery Recycling Bill." Retrieved from: http://waste360.com/state-and-local/california-considering-battery-recycling-bill.

147. Mathew Weaver, "Q&A: Battery Recycling," *The Guardian*, May 5, 2006. Retrieved from: http://www.theguardian.com/world/2006/may/05/qanda.recycling.

148. http://www.bebat.be.

149. http://no-burn.org/downloads/ZW percent20Flanders.pdf.

150. http://ec.europa.eu/environment/enveco/taxation/pdf/ch13_batteries.pdf.

151. http://www.globalpsc.net/wp-content/uploads/2012/08/GlobalPSC_Battery_PS_Belgium__Switzerland_0812.pdf.

152. http://www.epbaeurope.net/recycling.html.

153. http://www.bebat.be/en/figures.

154. Container Recycling Institute (2009). "Keep American Beautiful: A History." Retrieved from. http://toolkit.bottlebill.org/opposition/KABhistory.htm.

155. Robert G. Hunt, William E. Franklin, and R. G. Hunt, "LCA—How It Came About," *The International Journal of Life Cycle Assessment* 1(1) (1996): 4–7.

156. *Burlington Free Press* (2011). "Vermont's Bottle Bill, Once First in the Nation, Now Facing Serious Effort at Repeal." Retrieved from: http://www.bottlebill.org/news/articles/2011/VT-1-30-VTsBBOnceFirst.htm.

157. Container Recycling Institute (2013). "Bottle Bills in the USA." Retrieved from: http://www.bottlebill.org/legislation/usa.htm.

158. *Burlington Free Press* (2011). "Vermont's Bottle Bill, Once First in the Nation, Now Facing Serious Effort at Repeal." Retrieved from: http://www.bottlebill.org/news/articles/2011/VT-1-30-VTsBBOnceFirst.htm.

159. C. Morawski and R3 Consulting Group (2009) "Evaluating End-of-Life Beverage Container Management Systems for California." Retrieved from: http://www.bottlebill.org/assets/pdfs/pubs/2009-BeverageSystemsCalifornia.pdf.

160. Serena Ng, "High Costs Put Cracks in Glass-Recycling Programs," *Wall Street Journal*, April 22, 2015.

161. The figure follows a somewhat different one suggested in a publication of the MacArthur Foundation. See: https://www.ellenmacarthurfoundation.org/assets/downloads/publications/Ellen-MacArthur-Foundation-Towards-the-Circular-Economy-vol.1.pdf.

162. http://www.johnsoncontrols.com/content/us/en/products/power-solutions/responsible-recycling/where.html.

163. http://www.johnsoncontrols.com/content/us/en/products/power_solutions/global_battery_recycling/.

164. E. Blanco and K. Cottrill, "Closing the Loop on a Circular Supply Chain," *Supply Chain Management Review*, September/October 2014.

165. http://www.johnsoncontrols.com/content/us/en/products/power-solutions/responsible-recycling/how.html.

166. http://www.johnsoncontrols.com/content/us/en/products/power-solutions/responsible-recycling/why.html.

167. http://www.leadforlead.com/lead-prices/lme-lead-prices.html.

168. http://www.reuters.com/article/us-metals-lead-environment-idUSBRE82P0HC20120326.

169. http://www.indexmundi.com/minerals/?product=lead.

170. "In the Bin: Recycling in America," *The Economist*, April 22, 2015.

171. David Gelles, "Big Companies Put Their Money Where the Trash Is," *The New York Times*, November 28, 2015. Retrieved from: http://www.nytimes.com/2015/11/29/business/energy-environment/big-companies-put-their-money-where-the-trash-is.html.

172. http://www.environmentalleader.com/2014/10/17/zero-interest-loans-to-develop-recycling-infrastructure-available/.

173. Kimberly-Clark (2010). Supporting Local Economies. Retrieved from: http://www.sustainabilityreport2010.kimberly-clark.com/people/supporting-local-economies.asp.

174. Ibid.

175. Dienst Centraal Milieubeheer Rijnmond.

176. http://www.deltalinqsenergyforum.nl/documents/def-juni percent202012/1001855 percent20- percent20Strategic percent20position percent20paper percent20- percent20development percent20CO2 percent20hub percent20Rotterdam.pdf.

177. http://projet.ifpen.fr/Projet/upload/docs/application/pdf/2013-01/session_2_2.pdf.

178. http://www.omafra.gov.on.ca/english/crops/facts/00-077.htm.

179. http://www.the-linde-group.com/en/clean_technology/clean_technology_portfolio/co2_applications/greenhouse_supply/index.html.

180. http://ccs-roadmap.ecofys.com/index.php/History_of_CCS_in_the_Netherlands.

181. http://www.rotterdamclimateinitiative.nl/documents/CO2 percent20network percent20approch.pdf.

182. http://energy.gov/fe/science-innovation/oil-gas-research/enhanced-oil-recovery.

183. http://www.rotterdamclimateinitiative.nl/documents/CO2 percent20network percent20approch.pdf.

184. http://www.epa.gov/climatechange/ccs/.

185. http://news.stanford.edu/news/2012/june/carbon-capture-earthquakes-061912.html.

186. H. Nguyen, M. Stuchtey, and M. Zils, "Remaking the Industrial Economy," *McKinsey Quarterly*, February 2014.

187. T. Chilton, S. Burnley, and S. Nesaratnam, "A Life Cycle Assessment of the Closed-Loop Recycling and Thermal Recovery of Post-Consumer PET." *Resources, Conservation and Recycling* 54 (2010): 1241–1249.

188. Novelis (2013). The Recycling Process. Retrieved from: http://www.novelis.com/en-us/Pages/The-Recycling-Process.aspx.

189. "In the Bin: Recycling in America." *The Economist*, April 22, 2015.

190. http://www.calrecycle.ca.gov/Publications/Documents/BevContainer percent5 C2011024.pdf.

191. http://www.sciencedirect.com/science/article/pii/S0921344911002217.

192. http://www.coca-colacompany.com/sustainabilityreport/world/water-stewardship.html.

193. http://www.theguardian.com/environment/2011/dec/29/japan-leads-field-plastic-recycling?newsfeed=true.

194. http://www.environmentalleader.com/2014/02/05/epas-toxic-substances-rules-discourage-recycling/.

195. Maxine Perella, "LEGO: How the Signature Brick is Going Green," *The Guardian*, April 11, 2014). Retrieved from: https://www.theguardian.com/sustainable-business/lego-design-sustainability-circular-economy. Accessed August 2014.

Notes to Chapter 8

1. https://www.jfklibrary.org/Research/Research-Aids/Ready-Reference/RFK-Speeches/Remarks-of-Robert-F-Kennedy-at-the-University-of-Kansas-March-18-1968.aspx.

2. Owen Pritchard, "Does Nike's New Making App Place Sustainability at the Forefront of Design?" *The Guardian*, July 17, 2013.

3. http://www.design.caltech.edu/Research/Imprecise/Reading_List/Ch02_90e.pdf.

4. Jason McLennan, *The Philosophy of Sustainable Design*, (Kansas City, MO: Ecotone Publishing Company, 2004).

5. *Packaging World* (2009). "Beverage Bottles Lighten Up." Retrieved from: http://www.packworld.com/newsletters/ppr-05-14-09.html.

6. Robert G. Hunt, William E. Franklin, and R. G. Hunt, "LCA—How it came about," *The International Journal of Life Cycle Assessment* 1, no. 1 (1996): 4–7.

7. https://www.apple.com/environment/pdf/Apple_Environmental_Responsibility_Report_2015.pdf.

8. Nike (2014). "Nike Sustainability Performance Summary." Retrieved from http://www.nikeresponsibility.com/report/uploads/files/FY12-13_NIKE_Inc_CR_Report.pdf.

9. Owen Pritchard, "Does Nike's New Making App Place Sustainability at the Forefront of Design?" *The Guardian*, July 17, 2013.

10. https://www.greenbiz.com/news/2002/09/16/eco-intelligence-nike-transforms-textile-industry.

11. Nike (2009). "Nike Corporate Responsibility Report. FY07-09."

12. Nike (2009). "Nike Corporate Responsibility Report. FY10-11."

13. http://www.sustainablebusiness.com/index.cfm/go/news.display/id/22816.

14. Kimberley Clark was attacked during from 2004 through 2009 by Greenpeace for destroying old-growth forests to get raw material for their throwaway products—Kleenex, Scott tissues, Huggies, and Pull-Ups.

15. LEGO was attacked for distributing toys in Shell stations. Shell was accused of drilling in the Arctic, creating a danger of oil spills. See https://www.youtube.com/watch?v=qhbliUq0_r4.

16. R. R. Henderson, R. Locke, C. Lyddy, and C. Reavis (2009). "Nike Considered: Getting Traction on Sustainability." MIT Sloan School of Management White Paper.

17. https://www.greenbiz.com/blog/2012/05/07/nike-sustainability-goals-supply-chain.

18. http://www.nikeresponsibility.com/report/content/chapter/our-sustainability-strategy.

19. http://www.adidas-group.com/media/filer_public/2013/07/31/ag_individual_roadmap_november_18_2011_en.pdf.

20. http://www.adidas-group.com/media/filer_public/2013/08/26/environmental_statement_2007_english.pdf.

21. http://www.adidas-group.com/en/sustainability/products/materials/.

22. http://www.bloomberg.com/bw/articles/2012-03-15/is-nikes-flyknit-the-swoosh-of-the-future.

23. Ibid.

24. http://www.nytimes.com/2010/09/19/science/earth/19clean.html?_r=0.

25. Bryan Walsh, "Greener Dishwashing: A Farewell to Phosphates," *Time*, November 13, 2010. Retrieved from: http://www.time.com/time/printout/0,8816 ,2030878,00.html.

26. Sierra Club (2006). "Washington State Phosphate Ban First in Nation: Eliminating Phosphates from Dishwashing Detergents 'Cleans Dishes While Saving Fishes.'" Retrieved from: http://www.waterplanet.ws/phosphates/Site/Media/ Entries/2006/3/27_Washington_state_phosphate_ban_first_in_nation.html.

27. Mireya Navarro, "Cleaner for the Environment, Not for the Dishes," *The New York Times*, September 18, 2010. Retrieved from: http://www.nytimes.com/ 2010/09/19/science/earth/19clean.html?_r=0.

28. Ibid.

29. Ibid.

30. *Consumer Reports* (2013). "Cascade and Finish Top Our Tough Tests." Retrieved from: http://www.consumerreports.org/cro/magazine/2013/10/find-the-best-dishwasher-detergent/index.htm.

31. Seventh Generation (2009). "Improved Products." Retrieved from: http:// www.2009.7genreport.com/products/improved.php.

32. EPA (2000). "1,4-Dioxane (1,4—Diethyleneoxide)." Retrieved from: http:// www.epa.gov/ttnatw01/hlthef/dioxane.html.

33. Seventh Generation (2009). "Improved Products." Retrieved from: http:// www.seventhgeneration.com/mission/product-philosophy/improved-products -2009.

34. http://www.sciencemag.org/news/2016/05/us-panel-releases-consensus-geneti cally-engineered-crops.

35. Alan Boyle, "Scientists and Public at Odds over Climate, GMOs and More," NBC News, January 29, 2015. Retrieved from: http://www.nbcnews.com/science/ science-news/survey-shows-scientists-public-odds-over-climate-gmos-more -n296231.

36. Walgreens (2012). "Walgreens Introduces the 'Ology' Brand of Healthy Home Products." Retrieved from: http://news.walgreens.com/article_print.cfm?article _id=5666.

37. CTL, "Building Supply Chains That Deliver Sustainability," 2010 Crossroads, MIT, Cambridge, MA, March 25, 2010.

38. CTL, "Supply Chains in Transition: The Driving Forces of Change," 2012 Crossroads, MIT, Cambridge, MA, June 28, 2012.

39. Interview with Carlos Navarros, Charlene Wall-Warren, and Leta LaRuch, BASF Canada, April 8, 2016.

40. https://www.basf.com/documents/corp/en/sustainability/management-and -instruments/sustainable-solution-steering/BASF_Brochure_Sustainable_Solution _Steering.pdf.

41. https://www.greenbiz.com/article/basfs-new-strategy-greener-supply-chain.

42. https://www.basf.com/documents/corp/en/investor-relations/calendar-and -publications/presentations/2015/151001_BASF_SRI.pdf.

43. https://www.basf.com/documents/corp/en/sustainability/management-and -instruments/sustainable-solution-steering/BASF_Booklet_Sustainable_Solution _Steering.pdf.

44. Ibid.

45. Interview with Carles Navarro, Charlene Wall-Warren, and Leta LaRuch, BASF Canada, April 8, 2016.

46. Interview with Cynthia Wilkinson, 2013.

47. Laura Northrup, "How the Stupid Shipping Gang Sends a Bottle of White Out," *Consumerist*, August 21, 2012. Retrieved from: http://consumerist.com/ 2012/08/21/how-the-stupid-shipping-gang-sends-a-bottle-of-white-out/.

48. Laura Northrup, "Amazon Makes Sure Sharpie Shipment Arrives Very, Very, Very Safely," *Consumerist*, July 3, 2012. Retrieved from: http://consumerist.com/ 2012/07/03/amazon-makes-sure-sharpie-shipment-arrives-very-very-very-safely/.

49. Laura Northrup, "Macy's Includes Free Mug in My Box of Air Pillows," *Consumerist*, May 20, 2013. Retrieved from: http://consumerist.com/2013/05/20/ macys-includes-free-mug-in-my-box-of-air-pillows/.

50. Interview with Cynthia Wilkinson, 2013.

51. http://wwd.com/business-news/financial/amazon-walmart-top-ecommerc e-retailers-10383750/.

52. *Packaging World* (2013). "Staples Deploys on-Demand, Custom Case Making." Retrieved from: http://www.packworld.com/machinery/converting -machinery/staples-deploys-demand-custom-case-making.

53. Ibid.

54. Break-pack orders are orders in which the customer wants less than a full case of a product. They require workers at the distribution center to "break" a case and pack one or more different items into a separate (usually smaller) box.

55. Maida Napolitano, "Staples: Smart Packaging, Happy Customers, Healthy Planet," *Modern Material Handling*, June 1, 2013. Retrieved from: http://www .mmh.com/article/staples_smart_packaging_happy_customers_healthy_planet.

56. Staples piloted Packsize equipment at a single fulfillment center in Orlando, Florida, in early 2011, according to a Staples/Packsize case study.

57. Interview with Cynthia Wilkinson, 2013.

58. Prior to working with Packsize, Staples' fulfillment centers stocked between 7 and 14 different box options and kept half a truckload to a full truckload of each on hand. With all boxes drawing from the same stock, centers using the Packsize machines have been able to reduce their total cardboard storage to less than two truckloads (Staples-Packsize Joint Press Release 2013).

59. DC Velocity 2013.

60. Staples/Packsize Joint Press-Release (2012). "Staples Delivers Custom Box Sizes with Every Order for More Convenience, Reduced Waste."

61. ECORYS (2010). "Freight Transport for Development, A Policy Toolkit." Cambridge Systematics, Retrieved from: http://www.ppiaf.org/freighttoolkit/sites/default/files/casestudies/Walmart.pdf.

62. Walmart News Archive (2006), http://news.walmart.com/news-archive/2006/11/01/wal-mart-unveils-packaging-scorecard-to-suppliers. Accessed July 2014.

63. "Walmart 2014 Sustainability Report." http://www.corporatereport.com/walmart/2014/grr/environment_packing_materials.html. Accessed July 2014.

64. Environmental News Network (2013). Amazon Promotes "Frustration-Free Packaging Initiative." Retrieved from: http://www.enn.com/business/article/46770.

65. Ibid.

66. Amazon (n.d.). "About Amazon Certified Frustration-Free Packaging." Retrieved from: http://www.amazon.com/gp/help/customer/display.html?ie=UTF8&nodeId=200285450.

67. Amazon (2013). "Amazon Frustration-Free Packaging Letter to Customers." Retrieved from: http://www.amazon.com/gp/feature.html/ref=amb_link_84595831_1?ie=UTF8&docId=1001920911&pf_rd_m=ATVPDKIKX0DER&pf_rd_s=merchandised-search-5&pf_rd_r=0MGZCPER0HQ4B2MPYNDW&pf_rd_t=101&pf_rd_p=1721461822&pf_rd_i=5521637011. Accessed July 2014.

68. Stephanie Clifford, "Packaging is All the Rage, and Not in a Good Way," *The New York Times*, September 7, 2010. Retrieved from: http://www.nytimes.com/2010/09/08/technology/08packaging.html?_r=0.

69. Ibid.

70. GreenBlue (2014). "History." Retrieved from: http://www.greenblue.org/about/history/.

71. GreenBlue (2014). "COMPASS: Comparative Packaging Assessment." Retrieved from: http://www.sustainablepackaging.org/content/?type=5&id=compass-comparative-packaging-assessment.

72. Seventh Generation (2014). "Supply Chain Sustainability and Life Cycle Assessment." Presentation at MIT.

73. Pouches for automatic dishwasher packs and laundry powder packs are able to be recycled because they are solid pouches, unlike the liquid hand wash and dish washer soap.

74. Seventh Generation (2012). "Corporate Consciousness Report." Retrieved from: http://2013.7genreport.com.

75. Kao (2012). "Attack Changed the History of Laundry Detergent." Retrieved from: http://www.kao.co.jp/rd/eng/products/household/details.html/.

76. Japan for Sustainability (2012). "Consumer Driven Policy—Making Good Products with Integrity: Toward a Sustainable Japan—Corporations at Work," Article Series No. 31. Retrieved from: http://www.japanfs.org/en_/business/corporations31.html.

77. Kao promotional materials called it "a size that can be carried easily with one hand."

78. M. Fujiwara (2011). "Innovation by Defining Failures under Environmental and Competitive Pressures: A Case Study of the Laundry Detergent Market in Japan." Asia Research Center: Denmark.

79. Soon Neo Lim, "Even with Soap, Less Can Be More: Marketing: Super-concentrated Detergents in Recyclable Packages Have Hit West Coast Stores. They Already Command 90% of the Japanese Market," *Los Angeles Times*, December 26, 1990. Retrieved from: http://articles.latimes.com/1990-12-26/business/fi-6641_1_super-concentrated-detergent/.

80. About.com (2012). "Tide Laundry Detergent through the Decades." Retrieved from: http://laundry.about.com/od/laundrydetergents/ss/Tide-Laundry-Detergent-Through-The-Decades_4.htm.

81. Ibid.

82. I. Breskin, "Consumers Resist Increased Liquid Concentration," *Chemical Week* 156, no. 3 (1995): 39.

83. Ibid.

84. Edward Humes. *Force of Nature: The Unlikely Story of Wal-Mart's Green Revolution* (New York: HarperBusiness, 2011).

85. Kathy Claffey, "P&G's Detergent Concentration Shift." Presentation at MIT CTL annual Crossroads conference (2010).

86. P&G, CTL. "Building Supply Chains That Deliver Sustainability." 2010 Crossroads.

87. Walmart (2008). "Walmart to Sell Only Concentrated Products in Liquid Laundry Detergent Category by May 2008." Retrieved from: http://news.walmart.com/news-archive/2007/09/26/-to-sell-only-concentrated-products-in-liquid-laundry-detergent-category-by-may-2008.

88. Awareness Into Action (2011). "Save More. Live Better: Wal-Mart's 360 Approach: Reducing Waste and Switching to Sustainable Technologies to Save Money and Increase Profits." Retrieved from: http://www.awarenessintoaction.com/whitepapers/-Supply-Chain-Packaging-Scorecard-sustainability.html.

89. http://www.bbc.com/news/business-29543834.

90. Dell (2014). "Green Packaging & Shipping: Bamboo." Retrieved from http://www.dell.com/learn/us/en/uscorp1/corp-comm/bamboo-packaging?c=us&l=en&s=corp&cs=uscorp1.

91. Interview with Oliver Campbell, 2014.

92. http://www.bbc.com/news/business-29543834.

93. See: www.ecovativedesign.com.

94. http://www.plasticsnews.com/article/20131112/NEWS/131119978/sealed-air-reopening-iowa-plant-to-make-fungi-based-packaging.

95. Joint Nature Conservation Committee, DEFRA, U.K. (2014). "Mushrooms Wrap Up Plastic Packaging." Retrieved from: http://jncc.defra.gov.uk/page-5784. Accessed July 2014.

96. Dell (2014). "Green Packaging & Shipping: Mushroom Packaging." Retrieved from: http://www.dell.com/learn/us/en/uscorp1/corp-comm/mushroom -packaging.

97. http://www.bbc.com/news/business-29543834.

98. http://i.dell.com/sites/doccontent/corporate/corp-comm/en/Documents/fy15 -cr-report.pdf.

99. http://iowapublicradio.org/post/biomaterials-breathe-new-life-vacant -cryovac-plant.

100. http://www.plasticsnews.com/article/20131112/NEWS/131119978/sealed -air-reopening-iowa-plant-to-make-fungi-based-packaging.

101. http://www.nhtsa.gov/fuel-economy.

102. http://www.sgtorrice.com/files/Pages/News/2015-Regional-Standards -Cooling-Heating%20Products-rev1.pdf.

103. https://www.energystar.gov/ia/products/lighting/cfls/downloads/EISA _Backgrounder_FINAL_4-11_EPA.pdf.

104. Lucas Davis and Gilbert Metcalf, "Does Better Information Lead to Better Choice? Evidence from Energy Efficiency Labels," NBER Working Paper No 20720, November 2014.

105. Chris Mooney, "Why It's Not Okay to Have a Second Refrigerator," *Washington Post*, November 26, 2014.

106. Joanna Mauer, Andrew deLaski, Steven Nadel, Anthony Fryer, and Rachel Young, "Better Appliances: An Analysis of Performance, Features, and Price as Efficiency Has Improved," American Council for an Energy Efficient Economy Report No. A132, May 2013.

107. http://www.consumerreports.org/cro/news/2011/03/come-on-new-yor k-times-washers-can-be-green-and-efficient/index.htm.

108. https://www.energystar.gov/index.cfm?c=monitors.lcd.

109. See Table 2-1 in the US EPA Trends report: http://www.fueleconomy.gov/ feg/pdfs/420r13011_EPA_LD_FE_2013_TRENDS.pdf.

110. Dana Oliver, "Dry Shampoo: The Dos and Don'ts of Skipping the Sud," *Huffington Post*, April 6, 2014. Retrieved from: http://www.huffingtonpost .com/2012/04/06/dry-shampoo_n_1395302.html.

111. Unilever Sustainable Living (2014). "Reducing GHG in Consumer Use." Retrieved from: http://www.unilever.com/sustainable-living-2014/reducing-en vironmental-impact/greenhouse-gases/reducing-ghg-in-consumer-use/. Accessed August 2014.

112. UN Global Compact Report (2012). "Michelin Performance and Responsibility." Retrieved from: http://unglobalcompact.org/system/attachments/21304/ original/PRMdata_Grenelle2_2012-Registration-Document.pdf?1365610917.

113. http://shradertireandoil.com/blog/10-reasons-to-convert-to-michelin-x-one -tires.

114. Carbon Disclosure Project, CDP 2013 Investor CDP 2012 Information Request BASF SE.

115. https://www.basf.com/documents/corp/en/about-us/publications/reports/2014/BASF_Report_2013.pdf.

116. BusinessWire (2005). "GE Launches Ecomagination to Develop Environmental Technologies; Company-Wide Focus on Addressing Pressing Challenges. Retrieved from: http://www.businesswire.com/news/home/20050509005663/en/GE-Launches-Ecomagination-Develop-Environmental-Technologies-Company-Wide#.U8UcCFa7Awc.

117. http://www.greentechmedia.com/articles/read/natural-gas-at-heart-of-ges-10b-ecomagination-boost.

118. GE (2014). "GE Renews Ecomagination Commitments." Retrieved from: http://www.genewscenter.com/Press-Releases/GE-Renews-Ecomagination-Commitments-454d.aspx. Accessed July 2014.

119. Sheila Bonini and Steven Swartz, "Bringing Discipline to Your Sustainability Initiatives," *McKinsey & Company, Sustainability & Resource Productivity*, August 2014.

120. http://www.latimes.com/business/la-fi-hy-elon-musk-defends-subsidies-20150601-htmlstory.html.

121. Tim Higgins and Charles Rollet, "Tesla Sales Fall to Zero in Hong Kong after Government Tax Break is Slashed," *Wall Street Journal*, July 9, 2017.

122. Marty Padgett, "Toyota Prius: A Brief History in Time," *Green Car Reports*, September 10, 2008. Retrieved from: http://www.greencarreports.com/news/1014178_toyota-prius-a-brief-history-in-time.

123. https://www.fueleconomy.gov/feg/Find.do?action=sbs&id=37825&id=37626.

124. For example, assuming a 13-years life for the average US car (see: https://en.wikipedia.org/wiki/Car_longevity), the number of miles required to break even are 2.6 times higher if the discount rate is 3 percent and 4.7 times higher at a discount rate of 5 percent.

125. Slate (2008). "Tank vs. Hybrid." Retrieved from: http://www.slate.com/articles/health_and_science/the_green_lantern/2008/03/tank_vs_hybrid.html.

126. Chris Demorro, "Prius Outdoes Hummer in Environmental Damage," *The Recorder*, March 7, 2007. Retrieved from: http://www.freerepublic.com/focus/f-news/1904448/posts.

127. Ibid.

128. http://pacinst.org/app/uploads/2013/02/hummer_vs_prius3.pdf.

129. https://thinkprogress.org/prius-easily-beats-hummer-in-life-cycle-energy-use-dust-to-dust-report-has-no-basis-in-fact-58001d2e5658.

130. http://www.thecarconnection.com/tips-article/1010861_prius-versus-hummer-exploding-the-myth.

131. T. Nonaka and M. Nakano, "Study of Popularization Policy of Clean Energy Vehicles Using Life Cycle Assessment." *Next Generation Infrastructure Systems for Eco-Cities* (Shenzhen, 2010), pp. 1–6.

132. http://www.pnas.org/content/108/40/16554.abstract.

133. Mike Ramsey, "Ford Projects Up to 20% Mileage Gain in F-150," *Wall Street Journal*, September 30, 2014.

134. http://www.livescience.com/22277-energy-footprint-cars-ria.html.

135. J. Sullivan, R. Williams, S. Yester, E. Cobas-Flores et al., "Life Cycle Inventory of a Generic US Family Sedan Overview of Results USCAR AMP Project," SAE Technical Paper 982160, 1998, doi:10.4271/982160.

136. S. Raykar, "Analysis of Energy Use and Carbon Emissions from Automobile Manufacturing," A thesis in the MIT Department of Mechanical Engineering, June 2015. https://dspace.mit.edu/handle/1721.1/100098.

137. http://www3.epa.gov/ttncatc1/dir1/fnoxdoc.pdf.

138. John German, "Volkswagen's Defeat Device Scandal." Transportation Economics, Energy and the Environment Conference, The Michigan League, Ann Arbor, October 30, 2015. Lecture. Retrieved from: https://www.youtube.com/watch?v=swBvfSy4BMo&feature=youtu.be. Accessed March 11, 2016.

139. Guilbert Gates, Jack Ewing, Karl Russell, and Derek Watkins, "How Volkswagen Is Grappling with Diesel Deception," *The New York Times*, updated March 16, 2017. Retrieved from: http://www.nytimes.com/interactive/2015/business/international/vw-diesel-emissions-scandal-explained.html?_r=0.

140. http://www.bbc.com/news/business-34324772.

141. http://fortune.com/2015/09/23/volkswagen-stock-drop/.

142. http://www.roadandtrack.com/car-culture/news/a27809/volkswagen-diesel-scandal-could-lead-to-48-billion-in-fines/.

143. http://www.wsj.com/articles/volkswagen-faces-south-korean-ban-on-vehicle-sales-1470105191.

144. Aruna Viswanatha, William Boston, and Mike Spector, "US Indicted Six Volkswagen Executives in Emissions Scandal," *Wall Street Journal*, January 11, 2017. Retrieved from: http://www.wsj.com/articles/volkswagen-pleads-guilty-in-u-s-emissions-scam-1484159603.

145. David Rogers, "Rising Global Middle Classes Pose Huge Resource Threat," *Global Construction Review*, May 8, 2014.

146. Herman Miller (2013). "Aeron Disassembly for Recycling." Retrieved from: http://www.hermanmiller.com/content/dam/hermanmiller/documents/environmental/recycling/Aeron_Chairs_Recycling_Instructions.pdf.

147. Herman Miller (n.d.). "Mirra Seating Material Content and Recyclability." Retrieved from: http://www.hermanmiller.com/content/dam/hermanmiller/documents/environmental/other/Material_Content_and_Recyc-Mirra.pdf.

148. Herman Miller (2013). "Awards and Recognitions: Product." Retrieved from: http://www.hermanmiller.com/about-us/who-is-herman-miller/awards-and-recognition/product.html.

149. Herman Miller (2013). "rePurpose Program." Retrieved from: http://www.hermanmiller.com/about-us/our-values-in-action/environmental-advocacy/repurpose-program.html.

150. Lorna Thorpe, "Steelcase 'Closes the Loop' on Textile Waste," *The Guardian*, May 16, 2013. Retrieved from: http://www.theguardian.com/sustainable-business/steelcase-closes-loop-textile-waste. Accessed August 2014.

151. In 2015 EMC was acquired by Dell in the largest deal in tech history.

152. EMC (2013). "Material and Resources Use." Retrieved from: http://www.emc.com/corporate/sustainability/sustaining-ecosystems/eol.htm.

153. Ibid.

154. Interview with Benjamin Ezra, Principal Program Manager of EMC's Global Product Take Back, 2013.

155. Interface Flor (2007). RePrise Collection Brochure. Interface products.

156. Integral. Ray Anderson's Personal and Company Vision. Retrieved from: http://www.integral.org.au/ray-andersons-personal-and-company-vision.

157. Ray Anderson, *Mid-Course Correction: Toward a Sustainable Enterprise: The Interface Model* (White River Junction, VT: Chelsea Green Publishing Company, 1998).

158. Lorna Thorpe, "InterfaceFlor—Closing the Loop in the Manufacturing Process," *The Guardian*, May 26, 2011. Retrieved from: http://www.theguardian.com/sustainable-business/closing-loop-manufacturing-process-reduce-waste.

159. YouTube (2012). "I AM Mission Zero." Retrieved from: http://www.youtube.com/watch?v=chPD3g4dMJI.

160. Carpet Recovery (2008). "Carpet Cycle, InterFace Flor Named CARE Recyclers of the Year." Retrieved from: http://www.carpetrecovery.org/070509_CARE_Conference.php.

161. It is important to note that the service model was not quickly adopted by customers and took many years of work before there was adoption of this changed model for carpet use.

Notes to Chapter 9

1. http://fortune.com/2015/10/14/whole-foods-retail-software/.

2. Lucy Atkinson, "'Wild West' of Eco-Labels: Sustainability Claims are Confusing Consumers," *The Guardian*, July 4, 2014. Retrieved from: http://www.theguardian.com/sustainable-business/eco-labels-sustainability-trust-corporate-government.

3. http://www.iso.org/iso/environmental-labelling.pdf.

4. James Kantor, "Does Carbon Labeling Confuse Consumers?" *The New York Times*, August 25, 2009. Retrieved from: http://green.blogs.nytimes.com/2009/08/25/does-carbon-labeling-confuse-consumers/.

5. Ibid.

6. Ibid.

7. Virginie Helias, Director, Sustainable Brand Development, P&G. Presentation at the MIT CTL Environmentally Sustainable Supply Chains Roundtable, Cincinnati, Ohio, January 13, 2015.

8. Ian Quinn, "'Frustrated' Tesco Ditches Eco-Labels," *The Grocer*, January 28, 2012. Retrieved from: http://www.thegrocer.co.uk/companies/supermarkets/tesco/frustrated-tesco-ditches-eco-labels/225502.article.

9. Cone Communications (2013). "2013 Cone Communications/Echo Global CSR Study." Retrieved from: http://www.conecomm.com/global-csr-study. Accessed April 1, 2015.

10. Stacy Mitchell, "Walmart's Promised Green Product Rankings Fall off the Radar," *Grist*, November 22, 2011. Retrieved from: http://grist.org/business-technology/2011-11-21-walmart-promised-green-product-rankings-fall-off-radar/.

11. http://www.marketingcharts.com/traditional/how-important-is-green-to-consumers-38073/.

12. E. Golan, et al., "Economics of Food Labeling," *Journal of Consumer Policy* 24 (2001): 117–184.

13. Ecolabel Index Website (2013). "Ecolabel Index: About." Retrieved from: http://www.ecolabelindex.com/about/.

14. Ecolabel Index Website (2014). "Ecolabel Index: Ecolabels." Retrieved from: www.ecolabelindex.com/ecolabels/.

15. Interview with Dr. Anastasia O'Rourke, September 12, 2012.

16. http://sinsofgreenwashing.org/index35c6.pdf, p. 20.

17. M. Delmas and L. Grant, "Eco-Labeling Strategies and Price-Premium: The Wine Industry Puzzle," *Business and Society* 53, no. 1 (2010): 6–44.

18. D. Gromet, et al. "Political Ideology Affects Energy-Efficiency Attitudes and Choices," *Proceedings of National Academy of Sciences of the United States of America* 110, no. 23 (2013): 9314–9319.

19. S. Yang, et al, "Consumer Willingness to Pay for Fair Trade Coffee: A Chinese Case Study," *Journal of Agricultural and Applied Economics* 44 (2012): 21–34.

20. Ibon Galarraga and Anil Markandya, "Economic Techniques to Estimate the Demand for Sustainable Products: A Case Study for Fair Trade and Organic Coffee in the United Kingdom." *Economia Agraria y Recursos Naturales* 4, no. 7 (2004): 109–134.

21. T. B. Bjørner, L. G. Hansen, and C. S. Russell, "Environmental Labeling and Consumers' Choice—An Empirical Analysis of the Effect of the Nordic Swan," *Journal of Environmental Economics and Management* 47 no. 3 (2004): 411–434.

22. Ibid.

23. http://www.sustainablebrands.com/news_and_views/stakeholder_trends_insights/sustainable_brands/eu_study_finds_sustainability_understa.

24. Interview with Keith Sutter, January 31, 2013.

25. http://www.nielsen.com/us/en/press-room/2014/global-consumers-are-willing -to-put-their-money-where-their-heart-is.html. Accessed June 17, 2014.

26. Edgar Blanco and Yossi Sheffi, "Green Logistics," in Yan Bouchery, Tarkan Tan, Jan Fransoo, and Charles Corbett (eds.), *Sustainable Supply Chains* (New York: Springer-Verlag, 2016).

27. Phillip Nelson, "Information and Consumer Behavior," *Journal of Political Economy*, 78(2) (1970): 311–329.

28. M. Darby and E. Karni, "Free Competition and the Optimal Amount of Fraud" *Journal of Law and Economics* 16, no. 1 (1973): 67–88.

29. Ibid.

30. Pier Luigi Sigismondi, Chief Supply Chain Officer, Unilever, Visit and Presentation at MIT, September 27, 2013.

31. Unilever HBR case study, http://www.hbs.edu/faculty/Pages/item.aspx ?num=41262.

32. R. Henderson and F. Nellemann (2011). "Sustainable Tea at Unilever." Harvard Business Case study.

33. Nicholas Institute for Environmental Policy Solutions (2010). "An Overview of Ecolabels and Sustainability Certifications in the Global Marketplace." Duke University.

34. http://www.rainforest-alliance.org/marketing/marks.

35. Nordic Ecolabelling (2014). "The Nordic Ecolabel—The Official Ecolabel in the Nordic Countries." Retrieved from: http://www.nordic-ecolabel.org/about/.

36. Interview with Keith Sutter, Senior Product Director for the Sustainability arm of Johnson & Johnson, March 6, 2013.

37. Interview with Ann Bailey, 2012.

38. Energy Star website (2013). "How a Product Earns the ENERGY STAR Label." Retrieved from: http://www.energystar.gov/index.cfm?c=products.pr _how_earn.

39. EPA (2012). "Energy Star Products: 20 Years of Helping America Save Energy, Save Money and Protect the Environment." Retrieved from: http://www.energystar .gov/ia/products/downloads/ES_Anniv_Book_030712_508compliant_v2.pdf.

40. Ibid.

41. http://www.forbes.com/2004/05/18/cz_jf_0518mpg.html.

42. EPA (2010). "Environmental Protection Agency Fuel Economy Label: Literature Review." Environmental Protection Agency and Department of Transportation, Retrieved from: http://www.epa.gov/fueleconomy/label/420r10906.pdf.

43. GPO (2007). "The Energy Independence and Security Act of 2007." Retrieved from: http://www.gpo.gov/fdsys/pkg/BILLS-110hr6enr/pdf/BILLS-110hr6enr.pdf.

44. EPA (2013). "Green Vehicle Guide: About the Ratings." Retrieved from: www.epa.gov/greenvehicles/Aboutratings.do.

45. EPA (2013). "Emission and Fuel Economy Test Data." Retrieved from: http:// www.epa.gov/otaq/testdata.htm.

46. More information is available at US Department of Energy (2013). "Gasoline Vehicles:LearnMoreAbouttheNewLabel."Retrievedfrom:www.fueleconomy.gov/ feg/label/learn-more-gasoline-label.shtml.

47. http://www.consumer.ftc.gov/articles/0072-shopping-home-appliances -use-energyguide-label.

48. Lucas Davis and Gilbert Metcalf, "Does Better Information Lead to Better Choices? Evidence from Energy-Efficiency Labels," NBER Working Paper 20720, November 2014. Retrieved from: http://www.nber.org/papers/w20720.

49. Joanna Mauer, Andrew deLaski, Steven Nadel, Anthony Fryer, and Rachel Young, "Better Appliances: An Analysis of Performance, Features, and Price as Efficiency Has Improved," American Council for an Energy Efficient Economy, Report Number A132, May 2013.

50. Stephanie Strom, "Has 'Organic' Been Oversized?" *The New York Times*, July 7, 2012. Retrieved from: http://www.nytimes.com/2012/07/08/business/organi c-food-purists-worry-about-big-companies-influence.html?pagewanted=all&_r =0.

51. Kimberly Kindy and Lyndsey Layto, "Integrity of Federal 'Organic' Label is Questioned," *Washington Post*, July 3, 2009. Retrieved from: http://articles .washingtonpost.com/2009-07-03/news/36836942_1_organic-label-organic -products-usda-organic.

52. Ibid.

53. Megan Riesz, "Apple Pulls Out of Eco-Friendly Certification, Insists It's Already Green," *Christian Science Monitor*, July 11, 2012. Retrieved from: http:// www.csmonitor.com/Innovation/2012/0711/Apple-pulls-out-of-eco-friendly -certification-insists-it-s-already-green.

54. Philip Elmer-DeWitt, "What Apple Lost by Dropping EPEAT Green Certification" *Fortune*, July 7, 2012. Retrieved from: http://fortune.com/2012/07/07/wha t-apple-lost-by-dropping-epeat-green-certification/.

55. EPA (2010). "Electronic Product Environmental Assessment Tool (EPEAT)." Retrieved from: http://www.epa.gov/epp/pubs/products/epeat.htm.

56. Ecolabel Index (2013). "Ecolabels: EPEAT." Retrieved from: http://www .ecolabelindex.com/ecolabel/epeat.

57. Megan Riesz, "Apple Pulls Out of Eco-Friendly Certification, Insists It's Already Green," *Christian Science Monitor*, July 11, 2012. Retrieved from: http:// www.csmonitor.com/Innovation/2012/0711/Apple-pulls-out-of-eco-friendly-ce rtification-insists-it-s-already-green.

58. Josh Lowensohn, "Apple Reverses Course, Re-Ups with EPEAT Green Standard," *CNET*, July 13, 2012. Retrieved from: http://news.cnet.com/8301-13579 _3-57472035-37/apple-reverses-course-re-ups-with-epeat-green-standard/.

59. Michael McCoy, "Spread of Ecolabels Vexes Cleaning Product Makers," *Chemical and Engineering News* 91, no. 4 (2013): 10–15.

60. Jonathan Bardelline, "Seventh Generation, NatureWorks First to Earn USDA Biobased Label," *GreenBiz*, April 7, 2011. Retrieved from: http://www.greenbiz

.com/news/2011/04/07/seventh-generation-natureworks-among-first-earn-usda -biobased-label.

61. M. Delmas and L. Grant, "Eco-Labeling Strategies and Price-Premium: The Wine Industry Puzzle," *Business and Society* 53, no. 1 (2010): 6–44.

62. D. Gromet, et al. "Political Ideology Affects Energy-Efficiency Attitudes and Choices," *Proceedings of National Academy of Sciences of the United States of America* 110, no. 23 (2013): 9314–9319.

63. http://www.businessweek.com/articles/2014-02-04/mcdonald-s-wants-you-to -watch-how-mcnuggets-are-made#r=shared.

64. McDonald's Chicken McNuggets are small pieces of chicken meat that have been battered and deep-fried.

65. Clorox (2013). Green Works All-Purpose Cleaner. Retrieved from: http:// www.greenworkscleaners.com/products/all-purpose-cleaner/ingredients/.

66. Clorox (2013). Clean-Up Cleaner + Bleach. Retrieved from: http://www.clorox .com/products/clorox-clean-up-cleaner-bleach/.

67. http://www.harvestmark.com/latest-news/press-releases/driscoll%27s -completes-key-milestones-in-clamshell-traceability-program.aspx.

68. http://www.essentialretail.com/news/in-store/article/52f8bd1577911-tesco -lotus-reports-benefits-of-qr-code-technology.

69. http://www.packwebasia.com/production/labels/3068-a-thai-retail-first -tracing-products-with-tesco-lotus-qr-code-system.

70. http://www.top10produce.com/meet_the_growers.

71. http://oregonstate.edu/ua/ncs/archives/2009/feb/pilot-project-consumers-can -track-their-fish-meet-fishermen-bar-code-system.

72. http://www.idigitaltimes.com/buycott-app-how-does-app-help-boycott -companies-357680.

73. Andrew Martin and Elizabeth Rosenthal, "Cold-Water Detergents Get a Cold Shoulder," *The New York Times*, September 16, 2011.

74. http://cdn.pg.com/-/media/PGCOMUS/Documents/PDF/Sustanability_PDF/ sustainability_reports/PG2015SustainabilityReport.pdf?la=en-US&v=1-20160 5111505.

75. P&G Press Release, "P&G 'Take a Load Off" Campaign, Together with Actress Vanessa Lachey, Empowers Consumers Nationwide to Switch to Cold Water Laundry Washing This Earth Day," April 2, 2012. Retrieved from: http:// news.pg.com/press-release/pg-corporate-announcements/pg-take-load-campaig n-together-actress-vanessa-lachey-empow.

76. http://www.purexlaundry.ca/products/detergents/coldwater. Accessed January 2015.

77. Andrew Martin and Elizabeth Rosenthal, "Cold-Water Detergents Get a Cold Shoulder," *The New York Times*, September 16, 2011.

78. Ibid.

79. Ibid.

80. http://www.iprefer30.eu/partners.

81. http://www.businessforpost-2015.org/goal-13-combat-climate-change/.

82. http://walmartstores.com/download/4887.pdf.

83. http://www.businessinsider.com/does-freezing-your-jeans-kill-bacteria -2014-5.

84. Sadie Whitelocks, "Should Real Denim Wearers Ever Wash Their Jeans? Levi's CEO Boasts that He Hasn't Cleaned His 501s for a Year," *Daily Mail*, May 21, 2014. Retrieved from: http://www.dailymail.co.uk/femail/article-2635085/ I-know-sounds-totally-disgusting-Levis-CEO-admits-washed-jeans-YEAR.html.

85. http://us.pg.com/sustainability/environmental_sustainability/brand_efforts.

86. Jessica Lyons Hardcastle, "Tide's Hotel Laundry System Reduces Water Use 40%," *Environmental Leader*, April 29, 2015.

87. Boots (2010). A Holistic Approach to Sustainable Products. The original source is no longer online. Information available at: https://greenlab.mit.edu/sites/ default/files/documents/ Life%20cycle%20analysis.pdf), which shows the 93 percent figure mentioned in the text in graphical form.

88. Ibid.

89. Ethical Corporate (2008). "Carbon Labels—Green Mark Too Far?" Retrieved from: http://www.ethicalcorp.com/business-strategy/carbon-labels-gree n-mark-too-far.

90. Unilever (2014). "Project Sunlight." Retrieved from: https://www.project sunlight.us/?utm_source=google&utm_medium=online+search&utm_term =project+sunlight&utm_campaign=R-Project-Sunlight_Nov2065project +sunlight&utm_campaign=R-Project-Sunlight_Nov2013&gclid=CjwKEA jwns6hBRDTpb_jkbTv1UYSJACBhberyg42OMp20lakUSvklECI4PxEJD4 oq7ulC0YAsYx6JBoC-hzw_wcB&gclsrc=aw.ds.

91. https://www.basf.com/documents/corp/en/about-us/publications/reports/ 2015/BASF_Report_2014.pdf.

92. https://www.basf.com/documents/it/publications/BASF_Report_2014.pdf.

93. https://www.basf.com/documents/corp/en/about-us/publications/reports/ 2015/BASF_Report_2014.pdf.

94. https://www.basf.com/en/company/sustainability/management-and -instruments/sustainable-solution-steering.html.

95. See chapter 4 for further explanation of Grenelle I and II.

96. Institut RSE Management (2012). "The Grenelle II Act in France: a Milestone Towards Integrated Reporting." Archived at: https://www.yumpu.com/en/ document/view/38199171/the-grenelle-ii-act-in-france-a-milestone-towards -capital-institute.

97. BSR (2012). "The Five W's of France's CSR Reporting Law. BSR Special Report."

98. https://www.basf.com/us/en/company/sustainability/environment/water.html.

99. Al Bredenberg, "At Logistics Giant UPS, Sustainability Is about ... Logistics," *IMT Green & Clean Journal*, October 1, 2012. Retrieved from: http://news .thomasnet.com/green_clean/2012/10/01/at-logistics-giant-ups-sustainability-is -about-logistics/.

100. http://www.greenbiz.com/blog/2013/08/19/why-cdp-gri-djsi-stand-out -among-sustainability-frameworks.

101. KPMG (2011). "KPMG International Survey of Corporate Responsibility Reporting." Retrieved from: http://www.kpmg.com/US/en/IssuesAndInsights/ ArticlesPublications/Documents/corporate-responsibility-reporting-2011.pdf.

102. http://www.environmentalleader.com/2015/03/10/gri-cdp-streamlin e-sustainability-reporting/.

103. Oscar Wild, *The Importance of Being Earnest* (1895).

104. http://www.cbc.ca/news/canada/10-worst-household-products-for-green washing-1.1200620.

105. Ibid.

106. Cone Communications (2013). "2013 Cone Communications/Echo Global CSR Study." Retrieved from: http://www.conecomm.com/global-csr-study. Accessed April 1, 2015.

107. Megali Delmas and Vanessa Burbano, "The Drivers of Greenwashing," *California Management Review* 54, no. 1 (2011): 64–87.

108. Paul Nastu, "Fiji Water Releases Carbon Footprint of Products, Challenges Industry," *Environmental Leader*, April 9, 2008. Retrieved from: https://www .environmentalleader.com/2008/04/fiji-water-releases-carbon-footprint-of -products-challenges-industry/.

109. Fiji (2009). Press Releases. Retrieved from: http://www.fijiwater.com/2009/ fiji-water-foundation-plants-forest/.

110. CSR Wire (2008). "Fiji Water Becomes First Bottled Water Company to Release Carbon Footprint of Its Products." Retrieved from: http:// www.csrwire.com/press_releases/15107-FIJI-Water-Becomes-First-Bottled- Water-Company-to-Release-Carbon-Footprint-of-Its-Products.

111. http://www.fastcompany.com/1714334/fiji-water-sued-over-carbon-credi t-greenwashing.

112. Court proceedings of Ayana Hill v. Roll International Corporation, Court of Appeal of California, May 26, 2011.

113. SC Johnson & Co. (2011). Press Release: "SC Johnson Settles Cases Involving Greenlist Labeling." Retrieved from: http://www.scjohnson.com/en/press -room/press-releases/07-08-2011/SC-Johnson-Settles-Cases-Involving -Greenlist-Labeling.aspx.

114. SC Johnson & Co. (2008). Press Release: "Don't Let the Blue Fool You." Retrieved from: http://www.scjohnson.com/en/press-room/press-releases/ 01-17-2008/Don%E2%80%99t-Let-The-Blue-Fool-You.aspx.

115. Vanessa O'Connell, "'Green' Goods, Red Flags," *Wall Street Journal*, April 24, 2010. Retrieved from: https://www.wsj.com/articles/SB1000142405270230 45069045751802107583367310.

116. http://www.scjohnson.com/en/commitment/focus-on/greener-products/greenlist.aspx.

117. "PepsiCo Agrees to Acquire Naked Juice Company." Press release: http://www.prnewswire.com/news-releases/pepsico-agrees-to-acquire-naked-juice-company-56477082.html.

118. Jessica Lyons Hardcastle, "Pepsi Pays $9M, Removes 'All Natural' Naked Juices Label," *Environmental Leader*, July 29, 2013.

119. *Consumer Reports* (2012). "FTC Issues Revised Green Guides." Retrieved from: http://www.consumerreports.org/cro/news/2012/10/ftc-issues-revised-green-guides/index.htm#.

120. FTC (2012). "Green Guides—Part 260—Guides for the use of Environmental Marketing Claims." Federal Trade Commission.

121. Ibid.

122. EPA (2010). "EPA Comments on Proposed Revisions to Green Guides." Retrieved from: http://ftc.gov/os/comments/greenguiderevisions/00288-57070.pdf.

123. http://fairworldproject.org/blogs/rainforest-alliance-is-not-fair-trade/.

124. http://www.rainforest-alliance.org/sites/default/files/publication/pdf/ra-certification-cocoa-cote-divoire-cosa.pdf.

125. Terrachoice (2010). "The Sins of Greenwashing." Underwriters Laboratories.

126. Ibid.

127. Joel Makower, "Is TerraChoice Greenwashing?" *GreenBiz*, November 10, 2010. Retrieved from: http://www.greenbiz.com/blog/2010/11/01/terrachoice-greenwashing.

128. Ibid.

129. Interview with Kathrin Winkler, December 5, 2013.

130. https://www.youtube.com/watch?v=uRGiGbX9lIo.

131. James Hamblin, "A Brewing Problem," *The Atlantic*, March 2, 2015.

132. http://www.motherjones.com/blue-marble/2014/03/coffee-k-cups-green-mountain-polystyrene-plastic.

133. http://www.sciencedirect.com/science/article/pii/S0959652609001474.

134. http://www.keuriggreenmountain.com/~/media/Sustainability/PDF/ReportsDisclosures/Keurig_Fiscal2014_SustainabilityReport.ashx.

135. http://www.sciencedirect.com/science/article/pii/S0959652609001474.

136. *The Economist* (2010). "The Other Oil Spill." Retrieved from: www.economist.com/node/16423833.

137. Lian Pin Koh, Jaboury Ghazoul, Rhett A. Butler, et al., "Wash and Spin Cycle Threats to Tropical Biodiversity," *BIOTROPICA* 42, no. 1 (2010): 62–71.

138. Rhett A. Butler, "Blackwashing by NGOs, Greenwashing by Corporations, Threatens Environmental Progress," Mongabay.com, November 12, 2009.

139. Oliver Balch, "Sobering results for drinks giant Diageo reveal problems of sustainability targets," *The Guardian*, September 3, 2015.

140. Eric M. Lowitt and Jim Grimsley, "Hewlett-Packard: Sustainability as a Competitive Advantage," Accenture Case Study, May 2009.

141. Stephanie Rosenbloom and Michael Barbaro, "Green-Light Specials, Now at Walmart," *The New York Times*, January 24, 2009.

Notes to Chapter 10

1. http://corporate.marksandspencer.com/aboutus/our-heritage.

2. https://about.futurelearn.com/blog/ms-innovation/.

3. Just-style (2009). "Sir Stuart Rose's Five Years as M&S Chief." Retrieved from: http://www.just-style.com/analysis/sir-stuart-roses-five-years-as-ms-chief_id105959 .aspx.

4. http://www.theguardian.com/environment/2007/apr/15/fashion.ethicalliving.

5. http://www.yellowbridge.com/onlinelit/daodejing64.php.

6. Nina Kruschwitz, "How an 'Abundance Mentality' and a CEO's Fierce Resolve Kickstarted CSR at Campbell's Soup," *MIT Sloan Management Review*, August 14, 2012. Retrieved from: http://sloanreview.mit.edu/article/how-an-abundance -mentality-and-a-ceos-fierce-resolve-kickstarted-csr-at-campbell-soup/.

7. Dina Gerdeman, "Pulling Campbell's Out of the Soup," *HBS Working Knowledge*, March 22, 2013. Retrieved from: http://hbswk.hbs.edu/item/7133.html.

8. Google Finance (2014). Campbell Soup Company. Retrieved from: https:// www.google.com/finance?cid=5433.

9. Dina Gerdeman, "Pulling Campbell's Out of the Soup," *HBS Working Knowledge*, March 22, 2013. Retrieved from: http://hbswk.hbs.edu/item/7133.html.

10. CSRWire (2008). "Campbell Appoints David Stangis Vice President Corporate Social Responsibility." Retrieved from: http://www.csrwire.com/press_releases/ 13934-Campbell-Appoints-David-Stangis-Vice-President-Corporate-Social -Responsibility-.

11. Sustainable Plant (2013). "Campbell Soup's Aggressive Waste Reduction Initiatives." Retrieved from: http://www.sustainableplant.com/2013/09/campbell -soup-s-aggressive-waste-reduction-initiatives/.

12. http://www.campbellcsr.com/planet/ and web pages therein.

13. Sustainable Plant (2013). "Campbell Soup's Aggressive Waste Reduction Initiatives." Retrieved from: http://www.sustainableplant.com/2013/09/campbell -soup-s-aggressive-waste-reduction-initiatives/.

14. Nina Kruschwitz, "How an 'Abundance Mentality' and a CEO's Fierce Resolve Kickstarted CSR at Campbell's Soup," *MIT Sloan Management Review*, August 14, 2012. Retrieved from: http://sloanreview.mit.edu/article/how-an

-abundance-mentality-and-a-ceos-fierce-resolve-kickstarted-csr-at-campbell-soup/.

15. Vijay Kanal, "Just How Important is the CEO to Sustainability?" *GreenBiz*, January 31, 2011. Retrieved from: http://www.greenbiz.com/blog/2011/01/31/just-how-important-ceo-sustainability.

16. http://graphics.eiu.com/upload/eb/Enel_Managing_for_sustainability_WEB.pdf.

17. Marc Gunther, "Why eBay is a Green Giant," *GreenBiz*, February 16, 2010. Retrieved from: http://www.greenbiz.com/blog/2010/02/16/why-ebay-green-giant.

18. Interview with Lori Duvall, Global Director of Green, eBay, April 5, 2013.

19. *San Diego Union-Tribune* (2009). "Whitman Says She'd Suspend 'Green Initiative.'" Retrieved from: http://www.utsandiego.com/news/2009/sep/24/whitman-says-shed-suspend-8216green8217-initiative/.

20. Marc Gunther, "Why eBay is a Green Giant," *GreenBiz*, February 16, 2010. Retrieved from: http://www.greenbiz.com/blog/2010/02/16/why-ebay-green-giant.

21. Ibid.

22. Tina Casey, "eBay Bets on Bloom Energy for Green Data Center," *Triple Pundit*, June 25, 2012. Retrieved from: http://www.triplepundit.com/2012/06/ebay-will-use-bloom-energy-biogas-fuel-cells/.

23. http://tech.ebay.com/blog-post/introducing-our-salt-lake-city-data-center-advancing-our-commitment-cleaner-greener.

24. Interview with Lori Duvall, Global Director of Green, eBay, April 5, 2013.

25. Interview with Caitlin Bristol, Global Manager of Green, eBay, April 4, 2013.

26. Interview with Mark Buckley, Staples, December 8, 2013.

27. Dogwood Alliance (2007). "Corporate Campaigns: Working in the Marketplace to Defend Communities & The Environment." Presentation retrieved from: http://www.powershow.com/view/114265-NjAwZ/Corporate_Campaigns_Working_in_the_Marketplace_to_Defend_Communities_powerpoint_ppt_presentation.

28. Staples (2002). "Staples Appoints Mark Buckley Vice President of Environmental Affairs." Retrieved from: http://staples.newshq.businesswire.com/press-release/staples-appoints-mark-buckley-vice-president-environmental-affairs#axzz2lg9BwFRY.

29. EPA (2007). "Interview with Energy Champion: Mark Buckley." Retrieved on June 21, 2016 from: http://www.epa.gov/climateleadership/documents/staples_interview.pdf.

30. Ibid.

31. Staples (2014). "Making More Sustainable Choices: Overview." Retrieved from: http://www.staples.com/sbd/cre/marketing/staples_soul/environment.html.

32. Interview with Keith Sutter, Senior Product Director for the Sustainability arm of Johnson & Johnson, March 6, 2013.

33. Interviews with Tony Dunnage, Group Environmental Engineering Manager, Unilever, February 5, 2013; Jessie Sobel, North American Sustainability Manager, Unilever, May 31, 2013.

34. Stephan Schmidheiny, *Changing Course: A Global Business Perspective on Development and the Environment* (Geneva: World Business Council for Sustainable Development, 1992).

35. https://bus.wisc.edu/knowledge-expertise/newsroom/press-releases/2015/09/10/financial-losses-stemming-from-reputation-damage-theres-an-insurance-policy-for-that.

36. http://nbs.net/wp-content/uploads/NBS-Long-Term-Thinking-ER.pdf.

37. https://www.unilever.com/news/press-releases/2015/Unilever-sees-sustainability-supporting-growth.html.

38. http://www.sustainablebrands.com/digital_learning/slideshow/brand_innovation/how_inform_justify_expand_product_portfolio_shift_favor_.

39. Muhtar Kent and Carter Roberts, "Ensuring There's Water for all," *Politico*, July 15, 2013.

40. Lauren Hepler and Barbara Grady, "Environment as Economic Threat: How Sustainability Redefines Risk," *GreenBiz*, February 4, 2015.

41. Eliza Roberts and Brooke Barton, "Feeding Ourselves Thirsty: How the Food Sector is Managing Global Water Risks" *Ceres Report*, May 2015, p. 46.

42. Trucost (2012). "New PUMA Shoe and T-shirt Impact the Environment by a Third Less than Conventional Products." Retrieved from: http://www.trucost.com/news/156/new-puma-shoe-and-t-shirt-impact-the-environment-by-a-third-less-than-conventional-products.

43. World Wildlife Federation Global (2008). "Unsustainable Cattle Ranching." Retrieved from: http://wwf.panda.org/what_we_do/where_we_work/amazon/problems/unsustainable_cattle_ranching/.

44. Unfortunately, despite repeated requests, TruCost refused to discuss their methodology, leaving the author wondering how they had derived their numbers.

45. PUMA (2011). PUMA's Environmental Profit and Loss Account for the year ended 31 December 2010. Retrieved from: http://glasaaward.org/wp-content/uploads/2014/01/EPL080212final.pdf.

46. Interview with Stefan Seidel, Deputy Head of PUMA Safe Global, February 21, 2014.

47. https://b8f65cb373b1b7b15feb-c70d8ead6ced550b4d987d7c03fcdd1d.ssl.cf3.rackcdn.com/cms/reports/documents/000/001/132/original/CDP_Carbon_Price_report_2016.pdf?1474899276.

48. Nina Kruschwitz, "Who's the Real Audience for Sustainability Efforts?" *MIT Sloan Management Review*, February 24 2013, reprint 54305, p. 4.

49. The phrase is often attributed to Abraham Lincoln responding to critics who blamed him for violating the US Constitution when he suspended habeas corpus during the American Civil War (see: https://en.wikipedia.org/wiki/The

_Constitution_is_not_a_suicide_pact). However, the exact phrase "'suicide pact" was used by Justice Jackson. His exact quote is: "There is danger that, if the court does not temper its doctrinaire logic with a little practical wisdom, it will convert the constitutional Bill of Rights into a suicide pact." See http://www.nytimes .com/2002/09/22/weekinreview/the-nation-suicide-pact.html.

50. Naturally, environmentalists could use this same analogy to say that there are considerations more important than business principles. They would assert that just as the constitutional rights of individuals are subservient to long-term societal survival (Justice Jackson's dissenting view), so, too, the rights of individual businesses are subservient to long-term societal survival.

51. Best Food Forward (2012). "Will the PUMA Leather Ban Deliver Real Environmental Gains?" Retrieved from: http://www.bestfootforward.com/ industry-insights/blog/2012/09/14/will-puma-leather-ban-deliver-real-environ mental-gains/.

52. Interview with Scott Wicker, UPS.

53. UPS (2014). "Alternative Fuel and Advanced Technology." Retrieved from: http://www.responsibility.ups.com/Environment/Alternative+Fuels.

54. http://www.pressroom.ups.com/Fact+Sheets/UPS+Fact+Sheet.

55. Interview with Scott Wicker, UPS.

56. Diane Cardwell, "UPS Agrees to Buy 46 Million Gallons of Renewal Diesel," *The New York Times*, July 30, 2015. Retrieved from: http://www.nytimes.com/2015/ 07/30/business/ups-agrees-to-buy-46-million-gallons-of-renewable-diesel.html.

57. *The Economist* (2008). "Just Good Business," Special Report: Corporation Social Responsibility. January 19, 2008.

58. Jeanne C. Meister and Karie Willyerd, "Mentoring Millennials," *Harvard Business Review*, May 2010.

59. *Bloomberg Businessweek* (August 20, 2006). "Passion for the Planet." Retrieved from: http://www.businessweek.com/stories/2006-08-20/a-passion-for -the-planet.

60. Ere.net Recruiting Intelligence. Retrieved from: http://www.ere.net/2013/05/20/ why-you-cant-get-a-job-recruiting-explained-by-the-numbers/.

61. http://www.inc.com/magazine/201204/tom-foster/the-undiluted-genius-of -dr-bronners.html.

62. Design Council (2006). "Green & Black's: How to Design Your Way to 789% Sales Growth: the Rise and Rise of Green & Black's." Retrieved from: http:// www.designcouncil.org.uk/publications/design-council-magazine-issue-1/ case-studies/green-and-blacks/.

63. Ben Cooper, "Ethical Brands—How Green & Black's Struck Chocolate Gold," Ethical Corporation, May 5, 2009. Retrieved from: http://www.ethicalcorp.com/ business-strategy/ethical-brands-how-green-blacks-struck-chocolate-gold.

64. Dell (2012). "Dell 2020 Legacy of Good." Retrieved from: http://i.dell.com/ sites/doccontent/corporate/corp-comm/en/Documents/2020-plan.pdf.

65. Business Wire (2006). "Dell Tackles Energy Efficiency from Desktop to Data Center." Retrieved from: http://www.businesswire.com/news/home/2006120400 5910/en/Dell-Tackles-Energy-Efficiency-Desktop-Data-Center#.UvQGVP3TLd4.

66. Ariel Schwartz, "Walmart Plans to Cut 20 Million Metric Tons of Greenhouse Gas Emissions from Supply Chain," *Fast Company*, February 25, 2010. Retrieved from: http://www.fastcompany.com/1563121/walmart-plans-cut-20-million-metric -tons-greenhouse-gas-emissions-supply-chain.

67. http://news.walmart.com/news-archive/2015/11/17/walmart-marks -fulfillment-of-key-global-responsibility-commitments.

68. http://www.nestle.com/csv/water/water-efficiency.

69. http://www.ghgprotocol.org.

70. http://sustainability.baxter.com/environment-health-safety/environmental -performance/ghg-emissions-across-value-chain.html.

71. http://fortune.com/2013/08/15/carlos-brito-brewmaster-of-the-universe/.

72. http://www.triplepundit.com/2013/03/anheuser-busch-inbev-met-three-year -environmental-goals/.

73. http://www.ab-inbev.com/social-responsibility/environment/management -system.html.

74. http://www.environmentalleader.com/products/anheuser-busch-inbev -accountability-through-metrics-vpo/.

75. Ibid.

76. WCBSD (2010). "People Matter: Linking Sustainability to Pay." World Business Council for Sustainable Development Issue Brief.

77. Ibid.

78. SC Johnson (2013). "Our Greenlist Process: Better Products for Better Information." Retrieved from: http://www.scjohnson.com/en/commitment/focus-on/ greener-products/greenlist.aspx.

79. WCBSD (2010). "People Matter: Linking Sustainability to Pay." World Business Council for Sustainable Development Issue Brief.

80. Anca Novacovici, "Linking Sustainability Performance to Compensation: A Must for Success," *Huffington Post*, October 8, 2013. Retrieved from: http:// www.huffingtonpost.com/anca-novacovici/post_5817_b_4060647.html.

81. V. G. Narayanan and Ananth Raman, "Aligning Incentives in Supply Chains." *Harvard Business Review* 82, no. 11 (2004): 94–102.

82. WCBSD (2010). "People Matter: Linking Sustainability to Pay." World Business Council for Sustainable Development Issue Brief.

83. National Environmental Education Foundation (2010). "The Business Case for Environmental and Sustainability Employee Education." Retrieved from: https://microedge.com/~/media/Files/PDF/WhitePapers/The_Business_Case_for _Sustainability_Employee_Engagement.ashx.

84. Ellen Weinreb, "The Pros & Cons of Linking Sustainability Successes with Bonuses," *GreenBiz*, January 11, 2012. Retrieved from: http://www.greenbiz.com/blog/2012/01/11/pros-cons-linking-sustainability-successes-bonuses?page=0%2 C0.

85. https://books.google.com/books?id=147UhaLQrPQC&pg=PT97&lpg=PT97 &dq=bonus+johnson+greenlist&source=bl.

86. Interview with Steve Lovejoy, 2014.

87. Ceres (2012). "The Road to 2020: Corporate Progress on the Ceres Roadmap for Sustainability." Retrieved from: https://www.ceres.org/resources/reports/gaining-ground-corporate-progress-ceres-roadmap-sustainability.

88. Glass Lewis (2012). "Greening the Green." Retrieved from: http://www.glasslewis.com/blog/glass-lewis-publishes-greening-the-green-2012-linking-executive-compensation-to-sustainability/.

89. http://www.wri.org/blog/2009/12/fact-sheet-are-you-ready-lacey-act.

90. http://ec.europa.eu/finance/company-reporting/non-financial_reporting/index_en.htm.

91. https://www.sec.gov/rules/interp/2010/33-9106.pdf.

92. http://sustainability.thomsonreuters.com/2014/12/13/executive-perspective-corporate-sustainability-reporting-world-today/.

93. The Clean Air Act is a combination of several US acts (1955, 1963, and 1967). See: EPA (2013). "History of the Clean Air Act." Retrieved from: http://www.epa.gov/air/caa/amendments.html.

94. EPA (2014). "Setting Emissions Standards Based on Technology Performance." Retrieved from: http://www.epa.gov/air/caa/standards_technology.html.

95. Ibid.

96. EPA (2014). "EPA Sets Tier 3 Motor Vehicle Emission and Fuel Standards." Retrieved from: http://www.epa.gov/otaq/documents/tier3/420f14009.pdf.

97. EPA (2010). "40th Anniversary of the Clean Air Act." Retrieved from: http://www.epa.gov/air/caa/40th.html.

98. Michael Greenstone, John A. List, and Chad Syverson (2012). "The Effects of Environmental Regulation on the Competitiveness of US Manufacturing. National Bureau of Economic Research." NBER Working Paper No. 18392.

99. Elisabeth Rosenthal, "By 'Bagging It,' Ireland Rids Itself of a Plastic Nuisance," *The New York Times*, January 31, 2008. Retrieved from: http://www.nytimes.com/2008/01/31/world/europe/31iht-bags.4.9650382.html.

100. http://ec.europa.eu/clima/policies/ets/index_en.htm.

101. Brad Plumer, "Europe's Cap-and-Trade Program is in Trouble. Can it be fixed?" *Washington Post*, April 20, 2013. Retrieved from: https://www.washingtonpost.com/news/wonk/wp/2013/04/20/europes-cap-and-trade-program-is-in-trouble-can-it-be-fixed/?utm_term=.bc345a9e685f.

102. http://ec.europa.eu/environment/waste/rohs_eee/index_en.htm.

103. http://www3.epa.gov/epawaste/hazard/refdocs.htm.

104. Christine Harvey, "Dusky Gopher Frog Habitat Designated in St. Tammany Parish," *The Times-Picayune*, June 15, 2012. Retrieved from: http://www.nola.com/environment/index.ssf/2012/06/dusky_gopher_frog_habitat_desi.html.

105. Ibid.

106. Kim Chatelain, "Frog's 'Critical Habitat' Not Abuse of Federal Power, Court Rules," *The Times-Picayune*, July 5, 2016. Retrieved from: http://www.nola.com/crime/index.ssf/2016/07/court_frogs_critical_habitat_n.html.

107. NOAA Fisheries (2014). "Endangered Species Act." Retrieved from: http://www.nmfs.noaa.gov/pr/laws/esa/.

108. http://corporate.walmart.com/newsroom/company-facts.

109. Stephanie Rosenbloom and Michael Barbaro, "Green-Light Specials, Now at Wal-Mart," *The New York Times*, January 24, 2009. Retrieved from: http://www.nytimes.com/2009/01/25/business/25walmart.html?pagewanted=1&_r=0&ref=sustainableliving.

110. Ann Zimmerman, "Wal-Mart Boss's Unlikely Role: Corporate Defender-in-Chief," *The Wall Street Journal*, July 26, 2005.

111. Amanda Little, "Al Gore Takes his Green Message to Wal-Mart Headquarters," *Grist*, July 20, 2006. Retrieved from: http://grist.org/article/gore-walmart/.

112. Andrew Clark, "Is Wal-Mart Really Going Green?" *The Guardian*, November 6, 2006. Retrieved from: http://www.theguardian.com/environment/2006/nov/06/energy.supermarkets.

113. http://business.edf.org/projects/featured/sustainable-supply-chains/edf-and-walmart-partnership-timeline/.

114. Stephanie Rosenbloom and Michael Barbaro, "Green-Light Specials, Now at Wal-Mart," *The New York Times*, January 24, 2009. Retrieved from: http://www.nytimes.com/2009/01/25/business/25walmart.html?pagewanted=1&_r=0&ref=sustainableliving.

115. Diane Regas, "Walmart, EDF and 3 Reasons to Think Bigger on Collaboration," *GreenBiz*, March 10, 2016. Retrieved from: https://www.greenbiz.com/article/walmart-edf-and-3-reasons-think-bigger-collaboration.

116. Stacy Mitchell, "Walmart's Promised Green Product Rankings Fall off the Radar," *Grist*, November 22, 2011. Retrieved from: http://grist.org/business-technology/2011-11-21-walmart-promised-green-product-rankings-fall-off-radar/.

117. Interview with Michelle Harvey, EDF, Bentonville Office.

118. Interview with Jon Johnson, The Sustainability Consortium.

119. Stephanie Clifford, "Unexpected Ally Helps Wal-Mart Cut Waste," *The New York Times*, April 13, 2012. Retrieved from: http://www.nytimes.com/2012/04/14/business/wal-mart-and-environmental-fund-team-up-to-cut-waste.html.

120. YouGov BrandIndex (2013). "Countries." Retrieved from: http://www.brandindex.com/countries.

121. Stephanie Clifford, "Unexpected Ally Helps Wal-Mart Cut Waste," *The New York Times*, April 13, 2012. Retrieved from: http://www.nytimes.com/2012/04/14/business/wal-mart-and-environmental-fund-team-up-to-cut-waste.html.

122. Google Finance. Wal-Mart Stores, Inc.—NYSE:WMT. Retrieved from: https://www.google.com/finance?q=NYSE:WMT&sa=X&ei=ENjBUaqNDa 620AGW-4GwCw&ved=0CC8Q2AE.

123. Scott Poynton, "Dancing With Devils," *Huffington Post Green*, March 18, 2011. Retrieved from: http://www.huffingtonpost.com/scott-poynton/dancing -with-devils_b_837442.html?view=print&comm_ref=false.

124. Interview with Scott Poynton, founder of TFT, November 15, 2013.

125. TFT (2013). "Palm Oil Group." Retrieved from: http://www.tft-forests.org/ product-groups/pages/?p=6277.

126. Greenpeace (2010). "Sweet Success for Kit Kat Campaign: You Asked, Nestlé has Answered. Retrieved from: http://www.greenpeace.org/international/ en/news/features/Sweet-success-for-Kit-Kat-campaign/.

127. Food Navigator (2013). "Nestlé Releases Deforestation Guides for Commodity Sourcing." Retrieved from: http://www.foodnavigator.com/Market-Trends/ Nestle-releases-deforestation-guides-for-commodity-sourcing.

128. EDF & GEMI (2008). "Guide to Successful Corporate-NGOP Partnerships." Retrieved from: http://www.gemi.org/resources/gemi-edf%20guide.pdf.

129. http://www.cjr.org/the_observatory/nyt_obscures_wal-mart_edf_link.php.

130. EDF (2013). Why EDF celebrates Walmart's environmental gains. Retrieved from: http://www.edf.org/blog/2013/11/14/why-edf-celebrates-walmarts -environmental-gains.

131. Stacy Mitchell, "EDF Sells Green Cred to Walmart for the Low, Low Price of $66 million," *Grist*, November 6, 2013. Retrieved from: http://grist.org/ business-technology/edf-sells-green-cred-to-walmart-for-the-low-low-price-of -66-million/.

132. http://www.tft-earth.org/who-we-work-with/members/.

133. Greenpeace (2013). "Certifying Destruction: Why Consumer Companies Need to Go Beyond the RSPO to Stop Forest Destruction." Retrieved from: http:// www.greenpeace.org/international/en/publications/Campaign-reports/Forests -Reports/Certifying-Destruction/.

134. Leon Kaye, "More Brands Dump Sustainable Forest Initiative's Paper Certification Program," *Triple Pundit*, May 2, 2013. Retrieved from: http:// www.triplepundit.com/2013/05/sustainable-forest-initiative-program/.

135. ForestEthics (2013). "Expose 'Sustainable' Forestry Initiative's Greenwash." Retrieved from: http://forestethics.org/sustainable-forestry-initiative.

136. ForestEthics (2013). "Why is 3M Stuck on SFI: Because it Greenwashes its Forest Destruction." Retrieved from: http://action.forestethics.org/ea-action/ action?ea.client.id=1818&ea.campaign.id=22952&ea.tracking.id=web.

137. National Coffee Association (2013). "Coffee Reporter News: NCA Creates Sustainability Task Force." Retrieved from: http://www.ncausa.org/custom/headlines/headlinedetails.cfm?id=889&returnto=1.

138. Starbucks (2014). "Ethically Sourced Cocoa." Retrieved from: http://www.starbucks.ph/responsibility/ethical-sourcing/cocoa-sourcing.

139. Starbucks (2013). "Our Relationships: Cultivating Change—One Relationship at a Time." Retrieved from: http://www.starbucks.com/responsibility/learn-more/relationships.

140. Interview with Jeanette Skjelmose, IKEA.

141. http://www.ft.com/cms/s/2/8e42bdc8-0838-11e4-9afc-00144feab7de.html.

142. National Environmental Education Foundation (2009). "The Engaged Organization: Corporate Employee Environmental Education Survey and Case Study Findings." Business & Environment Research Report.

143. Ibid.

144. Stonyfield Farm (2013). Mission Action Program Teams. From the Inside Out, 2013 version of Stonyfield website.

145. Stonyfield Farms Blog (2012)."Walking the Talk: Stonyfields' MAP Team Adds Light Tubes." Retrieved from http://www.stonyfield.com/blog/map_series_light-tubes/.

146. National Environmental Education Foundation (2009). "The Engaged Organization: Corporate Employee Environmental Education Survey and Case Study Findings." Business & Environment Research Report.

147. Ibid.

148. The Frances Hesselbein Leadership Institute (2002). "Profits with a Conscience." Retrieved from: http://www.hesselbeininstitute.org/knowledgecenter/journal.aspx?ArticleID=115.

149. *Mother Nature Network* (2010). "Interview with Stonyfield CEO Gary Hirschberg: 'Everybody can win.'" Retrieved from: http://www.mnn.com/lifestyle/responsible-living/blogs/interview-with-stonyfield-ceo-gary-hirshberg-everybody-can-win.

150. Jen Boynton, "Scaling Stonyfield Yogurt," *Triple Pundit*, April 18, 2012. Retrieved from: http://www.triplepundit.com/2012/04/economics-stonyfield-yogurt/.

151. Asa Bennett, "Q&A: Green & Black's Co-founder Jo Fairley," *London Loves Business*, April 28, 2013. Retrieved from: http://www.londonlovesbusiness.com/entrepreneurs/famous-entrepreneurs/qa-green-and-blacks-co-founder-jo-fairley/5382.article.

152. In 2010, Kraft acquired Cadbury for $19.6 billion.

153. Rebecca Smithers, "Green & Black's Meets Fairtrade Pledge," *The Guardian*, March 8, 2011. Retrieved from http://www.theguardian.com/environment/2011/mar/08/green-blacks-fairtrade-pledge.

154. Asa Bennett, "Q&A: Green & Black's Co-founder Jo Fairley," *London Loves Business*, April 28, 2013. Retrieved from: http://www.londonlovesbusiness.com/entrepreneurs/famous-entrepreneurs/qa-green-and-blacks-co-founder-jo-fairley/5382.article.

155. Rebecca Smithers, "Green & Black's Meets Fairtrade Pledge," *The Guardian*, March 8, 2011. Retrieved from http://www.theguardian.com/environment/2011/mar/08/green-blacks-fairtrade-pledge.

156. Cahal Milmo, "Cadbury Deal Turns Sour for Green & Black's," *The Independent*, January 18, 2011. Retrieved from: http://www.independent.co.uk/news/business/analysis-and-features/cadbury-deal-turns-sour-for-green-amp-blacks-2187044.html.

157. http://www.foodbusinessnews.net/articles/news_home/Business_News/2016/09/Mondelez_keys_in_on_three_grow.aspx?ID={506125E7-CEBF-4179-B15C-B471BDBFCBD2}&cck=1.

158. Dell (2014). "Dell Reconnect: Donate Any Brand of Computer to Goodwill." Retrieved from: http://www.dell.com/learn/us/en/uscorp1/corp-comm/us-goodwill-reconnect.

159. Sustainable Brands (2012). "Accelerating Reduction: EMC Advances Practice on Climate-Stabilizing Targets." Retrieved from: http://www.sustainablebrands.com/news_and_views/new-metrics/accelerating-reduction-emc-advances-practice-climate-stabilizing-targets.

160. Interview with EMC.

161. EMC (2012). "Key Performance Indicators Dashboard." Retrieved from: http://www.emc.com/collateral/sustainability/emc_sustainability_kpi_dashboard.pdf.

162. EMC (2014). "Efficient Products." Retrieved from: http://www.emc.com/corporate/sustainability/sustaining-ecosystems/products.htm.

163. Richard Murphy, "The race to Remove Toxic Chemicals from Mission Critical Systems," *The Guardian*, September 10, 2015.

164. Ibid.

165. Email correspondence with Mike Barry, Director of Plan A, Marks and Spencer, April 28, 2017.

166. http://www.ethicalcorp.com/business-strategy/marks-spencer-grade-progress.

167. http://corporate.marksandspencer.com/media/press-releases/archive/2007/15012007_marksspencerlaunchesplana200mecoplan.

168. "Sir Stuart Rose on the Changing Role of Business Leaders," *The Guardian*, March 29, 2012. Retrieved from: http://www.theguardian.com/sustainable-business/sir-stuart-rose-changing-role-business-leaders.

169. Ibid.

170. Marks & Spencer (2007). "Marks & Spencer Launches 'Plan A'—200m Euro 'Eco-plan.' Retrieved from: http://corporate.marksandspencer.com/media/press-releases/archive/2007/15012007_marksspencerlaunchesplana200mecoplan.

171. http://ethicalperformance.com/PDFs/2007_hwdb_report.pdf.

172. Interview with Mike Barry, Director of Sustainable Business (Plan A), Marks & Spencer, November 3, 2015.

173. Jenny Purt, "M&S: Supply Chain Champions of Sustainable Business," *The Guardian*, January 10, 2013. Retrieved from: http://www.theguardian.com/sustainable-business/marks-and-spencer-supply-chain-sustainable-business.

174. Marks & Spencers (2012). "The Key Lessons from the Plan A Business Case." Retrieved from: http://corporate.marksandspencer.com/documents/publications/2012/plan_a_report_2012.pdf.

175. http://www.carbontrust.com/news/2014/09/sustainability-leaders-munish-datta-head-of-facilities-management-plan-a-marks-and-spencer.

176. https://dspace.lib.cranfield.ac.uk/bitstream/1826/6824/1/Embedding_Corporate_Responsibility_and_Sustainability.pdf.

177. http://www.accountability.org/about-us/news/cr-leaders-corner/mike-barry.html.

178. http://www.accountability.org/about-us/news/cr-leaders-corner/mike-barry.html.

179. https://www.cdp.net/CDPResults/carbon-pricing-in-the-corporate-world.pdf.

180. http://corporate.marksandspencer.com/investors/e911816df3514e579caf373c9fde82c0.

181. http://www.greeneventbook.com/wp-content/uploads/2015/05/pas-2060-specification-for-the-demonstration-of-carbon-neutrality.pdf.

182. http://corporate.marksandspencer.com/investors/233f6addda26424e84e818831c2a7e68.

183. Email correspondence with Mike Barry, Director of Sustainable Business (Plan A), Marks & Spencer, April 28, 2017.

184. Rob Bailes, "Sustainability Commercialized: Marks & Spencer—Helping Suppliers Get with the Plan," *Ethical Corporation*, September 2012. Retrieved from: http://www.ethicalcorp.com/business-strategy/sustainability-commercialised-marks-spencer-helping-suppliers-get-plan.

185. Interview with Mike Barry, Director of Sustainable Business (Plan A), Marks & Spencer, November 3, 2015.

186. Civilsociety.co.uk (2013). "M&S and Oxfam Voted Most Admired Charity-Corporate Partnership." Retrieved from: http://www.civilsociety.co.uk/fundraising/news/content/16061/mands_and_oxfam_voted_most_admired_charity-corporate_partnership.

187. http://www.greeneventbook.com/wp-content/uploads/2015/05/pas-2060-specification-for-the-demonstration-of-carbon-neutrality.pdf.

188. http://www.environmentalleader.com/2013/06/12/marks-spencer-sustainability-report-beats-water-goal-delays-transport-target/.

189. https://www.forbes.com/sites/kathryndill/2015/01/21/the-worlds-most-sustainable-companies-2015/#70200f357594.

190. http://corporate.marksandspencer.com/media/press-releases/2014/plan-a-report-launches-new-2020-eco-and-ethical-plan-for-mands.

191. http://ethicalperformance.com/PDFs/M&Showwedo.pdf.

192. *Business Green* (2013). "M&S Plan A Sustainability Savings Reach 135m Euro." Retrieved from: http://www.businessgreen.com/bg/news/2273234/m-s-plan-a-sustainability-savings-reach-gbp135m.

193. Decision Technology (2012). "Brand Personality." Retrieved from: http://www.dectech.co.uk/brand2012/BrandPersonality2012.pdf.

Notes to Chapter 11

1. *Huffington Post* (2012). "Dr. Bronner's Magic Soap CEO Has Hemp Protest Cut Short by Police with Power Saw." Retrieved from: http://www.huffingtonpost.com/2012/06/11/dr-bronners-magic-soap-ce_n_1586740.html.

2. Margaret Ely, "Dr. Bronner's Magic Soaps CEO Arrested in Hemp Protest," *Washington Post* June 11, 2012. Retrieved from: http://articles.washingtonpost.com/2012-06-11/local/35459696_1_hemp-oil-hemp-food-industrial-hemp.

3. Stopthedrugwar.org (2001). "Hemp Taste-Test Demonstrations Target DEA Offices Across the Country, Protests Held in 76 Cities." Retrieved from: http://stopthedrugwar.org/chronicle-old/214/tastetests.shtml.

4. NORML (2009). "David Bronner Among Those Arrested for Planting Hemp at DEA HQ." Retrieved from: http://blog.norml.org/2009/10/13/dr-bronner-among-those-arrested-for-planting-hemp-at-dea-hq/.

5. Margaret Ely, "Dr. Bronner's Magic Soaps CEO Arrested in Hemp Protest," *Washington Post* June 11, 2012. Retrieved from: http://articles.washingtonpost.com/2012-06-11/local/35459696_1_hemp-oil-hemp-food-industrial-hemp.

6. Dr. Bronner's (2013). "Dr. Bronner's Timeline." Retrieved from: http://www.drbronner.com/timeline.php.

7. https://www.drbronner.com/our-story/timeline/read-the-moral-abcs/.

8. http://www.votehemp.com/PDF/renewal.pdf.

9. Tom Foster, "The Undiluted Genius of Dr. Bronner's," *Inc.*, April 2012. Retrieved from: https://www.inc.com/magazine/201204/tom-foster/the-undiluted-genius-of-dr-bronners.html.

10. North American Industrial Hemp Council, Inc. (2013). "Distinguishing Hemp from its Cousin?" Retrieved from: http://naihc.org/hemp_information/content/hempCharacter.html.

11. *Huffington Post* (2012). Dr. Bronner's Magic Soap CEO Has Hemp Protest Cut Short by Police with Power Saw. Retrieved from: http://www.huffingtonpost.com/2012/06/11/dr-bronners-magic-soap-ce_n_1586740.html.

12. Interview with Michael Milam, COO, Dr. Bronner's, April 2013.

13. Dr. Bronner's (2013). "Dr. Bronner's Timeline." Retrieved from: http://www.drbronner.com/timeline.php.

14. Interview with Michael Milam, COO, Dr. Bronner's, April 5, 2013.

15. All One God Faith/Dr. Bronner's vs. ESTÉE LAUDER, et. al. (2008). Joint Initial Case Management Conference Statement. Superior Court of the State of California for the County of San Francisco.

16. Law 360 (2012). "Judge Defers to USDA in Dr. Bronner's False Ad Suit." Retrieved from: http://www.law360.com/articles/368154/judge-defers-to-usda-in -dr-bronner-s-false-ad-suit.

17. Tom Foster, "The Undiluted Genius of Dr. Bronner's," *Inc.*, April 2012. Retrieved from: https://www.inc.com/magazine/201204/tom-foster/the-undiluted -genius-of-dr-bronners.html.

18. Law 360 (2012). "Judge Defers to USDA in Dr. Bronner's False Ad Suit." Retrieved from: http://www.law360.com/articles/368154/judge-defers-to-usda-in -dr-bronner-s-false-ad-suit.

19. https://books.google.com/books?id=jsmcAue0TxIC&pg=PA119&lpg =PA119&dq=Constructive+Capitalism+bronner&source=bl&ots=yFuvi1JHmS &sig=tnQQGE99_-MGaPGY81H-sKgXCFQ&hl=en&sa=X&ved=0ahUKEwjw 0aK44eDLAhUG1GMKHa-5DsYQ6AEIMzAJ.

20. Tom Foster, "The Undiluted Genius of Dr. Bronner's," *Inc.*, April 2012. Retrieved from: https://www.inc.com/magazine/201204/tom-foster/the-undiluted -genius-of-dr-bronners.html.

21. Ibid.

22. Interview with David Bronner, Dr. Bronner's, April 5, 2013.

23. Ramon Casadesus-Masanell, Michael Crooke, Forest Reinhardt, and Vishal Vasishth, "Households' Willingness to Pay for "Green" Goods: Evidence from Patagonia's Introduction of Organic Cotton Sportswear," *Journal of Economics & Management Strategy* 18, no. 1 (Spring 2009): 203–233.

24. Jacob Gordon, "The TH Interview: Yvon Chouinard, founder of Patagonia (Part One)." *TreeHugger*, February 7, 2008. Retrieved from: http://www.treehugger .com/treehugger-radio/the-th-interview-yvon-chouinard-founder-of-patagonia -part-one.html.

25. Matilda Lee, "Patagonia: the Anti-Fashion Fashion Brand," *The Ecologist*, October 4, 2011. Retrieved from: http://www.theecologist.org/green_green_ living/clothing/1078046/patagonia_the_antifashion_fashion_brand.html.

26. One Percent for the Planet (2013). "History: Timeline." Retrieved from: http://onepercentfortheplanet.org/about/history/.

27. Patagonia.com (2013). "One Percent for the Planet." Retrieved from: http:// www.patagonia.com/us/patagonia.go?assetid=81218&ln=450.

28. Amy Roach Partridge, "Going Green: A Winning Warehouse Strategy," *Apparel*, June 30, 20111. Retrieved from: http://apparel.edgl.com/case-studies/ Going-Green–A-Winning-Warehouse-Strategy74011.

29. "Measuring Footprints," *Fast Company*, April 1, 2008. Retrieved from: http://www.fastcompany.com/756443/measuring-footprints.

30. http://www.patagonia.com/product/mens-windsweep-3-in-1-rain-jacket/28090.html?dwvar_28090_color=FGE&cgid=mens-jackets-vests-system#start=1.

31. http://www.patagonia.com/footprint.html.

32. Interview with Reed Doyle, Seventh Generation.

33. Stonyfield Farm (2014). "Stonyfield Source Map." Retrieved from: http://www.stonyfield.com/sourcemap/.

34. Ariel Schwartz, "Stonyfield Creates an Interactive Sourcing Map for its Yogurt Ingredients," *Fast Company*, June 13, 2014. Retrieved from: http://www.fastcoexist.com/3031819/stonyfield-creates-an-interactive-sourcing-map-for-its-yogurt-ingredients.

35. Patagonia.com (2013). Sewing Factory: Arvind Ltd. For more on the relationship between the companies see: Wayne Visser, *The Age of Responsibility: CSR 2.0 and the New DNA of Business* (Wiley, 2011).

36. Patagonia.com (2013). Sewing Factory: Arvind Ltd., photographs 15 and16.

37. http://www.ewg.org/research/poisoned-legacy/where-consumers-encounter-pfcs-today.

38. http://www.ncceh.ca/sites/default/files/Health_effects_PFCs_Oct_2010.pdf.

39. https://books.google.com/books?id=SMqF2zTuKjcC&pg=PA92&lpg=PA92&dq=pfoa+footprint+chronicles+Patagonia.

40. Jeffrey Hollender and Bill Breen, *The Responsibility Revolution: How the Next Generation of Businesses Will Win* (New York: John Wiley & Sons, 2010), p. 93. https://books.google.com/books?id=SMqF2zTuKjcC&pg=PA92&lpg=PA92&dq=pfoa+footprint+chronicles+Patagonia.

41. Ecouterre (2012). "Greenpeace Detects Chemicals in Popular Outerwear Brands." Retrieved from: http://www.ecouterre.com/greenpeace-detects-high-concentrations-of-toxic-chemicals-in-popular-outerwear-brands/.

42. http://www.greenpeace.org/romania/Global/romania/detox/Chemistry%20for%20any%20weather.pdf.

43. http://m.greenpeace.org/international/en/mid/news/Blogs/makingwaves/detox-outdoors/blog/54178/.

44. http://www.thecleanestline.com/2015/09/our-dwr-problem-updated.html.

45. http://m.greenpeace.org/international/en/mid/news/Blogs/makingwaves/detox-outdoors/blog/54178/.

46. http://www.greenpeace.org/romania/Global/romania/detox/Chemistry%20for%20any%20weather.pdf.

47. http://www.thecleanestline.com/2015/09/our-dwr-problem-updated.html.

48. The weight of the jacket as cited in http://sectionhiker.com/patagonia-torrentshell-rain-jacket-review/.

49. Estimate based on Greenpeace measurement of 196 micrograms/m$\wedge$2 and rough estimate that a jacket is about 1 m$\wedge$2 in being 1 meter in circumference times less than 2/3 meter long with sleeves needing about 1/2 x 2/3 meters of

cloth. See http://www.greenpeace.org/romania/Global/romania/detox/Chemistry%20for%20any%20weather.pdf.

50. http://www.patagonia.com/blog/2015/03/our-dwr-problem/.

51. http://www.thecleanestline.com/2015/09/our-dwr-problem-updated.html.

52. Ibid.

53. Jen Boynton, "How Patagonia, Levi Strauss Connect with Consumers Through Sustainability," *Triple Pundit*, January 30, 2013. Retrieved from: http://www.triplepundit.com/2013/01/patagonia-levi-strauss-customer-engagemen-sustainability-initiatives/.

54. Mat McDermott, "Sustainable Apparel Coalition Plans Industry-Wide Eco-Index," *TreeHugger*, March 1, 2011. Retrieved from: http://www.treehugger.com/style/sustainable-apparel-coalition-plans-industry-wide-eco-index.html.

55. Patagonia (2013). "Footprint Chronicles Mini-profile for Maxport JSC." Retrieved from: http://www.patagonia.com/us/footprint/suppliers-map/.

56. Erica Plambeck, Hau L. Lee, and Pamela Yatsko, "Improving Environmental Performance in Your Chinese Supply Chain," *MIT Sloan Management Review*, Winter 2012. Retrieved from: http://sloanreview.mit.edu/article/improving-environmental-performance-in-your-chinese-supply-chain/.

57. Hau Lee, Erica Plambeck, and Pamela Yatsko, "Incentivizing Sustainability in Your Chinese Supply Chain," *The European Business Review*, May-June 2012. Retrieved from: http://www.europeanbusinessreview.com/?p=3446.

58. Erica Plambeck, Hau L. Lee, and Pamela Yatsko, "Improving Environmental Performance in Your Chinese Supply Chain," *MIT Sloan Management Review*, Winter 2012. Retrieved from: http://sloanreview.mit.edu/article/improving-environmental-performance-in-your-chinese-supply-chain/.

59. Hau Lee, Erica Plambeck, and Pamela Yatsko, "Incentivizing Sustainability in Your Chinese Supply Chain," *The European Business Review*, May-June 2012. Retrieved from: http://www.europeanbusinessreview.com/?p=3446.

60. "Measuring Footprints," *Fast Company*, April 1, 2008. Retrieved from: http://www.fastcompany.com/756443/measuring-footprints.

61. Patagonia Sustainability Review, November 2012. Retrieved from: http://sustainablesv.org/ecocloud/index.php/topics/integrating-sustainability/sustainability-initiatives/companies/Patagonia.

62. "Patagonia to Place bluesign Requirement on Suppliers," *Inside Door*, August 9, 2011. Retrieved from: http://www.insideoutdoor.com/News/08.09.11.Patablue.htm. Accessed July 1, 2013.

63. The Cleanest Line (2011). "Don't Buy This Jacket Ad." Retrieved from: http://www.thecleanestline.com/2011/11/dont-buy-this-jacket-black-friday-and-the-new-york-times.html.

64. ebay (2011). "Inside the Partnership: Patagonia + eBay." Retrieved from: http://green.ebay.com/greenteam/blog/Inside-the-Partnership-Patagonia-eBay/7797.

65. ebay (2013). "Join us in the Common Threads Partnership." Retrieved from: http://campaigns.ebay.com/patagonia/join/.

66. Ibid.

67. Results from searching eBay.com on November 5, 2013 using keyword "Patagonia jacket."

68. ebay.com listing "http://www.ebay.com/itm/Patagonia-MARS-R2-Large-Alpha-Green-SEALS-SOF-DEVGRU-/251371747209?pt=LH_DefaultDomain_0&hash=item3a86ec7789."

69. Tim Smedley, "Can Patagonia and eBay Make Shopping More Sustainable?" *The Guardian*, May 13, 2013. Retrieved from: http://www.guardian.co.uk/sustainable-business/patagonia-ebay-making-shopping-more-sustainable.

70. Patagonia (2013). "Common Threads: eRecycle." Retrieved from: http://www.patagonia.com/us/common-threads/recycle.

71. Jan Lee, "Patagonia Launches Resale Outlets for Pre-Loved Items" *Triple Pundit*. October 23, 2013. Retrieved from: http://www.triplepundit.com/2013/10/patagonia-launches-resale-outlets-pre-loved-items/.

72. Interview with eBay.

73. http://www.adweek.com/news/advertising-branding/patagonia-taking-provocative-anti-growth-position-152782.

74. Seventh Generation headquarters visit. See also https://en.wikipedia.org/wiki/Seven_generation_sustainability.

75. Seventh Generation (2013). "About." Retrieved from: http://www.seventhgeneration.com/about.

76. Vtdigger (2011). "Seventh Generation named 2011 United Nations Leader of Change." Retrieved from: http://vtdigger.org/2011/10/20/seventh-generation-named-2011.united-nations-leader-of-change/.

77. Seventh Generation headquarters visit, December 17, 2012.

78. Retrieved from http://www.seventhgeneration.com/ingredients.

79. Seventh Generation (2013). "Future Tense: 2012 Corporate Consciousness Report." Retrieved from: http://2013.7genreport.com/2012_Corporate_Responsibility_Report/#/1/. Accessed May 2015.

80. http://www.jeffreyhollender.com/?p=2806.

81. Seventh Generation headquarters visit, December 17, 2012.

82. Ibid.

83. Ibid.

84. RP Siegel, "Radical Transparency: Seventh Gen's Hollender Puts His Money on the Truth," *Triple Pundit*, July 29, 2010. Retrieved from: http://www.triplepundit.com/2010/07/radical-transparency-seventh-generations-jeffrey-hollender-puts-his-money-on-the-truth/.

85. Seventh Generation headquarters visit, December 17, 2012.

86. PDMA (2013). "Materials Selection for Sustainable Design: Sustainable Innovation Webinar," led by Martin Wolf of Seventh Generation. Retrieved from: http://www.pdma.org/p/cm/ld/fid=831.

87. *Huffington Post* (2010). "Erin Brokovich, Seventh Generation Launch Million Baby Crawl Campaign." Retrieved from: http://www.huffingtonpost.com/2009/10/23/erin-brockovich-seventh-g_n_331935.html.

88. American Sustainable Business Council (2013). "ASBC Announces 'Companies for Safer Chemicals Coalition.'" Retrieved from: http://asbcouncil.org/node/1421.

89. Danielle Sacks, "Jeffrey Hollender: Seventh Generation, Triple Bottom Line Entrepreneur," February 2, 2010, *Fast Company*. Retrieved from: http://www.fastcompany.com/1535762/jeffrey-hollender-seventh-generation-triple-bottom-line-entrepreneur.

90. YouTube (2010). "Detergent Industry Phosphate Ban Will Result in Less Water Pollution." Retrieved from: http://www.youtube.com/watch?v=FAnlsydCqQM.

91. *Huffington Post* (2010). "Erin Brokovich, Seventh Generation Launch Million Baby Crawl Campaign." Retrieved from: http://www.huffingtonpost.com/2009/10/23/erin-brockovich-seventh-g_n_331935.html.

92. https://en.wikipedia.org/wiki/Million_Man_March.

93. Environmental Protection Agency (EPA) (2012). "Toxic Substances Control Act (TSCA)." Retrieved from: https://www.epa.gov/laws-regulations/summary-toxic-substances-control-act.

94. Seventh Generation Blog (2013). "Where Do You Stand on Toxic Chemical Reform?" Retrieved from: http://www.seventhgeneration.com/learn/blog/where-do-you-stand-toxic-chemical-reform.

95. Environmental Leader (2013). "The Chemical Safety Improvement Act: Potential Implications for Industry." Retrieved from: http://www.environmentalleader.com/2013/09/03/the-chemical-safety-improvement-act-potential-implications-for-industry/.

96. http://www.seventhgeneration.com/transforming-commerce/statement-chemical-safety-21st-century-act.

97. Seventh Generation headquarters visit, December 17, 2012.

98. Ibid.

99. Transworld Business (2012). "Patagonia's New Plant-Based Wetsuits and Goal to End Neoprene's Use Across Surf." Retrieved from: http://business.transworld.net/116138/features/jason-mccaffrey-on-patagonias-new-ecological-wetsuit-material/.

100. http://www.unilever.co.uk/media-centre/pressreleases/2015/Unilever-sees-sustainability-supporting-growth.aspx.

101. Sustainable Brands (2015). "The New Financial Metrics of Sustainable Business: A Practical Catalog of 20+ Trailblazing Case Studies." Retrieved from: http://www.wespire.com/press-room/the-new-financial-metrics-of-sustainable-business-a-practical-catalog-of-20-trailblazing-case-studies/. Accessed November 15, 2015.

102. Scheherazade Daneshkhu and David Oakley, "Paul Polman's Socially Responsible Unilever Falls Short on Growth," *Financial Times*, February 9, 2015.

103. Milton Friedman, "The Social Responsibility of Business is to Increase its Profits," *The New York Times*, September 13, 1970.

104. Edward Freeman, *Strategic Management: A Stakeholder Approach* (Boston: Cambridge University Press, 1984). Since 2010, Cambridge University Press has offered a new print-on-demand edition.

105. http://scholarship.law.wm.edu/cgi/viewcontent.cgi?article=1058&context=wmblr#page=11.

106. See for example, the court opinion in eBay vs. Newmark in http://www.litigationandtrial.com/2010/09/articles/series/special-comment/ebay-v-newmark-al-franken-was-right-corporations-are-legally-required-to-maximize-profits/. See also the article by Leo E. Strine, Jr., Chancellor of the Delaware Court of Chancery, in http://wakeforestlawreview.com/2012/04/our-continuing-struggle-with-the-idea-that-for-profit-corporations-seek-profit/.

107. Martha Groszewski Interview with Casadesus-Masanell, Reinhardt, and Freier, Ventura, California, October 29, 2002. Cited in Ramon Casadesus-Masanell, Michael Crooke, Forest Reinhardt, and Vishal Vasishht, "Households' Willingness to Pay for 'Green' Goods: Evidence from Patagonia's Introduction of Organic Cotton Sportswear," *Journal of Economics & Management Strategy* 18, no. 1 (Spring 2009): 203–233.

108. *Businessweek* (2010). "Maryland Passes 'Benefit Corp.' Law for Social Entrepreneurs." Retrieved from: http://www.businessweek.com/smallbiz/running_small_business/archives/2010/04/benefit_corp_bi.html. Accessed July 2014.

109. Benefit Corporation, "State by State Status of Legislation." Retrieved from: http://benefitcorp.net/policymakers/state-by-state-status. Accessed September 2017.

110. http://www.cleanyield.com/when-b-corp-met-wall-street/.

111. http://bcorporation.eu/blog/italian-parliament-approves-benefit-corporation-legal-status.

112. B-Lab (2014). "How to Become a B Corp." Retrieved from: http://www.bcorporation.net/become-a-b-corp/how-to-become-a-b-corp. Accessed July 2014.

113. Benefit Corp Information Center (2014). "Find a Benefit Corp." Retrieved from: http://www.benefitcorp.net/find-a-benefit-corp. Accessed July 2014.

114. B Lab (2017). "Find a Benefit Corp." Retrieved from: http://www.bcorporation.net/community/find-a-b-corp. Accessed September 2017.

115. B-Lab (2014). "How to Become a B Corp." Retrieved from: http://www.bcorporation.net/become-a-b-corp/how-to-become-a-b-corp. Accessed July 2014.

116. Ryan Honeyman, "What's the Difference Between Certified B Corps and Benefit Corps?" *Triple Pundit*, August 26, 2014. Retrieved from: http://www.triplepundit.com/2014/08/whats-difference-certified-b-corps-benefit-corps/.

117. https://www.bcorporation.net/community/patagonia-inc.

118. Mat McDermott, "Patagonia Becomes a California Benefit Corporation," *TreeHugger*, January 3, 2012. Retrieved from: http://www.treehugger.com/corporate-responsibility/patagonia-becomes-california-benefit-corporation.html.

119. Patagonia (2017). http://www.patagonia.com/b-lab.html. Accessed September 2017.

120. https://www.drbronner.com/impact/corporate-responsibility/benefit-corpora tion-status/.

121. https://www.drbronner.com/impact/corporate-responsibility/b-corps -certification/.

122. https://www.bcorporation.net/community/seventh-generation.

123. https://www.seventhgeneration.com/transforming-commerce/seventh -generation-receives-b-corp-recertification.

124. Anne Field, "More About Seventh Generation's $30M Infusion From Al Gore," *Forbes*, October 12, 2014. Retrieved from: http://www.forbes.com/sites/ annefield/2014/10/12/more-about-seventh-generations-30-million-infusion-from -al-gore/.

125. Beth Kowitt, "Seventh Generation CEO: Here's How the Unilever Deal Went Down," September 20, 2016. Retrieved from: http://fortune.com/2016/09/20/ seventh-generation-unilever-deal/.

126. http://www.benjerry.com/about-us/b-corp.

127. https://www.drbronner.com/impact/corporate-responsibility/benefi t-corporation-status/.

128. Seventh Generation (2013). "Future Tense: 2012 Corporate Consciousness Report." Retrieved from: http://2013.7genreport.com/2012_Corporate_Responsi bility_Report/#/1/. Accessed May 2015.

Notes to Chapter 12

1. One exception, at least regionally, is described in chapter 13.

2. Dr. Bronner's (2013). "Dr. Bronner's Demonstrates that Palm Oil can be Produced Sustainably under Fair Trade and Organic Certification." Retrieved from: https://www.drbronner.com/media-center/united-states/press-releases/dr-bronner s-demonstrates-that-palm-oil-can-be-produced-sustainably-under-fair-trade-and- organic-certification/.

3. Sustainable Brands (2013). "Unilever Pledges 100% Traceable Palm Oil by End of 2014." Retrieved from: http://www.sustainablebrands.com/news_and_views/ food_systems/mike-hower/unilever-promises-100-palm-oil-will-be-traceable -known-source.

4. https://www.unilever.com/Images/unilever-palm-oil-position-paper-may-2016 _tcm244-481753_en.pdf.

5. http://www.rainforest-alliance.org/sites/default/files/publication/pdf/palm-oil -faq.pdf.

6. Joost Vogtländer, Pablo Van der Lugt, and Han Brezet, "The Sustainability of Bamboo Products for Local and Western European Applications. LCAs and Land-Use," *Journal of Cleaner Production* 18, no. 13 (2010): 1260–1269.

7. Interview with Oliver Campbell, Director of Procurement Packaging, Dell, April 18, 2014.

8. Nina Kruschwitz, "How Dell Turned Bamboo and Mushrooms Into Environmental- Friendly Packaging," interview with John Pflueger (Dell), *MIT Sloan Management Review*, July 17, 2012, reprint number 54105, p. 12.

9. Fiona Graham, "'Air' Plastic and Mushroom Cushions—Dell Packages the Future," BBC News, October 10, 2014. Retrieved from: http://www.bbc.com/news/business-29543834.

10. The quote is usually attributed to Yogi Berra but some sources assign it to Chuck Reid. See: http://wiki.c2.com/?DifferenceBetweenTheoryAndPractice.

11. http://i.dell.com/sites/doccontent/corporate/corp-comm/en/Documents/fy15-cr-report.pdf.

12. https://books.google.com/books?id=gRS0WkCRiKsC&pg=PA85&lpg=PA85&dq=stonyfield+%22educate+consumers+and+producers+about+the+value+of+protecting%22&source=bl&ots=jEH3ocg7nz&sig=UFnczQuBrMhjmZvaZHByS0ST2n8&hl=en&sa=X&ved=0CB8Q6AEwA2oVChMI9qWrv7_YxgIVhnY-Ch34FQ46.

13. http://www.nofany.org/organic-certification/dairy/livestock-certification/dairy-transition.

14. Mercola (2006). "Stonyfield Rebuttal." Retrieved from: http://www.mercola.com/20061205/stonyfield/index.htm.

15. http://blog.seacoasteatlocal.org/2008/03/20/gary-hirshberg-founder-of-stonyfield-farm-at-riverrun-bookstore-in-portsmouth-7pm-tonight-march-20/ and http://www.michaelprager.carr-jones.com/Trader-Joes-Stonyfield-Farms-Organic-Valley-Pat-Hayes-yogurt-milk.

16. Joel Makower, "Exit Interview: Nancy Hirshberg, Stonyfield Farm," *GreenBiz*, May 6, 2013.

17. Mercola (2006). "Stonyfield Rebuttal." Retrieved from: http://www.mercola.com/20061205/stonyfield/index.htm.

18. Michael Prager blog (2011). "Where Stonyfield Buys, and Sells." Retrieved from: http://michaelprager.com/Trader-Joes-Stonyfield-Farms-Organic-Valley-Pat-Hayes-yogurt-milk.

19. Mercola (2006). "Stonyfield Rebuttal." Retrieved from: http://www.mercola.com/20061205/stonyfield/index.htm.

20. Ilan Brat, "Hunger for Organic Foods Stretches Supply Chains," *Wall Street Journal*, April 3, 2015.

21. Just Food (2009). "The Just-Food Interview—Dominic Lowe, Green & Black's." Retrieved from: http://www.just-food.com/interview/the-just-food-interview-dominic-lowe-green-blacks_id107060.aspx.

22. No Limit, Just a Line (2010). "Fair Trade Chocolate ... Deliciously Right!" Retrieved from: http://nolimitjustaline.blogspot.com/2010/01/after-having-mad-craving-for-chocolate.html.

23. David Goodman, "Culture Change," *Mother Jones*, January/February 2003. Retrieved from: http://www.motherjones.com/politics/2003/01/culture-change.

24. Rebecca Burn-Callander, "'I wish I'd Never Sold Green & Blacks to Cadbury,'" *The Telegraph*, October 24, 2015. Retrieved from: http://www.telegraph .co.uk/finance/newsbysector/retailandconsumer/11951398/I-wish-Id-never-sold -Green-and-Blacks-to-Cadbury.html.

25. Unilever (2014). "General FAQs." Retrieved from: http://www.unilever.com/ investorrelations/shareholder_info/shareholderfaqs/general/.

26. Unilever (2012). "General FAQs." Retrieved from: http://www.unilever.com/ investorrelations/shareholder_info/shareholderfaqs/general/.

27. https://www.unilever.com/Images/uslp-progress-report-2012-fi_tcm13 -387367_tcm244-409862_en.pdf.

28. https://www.unilever.com/about/who-we-are/about-Unilever/.

29. Clayton Christensen, *The Innovator's Dilemma: When New Technologies Cause Great Firms to Fail* (Boston, MA: Harvard Business School Press, 2013; reprint edition).

30. http://added-value.com/danones-recipe-for-sustainable-innovation/.

31. http://laundry.reviewed.com/news/new-green-laundry-detergent-wears-a -familiar-label.

32. https://www.unilever.com/sustainable-living/the-sustainable-living-plan/ reducing-environmental-impact/sustainable-sourcing/our-approach-to-sustainable -sourcing/sustainable-soy-and-oils.html.

33. David Gelles, "Unilever Finds That Shrinking Its Footprint Is a Giant Task," *The New York Times*, November 21, 2015.

34. Ibid.

35. Based on a market price of $9.54 per bushel on March 29, 2016. http:// www.indexmundi.com/commodities/?commodity=soybeans.

36. http://civileats.com/2015/09/25/unilever-turns-its-attention-to-farm-runoff -with-sustainable-soy-effort/.

37. http://unitedsoybean.org/article/sustainable-practices-make-cents-for-iowa -farmers/.

38. David Gelles, "Unilever Finds That Shrinking Its Footprint Is a Giant Task," *The New York Times*, November 21, 2015.

39. http://unitedsoybean.org/article/sustainable-practices-make-cents-for-iowa -farmers/.

40. http://civileats.com/2015/09/25/unilever-turns-its-attention-to-farm-runoff -with-sustainable-soy-effort/.

41. Ibid.

42. http://unitedsoybean.org/article/sustainable-practices-make-cents-for-iowa -farmers/.

43. David Gelles, "Unilever Finds That Shrinking Its Footprint Is a Giant Task," *The New York Times*, November 21, 2015.

44. Ibid.

45. Ibid.

46. http://farmprogress.com/story-iowa-leads-corn-soybean-acres-year-14-61324.

47. David Gelles, "Unilever Finds That Shrinking Its Footprint Is a Giant Task," *The New York Times*, November 21, 2015.

48. Will Nichols, "Case Study: Unilever Reveals Secrets of Zero Waste Campaign," *BusinessGreen*, April 17, 2013. Retrieved from: http://www.businessgreen .com/print_article/bg/feature/2242656/case-study-unilever-reveals-secrets-of-zero -waste-campaign.

49. Ibid.

50. Ibid.

51. Oliver Laasch and Roger Conaway, *Principles of Responsible Management, Global Sustainability, Responsibility and Ethics* (Stamford, CT: Cengage Learning, 2015), p. 170. http://books.google.com/books?id=0uLKAgAAQBAJ&pg =PT190&lpg=PT190&dq=clorox+business+units&source=bl&ots=9kXt81YSG P&sig=igHPRUCy6coHIV-UrNvx-SV5S2o&hl=en&sa=X&ei=HN7fU4KE M4risAS-iIDICw&ved=0CCcQ6AEwADgK#v=onepage&q=clorox%20business %20units&f=false.

52. Joel Makower, "Clorox Aims to Show that 'Green Works,'" *GreenBiz*, January 12, 2008. Retrieved from: http://www.greenbiz.com/blog/2008/01/12/clorox-aims -show-green-works.

53. http://www.environmentalleader.com/2008/08/17/nad-tells-clorox-to-clean -up-ads/.

54. Jane L. Levere, "In an Overhaul, Clorox Aims to Get Green Works Out of Its Niche," *The New York Times*, April 21, 2013. Retrieved from: http://www.nytimes .com/2013/04/22/business/media/cloroxs-green-works-aims-to-get-out-of-the -niche.html?_r=0.

55. Tilde Herrera, "Why Clorox Made the Leap from Bleach to Green Works," *GreenBiz*, February 3, 2011. Retrieved from: http://www.greenbiz.com/news/ 2011/02/03/why-clorox-made-leap-bleach-green-works.

56. Jane L. Levere, "In an Overhaul, Clorox Aims to Get Green Works Out of Its Niche," *The New York Times*, April 21, 2013. Retrieved from: http://www.nytimes .com/2013/04/22/business/media/cloroxs-green-works-aims-to-get-out-of-the -niche.html?_r=0.

57. GreenWorks (2014). Website: What's New. Retrieved from: https://www.green workscleaners.com/whats-new/.

58. Tilde Herrera, "Why Clorox Made the Leap from Bleach to Green Works," *GreenBiz*, February 3, 2011. Retrieved from: http://www.greenbiz.com/news/ 2011/02/03/why-clorox-made-leap-bleach-green-works.

59. Joel Makower, "Clorox Aims to Show that 'Green Works,'" *GreenBiz*, January 12, 2008. Retrieved from: http://www.greenbiz.com/blog/2008/01/12/clorox-aims -show-green-works.

60. Joel Makower, "Exit Interview: Nancy Hirshberg, Stonyfield Farm," *GreenBiz*, May 6, 2013.

61. Stonyfield Farm. "Stonyfield Farm and the SmartWay Partnership." Retrieved from: https://www.northeastdiesel.org/pdf/2013partnersmeeting/ReneeSherman .pdf. Accessed April 18, 2016.

62. http://www.mnn.com/lifestyle/responsible-living/blogs/interview-with -stonyfield-ceo-gary-hirshberg-everybody-can-win.

63. Interview with David Bronner, April 5, 2013.

64. http://www.aeb.org/farmers-and-marketers/industry-overview/31-farmers -marketers.

65. http://www.organicauthority.com/57-major-food-companies-switching-to -cage-free-eggs-list/.

66. http://news.walmart.com/news-archive/2016/04/05/walmart-us-announces -transition-to-cage-free-egg-supply-chain-by-2025.

67. Tara Duggan, "What Does 'Cage-Free' Really Mean, Exactly?" *San Francisco Chronicle*, April 14, 2016. Retrieved from: http://www.sfchronicle.com/food/ article/What-does-cage-free-really-mean-exactly-7249746.php.

68. http://www.techtimes.com/articles/147562/20160406/walmart-commits-to -sell-cage-free-eggs-by-2025.htm.

69. http://www.organicauthority.com/57-major-food-companies-switching-to -cage-free-eggs-list/.

70. http://www.bloomberg.com/news/articles/2016-04-05/wal-mart-will-sell-100 -cage-free-eggs-by-2025-in-industry-shift.

71. Henry Gass, "Walmart Makes Good on its Massive Clean Energy Promises," *Christian Science Monitor*, November 6, 2015. Retrieved from: http://www .csmonitor.com/USA/USA-Update/2015/1106/Walmart-starts-to-make-good-on -massive-clean-energy-promises?cmpid=addthis_email#.

72. Christopher Helman, "How Walmart Became A Green Energy Giant, Using Other People's Money," *Forbes*, November 4, 2015. Retrieved from: http://www .forbes.com/sites/christopherhelman/2015/11/04/walmarts-everyday-renewable -energy/#167d46144894.

73. Alexandra Alter, "Yet Another 'Footprint' to Worry About: Water," *Wall Street Journal*, February 17, 2009. Retrieved from: http://online.wsj.com/article/ SB123483638138996305.html.

74. Lauren Hepler, "9 Supply Chain Tech Companies You Should Know," *GreenBiz*, October 15, 2015. Retrieved from: http://www.greenbiz.com/article/9-supply -chain-tech-companies-you-should-know.

75. Andrew Winston, "How Target is Taking Sustainable Products Mainstream," *Harvard Business Review*, August 4, 2015. Retrieved from: https://hbr.org/2015/08/ how-target-is-taking-sustainable-products-mainstream.

76. Mat McDermott, "Sustainable Apparel Coalition Plans Industry-Wide Eco-Index," *TreeHugger*, March 1, 2011. Retrieved from: http://www.treehugger .com/style/sustainable-apparel-coalition-plans-industry-wide-eco-index.html.

77. Sustainable Apparel Coalition Website (2014). "About Us." Retrieved from: http://www.apparelcoalition.org/overview/.

78. Sustainable Apparel Coalition Website (2014). "Membership." Retrieved from: http://www.apparelcoalition.org/overview/.

79. Mary Mazzoni, "The Higg 2.0 Index and the Journey to an Industry-Wide Sustainable Apparel Standard," *Triple Pundit*, February 19, 2014. Retrieved from: http://www.triplepundit.com/special/sustainable-fashion-2014/higg-2-0-index -journey-industry-wide-sustainable-apparel-standard/.

80. https://outdoorindustry.org/research-tools/business-supply-chain-tools/ higg-index/.

81. Tim Smedley, "Can Patagonia and eBay Make Shopping More Sustainable?" *The Guardian*, May 13, 2013. Retrieved from: http://www.guardian.co.uk/ sustainable-business/patagonia-ebay-making-shopping-more-sustainable.

82. Sustainability Apparel Coalition Website (2012). "Higg Index." Retrieved from: http://www.apparelcoalition.org/higgindex/.

83. Tim Smedley, "Can Patagonia and eBay Make Shopping More Sustainable?" *The Guardian*, May 13, 2013. Retrieved from: http://www.guardian.co.uk/ sustainable-business/patagonia-ebay-making-shopping-more-sustainable.

84. Kohl's (2013). "Corporate Social Responsibility Report."

85. Tim Smedley, "Can Patagonia and eBay Make Shopping More Sustainable?" *The Guardian*, May 13, 2013. Retrieved from: http://www.guardian.co.uk/ sustainable-business/patagonia-ebay-making-shopping-more-sustainable.

86. http://www.outdoorindustry.org/responsibility/resources/casestudies.html.

87. Raz Godelnik, "Interview: New Tool Will Measure Sustainability Across Apparel Supply Chains," *Triple Pundit*, July 27, 2012. Retrieved from: http:// www.triplepundit.com/2012/07/interview-sustainable-apparel-coalitions-executive -director-new-higg-index/. The index was released in 2017. See: http://apparel coalition.org/the-higg-index/.

88. Interview with Jill Dumain, Director of Environmental Strategy, Patagonia, April 8, 2013, at Patagonia headquarters.

89. Tim Smedley, "Can Patagonia and eBay Make Shopping More Sustainable?" *The Guardian*, May 13, 2013. Retrieved from: http://www.guardian.co.uk/ sustainable-business/patagonia-ebay-making-shopping-more-sustainable.

90. Raz Godelnik, "Interview: New Tool Will Measure Sustainability Across Apparel Supply Chains," *Triple Pundit*, July 27, 2012. Retrieved from: http://www .triplepundit.com/2012/07/interview-sustainable-apparel-coalitions-executive -director-new-higg-index/.

91. Leon Kaye, "Five Global Companies Pledge Cooperation on Bioplastic," *Triple Pundit*, June 12, 2012. Retrieved from: http://www.triplepundit.com/2012/06/ coca-cola-nike-heinz-plantbottle-cooperation-bioplastic/.

92. http://bioplasticfeedstockalliance.org/who-we-are/.

93. http://www.environmentalleader.com/2014/06/11/ford-heinz-test-tomatoes -for-vehicle-use/.

94. http://bioplasticfeedstockalliance.org/news-title-6/.

95. PETA (2013). "Cosmetics and Household-Product Animal Testing." Retrieved from: http://www.peta.org/issues/animals-used-for-experimentation/cosmetic-house hold-products-animal-testing.aspx.

96. Management Exchange (2012). "Innovation in Well-Being—The Creation of Sustainable Value at Natura." Retrieved from: http://www.managementexchange .com/story/innovation-in-well-being.

97. United Nations Development Program (2007). "Case Study: Natura's Ekos: Perfume Essences Produce Sustainable Development in Brazil." Private Sector Division, Partnerships Bureau Report.

98. G. Jones and R. Reisen de Pinho, "Natura: Global Beauty Made in Brazil," Harvard Business School, Case Study 9-807-029.

99. Management Exchange (2012). "Innovation in Well-Being—The Creation of Sustainable Value at Natura." Retrieved from: http://www.managementexchange .com/story/innovation-in-well-being.

100. Luciana Hashiba, "Innovation in Well-Being—The Creation of Sustainable Value at Natura." Management Innovation Exchange. Retrieved from: http:// www.managementexchange.com/story/innovation-in-well-being. Accessed August 2013.

101. Oliver Balch, "Natura Commits to Sourcing Sustainably from Amazon," *The Guardian*, March 18, 2013. Retrieved from: http://www.theguardian.com/ sustainable-business/natura-sourcing-sustainably-from-amazon.

102. Leon Kaye, "Brazil's Natura Cosmetics Now the World's Largest B Corp," *Triple Pundit*, December 29, 2014. Retrieved from: http://www.triplepundit .com/2014/12/brazils-natura-cosmetics-now-worlds-largest-b-corp/.

103. In US-dollar terms, the company would be twice that size had the Brazilian real not tumbled by over 50 percent relative to the US dollar between the end of 2011 and the end of 2015.

104. Oliver Balch, "Natura Commits to Sourcing Sustainably from Amazon," *The Guardian*, March 18, 2013. Retrieved from: http://www.theguardian.com/ sustainable-business/natura-sourcing-sustainably-from-amazon.

105. Andrea Pereira de Carvalho and Jose Carlos Barbieri, "Innovation and Sustainability in the Supply Chain of a Cosmetics Company a Case Study," *Journal of Technology Management and Innovation* 7, no. 2 (2012): 144–156.

106. ZDNet (2013). "Apple Boosts R&D Spend, Now 3 Percent of Revenue." Retrieved from http://www.zdnet.com/apple-boosts-r-and-d-spend-now-3-percent -of-revenue-7000014515/. Accessed July 2013.

107. Wiki Invest (2014). Retrieved from http://www.wikinvest.com/stock/ L'oreal_(LRLCY).

108. Sustainable Brands (2014). "Natura Asks: Why Do You Need What You Don't Need?" Retrieved from http://www.sustainablebrands.com/news_and_views/ design_innovation/packaging/mathieu-jahnich/natura-asks-why-do-you -need-what-you-dont.

109. Global Cosmetic Industry (2010). "A Lesson in Sustainability: Natura's Markos Vaz." Retrieved from: http://www.gcimagazine.com/business/management/sustainability/101888568.html.

110. Ibid.

111. United Nations Development Program (2007). "Case Study: Natura's Ekos: Perfume Essences Produce Sustainable Development in Brazil." Private Sector Division, Partnerships Bureau Report.

112. Natura (2014). "Sustainability: Active Ingredient Certification Program." Retrieved from: http://www.natura.net/port/cosmoprof/ing/sustentabilidade.asp.

113. Andrea Pereira de Carvalho and Jose Carlos Barbieri, "Innovation and Sustainability in the Supply Chain of a Cosmetics Company a Case Study," *Journal of Technology Management and Innovation* 7, no. 2 (2012): 144–156.

114. Leonardo Liberman, Sergio Garcilazo, and Eva Stal, *Multinationals in Latin America: Case Studies* (London: Plagrave McMillan, 2014). https://books.google.com/books?id=u2QYDAAAQBAJ&pg=PA57&lpg=PA57&dq=ekos+higher+prices&source=bl&ots=cW0AdDNsgL&sig=gY93yRBRxF3VVr-86sDXReJVmDk&hl=en&sa=X&ved=0ahUKEwior-vL1MbNAhVDXR4KHeeHD-cQ6AEIHjAA#v=onepage&q&f=false.

115. Global Cosmetic Industry (2010). "A Lesson in Sustainability: Natura's Markos Vaz." Retrieved from: http://www.gcimagazine.com/business/management/sustainability/101888568.html.

116. United Nations Development Program (2007). "Case Study: Natura's Ekos: Perfume Essences Produce Sustainable Development in Brazil." Private Sector Division, Partnerships Bureau Report.

117. C. Boechat and R. Mokrejs Paro (2007). "Natura's Ekos: Perfume Essences Produce Sustainable Development in Brazil," *GIM UNDP Case Study Database, New York*.

118. Oliver Balch, "Natura Commits to Sourcing Sustainably from Amazon," *The Guardian*, March 18, 2013. Retrieved from: http://www.theguardian.com/sustainable-business/natura-sourcing-sustainably-from-amazon.

119. United Nations Development Program (2007). "Case Study: Natura's Ekos: Perfume Essences Produce Sustainable Development in Brazil." Private Sector Division, Partnerships Bureau Report.

120. Ibid.

121. H. L. Lee, V. Padmanabhan, and S. Whang, S. "Information Distortion in a Supply Chain: The Bullwhip Effect," *Management Science* 43, no. 4 (1997): 546–558.

122. Interview with Rodrigo Brea, Natura.

123. Bruce Watson, "Natura Joins B Corps: Will Other Big Business Embrace Sustainability Certificaiton?" *The Guardian*, December 12, 2014. Retrieved from: http://www.theguardian.com/sustainable-business/2014/dec/12/b-corps-certification-sustainability-natura.

124. http://www.cleanyield.com/when-b-corp-met-wall-street/.

125. Ibid.

126. http://www.furriela.adv.br/en/?artigos=teste-artigos-novos.

127. Natura (2014). Deutsche Bank Access Global Consumer Conference. Retrieved from: http://natura.infoinvest.com.br/enu/4781/Natura_DB_2014VFinal .pdf.

128. "Responsible Supply Chain." Presentation by João Paulo Ferreira, Supply Chain Vice President, Natura.

129. Luciana Hashiba, "Innovation in Well-Being—The Creation of Sustainable Value at Natura." Management Innovation Exchange. Retrieved from: http:// www.managementexchange.com/story/innovation-in-well-being. Accessed August 2013.

130. Geoffrey Jones and Ricardo Reisen De Pinho 2012). "Natura: Global Beauty Made in Brazil." Harvard Business School, Case Study 807-029.

131. Ibid.

132. Cosmetic Design (2004). "Euromonitor Publishes Brazil Market Report as Natura Prepares for IPO." Retrieved from http://www.cosmeticsdesign.com/ Market-Trends/Euromonitor-publishes-Brazil-market-report-as-Natura-prepares -for-IPO. Accessed July 2014. The reported sales prior to the IPO were of R$1 billion. An exchange rate of 0.44 reals per USD was used to quote this number.

133. Management Exchange (2012). "Innovation in Well-Being—The Creation of Sustainable Value at Natura." Retrieved from: http://www.managementexchange .com/story/innovation-in-well-being.

134. https://www.google.com/search?q=natura+cosmeticos+market+cap&ie=utf -8&oe=utf-8.

135. *Forbes* (2014). "Natura Cosmeticos." Retrieved from: http://www.forbes .com/companies/natura-cosmeticos/.

Notes to Chapter 13

1. *The Telegraph* (2013). "Procter & Gamble Brings Back Former CEO AG Lafley to Revive Growth." Retrieved from: http://www.telegraph.co.uk/finance/newsby sector/retailandconsumer/10078775/Procter-and-Gamble-brings-back-former -CEO-AG-Lafley-to-revive-growth.html.

2. P&G (2013). "A.G. Lafley Rejoins Procter & Gamble as Chairman, President and Chief Executive Officer." Retrieved from: http://news.pg.com/press-release/pg -corporate-announcements/ag-lafley-rejoins-procter-gamble-chairman-president -and-chi.

3. Amy Rush-Imber, "Armstrong CEO's Mandate: Growth, Innovation, Branding," *Floor Covering Weekly*, February 20, 2014. Retrieved from: http://www .floorcoveringweekly.com/main/topnews/armstrong-ceos-mandate-growth -innovation-branding-10488.aspx.

4. http://www.bain.com/consulting-services/strategy/fundamentals-of-growth .aspx.

5. See also, for example, Myron Gordon and Jeffrey Rosenthal, "Capitalism's Growth Imperative," *Cambridge Journal of Economics* 27, no. 1 (2003): 25–48.

6. http://www.multpl.com/world-gdp/table/by-year.

7. https://www.google.com/search?q=2020+worl+population&ie=utf-8&oe =utf-8.

8. http://www.oecdobserver.org/news/fullstory.php/aid/3681/An_emerging _middle_class.html.

9. PWC 17th Annual Global CEO Survey, https://www.pwc.com/gx/en/ sustainability/ceo-views/assets/pwc-ceo-summary-sustainability.pdf.

10. http://www3.epa.gov/climatechange/ghgemissions/global.html.

11. http://www.esrl.noaa.gov/gmd/ccgg/trends/full.html.

12. Ratios computed from figures in http://www.iea.org/publications/freepubli cations/publication/KeyWorld_Statistics_2015.pdf.

13. http://www.aip.org/history/climate/summary.htm.

14. http://www.ipcc.ch/report/ar5/wg1/.

15. https://en.wikipedia.org/wiki/List_of_scientists_opposing_the_mainstream _scientific_assessment_of_global_warming.

16. http://www.bloomberg.com/news/articles/2015-02-27/54-of-india-is-facing -high-water-stress-from-over-usage.

17. http://www.un.org/waterforlifedecade/scarcity.shtml.

18. Estimated global water volume. Retrieved from: http://water.usgs.gov/edu/ gallery/global-water-volume.html.

19. http://www.slideshare.net/SyngentaCommunications/our-industry-2014.

20. http://www.ab-inbev.com/content/dam/universaltemplate/abinbev/pdf/ investors/annual-and-hy-reports/2014/AB_InBev_AR14_EN_financial.pdf.

21. http://www.climate.org/topics/climate-change/beer-climate-change.html.

22. http://thinkprogress.org/climate/2014/06/07/3446248/climate-change-beer -water/.

23. https://www.edf.org/climate/climate-change-impacts.

24. http://www.climate.org/topics/climate-change/beer-climate-change.html.

25. See, for example, Naomi Klein, *This Changes Everything: Capitalism vs. The Climate* (New York: Simon and Schuster, 2014).

26. http://www.historic-uk.com/HistoryUK/HistoryofBritain/Great-Horse -Manure-Crisis-of-1894/.

27. David White, "The Unmined Supply of Petroleum in the United States," *Transactions of the Society of Automotive Engineers* 14, part 1 (1919): 227.

28. Calculated from data from https://www.eia.gov/cfapps/ipdbproject/iedindex3 .cfm?tid=5&pid=57&aid=6&cid=regions&syid=1980&eyid=2015&unit=BB and https://www.eia.gov/cfapps/ipdbproject/iedindex3.cfm?tid=5&pid=5&aid=2 &cid=regions&syid=1980&eyid=2014&unit=TBPD.

29. Ibid.

30. Rick Wartzman, "The Long View: Why 'Maximizing Shareholder Value' is on its Way Out," *TIME*, September 25, 2013. Retrieved from: http://business.time.com/2013/09/25/the-long-view-why-maximizing-shareholder-value-is-on-its-way-out/.

31. Peter Drucker, *Managing for the Future* (Oxford: Butterworth-Heinemann, 1992).

32. https://www.rand.org/pubs/commercial_books/CB367.html.

33. http://www.eluniversal.com/nacional-y-politica/160227/water-shortage-is-the-major-environmental-risk-in-2015-in-venezuela.

34. Ron Grech, "Joining Forces Against 'Eco-terrorism,'" *The Daily Press (Timmins)*, June 10, 2015. Retrieved from: http://www.timminspress.com/2015/06/10/joining-forces-against-eco-terrorism.

35. Tyler Elm, "6 tips to Survive a Misinformation Campaign," *GreenBiz*, June 11, 2015.

36. Antony Oliver, "Profits versus Planet" *The New Civil Engineer*, November 19, 1998. Retrieved from: http://www.nce.co.uk/profits-versus-planet/851614.article.

37. H. Jeff Smith, "The Shareholders vs. Stakeholders Debate" *Sloan Management Review*, Summer 2003. Retrieved from: http://sloanreview.mit.edu/article/the-shareholders-vs-stakeholders-debate/. Accessed July 15, 2003.

38. http://www.energy.alberta.ca/oilsands/791.asp.

39. http://www.pnas.org/content/111/9/3209.full.pdf.

40. http://www.ncbi.nlm.nih.gov/pmc/articles/PMC2679626/.

41. http://www.economist.com/news/science-and-technology/21615488-new-technologies-are-being-used-extract-bitumen-oil-sands-steam.

42. http://www.ncbi.nlm.nih.gov/pmc/articles/PMC2679626/.

43. http://www.desmogblog.com/sites/beta.desmogblog.com/files/TarSands_TheReport%20final.pdf.

44. Tim McDonnell, "There's No Hiding from Tar Sands Oil," *Mother Jones*, December 15, 2011. Retrieved from: http://www.motherjones.com/environment/2011/12/theres-no-hiding-tar-sands-oil.

45. http://www.forestethics.org/major-companies-act-to-clean-up-their-transportation-footprints.

46. "Alberta's Oil Sands: The Facts," January 2014. Retrieved from: http://www.oilsands.alberta.ca/FactSheets/Albertas_Oil_Sands_The_Facts_Jan_2014.pdf.

47. http://www.alternativesjournal.ca/community/reviews/tar-sands-dirty-oil-and-future-continent?PageSpeed=noscript.

48. Colby Cosh, "Don't Call Them 'Tar Sands,'" *Maclean's*, April 3, 2012. Retrieved from: http://www.macleans.ca/news/canada/oil-by-any-other-name/.

49. http://www.environmentalleader.com/2010/08/30/walgreens-gap-levi-join-oil-sands-fuel-boycott/.

50. Tim McDonnell, "There's No Hiding from Tar Sands Oil," *Mother Jones*, December 15, 2011. Retrieved from: http://www.motherjones.com/environment/2011/12/theres-no-hiding-tar-sands-oil.

51. http://www.environmentalleader.com/2010/08/30/walgreens-gap-levi-join-oil -sands-fuel-boycott/.

52. http://www.cbc.ca/news/canada/edmonton/not-boycotting-oilsands-3-u-s -firms-say-1.945517.

53. Ibid.

54. http://www.tradingeconomics.com/china/disposable-personal-income.

55. http://www.chinability.com/Rmb.htm.

56. 100-fold in terms yuan or RMB (the Chinese currency); "only" 25-fold in dollar terms.

57. http://www.tradingeconomics.com/china/disposable-personal-income.

58. Helen Wang, "The Biggest Story of Our Time: The Rise of China's Middle Class," *Forbes/Business*, December 21, 2011. Retrieved from: http://www.forbes .com/sites/helenwang/2011/12/21/the-biggest-story-of-our-time-the-rise-of-chinas -middle-class/.

59. http://www.livescience.com/27862-china-environmental-problems.html.

60. http://www.economist.com/blogs/analects/2013/03/water-pollution.

61. http://www.ipsnews.net/2012/07/china-battles-desertification/.

62. Edward Wong, "Air Pollution Linked to 1.2 Million Premature Deaths in China," *The New York Times*, April 1, 2013. Retrieved from: http://www.nytimes.com/ 2013/04/02/world/asia/air-pollution-linked-to-1-2-million-deaths-in-china.html.

63. http://www.worldlifeexpectancy.com/country-health-profile/china.

64. http://www.economist.com/news/china/21677267-new-study-casts-new -light-chinas-progress-noodles-longevity.

65. http://www.mckinsey.com/global-themes/urbanization/preparing-for-chinas -urban-billion.

66. Gary Gereffi, and Stacey Frederick (2010). "The Global Apparel Value Chain, Trade and the Crisis: Challenges and Opportunities for Developing Countries." World Bank Policy Research Working Paper 5281. Retrieved from: http://www -wds.worldbank.org/external/default/WDSContentServer/WDSP/IB/2010/04/27/ 000158349_20100427111841/Rendered/PDF/WPS5281.pdf.

67. Alessandro Nicita, "Who Benefits from Export-led Growth? Evidence from Madagascar's Textile and Apparel Industry." *Journal of African Economies* 17, no. 3 (2008): 465–489.

68. Alessandro Nicita and Susan Razzaz (2003). "Who Benefits and How Much? How Gender Affects Welfare Impacts of a Booming Textile Industry." World Bank, Policy Research Working Paper 3029, Washington, DC. Retrieved from: https:// openknowledge.worldbank.org/bitstream/handle/10986/18227/multi0page.pdf ?sequence=1&isAllowed=y.

69. http://www.nrdc.org/living/stuff/green-fashion.asp.

70. Steven Greenhouse, "Some Retailers Rethink Their Role in Bangladesh," *The New York Times*, May 1, 2013.

71. Nazli Kibria, "Becoming a Garments Worker: The Mobilization of Women into the Garments Factories of Bangladesh," Occasional Paper 9, March 1998, UN Research Institute for Social Development. Available at:http://www.unrisd.org/unrisd/website/document.nsf/0/523115d41019b9d980256b67005b6ef8/$FILE/opb9.pdf.

72. Interview with Gary Niekerk, Director of Global Citizenship, Intel, July 23, 2012.

73. http://news.stanford.edu/news/2014/february/kolstad-carbon-tax-022814.html.

74. http://www.euractiv.com/cap/fao-report-links-high-food-price-news-516502.

75. Interview with Mike Barry, Director of Sustainable Business (Plan A), Marks & Spencer, November 3, 2015.

76. David Giles, "Unilever Finds that Shrinking its Footprint is a Giant Task," *The New York Times*, November 21, 2015. Retrieved from: http://www.nytimes.com/2015/11/22/business/unilever-finds-that-shrinking-its-footprint-is-a-giant-task.html?_r=0.

77. Ibid.

78. https://www.law.cornell.edu/wex/bright-line_rule.

79. http://www.npr.org/sections/thesalt/2015/06/12/411779324/organic-farmers-call-foul-on-whole-foods-produce-rating-system.

80. http://www.wholefoodsmarket.com/responsibly-grown/produce-rating-system.

81. Stephanie Strom, "Organic Farmers Object to Whole Foods Rating System," *The New York Times*, June 12, 2015. Retrieved from: http://www.nytimes.com/2015/06/13/business/organic-farmers-object-to-whole-foods-rating-system.html.

82. http://www.npr.org/sections/thesalt/2015/06/12/411779324/organic-farmers-call-foul-on-whole-foods-produce-rating-system.

83. http://graphics8.nytimes.com/packages/pdf/business/JohnMackeyLetter.pdf.

84. http://www.wholefoodsmarket.com/blog/clarifying-tenets-responsibly-grown.

85. Stephanie Strom, "Organic Farmers Object to Whole Foods Rating System," *The New York Times*, June 12, 2015. Retrieved from: http://www.nytimes.com/2015/06/13/business/organic-farmers-object-to-whole-foods-rating-system.html.

86. http://www.ccof.org/press/ccof-and-whole-foods-market-announce-adjustments-responsibly-grown-ratings.

87. http://www.wholefoodsmarket.com/blog/update-our-responsibly-grown-ratings-system.

88. Stephanie Strom, "Organic Farmers Object to Whole Foods Rating System," *The New York Times*, June 12, 2015. Retrieved from: http://www.nytimes.com/2015/06/13/business/organic-farmers-object-to-whole-foods-rating-system.html

89. http://www.wholefoodsmarket.com/blog/update-our-responsibly-grown-ratings-system.

90. http://www.wholefoodsmarket.com/blog/clarifying-tenets-responsibly-grown.

91. Stephanie Strom, "Organic Farmers Object to Whole Foods Rating System," *The New York Times*, June 12, 2015. Retrieved from: http://www.nytimes.com/2015/06/13/business/organic-farmers-object-to-whole-foods-rating-system.html.

92. http://www.telegraph.co.uk/news/earth/countryside/9727128/The-Great-Smog-of-London-the-air-was-thick-with-apathy.html.

93. http://news.bbc.co.uk/2/hi/europe/1371142.stm.

94. http://www.aqmd.gov/home/library/public-information/publications/50-years-of-progress.

95. https://www3.epa.gov/airmarkets/progress/reports/index.html.

96. Theodore Panayotou (2000). "Globalization and Environment," Center for International Development at Harvard University, No. 53. Accessible at http://www.hks.harvard.edu/var/ezp_site/storage/fckeditor/file/pdfs/centers-programs/centers/cid/publications/faculty/wp/053.pdf.

97. https://www.gov.uk/government/uploads/system/uploads/attachment_data/file/69195/pb13390-economic-growth-100305.pdf.

98. http://www.bloomberg.com/news/articles/2014-04-24/china-enacts-biggest-pollution-curbs-in-25-years.

99. Edward Wong and Chris Buckley, "Chinese Premier Vows Tougher Regulation on Air Pollution," *The New York Times*, March 15 2015. Retrieved from: http://www.nytimes.com/2015/03/16/world/asia/chinese-premier-li-keqiang-vows-tougher-regulation-on-air-pollution.html.

100. http://cspc.nonprofitsoapbox.com/storage/documents/Fellows2008/Whittemore.pdf.

101. https://www.oxfamamerica.org/publications/prep-value-chain-climate-resilience/.

102. http://www.independent.co.uk/environment/climate-change/greenland-reaps-benefits-of-global-warming-8555241.html.

103. Costas Paris, "Chinese Shipping Group Cosco Planning Regular Trans-Arctic Sailings," *Wall Street Journal*, October 29, 2015. Retrieved from: http://www.wsj.com/articles/chinese-shipper-cosco-to-schedule-regular-trans-arctic-sailings-1446133485?alg=y.

104. http://www.npr.org/2013/08/21/209579037/why-millennials-are-ditching-cars-and-redefining-ownership.

105. http://americasmarkets.usatoday.com/2014/04/23/little-car-love-among-urban-millennials/.

106. http://www.huffingtonpost.ca/2013/01/18/generation-y-consumerism-ownership_n_2500697.html.

107. http://www.bbc.com/news/world-europe-32929962.

108. http://news.discovery.com/human/population-boom-110729.htm.

109. http://www.technologyreview.com/news/530866/un-predicts-new-global-population-boom/.

110. https://hbr.org/2012/06/captain-planet.

111. The Guardian (2012). Unilever's Paul Polman: challenging the corporate status quo. Retrieved from: http://www.theguardian.com/sustainable-business/paul-polman-unilever-sustainable-living-plan.

112. Unilever (2014). "Unilever Sustainable Living Plan." http://www.unilever.com/sustainable-living-2014/.

113. http://www.vodppl.upm.edu.my/uploads/docs/CMR_Starbucks_NGOs.pdf.

114. http://corporate.walmart.com/_news_/news-archive/2009/07/16/walmart-announces-sustainable-product-index.

115. Jessica Shankleman, "Tim Cook Tells Climate Change Sceptics to Ditch Apple Shares," *The Guardian*, March 3, 2014. Retrieved from: http://www.theguardian.com/environment/2014/mar/03/tim-cook-climate-change-sceptics-ditch-apple-shares.

116. http://www.ecowatch.com/apple-to-clean-up-act-in-china-with-huge-investments-in-renewable-ener-1882109614.html.

117. https://www.apple.com/environment/pdf/Apple_Environmental_Responsibility_Report_2016.pdf.

118. http://blogs.wsj.com/digits/2015/05/10/apple-expands-renewable-energy-goal-to-cover-supply-chain/.

119. http://www.greencarreports.com/news/1077568_2012-toyota-prius-c-yes-your-gas-mileage-will-vary.

120. http://www.ab-inbev.com/content/dam/universaltemplate/abinbev/pdf/sr/download-center/2014_GSR_REPORT_Environment.pdf.

121. http://www.triplepundit.com/2015/06/what-weve-learned-about-collective-action-on-water-stewardship/

122. Ibid.

123. https://translate.google.com/translate?hl=en&ie=UTF8&prev=_t&sl=pt-BR&tl=en&u=https://www.google.com/url%3Fq%3Dhttps://www.embrapa.br/en/busca-de-noticias/-/noticia/2581020/prefeitura-de-jaguariuna-lanca-programa-bacias-jaguariuna%26sa%3DU%26ved%3D0CBQQFjAAahUKEwjSrKm8iILJAhUPzmMKHZcpBD0%26sig2%3DNqx2rfG5Z7DHdmjCXeuIxQ%26usg%3DAFQjCNHKnGFIKXWhbadTlIgyk9rwC1BUQA.

124. http://creativity-online.com/work/ambev-cyan-bank-water-project/23542.

125. https://www.rita.dot.gov/bts/sites/rita.dot.gov.bts/files/publications/national_transportation_statistics/html/table_01_50.html.

126. Corynne Jaffeux and Philippe Wieser, *Essentials of Logistics and Management*, 3rd Ed. (Boca Raton, FL: CRC Press, 2012), p. 253.

127. The World Bank, "Merchandise Trade (% of GDP) Tables from 1981–2014." Retrieved from: http://data.worldbank.org/indicator/TG.VAL.TOTL.GD.ZS.

128. http://www.roadandtrack.com/new-cars/news/a4173/news-peterbilt-cummins-tractor-trailer-fuel-economy/.

129. Kristen Leigh Painter, "The 787 Dreamliner's Fuel Efficiency Makes Tokyo Possible for Denver," *The Denver Post*, November 9, 2012; updated April 30, 2016. Retrieved from: http://www.denverpost.com/ci_21968731/787-dreamliners -fuel-efficiency-makes-tokyo-possible-denver.

130. http://www.maersk.com/en/hardware/triple-e/efficiency.

131. https://people.hofstra.edu/geotrans/eng/ch8en/conc8en/fuel_consumption _containerships.html.

132. http://www.claimsjournal.com/news/national/2014/05/01/248279.htm.

133. http://www.cumminspowersouth.com/pdf/F-1607-LowEmissionsBrochure -en.pdf.

134. Raytheon Inc., "Alternate Cleaning Technology." Technical Report Phase II. January-October 1991.

135. Michael Porter and Claas van der Linde, "Towards a New Conception of Environment-Competitive Relationships," *The Journal of Economic Perspectives* 9, no. 4 (1995): 97–118.

136. http://cnsnews.com/news/article/ford-introduces-new-f-150-made -aluminum.

137. http://www.environmentalleader.com/2015/11/02/ge-aviation-invests-200m -to-build-ultra-lightweight-materials/.

138. http://newsfeed.time.com/2013/03/25/more-people-have-cell-phones-than -toilets-u-n-study-shows/.

139. Tim Worstall, "Africa Might Just Skip the Entire PC Revolution," *Forbes*, August 17, 2011. Retrieved from: http://www.forbes.com/sites/timworstall/2011/ 08/17/africa-might-just-skip-the-entire-pc-revolution/.

140. https://interactivemap.marksandspencer.com/.

141. Conversation with Philippe Cochet, GE's Chief Productivity Officer.

142. http://newsfeed.time.com/2013/03/25/more-people-have-cell-phones-than -toilets-u-n-study-shows/.

143. OECD (2014). "The State of Play on Extended Producer Responsibility (EPR): Opportunities and Challenges," Issues Paper. Retrieved from: http://www .oecd.org/environment/waste/Global%20Forum%20Tokyo%20Issues%20Paper %2030-5-2014.pdf.

144. http://www.emc.com/corporate/sustainability/sustaining-ecosystems/eol .htm.

145. David Rogers, "Rising Global Middle Classes Pose Huge Resource Threat," *Global Construction Review*, May 8, 2014. Retrieved from: http://www.global constructionreview.com/trends/rising-global-middle-classes8-pose-huge100/.

146. Jo Confino, "Unilever: The Highs and Lows of Driving Sustainable Change," *The Guardian*, April 22, 2013. Retrieved from: http://www.theguardian.com/ sustainable-business/blog/unilever-driving-sustainable-change.

147. http://media.corporate-ir.net/media_files/irol/10/100529/AR11/nike-sh -2011/mark_parker_letter.html.

Table of Thanks

As mentioned in the preface, this book, which is based mostly on primary research, benefited from the generous contribution of insights and stories from nearly 300 executives and experts. Hopefully, I did not forget too many of them, because their hospitality, openness, and helpfulness not only made the research possible, but also made it fun. (Note: The titles mentioned are those in effect during the time of my interactions with them.)

Company	Name	Title
AB InBev	Ezgi Barcenas	Global Manager, Beer & Better World
AB InBev	Sabine Chalmers	Chief Legal & Corporate Affairs Officer
AB InBev	Danillo Figueiredo	Global Director of Supply Chain Integration
AB InBev	Gary Hanning	Director of Global Barley Research
AB InBev	Rolim Ricardo	Vice President Global Sustainability
AB InBev	John Rogers	Global Director of Agricultural Development
AB InBev	Hugh "Bert" Share	Senior Global Director, Beer & Better World
ADEME	Olivier Réthoré	LCA Project Manager
Aoyama Gakuin University	Tomomi Nonaka	Assistant Professor
ASICS	Jimmy Adames	Sustainability & Social Responsibility Manager

Company	Name	Title
ASICS	Brian Johnston	CSR and Sustainability Specialist
Association Bilan Carbone	Simon Dely	Project Manager, Methodology
B Lab	Jay Coen Gilbert	Cofounder
B Lab	Stephanie Nieman	Director, Developed Market Standards
BASF	Andreas Backhaus	Senior Vice President of Global Supply Chain
BASF	Robert Blackburn	Senior Vice President & Head Global Supply Chain
BASF	Inga-Lena Darkow	Global Business Analytics, Senior Manager Programs
BASF	Paul Devoy	Supply Chain Director, Chemical Intermediates North America
BASF	Noora Miettinen	GSB/SD—Global Supply Chain Strategy Development, Supply Chain Models
BASF	Carles Navarro	Managing Director, Country Cluster Head Iberia, former president of BASF Canada
BASF	Andrew O'Connor	Global Director of Supply Chain Strategy Development
BASF	Scott Stussi	Senior Expert, Supply Chain Strategy
BASF	Oleta LaRush	Manager of Communications
BASF	Charlene Wall-Warren	Director, Sustainability
Better Cotton Initiative	Ruchira Joshi	Programme Director—Demand
Boeing	Stephen Robbins	Enterprise Supply Chain Logistics—SDC Traffic
Boston Herald	Adriana Cohen	Talk Show Host and Columnist
Boston Scientific	David Sapienza	Vice President Operations
Boston Scientific	Leonard Sarapas	Corporate Director, Environmental Health & Safety

Company	Name	Title
BP	George Huff	Technical Advisor
BP	James Simnick	Technical Advisor
Carbon Disclosure Project	Dexter Galvin	Head of Supply Chain
Carbon Trust	Martin Barrow	Associate Director, Head of Footprinting
Cementos Argos	Maria Isabel Echeverri Carvajal	Vice President of Sustainability
Cemex	Daniel Huerta	Builders Segment Pricing Manager
Cemex	Maria Verdugo	Procurement Model Evolution and Communication Manager
Chiquita	Ana Lucia Alonzo	Director, Continuous Improvement and Sustainability
Cintas	Melanie Boyle	Corporate Communications Manager
Cintas	Pamela Brailsford	Senior Director of Supplier Diversity and Sustainability
Cintas	Dave Wheeler	Senior Vice President Global Supply Chain
Columbia University/ PeerAspect	Scott Kaufman	Adjunct Professor/CEO
Cradle to Cradle	Will Duggan	Senior Writer and Communications Director
Cradle to Cradle	Bridgett Luther	President and Founder
Delhaize	Lou DeLorenzo	Director, Supply Chain Services
Delhaize	George Parmenter	Manager of Sustainability
Dell	Steve Bagnaschi	Fulfillment Senior Manager
Dell	Oliver Campbell	Director, Procurement & Packaging Innovation
Dell	Lori Chisum	Program Manager

Company	Name	Title
Dell	David Lear	Vice President, Corporate Sustainability
Dell	Michael Murphy	Executive Director, Product Compliance
Dell	Scott O'Connell	Director, Environmental Affairs
Dell	Deborah Sanders	Director, Services IT Portfolio
DHL	Björn Hannappel	Senior Expert, GoGreen
Dow AgroSciences	Joshua Merrill	Global Supply Chain Manager
Dr. Bronner's Magic Soap	Bernardo Andrade	Manufacturing and Warehouse Specialist
Dr. Bronner's Magic Soap	David Bronner	CEO
Dr. Bronner's Magic Soap	Mike Bronner	President
Dr. Bronner's Magic Soap	Trudy Bronner	Chief Financial Officer
Dr. Bronner's Magic Soap	Michael Milam	Chief Operations Officer
eBay	Caitlin Bristol	Senior Manager, Global Impact
eBay	Lori Duvall	Global Director, Green
eBay	Prakash Muppirala	Director, Product Development, Managed Marketplaces
ecoATM	Mark Bowles	Founder
Ecodesk	Remy Leaf	Account Executive
Ecodesk	Nick Murry	Chief Sustainability Officer
Ecolabel Index	Anastasia O'Rourke	Cofounder
EcoVadis	Geoffrey Carbonnel	CSR Ratings Operations Manager
EcoVadis	Pierre-Francois Thaler	Cofounder, Co-CEO
EMC	Ezra Benjamin	Principal Program Manager, Global Product Take Back

Company	Name	Title
EMC	Alyssa Caddle	Consultant Program Manager
EMC	Maria Gorsuch-Kennedy	Principal Program Manager
EMC	Matt Mills	Principal Program Manager
EMC	Michael Norbeck	Principal Program Manager
EMC	Katie Schindall	Consultant Program Manager
EMC	Kathrin Winkler	Senior Vice President, Corporate Sustainability, and Chief Sustainability Officer
Environmental Defense Fund	Michelle Harvey	Director, Supply Chain
Environmental Defense Fund	Jason Mathers	Director
Environmental Defense Fund	Michael Reading	Manager, Corporate Partnerships
Environmental Defense Fund	Elizabeth Sturcken	Managing Director, Corporate Partnerships
EPFL	Naoufel Cheikhrouhou	Professor of Supply Chain Management
EPFL	Dimitri Weideli	Master's Student
Fair Trade USA	Todd Stark	Chief Operations Officer
Fiat Chrysler	Mary Gauthier	Head, Sustainability Communications
Fiat Chrysler	Bill Hall	Head of Sustainability
Fiat Chrysler	Michael Palese	Corporate Communications Strategy/ Litigation Communications
Fiat Chrysler	Todd Yaney	Supply Chain Sustainability Manager
Flextronics	Tom Linton	Chief Procurement and Supply Chain Officer
Forest Stewardship Council	Phil Guillery	Systems Integrity Director
Freelance	Matt Casey	Freelance journalist

Company	Name	Title
GENCO	Gregor Thompson	Managing Director
General Electric	Philippe Cochet	Chief Productivity Officer
General Mills	Joel LaFrance	Supply Chain Visibility Lead
General Mills	Kathy Rodriguez	Demand Planning Manager
General Motors	Bill Hurles	Executive Director of Supply Chain
General Motors	David Tulauskas	Director, Sustainability
GeoTraceability	Pierre Courtemanche	CEO
Green River	Benjamin Tucker	Director of Products
Green Seal	Linda Chipperfield	Vice President, Marketing & Communications
Greenpeace	Femke Bartels	Global Forest Network Director
Greenpeace	Lasse Bruun	Senior Campaigner
Greenpeace	Suzanne Kröger	International Project Leader
Greenpeace	Alexander Navarro	Global Digital Strategist
HP	Tom Etheridge	LCA Program Manager
HP	Judy Glazer	Director of Social and Environmental Responsibility
Ian Midgley Associates	Ian Midgley	Managing Director
IKEA	Kelly Deng	Senior Auditor
IKEA	Greg Priest	Head of Sustainability Policy
IKEA	Jeanette Skjelmose	Sustainability Manager
IKEA	Brigitte Warren	Sustainability Compliance Manager
Intel	Dawn Graunke	Supply Chain Regulatory Manager
ISEAL Alliance	Helen Ireland	Innovation Manager
ITC	Ashesh Ambasta	Executive Vice President and Head of Social Investments

Company	Name	Title
Johnson & Johnson	Philip Dahlin	Global Director of Sustainability
Johnson & Johnson	Thomas LaVake	Director
Johnson & Johnson	Keith Sutter	Worldwide Director of Sustainability
Kao	Akikazu Sato	Manager Corporate Strategy
Kao	Masaki Tsumadori	Vice President, Global Research and Development
Kao	Takashi Matsuo	Research Fellow
Kao	Shirasaki Yoshitsugu	Environmental Director
Li & Fung	Pamela Mar	Director of Sustainability
LKAB	Stina Eriksson	Sustainability Manager
LKAB	Magnus Johansson	Senior Advisor Sustainable Purchasing
LOGyCA	Vivian Rangel Castelblanco	Researcher
Lowe's	Steve Palmer	Vice President of Transportation
Maersk Line	Lee Kindberg	Director, Environment and Sustainability
Malaysia Institute for Supply Chain Innovation	Asad Ata	Assistant Professor
Malaysia Institute for Supply Chain Innovation	David Gonsalvez	CEO & Rector
Marine Stewardship Council	Titia Sjenitzer	Senior Supply Chain Standards Manager
Marks & Spencer	Mike Barry	Director of Sustainable Business (Plan A)
McDonald's	Cindy Jiang	Senior Director, Worldwide Food Safety, Quality and Nutrition
Michelin	Gerald Bourlon	Executive Vice President of Logistics and Customer Service

Company	Name	Title
Middlebury College	Bill Baue	Corporate Sustainability Architect
Mitsubishi Electric	Mark Foscoe	Group Logistics Manager
MIT	Tony Craig	Postdoctoral Associate
MIT	Courtney DeSisto	Intern
MIT	Suzanne Glassburn	Counsel
MIT	Suzanne Greene	LEAP Program Manager
MIT	Jeremy Gregory	Research Scientist
MIT	Jason Jay	Director of Sustainability Initiative
MIT	Randolph Kirchain	Principal Research Associate, Material Systems Lab
MIT	Christopher Knittel	Professor of Management
MIT	Yin Jin Lee	Doctoral Student
MIT	Reed Miller	Master's Student
MIT	Gregory Morgan	General Counsel
MIT	Elsa Olivetti	Assistant Professor, Material Science and Engineering
MIT	Noelle Eckley Selin	Associate Professor, Earth and Planetary Science
MIT	Josué Velázquez	Research Associate, Center for Transportation and Logistics
National Organic Program	Miles McEvoy	Deputy Administrator
Natural Resource Defense Council	Adrian Martinez	Project Attorney
Natura	Emiliano Barelli	Senior Manager, Packaging R&D
Natura	Rodrigo Brea	Distribution and Customer Service Director
Natura	Thais Ferraz	Sustainability Manager

Company	Name	Title
Natura	Alessandro Mendes	R&D Director
Natura	Juliana Pasqualini	Sustainability Coordinator
Natura	Angela Pinhati	Supply Chain Director
Natura	Sergio Talocchi	Reverse Logistics and Recycled Materials Manager
Natura	Romulo Zamberlan	Packaging Development Manager
New Britain Palm Oil	Simon Lord	Managing Director
New Britain Palm Oil	Petra Meekers	Group Sustainability Manager
Niagara Bottling	Ashley Dorna	Executive Vice President, Supply Chain
Niagara Bottling	Rali Sanderson	Executive Vice President, Procurement
Nike	Laura Adams	Open Innovation Director
Nike	Agata Ramallo Garcia	Senior Director, Global Sourcing
Nike	Santiago Gowland	General Manager, Sustainable Business & Innovation
Nike	Hannah Jones	Chief Sustainability Officer
Nike	Stephani Kobayashi Stevenson	University Relations Manager
Novozymes	Peter Brond	Senior Manager
Novozymes	Adam Monroe	President
Pacific Gas & Electric	Debora Bonner	Supply Chain Sustainability Manager
Packsize	Brandon Brooks	Global Vice President of Strategy and Marketing
Patagonia	Cara Chacon	Vice President, Social and Environmental Strategy
Patagonia	Jill Dumain	Director of Environmental Strategy
Patagonia	Betsy Held	Paralegal

Company	Name	Title
Patagonia	Brett Krasniewicz	Materials R&D Manager
Patagonia	Elissa Foster	Senior Manager of Product Responsibility
Patagonia	Elisabeth Mast	Director of Sourcing
Patagonia	Vincent Stanley	Vice President, Marketing and Communications
PepsiCo	Tim Carey	Senior Director, Sustainability
Petrobas	Janine Cardoso Senna	Senior Engineer
Pfizer	Jim Cafone	Vice President of Supply Operations
Port of Long Beach	Robert Kanter	Managing Director
Port of Los Angeles	Chris Cannon	Director of Environmental Management
Port of Los Angeles	Christopher Patton	Environmental Affairs Officer
Procter & Gamble	Sergio Barbarino	Research Fellow
Procter & Gamble	Andrew Byer	Associate Director, Supply Network
Procter & Gamble	Kathy Claffey	Global Fabric & Home Care Supply Network Operations
Procter & Gamble	James McCall	Global Product Supply Sustainability Leader
Procter & Gamble	Forbes McDougall	Corporate Waste Strategy Leader
Procter & Gamble	Stefano Zenezini	Vice President, Global Product Supply Beauty Sector
PUMA	Adam Brennan	Sustainability Project Manager
PUMA	Reiner Hengstmann	Global Director, Sustainability & Compliance
PUMA	Stefan Seidel	Head of Corporate Sustainability
Rainforest Alliance	W. Robert Beer	Director, SmartWood Program
Ralph Lauren	Jay Kimpton	Vice President—Global Supply Chain PMO

Company	Name	Title
Ralph Lauren	Russ LoCurto	Senior Vice President, Operations
Ralph Lauren	Dania Nasser	Business Operations and Compliance Counsel
Ralph Lauren	Sejung Park	Director, Program Management Office
Ralph Lauren	John Zomberg	Senior Manager of Supply Chain Finance
Schlumberger	Sarah Bruce Courtney	Global Supplier Manager
Seventh Generation	Jim Barch	Director of R&D
Seventh Generation	Clement Choy	Senior Director of R&D
Seventh Generation	Tim Fowler	Senior Vice President of R&D
Seventh Generation	John Henry Siedlecki	Senior Brand Manager
Seventh Generation	Peter Swaine	Director of Sourcing
Seventh Generation	Martin Wolf	Director of Sustainability & Authenticity
Seventh Generation	Reed Doyle	Director of Corporate Social Responsibility
Siemens	Arnd Hirschberg	CPO, Process Industries and Drives
Siemens	Georg Schroeder	Supply Chain Management, Executive Relations
Siemens	Matthias Weirdinger	Vice President of Human Resources
Siemens	Dirk Weiss	Executive Assistant
Siemens	Barbara Kux	Chief Sustainability and Supply Chain Officer
Sierra Club	Gina Coplon-Newfield	Director of Electric Vehicles Initiative
Sierra Club	Michael Marx	Senior Campaign Director, Beyond Oil Campaign
Sierra Club	Lucy Page	Campaigner
Sourcemap	Leo Bonanni	Founder and CEO
Sprint	Amy Hargroves	Director, Corporate Responsibility and Sustainability

Company	Name	Title
Stanford University	Hau Lee	Thoma Professor of Operations, Information, and Technology
Staples	Mark Buckley	Vice President Environmental Affairs
Staples	Cynthia Wilkinson	Director of Supply Chain Sustainability
Starbucks	Julie Anderson	Senior Manager, Global Impact
Starbucks	Kelly Goodejohn	Director of Social Impact and Public Policy
Starbucks	Steve Lovejoy	Senior Vice President, Global Supply Chain
Starbucks	Deverl Maserang	Executive Vice President, Global Supply Chain Organization
Texas Organic Cotton Marketing Cooperative	Anita Morton	Customer Service Coordinator
Texas Organic Cotton Marketing Cooperative	Kelly Pepper	Manager
The Forest Trust	Sonia Lieberherr	Program Manager
The Forest Trust	Scott Poynton	Founder
The Sustainability Consortium	Mike Faupel	Chief Operating Officer
The Sustainability Consortium	Nicole Hardiman	Senior Research, Pulp, Paper, and Forestry Sector
The Sustainability Consortium	Jonathan Johnson	Professor (University of Arkansas) and Academic Director
The Sustainability Consortium	Sarah Lewis	Managing Director of Members and Implementation
The Sustainability Consortium	Christy Slay	Director of Research
This Fish	Eric Enno Tamm	Co-Founder and General Manager
TJX	John Bauer	Executive Vice President, Chief Logistics Officer

Company	Name	Title
TJX	Laurie Lyman	Vice President, Logistics Development
TJX	Brenna Zimmer	Assistant Vice President, Environmental Sustainability Director
Trucost	Richard Mattison	CEO
Trucost	James Salo	Head of Data Strategy and Operations
Unilever	Karime Abib	Global Logistics Program Officer
Unilever	Stella Constantatos	Logistics Development Manager
Unilever	Giovanni Dal Bon	Strategic Logistics Director
Unilever	Flip Dötsch	Global Head of Procurement Communication
Unilever	Tony Dunnage	Group Director of Manufacturing Sustainability
Unilever	Maeve Hall	Group Manufacturing Sustainability Manager
Unilever	Derek Harkin	Global Manufacturing Technology Manager
Unilever	Wendy Herrick	Vice President, Supply Chain USA
Unilever	David Lovejoy	Group EHS Director
Unilever	John Maguire	Engineering Director Africa
Unilever	Pier Luigi Sigismondi	Chief Supply Chain Officer
Unilever	Jessica Sobel	Senior Manager, Sustainable Living and Strategic Initiatives
Unilever	Scott Spoerl	EHS Group Operations Director Operations Manager
Unilever	Kyle Stone	Supply Chain Manager
Unilever	Georgia Szewczak	Quality Director
Universidad Politécnica de Madrid	Eva Maria Ponce Cueto	Professor

Company	Name	Title
University of Pau/ Université Paris Dauphine	Gisele Bilek	Ensignmant Chercheur
University of São Paulo	Claudio Barbieri de Cunha	Professor e Pesquisador
UPS	Gina Hutchins	Global Executive Talent Director
UPS	Randy Stashick	President of Engineering
UPS	Roger Whitson	Managing Director, Customer Solutions
UPS	Scott Wicker	Vice President of Global Plant Engineering and Sustainability
Walmart	Elizabeth Fretheim	Senior Director, Supply Chain Sustainability
Walmart	Katherine Neebe	Director of Sustainability
Walmart	Tracy Rosser	Senior Vice President, Transportation and Supply Chain
Walmart	Jeff Smith	Senior Director of Logistics, Maintenance, and Purchasing
Walmart	Chris Sultemeier	Executive Vice President, Logistics
Walmart	Andrea Thomas	Senior Vice President, Sustainability
Walmart	John Visser	Senior Director of International Logistics
Waters	Andrew Pastor	Global Product Stewardship Specialist
World 50	Phillip Barlag	Executive Director, General Counsel
World 50	Steve Walker	Director, Sustainable Supply Chain Initiative

Index